W9-ARI-642

EAST HAMPTON FREE LIBRARY

East Hampton, New York

in memory of

MARJORIE STEELE

Presented by

Walnut Hall Foundation

COMMON LANDSCAPE OF AMERICA, 1580 TO 1845

Common Landscape of America, 1580 to 1845

JOHN R. STILGOE

YALE UNIVERSITY PRESS

NEW HAVEN AND LONDON

c.1

973
Sti

Published with assistance from the Mary Cady Tew Memorial Fund.

Copyright © 1982 by Yale University.
All rights reserved.
This book may not be reproduced, in whole
or in part, in any form (beyond that
copying permitted by Sections 107 and 108
of the U.S. Copyright Law and except by
reviewers for the public press), without
written permission from the publishers.

Designed by Sally Harris
and set in Baskerville type by
The Composing Room of Michigan, Inc.
Printed in the United States of America by
Halliday Lithograph, West Hanover, Mass.

Library of Congress Cataloging in Publication Data

Stilgoe, John R., 1949–
   Common landscape of America, 1580 to 1845.

   Bibliography: p.
   Includes index.
   1. Land settlement—United States—History.
2. United States—Civilization. 3. Landscape—
United States—History. 4. United States—
Social conditions—To 1845. I. Title.
E169.1.S85   973   81-16367
ISBN 0-300-02699-4   AACR2

10 9 8 7 6 5 4 3 2 1

8/30/82
BKh
29.95

for Mary Ann

C O N T E N T S

What follows is an analysis of landscape, specifically the landscape made by Americans between 1580, when the Spanish colonists crossed the Rio Grande and began shaping the land previously explored and claimed by the *conquistadores*, and 1845, when pioneers moving west from Indiana and Illinois encountered the open prairie. Traditional landscape extended from the Rio Grande north to the Arkansas River, and from the Atlantic coast to the French settlements just west of the Mississippi. Within that vast area lay several distinctly regional variations of the western European landscape cherished by most colonists. After the American Revolution a thin veneer of national form reached out across all but the Spanish-shaped land. Beneath the veneer endured a complex and decidedly traditional arrangement of space and structure derived from the heritages of agriculture and artifice. Americans loved the construct of traditionally shaped space and structure—and its thin overlay of innovative, national form—and judged wilderness and cityscape against them.

In this study, *common* means not rude or vulgar but belonging to a people. Common design is that design understood and agreed upon by all, and passed from one generation to another, usually by example. Transmission by example is of great importance; the builders who created and maintained the American landscape until 1845 learned mostly from one another, in part by listening and reading but chiefly by duplicating and improving one another's spaces and structures. Just as contemporary children learn without books—and sometimes with no spoken instruction—to build snowmen and sandcastles, so Americans learned by looking. Few professional designers worked in the colonies and the early Republic; most chose to remain in European cities and practice an essentially book-learned, urban design. Out of the rural areas of Europe, where new ideas came so slowly that as late as the early seventeenth century the adjectives *late medieval* and *early modern* best describe the attitudes of the people, came most of the settlers of the North American colonies, especially those settlers intending to farm. City dwellers often arrived intending to make towns and cities, and their standards and structures differentiated them from the bulk of the population. Landscape objectified the dominant design thinking in North America until the 1850s, and for decades after it reflected the design standards by which most Americans evaluated wilderness and cityscape. Landscape objectified *common sense*, not the doubtful innovation of professional designers.

Any analysis of 265 years of building throughout such a vast region must necessarily emphasize the relation of particular landscape constituents to the larger construct, not the intricate evolution of each artifact. Readers interested in the history of particular landscape constituents will find extensive citations in the bibliography, if such citations exist. Not every space and structure and other artifact selected for examination here has attracted scholarly interest, largely because familiarity makes many landscape constituents invisible. Prolonged visual analysis of the contemporary man-made American environment raises questions about the origins and meanings of many individual elements, and often the answers can be found only by interviewing hundreds of people knowledgeable about the history of their land and structures. This book delineates the important patterns of common building that still reveal themselves to careful observers, and it seeks to explain their development and meaning.[1]

ACKNOWLEDGMENTS

Many people made suggestions concerning this book. Especially, I thank my friend John Brinckerhoff Jackson, and my colleagues in the Department of Landscape Architecture and the Department of Visual and Environmental Studies. Daniel Aaron, Eduard Sekler, and Carl Steinitz all offered helpful advice, and Loeb Library reference librarian Christopher Hail provided thoughtful assistance. To my students I am indebted for questions and requests for examples, and to Judy Metro and Alexander Metro of Yale University Press, for thorough editing and gracious understanding of stylistic peculiarity. Above all, I thank my wife, for assistance and support in a thousand ways.

LANDSCAPE

*I like to have a man's knowledge comprehend more
than one class of topics, one row of shelves.
I like a man who likes to see a fine barn
as well as a good tragedy.*[1]

Ralph Waldo Emerson
Journal
1828

Living roland at *landschaft* center. From Mejborg, *Das Bauernhaus im Herzogthum Schleswig*.

andscape is a slippery word. It means more than scenery painting, a pleasant rural vista, or ornamental planting around a country house. It means shaped land, land modified for permanent human occupation, for dwelling, agriculture, manufacturing, government, worship, and for pleasure. A landscape happens not by chance but by contrivance, by premeditation, by design; a forest or swamp or prairie no more constitutes a landscape than does a chain of mountains. Such land forms are only wilderness, the chaos from which landscapes are created by men intent on ordering and shaping space for their own ends. But landscapes always display a fragile equilibrium between natural and human force; terrain and vegetation are moulded, not dominated. When men wholly dominate the land, when they shroud it almost completely with structure and chiseled space, landscape is no longer landscape; it is cityscape, a related but different form. Landscape is essentially rural, the product of traditional agriculture interrupted here and there by traditional artifice, a mix of natural and man-made form.[2]

Contemporary Americans recall landscape with vague delight and understanding, remembering it as space objectifying a traditional social order. What keeps alive the half-imagined memory? Antique illustrations like those of Currier and Ives, nostalgic advertisements equating rural space with health, unadulterated food, and family serenity, and—most importantly—tens of thousands of vestigial remains of former landscapes now transformed into urban or suburban space and dominated by new structures, juxtapositions, and patterns. One-room schoolhouses, and centrally placed meetinghouses, covered bridges and corncribs, lighthouses and Pennsylvania bank barns, meadows and gristmills, factory villages and walled-in graveyards, tiny cornfields and right-angle section lines, country fairgrounds and crossroads churches, farmhouse ells and abandoned iron furnaces, rural camp-meeting grounds and other vestiges of landscape still sway the national imagination by subtly informing judgments about windowless factories, rows of identical houses, interstate highways, strips of franchised commercial development, garden apartments, looming storage sheds, sprawling schools, and acres upon acres of scattered machinery taller than houses, mysterious complexes of metal buildings, and half-understood spaces surrounded by no-trespassing signs. Americans speak glibly enough of a national landscape characterized and dominated by such twentieth-century forms and lament the roadside homogeniety of structure and space without understanding that the United States owns not only the

3

contemporary, dramatically intricate and perplexing "national land-scape" but thousands of smaller, more traditional places still charac-terized by the old equilibrium. Because of their lack of understanding, Americans grow increasingly wary of new manipulations of space. They champion zoning regulations, conservation of wooded and agricultural land as open space, and the preservation, restoration, and adaptive reuse of old buildings. Environmental impact legislation and explorations of scenic quality slow the development of swamps, farms, and miscellane-ous vacant lots, proving the bane of designers and speculators while vaguely reassuring the general public that change is slower now and less likely to be destructive of meaningful, traditional space. Hesitantly, and sometimes emotionally, Americans are discovering the meaning and sig-nificance of landscape by scrutinizing landscape vestiges.

Implicit in the landscape of tradition are two dichotomies, one be-tween husbandry and artifice and one between common and profes-sional design. Agriculturists have long distrusted miners, millers, and other proponents of manufacturing; in a land where once nine of every ten people worked in agriculture, it is not surprising that much of our national heritage sublty emphasizes the good life of husbandry and the beauty and rightness of space shaped for farming. Equally significant in American culture is the tension between common and professional build-ers; while well-read men who understood the new theories of geog-raphy, mercantile capitalism, representative government, and innovative design sometimes directed colonization, people much less literate and far more traditional actually shaped the land. Very few cartographers and surveyors and spatial theorists migrated to the New World; men like William Penn were as rare as his finely drawn plan for Philadelphia, and even he did not stay to watch his plan take form. Although the wilder-ness was occasionally mapped and platted and otherwise ordered by literate professionals familiar with innovative ideas, almost invariably it was shaped by tradition, by husbandmen eager to plant old-country crops in fields shaped according to old-country standards, by housewives determined to process crops in traditional kitchens and kitchen ells and to feed poultry and grow vegetables in traditional farmyards. Artifice developed according to tradition too. Millers and smiths thought care-fully before abandoning established businesses for New World planta-tions, but when they arrived they shaped the land and erected ma-chinery as their fathers had taught them. From the late sixteenth century to the end of the eighteenth, agriculturists and artificers distrusted each other but worked together to shape the wilderness into useful space.

For two centuries, common knowledge governed American spatial design. Common knowledge is neither folk nor literate but a complex mixture of both the "little tradition" transmitted by generations of half-literate peasants and the "great tradition" of the literate, innovative minority of scholars, rulers, and merchants, and of professional designers such as surveyors and architects.[3] Husbandry was more closely tied to the folk tradition than was artifice, but neither depended for success on constant technical innovation. After a brief period of adjustment to North American weather and soil, husbandmen shaped the ground with little regard for subsequent Old World agricultural invention. Artificers proved even less open to innovation and by the middle of the eighteenth century often struck European visitors as old-fashioned and ignorant. Colonial clergymen and merchants exchanged letters and books with European friends, of course, and some knew the latest fashions in Madrid and London, but husbandmen and artificers nurtured the wisdom of the past and applied its dictates to the land.

Common knowledge inspired and restricted the leaders of the new United States. Even the best educated of them had unconsciously assimilated the tenets of common spatial design; after all, almost all the land they saw was either wilderness or objectified common thinking about farm location, housebuilding, or mill-siting. When Congress "ordered" the "back country" after 1785 with a national-scale rectilinear survey, it codified the common moulding of space that had served Americans for almost 200 years. Jefferson and other intellectuals proposed innovations, but Congress almost invariably defeated them. All the vastness west of the Appalachian Mountains was quickly and simply ordered to encourage every sort of common building.

Not until the first years of the nineteenth century did professional designers make significant contributions to the shaping of American wilderness. Turnpike and canal corporations employed skilled engineers—when they could find them—to plan and build gradients and channels, and railroad companies employed them too, in the 1830s and 40s. By 1850 expansion-minded cities and states competed with corporations in employing innovative builders who understood mathematical formulas as well as shovels and wood beams. But until the Civil War, even the engineers built chiefly in wood and stone, materials well known to countless untrained but ingenious men who frequently outperformed the best-educated products of American and European technical schools. The war fueled changes already evident by the late 1840s, however, and by its close thousands of men were "hands," laboring at simple jobs that produced intricate monuments like long-distance railroads and multistory factories. Shaping was no longer always intelligible to farmers

and artisans, and thoughtful observers began to worry even as they
marveled.

In the first half of the nineteenth century husbandry became farming
and artifice became industry. Both transitions derived from more accessible printed information, better schooling, and experiment. Agriculture
changed far more slowly than artifice. Husbandmen relied on traditional
techniques until new processes proved better, and proof was years in
coming. Steam power transformed artifice, and massive capital investment made the changes permanent. Families continued to own and
manage farms, but corporations owned railroads and factories and
placed them under the direction of skilled supervisors. Farmers owned
their tools and their labor, but factory workers did not; by 1860 the
hands no longer always understood their place in the large enterprises in
which they were employed—they knew only their wages. When they
lamented their condition, they recalled the good life left behind on
farms or in small towns away from railroads. Reverie ignored the
backbreaking drudgery of farming, but it stimulated the imagination of
urban writers and illustrators. By 1870 the farm objectified the good life
and epitomized "pure America."

Farming and industry combined to subdue the nation's newly discovered prairie wilderness. Old fears of Indians and wild beasts eased with
the perfection of the revolver and repeating rifle, and windmills, steel
plows, and barbed wire made the prairie bloom almost overnight. In the
East, among the sprawling, increasingly crowded, ever more frantic industrial cities, particularly acute and sensitive observers discerned the
end of landscape and the fragility of the ideals and traditions that had
produced it. No image better captures their distrust of urbanization and
industrialization than Thoreau's 1849 notice in *A Week on the Concord and
Merrimack Rivers* that the great dams erected in manufacturing cities
impounded water so far upstream that farmers supposedly distant from
the centers of industry watch as their meadows flood and get destroyed.[4]
The gathering power of industrialized urbanism drove many of the
writers into the past or into the wilderness of woodlots; Hawthorne
wrote about the colonial era and Thoreau described the woods around
Walden Pond. In their haste to ignore and dismiss the new space ordered by industry and urban growth, most discovered a new meaning in
wilderness. No longer was wilderness the evil so distrusted by colonial
clergymen and the few nineteenth-century writers like Hawthorne who
knew the old significance of forest chaos. Suddenly it was a pure force
able to invigorate men and women sensitive enough to see it with their
whole spirits; Emerson's transcendentalism accepted the healthful influ-

ence of the woodlot wilderness and announced it to people still wary of
unshaped space but already weary of urban manufacturing. Not for decades, however, was the transformation of wilderness complete; too many
people remembered the wilderness as the objectification of chaotic evil.

WILDERNESS

Snow White, according to the old German folktale, so threatened the
ugly queen that a huntsman was ordered to drag her into the forest, put
her to death, and cut out her lungs and liver. In the folk imagination of
the Middle Ages the forest is the logical setting for such atrocity. After
all, it is a great chaos, the lair of wild beasts and wilder men, where order
and shaping are not, where hapless peasants are first *be-wildered*, then
seduced into all manner of sin. The very vastness of the disorder leaches
away the peasant's reserve of reason and self-control; he confuses freedom with license and succumbs to the animal appetites latent in all men
and restrained only by society. No one in the Middle Ages feared woodlots and copses, the discrete, knowable places within larger cultivated
areas. They dreaded wilderness.[5]

The peasant attitude owed something to the Bible but far more to the
Old Religion, to the substructure of belief that underlay the veneer of
Christianity well into the early modern era. Missionaries described the
wilderness in which the Israelites found every kind of demon, the *sair*, or
hairy satyr, the howling dragon they called the *tan*, and *lilith*, the winged
female monster of the night. In the spirit Azazel, Jews discovered a
collective figure for all the furies of the wild, for the gods who contested
with their own for control of their space and their souls. The biblical
wilderness was indeed bewildering, a place where man strayed from the
holy path and slid into temptation and blasphemy. But it was sometimes
a place of punitive preparation for salvation, an area free from the
temptations of cities and almost the favored ground of God. It was the
scene of His covenant with Israel, of the visions of Jacob and Ezekiel, of
John the Baptist's witness, and of Christ's triumph over the Devil.
Church fathers introduced its dual nature to tribes well schooled in
wilderness life, and compared the barren desert with the wild vastness of
forest. But their sermons concerned salvation, not wilderness depiction,
and for centuries pagan imaginings dominated their listeners' understanding of wild land.[6]

In western and northern Europe, where peasants worshiped trees and
groves of trees, missionaries encountered the full force of the Old Religion. Across Scandinavia, tribespeople believed that trees had souls and

were human ancestors; in German lands they knew that elves lived under oaks and elders and that firs must not be uprooted lest the sprites beneath be disturbed; in Bohemia they understood that hawthorn branches frightened away the witches attracted to walnut trees. Tree veneration focused on conifers and such other evergreens as mistletoe and holly because their constant greenness reassured people that the coming of spring was certain. The Old Religion proved too strong to denounce and too potent to ignore; it drew strength from Christian attack and its endurance taxed the patience of missionaries everywhere. As late as 1386, when Grand Duke Jagello proclaimed Lithuania a Christian land and his more conservative subjects retreated into the forests to worship holly, Christians sometimes doubted the certainty of the church's victory over the powers of darkness. Even as the Age of Discovery began, that half-known power still overshadowed the power objectified in church buildings, crosses, and sacraments. It was in a dark wood that Dante lost his way and discovered the entrance to Hell. It was in a deep forest that Red Riding Hood strayed from the path to search for wildflowers and met the wolf. In the wilderness the medieval Christian—courtier and peasant—confronted the Old Religion.[7]

Medieval peasants understood wilderness in half-pagan, half-Christian terms. Few if any spoke of Pan, at least to any hearer educated enough—or brave enough—to enter their words in writing. Instead they confused Pan with Satan and related hoary tales like those of the "wild hunt." On moonless nights, and especially on Walpurgisnacht (May Day eve), Satan and his hounds coursed through the forest, pursuing with a terrible roaring and baying all the wild creatures and any humans unlucky enough to stumble in their way. Saint Paul's warning to "refuse profane and old wives' fables" did nothing to stop the continual retelling of such tales because the peasants saw in them the murky outlines of larger, perfectly Christian truth.[8] Satan lived, and it seemed only natural that he lived most comfortably in the wilderness, incarnate in disorder and terror.

Christianity destroyed the ancient oneness of man and nature. Whatever the Old Religion was, and it is known now almost entirely in descriptions composed by its enemies, its tenets derived from that oneness. Seasonal change, successful hunts, bountiful harvests, deaths in winter storms, even the continual collisions of man with beast explained man's niche in a larger order of things. Christianity, along with agriculture and artifice, wrenched man from his niche and made him sometime master of the earth. Agriculture and artifice made him ever less familiar with the wild, until he was no longer "at home" in it, until he recognized it as wild, as a place other than his own. As his belief in Satan grew and his familiarity with the forest lessened, the medieval peasant peered about a world teeming with supranatural beings respected in years gone by. At dusk, by the chimney corner and in the shadows of his doorway, he recalled the former respect once accorded to beings he now scorned. He thought of spriggans, of *gwragedd annwn, sidhe, hyter, ghillie dhu, cluricaun, fir darrig, witchtlein, kobold, coblynau, daugars, fachan,* and selkies, and of hundreds more now-nameless minions of the old gods his priest called devils.[9] Away from the centers of Christendom, beyond the royal highway, creatures of the Old Religion tormented pious clerics and travelers who knew that husbandmen still honored the helpful spirits of ages past—and feared the malignancies of those turned demons by Christian scorn.

A great tree of life symbolized the chief tenets of the Old Religion. Rooted in the underworld of death, it soared to the heavenly home of powerful gods like Freyr and Freyja, linking the world of men with the worlds of shadow and of divinity. Odin and Thor were gods of war, courage, and strength, but Freyr and Freyja were brother and sister of fertility. To them peasants sacrificed in the hope of having healthy children, good harvests, and bountiful hunts and catches. Scores of land spirits served the two fertility gods, and it was they that survived longest into the Christian era, as agriculture became progressively more important than hunting and pillaging, and as men deserted forests for fields. Peasants across northern Europe learned more and more about the New Religion, the religion that substituted for the living, blossoming tree of life a cross of hewn wood. Christianity was clearly a religion of settled land, not chaotic wastes and forests, and when peasants and travelers entered the wilderness they knew all too clearly that they entered the last domain of scorned and perhaps still powerful gods and demigods. As long as such beings lived, Christians feared.

Lithuanian pagans threatened Christian travelers as late as 1547, when the Old Religion bloomed once again, terrifying rural Catholics and Protestants who were warring over biblical interpretation and ecclesiastical practice. The Reformation nurtured religious insecurity along with religious oddity, and everywhere on the fringes of civilized Christian Europe peasants succumbed to half-dormant respect for old gods, particularly those ensuring fertility. "Idolaters are still to be found in the forests," wrote Sigmund Herberstein in his 1557 *Description of Moscow and Muscovy,* "and Russian monks or hermits often go to them there and strive to turn them to the true faith, even unto this day."[10] Jesuits preaching later in the century in parts of the kingdom of Seville found people who fed on acorns, lived in caves and huts, and "resembled Indians rather than Spaniards." Seventeenth-century Englishmen distrusted what they called "the dark corners" of the British Isles, the little-known vales of Cornwall where men spoke Gaelic, the mountains of Wales, the far highlands and islands of Scotland, "the utmost skirts of the north" in the words of one impassioned member of Parliament in 1628, "where the prayers of the common people are more like spells and charms than devotions." Satanism acquired spatial significance in the imagination of pious Christians. It suffused the wilderness that nourished it. John Dury, who traveled beyond the utmost northern skirts to Sweden in 1636, wrote home to England about the colonization of North America. "Is not there more hope to do good to Christianity in building up the waste places here and hereabout in Europe than in laying new foundations without settled ground?" he asked a New World-minded friend.[11] Dury had good reason to wonder. Well into the eighteenth century, people in the Scandinavian Alps worshiped the Norse god Thor and honored Thursday as a holy day—Thor's Day. Away from the world of pious Christians lay the wilderness that hid the shadowy power of Satan and the older gods from the penetrating scrutiny of the Christian clerics.

To Anglo-Saxons the words *wylder ness* identified the nest or lair of a wild beast, not the chaotic mountains or forest or rolling waste denoted by the early modern *wilderness.* In the sixteenth century, mountains like the Harz and Alps, forests like the Schwarzwald, steppes like the barrens of Hungary, swamps like the Rijnland of Holland, even heaths like the uplands of Scotland terrified peasants and nobles alike. They objectified a test of faith, a contest between the faith abandoned a short while before and a newer faith objectified in carefully shaped land. Bewilderment meant encountering the dragons and great worms of age-old tale, and it meant fighting off wolf packs, boars, and bears. It meant confronting the fragmented former oneness of man and nature, and it meant knowing the true fragility of civilized order. *Wilderness* identified those spaces beyond human control, the spaces of bewilderment, the spaces of *heathen.*[12]

On the Continent, wilderness often meant a rugged stretch of country untouched by agriculturalists and unpoliced by anyone; frequently it connoted a mountainous forest, like those that inspired so many late medieval and early modern painters. But wilderness varied according to time of day and season of the year; the half-known woodlot presented a different face on a clear July afternoon than at dusk in January at the beginning of a snowstorm. Even in England, where by the sixteenth century many great forests had been almost destroyed by peasants seeking arable land, firewood, and timber, the implications of wilderness remained extremely powerful. The fens, for example, tormented travelers; even where no trees blocked the view across the bogs and swamps, people feared quicksand and mire, and the creatures commonly believed to writhe in them. Fen creatures had no precise name in England, but Scots classified them as kelpies or water horses. Folktales describing the habitats of such creatures make clear the early modern understanding of wilderness as that land or water beyond civilized, Christian control.

Scots believed in kelpies and water horses as firmly as the Irish believed in *pooka* and *piast* and Scandinavians believed in *soe-orm* and *skrimsl.* Water creatures took two forms; the smaller sort inhabited shallow streams and ponds, while the larger, perhaps the last surviving zeuglodons, claimed deep lakes and lochs. Peasants fishing, crossing fords, or gathering driftwood chanced encountering one sort or another. In 1527, one Scottish historian noted that "out of Garloch, a loch of Argyle, came a terrible beast as big as a greyhound, puted like a gander, and struck down great trees with the length of his tail; and slew three men quickly who were hunting." As late as 1645 a mapmaker identified Loch Lomond as having "fish without fin," but determined that "the fish which they speak of as having no fins are a kind of snake and therefore no wonder."[13] Local people failed to stop wondering, however, and in 1773, on the island of Rasay, one told Boswell and Johnson about a sea horse that devoured a man's daughter. "He did not laugh when he told us this story," Boswell recorded, nor did other inhabitants of the utmost skirts of the north laugh when they told Londoners about "Each Uisge," the water horse.[14] Such creatures of wilderness swallowed hapless boaters and slithered ashore to eat innocent peasants. Until saints or determined men eradicated them, no person felt wholly safe near the shore, let alone upon the water.

A fen, bog, or loch is not easily known. Although travelers may easily scan the surface of such open wilderness, the depths conceal terrors as frightful as the most loathesome creature of any imagination, the squat, squalid thing that personifies the beast still snuffling about in human unconsciousness, the thing that goes bump in the night. Watery wilderness shelters such creatures, and like all other wilderness, forever threatens to overwhelm the land ordered and shaped by man. Wilderness is the spatial correlative of unreason, or madness, of the unhuman anarchy that informs so many folktales emphasizing the ephemeral stability of Christianity, society, and agriculture. In the early modern imagination, wilderness is the sea cascading into polder, the heath fire engulfing wheat fields, the earthquake swallowing houses, the forest or loch concealing the wolf, fish without fin, and the *loup-garou.*

LANDSCHAFT

The antithesis of wilderness is landscape, the land shaped by men. Originally the word was German—*landschaft*—and meant something other than it does today. A landschaft was not a town exactly, or a manor or a village, but a collection of dwellings and other structures crowded together within a circle of pasture, meadow, and planting fields and surrounded by unimproved forest or marsh. Like the Anglo-Saxon *tithing* and the Old French *vill*, the word meant more than an organization of space; it connoted too the inhabitants of the place and their obligations to one another and to the land. The idea of a landschaft, of a traditional landscape, is very old. An Egyptian hieroglyph captures it in abstract form and distinguishes it from a town.[15]

The essence of a landschaft in ancient and medieval thought is the intimate relation of fields and clustered structures. In the landschaft, fields and structures share equal importance, but in the town no such equality exists. Indeed the fields are forgotten, and buildings and streets dominate the land. Traditionally, then, landschaft implied an agricultural community and a smallness of scale unknown in towns.[16]

Smallness was both absolute and subjective in the typical medieval landschaft. The twelve- to fifteen-square-mile area was home to perhaps 300 people, satisfying almost all their wants and recognizing every rod of ground as vitally important. Meadows, arable fields, and pastures produced more than food; they gave identity to each inhabitant. The

common fields, expanses of wheat, rye, or barley plowed at the same time, planted to the same crops, harvested at the same moment, and opened at the same time for stubble grazing objectified community purpose, strength, and traditional skill. Each spring the men yoked together all the landschaft oxen to pull the community plow across the land of all; the most respected husbandman was he who best kept the corporate tradition, who best husbanded the old wisdom of agriculture. The innovator with new seeds, equipment, and techniques was distrusted and forbidden any opportunity to experiment, even on those portions of the great fields to whose produce he was entitled. The strips, as husbandmen called the portions, existed as private property only in the sense that they belonged to a *seignior* or noble; otherwise they were almost public. Some landschaft councils assigned them each year by lottery, but in most they were allotted year after year to the same families. A householder might buy or lease another's right to a strip or strips, but he could not buy or sell any piece of a common field any more than he could fence off his strips. The fields objectified the corporate identity of the landschaft householders, and to cut up one or all was akin to destroying the social compact.[17] Small as the landschaft actually was, and tiny as it seemed when wilderness danger beset its inhabitants, its wholeness gave it strength.

Within the encircling ring of common fields stood the landschaft shelters, the houses and dwellings that announced and reinforced the status of their inhabitants. Early modern Europeans cherished houses and yards as stays against confusion and catastrophe; they understood the distinction between *house* and *dwelling*. By medieval and early modern legal and popular definition, a dwelling is a temporary habitation, a rude

shelter thrown up by charcoal burners, shepherds, peat diggers, or agricultural laborers who neither own nor lease land. A typical cottage
existed only as a rough framework of light timber covered with a low-
quality sheathing; reeds, wattle-and-daub, thatch, divot (turf or sods), or
mud. It lacked a loft, paved floor, and (usually) interior partition walls;
poultry and other small livestock owned by the cotter slept in one corner
of the dank, dark chamber, in the center of which burned a tiny fire, its
smoke escaping through a hole in the roof or through a door or *window*.
A house, on the other hand, objectified permanence not only in its larger
size and stone fireplace and chimney but because its frame and covering
endured much longer.[18] Stone walls and heavy rafters supported a
thatch or tile roof, under which lay an upper-story sleeping loft above
one or more rooms. A cotter expected to vacate his dwelling sooner or
later, perhaps to carry its main structural components away with him to a
new place of occupation; no householder expected to move. Although
householders occasionally carted the frames of their houses from one
landschaft to another, all expected to remain on what they called their
steads, that complex of structure and space remembered now in English
words like *homestead* and *farmstead.*

Steads varied in form across central and western Europe, but the
essential pattern, a rough rectangle made by buildings and fences, extended from the Danube to the British Isles. The house comprised one
edge of the enclosure; a small stable and cow-house formed another.
Sometimes a granary and smaller structures like dovecotes completed
the third side, and several tiny dwellings, the cottages of laborers engaged by the householder, completed the enclosure on prosperous holdings. Walls or fences usually closed any intervening openings. A stead
might be imposing, carefully made of stone or heavy timber and including a number of cottages adjacent to its house, or it might be tiny. But
within its walls lay the yard, the *hof,* the *cour,* the focus of agricultural
activity other than planting, and just beyond lay the kitchen garden and
perhaps several fruit trees.[19] Having a stead, a house and yard, meant
having some fragment of outdoor space secured from chaos and made
profitable; for all that the poor widow of Chaucer's "Nun's Priest's Tale"
lives in a cottage, she contrives such a space: "A yeerd she hadde, enclosed al aboute/With stikkes, and a drye dych withoute,/In which she
hadde a cok." Of course, even the virtuous widow understood that her
yard, like her dwelling, might be swept away at the whim of her landlord,
but her modest enclosure emphasizes her attachment to a particular
locale, to the land near her husband's grave.[20] Holding a house and yard
and fulfilling its responsibilities to the landschaft enabled a family to

hold its spatial and social position indefinitely, the dream of every cottager.

Acquiring a stead proved very difficult; for centuries, most European peasants expected to be landless. Families who did not inherit a stead might, through vast sacrifice and great good luck, accumulate enough capital to acquire the right to hold one, but such deeds became rarer with every passing generation. Such an acquisition greatly enhanced the family's social and political status; its head became a householder with voting rights, rights to common pasture, timber, and arable ground, and other rights *owned by the stead*. A particular stead might have the rights to cut six large trees each year in the common woodlot, or take two cartloads of stone each spring from the landschaft "waste." Householders frequently transferred such ancient customary rights among one another, but they did so temporarily; no householder could permanently alienate rights owned by his stead or escape the peculiar responsibilities belonging to his stead. Householders sometimes contracted with cottagers to fulfill the duty to work eight days each autumn in the lord's woodlot or give four days each spring to brush-cutting, but they could not evade the tasks unless their lord converted the duties into monetary payments. A householder consequently knew his social and political position in the landschaft as clearly as he knew his spatial location; as long as he carried out his duties, his future remained far more certain than that of cottagers.

If a householder committed some heinous crime, like heresy or returning a judicial verdict contrary to evidence, his neighbors and lord punished him. They deprived him of his franchise and other political privileges, and then often pulled down his house and plowed up his yard. Breaking down the house broke the man, and unless his neighbors imprisoned or executed him, he and his family wandered from landschaft to landschaft, becoming creatures of wilderness. Few broken men trudged across early modern Europe; householders cherished landschaft unity and knew the penalties of wickedness too well to transgress the law. Breaking down a cottage carried far less significance; courts punished the cottager's person, not the dwelling owned by his landlord, who was free to demolish it almost as he pleased. The distinction between house-breaking and cottage-breaking surfaced in criminal law. To unjustly break a house, to smash it to gain entry for robbery, carried heavy penalties largely because breaking the house attacked the political rights of its holder while simultaneously upsetting the body politic founded upon the rights and responsibilities owned by every stead. Even trespass threatened more than the spatial integrity of the yard; land unjustly occupied or used by another person confused titles and political constructs almost as certainly as house-breaking.[21] In an age of chronic shortages, economic fluctuation, pestilence, and religious turmoil, holding a stead offered almost the only security. No wonder Europeans cherished their steads and revealed their love of them by naming them. Every stead had a unique identity worthy of a proper name and deserving the most valiant defense possible.

Supernatural evil assaulted steads, and especially houses, throughout the early modern era, and householders repelled it as effectively as possible. Across Britain, for example, householders protected doorways and fireplaces with carved figures or posts. Witches and other malignities entered a house most often by a door or by the chimney and gained power over its inhabitants by passing completely through the structure, from doorway to fireplace to chimney-top. Prudent householders erected a carved representation of some pre-Christian fertility spirit at one or both sides of the doorway, or else carved a "witch post" along one side of the hearth. Rowan wood, the wood that delighted the Old Religion god Thor, struck most householders as the best repellent of witches, and often they carved it with Saint Andrew's crosses and had the local priest set it in place. Carved figures represented a curious mix of pagan and Christian iconography and sometimes appeared in pairs, a male figure guarding one side of the doorway and a female one protecting the other. Respect for antique figures and posts endured well into the eighteenth century, especially in Wales, and householders building new houses in the 1730s chose to protect doorways and fireplaces by carving new posts.[22] Nighttime intrusion frightened householders trying to sleep, and their fear caused lawmakers to make breaking and entering a house *in the nighttime* a crime deserving harsher penalties than simple house-breaking.

House and stead defense concerned English householders in the late sixteenth century because nobles began enclosing the common fields for use as sheep pasture, and so terminating the long-term leases that made small-scale landschaft agriculture practical. Cottagers, of course, had little recourse. Whole groups of them left their tiny dwellings. But despite having secure houses and yards, householders learned the perils of depending on the system of common-land use and bitterly opposed enclosure. Parliament addressed enclosure cruelties early in 1589, in "An Act Againste Erecting and Maintaining of Cottages," by forbidding anyone to build or cause to be built a cottage without a four-acre yard, "to be continually occupied and manured therewith so long as the same cottage shall be inhabited," unless the occupants be miners or brickmakers, or the dwelling sited in a town to shelter a craftsman. Parliament also excluded "any cottage to be made within a mile of the sea" or "in any forest, chase, warren, or park, and those sheltering shepherds or "a poor, lame, sick, aged, or impotent person."[23] No legal document more clearly indicates the extraordinary importance attached to the stead. As the colonization era matured, the traditional landschaft appeared more and more inviting, and the meaning of the house and yard attracted increased attention not only from the landless cottagers but also from the householders impoverished by enclosure.

The form of the landschaft, fields surrounding a cluster of houses, derived from spatial economics, but medieval and early modern inhabitants, like their less advanced counterparts today, failed to realize it. Across the present, unmechanized agricultural world, in back-country Africa, South America, and southwestern Asia, peasants know a landschaft form much like that of early modern Europe, a small nucleus of houses and other structures encompassed by the *täglich lande,* or daily lands (the garden plots, orchards, and fields requiring daily attention), a second ring of fields worked less intensively and usually planted to rye or other cereals, a third of meadow hayed once or twice a summer, and a fourth of pasture. Variations in soils and climate along with other local circumstances ensure that no landschaft had or has perfectly concentric zones of cultivation, and in warm climates the ring of meadow is often lacking because hay is unnecessary as winter fodder. The general pattern, determined chiefly by the walking time from housing cluster to fields, is similar, however, and in parts of Europe the medieval form survives almost intact, although fields are no longer commonly owned and worked. In isolated areas of Brittany, Portugal, Spain, and Sicily, farmers still live in grouped houses and walk out each day to fields. They understand that crops requiring frequent, time-consuming care—vegetables and fruits especially—must be near the houses, lest men lose hours every week trudging from houses to fields and home again.[24] Medieval and early modern *landschaften* were small in area because their inhabitants walked out from a central point. When the landschaft population grew so numerous that the outermost fields proved uneconomical because they were too distant, younger men and their families left to establish a new landschaft in the wilderness abutting the old, or else left for cities. The medieval and early modern landschaft, therefore, existed as a strictly pedestrian place.

Landschaften otherwise varied from region to region, partly as a function of agriculture, partly too as a result of cultural decisions. In parts of Scandinavia, for example, landschaften evidenced the importance of sunlight. *Skolstifte* fields angled away from the sun's orbit, so that each—and each dwelling too—received as much sunlight as possible. In Wales the clustered form was little known, at least away from the English border where military necessity was not so pressing. Like the Irish, the Welsh devoted themselves to stock raising and required acres of pasture about their dwellings. Elsewhere in the British Isles, especially in pastoral Scotland and in grain-raising Kent, husbandmen lived on free-standing holdings scattered along hillsides and valleys. In German forests some landschaften were closely nucleated while others straggled along narrow roads. The ideal and most common landschaft form, however, was the concentric type evident in central England, much of France and the northern German states, in Italy, Austria, and far into the east. At its fringe stood a windmill or water mill perhaps, sited on a promontory or waterfall, and beyond that bastion of artifice, only the wilderness of forest, mountain, or steppe, or the fringe fields of the neighboring landschaft.

At its center stood a roland, the objectified essence of landschaft. Rolands predated Christianity, but the new religion incorporated them and their significance; order mattered as much to missionary priests as it did to peasants enduring incursions of wildness. Pagans occasionally clustered their dwellings about great single trees, but more often they marked the focus of their settlements with simple staffs hewn from stone or tree trunks. Christianity replaced many of them with large crosses, but the older form and old notions of tree-of-life fertility survived. A hewn roland represented the pruning of the tree of life and objectified the artificiality of the fields made from wilderness. Miters, scepters, and maces—perhaps even the patrolman's nightstick—derive from the Christianized pagan symbol of imposed order that dominated the typical late medieval landschaft.

Trees and staffs suggested the once-potent efficacy of the Old Religion of unhewn trees, and pious Christians periodically sought to replace them with crosses less likely to inspire Satanic May-day frolics. Reforming clergymen despised the use of rolands as May-poles, but to no avail. The English, lamented one angry and determined cleric in 1660, cavorted about the beribboned shafts, "doting on old superstition, profane customs, returning with the dogs of the world to lick up that filth which seemingly they had long since vomited up." Old Religion ceremony (or filth) involved fertility rites, drunkenness, licentious procreation, general surrender to sexuality, and a variety of other "rogueries." Throughout the sixteenth century Christians confronted a resurgence of despicable celebrations, some of which revolved about the roland. Calvinists in particular moved against "superstition"; in Scotland they mounted a vigorous attack on celebrations of Christmas and Midsummer, and on other festivals involving singing, dancing, plays, and bonfires. Catholics too sought to diminish their importance and like their Protestant enemies had only intermittent success. In an age of spiritual uncertainty the old fertility customs acquired enhanced meaning.[25]

On most days, however, the roland epitomized Christian order, for it marked the landschaft hierophany, the place where Christian Heaven touched the wilderness-slaying Christian place made by agriculture and artifice. It objectified the "peace of the market," the rule of holy law, and it objectified too a centripetal view of things. "They love only their own region," wrote a seventeenth-century landschaft priest about his parishioners. "They are not interested in the news or the fashions of other parts, but are quite detached from everything that happens in the rest of the world."[26] The roland was indeed an *axis mundi,* a shaft about which a small, almost self-sufficient world continuously revolved.

In the late Middle Ages every landschaft objectified far more than agricultural economics. Each was for its inhabitants a representation of the world because each was the world. Few men and fewer women left their native landschaft, for they could not desert their livestock. If they did travel they usually visited a contiguous landschaft much like their own but for them lacking the richness of association to which they were accustomed. At home every spot was invested with meaning—the meadow where someone saw the Devil at the edge of the forest, the houses of the well-off and the hovels of the poor, the hill struck twice by lightning long ago. Every landschaft mirrored a social, political, and economic order, the hierarchical structure of the universe, and the uneasy truce between the Old Religion and Christianity. Each was so uncritically accepted as the emblem of all order that each was thought natural. After all, only rare adventurers compared their landschaften with others very different. Wilderness dangers of this world and the other forestalled would-be explorers.

In the folk imagination a landschaft nurtures and reinforces character. Folktales detailing the wilderness adventures of landschaft inhabitants stress that the adventurers discover good or evil according to their natures. Helpful, obedient, self-sacrificing children, those who have internalized the group values that ensure landschaft order, discover piles of silver, magic herbs, or other treasure after triumphing over witches and dwarfs, and return home wiser and richer. Selfish, misbehaved children and beautiful but self-centered maidens—the figures of most folktales concerning wilderness catastrophe—find ashes, dragons, and sex fiends and are punished or destroyed, or else converted by the evildoers of the wild.[27] Implicit in most tales is a clear understanding of the role of landschaft space and social order in moulding the character of every landschaft resident. Only the inhabitants most committed to corporate values proved strong enough to desert shaped land for wilderness, and then only for a day or two. Others did best to stay home.

Sometimes, of course, chaos intruded upon order. Any field left untilled grew up at once in weeds and brush, and wolves and wild boars foraged among sheepfolds and fields, occasionally slaying a husbandman trudging homeward after dusk. But it was the human evil of the forest and mountain that people feared too, eldritch hermits who honored goety, rape, and theft and who snatched children for unspeakable purposes. Gypsies with lurchers, crazed magicians, and countless vagabonds, especially those organized in bands, terrorized the whole of rural Europe. Bandits like the infamous Hulin, who roamed with his followers from Normandy to Franche Comte late in the eighteenth century, were the last in a long line of forest lurkers who delighted in surprise attacks launched from mysterious hideouts. Respectable people bolted their doors and windows at nightfall and prayed for deliverance from the supranatural creatures and human criminals they linked with impenetrable thickets, twilit ravines, and bewilderment.[28] Darkness was like forest gloom. It concealed and emboldened the sinister roamers who made landschaft life a torment of expectancy.

Peasants hesitated before chasing roving cattle or investigating eerie noises beyond the farthest fields. They feared the bewilderment that began with simple spatial disorientation and climaxed in spiritual death, but they feared encounters with wild folk too. Wild folk were popularly believed to be long-bewildered humans or manlike beasts; peasants cared little for distinctions. The descriptions recorded by clerics and other examiners suggest now that many wild folk were mentally retarded castoffs forced to subsist by hunting and robbing, sometimes in company but most often alone, or else were criminals exiled from landschaften. In an age without asylums and with few prisons, such unfortunates wandered freely in the wilderness. In the mountains of Central Europe and Wales they were particularly numerous and especially feared, but everywhere pious people thought them possessed or confused them with ogres and child-devouring ghouls or credited them with diabolical powers. Female wild folk counterfeited voluptuous maidens and entangled plowmen in erotic sin; males felled trees at will or led the Wild Hunt.[29] Shakespeare's Caliban is perhaps the most famous wild man in early modern literature, but there are many others, Spenser's Sir

Satyrane, for example, and Milton's Comus. The wild folk of drama and poetry are descended from the wild folk whom peasants knew and feared as Satan's bastards or victims of bewilderment beyond the land-schaft fringe.

Until well into the seventeenth century, peasants peered at the wilderness through the prism of bewilderment and chaos. Every sort of experience beyond the farthest field was distorted by the certainties attendant upon losing one's way. Huntsmen and woodcutters who understood devious paths and trackless reaches of forest were never entirely trusted by their stay-at-home neighbors. No one knew when a woodcutter or charcoal burner might suddenly succumb to the temptations successfully resisted for years. In the landschaft of folktale such half-trusted characters live not in the dwelling cluster inhabited by husbandmen but at the edge of the landschaft, at the interface of field and wilderness. Their solitary huts, like the isolated windmill or water mill, stood in the shadowy interface of landschaft and wilderness chaos.

A typical landschaft consequently objectified order not only in its intricate arrangement of dwellings and fields and mills and pastures but in its juxtaposition with chaos. Wild folk only sharpened the peasant view of landschaft as comfortable order, and until the blossoming of *strassen-romantik* ("the romance of the road") personified the uncertainties beyond the edge.

ROADS

Princes and kings intent on consolidating their rule by unifying their realms shattered the old integrity of landschaft space and social order. From the fifteenth century onward, at first hesitantly and then decisively, they made forests and other wastes safe for travel. Pacification through road-building proceeded unevenly, but by the close of sixteenth century rural people sensed new possibilities for adventure and profit. The concern for good roads—and overseas exploration—developed as slowly as political unity and long-distance overland commerce, but eventually it modified the popular distrust of the wilderness. Sixteenth-century Europeans saw the road not as good or evil but as enticingly mysterious.[30] Their fascination with it found expression in strassen-romantik, in ballads about the joys of wandering, and most importantly, in wandering itself, for the roads that passed from landschaft into wilderness promised excitement and fortune. Folktale after folktale begins with a plowman or craftsman accosted by a traveler on the highway and lured into adventure.

Unlike the path between fields, garden plots, or dwellings, which belonged to its abutters and was limited in use, the highway belonged to wayfarers and to the king. It clearly expressed an authority greater than that of landschaft householders, for it promised protection from wilderness danger. Highway robbery was infinitely more than theft by violence—it affronted and mocked royal power and disrupted the new order of the road. By any name, *camino real, Reichstrasse,* and *route royale,* the king's highway was a new sort of space. Each landschaft on the long-distance road was commanded to maintain its share of roadbed in order that armies, couriers, and traders might not be delayed. Along the highway flowed wealth greater than that of any landschaft, and self-sufficiency vanished as cities and large towns drained surrounding regions of talent and produce and flooded landschaften with fashionable goods. Local values too contested with those of the highway; the peddler prized an honesty unthinkable to the husbandman. Economic and social conflict grew as roads became safer and smoother, and as carts, wagons, and finally coaches replaced packhorses. No longer was a stranger a distrusted oddity to be cautiously welcomed or warned away from a landschaft but an expected figure in—but not of—any landschaft intersected by a long-distance road.

Highways seemed to most peasants to be half-landschaft and half-wilderness. On the one hand they existed by royal decrees and received intermittent maintenance; quite clearly they expressed intention. On the other, they supported what most European husbandmen called "the traveling folk," a shadowy host of people without place. Wild folk, of course, had no specific place on earth—only the vague run of the wilderness. But road people confined themselves, at least most of the time, to the road and moved about with little apparent reason. By the seventeenth century they included swarms of traveling entertainers (some organized in bands large enough to be termed circuses) dragging with them exotic animals and more exotic customs. As of old there were pilgrims, of course, and wandering clerics, and traveling scholars too, the last spreading the new significance of printed literature. Discharged soldiers roamed the roads, seeking employment and adventure and now and then descending on a landschaft to loot and kill. Beggars and exiled peasants and refugees from growing religious persecution stumbled along the roads and mixed freely among the merchants, traveling apprentices, royal couriers, tax collectors, armies, and those grown weary of landschaft order.[31]

Although professional itinerants often claimed residence in some city or town along the road they usually had only the road as home. Theirs was a new view of the countryside, for they saw only what was visible from the road and they used only what was immediately accessible from it. Increasingly the roadside adapted to their needs. First came inns, and stables for pack animals; then corrals for driven herds; then bridges for wagons freighted with precious ores and with smelted metals; then toll gates to tax the growing traffic. Eventually directional signs and mileposts made asking directions unnecessary even after dark, and great rows of trees to shade marching armies lined the shoulders. It was at this time that *vill*, the French and English synonym for *landschaft*, was replaced by *village*, a new word emphasizing the cluster of structures at the center of the landschaft.[32] Travelers cared for good inns, blacksmith shops, and other structures in which they had business, not for fields and meadows and pastures.

The wayfarer was, for the sedentary inhabitants of the landschaft, personified other, that against which they evaluated themselves. In the days when roads were so few and so dangerous that traveling was almost unknown, adolescents had only their parents and adult neighbors as models. The absence of different values and exotic behavior made internalization of landschaft values fairly simple, and only when travelers provided new standards to any youth astute enough to linger about the inn or stableyard after nightfall did socialization break down. Travelers were anonymous, without past and without place, and their larger experience was approached with a mixture of distrust and deference by adults and adolescents alike. The road introduced a marked change in personal relationships, one almost identical to the essence of urban life. Strangers met knowing they might not meet again, judged one another as types according to dress and occupation, and talked of things that mattered only to themselves. It was a rare carter who was deeply interested in the state of the crops, and a rarer husbandman who cared about the unsafe bridge thirty miles to the east, but traveler and native alike were interested in conversation, the traveler to pass his evening and the native to learn something of the broader world. However well liked and trusted the traveler, people forever suspected him as foreign. For all that the traveler's linear space lay in the landschaft, it smacked too much of wilderness-like disorder.

The wider world beyond the turn in the highway, beyond the farthest field and the wilderness edge—if the wilderness had not been cleared to provide additional arable or grazing land—made its presence felt in every landschaft. Old landholding customs disintegrated in the face of market agriculture, as elders subdivided common fields and sold lots to husbandmen who fenced in their land and often moved their families away from the dwelling clusters onto free-standing farms.[33] Market agriculture rewarded specialization and innovation in ways unknown to earlier generations of husbandmen, and countless changes in field size and crops testified to the overpowering urge to discard old ways. Industrious sons, deprived of any chance to practice any agriculture at all due to a growing shortage of land, left landschaften for new occupations in artifice, or on the highway, or in the burgeoning cities.

At the beginning of the sixteenth century only four European cities boasted populations of more than 100,000 people. Most so-called cities seemed villages when travelers compared them to Istanbul, Naples, Venice, and Paris; their tiny forms remained dominated by adjoining agricultural land or by ocean wilderness. Behind most houses extended some sort of garden space, and many householders enjoyed vegetables and fruit in season from their own plants. Only the rare late medieval mercantile town or city extended more than half a mile from its center, the church or cathedral that marked its ecclesiastical focus and the roland that pinpointed its civil axis mundi, but within the perimeter defined by new, often artillery-resistant walls pulsed a life almost invariably attractive to travelers from landschaften. Markets presented crafts beyond the imagination of plowmen, and religious festivals prompted great processions and week-long entertainments, all encapsulated in space seemingly free of natural forms and restraints. The narrow, twisting streets and alleys, or the rectilinear avenues newly laid out in expanding cities, nurtured few trees and fewer shrubs.[34] Man-made form, not natural vegetation, ruled urban space, even though city dwellers lived closely attached to the landschaften a few miles beyond their gates. Indeed no plants belonged in urban space. Curses like "May grass grow in your streets!" took their power from the terrible image of a deserted city, its streets regained by the wilderness.[35] Urban form—cityscape—attracted people away from landscape, although urbanites eventually hungered for the land of tradition they left behind.

Landscape

It was at this time, in the last years of the sixteenth century, that *landscape* entered the English language, imported from Holland along with Dutch scenery, or *landschap*, painting. By *landschap*, of course, the Dutch understood the traditional territorial *landschaft*, the houses surrounded by common fields and encircled by wildernesses of ocean or swamps. The English garbled the meaning, however, and *landschap* entered the language as *landskip* and meant at first only the Dutch paintings. Within two decades it was spelled as it now is, but it had acquired a far more complicated definition. By 1630 *landscape* denoted large-scale rural vistas, chiefly hilltop views of woods, villages, fields, and roads, dominated by the colors of vegetation and good soil—green and brown. It meant also large-scale ornamental gardens objectifying ideals of beauty and denoted still paintings of rural vistas. The English seemed fascinated with the new word and used it familiarly and loosely, to the confusion of dictionary compilers.[36] Quite evidently, the word captured in two syllables something most important.

Certainly the connotations of *landscape* were pleasing to an England caught in an age of change. The word invoked neat hedgerows, small ponds and copses, and cows grazing lazily near thatched farmhouses. It recalled a past age thought golden by people bound up in technological innovation, religious ferment, and overseas adventure. While *landscape* connoted agricultural stability, it connoted too the small, agriculture-dominated enterprises of artifice evident in but hardly intrusive in the countryside. Ironworks, mines, water mills, and other enterprises that disconcerted traditionalists seemed much less threatening in a large context of agricultural space. Even the city of London seemed manageable when viewed from afar, across an agricultural foreground. *Landscape* identified beloved, traditional space from which more sinister forms seemed less fearsome.

Highways and dramatic urban growth sharpened perceptions of space, and sensitive observers throughout the seventeenth century set off to discover landscape. Most of the great painters of the sixteenth and seventeenth centuries traveled either through their own countries or through others, particularly across Italy, and writers of topographical description, a genre that became more popular as explorers brought back tales of new places beyond the seas, wandered too. Many chose to closely describe every place in their home region by compiling vast "itineraries" or "perambulations" of counties, districts, and even kingdoms. In comparing one landscape with another they passed judgment on the aesthetic and functional worth of each. Implicit in their evaluations is a traditional, strongly agricultural bias: beautiful, useful landscapes are those made and maintained by husbandmen. Land shaped by artifice they ignored or condemned as ugly. Their topophilic aesthetics survived the Atlantic crossing, endured, and prosper today. They loved, and many Americans still love, landscape: space shaped for agriculture and gently punctuated by artifice and roads.

Of course, wilderness endured to bias men's judgments. Well into the nineteenth century, great expanses of wilderness interrupted eastern American landscape. Edmund Ruffin, along with many other southerners, worried about the gigantic quagmire that stretched some forty miles from Virginia into North Carolina. In 1837 Dismal Swamp remained as treacherous and unexplored as William Byrd found it more than a century before, when his boundary surveyors blundered about it for days. Ruffin discovered to his horror that the impenetrable swamp had become the last resort of great bears, wild cats, and wolves, all of which—along with fugitive slaves—now and then rampaged through the contiguous landscape before retreating to the shelter of the tree-covered mire. Along with Byrd, Ruffin proposed that the swamp be drained and made into agricultural land—shaped into landscape.[37]

Wilderness took other, more horrifying forms, even in the regions most shaped by people. Earthquakes tormented New Englanders throughout the seventeenth and eighteenth centuries, the one of 1727 prompting one clergymen to write two books describing the fragility of man-shaped spaces and structures. "In one ward of the city," wrote Cotton Mather of the 1726 earthquake that destroyed much of Palermo in Sicily, "a whole street gaped at once with a hideous and horrid noise; and from the chasm there issued out flames, which were mixed with calcined stones, and a torrent of burning brimstone, whereby in less than half an hour, the whole ward was consumed." Earthquakes like the 1692 shock that destroyed Port Royal in Jamaica and the one in 1755 that flattened the city of Lisbon in Portugal and muddied springs and wells across most of western Europe—and roiled the waters of Lake Ontario too, according to information subsequently gathered from trappers— reminded North American colonists that wilderness existed in the heart of towns. The great Missouri Territory earthquake of 1812, however, made the New England tremors unimportant and made the peace of shaped land infinitely sweeter. A series of gigantic convulsions toppled log houses, created lakes twenty miles long, split trees, buried prairies with several feet of water-carried sand, and showered farms with rocks and debris blasted up from the earth. Not many people died in the scantily populated frontier area, but the loss in agricultural land, houses, and livestock ruined the lives of many settlers. While the fear of being thrown "down quick into the pit" caused the previously impious settlers to turn from sinful ways, it caused too a pronounced migration from the region.[38] No traveler stared into the abysslike crevices marking the former site of Little Prairie without thinking of the wilderness temporarily quiet beneath the waving grass.

Subterranean wildness convinced Americans that Satan lurked just beneath farms and houses, and places of frequent tremors acquired fearsome reputations. In Connecticut, for example, the otherwise peaceful town of East Haddam suffered such frequent and powerful earthquakes throughout the eighteenth century that wise inhabitants recalled that the Indian name of the region, *Machemoodus,* meant "place of noises." The town clergyman remarked in 1729 that East Haddam was "a place where the Indians drove a prodigious trade at worshiping the devil" and remembered that years before, an aged Indian explained the tremors and eerie noises by saying that "the Indians' god was very angry because the Englishmen's God was come here." While the Puritan cleric wondered about "fire or air distressed in the subterraneous caverns of the earth," he remained suspicious of diabolical presences, and his suspicions endured well into the nineteenth century.[39] No matter how carefully the East Haddam townsfolk built their houses and shaped their stone walls, the intermittent convulsions toppled chimneys and opened fissures into the earth. The "moodus noises" awakening them at night and the convulsions heaving them from bed warned all Americans of the enduring potential of wilderness.

And always the ocean made people appreciate landscape. Sea serpents worried New England colonists, especially those unlucky enough to encounter them squirming off Cape Cod and other supposedly civilized places, and they frightened nineteenth-century fishermen too. Melville's *Moby-Dick* epitomizes the mid-nineteenth-century fascination with deep-sea creatures and with the idea of ocean as chaotic, mysterious wilderness. But even Melville wondered about creatures larger than the white sperm whale, and in 1851 confided to Hawthorne that "leviathan is not the biggest fish—I have heard of Krakens." Certainly something, giant squid or otherwise, lurked beneath the ocean surface and symbolized whatever submerged terrors tormented Melville and his contemporaries. For all his love of "nature," Thoreau distrusted the ocean lapping at Cape Cod beaches, noted that no one laughed when the lighthouse-keeper told of sharks, and marveled at the force half-hidden in the waves. "Serpents, bears, hyenas, tigers, rapidly vanish as civilization advances," he wrote after visiting the shore and the bodies cast up after a shipwreck, "but the most populous and civilized city cannot scare a shark far from its wharves." Thoreau described the ocean wilderness that almost drowned him in Plymouth Harbor as chaos itself.[40] As did Melville and others, Thoreau scorned the landscape-destroying monster of industrial urbanism, but he hated equally real wilderness—wilderness unlike the woodlots of safe, peaceful Concord.[41]

Until the middle of the nineteenth century, seekers of landscape moved on foot or horseback. Scarcely any difference in spatial perception separates Daniel Defoe's *A Tour through the Whole Island of Great Britain* of 1724 from William Cobbett's *Rural Rides* of 1830, or Timothy

Dwight's *Travels in New England and New York* of 1821 from Frederick Law Olmsted's *A Journey in the Back Country* of 1860. Dwight's experiences are typical. He paused to inquire into crops and wildflowers, to examine soils and ferries, to discover local history each evening at an inn, and to question farmers about their land. He gazed from hilltops on the landscape below, criticized houses and street arrangements, and now and then marveled at industrial enterprises nestled in ravines and crowding waterfalls. He enjoyed moments of "profound contemplation and playfulness of mind" only when gazing at landscape, at traditional rural space. For Dwight, horseback travel was a succession of minor discoveries and observations, of deciphering vague maps and vaguer directions, of stopping again and again to examine a barn or a run-down farm or any other constituent of landscape. His four-volume book chronicles self-paced searching after details and wholes, a searching that in 1860 Olmsted found conveniently only in the back-country South, away from railroads. Self-paced travel, what Thoreau called "walking" in an essay aimed at encouraging people to do it, vanished in the 1840s in Europe and in the eastern United States with the coming of the railroads and the popularization of railroad observation.[42]

Railroads epitomized the new industrial age that came to fruition only after the Civil War. Mines and factories grew larger and larger by the decade but in the 1840s dominated few rural regions. But expansion quickened with the coming of corporation-owned manufacturing towns such as Lowell in Massachusetts, with the dramatic growth of urban population that fueled industrial and commercial development, and— most importantly—with the perfecting of steam power. No longer did entrepreneurs locate mills and factories only near waterfalls; suddenly such structures, along with railroad trains, appeared almost everywhere, and the shriek of steam whistles floated over coastal towns and western farms along with black, acrid smoke. Had Americans not confronted other change, the new power of industry might have seemed less threatening. But suddenly new difficulties appeared. In the west, pioneers learned that the great forest ended somewhere in Illinois and that entire agricultural techniques were almost worthless on the prairie and plains. In the East, farmers no longer processed most of their harvest but shipped it on trains to urban manufacturing centers. Everywhere the family gave up some fraction of its importance to well-established schools and churches and social institutions. Abolition and talk of dis-union and rebellion frayed everyone's nerves. In 1845 Americans glanced backward, recalling the traditional space of the preindustrial age with satisfaction and half-consciously ordering the spatial aesthetics of the future.

What they remembered or thought they remembered blossomed in the prose, poetry, and painting of the American Renaissance, the creation of Emerson, Hawthorne, Kennedy, Thoreau, Melville, Bancroft, Prescott, Parkman, Fitz Hugh Lane, Martin Johnson Heade, and others. What had been—the land shaped between 1580 and 1845 in accordance with local, then regional, and finally national understanding of vernacular tradition—informs their work, making it "romantic" in both setting and tone. But the land as it was shaped cannot be discovered in artistry alone, because every artist interprets what he or she sees, adding and deleting details and juxtapositions according to personal whim or literary prototype. In order to discover the shapes of the past, one must read the shapes of the present as one reads a palimpsest, looking for details perhaps overshadowed by newer building and then ascertaining their evolution and contemporaneous meaning.

What vestiges are selected for examination here? Almost all are *common,* the creation of common people shaping and building according to orally transmitted or example-transmitted tradition. Only a few are the creation of professional designers; the building of monuments has been recounted frequently although such monuments were—and are—rare anywhere within the current bounds of the United States east of the Mississippi and south of the Arkansas, the area shaped between 1580 and 1845. Almost none are urban, partly because cities have received much careful attention of late, partly because cityscape is not landscape, but chiefly because the vast amount of American space shaped between 1580 and 1845 was not urban—and is still not urban. The vestiges examined in this book constitute a theory of landscape, a theory in the sense of *theoria,* the ancient Greek word meaning a spectacle, something seen. Taken together, they are landscape. Mixed with subsequent forms and spaces, they are the contemporary confusion called "the man-made environment."

PLANTING

*And yet, as soundly and contentedly as I had slept,
the sun itself had scarce got up before me, so
earnestly did I desire to take a view of the New
England shore, which now appeared as plain as
could be to us; and though it was a sight so much
desired, it looked to me with but a poor appearance:
a mighty wilderness of trees it looked like; and here
and there a little spot of clearer ground, that looked
like a plantation; and such the mariners informed
me that they were.* [1]

John Dunton
1686

Casa-corral with *torreón*, Cienega, New Mexico. (JRS)

obinson Crusoe colonized Desolation Island with a minimum of fuss and bother. After a lengthy sea journey he landed half-exhausted in a wilderness and, after a brief reconnaissance, selected a site for habitation. He discovered a healthful spot near fresh water, shade, and the sea, one offering "security from ravenous creatures, whether man or beast." His first dwelling was only a crude hut fenced about with a secure palisade, but soon he began to build more expertly and to shape the land on a grander scale. He captured goats, built a corral for them, and eventually fenced in a pasture. With the greatest care he rescued a few grains of barley and rice and after four years of hard labor looked with pride on well-fenced, well-tended arable fields and a full granary. He cultivated wild tobacco too, and grapes and melons, and learned to enjoy limes and lemons from his orchard. Soon he built a mill to grind his grain, and clay pots to preserve his flour and raisins. Within five years he was no longer a castaway but a planter, living comfortably on his own land, investigating the possibilities of slavery and practicing his religion freely. With his umbrella and dog, Crusoe walked about a miniature but very traditional landschaft.

The Life and Strange Surprizing Adventures of Robinson Crusoe is Daniel Defoe's chronicle of New World colonization.[2] By 1719 the permanence of Spanish and English settlements in North America was assured, and even stay-at-home Europeans understood the colonies as increasingly self-reliant. Agriculture made the colonies strong and prosperous. The farmer, announced Emerson in 1849, "changes the face of the landscape. Put him on a new planet and he would know where to begin."[3] Concord proved the statement true. At mid-nineteenth century Emerson looked around him at farms shaped from the wilderness—what Emerson called landscape—eight generations before by the husbandmen who planted Concord. Until the husbandmen arrived, the outposts of Spain and England were only temporary forts or fishing bases totally dependent on European supplies. Once the husbandmen felled or girdled the trees and opened the soil for sowing, however, the outposts took on a wholly new identity. In the language of the day they became plantations, and as Emerson noted, they prospered mightily because husbandmen, like Robinson Crusoe, knew where to begin and what to do next.

Most of the settlements of northern New Spain, the Tidewater South, and New England were agricultural from the beginning because their founders intended them to be permanent. Some the colonists carefully modeled after the traditional territorial landschaft of the Old World, and for many decades they feared the new roadless wilderness. Now and then, however, they devised novel arrangements of space. Their field patterns, dwelling arrangements, and structure types are as revealing of New World adaptations as they are of a remembered Old World order, but in the final analysis the first shaping of New World wilderness was distinctly agricultural, the work of husbandmen who knew with Robinson Crusoe that no settlement would survive if it could not feed itself.

CHIMAYO

North of Santa Fe, in the Santa Cruz Valley of the Sangre de Cristo Mountains, are several villages established at the close of the seventeenth century by viceroys determined to protect the larger mission town against surprise attack. Santa Fe, Albuquerque, and the great cities of California have all grown far beyond their original Spanish form, but Cundiyo, Truchas, Santa Cruz, Pojoaque, and especially Chimayo are little changed from the plantations they once were. Chimayo, in fact, seems at first a dilapidated illusion. It is the nation's last walled village and is still surrounded by small, irrigated fields.

It is a creature of *The Laws of the Indies,* a code that appeared in 1573, just as the *conquistadores* pushed north from Chihuahua into the Rio Grande country. New Spain was changing, and dream as they might of plunder and adventure beyond the Sierra Madre, men knew that the days of glory were gone. Everywhere disease had decimated the Indian population, and the *encomendero* class, deprived of its labor force, declined in size and influence. The lesser nobility was still powerful, but it too directed its attention away from mining and fortune hunting to smaller farming and ranching enterprises. The age of conquest passed and the age of consolidation began.[4] In the north, in the region vaguely known as San Felipe, Nueva Andalusia, or Nuevo Mexico, men discovered little adventure and even less gold. Warm, fertile soil, not loot, attracted the husbandmen who followed the explorers.

A newer attitude toward space found expression in *The Laws,* particularly in a chapter entitled "Royal Ordinances for the Laying Out of New Cities, Towns, or Villages." Seventy years of colonization experience and a wealth of old-country memories united in thirty-eight articles carefully describing the ideal settlement form. Perfection was a grid of streets crossing at right angles and arranged around a rectangular central plaza of about five-and-one-half acres. Set off at one end by a church and other ecclesiastical buildings and at the other end by such government structures as a town-council house, an arsenal, and a customhouse, the plaza was bordered by arcaded shops and houses, all uniformly built "for the sake of the beauty of the town" but arranged too as a "defense or fortress against those who might attempt to create disturbances or occupy" the place. Beyond the houses were the common pastures and woodlots, and the privately owned—not commonly held—fields assigned to each family. And beyond the cultivated land lay the dusty, disordered home of rattlesnakes and Indians, the wilderness called in Spanish *confusión*.

Amid the details, however, careful *estensión*-makers discerned omissions. The royal planners scarcely mentioned irrigation networks, common woodlots, and long-distance roads and all difficulties presented by future growth, particularly the disruption of agriculture as arable land is converted to houselots and other uses. Of course, *The Laws of the Indies* is only a compilation of 6,500 laws deemed most useful in the daily life of New Spain, and it warns its readers to recall laws not included and to follow the general statutes of Castile when the selection is silent or vague.[5] The planning ordinances are only an outline then, an attempt to codify the essential elements of a plantation. For most officials north of Chihuahua, the thirty-eight articles proved sufficiently detailed for all occasions, including the founding of Santa Fe and Albuquerque—and of Chimayo. It was the plantation that was important, not the wilderness around it or the roads that linked it with others, and it was the plantation that the ordinances—and tradition—concerned.

The ordinances endured because their eunomic presupposition was second nature to the settlers of New Spain. Many of the settlers, and especially the veterans of the wars against the Moors, Dutch, and Indians, accepted the military hierarchy of rank and the corollary assignment of privilege and booty. In the New World, however, even the lowliest infantryman determined that Indians, whatever their legal status as children of God, stood far beneath him, and vernacular Spanish quickly reflected his decision. At home the word *peon* meant a foot soldier far inferior in rank to a cavalryman, but in New Spain it soon applied only to Indian laborers.[6] Every soldier hoped to be a cavalryman, and the pressure of conquest helped promote many to that prestigious rank. When the time came to reward veterans with land grants, however, viceroys discovered that all enlisted men claimed mounted status, and with few exceptions officialdom gratified the masqueraders. Hierarchy—and eunomy—still ruled, but almost every adventurer rose one link on the chain of being.

Viceroys assigned land according to rank, allotting the *peonia* of 20 acres only to Indians, many of whom were already familiar with individually owned fields before the Spanish conquest. Most soldiers and civilian settlers received a *caballeria* of 106 acres in addition to their 1-acre village houselot, or *solare*. Officers were granted *estancias*, whose size depended on the livestock chosen by the grantee; a cattle *estancia* totaled 2,200 acres, while a sheep estancia incorporated 4,700 because sheep crop grass more closely. The nobility owned *haciendas*, estates comprised of estancias, *caballerias*, and *peonias*, and until the plagues of the mid-sixteenth century, usually worked such agglomerations with Indian serfs supervised by Spanish overseers.

Originally *hacienda* meant only property—a man might have a hacienda of wine, for example, or of mules—but the importance of landowning in New Spain skewed the connotation until the word defined only space. In the north of Mexico, where slight rainfall meant that every sheep or steer needed acres for grazing, haciendas were eventually measured in hundreds of square miles, although the lesser nobility contented itself with more manageable *ranchos* worked with far fewer laborers. Indeed social harmony seemed so dependent on accurate lot size and nomenclature that in 1567 the Viceroy Marques de Falces defined standards of measurement and codified the area of each type of holding.[7] If social hierarchy was to endure, the countryside had to reflect and reinforce it, and gradually trespassers and scofflaws surrendered acreage acquired by squatting, vague surveys, and fraud. Like the town-planning ordinances six years later, the viceroy's edicts are not completely detailed, but they indicate beyond doubt that everyone increasingly valued landownership as the prime indicator of social status and the chief support of economic rank.

The estensión was the key element in the countryside of northern New Spain. Haciendas and ranchos were far less common away from the pacified south, and in Coahuila, Chihuahua, and more northern provinces, the estensión, or traditional *landschaft* of clustered houses surrounded by common and privately owned fields, endured partly as a defensive military arrangement; the ordinances prescribe a palisade or ditch about newly erected houses. But even where the Indians were not a menace, the estensión proved the only solution to almost insurmountable problems of group resource allocation. Building timber, for example, was scarce, and the *monte*, or common woodland, was closely monitored so that every householder had enough wood for framing, roofing, and fencing. Like the monte, the *pastos comunes*, or common pasture, was strictly regulated too, so that during droughts all livestock might survive. The *estensión,* or *pueblo,* was more than houses and fields; it was an institution with recognized judicial and administrative powers that controlled common resources for the good of its members.[8]

Irrigation was the great test of its authority. Many settlers in New Spain learned about windy, semiarid climates in the old country, in Andalucia and the district surrounding Valencia, where agriculture without irrigation is impossible. Long before the Moorish conquest of southern Spain, the inhabitants had worked out intricate arrangements of canals and water rights, but the Arabs brought with them a finer expertise. For seven centuries they improved the networks of dikes and codified the informal distribution agreements; after the defeat and expulsion of the Arabs in the late fifteenth century, the victorious Spaniards retained their revisions. Eunomy was the crux of Moorish water law. Each landowner received water in proportion to his acreage although each awaited his turn, or *dula.* In a wet year there was enough water for all the gates to be open at once, but during a drought a man might receive his two- or four-hours' flow once every five days, perhaps beginning at midnight, perhaps at midday. Moorish words ordered the Spanish irrigation vocabulary; *acequia* ("irrigation ditch") was especially enduring, and in New Spain north of Chihuahua it and *dula* took on heightened meaning.

The Pueblo Indians produced corn, beans, squash, and cotton in quantities that so awed the Apaches and Navajos that eventually their tales of golden cities reached south, where the Spanish misinterpreted the significance of the golden grain. Indian agriculture depended on a coincidence of factors: early thaws, late frosts, the careful choice of seed, and, above all, adequate rainfall—so important that supplications for it preceded every sowing. Many Indians practiced *arroyo* flood-farming, hoping that spring rains would soak the gullies without the aid of ditches and dikes, and most worked some flat fields entirely dependent on rain. Late in the sixteenth century a prolonged drought made arroyo- and dry-farming impossible, and the Indians along the Rio Grande depended solely on irrigated fields.[9] The conquistadores, attracted by tales of wealth, understood the irrigation networks at once, and the settlers who followed sometimes incorporated them into their own systems. Across present-day New Mexico evolved a countryside of scattered estensiónes, each usually near an Indian settlement in accordance with the royal wish to provide pagans with Christian exemplars and each watered by an *acequia madre,* a mother ditch.

Prospective householders petitioned for membership in the estensión of their choice; the law required each applicant to own ten cows, four bulls, one mare, one brood sow, twenty ewes, six hens, and one rooster. Estensión elders evaluated each applicant's potential before turning him away or offering him a one-acre solare on which to build the house-outbuilding complex called a *casa-corral*, and an outlying *suerte*, either a *caballeria* or an *estancia*. Typical land grants were measured by the *huebra*, the amount of land plowed in one day by a husbandman and an ox team. The grants stipulated that each newcomer cultivate all or most of his land within one year, that after harvest he open it as common pasture, and that he allow only draft animals, not grazing livestock, on the arable part during the growing season in order to reduce the estensión need for fencing and the chance of crop damage. A suerte, therefore, was individually owned but collectively regulated, and possession of it endured only as long as the husbandman fulfilled his public obligations. If he let it lie fallow for four years it reverted to the community; if he absented himself from the estensión for more than three months without the councilmen's permission (and so neglected his responsibilities for fences, *acequias*, and the pastos comunes), he was automatically divested of all political privilege. To own a suerte was to accept responsibility for all *suertes*, and for all common land.[10] The estensión was not an assemblage of tiny autonomous fiefdoms but an intricate construct of simultaneously private and public spaces reflecting the privileges and responsibilities of community life. Householding conferred many privileges, from the life-giving dula to military security, but for every advantage there was a corresponding duty.

The Spanish of the Rio Grande brought with them a peculiar house type invented during the sixteenth century in central Mexico, where building timber was scarce and rainfall scant. *Adobe* derives from *atob*, the Arabic word for brick, but only a few Spanish houses were built of sun-dried mud bricks reinforced with straw. Instead, most were constructed of rough-hewn stone mortared and plastered with mud. Adobe and stone were available everywhere but presented difficulties in construction. Walls had to be extremely thick, and except in churches, arches were unknown; massive timber lintels capped windows and doors. Roof beams (*vigas*) were difficult to obtain away from the mountains, so house-building proceeded slowly, room by room. Each room was a complete unit, a sort of bay having its own door, window, and corner fireplace. Despite the explicit ordinance to the contrary, settlers chose to build asymmetrical, decidedly unstandardized houses, although most accepted a single-story height. Indian structures occasionally reached six and seven stories, but such massive projects proved too difficult for Spanish husbandmen. Still, however, the material and

method adapted perfectly to the northern New Spain climate and settlement process, although men found it necessary, of course, to periodically replaster the walls and roof lest the adobe bricks and mortar be
exposed and destroyed by infrequent rains—but the superb insulating
qualities of the walls offset the inconvenience. In summer the dark interiors remained cool, and in winter the great walls retained solar and
fireplace heat long into the night. As families grew, they added rooms at
slight expense and learned that the house type adapted to changes in
domestic industry too.[11] A house, the symbol of estensión membership
and responsibility, was in reach of most settlers almost immediately and
reflected every twist of its inhabitants' fortunes.

Despite its location in a cluster, the Spanish house was a private place.
In time many rooms reached around the solare, enclosing in a hollow
square a sort of patio that impressed non-Spanish visitors in later centuries. "Most of the apartments," remarked Josiah Gregg in 1848, "except the winter rooms, open into the patio; but the latter are most frequently entered through the sala, or hall, which, added to the thickness
of their walls and roofs, renders them delightfully warm during the cold
season, while they are perfectly cool and agreeable in summer."[12] Yankees were impressed too with the social climate of such houses, for behind the three-foot-thick walls or in the patio or yard, the Spanish
householder was hidden from the gaze of neighbors in a retreat of
private darkness where there was rest from public labor and responsibility.

Everywhere across northern New Spain the balance of public life and
private happiness, of estensión and house, implicit in the royal ordinances took form in the countryside. The ordinances were obeyed, not
always to the letter but in spirit at least, especially in the founding of
places intended to grow into cities. In 1706, one and one-half centuries
after the compilation appeared, Don Francisco Cuerba y Valdez certified
to the king of Spain and the viceroy of Mexico that he "founded a villa
on the margin and meadows of the Rio del Norte in a goodly place of
fields, water, pasturage, and timber . . . keeping in mind what is prescribed by His Majesty in his Royal Laws of the Recopilación, Book III,
Title VII." Don Francisco was pleased; thirty-five families had settled,
the church building was completed, "capacious and appropriate, with
part of the dwelling for the Religious Minister, the Royal Houses begun,
and the other houses of the settlers finished with their corrals, acequias
ditched and running, fields sowed—all well arranged and without any
expense to the Royal Treasury."[13]

Almost a century before, La Villa Real de la Santa Fe de San Francisco,
the Royal City of the Holy Faith of Saint Francis, was founded according

to the same ordinances only ninety miles north of Don Francisco's site. Santa Fe was planned with the additional help of another viceroy, who supplemented the ordinances by ordering that the councilmen of the new town "mark out for each resident two lots for house and garden and two *suertes* for vegetable gardens and two more for vineyards and for an olive grove, and four *caballerias* of land, and for the irrigation thereof the necessary water, obliging him to live thereon ten years continuously without absenting himself." The allotments were generous, but the residence requirement was stiff; Santa Fe was not for speculators or drifting adventurers but for husbandmen. Had it not been for the Indian revolt of 1680 the city might have retained its early symmetrical design, but the rebellion and eighteen-year desertion by the Spanish destroyed its original pattern. When the Spanish returned in force they resettled the town and established a network of estensiónes high in the Sangre de Cristo Mountains north of it. As with Santa Fe, they carefully sited and planned the mountain estensiónes, intending them to endure.

Chimayo is a perfect, if diminutive, example of the Spanish estensión. Before the Indian revolt, the Santa Cruz Valley was dotted with small ranchos and haciendas dependent on Indian labor and ordered about lonely, fortress-like compounds, some equipped with *torreónes*, high watchtowers with slitted windows. When families resettled the valley, they abandoned the ranchos and haciendas in favor of small landschaften laid out around rectangular plazas. The houses of Chimayo abut one another and in the seventeenth century had no windows or doors on their outside walls; from a distance the dwelling cluster appeared as a solid wall of adobe broken only by two portals. Chimayo measured roughly 420 by 330 feet and consisted of some forty houses, one or two stores, and a church, all facing a small plaza planted with trees, partially fenced off as a livestock corral, and crossed by an acequia. Beyond the rectangle of houses lay the suertes and common fields, all abutting the Rio Santa Cruz or an acequia.[14] Chimayo was a tiny expression of royal will and community purpose, its social and economic order manifest to any observer energetic enough to climb one of the nearby hills and look down upon its form.

Places like Chimayo changed slowly, and then only because some husbandmen moved onto their suertes to avoid the long walk from houses to fields. The arrangement of acequias, however, limited such out-migration, and most landowners usually remained in the cluster. Elders arranged the suertes along small rivulets or acequias; each bordered the water and stretched back to higher and drier ground. The soil next to the water was wet enough for vegetable and grain growing, and several

The west wall of houses, Chimayo. (JRS)

hundred yards away it was still moist enough to use as meadow. But a few hundred yards farther on the soil was almost dry, useful only as grazing land and then only for a limited number of animals. When a father died his children divided the suerte in the only possible way, lengthwise from wet soil to dry, each taking a strip including the three sorts of ground. After three, and sometimes only two generations, men found that inheritance and marriage left them owning several such strips scattered about the estensión. It was more practical to reside in the house cluster, near the *pastos comunes* and *monte,* and walk to a different strip each day than to settle on one and be at the edge of things.[15] For such reasons, and also because the adobe and stone houses were impossible to move and difficult to quickly replace, families preferred the nucleated pattern.

Settlers invested boundaries with great significance, partly owing to the scarcity of irrigated fertile land but chiefly because social status remained inextricably linked to the land. Giving possession of land was a ceremony of almost religious significance. The estensión mayor took a new settler to his suerte, led him along its borders, and then plucked from the ground a lump of sod, drove a stick through it, and presented it to the newcomer. The custom called "turf-and-twig" did more than ensure that at least once the grantee perambulated his bounds; it symbolized grazing, planting, and lumbering rights, the rights that bestowed identity and responsibility on the owner. The borders of large holdings, estancias and haciendas, were often vague, and men sometimes spoke in terms of measurement not related to bounds; *fanega,* for example, simply defined an area needing two bushels of seed wheat for complete broadcast sowing.[16] But smaller lots were far more carefully defined, especially after the Viceroy de Falces, convinced that "the proper method and procedure have not been completely enunciated for locating, setting up the boundaries, measuring, and giving possession" of the thousands of small lots upon which the hierarchical society of New Spain depended, announced his codification of measures. Six years later the royal ordinances specified careful "measuring by cord and ruler, beginning with the main square from which streets are to run" as the first step in settling a place. From the plaza to the farthest caballeria elders carefully bounded and measured every holding because land alone bestowed right, status, and estensión duty.[17]

The carefully ordered and delineated arrangement of space that objectified and reinforced hierarchical society was sanctified in countless ways by the Catholic faith. The plaza, or *zocala,* served not only as the place for socializing and trade and as a refuge for livestock during Indian attack; it was also the outdoor focus of such religious rites as the blessing of livestock on Saint Anthony's Day and the blessing of seed on May 15. Fiestas made every inhabitant aware of the zocala's centrality; about it revolved all ecclesiastical activity outside the church building, and from it emanated all ecclesiastical and civil order. Municipal authority extended five leagues outward from the zocala at Santa Fe, for example, and within the circle of roughly seventy-nine square leagues the councilmen had jurisdiction over all criminal and civil cases not involving Indians, and within the circle too every landowner enjoyed the protection of Santa Fe's patron saint. Even today, the men of isolated Spanish villages in New Mexico carry the statue of their patron saint about the fields during drought. The estensión objectified the complex relation of temporal order strengthened by divine blessing, and remnants of that relation endure.

Away from the zocala, church buildings, and close-built houses, beyond the suertes at the end of the acequias, lay the wilderness, the *soledad,* the confusión. Every estensión north of the Rio Grande exemplified order because it contrasted with the sterile chaos of arid terrain. The confusión was a place of wandering, thirst, loneliness, and death. Only in the estensión, in his house and in the plaza, and among his fields and those of his neighbors, could a man feel secure and know his place. Conquistadores carried the Spanish flag to present-day Michigan, Montana, and even to Alaska, but only where Spanish husbandmen shaped the confusión did the empire prosper.

NEW ENGLAND

Santa Fe was twenty years established when the first Englishmen took up permanent residence more than 2,000 miles to the northeast. Like their Spanish enemies, the English colonists accepted the necessity for agricultural settlements, for plantations, without hesitation. Before the *Arabella* anchored off the Massachusetts coast, John Winthrop had already sketched the perfect town plan on a blank page in his sea journal. Too many Puritans arrived in the fleet for his walled, hilltop plantation to be immediately practical, but his sentiments were characteristic. In their haste to civilize New England the English devoted little time to recording their concepts of planting or shaping the wilderness. Most of the settlers shared common memories of old-country landschaften in decay, memories that moulded their dreams and plans for the confusion they discovered away from the beach.[18] What little they did write they wrote after the fact.

Not until 1635 did an anonymous New Englander create an equivalent of Spain's royal ordinances, and then only because he distrusted the towns evolving so quickly around him. "The Ordering of Towns" is far less detailed than its Spanish counterpart but its theme is identical. Its author proposes a plantation of six concentric zones set within a territory six miles square; the meetinghouse, "the center of the whole circumference," is the point about which the ideal plantation is ordered.[19] Around it is a zone of houses, "orderly placed to enjoy comfortable communion," and beyond is a ring of common fields, where everyone works for the common welfare. Livestock is owned in common too and pastured beyond the common planting ground in a third ring of improved land. From the meetinghouse to the outer edge of the livestock pastures is only one and one-half miles, but that is the limit of initial colonization; within the seven-square-mile circle occurs all the pioneering activity. Unless any "men of great estate" choose to settle on the 400-acre lots reserved for such desired newcomers, the focus of daily life in the first years is the meetinghouse and the land immediately around it. Only after the settlement's survival is assured will the common fields be divided and apportioned among the householders, and further freeholds established in a fourth or fifth ring, among or beyond the 400-acre lots. Since the land committee "will not lay out any farmhouse about the whole town to be above two miles distant from the meeting," the final area of habitation is only thirteen square miles, one-third the area granted to the settlers. The remaining two-thirds, "the swamps and rubbish waste grounds," are regularly used but never occupied. Within the encircling zone of forest and swamp the colonists discover their common identity and objectify it in shaped land.

"The Ordering of Towns" implies that shaped space controls society. Certainly the eunomic assignment of land reinforces social hierarchy. Land is divided "in such manner as every man may have his due proportion, more or less according to his present or apparent future occasion of employment, and so the mean ones not be neglected." The fifth-circle freeholds in particular, averaging from thirty to forty acres of forest, arable, and meadow, are visible confirmations of their owners' status. "God Almighty in his most holy and wise providence has so disposed of the condition of mankind," Winthrop had preached aboard the *Arabella* in 1630, "as in all times some must be rich, some poor, some high and eminent in power and dignity, others mean and in subjection."[20] The ideal spatial arrangement, according to the essayist, ought to mirror the divinely sanctioned social hierarchy. The *town*, as the landscape like configuration of clustered dwellings and encircling fields became known in New England parlance, is the essayist's epitome of order objectified.

That the essayist's town remained the ideal at least until 1654 is certain because in that year appeared Edward Johnson's *Wonder-Working Providence of Sion's Savior in New England*, a sort of topographical history of the colonization enterprise. Johnson was fascinated with discovering the shapes of Bay Colony towns, and some, he was gratified to learn, nearly attained the essayist's ideal. He found his own town of Woburn four miles square, and Lynn almost rectangular. Cambridge at its founding was "compact closely within itself," and Roxbury was "somewhat like a wedge double-pointed." But Johnson described a changing settlement pattern. In 1654 few towns remained nucleated about their meetinghouses, and the compact clusters of houses had either disintegrated or else never materialized in the first place. Some communities, like Andover, which fined "outlivers" twenty shillings for each month they lived in houses beyond the nucleus, found that men no longer honored the ideal of "neighborly living," and others watched families build houses with no regard to centrality or overall pattern. Dorchester defied description: "The form of this town is almost like a serpent turning her head to the northward, over against Thompson's Island and the Castle; her body and wings being chiefly built on, are filled somewhat thick with houses, only that one of her wings is clipped, her tail being of such a large extent that she can hardly draw it after her." Johnson found "nothing delightful to the eye in any place" in Watertown either, where rivulets and springs prompted a scattered building pattern, or in Hingham, whose form "somewhat intricate to describe, by reason of the sea's wasting creeks, where it beats upon a mouldering shore" upset him.[21] For him the physical shape and layout of a town objectified its social and ecclesiastical condition. The more regular a town's outline, fields, and houselots, the more beautiful and innocent it is.

For those towns lacking orderly natural or man-made outlines, Johnson struggled to imagine them, finding forms on the land as Hamlet finds them in clouds. His figurative outlines become more and more strained as he attempts to bound towns no longer or never ordered about a meetinghouse but extending haphazardly into forest. It is no accident that the towns which he cannot define in even the most fanciful similes, Watertown and Hingham, for example, are those which experienced the most severe ecclesiastical and civil unrest. Dissension almost invariably derived from or produced spatial disintegration, and Johnson knew it, along with many other New England commentators. "Society in all sorts of human affairs is better than solitariness," wrote John Cotton two years before *Wonder-Working Providence*.[22] For years Cotton had preached against those New Englanders wishing to live away from meetinghouses, neighbors, and communal duties. In 1642 he mimicked the cry of the land-hungry: "If we could have large elbow-room enough, and meadow enough, though we had no religious ordinances, we can then go and live like lambs in a large place." His were only the first sermons against outliving, as he and other clergymen termed it. Bemoaning that "Land! Land! has been the idol of many in New England," Increase Mather asserted thirty-four years later that men's spatial requirements had mushroomed. The original settlers, he claimed, contented themselves with one acre per individual and twenty per family, but after two generations, he asked, "How many men since coveted after the earth, that many hundreds, nay thousands of acres, have been engrossed by one man, and they that profess themselves Christians, have forsaken churches and ordinances, and for land and elbow-room enough in the world?"[23] The answer, of course, was many. Husbandmen did hanker after freeholds far larger than those assigned to the first settlers, and groups requested larger grants for towns. For all their exhortations, and for all their improved examples of massacres by King Philip's Indians in 1676, the seventeenth-century clergy failed to sustain the ideal of the small-scale, nucleated town that inspired the earliest settlers. Men wanted elbow room, not clustered houses and outlying common or private fields.

"The Ordering of Towns" is a retrospective essay. The Spanish ordinances are solidly grounded in the theories of Vitruvius and his Renaissance disciple, Leon Alberti of Florence, and in the realities of a New World environment of scant resources, severe climate, and prospective population growth. The New England document has no discernible classical sources, but it is even more deeply rooted in folk and common memory in the days before enclosure when agriculture was a community enterprise and surpluses were rare. Its author had in mind the English vill of the late sixteenth century and before, where husbandmen lived in a cluster of houses near a church and where each held several widely scattered strips in two or three common fields. It was the disruption of such landschaften that sent so many rural Englishmen to London or to America, and it is perhaps understandable that the essayist envisioned in New England an agricultural utopia of a by-gone golden age in which perfect religion might flourish alongside perfect husbandry.[24] Unlike the Spanish theorists, however, he gave very little attention to the New World experience of English colonists. His essay did not guide later colonists and describes the settlements created by only a few of the earliest.

During the first years of settlement in the Plymouth and Bay colonies, planting was a deliberate enterprise. A group of husbandmen selected several of its wisest members during the sea journey or immediately upon arrival, and the men (the "selectmen" of New England political tradition) received permission from colony authorities to seek out a suitable location for a plantation. While their compatriots remained in temporary quarters in Plymouth or Boston, the men wandered about looking for a healthful place with fertile soil, plentiful fresh water, good building timber, and most importantly, some natural meadow, usually fresh-water but sometimes salt-water marsh. They then returned to the coast, received a grant of the land from the colony general court, and led their colleagues and their families into the interior. There the selectmen, sometimes assisted by a clerk and sometimes by a committee designated for the purpose, planned the sites of houses, houselots, and planting fields. If the group came from that part of England where common-field husbandry endured in practice or memory, and most groups did, they often laid out common fields around the nucleus of houselots. They took pains to recruit a clergyman and erect a meetinghouse at the earliest opportunity, and set in motion all the intricate workings of common-field law.[25] Not everything was English, however, for all that determined settlers tried to make it so. The climate spurred immediate changes in livestock husbandry—sheep, cattle, and horses could not be left unhoused during the winter—and in planting techniques. All sorts of wild animals also interfered with old-country agriculture; wolves devoured livestock and smaller creatures destroyed field crops. And finally, the indigenous grasses proved wholly unsuitable for grazing and haying; most were annuals, grazing livestock prevented them from reseeding, and all were low in nutritional value. From the beginning, then, the New England town was neither wholly English nor wholly American. Its general form usually derived from old-country experience, but many of its constituent features, livestock sheds and barns, fences, and carefully tended meadows and pastures, represented hasty adjustments to a new place.[26]

Englishmen were successful husbandmen from the start. They cleared the land of trees and brush and planted most of the familiar English grains along with the corn they learned about from the Indians. The smallpox epidemic of 1617 had decimated the native population, and the settlers established many towns next to Indian fields abandoned for nearly two decades, almost immediately useful as pasture and meadow, and, with only a little effort, as arable land planted to American crops like corn, pumpkins, and beans. The husbandmen eventually surmounted the problems posed by the poor native grasses too by importing seed from home and sowing it everywhere. English grass proved peculiarly adapted to New England; long after the native grass withered and the sharp frosts turned the trees orange and red, the imported grass remained green and supported ever larger flocks of sheep and herds of cattle.

Transplanted English husbandry, and especially transplanted English grass, worked so successfully that they led within four decades to the disintegration of the original town form introduced in Plymouth in 1620. The first colonists discovered a ready market for surplus livestock and produce among the settlers who followed them. Immigrants were desperate for livestock of any kind and for enough food to last them until their first harvest, and they paid high prices—and paid in cash—for whatever they bought. Out of very small beginnings, a single lamb or bag of grain perhaps, developed a market trade that strained early town layouts and agricultural practices to the breaking point. Husbandmen wanted larger and larger lots, both of arable and of meadow land, and they wanted to live on them to better supervise the livestock and crops and to avoid the long walk from the nucleus of houses. Most of all, however, they demanded an end to common fields and to relying on joint effort because innovation rewarded them with greater profits. Certainly older traditionalists balked at such changes but found they could do little to stop the trend.[27] In 1635 the Massachusetts General Court ordered that "no dwelling house shall be built above half a mile from the meetinghouse in any new plantation," but by 1640 it repealed the already flouted law. As New Englanders brought more and more land into cultivation they found an ever greater number of outlets for their produce. Husbandmen sent shingles, hoop-poles, and boards to England and the West Indies and supplied European fishing fleets with grain. They sent more lumber and grain to Caribbean plantations and began supplying lumber and produce to the growing population of New England craftsmen. Everywhere good land was at a premium, and industrious men, with a little luck, grew rich by working larger and larger holdings and by speculating in land.[28] Elbow room was not the product of sinful lust but of calculated investment.

Still, however, the early ideal of nucleated houses surrounded by outlying fields remained an integral part of planting. Groups continued to settle towns, and selectmen and land committees continued to apportion land eunomically, in ways that objectified social hierarchy on the ground. The meetinghouse remained the center of all man-made improvements; roads radiated from it, and before it lay a graveyard and a training field, where husbandmen mustered for military exercises. Around it too usually stood a few houses (almost always the parsonage) and as years passed and travel among towns became more common, an ordinary or inn. Until well into the eighteenth century the town continued to objectify more than social hierarchy and ecclesiastical control. Evidence of community effort marked it everywhere.

Near the center of most towns lay the clearest objectification of corporate effort: the "common" or "green," called in some towns the "meetinghouse lot" because of its proximity to the chief public structure. A green allowed the militia space in which to exercise and provided an area for hangings, outdoor religious assemblies, and—most importantly— livestock collection. A typical green covered only a few acres, far too small a space to graze the livestock owned by the townspeople. But every morning, as long as the tradition of common pasturing endured, children brought their family cow or horse to the green and left the animal in care of the town herdsman, who then led the herd to a distant piece of common ground. Late in the afternoon the herdsman returned with the livestock, and children came to the green to fetch home their own animals. Continual trampling left most greens anything but grass covered; most looked like wide, muddy paddocks, and only when common herding ended did some towns fence in their greens and rent them as pasture, using the income to maintain meetinghouses. But most towns ignored the open spaces, and as late as 1853 a traveler in Fairhaven, Vermont, dismissed the green as "an uneven and barren sand waste, lying open to the public, traversed by vehicles in all directions."[29] Even when abandoned by livestock, however, the green objectified the corporate spirit that shaped space and structure.

From 1620 to 1845 New England townspeople layed out, built, and maintained all the public "ways," or roads, and collectively erected the structures necessary for the common good. Bridges, stocks, whipping posts, and especially livestock pounds showed their builders' desire to establish in New England the revered landschaft order of the past and to retain some remnants of it many decades later. Across New England, men fenced their livestock inside pastures so that beasts might not wander into the meadows planted with precious English grass and into arable fields, or else they grazed them under the care of a town herdsman. As herds increased and individual husbandmen became more concerned about pedigrees, men kept their animals in private pastures and bred them carefully, sometimes with a prize bull maintained at town expense and sometimes with privately owned studs. Fencing pastures demanded great effort, but it freed husbandmen from fencing meadows and arable fields, and in New England such fields outnumbered pastures. The few owners careless enough to let their stock wander at will learned that their neighbors would capture them and confine them in the town-built livestock pound and levy fines. The New England town at first objectified traditional corporate effort and control intermixed with innovative enterprise, and long after the corporate effort decayed, remnants like the impounding of stray livestock in community pounds endured, reminding individuals that community good had once determined almost all activity, even milling.

Every town hoped to attract a miller by offering monopolies, mill seats, and grants of land, but every town expected to control its miller's activities. In 1640 the town of Scituate in Plymouth Colony offered thirty acres of upland and three or four of swamp plus the sole right to grind all the town's grain to anyone who would build a gristmill. Applicants learned that they would control the flow of water in whatever ponds they created, and that they could keep one-fourteenth of all the grain they ground and sell it as they wished. But the townsmen insisted that whoever accepted the offer complete his mill within seven years of the agreement and tend it faithfully for at least fourteen years thereafter.[30] In seventeenth-century New England towns, grist- and sawmills operated as public utilities, not entrepreneurial ventures. Millers—and blacksmiths—understood the delicate relation between their operations and community prosperity, and although they bickered about unjust restriction they accepted lifetimes of interference. When Charles Stockbridge accepted the Scituate milling offer he accepted continuous inspection and regulation by husbandmen assembled in "town meeting" to adjust private enterprise to community ends.

Corporate control extended to domestic life too. As in the estensión, householders permitted families to settle among them and build houses according to local ordinance; newcomers did not simply arrive, buy land, and begin clearing forest. Houses and fields took shape according to community will; elected selectmen banned wooden chimneys and thatch roofs as fire hazards, and land committees sited each family's acreage. The single-bay, story-and-a-half houses sheltered complex family orders answerable to the householders of the community; selectmen and clergy entered houses at will to see that rules governing domestic tranquility and religious instructions directed family life. Because outsiders might disrupt the delicate order of town life, householders forbade any family to shelter strangers for more than several days without the permission of the selectmen. Householders "warned out" poor wayfarers, for fear that such destitute drifters might become public charges. The modest houses offered snug refuge from winter storms and summer heat but they sheltered no one from public responsibility. Every householder kept his wife and children, and any adults who lived under his roof, in the knowledge of God and His laws and in continuous obedience to local regulation, or else his neighbors entered his house and corrected his error. The household, as a microcosm of the town, depended on mutual aid to maintain order, but every household order depended on the town for its existence.

Not surprisingly, New Englanders devoted painstaking attention to housebuilding, choosing to erect the massively framed structures tested by centuries of English use. In 1637 one colonist planned a house approximately thirty by eighteen feet, with heavily plastered wood chimneys at each end. "Be sure that all the doorways in every place be so high that any man may go upright under," he directed, but otherwise he trusted traditional knowledge and form, specifying that the windows "be not over large in any room and as few as conveniently may be," the frame "strong in timber, though plain and well braced," the sheathing "good oak-heart inch board" temporarily attached in anticipation of a brick facade a few years after. Finally, he specified, "I think it not best to have too much timber felled near the house place westward." What the future householder wanted, therefore, was an inward-focused house, a sure defense against human and animal enemies, against heavy snowfall

and cold, and against the biting west wind, as well as a useful agricultural
implement, complete with a cellar accessible to the outdoors, "so hereaf-
ter one may make comings in from without."[31] Housebuilding resembled the mostly traditional, sometimes innovative shaping of wilderness
into landschaft-life space. A completed house reinforced domestic order
and made recognizable the pains of *house-less-ness,* just as the town
emerging from forest made the wilderness all the more apparent.

As husbandmen felled trees and broke up ground for planting they
became aware of the wilderness at the edge of the fields. The dark,
impenetrable forest that informs so much public prose and poetry of
New England's first century went unnoticed by explorers such as Gos-
nold and Brereton, who saw nothing but promise in the open woods,
acres of strawberries, and river meadows they cursorily explored. Only
as towns began to appear did the wilderness motif take form too. A few
lines from Wallace Stevens's "Anecdote of the Jar" explains the cause:

> I placed a jar in Tennessee,
> And round it was, upon a hill.
> It made the slovenly wilderness
> Surround that hill.[32]

Stevens's jar is no more a Grecian urn than the emerging towns were
finished cities, but because it is an artificial construct it makes apparent
the previously unrealized wilderness. Without the artifact the wilderness
is formless, the hill is indistinguishable, and chaos does not exist because
it is everywhere. Puritans disliked the pathless forest because they entered it from open, ordered towns—and the more ordered the town the
more its inhabitants disliked the chaos around it. In the backcountry, in
Westfield and Northampton, clergymen and parishioners concerned
themselves less with the wilderness motif and more with town-making.
In late seventeenth-century Boston, however, clergymen preached sermon upon sermon about the wilderness a few miles west.

Nathaniel Hawthorne, who more than the Mathers and Wigglesworth
perpetuated the seventeenth-century equation of primeval forest with
moral wilderness, recognized in the nineteenth century that it was the
transition from streets and houses to dense forest which must terrify
Hester Prynne, Dimmesdale, and young Goodman Brown. Hawthorne
was not mistaken. The most casual examination of seventeenth-century
town plats reveals that the typical New England community fronted the
ocean or faced in upon itself. Roads gave access to outlying fields and
paralleled the forest; only a lonely few connected the towns. Samuel
Sewall was perfectly content to enjoy a pleasant view of a far-off town as

he rode his judicial circuit, but as late as 1704 he distrusted the closed-in connecting roads. Like other New Englanders, he was a creature of towns, of man-made order, and he understood the forest, like murder and witchcraft, as a threat to social and psychological stability. His fear derived in part from subtle conditioning by two generations of Puritan clergymen, who used the forest as the chief symbol of the infernal chaos latent in all men and restrained only by reason and society. But it also derived from his own limited experience. Like most New Englanders at the beginning of the eighteenth century, Sewall saw space in atomistic terms: that field belonged to Merritt, that woodlot to Jacobs.[33] The typical husbandman named his fields, bounded them, measured them, and wrote down his private perception of them in deeds when he sold them, but he rarely left them or the town of which they were a part. His business lay in cultivated places, or at the very fringe of the forest, getting timber or building stone.[34] Because he carefully enclosed his livestock, he rarely pursued a wandering sheep or cow into the forest. Wilderness indeed threatened husbandmen at ease in fields and inclined to respect any sort of tales about wild beasts, Indians, and the few English people demented enough to choose to live in it. Husbandmen possessed only towns and left the wilderness to the clergy and historians who brooded about it, to the occasional traveler who journeyed along the narrow paths from town to town, and to Satan himself.

Wildness threatened to engulf every New England town, regardless of how much men assembled to fell trees and cut brush. Usually the wildness had physical form, as it had in the Puritan town of Oyster Bay on Long Island. In the spring of 1672 the town elders ordered that every owner of a house lot appear "at the house of Anthony Wrights" in late July "for the cutting up of brush." Communal clearing of "rubbish waste grounds" like those described in "The Ordering of Towns" relieved Oyster Bay fears of wolves, Indians, and—perhaps—of the Devil popularly believed to hover with a host of "fiery flying serpents" just beyond the fields. Cotton Mather described the wilderness evil in *Wonders of the Invisible World,* a book he hurriedly published several months after an orgy of witchcraft, accusations, and executions struck the town of Salem. "The Devil, exhibiting himself ordinarily as a small black man," lamented Mather, "has decoyed a fearful knot of proud, froward, ignorant, envious and malicious creatures, to lift themselves in his horrid service, by entering their names in a book by him tendered unto them." No one noticed that four-fifths of the accused witches lived beyond the bounds of Salem Village and were somehow different (lacking in deference, perhaps, or adept at getting wealth) or that most accusers lashed out from jealousy. Everyone blamed the Satan of the forest, the mysterious force that seduced young girls and old men into signing the loathesome book.

Colonial New England focused not on the region claimed by England as New England, therefore, but on the towns laced with centripetal roads. Few maps of seventeenth-century towns survive, but those that do show the insular arrangement of houselots and fields suggested in "The Ordering of Towns."[35] In 1681, for example, Little Compton in Rhode Island had evolved as a scarcely modified landschaft, its houses and fields encircled by the forest. But its unnamed roads ran no farther than the most distant fields before turning along the civilized perimeter or ending at the forest edge. There was no chance in Little Compton for a European strassenromantik to develop; the roads led home, not on to cities, castles, and excitement. Adventure—and terror—lay beyond the road, in the pathless or almost pathless forest where the hardworking townspeople rarely ventured for fear of bewilderment. Off-the-road confusion surfaces again and again in New England accounts of men hopelessly lost only several miles from cultivated land. Several would-be Massachusetts militiamen tried a nighttime shortcut through a large woodlot in their own town in 1774, "and in them woods," one recorded later in his diary, "we got most confoundedly lost."[36] Such mishaps persisted into the nineteenth century and caused Thoreau to remark that "even country people, I have observed, magnify the difficulty of traveling in the forest, and especially among mountains. They seem to lack their usual common sense in this."[37] But Thoreau himself grew uncomfortable when houses and towns were far away; on desolate Cape Cod beaches and in Maine forests he lacked the certainty he knew among the woodlots of Concord. His predilection for hiking in woods near roads stemmed from the seventeenth-century preoccupation with the inward-turning ways and atomistic towns that two centuries later found expression in Hawthorne's fiction. The colonial New England town existed first of all as a perpetual motion machine, continuously guiding townspeople back to its center. Out-of-town travel never began as passive submission to an inviting road but as a deliberate breaking free of centripetal orbit.

Colonial New Englanders undertook travel most easily as a joint adventure; men enjoyed company on lonesome roads and when searching out locations for new towns. Last journeys, however, were invariably solitary. Unlike the Anglican, who had help from church and priest, the dying Puritan faced the afterlife alone. According to the clergy, life existed only as the threshold to salvation or damnation, and like the wayfarer in *Pilgrim's Progress*, wise New Englanders fixed their hearts on

Heaven. For those certain of their own election to grace, death perhaps seemed not especially traumatic, but for the thousands more who confronted an imminent meeting with the Devil, every neglected, disordered burying ground warned of the lonely chaos of death. Along with church organs and stained glass, the Puritans abandoned traditional graveyard design. Graves no longer faced east so that the dead might rise on Judgment Day with a minimum of twisting, and no one buried clergymen facing their parishioners in death as they had from the pulpit in life. For the discarded churchyard the colonists substituted a roughly walled piece of the poorest soil, sometimes but not always adjoining the meetinghouse. In 1648 the town of Roxbury paid its constable to wall and gate its burying ground but it ignored the placing of graves and subsequent upkeep. Despite a wide range of town officers (fence viewers, hog reeves, and tithing men among others) no one performed the old duties of sexton-gravedigger. As late as 1724, and perhaps long after, New Englanders valued graveyards more as meadows than as sacred spaces. The portal-like shape of the half-toppled, weed-grown stones may explain the patches of disorder. For New England Puritans, death was an opening on another world, through which the soul passed into eternity, and a corpse only a memento mori, a monument to the death overcome by the Puritans' covenanted God and, throughout the seventeenth century, a husk buried without graveside prayer.[38] Seventeenth- and eighteenth-century graveyards were *contrived* disorders that clearly warned everyone of the fiery, chaotic wilderness of Hell. Even gravestone epitaphs warned mortals to reform their sinful souls lest they suffer a worse fate than their corpses. At the center of almost every town lay a space as ambiguous and unfrequented as the surrounding uncivilized forest.

Graveyards were common, if not hallowed ground. Saint and sinner, clergyman and housewife lay buried in a space belonging to all townsmen and watched over by none. Common land played an integral part in every town economy from the 1620s to the Revolutionary era but its role changed with each generation of overseers. Early coastal towns reserved great tracts of salt marsh and forest for common use as meadow and timber supply, and some groups even transplanted and tried to maintain common-field agriculture too. Although traditional corporate husbandry did not last long, for generations householders used frequently the common "waste," the clay pits, hickory swamps, pastures, and meadows where each householder satisfied his need for chimney bricks, hoop-poles, and grass and hay. Rich and poor alike shared these public resource spaces until mid-seventeenth century, when industrious husbandmen began acquiring them, especially meadows and pastures, by purchase and encroachment. The vast amount of common land was destined to be divided among the householders anyway, and men jealously guarded the outlying forest and natural meadows while impatiently waiting for allotting day. Sons and grandsons received their allotments, as the decades passed, until only the reserved resource areas remained—and the stony, infertile ground so poor that land-assignment committees despaired of allotting them—and landless young men gathered together and "hived" off to begin new towns in the interior. But town after town slowly surrendered the reserved spaces to husbandmen eager to straighten lot lines or unify fragmented holdings acquired by purchase. By the middle of the eighteenth century, gores of common land dotted most New England towns, but the gores remained common only because no one wanted them.[39] Until community building projects exhausted their scanty resources, the gores provided building stone and sometimes building timber; thereafter selectmen and town meetings no longer interested in old ideals of corporate living ignored them. The frittering away of common land is of great significance because it marked the rise of self-sufficient husbandmen at the expense of the community-supported colonists who first cleared and planted the soil. The eighteenth-century agricultural poor had little chance to prosper in the New England towns because the wealthier farmers by then owned the once-common lands that formerly furnished firewood, hay, and other resources to all householders, the "men of great estate" mentioned in "The Ordering of Towns" and the "mean ones" remembered by John Winthrop when he explained God's hierarchical society. As the Revolution neared, stewardship of common land evolved into improvement of private property.

The prism of private ownership did not distort the vision of the town as a model of social order because the chaos of the surrounding forest lingered. As time and generations passed, the pathless intervals of forest separating the original settlements disappeared and one town's fields adjoined those of another. A new sort of frontier replaced the old, a frontier in the European sense. As long as town boundaries remained inexact and a succession of refined surveying instruments kept them uncertain until the late eighteenth century, men disliked settling or even owing the lots abutting them. Land clearing and other improvements along the fringe occurred only hesitantly, and until the nineteenth century boundary zones were characterized by unfelled trees or half-cut brush, since the danger of a boundary controversy and subsequent title disputes remained great. Despite annual perambulations by selectmen bent on protecting town boundaries, the narrow zones abutting them went unvisited by townspeople still guided by old centripetal roads. Place-names there were uncommon and town-meeting perceptions of the zones were dim. The narrow zones of vestigial wilderness reinforced the vision of a town as a discrete, special place focused inward upon itself.[40] Tocqueville remarked in 1839 that New England towns were topographically distinct: "Americans love their towns for much the same reason that highlanders love their mountains. In both cases the native land has emphatic and peculiar features." Only in this brief comment on the New England countryside does Tocqueville choose the term *cite;* elsewhere he uses *commune* when speaking of towns. His terminology is precise and his intention is unmistakable—it is the physical town, the *cite,* that the New Englander loves, not the political community or *commune.* [41] The weary traveler riding from Boston or New Haven, or even from a nearby town, knew he was home when he passed through the frontier of vestigial wilderness and gazed about at the objective correlative of his own social, political, and economic order.

The New England countryside was, therefore, a cellular countryside, and in time it nurtured a complementary aesthetic. "Beauty of prospect demands not only amplitude," declared Timothy Dwight in 1821, "but variety. A continued succession of hills and valleys, scarcely distinguishable from one another in appearance, though less wearisome than the uniformity of a spacious plain, is still remote from the exquisite scenery which forms the fine landscape." From 1790 to 1815 Dwight explored the towns of New England, and eventually he focused on town churches to explain his aesthetic of topographical beauty. "In almost every part of the country," he remarked, "except where the settlements are quite new, they are found at the distances of five, six, and seven miles; and with their handsome spires and cupolas, almost universally white, add an exquisite beauty to the landscape and perpetually refresh the eye of the traveler."[42] The finest space, then, is not the romantic cataract or mountain valley but the exquisite artifact of meetinghouse and surrounding town, the "clump of houses with a church" remarked more than a century later by Robert Frost.

Like Jacob's ladder, the New England meetinghouse existed as a hierophany, an axis linking earth with Heaven. Puritans almost invariably worshiped indoors, and in a land hostile to crucifixes, market crosses, and relics, the meetinghouse acquired a vernacular symbolic value despite the clergy's protest that it stand only as a shelter. New England houses usually reached only two stories—if that—before spreading horizontally in attached lean-tos and sheds. Only the meetinghouse grew

taller as generations passed and original theology decayed, adding galleries in the 1650s, turrets and belfries in later decades, and towers and
spires after 1699, dwarfing nearby houses and trees, and suddenly, in
the first years of the eighteenth century, ordering not only individual
towns but the landscape emerging from forest wilderness.

Town after town furiously debated the proper location for its meetinghouse; sometimes husbandmen struggled to locate the exact geographical center of the town, and in many towns opposing factions determined
to split into two wholly separate ecclesiastical-political entities, each with
its own meetinghouse. Sabbath-day travel difficulties alone do not explain the uproars although townsmen frequently complained about
six-mile wintertime walks to services. Rather, in every town, New Englanders wanted to reside near their only sacred center, near the roland
that marked their town from afar and epitomized architectural beauty
while objectifying the exalted religious meaning of their New World
errand in town building. In 1702 Cotton Mather deliberately chose a tiny
meetinghouse symbol to locate each New England town identified on his
"Exact Map of New England and New York." By then, New Englanders
had shaped some wilderness into landscape and could see, if not from
town to town, at least from hilltop to meetinghouse.[43] Meetinghouse
spires, brightly painted hierophanic rolands, made the cellular countryside intelligible to resident and traveler alike—and refreshed the eye.

For colonial New Englanders the word *town* was rich in peculiar spatial
significance. It denoted a self-governing, nearly self-sufficient agricultural community inhabiting a discrete, carefully bounded space shaped
from wilderness chaos and through continuous corporate effort maintained in equilibrium against the wild beasts and plants—and supernatural evils like witches—that threatened to overwhelm it. It connoted
the standard man-made constructs every New Englander thought absolutely necessary to town existence: communally built roads, bridges,
stocks and sometimes a gallows, and cattle pound, along with the green
used to temporarily enclose the town livestock. It connoted too the
natural resources jointly managed for the common good, the clay pits,
rock piles, woodlots, and—most importantly—the common pastures,
meadows, and arable fields. And finally, the word connoted a social and
spatial structure divinely inspired and focused on divinity, the divinity
symbolized so clearly in the meetinghouse and less clearly in such social
and economic structures as the hierarchy of families and the eunomic
technique of land assignment. Settlers in New Spain inhabited estensiónes that objectified a similar world view; they might have understood
the New England richness of *town*. But in Virginia, Maryland, and the

other southern Atlantic Coast colonies few transplanted English people understood the New England meaning, and by 1750, few cared to try.

TIDEWATER AND PIEDMONT

Virginia seduced the English. In 1705, one hundred and twenty years after the founding of Roanoke and almost a century after the establishment of Jamestown, Robert Beverly tried to understand how. The earliest explorers, he wrote in the first chapter of *The History and Present State of Virginia,* represented the country as "so delightful, and desirable; so pleasant, and plentiful; the climate, and air, so temperate, sweet, and wholesome; the woods, and soil, so charming, and fruitful, and all other things so agreeable, that Paradise itself seemed to be there, in its first native luster."[44] Paradise was more than a promotional metaphor intended to entice adventurers to the newly found place; it was the prism through which the English long viewed the Tidewater South. As late as 1666 George Alsop described that part of Virginia called Maryland in the same extravagant way. "Neither do I think there is any place under the heavenly altitude, or that has footing or room upon the circular globe of this world," he boasted, "that can parallel this fertile and pleasant piece of ground in its multiplicity, or rather Nature's extravagancy of a super-abounding plenty." Alsop was indeed smitten with Maryland. To him it clearly outshone any garden or any picture, but he chose the new painterly term to help describe it, asserting that "he, who out of curiosity desires to see the landskip of the creation drawn to the life, or to read Nature's universal herbal without book, may with the optics of a discreet discerning view Maryland dressed in her green and fragrant mantle of the spring." But Paradise, remarked Beverly four decades after Alsop wrote his glowing description, is not the best place to establish a colony. In such perfection everyone falls into temptation.

Virginia, by all seventeenth-century accounts and by most early eighteenth-century reports too, struck observers as a vast garden. Its breezes whispered one message over and over, seducing every wondering newcomer: "Dwell here, live plentifully, and be rich." The "endless succession of native pleasures" described by Beverly, good weather, shady groves, murmuring brooks, singing birds, and "an eternal fragrancy of flowers" made people indolent.[45] Beverly was not the first to note the insidious effects of natural bounty. In 1656 John Hammond affirmed "the country to be wholesome, healthy and fruitful; and a model on which industry may as much improve itself in, as in any other habitable part of the world; yet not such a lubberland as the fiction of the

Land of Ease, is reported to be, nor such a Utopia as Sir Thomas More has related to be found out."[46] Unlike northern New Spain and coastal New England, whose climate and topography made hard work necessary from the start and allusions to gardens rare, the Tidewater South promised colonists riches beyond belief.

Despite the Virginia Company's explicit instructions to found an agricultural settlement before searching for gold and other riches, the settlers of Jamestown erected only temporary shelters before scattering in quest of jewels and precious ores. They did, it is true, select a very defensible spot on the end of a peninsula and they did scatter some wheat almost at once, but the site was so heavily wooded and marshy that agriculture languished. The effort of felling trees and clearing brush proved too much for the gentlemen adventurers although many enjoyed the novelty of the first days' work. It is difficult to conceive of a less organized enterprise than the early colonization of Virginia. Not until 1608 did the adventurers learn about tree girdling from the Indians, and not for another year did they plant maize. Once they learned that no gold lay under the ground, most of the men wanted only to go home, and they slaughtered almost all the livestock they had brought with them in order to force the company to evacuate them. Not until 1612, in fact, did the settlement seem permanent; until then the English brought maize from the Indians and hunted with varying degrees of enthusiasm the plentiful wild game. A happy accident alone guaranteed the prosperity and permanence of Virginian colonization. John Rolfe discovered that tobacco would grow (with careful cultivation) and sell at a profit.

New England settlers benefited from the mistakes of the first Virginians, particularly from the mistakes of the company. New England and New Spain developed traditional, landschaft-like settlements because their settlers prized traditional agricultural and social orders only slightly tempered by innovation. In Virginia evolved a different sort of countryside, despite the early efforts of the company to coerce its settlers into raising tobacco as Englishmen at home had once raised wheat and other crops in common fields, but without the corporate decision making so important to the success of traditional landschaft agriculture. New Englanders innovated carefully because they understood the example of Virginian experimentation.

No one intended Virginia to be home to husbandmen controlling their own fields. The company hoped to profit from furs, precious minerals, and rare plants and to control its employees from London. When it eventually tried to profit from tobacco raising, it organized its Jamestown settlement in an almost feudal fashion; men lived in company-owned dwellings surrounded by company-owned fields, and worked for wages. Not surprisingly, the men devoted much time to leaning on their spades and hoes and to wandering about in search of the hallucinogenic plant they named Jamestown, or "Jimson," weed. Company-directed agriculture failed completely by 1616, and in that year the company directors determined that each man of good reputation might lease three acres of land and grow whatever he wished and send for a wife, if he had not done so already.[47]

To the pleasure and chagrin of the company, production of wheat, maize, and tobacco immediately increased; although it welcomed the larger harvest of foodstuffs, the growing output of tobacco competed with the harvest reaped from the company's fields. It tried to protect its stake in the tobacco business by offering each worthy man a four-room house and twelve acres of arable land on which he might plant wheat, maize, root crops, herbs, and anything else but tobacco. By 1618, however, no settler ignored the lucrative tobacco business, and the company, honoring contracts it had made in years before to encourage settlement, began assigning freeholds on which men raised whatever they wished—usually tobacco.

Virginia passed almost at once from nearly feudal to nearly modern agricultural enterprise, skipping entirely the period of common-field, landschaft-like husbandry and confusing its settlers and Europeans who learned about the colony. In Virginia, would-be settlers learned, husbandmen practiced market agriculture with no common responsibilities. Virginians so loved tobacco raising that now and then they went almost hungry; no one wanted to plant food crops, and no corporate body enforced what the English at home considered to be common sense agriculture. As the company slowly dissolved, Virginians devised with its aid the chief innovation of southern colonization. "Old planters," the settlers who arrived in Virginia under company rule and others who purchased one or more shares in the company, received the right to 100 acres of land at once and the right to 100 more in a year or two. Newcomers received 50 acres if they had paid their own fare across the Atlantic, and everyone received 50 acres for every man, woman, and child whose fare they paid. In time, Virginians called the 50-acre allotment a "headright" and decided that the system proved wonderfully effective in settling families.[48]

The company, and later the colony, granted only the headright; it left the location of the land to the discretion of the settler, and within months men began wandering in search of the best soil. Since neither body prescribed the shape of the allotment, men returned from the woods

and natural or Indian-cleared meadows and submitted all sorts of irregularly shaped plats to the recorders. Tobacco culture governed
where people settled, and the Virginian countryside quickly reflected
the difficulties of raising an unfamiliar crop in a new and increasingly
surprising land.

Tobacco perplexed Englishmen from the moment they began raising
it, and not for decades did they fully understand its culture. Tobacco
thrives only in the richest soil, so the colonists sought out virgin, black,
forested ground; they girdled the trees by hacking the bark from the
trunks (and so killing them) and spaded deeply in preparation for planting. Unlike most crops, tobacco is transplanted from seedbeds, a long
and laborious process. Since 10,000 tobacco seeds barely overflow a
teaspoon, preparing and sowing the seedbed made for a difficult task;
most colonists mixed the seed with fine ashes in order to sow it more
evenly. Once he transplanted the seedlings, the tobacco grower began
even more difficult tasks. Tobacco is subject to depredations by worms
and insects, and if its main stem is not broken at the proper moment its
prized leaves do not develop. The colonial tobacco grower spent almost
every day in his fields, cleaning his plants of pests, pruning them, and
hoeing weeds from around them. At harvest time he cut the leaves and
hung them to dry in curing barns. Several months later he packed them
in hogshead barrels and shipped them to England.[49]

Unfortunately for the grower, tobacco exhausted the soil in which it
grew. After four or five years, even the richest ground wore out, forcing
men to make new fields. Soil exhaustion puzzled the colonists because
Virginia's rich black earth proved so fertile that wheat grew strangely tall
but with tiny seedheads. Only when the ground was seasoned by a year's
tobacco planting was it suitable for wheat. But colonists generally ignored wheat and other foodstuffs when they profited so dramatically
from raising tobacco plants, and they grew only enough food for themselves, their families, and their servants and slaves if they chose not to
buy produce imported from New England. Most of their land they
planted to tobacco, and when the soil wore out they abandoned the acres
as otherwise worthless. By 1640 Virginia acquired the worn-out, scraggly
appearance for which Europeans and New Englanders so strongly condemned it.

Tobacco culture made men mobile and inclined to think in terms of
markets. Not only did colonists search out the best possible soil on which
to build their large or small operations; they continually looked for good
land to move to when their own wore out. The headright system contributed to the rage for "moving on" because the colony made no restric-

tions on where a man might locate, as long as no one already claimed it, and within two or three decades, men simply bought headrights for five shillings each and so avoided the complications of importing indentured servants.[50] Settlers wanted more than good soil, however. They knew that they must somehow profitably market their crop, and they coveted locations along estuaries and navigable rivers, where they built small wharves and sold their barrels of tobacco to merchant-ship captains or else consigned them to agents in London. The coastal plain, or Tidewater, extends almost 200 miles inland before reaching the "fall line" that blocks ocean-going ships. Everywhere east of the falls, tobacco growers scrambled for the choicest waterfront locations. Owners of large plantations communicated directly with ship captains, but even householders availed themselves of narrow inlets along which shallops cruised to freight tobacco cargoes to deep-draught ships. Large and small plantations and hundreds of householdings stretched along the banks; many large holdings extended a mile along the bank but reached inland only a few thousand yards.[51] For as long as the riverbank soil remained fertile, tobacco growers prospered and awaited the seasonal visits of merchant ships with pleased anticipation.

Tobacco growers ignored most other agricultural activities. Livestock husbandry suffered because the southern colonists firmly believed that horses, cattle, swine, and sheep could fend for themselves in the temperate climate and lush woods. Men turned out livestock to graze on native grasses and cane, and on the fallen leaves and acorns the colonists called "mast." Although conservative settlers warned that such stock would become almost wild, Virginia and later Maryland, the Carolinas, and Georgia made official the open-range system and required all settlers to fence in not their livestock but their fields of corn and other crops. At first a legal fence stood only four-and-a-half feet high, but the ability of forest-bred hogs to jump such barriers forced most settlers to erect the six-foot-high fences that became the legal standard across the Carolinas and Georgia, where livestock raising proved more economical than tobacco planting, once the colonists learned that beef, pork, and hides— and live animals too—sold at a profit in England, the West Indies, and sometimes in New England. Although the proprietors of South Carolina announced as early as 1674 that they "design to have planters there and not graziers," nothing officialdom did curtailed the growing popularity of livestock husbandry by men whose land seemed too poor for tobacco or lay too far from estuary docks. The colonists, remarked Nathaniel Shrigley in 1669, "feed not their swine or cattle, but kill them far out in the woods."[52] His observation of the emerging innovative southern system of raising livestock suggests what other writers explain. Across the inland Tidewater, and eventually in the Piedmont, developed a significantly different livestock husbandry that prompted a new attitude toward the land.

Cattle rustling perturbed settlers as early as the 1630s, and by 1671 herds of wild horses had become a nuisance in Maryland. Breeding cattle imported from Bermuda and elsewhere bred so rapidly that by 1682 one observer noted that some Carolina stock raisers owned herds of 700 or 800 head. Three decades later a Carolina resident claimed that cattle "have mightily increased since the first settling of the colony, about forty years ago. It was then reckoned a great deal to have three or four cows, but now some people have one thousand head, but for one man to have two hundred head is very common." More than warm winters and scarce predators explain the dramatic rise of the southern cattle industry. Despite the wild herds and the casual attitude of many colonists, southern livestock raising depended on the successful invention and use of the "cowpen," the small yard or pen in which the best stock lived in winter on corn blades and crab-grass hay (and at times on hay imported from New England) and which gave its name to what can otherwise best be called the cattle plantation. In early August 1733 the South Carolina *Gazette* advertised for sale "two hundred acres of land . . . on the north side of the river, joining a large savannah, very commodious for a cow-pen or hog-craul." By "cowpen," therefore, southerners understood a fenced-in enclosure, barn, and perhaps a dwelling on land owned by an individual, and a large surrounding acreage of savanna or forest over which the livestock ranged but which no one in particular owned.[53] The best cowpens lay between savanna land and cane swamps, the savanna used for summer grazing and the cane for winter, but many stood on ground cleared chiefly by firing the forest until wild grass replaced the trees.

A "cowpen keeper" or "cowpen manager" owned or operated the enterprise, usually with the assistance of black "cattle hunters," slaves who "hunted down" or "hunted up" the roving livestock for branding and slaughter. Perhaps the western word *buckaroo* derives not from the Spanish *vaquero* but from the Gullah *buckra;* perhaps not, but it connotes the hard-riding independence of well-mounted, well-equipped men who simply rode west and joined Indian tribes, as secure in the ways of the forest wilderness as their white masters, and almost as loosely tied to the land.[54] Livestock husbandry indeed made the English familiar with the wilderness, and it introduced them to using—and misusing by overgrazing—land they did not own. When more and more settlers arrived in an area, a cowpen keeper sold his crude buildings and fenced-in enclosure and moved west, leaving behind land fit only for hard-scrabble crop raising. He thought little of improving the land he did not own and cared only for his herd, his movable hacienda of wealth.

Householders owning only 50 or 100 or 200 acres did not build for permanence either, because they knew that tobacco would exhaust their soil and force them to move on. Manuring tobacco fields by temporarily enclosing cattle on them failed; the plants acquired the taste of manure. Fields, dwellings, barns, and fences soon reflected the transiency of their builders. Initially, southerners built barns as solidly as New Englanders erected theirs a few years later, but they quickly learned that they had no traditional need for barns at all. Livestock that wintered in the forest required no shelters or even much hay that necessitated storage structures, and Virginians and other southerners stored their small grain harvests in simple sheds. But southerners did need structures for curing tobacco, and once they discovered that tobacco cures best when air flows among the leaves, they experimented in building barns with loosely jointed sideboards. Since the crude frames carried little weight and the roofs rarely supported snow, the southern-devised tobacco barn, like the small stables reserved for saddle horses and milk cows, struck Europeans and northern colonists as stupidly flimsy. Southerners experimented with hastily built dwellings too, designing them primarily as shelters from rain and sun. The typical southern dwelling had a crude chimney at each gable end and split along an open-air corridor called a "dogtrot." Clearly the southern barn resembled the southern dwelling, and southerners invented terms that described parts of both even as they puzzled visitors. They called each side of a dogtrot dwelling a "pen," for example, not a "bay" or "room," and none of the common terms ever connoted permanence. By the middle of the seventeenth century, poorer householders learned to throw up rough curing barns and dwellings and then burn down the structures for their nails when soil exhaustion forced a move to new land. Also it is not surprising that the householders devoted very little attention to building enduring fences or that they invented an easily erected if otherwise poor quality fence. The worm- or snake-fence enclosed arable fields everywhere in the southern colonies by the early eighteenth century. Southerners knew that logs were plentiful and easily split into rails and that the rails could be piled up on one another and arranged in a self-supporting zigzag structure. Worm-fences fascinated European travelers such as Hugh Jones, who described them in 1753 as "made of rails supporting one another very firmly in a particular manner" for all that they needed no posts or postholes.[55]

Southern colonists knew as well as critical outsiders that worm-fences wasted vast quantities of wood, occupied far more ground than a typical post-and-rail fence, and encouraged weeds and the animals that live in weeds, but they firmly believed that the zigzag fences, like the rough barns and dwellings, provided the most satisfactory response to the transient lifestyle their builders loved. Building permanent structures and fences, like nurturing soil fertility, made no sense when rich land lay everywhere and seemed almost free.

Southerners nevertheless recognized the house as the key to land-ownership. As early as 1648 the governor and council of Virginia confronted the problems of soil exhaustion and a transient populace. That year the burgesses petitioned on behalf "of the great and clamorous necessities of divers of the inhabitants occasioned and brought upon them through the mean produce of their labors upon barren and over-wrought grounds and the apparent decay of their cattle and hogs for want of sufficient range," and the governor granted the dissatisfied landowners permission to "remove and seat upon the north side of Charles River and Rappahanock River." Until 1666 *seat* and *plant* were vague terms; in that year the assembly resolved that "building a house and keeping a stock one whole year upon the land shall be accounted seating; and that clearing, tending, and planting an acre of ground shall be accounted planting."[56] Even in 1648, however, the landowners understood that everyone expected them to occupy and work the land granted to them, and that the clearest evidence of occupation and use was the building of a residence. It was in these years that squatting became so prevalent; in the absence of regularly surveyed plats, the building of a dwelling and the planting of a few acres established a husbandman as a *householder* with all attendant rights.

In the first decades of settlement the structures, fences, and fields of the householders differed only slightly from those of men owning many hundreds or thousands of acres. By the 1750s most similarities had vanished. A *planter* worked his land with slaves and hired help and ordered his *plantation* about a large house he called the *big house; householders* cultivated their few headrights of land themselves and dreamed of building plantations in the backcountry. With its columns and white paint the big house remains the dominant emblem of the antebellum South; it figures in novels such as John Pendleton Kennedy's *Swallow Barn* of 1832 and in countless letters written by European and northern observers. But only a rare big house ever attained the now romanticized ideal. Throughout the eighteenth century most were small, two-story structures built of roughly squared logs and sometimes covered with boards whitewashed against rain and insects. A big house acquired its magnificence by comparison with the dogtrot dwellings of householders and by the proximity of cramped slave cabins. A big house objectified the hierarchical order of southern colonial society, and it spoke forcefully of an economic order as eunomic as those of New Spain and New England.[57]

Late in the eighteenth century George Mason of Virginia recalled the complex economic order that focused on his father's big house. "My father had among his slaves carpenters, coopers, sawyers, blacksmiths, tanners, curriers, shoemakers, spinners, weavers and knitters, and even a distiller," he began. "His woods furnished timber and plank for the carpenters and coopers, and charcoal for the blacksmith; his cattle killed for his own consumption and for sale supplied skins for the tanners, curriers, and shoemakers, and his sheep gave wool and his fields produced cotton and flax for the weavers and spinners, and his orchards fruit for the distiller. His carpenters and sawyers built and kept in repair all the dwelling houses, barns, stables, plows, harrows, gates, etc., on the plantations and the out-houses at the home house." Mason noted the role of coopers in making tobacco hogsheads, of blacksmiths in "making and repairing plows, harrows, teeth chains, bolts" and other metal objects, and of spinners in making clothes. "All of these operations were carried on at the home house," he concluded, and slaves distributed the products to whatever fields and craft areas required them.[58] The Mason plantation depended on more slaves than most others, but its master's efforts toward self-sufficiency were typical; the planter who devised an inward-turning, self-reliant society and economy on his own land hedged his tobacco-growing enterprise against the fluctuations of the European market. He was—unlike the householder keeping most of his land in tobacco and buying his supplies from planters or the few craftsmen in the few towns—almost independent, and sometimes imagined he was.

Owners of large plantations often compared their estates to English manors, but the comparison is incorrect. The medieval English manor was a self-sufficient operation only fitfully engaged in a market economy. Its lord had only very limited power over the husbandmen and their families and frequently had difficulty exercising it. In Eastern Europe, beyond the knowledge of the southern plantation owners, a different system thrived, one based on a serfdom that amounted, like that of the New Spain hacienda order, to slavery. But even in Poland, Transylvania, and Russia, very few manorial enterprises depended intimately on wholesale markets, and only a rare lord personally and daily supervised his serfs. Most, like the owners of the haciendas, visited their manors rarely if at all, and left their operation to stewards or overseers charged with collecting rents and other duties from the serfs and directing the serfs' service in the lord's fields.[59] The large plantations of Virginia and Maryland, and later of South Carolina, Georgia, and more western regions, resulted chiefly from rapid experimentation in land clearing, from the "peculiar institution" of slavery, and from a devotion to market agriculture, not love of tradition.

After a century of colonization, typical large Tidewater plantations focused on the big house, slave cabins, and a collection of other structures—stable, barns for tobacco and other crops, hen house, milk house, smokehouse, dovecote, and often a kitchen house. The cluster of slave cabins, the "quarter" as it became known, was the hub of activity except when the slaves worked in the fields, but it attracted little notice from most whites. Early in the nineteenth century James Kirk Paulding discovered a collection of whitewashed and clean cabins on one plantation he visited and claimed that they exhibited such an appearance of comfort that he reconciled himself somewhat to slavery.[60] On almost every plantation, however, the slave cabins struck non-southerners as neither well-built nor well-maintained. Many plantation owners had their slaves build their own dwellings, and the cabins resembled the huts of West Africa. Other owners put up small frame structures or else opted for log cabins; only a very few built cozy houses of brick or stone equipped with solid chimneys and interior walls. But always in the seventeenth and eighteenth centuries the quarter stood intimately near its big house, although an occasional planter like Jefferson located his slave cabins out of sight and sound. At the beginning of the nineteenth century some guilt-ridden owners of large plantations began locating their slave cabins half a mile or more from their own residences and installing an overseer, usually a white, in a house nearby.

As many observers remarked, most large plantations seemed almost self-sufficient except for markets. The largest, like Jefferson's, were almost communities in themselves, covering 3,900 acres, laced with twenty miles of roads, and home to 200 people, most of them slaves. Jefferson's slaves, like Mason's, included more than ignorant laborers; among them were carpenters, masons, cabinetmakers, blacksmiths, and other experts.[61] On smaller plantations the number of skilled hands decreased with the total work force, but specialization remained the rule. Elderly slaves supervised children or worked at crafts, often away from their master's plantation, but they and the field hands were invisible to most white commentators until just before the Civil War, and their cabins were too. Quarters and slaves went unnoticed.

Slavery presented two spatial difficulties, especially to owners of large holdings. The size of a plantation depended first on the time it took the slaves to walk from their cabins to the most distant fields. Most planters permitted no quarter-to-field walks that lasted more than one hour, and often chose to relocate some or all slave cabins rather than lose the working time of their slaves. Unlike many planters in Haiti and elsewhere in the Caribbean, American slaveowners seemed to have distrusted the political consequences of very large quarters. They preferred, although how early is difficult to ascertain, to hire a second or even a third overseer and disperse their slaves among several settlements to shorten walking times and to defuse potentially explosive congregations of blacks.[62] The typical slaveowner supervised only a handful of slaves who lived close to his big house, but the dispersed settlement of slaves owned by masters of large plantations perhaps spared all whites, small and large slaveowners and those who owned none, from the grisly rebellions that shook Haiti and other island colonies in later decades.

Slavery may or may not have been profitable in the long run, but most planters thought it was and applied its principles to raising crops other than tobacco. About 1647 South Carolina colonists began experimenting with rice and indigo culture, and eventually with cotton growing too. Such crops, and later wheat (which replaced tobacco as a major cash crop in the Tidewater around 1730) and in Louisiana sugar cane, proved admirably adapted to the slave system because all demanded large work forces in the field and all required year-round cultivation and intricate processing. Wherever the soil was rich there soon sprouted tobacco or cotton—and clumps of slave cabins. Younger sons of slaveowning planters and other whites with loose capital pushed farther and farther west, searching out new spots on which to site plantations. Tidewater planters hesitated at first to sell precious field slaves but, as the coastal land wore out, more and more of the "old comers" supported their large houses and indulgent lifestyles by selling crops of young slaves to labor-hungry westerners. Backcountry planters bought eagerly, for they yearned to duplicate and surpass the Tidewater splendor they half-remembered and half-imagined. In field arrangements, house styles, slave quarters, and wharves along rivers, the new-made plantations of Alabama, Mississippi, and Kentucky mimicked those of the East.[63]

Plantations were only cherished dreams for householders too poor to buy great tracts of western land and "passels" of slaves. Such people moved west too, but they retreated to the Piedmont, to the hills and hollows where they discovered scraps of fertile, wooded land, planted a few acres of corn for bread and whiskey, loosed their razorbacked hogs into the forest, and varied their diet with game. By the early nineteenth century, travelers found two Souths—one of low-country plantations and one of the "hollers"—but more than memories of "Old Virginny" and "North Kerliner" tied them together.

Plantations and slavery combined to make villages, or "towns" as the southerners called them, uncommon everywhere in the South. By *town* southerners understood something very different from the New England concept; they thought of a town as a collection of stores, shops, offices, and houses occupied by wholesale and retail merchants, craftsmen, physicians and attorneys, and their families. In the southern imagination, agriculturists belonged in town only on market day; the rest of the week or month they devoted to their more or less self-reliant holdings. It took several decades for the peculiar definition and concept of *town* to evolve, however, and at first southerners were convinced that old-country-style towns were desirable. "We think it fit," noted Governor Culpepper as late as 1680, "that houses and buildings be so contrived together, as to make if not handsome towns, yet compact and orderly villages; that this is the most proper, and successful manner of proceedings in the new plantations, besides those of former ages, for example of the Spaniards in the West Indies, do fully instance." Military and ecclesiastical necessity supported residence in village-like towns, and Virginians and other southerners understood it—in theory. After the Indian massacres of 1622 the military disadvantages of dispersed settlement appeared so obvious that the assembly ordered that dwellings be clustered in neighborhoods, and one clergyman after another castigated southern colonists for neglecting to build churches and schools. In 1662 one anonymous cleric lamented "a heap of evil consequences of their scattered planting," but chief among them he ranked the settlers' lack of religious communion. He proposed that most families live in towns and that wealthy planters build townhouses and only occasionally leave them for their plantations. Slaves, except for one or two left to safeguard valuables, would live with their masters at the townhouses every Saturday afternoon and Sunday. Such a scheme was wholly impractical and planters knew it, but the colony governments tried again and again to establish towns. In 1662 and again in 1680, Virginia acted to create towns at the mouth of most large estuaries, and proposed that tobacco be consigned from them and all imported merchandise be inspected and taxed there.[64] Assemblymen specified town plans accurately enough (brick houses forty feet long by twenty wide arranged in a square or another orderly pattern) but little came of the orders. Even the 1680 offer of half an acre free in any of the new towns to anyone willing to settle attracted only a few craftsmen to several of the more promising sites; most of the proposed towns did not materialize at all. By 1710 Charleston and Williamsburg were scarcely more than large villages, although both hosted seasonal political assemblies and Williamsburg boasted a college. The dearth of towns, and the poor progress of the few that survived, irritated royal governors, who could not conceive of a countryside without prosperous villages. A few southerners agreed with them but most accepted the absence of towns without qualm. In 1785 Thomas Jefferson summarized the situation. "Our country being much intersected with navigable waters, and trade brought generally to our doors, instead of our being obliged to go in quest of it," he wrote in *Notes on the State of Virginia,* "has probably been one of the causes why we have no towns of any consequence."[65] Jefferson's book includes no other reasons, which is curious indeed since many other places intersected by navigable estuaries and rivers, most notably Holland, supported thriving towns. Direct trade with Europe and other markets accessible by water was perhaps not even the chief reason why the Tidewater had so few towns despite the efforts of royal governors and occasionally interested assemblies.

The few merchants and craftsmen who located in new towns quickly discovered that their local markets were closely circumscribed. Most large plantations scarcely needed them; slave artisans produced tools and other equipment necessary in daily agricultural activity, and the planters purchased what they could not produce from merchant captains offering for sale the latest in London finery. Householders were frequently too few or too scattered to support the townspeople, and poor roads made travel difficult. Planters typically concerned themselves with building roads from their plantations to the nearest shipping wharf, which they often sited at the edge of their own holdings. Householders usually brought their crops to the larger plantations too because the owners of large plantations often acted as agents for men producing only a barrel or two of tobacco or some other crop. Most roads ran at right angles to the estuaries and rivers, then, and most followed ridges rather than crossing valleys, because householders "rolled" tobacco to wharves, despite its being brutal work.[66] They pierced a great hogshead of tobacco on each end with an axle and harnessed the ends of the axle to a horse or two. The barrel revolved about the axle well enough but could not be rolled across a stream; thus the water leaked in and destroyed the leaves. Roads therefore snaked along one ridge after another, and over a rare rough bridge, until they terminated at a wharf. They linked householdings of all sizes with neighboring plantations, not with nearby towns, and made men aware of the impracticality of long-distance land travel, especially during storms. The preferred short-distance route almost always lay over water, at least in the Tidewater, and not until settlement in the Piedmont was well advanced did men try to improve the roads leading to the fall line. There was no existing network of roads into which towns might be fitted, and by 1662 southerners abandoned all hope of rearranging what few rough roads had once seemed likely to nourish towns.

Almost from the beginning, too, the Tidewater—and later the Piedmont—evolved substitutes for town life, particularly for town socializing. Different social groups created their own substitutes, and by mid-eighteenth century the southern countryside objectified the hierarchical nature of southern social order. Most slaves, of course, lived confined to their masters' plantations, and for them the quarters became almost the only place for public life. Many slave cabins fronted on an open courtyard or packed-earth street in which slaves did domestic chores together and relaxed in the evening. Whites, however, created a wide variety of substitute towns and enjoyed themselves immensely.

Wealthy planters favored parties and visits at nearby plantation houses. Southern hospitality derived in part from the scarcity of long-distance roads and travelers; prosperous families welcomed old friends and travelers until shortly before the Civil War, when all southerners suspected outsiders of abolitionism. The most generous hospitality, however, they reserved for wealthy neighbors, and most of the wealthy, like William Byrd of Westover Plantation, who recorded his activities in a diary, indulged in a continual round of visits and other at-home entertainments. In summer, when malaria and other plagues struck down families whose plantations lay near swamps, wealthy planters and their dependents abandoned their plantations to slaves and overseers and relaxed in small townhouses in Charleston and other healthier places. There men engaged in politics and women visited constantly with one another until the season of danger passed.[67] In later years many southerners traveled to escape the heat and plagues by sailing to Europe or, in the early nineteenth century especially, by visiting the summer resorts of New York and New England.

Other, more formal activities offered opportunities for socializing. The Anglican Church services held at isolated locations attracted the wealthy but not only for religious reasons; at least occasionally families congregated to exchange gossip and news and visits, for not all parishes held weekly services. No one intended to reserve Anglican services for the wealthy planters. They became so by default. The Anglican service is a read service, and by late in the seventeenth century literacy across the southern colonies had become an upper-class trait because householders usually lived far from the few schools. Wealthy parents employed tutors, often New Englanders, to instruct their children, and gradually the householders deserted the Anglican denomination in favor of the orally oriented Baptist and Methodist ones or in favor of none at all, as more than one cleric lamented as he looked about at the frivíolity—or godlessness—about him.

Horse racing engaged the attention of all white southern colonists, but only the planters institutionalized it. In 1673 a tailor named James Bullock was fined 100 pounds of tobacco for racing his horse; the court concluded that horse racing was a "sport for gentlemen alone." Annual races closed to all but the wealthy became a feature of social life throughout the southern colonies.[68] Usually the planters located the racecourses on worn-out land and provided few shelters or other amenities. But the seasonal races offered a relief from boredom and were well attended—as the Kentucky Derby still is.

Householders, especially when they lived close enough together to outnumber the owners of large plantations, created a variety of town substitutes too. Military musters provided an occasional opportunity for men to assemble under their wealthy officers and for their families to visit, and convenings of courts provided a similar chance for socializing and business dealing. In some counties courts met once a month, usually at some isolated courthouse near the geographical center of the county. Men arrived to register headrights and deeds, to sue and be sued, and to watch criminal proceedings. Less often elections created an even greater enthusiasm and prompted fistfights and speeches.[69] No one consciously intended musters and court days as substitutes for town life, but they provided most of the delights, including the opportunity to shop among peddlers, to trade horses, and to make love.

The crossroads store functioned as the most important town substitute for smallholders after the middle of the eighteenth century. In hilly regions where large plantations were few and householdings were numerous, enterprising peddlers and other men established small stores along the more frequented roads. They sold the few items householders could not make for themselves (rifles, traps, iron tools) or grow, and they sold a few small luxuries too, like hair ribbons. More importantly, the crossroads storekeepers acted as agents for the sale of agricultural produce. They assembled large lots of tobacco, and in later decades, of cotton and arranged to ship it to a Tidewater or Gulf Coast quay, or even to London. Because storekeepers dealt in lots larger than any household-

Crossroads store, North Carolina. (JRS)

er produced, they often received a better price than any householder obtained, and even after subtracting their commission, they passed along increased profits to growers, who then spent their income at the store. Storekeepers extended credit as well, usually in the form of merchandise bought against the next season's harvest but sometimes in cash to finance purchases of land or animals. Above all, storekeepers operated social centers.[70] They sold liquor and accommodated travelers, and many kept post offices, where householders gathered for letters and newspapers.

Storekeepers quickly learned the significance of their social and economic position; many entered politics on the strength of their front-porch and stove-side oratory, and many others accumulated great tracts of land as they foreclosed on mortgages, and so graduated into the order of wealthy planters. Except in Tidewater and backcountry regions dominated by plantations, crossroads stores provided almost all "town" excitement. The stores gradually became the popularly accepted foci of

local social and economic activity and eventually gave their owners'
names to the intersections, or "corners," they abutted. Natives used them
as landmarks to direct travelers and defined neighborhoods about them.

More than any other feature of the man-altered environment, southern roads offered all colonists, but particularly householders, space for
social interaction. Friends met friends on the way to isolated churches or
courthouses or on the way to crossroads stores, and local residents encountered the infrequent long-distance traveler. Even in regions dotted
with stores, the peddler, usually a fast-talking, sharp-dealing northerner,
brought news and novel merchandise and attracted swarms of people in
every hollow. On the better stretches of road young men held informal
horse races, and friends stopped everywhere to sit under trees and conduct business. Southerners treated their roads as extensions of church,
courthouse, and store, seeing in them the potential for excitement that
northern city dwellers found in streets. Strangers, especially Europeans
and "Yankees," failed to understand the extraordinary importance of
the road in southern culture because they searched for the towns or
hamlets so uncommon south of Pennsylvania and ignored the roads and
waterways that substituted for towns.

Backcountry southerners intimately familiar with the eastern estuary
settlement pattern and the easy comradeship of road travel discovered in
western rivers the almost perfect synthesis of natural and man-made
highways. Keelboats and flatboats, and later steamboats, made the western river system into a vast highway network focused on New Orleans.
To northern eyes, the western South, even in the 1850s, lacked most
"standard" features of spatial order, but a few discerning strangers discovered the magnificent utility of navigable rivers reaching plantations
equipped with private docks. One northerner remarked how a great
steamboat suddenly slowed and stopped at a "landing" among the trees.
The ship's first officer "appeared with a box of raisins under his arm,
and walked up to a solitary house at some distance from the shore," the
observer continued. "He was met at the door by an old gentleman and
his wife, to whom he gave the box and a newspaper, and, after a
moment's chat, he returned on board, gave the necessary orders, and we
were soon on our way again."[71] Such door-to-door service provided by
600-ton, 200-passenger floating villages made towns and even hamlets
superfluous and enabled curious travelers to observe the South in comfort.

Throughout the colonial period and until 1850, outsiders criticized
the culture and countryside of the Tidewater and the Piedmont. Very
often travelers were disgusted by the condition of the slaves and by the

manners of the slaveowners, but their disgust was reinforced by their distaste for southern agriculture. In the minds of many visitors, and in the minds of some residents too, the colonists had destroyed the promise of the southern garden.

Europeans in particular faulted southerners for abusing the soil. As early as 1666 John Clayton complained to the Royal Society that Virginians too quickly abandoned land worn out by tobacco planting. Even if manure did flavor tobacco planted over it, he argued, nothing prevented composted material, especially muck dug out of swamps, from being carefully applied to the fields. Clayton complained too that the colonists refused to drain swamps partly because they felt that the resulting land would be too poor for tobacco and partly because they preferred the labor of clearing more forest upland. Despite a successful demonstration—which he accomplished only because a planter's wife wanted to experiment—his neighbors refused to drain additional swamps or apply muck to worn-out fields. Clayton was deeply annoyed by the appearance of the plantations; he claimed that 200 or 300 acres of intensively worked land would produce, with proper fertilizing, more of all crops than a 3,000-acre plantation cultivated in the usual way.[72] Until the colonists reformed their ways, he noted, the fertility of the soil would be wasted.

By the mid-seventeenth century no one denied Clayton's conclusions. The old fields abandoned after successive crops of tobacco and then of wheat or maize did not simply lie fallow before growing up in brush and trees. They suffered remarkable erosion from severe thunderstorms and frequently turned into corrugated mazes of deep gullies, useless even as grazing land and dangerous to cross on horseback. Most colonists simply ignored the eroded fields and moved on to clear more virgin land. Not surprisingly then, travelers from places where families worked fields differently and carefully restrained livestock from wandering at large in forests described southerners as callous indeed.

More than a century after Clayton's suggestions and annoyance, a professionally trained German forester and farmer rode through the Tidewater and Piedmont. Johann David Schoepf carefully scrutinized the agricultural practices prevalent in the newly independent states and he, like Clayton, grew disturbed by what he found. He noted that the countryside changed dramatically as he moved south from Pennsylvania into Maryland and Virginia. "It was a matter of no little astonishment to see so much waste or new-cleared land," he remarked of Virginia, "having just come from the very well settled and cultivated regions of Pennsylvania and Maryland." Schoepf examined the soil and wild plants and animals, and concluded, as had the English colonists nearly two centuries before, that the South seemed extremely fertile, well-watered, and blessed with a useful climate. With amazement, however, he recorded how little the southerners knew about manure or about the growing and cutting of hay for saddle horses and milk cows. "Wheat, pease, and other straw is cast out as useless," he wrote, knowing how such information would astonish his German readers, "and during the war, when Pennsylvania and Maryland teamsters came by with the army, the people of this region made the important and new discovery that horses eat small-cut straw, and I was asked in all seriousness whether our German horses condescend to this sort of feed." Schoepf was puzzled by slavery, by the absence of towns, by mystifyingly crooked, wretchedly kept roads, and by exorbitantly priced inns, but the extraordinary condition of the land worried him most.[73] According to his own agricultural tradition the shaped land objectified only stupidity and sloth.

At least some southerners agreed with the outsiders' views. In 1833 John Craven recalled the state of agriculture in central Virginia at the close of the eighteenth century. Craven was an innovative farmer whose new methods had proved a great success; perhaps his report of what he discovered when he moved onto his plantation is biased by his success, but his comments are similar to those made by others. Late in the eighteenth century he wrote in a lengthy letter in the *Farmers' Register,* "The whole face of the country presented a scene of desolation that baffles description—farm after farm had been worn out, and washed and gullied, so that scarcely an acre could be found in a place fit for cultivation." The term Craven chose to describe the land was *butchered,* and he linked the butchering to the traditional practice of abandoning worn-out land for new, even if the new land lay beyond the mountains in Kentucky, Tennessee, or Mississippi. The land "wore the most haggard, frightful, poverty-stricken appearance imaginable," he continued, "never having had upon it either plaster or clover, or, as one might naturally judge from its looks, vegetation of any kind." Craven did apply plaster to add lime to the soil, and he planted clover and ploughed deeply; in short he was the model planter inspired and educated by Edmund Ruffin, the editor of the *Register.*[74] But most southerners, especially the illiterate and scarcely literate smallholders, scoffed at Ruffin's ideas if they heard of them at all. Usually men preferred to move on, into the regions directly to the west or else to the southwest. Alabama, Mississippi, and East Texas were explored and settled by men searching for fertile land in quantities large enough to support the market agriculture of tobacco and especially of cotton. Men like Craven, who stayed behind and tried to restore the land, were few. The great Tidewater plantations began to decay in many regions before the Revolution, and many planters survived on the profits of slave breeding and the income from new plantations in the West.

Whitney's invention of the cotton gin in 1793 restored vitality to the slave system and made practical the growing of short-staple cotton, a variety which is difficult to clean by hand but which grows well on upland soils. The plantation system and its spirit spread westward and forced householders into the less fertile hill country everywhere, into the hollers, or hollows, where they subsisted on scanty crops and brewed liquor for home consumption and cash income.[75] The spirit of moving on to better land, of abandoning ill-used ground for fertile virgin land, moved westward too. Slavery—once abolished in the North—symbolized for travelers the southern error, but something else lay at the root of the European and northern distrust of the southern landscape. Certainly the abused land worried outsiders riding along the rutted roads or staring outward from steamboat decks, but the fear of that blighted landscape spreading over the fertile, virgin land coveted by westward-moving northerners sparked strident criticism throughout the pre-Civil War years. Outsiders focused their anger on abused slaves and eroded, abandoned fields, but the very alienness of the southern landscape unnerved them more. Even Pennsylvanians unaccustomed to villages or nucleated towns wondered at abandoned plantations and acres of brush.[76] However much a garden the South had been in the early seventeenth century, it pleased no visitor by the 1850s. Instead it seemed only a waste produced by sinister ideas of land use and social order, ideas objectified in isolated plantations, tumbledown houses, floating villages, and all-important roads. Southerners trapped in export agriculture and the slavery system could do little to change their peculiar landscape but most refused even to explain it, especially to outsiders whose spatial vocabulary made explanation almost impossible. Not even Pennsylvanians understood the southern man-made environment.

Prelude

William Penn's "holy experiment," the vast enterprise called Pennsylvania, was the last colony conceived according to tradition. Penn envisioned an Old World order transplanted across the Atlantic, a landscape of baronies, manors, and tightly nucleated agricultural villages, but he knew the lessons of the Tidewater and New England too. His plans did not come to fruition. A uniquely different landscape emerged from the chaos of wilderness, a landscape marked by tradition but accented by innovation.

In the years following 1680 a multitude of colonists accepted Penn's offer of fertile, inexpensive land and religious toleration. Families arrived from England, the north of Ireland, the German principalities, Wales, and France and joined the Swedes already resident in the southeastern corner of the grant. The different groups brought with them religious differences but very little rancor, and most found the others good neighbors, if at times difficult to understand. Pennsylvania was populated by upwardly mobile smallholders who clearly perceived their narrowly defined futures in Europe, and who sold their land and most of their movable possessions to support the gamble for a better life in the New World. All but a few distrusted community control of public and private resources because that control had slowly impoverished them as Europe moved closer to an agricultural economy dependent on markets dominated by large landowners.[77] The colonists of Pennsylvania were sometimes the religiously persecuted and sometimes the political outcasts, but almost always they were the innovators of their former landschaft or region. They wanted land to work as they wished to work it, and Penn provided the opportunity.

Until about 1700, Penn's land-assignment practices forestalled any mass scattering to the most fertile land. Immigrants entered the colony through Philadelphia and at first were assigned farms which focused on villages. Penn insisted that settlers live in towns, "so that the neighbors may help one another in a Christlike manner and praise God together, and that they may accustom their children to do the same." He thought that about ten families should comprise a "township" or "village," and that the total area of their holdings should amount to about 5,000 acres. Penn insisted that his surveyors plat out the townships before anyone settled the land, and for about two decades his measurers successfully ordered the land. As in New England, survey preceded settlement, and newcomers discovered bounded lots.[78] There, however, the parallel stopped. Pennsylvania was not New England.

Penn understood that farming was no longer a corporate enterprise dependent on common fields but an individualistic one which thrived on innovation. His villages were really only arrangements of free-standing farms and were designed to foster neighborliness and good citizenship, not husbandry. Newtown Township in Bucks County is a case in point. Each of the fifteen landowners possessed a narrow neck of land abutting the forty-acre rectangular common at the center of the township. There, according to Penn's intentions, he would build a house and outbuildings, and eventually a store or shop if he was so inclined. At the opposite end of the necks the holdings broadened, so that each owner had the advantages of neighbors and of an integrated farm. Such an agreement of

space precluded, of course, additional settlers because the farms wholly
enclosed the common. Penn knew that the holdings, which averaged
about 250 acres each, would require years of labor to clear and till, but
he knew too that they were certainly large enough to support their
occupants. Not only could a landowner raise enough produce for his
family's needs, but he could raise a good deal more for market. Pennsylvania never knew an era of subsistence farming.[79] Almost from the first
year, its inhabitants sold part of every crop they raised.

Despite being aware of the new spirit in agriculture, Penn underestimated the individuality of the settlers. Most were satisfied with the land
they bought; the soil of Pennsylvania, whatever its specific class, is generally good and, in comparison with most New England soil, excellent.
Most too were satisfied with the governing of the colony, although now
and then irked by Penn's insistence on quitrents and often unwilling to
pay them. They were not usually frightened of the Indians either, and so
they chose to live not in the narrow necks of their farms but in the center
of the broader wedges. There most fields were equidistant from the
barnyard and men lost little time traveling from one crop to the next.
Often a clear, constant spring or stream attracted the landowner, or a
spot of particularly rich soil. Officially constituted community served
little purpose, and soon men tired of the townships.

By 1720 the process of settlement exceeded the control of the surveyors and the recorders of deeds. Men struck westward in search of
the best soil, found likely places, and squatted on them. The Penn family
tried to accommodate its plans to those of the settlers by ordering that
any lot presented for recording have only four corners and by allowing
squatters to buy their land, but such measures came too late. Lots as
irregular as any Tidewater plantation, with twenty or thirty corners and
stretched along streams or rivers, were recorded, and many squatters
wanted deeds only to protect themselves from others. In the backcountry, away from the colony government, groups of squatters elected tri-
bunals to adjudicate boundary disputes, and slowly there emerged a
sectional division in the countryside something like that between Tidewater and Piedmont, but reversed. In eastern Pennsylvania ordered
townships and small farms were common, but farther west, beyond the
Brandywine River, farms were larger and more scattered and ordered
townships were almost unknown.[80] Much of the confusion resulted directly from land speculation, despite Penn's early ruling that no one
might own more than 500 acres. As the eighteenth century passed, however, more and more men bought large tracts to sell to immigrants or to
colonists moving west from too-small farms. By 1740, scarcely sixty years

after the official opening of the colony, the settled land appeared prosperous but not obviously orderly.

Like the southern colonists, Pennsylvanians were content to live without villages or towns. Craftsmen journeyed from one farm to the next, and churches stood at crossroads near the centers of their congregations. The landscape was not southern in arrangement, however, because the farmers needed market towns; none traded with a merchant captain docked at the edge of his farm. Philadelphia was the preeminent market for most of the colony, and until settlement reached westward enough, men depended on roads for communication. Under the best conditions a heavily laden wagon traveled about thirty miles in one day, and gradually there emerged a number of large market towns, each at the center of a trading circle roughly sixty miles in diameter but modified according to topography. Lancaster, York, and Carlisle depended on wagon transportation and were decidedly secondary in importance to Philadelphia, but they provided farmers with wholesale and retail markets. Baltimore developed as a rival of Philadelphia only after Pennsylvanians settled far enough west to make use of the river links to the south. The typical farmer, then, felt little or no need for a village or even a large town; what he did need, and what he earnestly petitioned for when he lived in a region too new to have one, was a wholesale market town—almost a city.

The Penns consistently emphasized the power of county government. Had they done otherwise, perhaps villages or territorial units like the New England town would have become popular. Instead evolved the *hamlet,* an unincorporated, haphazardly arranged collection of houses, a store or two, perhaps a blacksmith shop or the shop of some other craftsman, and a church building. The hamlet was more than the southern crossroads store because Pennsylvania farmers needed more services than self-sufficient plantation owners and had more ready capital than southern householders. Two or three dozen prosperous farm families supported several full- or part-time craftsmen and a storekeeper or two, and they looked to the hamlet as a place of socializing, buying and selling in small amounts, and for exchanging news. But the hamlet was not the center of their world. Centrality lay in the barnyard, for it was the farm that dominated the Pennsylvania landscape.

Almost every traveler across Pennsylvania remarked on the farms, and Europeans and New Englanders frequently marveled at the distances between them. "People live so far apart," commented Gottlieb Mittelberger in 1756, "that many have to walk a quarter or a half-hour just to reach their nearest neighbor."[81] Mittelberger understood that more than simple land hunger dictated the settlement pattern. Unlike southern tobacco growers, Pennsylvania agriculturists intended to reside permanently on their land in order to nurture it from one decade to the next. They needed large acreages for reasons other than soil exhaustion.

Europeans colonized North America at a critical time, during the era of agricultural modernization, a time marked not only by technological innovation but by economic and social change too, a time when husbandmen revised their ideas about space. The spatial effects of modernization derived chiefly from the perfecting of individualistic, market-oriented agriculture. In the Tidewater and the Piedmont, new crops and new soil conditions fostered the rapid development of change-oriented thinking, but in Pennsylvania too agriculturists adapted quickly to concepts retarded in Europe—and in New England, although much less completely—by the landschaft agricultural and spatial order. European travelers in the coastal colonies wondered about the new social and economic order so clearly objictified in the new shaping of space.

In the years between the planting of Chimayo and the settlement of middle Pennsylvania, settlers' spatial horizons simultaneously contracted and expanded. No longer was the traditional close-knit community—the colonial version of the old-country landschaft—of central importance in their lives although it occasionally served as a standard by which they judged new settlements. Even in the towns of New England, where the memory of the spatially distinct, corporately managed community remained strong until the middle of the eighteenth century, men looked with far more love at their own holdings than at the larger cultivated space they called the "town." Across the Tidewater, Piedmont, and Pennsylvania their bias was even more pronounced, and there *plantation* ceased to mean a new-born community and became an individual holding. The farm—the *plantation* of the late eighteenth century—acquired a wholly new significance in the New World east of New Spain.[82] Corporate space existed no longer according to tradition and group boundaries but by political act and maintenance. Away from New England the only immediately discernible communities were counties so lacking in spatial discreteness that European commentators despaired of describing them to Old World readers familiar only with the decayed landschaften called villages.

Had the Europeans spent less time on the road and more time visiting, they might have learned the new meaning of shaped space. In Pennsylvania and the other Middle Colonies, across the Tidewater and Piedmont, and even in western New England, the early modern European landschaft evolved into a distinctly American space: the neighborhood.

Before it defined a place, the word *neighborhood,* like *knighthood* and *fatherhood,* defined a way or condition of life, "the general character of living together in a rural village," according to Ferdinand Tönnies. The continuous meeting of the villagers, their cooperation and like thinking, produced a bond almost as strong as kinship. From the sixteenth century on, as the experience of living in large towns and cities became more common in Western Europe, *neighborhood* began to connote a spatial arrangement as well.[83] In 1597 Francis Bacon remarked that friendship is destroyed in large cities but strengthened in neighborhoods; his use of the word was almost experimental, however, and two centuries later in *The Spectator,* Richard Steele still felt obliged to define the word's newer meaning. He believed that "the men formed for society, and those little communities which we express by the word neighborhoods" make the most congenial companions because they are neither too active to be happy in private life nor too withdrawn to avoid public responsibility. Cotton Mather shared Steele's 1711 vision of small communities enjoying the best of public and private happiness. A year earlier he exhorted American do-gooders to reform their neighborhoods: "Methinks, this excellent zeal should be carried into our neighborhoods. Neighbors, you stand related unto one another; and you should be full of devices, that all the neighbors may have cause to be glad of your being in the neighborhood."[84] Like Bacon and Steele, Mather understood the subtle spatial connotations of neighborhood, and other colonists eventually acquired his understanding.

To most eighteenth-century Americans, *neighborhood* identified that space beyond their own property in which they had vital interests, close knowledge, and frequent reason to travel. Each family understood the neighborhood center to be its own house, farmyard, and fields, and the neighborhood circumference to be the limit of the family's other frequent concerns. In practice, neighborhood meant the familiar area within one-hour's walk from the family residence. In New England, *neighborhood* often coincided with town, but in the South, Middle Colonies, and on the frontier it connoted an area measured always from each householding and almost never from some sort of roland, civil or ecclesiastical.

A rural neighborhood, then, encompassed about fifty square miles, an extraordinarily large area by European and seventeenth-century New England standards. But there was another characteristic, too, for Europeans struggling to understand the man-altered environment of the southern and Middle colonies. The traditional landschaft and the typical New England town had single centers, foci of religion, trade, and dwelling; the rural neighborhood had several. Sometimes a crossroads store stood beside a church or meetinghouse, but often the religious centers of the neighborhood were several miles removed from the center of business. Occasionally the neighborhood mill stood adjacent to the store or to one of the meetinghouses, but usually it stood isolated beside the most regular waterfall.[85] By 1770 all except New Englanders found it useless to think of discrete settlements focused about single centers, to recall visions of the traditional landschaft remembered in New England's "Ordering of Towns" and the dreams of southern governors. The old ideal and reality of space coterminous with small, self-sufficient communities dissolved before social, economic, and political energy unknown two generations before. Even in New Spain the estensión began to fragment in the face of individualistic, market-oriented agriculture.

On July 4, 1776, the would-be Republic possessed several clearly identified cultural regions, each rapidly evolving in its own way from seventeenth-century beginnings and each displaying pronounced, peculiar characteristics. Hatred of British imperialism temporarily united the regions; beneath a towering elm—which thereafter enjoyed an almost sacred status—on a New England town common, a Virginian plantation owner took charge of the Army of Independence. War brought Rhode Islanders to Pennsylvania and Carolinians to New Hampshire, but the soldiers judged built spaces and forms according to those of "home." Local, neighborhood standards, almost invariably transmitted orally and by example, shaped building.

When the Revolution succeeded and the new national government hesitantly embarked on federal, not regional or local projects, Americans discovered the extraordinary power of custom objectified in regional man-made forms. National design began as a thin veneer overlaying pronounced regional differences, and so it remained for decades. Enlightenment innovation almost withered in the still-dominant shadow of traditional, if regionally diverse, common building.

Starrucca Viaduct, Susquehanna, Pennsylvania. (JRS)

NATIONAL DESIGN

It is only necessary to discover the want of a bridge, or a canal, to insure an effort, and commonly a successful one, to bring it into existence.[1]

James Fenimore Cooper
Notions of the Americans
1829

veryone recognizes checkerboard America. Like a great geometrical carpet, like a Mondrian painting, the United States west of the Appalachians is ordered in a vast grid. Nothing strikes an airborne European as more typically American than the great squares of farms reaching from horizon to horizon.

Only the fields are noticeable from 20,000 feet. At lower altitudes flyers discern among them the scattered farmsteads connected by ruler-straight gravel and blacktop roads. They marvel at the pattern and scrutinize the fields and farmsteads, wondering what crops show up so yellow at midsummer and worrying that the farmers might be lonely. Few look closely at the lines that hatch the countryside below; the lines seem accidental, the result of pastures abutting wheat fields and the building of roads. Almost no one perceives the regular spacing of the lines or guesses that the lines predate the fields and structures.

Section lines, like lines on graph paper, made the grid and make it still. They objectify the Enlightenment in America. Late in the eighteenth century they existed only in surveyors' notebooks and on the rough maps carefully stored in federal land office drawers. Here and there a blazed tree or pile of stones marked an intersection, but otherwise the lines existed only as invisible guides. Not until farmers settled the great rectangles platted by the surveyors and began shaping the land did the lines become more than legal abstractions of boundaries. Along them farmers built fences to mark their property limits and to divide livestock from corn, and along many they built roads too. Now and then a histori-cally minded flyer, often a foreigner intrigued by the geometric regu-larity of the countryside below, swoops down and hedgehops above a section line, following it as Wolfgang Langeweische did in 1939. "First it was a dirt road, narrow between two hedges, with a car crawling along it dragging a tail of dust. Then the road turned off, but the line went straight ahead, now as a barbed wire fence through a large pasture, with a thin footpath trod out on each side by each neighbor as he went, week after week, year after year, to inspect his fence. Then the fence stopped, but now there was corn on one side of the line and something green on the other."[2] On and on Langeweische flew, following the half-abstract, half-physical line across pasture land and arable, through a small town, and on into farms again. "When I climbed away and resumed my course," he remarked half-wonderingly, "I left it as a fence which had cows on one side and no cows on the other. That's a section line."[3] Like many amateur pilots, Langeweische appreciated section lines because they run rigidly north–south, east–west; despite being an eighteenth-century creation, they are a superb navigational aid. Nothing man has built into the American wilderness is more orderly.

On the ground, only the most perceptive travelers consciously recognize section lines. Here and there a hilltop offers a view of lines and right-angle intersections, but elsewhere the grid is masked by the slightly rolling topography that characterizes most of the Middle West. Farmers and other inhabitants of the grid country think nothing of the straight roads and property lines they have inherited from their forbears. Not until they drive east, into the coastal states and Kentucky, Vermont, and Tennessee, are they suddenly aware that behind them lies a landscape of more obvious order. All at once they recognize the absence of the geometrical structure that shapes their space, colors their speech, and subtly influences their lives, and they perceive the dominance of older, distinctly regional landscape skeletons.

MERCANTILE CITIES

William Penn introduced the grid to the English colonies in 1681, when he directed his agents and surveyors to lay out a city in Pennsylvania. Philadelphia was a city by intention, not accident, and it was markedly different from the few other large towns along the coast. Penn did not invent the urban grid—the towns of northern New Spain were ordered about a plaza and streets intersecting at right angles, and nine years before Philadelphia, Charleston in South Carolina was laid out "into regular streets"—but he emphasized the grid above walls, meeting-houses, and public squares. From the beginning, its streets defined and distinguished Philadelphia.

Until the 1740s colonial space struck visitors as simply rural. Only Boston, Newport, New York, Charleston, and above all Philadelphia broke the uniformity of farming settlements. As late as the 1690s, even Boston scarcely impressed visiting Europeans, although it was the center of most New England shipping, the seat of the Bay Colony government, and frequently compared by its inhabitants to the "city of London."[4] But at the close of the seventeenth century, Philadelphia promised only an imminent urbanity; Boston seemed certain to retain its place as the foremost English "merchandise" town.

The city upon a hill envisioned by John Winthrop began as an agricultural settlement on a peninsula. Like all other New Englanders, its inhabitants occupied themselves with allocating house lots and planting land, and with regulating the use of common pasture, meadow, and woods. Two years after its founding, approximately forty houses, each surrounded by a vegetable garden and some already dignified by sapling fruit trees, clustered haphazardly about a meetinghouse. Bostonians worried about growing enough food for themselves and focused their attention on the poor soil and the daily adventure of agriculture in a new place and a new climate.[5] Even as more and more immigrants landed at Town Cove and sought food, shelter, and seed, Bostonians behaved as did most other New Englanders, shaping the land and ordering society.

Seventeen years later 315 houses and 45 additional buildings bespoke Boston's new role. England's Civil War reduced immigration to a trickle after 1642 and deprived Bostonians of their entrepôt livings. All at once citizens discovered the necessity of locating new markets, and they directed their attention to the West Indies and Europe. At first Bostonians captured only the coasting trade, bringing lumber and cattle and cod from New Hampshire and the Grand Banks to the hungry plantations of the southern colonies and the West Indies, and carrying home molasses.[6] The trade prospered as New England's agricultural settlements produced larger and larger surpluses, and the Bostonians built larger ships and sailed for the Portuguese Islands, England, and the European continent in what became known as the triangular trade. Within two decades of the closing of immigration, Boston was something that other New England settlements except Newport were not, although exactly what puzzled visitors and natives alike. It was easy enough to see the physical differences, however, and traveler after traveler remarked on them.

Commerce weaned Bostonians from agriculture, and soon they jammed houses and other structures so closely together that houselot gardening almost vanished, at least near the waterfront. Craftsmen worked frantically erecting houses for newcomers like William Rix, who commissioned a one-room house, sixteen feet long and fourteen wide, with a cellar and loft, clapboarded walls and roof, and a timber chimney. It was an impossibly small house for a family man who made his living by weaving, and Rix requested a second structure to house his loom and other tools. Compared with Governor Winthrop's "mansion," Rix's house was simple indeed, a clear objectification of Puritan hierarchical society. But the loom-shed acquired a special significance because it revealed that Rix did not farm full time and that his specialized occupation kept him busy enough to require and support a specialized structure.[7] Craftsmen like Rix understood the necessity for specialized workspace, and Boston's carpenters, brickmakers, limeworkers, masons, sawyers, brewers, bakers, coopers, tanners, butchers, smiths, shipwrights, sailmakers, ropemakers, joiners soon produced structures of every sort, each type adapted to a particular calling.

Weavers and other craftsmen bought most of their food and raw materials from husbandmen who lived in outlying agricultural settlements and who walked to Boston filled with anticipation not only of profits but of excitement. In Boston they exchanged their produce for cash or services or else bartered it for imported or manufactured items impossible to obtain in their home settlements. Retail shops blossomed along the narrow, twisting streets, catering mostly to Bostonians but also to countrymen. "The town is full of good shops well furnished with all kinds of merchandise," remarked one inhabitant, and it was filled with shoppers too. By 1680 Boston supported twenty-four silversmiths, a sure sign of growing prosperity.

Six years after the founding of Boston the selectmen ordered that two "street ways" be laid out to accommodate the townspeople. Never again, however, did the town pay much attention to its growing traffic problem. More and more frequently it temporarily solved access problems by empowering individuals to open streets at their own cost; at the time the policy seemed sound. Boston received a new street or two, and the undertakers realized a profit by selling the abutting lots. Not surprisingly, such streets were narrow and crooked, but their very irregularity produced a wealth of changing views and surprises.[8] That Bostonians thought in terms of streets rather than roads or ways is significant because in the late sixteenth century *street* had already acquired richly evocative connotations. The word no longer meant merely a road or cartway but a passage in a city or town, a pathway through the verticality made by houses and other structures, and often bordered with pedestrian sidewalks. Even more than the king's highway, a street promised excitement and activity, and particularly the likelihood of meeting strangers, because *street* connoted above all else half-controlled urban chaos. Seventeenth-century Bostonians understood the connotation very well indeed, for as early as the 1650s their streets, in the words of one observer, were "full of girls and boys sporting up and down, with a continued concourse of people." Strangers of every sort thronged the streets: newly arrived immigrants waiting while their representatives selected fertile sites for settlements, seamen from English ships, merchants from other colonies, and countrymen from nearby towns. Whether the strangers tarried for only several days or decided to settle permanently in the port, Bostonians usually made them welcome because almost always they paid in cash for whatever goods and services they obtained. Unlike the ideal space specified in "The Ordering of Towns," the town's built environment quickly adapted to a continuous concourse of strangers. Boston was a place of exciting streets, not of roads and lanes.

Unlike most other New England settlements, Boston—and later Newport—acquired two spatial foci, and then several more. In its earliest years Boston focused on its meetinghouse, and because of its almost island-like site, no settlement more closely resembled the concentric utopia described in "The Ordering of Towns." Within one or two years, however, a second focus challenged the meetinghouse hierophany. Town Cove made a natural landing place, where deep water closely abutted the shore and where islands and headlands sheltered anchored ships from storms. William Wood foresaw that its deep harbor would make Boston the "chief place for shipping and merchandise" in New England, and other seventeenth-century visitors agreed.[9] Bostonians proved Wood correct. They built their first wharf at Town Cove, and then another, and then several more, until by 1645 fifteen wharves jutted into the harbor. Waterfront matters preoccupied the town elders, who ordered that piers be kept clear of buildings, that "no annoying things be left or laid about the sea shore" to decay and smell, and that two privies be erected at the wharves for the convenience of strangers. Bostonians rapidly grew too numerous for a single meetinghouse, and their clergy determined to split into separate "churches" or congregations, each of which erected its own meetinghouse. By 1680 Boston lacked the single religious hierophany that characterized almost all other New England settlements. Its jammed streets converged on an ever more congested—and ever more exciting—waterfront. Ministers warned of the evils of greed but their sermons failed to distract the people's attention from worldly matters.

New Amsterdam, Newport, and later Charleston struggled to emulate successful Boston, but not for decades did they achieve even a measure of Boston's prosperity or a semblance of Boston's excitement. Nevertheless, in each town wise men insisted that waterfronts receive increasing capital investment and scrutiny; shortly after 1680, for example, a group of Newport men built Long Wharf, a structure that surpassed even Boston's most handsome piers. In each town the public treasury supplemented private investment in anything that quickened commerce—bridges, ship channels, drainage ditches, and even fortifications. Growth proceeded particularly haphazardly in Boston and Newport and was only slightly more orderly in New Amsterdam and Charleston. Invariably, people considered first the immediately needed improvement, and as Charleston soon proved, the art of city planning scarcely coped with the economic and social forces that made and remade Boston's appearance every other decade.

Like Chimayo, Charleston was a walled town.[10] South Carolina's En-

glish proprietors worried about Indian attack but they especially feared
raids by Spanish warships. In 1680 they agreed that "a pallisade around
the town with a small ditch is sufficient fortification against the Indians,"
but the inhabitants of Charleston thought more grandly. The year 1704
found them building "forts, half moons, platforms, entrenchments,
flankers and parapets, sally ports, a gate and a drawbridge and blind."
When Edward Crisp surveyed the city around 1711, the complicated
battlements mounted eighty-three cannon that jutted from bastions of
every sort; two years later the walls and guns served their purpose in a
difficult Indian war. In peacetime, however, they proved an expensive
handicap. Early eighteenth-century fortifications withstood cannon fire
out of sheer massiveness, and engineers were hard pressed to design
effective walls that were easily thrown down to permit urban expansion.
Walls thick enough and intricate enough to turn back combined artillery
and infantry assaults or bombardment from warships drained Charleston of capital that might otherwise have built merchant ships, wharves,
and warehouses. And the walls constricted the uninhibited laying of
streets and erecting of houses and shops that so pleased Bostonians, who
were building according to commonly accepted tradition—and innovation.

In 1710 Charleston was two cities. Its perimeter was distinctly military,
almost medieval in its complexity. Its core was rigidly ordered for
growth in response to Lord Ashley's directive to plat the land "into
regular streets, for be the buildings never so mean and thin at first, yet as
the town increases in riches and people, the void places will be filled up
and the buildings will grow more beautiful." Ashley's 1672 instructions
produced—after several decades—a walled town "laid out into large and
capacious streets" in the words of one visitor, lined with structures built
chiefly of cypress and mahogany and roofed with tiles according to
Barbados practice. Living costs were high in Charleston, perhaps because of the continuing investment in the walls, and they became higher
still after a great fire destroyed many of the structures in 1698. By 1717,
however, the place was beginning to prosper, and its inhabitants agreed
to demolish the cumbersome walls erected only six years before. They
needed room for change.

The walls of Charleston objectified the crucial weakness of urban design theory from the fifteenth to the very early eighteenth century.
Burghers and designers first expected town form to mirror a static social, political, economic, and religious order before it reinforced and
nurtured it. Absence of form distressed more observers than the shape-
imagining Edward Johnson, but form proved difficult to achieve (and

nearly impossible to maintain) in an era of social and economic change. The ideal settlements proposed in the Spanish Royal Ordinances and the New England town-ordering essay are essentially static; scant attention is given to their eventual expansion. As the seventeenth century progressed, city dwellers desperately needed an urban form adaptable to change, but designers remained obsessed with outdated but "perfect" forms—especially the circle—and with defensive walls that ensured an orderly perimter at least.[11] As late as 1699 Governor Nicholson of Virginia, having failed to create a perfect town at Annapolis during his governorship of Maryland, tried again in his new colony. Today Annapolis objectifies his obsession with such pure forms as circles and straight streets, but it was at Williamsburg that the governor's outdated attempt to stress form over use made its greatest impact. Nicholson, remarked Robert Beverly in *The History and Present State of Virginia,* "flattered himself with the fond imagination of being the founder of a new city. He marked out the streets in many places so that they might represent the figure of a 'W' in memory of his late Majesty King William." Beverly owned land at Jamestown, and perhaps he resented the moving of the capital, but his description parallels that of Hugh Jones, who remarked in 1724 that Nicholson laid out the town "in the form of a cypher, made of a 'W' and 'M' for William and Mary."[12] Whatever the intended form, however, the irritated citizens of Williamsburg convinced Nicholson to lay out straight streets. Annapolis and Williamsburg, like most southern towns, never amounted to much, and it may well be that their curious street patterns prevented necessary expansion and the assembling of large lots. Even more than Charleston, they objectified out-of-date professional design.

It was a Dutch engineer and city planner, Simon Stevin of The Hague, who deciphered the contradictions in seventeenth-century town-planning theory. Like so many of his countrymen, Stevin immersed himself in mercantile economics (he popularized double-entry book-keeping in Western Europe) but his business sense clashed with his training in military engineering. Eventually he devised a compromise solution to design problems bedeviling city fathers intent on military protection and economic growth. He discarded the old notions of circles and other ideal forms and substituted for them the concept of symmetry. Stevin's ideal city is a rectangle, walled to be sure, but ordered by a grid of streets intersecting at right angles. Instead of one, it has several foci: a cathedral square, a palace for its prince, several small squares intended as neighborhood marketplaces, and a waterfront devoted to commerce.[13] Little of Stevin's ideal design was new in 1630; it synthesized plans and

designs known, although only theoretically, since 1500. Stevin's insight
lay first in his understanding that a grid of streets might be extended in
any direction with little modification of the encompassing walls, and that
a grid allowed for major changes anywhere within the walls. Stevin's
ideal city is not, therefore, a static form like the ideal Spanish estensión
or ideal New England town focused on a single central plaza or meetinghouse. Rather it is engineered to accept and order change, and especially to order growth. Far more importantly, however, Stevin explicitly
recognized the evolving nature of society, not only in the Netherlands
but elsewhere. Mercantile capitalism was slowly destroying the old order
of hierarchy and eunomy objectified in so many *landschappen,* and the
grid town seemed to him—and to many successors—perfectly adapted to
a new way of life.

Penn probably knew nothing of Stevin's essays and designs, but there
is no dismissing the striking similarity between his plan of Philadelphia
and the Dutch engineer's plans for an ideal city. Like Stevin, Penn seems
to have understood the changing nature of society, and for all that the
proprietor of Pennsylvania may have learned from the grid-street plans
submitted in the competition to rebuild London after the Great Fire of
1666, Philadelphia's pattern derived in large measure from the spirit of
an era of change.[14]

In the beginning Penn intended to lay out Philadelphia as an agricultural village in which every purchaser of 500 acres of planting land
would be entitled to a houselot of 10 acres. Almost immediately, however, Penn abandoned the scheme and determined to build a mercantile,
not an agricultural, town. He instructed his surveyors to find a site
"where most ships may best ride, of deepest draught of water, if possible
to load or unload at the bank or key side," and only afterward noted that
the site ought to be healthy and fertile too. Philadelphia's waterfront
preoccupied Penn. He ordered that no house be located closer to the
shore than a quarter mile in order that streets and warehouses might be
built without hindrance, and he stressed that each waterfront lot have at
least 800 feet of shore. When Penn arrived at Philadelphia in 1682 he
immediately extended the grid of streets to the bank of the Schuylkill, so
that the city had *two* waterfronts. He concerned himself less with the
inland or "backward" part of the city, although he specified that every
house be seated in the middle of its lot, so that the city "may be a green
country town, which will never be burnt, and always be wholesome," and
he located a great square of ten acres at the center (for a meetinghouse,
government hall, markethouse, and schoolhouse—and perhaps for his
own residence) and a lesser square of eight acres in each of the four

quarters of the city (for marketplaces). Between the waterfronts, however, Philadelphia's most striking feature was its grid of streets.[15] Nine great streets ran from "front to front," all crossed at right angles by twenty-one others. All were fifty feet wide, except for High and Broad streets, whose hundred-foot widths convinced newcomers that Philadelphia seemed destined for an urban greatness far beyond that of Boston or indeed most European cities.

Penn's surveyors platted only 1,280 acres, and at first the city's straggling appearance disappointed visitors. Within three years, however, 600 houses lined the streets nearest the city axis, and the waterfronts, particularly the Delaware one, flourished. A new dock 300 feet square jutted into the river, and near it stood the shops and houses of all manner of craftsmen from shoemakers and glaziers to brickmakers and woodturners. By 1685 men thought nothing of building in brick and had begun work on a great brick meetinghouse. Such furious activity resulted in part from steady immigration; Pennsylvania attracted settlers from England and its colonies as well as from elsewhere in Europe. The newcomers often discovered a place for themselves in Philadelphia, especially if they knew a useful trade, and never began farming. But much of the growth came from Penn's understanding of the city's mercantile function; twice a week great markets convened at the central square, and twice each year a great fair attracted husbandmen and traders from across the growing colony.[16] Penn's emerging road system brought more and more produce to Philadelphia for sale and transshipment to Europe or other colonies and offered quick access to the interior for imported goods. Like Stevin's ideal city, Philadelphia reached both to a developing backcountry and to the world of ocean commerce. Soon traffic jammed its great straight streets.

For fifteen years Penn's original plans directed the city's growth. Vine Street, Chestnut Street, Strawberry Street, and the other two-mile-long streets that linked the two waterfronts ordered visitors' impressions of the city while channeling traffic and real estate development. But around the turn of the century several canny inhabitants exploited the potential for common development implicit in Penn's grand design. They subdivided the great houselots and snaked narrow alleys down the middle of blocks; the modifications provided landowners with additional access and the possibility of selling or renting "streetfront" property. Gabriel Thomas, who had arrived in Philadelphia in 1681, described the subdivision process in 1698. He found "very many lanes and alleys" between Front Street and Second Street on the Delaware waterfront and decided that the narrow ways represented Philadelphia industry as

much as the great streets. Thomas was no doubt pleased with the 2,000
brick houses he saw about him, most "three stories high, after the mode
in London," and with the many warehouses and shops, and like most
other commentators on the city's appearance and character emphasized
the citizens' accomplishments rather than such serious shortcomings as
unpaved and miry streets. Penn's great grid guided the growth of the
city well into the eighteenth century but within its framework landowners
experimented with other designs.

Benjamin Franklin encountered the grid on his arrival in Philadelphia
in 1721, when he walked away from the dock in search of a meal and
bought the famous three pennyworth of bread, which he carried under
his arms. "Thus I went up Market Street as far as Fourth Street, passing
by the door of Mr. Read, my future wife's father, when she, standing at
the door, saw me, and thought I made—as I certainly did—a most awkward, ridiculous appearance," he wrote fifty years later in his *Autobiography*. "Then I turned and went down Chestnut Street and part of Walnut Street, eating my roll all the way, and coming round, found myself
again at Market Street wharf."[17] Franklin's first walk typifies the experience of so many other new arrivals guided by the great grid into a city
intimately familiar with strangers.

Philadelphia, as Franklin discovered, prospered without a center. Instead of focusing on the great square (Penn never did settle in the city he
designed) it focused on nodes of activity. Its waterfronts, of course,
became its most active places but even they were only conglomerations of
particularly active wharves and warehouses and craftsmens' shops and
taverns. In Philadelphia, and in Boston, New York, and even in Charleston and Newport too, the tavern became the focus of many men's daily
activities. Even the sober (and frugal) Franklin spent much of his time in
the street corner taverns, the common-designed hubs of Philadelphia
life.

Taverns, like tavern-goers, were of many sorts. The worst were the
grogshops that clustered near the wharves and served seamen, fishermen, and apprentices looking for a few minutes' excitement. City authorities recognized the necessity for such places; waterfront taverns
acted as informal hiring halls for seamen looking for ships and for
country lads looking to become seamen, they provided lodging for seamen looking for honest employment, and most importantly, they helped
confine rowdy individuals to the dockside. Despite occasional knifings
and brawls—and the intermittent scandals of harlotry—the grogshops
were rarely molested by the authorities although from time to time reforming clergymen denounced them. The better variety catered to visit-

ing husbandmen and small-time traders; their landlords offered hot food and crowded beds and the potential excitement that stimulated countrymen's imaginations. Bostonians visited the more respectable taverns in order to play shuffleboard and to bowl and to check for letters and parcels deposited by arriving ship captains. Despite crackdowns, tavern excitement persisted. In 1664 Boston's apprentices and other young people were charged with "taking their opportunity by meeting together in places of public entertainment, to corrupt one another by their uncivil and wanton carriages, rudely singing and making a noise to the disturbance" of landlords and other guests. New Yorkers loved tavern life even more than the apprentices of Boston, and in 1680 Governor Andros repeated the assertion made by Governor Stuyvesant in 1648: one-quarter of the city's houses functioned as "taverns for the sale of brandy, tobacco, and beer." Grogshops and other taverns of ill repute prospered in New York and other colonial cities because wealthy businessmen and government officials frequented their better competition. The Bunch of Grapes, King's Arms, and Blue Anchor in Boston lay away from the waterfront and hosted countless public meetings of men asked to close taverns. City fathers sipped their ale and did nothing.

Philadelphia boasted every sort of tavern soon after its founding and each type prospered with the city's growth. On his first day in the city Franklin was warned to avoid the Sign of the Three Mariners and was directed by a young Quaker to the Crooked Billet. In later years Franklin frequently conducted his business at taverns like the reputable one "at the corner of Third Street" where he discussed setting up a printing establishment with the colony governor. In each of the cities, but especially in Philadelphia where one streetcorner was very like another, taverns came to order men's activities. By 1750 the privately owned tavern serving the general public played a key role in town life.[18] It helped define urban neighborhoods and nurtured the fellowship nostalgically recalled by city dwellers only a few years removed from tiny old-country landschaften—and New World agricultural settlements.

Philadelphia's waterfront, mid-block streets, and busy taverns existed for men like Franklin, men who hoped to rise by hard work and good luck to higher and higher social positions. Unlike the eunomic New England and southern landscapes, Philadelphia's space was essentially isonomic: land was apportioned without regard for a person's religious or social standing. Whatever he was—except a criminal—a man might buy as much land as he could afford. Boston and Newport tried in their first decades to maintain the practice of inviting selected newcomers to settle and warning out undesirables, but Philadelphia accepted all arrivals. Franklin found there a freer political climate and certainly a more flexible economy. It was the perfect place for a young man to set up as a printer in competition with two others and to advance to owning a stationery shop and eventually to attaining public office. One man was as good as another in Philadelphia, just as one street was good as the next. An industrious man might make any streetcorner a node of business activity for six months or sixty years; the grid nourished all men equally.

Philadelphia spawned cities across Pennsylvania. Some, like Lancaster sixty miles to the west, were at least partly the creation of Penn himself but many others, Reading, Allentown, York, and Pittsburgh, for example, were platted by men whose only standard of urban beauty and efficiency was Philadelphia. A grid of streets was quick and simple to survey and easy to extend; across the new West, at Cincinnati, Louisville, Lexington, and scores of other places, men surveyed the grid and saw that it was good. It touched men's imagination in a way best defined in 1794 by one Cincinnati resident. "Curved lines, you know," remarked Daniel Drake, "symbolize the country, straight lines the city."[19] Straightness—artificiality to be more precise—was the standard by which everyone judged urban form. Into the twentieth century, people expected urban form to objectify the heady artificiality of city life and they found no better form than Penn's grid.

The city's 1,280 rectilinear-ordered acres comprised only a tiny fragment of Pennsylvania but they were clearly defined and understood as something special. Around unwalled Philadelphia existed a boundary as evident as Charleston's cumbersome walls, a clear definition of the meeting of urban and rural space. That border, where straight streets ended or became crooked roads, was not nearly so obvious at Boston, Newport, and New York, but eighteenth-century people understood its significance just the same. It separated the realm of agriculture from the realm of commerce and artifice. Town and city dwellers depended on husbandmen for their daily food and for export commodities, but little in the urban fabric announced the dependency. Here and there a stockyard or granary bespoke the link with the agricultural backcountry but elsewhere all seemed different, and visiting husbandmen learned that city folk laughed at their rude clothes while selling them merchandise. The colonial city objectified a nonagricultural order, one like wilderness, against which landscape and its order might be compared.

Colonial cities remained small, in both size and population, and even Philadelphia seemed only a tiny interruption in land shaped for agriculture. Away from the crowded waterfront, where scarcity of building land made every foot of dry soil extremely expensive, city dwellers enjoyed (sometimes) a small yard graced with a fruit tree, and many continued to keep a stall-fed cow or two, along with poultry. Despite the best efforts of city fathers to protect children and property, hogs wandered along the streets, eating whatever offal they discovered and now and then interfering with pedestrian movement. Beyond the high-priced land, householders enjoyed even larger lots and planted gardens in order to enjoy fresh vegetables in summer. Now and then a traveler wondered where landscape ended and cityscape began because some of the houses in the vague interface sheltered men who worked part-time at agriculture, and part-time at urban crafts like boatbuilding. Somewhere along the road from "the country," travelers entered "the city," but only where the city boasted a grid of straight streets did travelers see anything like a clear edge. Otherwise they drifted through the zone no one called suburban but in which builders combined the agriculture-based shapes and structures with the spaces and buildings derived from commerce. No fortifications and gates marked the division between rural and urban space.

GRID

May 20, 1785, is a momentous date in United States history. On that day Congress authorized the surveying of the western territories (the "backland," as the Congressmen called them during the lengthy debates) into six-mile-square townships. Each township, Congress directed, would be bounded by lines running due north–south and east–west; other parallel lines would divide each township into thirty-six square sections of 640 acres each. The Land Ordinance of 1785 began in compromises that truly satisfied no one, but with minor revisions it determined the spatial organization of two-thirds of the present United States.[20] The Ohio farmer of 1820—and much later the Wyoming rancher and the California fruit grower—settled and shaped wilderness surveyed according to the traditional and Enlightenment optimism that translated the *urban* grid of Philadelphia onto land destined for agriculture.

As early as 1638 the anonymous author of "The Ordering of Towns" suggested that the ideal New England town form ought to be a square six miles on a side. But as Edward Johnson noted two decades later, New England towns were almost always irregularly shaped and almost never thirty-six miles in area. Nevertheless, the six-mile-square town persisted in New England thinking as an attractive epitome of the cherished landschaft of memory and as a practical size for a meetinghouse-focused settlement, although the square shape itself received less support; in 1656, for example, the settlers of the town-to-be of Groton petitioned the Massachusetts General Court that "they be not strictly tied to a square form in the line laying out." Southerners honored the square shape mostly in theory. Virginia did order as early as 1701 that frontier plantations be platted in squares of 200 acres, and a North Carolina law of 1715 required newly acquired tracts to be surveyed in squares. As in Pennsylvania and New York, however, square lots and square townships proved rare exceptions to the rule of irregularity.[21] New England's anonymous essayist knew the square's geometric simplicity but underestimated men's love of good soil.

Square lots and square townships presumed surveyors familiar with the rudiments of geometry, and throughout the seventeenth century few such men lived in the colonies. English surveyors had enough to do measuring and platting the fields enclosed by landlords, and few accepted the uncertain rewards of colonial work. Many colonists distrusted surveying anyway, thinking of it as a sort of evil magic that trapped their land in a web of invisible lines drawn by a mysterious figure knowing things beyond common knowledge. Aside from the professionals employed by proprietors like Penn, therefore, most American surveyors were self-taught. Whether European-trained or self-educated, however, most "measurers" blundered frequently and repeatedly, particularly when they calculated the area of irregularly shaped lots originally bounded by husbandmen. Sometimes they measured perimeters, divided by four, and squared the result, certain that any shape could be analyzed as a square. Usually they lacked perspective too and failed to understand that a tract encompassing a hill has a greater area than a level one. Now and then a husbandman tried to measure his own or his neighbors' fields with homemade instruments and blundered worse than the more practiced amateur surveyors. By the eighteenth century, land records and boundaries confused husbandmen and judges in every colony.[22] Colonial theorists honored the square township and the square plantation and farm chiefly because the square was simpler to bound and assess than the irregular tracts, and because it was easier to visualize than the forms painstakingly recorded in land conveyances and deed books.

A simple but brilliant surveying innovation popularized squares in every colony, although only late in the eighteenth century. Edmund Gunter, an English surveyor who died in 1626, invented and promoted "Gunter's chain," a surveying chain of 100 links of 0.66 feet each. The chain is therefore 22 yards long, and if an acre is described as 10 square chains, 640 acres fit precisely in a square mile of ground. No mathematical ratio is more important in the American Enlightenment landscape. Gunter synthesized the "customary" English system of land measurement—the traditional acre and the mile—and the increasingly useful decimal system.[23] The hybrid proved particularly adapted to the square shape, and colonists gradually understood its significance. Slowly and deliberately surveyors adopted the new way of platting land.

Settlers had long assumed that topography indicated the best outlines for future towns and lots, and most tracts conformed to soil types, elevations, and water frontage. Squareness mandated a departure from this so-called natural practice, and for decades settlers hesitated before choosing a tract congruent with fertile soil or open grassland and one clearly and permanently surveyed in a square. As the manifest advantages of Gunter's system grew more and more familiar to settlers taking up new lots in the unsettled areas of the colonies, however, settlers gave less consideration to irregularly shaped lots, and in 1784 the new states of Massachusetts and New York embarked on great experiments in opening land for settlement. Both state legislatures insisted on square townships, as square as surveyors could plat them without wholly ignoring such important natural features as rivers. The old reliance on natural edges and shapes passed; legislatures charged surveyors with creating a graph-paper-like skein of townships across the District of Maine and western New York. New York specified that each township be six miles square and numbered in order of creation. Slowly everyone accepted Gunter's chain as the finest—and only—standard of land measurement.

New York, like Massachusetts, Connecticut, the Carolinas, and several other states, intended to reward its discharged soldiers with gifts of land, and surveying by squares seemed the quickest and surest way to provide the allotments. Neither eunomy nor isonomy governed the assignment of lots in New York's "military townships." Enlisted men received 200 acres each and, in a fashion reminiscent of New Spain, commissioned officers received proportionately more according to their rank. But the legislature included an element of chance too. Surveyors numbered each lot and a land officer drew numbers at random; some men received tracts of the best soil, and others found themselves with stony ground.[24] For many years the military townships were only partially settled. Not every recipient chose to improve his lot or even settle on it, and many sold their allotments to real estate speculators. When Timothy Dwight rode through the region in 1804, however, he saw at once that the townships had peculiar characteristics.

New York's surveyors ordered only the township outlines and the boundaries of lots. Everything else—roads, meetinghouse locations, and schoolhouse sites—they left to the residents. Dwight decided that the townships looked much like those farther east but he was struck by their names. In the military townships, he remarked, "they are chiefly derived from ancient heroes. This may be considered as characteristical of the nature of the grant, and the spirit of those to whom it was made." As he rode along, however, he marveled at additional categories of names (Homer, Virgil, Ovid, Milton, and Dryden, and Unanimity, Frugality, Perseverance, Sobriety, Enterprise, Industry, Economy, and Regularity, for example) and he finally concluded that "all these could not have come together by a common means, nor by the exercise of that ingenuity which falls to the share of ordinary men."[25] Dwight's observation was correct. The New York legislature had ordered its surveyors to name the townships, and the men had, as regularly as they had measured. Unlike the other townships and counties everywhere in the new nation, the military townships of New York, like the newly platted square townships of the District of Maine, derived from large-scale planning. As their names implied, one was like another in the eyes of their delineators, and Dwight, whose exquisite spatial form remained a meetinghouse surrounded by closely grouped houses, vaguely distrusted the similarity still apparent only in identical boundary shapes and linked names.

New York's military townships turned out larger than six miles square; political compromise dictated more acreage than originally intended. But the grid was tested. The legislators of New York anticipated the spatial tinkering of Congress, although only by a year, and presented a prototype to the nation.

Independence and confederation brought the backlands to the immediate attention of Congress because the nation was so short of funds that the sale of the western lands to individual farmers seemed to be the only solution to imminent bankruptcy. With several minor exceptions (particularly Connecticut's Western Reserve in Ohio) the states ceded all their western lands and claims to land to the federal government. Congress understood that thriving settlements would guarantee the nation's western border, and it quickly established a committee to research the best means of surveying unsettled lands.

Thomas Jefferson chaired the committee composed of two other southerners and two New Englanders, and he drafted the committee's report. Jefferson was strongly attached to the square form; between 1777 and 1779 he suggested that every Virginia county be divided for school-support purposes into townships five or six miles square. By 1784 his thoughts had matured, largely because of the decimal system he successfully applied to the new national currency. He convinced his committee colleagues that the backlands ought to be ordered in "hundreds," ten-geographical-mile-square townships bounded by lines running north–south and east–west and divided into 100 lots of 850 acres each. The hundreds would march across the whole Northwest Territory and comprise ten new territories. Jefferson proposed calling that territory near the Lake of the Woods Sylvania, that near the sources of seven large rivers, Metropotamia, that near many large and small rivers, Polypotamia, and so on.[26] Why he chose geographical miles rather than the statute miles on which Gunter's chain is based is a mystery, although since sixty geographical miles constitute each degree of latitude he perhaps thought them more regular. Jefferson's report is a model example of Enlightenment abstraction, a perfect scheme for ordering a wilderness tabla rasa. Congress did not like it at all.

What emerged as law on May 20, 1785, was a compromise, not only between northern and southern settlement ideas but between the traditional English and newfangled metric systems too. The law called for townships six statute miles square divided into thirty-six lots of 640 acres each; lines of longitude and latitude determined the alignment lines. Timothy Pickering took immediate exception to the last point, and remarked that meridians, unlike lines of latitude, converge near the poles. "Mathematical accuracy in actual surveys may not be expected," he told more than one Congressman in regard to Jefferson's ideas of geographical miles and hundreds, "but a difference of six hundred yards in ten miles must surely produce material errors."[27] Common sense did not prevail, however, and Congress ignored Pickering's clearly explained warnings. Square forms based on lines of latitude and longitude captured the imagination of Congress, and within a year of the bill's enactment into law surveyors in Ohio platted the first townships. Everyone ignored Jefferson's grandiose schemes.

Congress revised the law, although only slightly, in 1796 and again in 1810, chiefly to stymie land speculation by wealthy men who bought whole sections and sometimes whole townships, subdivided them, and sold them to poor farmers at great profits. Most southern Congressmen preferred the remedy of smaller sections; they proposed halving the minimum sale lot to 320 acres. Northern representatives, particularly New Englanders, suggested that townships be sold as wholes. The sectional controversy stemmed largely from ideas about land settlement and land shaping.[28] Southern Congressmen realized that their constituents sought out the best farm sites as they always had, by individual search. Northern representatives understood that their constituents preferred to settle in groups and often combined to purchase an entire township. For several years every other township was surveyed into sections to accommodate the southern pioneers, and its abutters were left undivided to accommodate northerners. Eventually, however, Congress determined that every township ought to be subdivided because a collection of sections could be purchased as easily as a township, but in smaller sections. Throughout the nineteenth century the size of sections decreased, first to 320 acres, then to 160, then to 80, and finally to 40, as Congress tried to assist poorer and poorer families. Each reduction exemplified the advantages of Gunter's chain and the six-mile-square township. The 640-acre section was easily subdivided into smaller lots of whole acres by surveyors not completely at ease with geometric formulas.

By 1820 the grid concept was permanently established in the national imagination, and westward-moving adventurers understood its characteristics. In each township the thirty-six sections were numbered in boustrophedonic order beginning with the northeast section, an effective but ancient vernacular way of designating lots. *Boustrophedonic* means "as the plow follows the ox," and the oscillating rows of numbered lots owe nothing to eighteenth-century rationalism. Rather they distinctly indicate the important substructure of traditional practice that shaped the innovative geometrical order: 640-acre sections and six-mile-square townships derived from invention tempered by common custom. Agriculturists exploring the newly surveyed territories discovered that townships, like sections, were numbered too, in north–south "ranges" of townships numbered from the western borders of the old colonies. Geometry and tradition simplified the locating and identifying of any specific tract of land; a farmer merely told a government land officer that he wanted to buy section number twelve in township number three in range number four in the Ohio Territory, and the official accepted his money and issued a deed. No farmer paid surveyors and few worried about titles, boundaries, and lots.[29] Federal maps and records ordered every rod of ground.

As settlers poured west they discovered the grid's very real limitations. Congress had worried about the lack of foci in the townships but had determined only that the sixteenth section, located roughly at the center, be reserved for the support of schools. It was impossible to locate a single schoolhouse on the section and expect children to attend from the corner sections, and most groups of settlers rented or sold the section to help support several crossroads schools scattered throughout the township. New England congressmen disliked the lack of provision for a central meetinghouse site and predicted that settlers would fall into sin, living as they did without religious centers and neighborhoods. They clashed with southern representatives who considered schools and meetinghouses far less important and said so as loudly as the southern pioneers who occupied sections or subsections in townships partly settled by northerners. As early as the 1830s Americans recognized the grid as a proven solution to vexing regional differences that dated to colonial times.

Settlers discovered too that Congress had forgotten to specify the location of public roads. The first trails wandered across the backlands just as colonial roads meandered, but settlers acquiring sections soon insisted that roads follow the section lines to forestall boundary quarrels and demarcate easily cultivated square and rectangular fields. But the dramatic popular decision condemned frontier families to laying out and maintaining seventy-two miles of perfectly straight roads per township and sacrificing privately owned land for rights of way. Diagonal travel, from section one to section thirty-six, for example, irritated settlers from the beginning because no roads directly linked township corners. Newcomers from New England and the Middle States resigned themselves to "taking the long way around," but southerners quietly accepted the long distances and enjoyed racing on the straight roads. Local, common agreement on road alignment made obvious and permanent the federal-mandated rectilinear order.

Roads followed section lines and section lines followed the compass. Surveyors gave no thought to avoiding natural obstacles or approaching natural resources, and as more than one anti-grid congressman had argued in the 1784 and 1796 debates, many settlers suffered permanently. Roads led deliberately and directly through swamps and over hilltops, tiring horses and infuriating drivers. Farmers discovered that some sections were well watered and that others were separated from useful ponds and springs by only several yards. Had the surveyors been allowed to modify the straight lines—even slightly—many sections would have been far more valuable. As it turned out, in Ohio and later in Kansas and later in Oregon, some sections were totally dry and others were almost wholly submerged by lakes and swamps.[30] More than one pioneer wrote east to say that on-the-spot inspection was the only way to choose a section, even in a township or county known to be fertile.

Only when they reached a navigable river or a reserve ceded to an Indian tribe did the surveyors follow orders to skew their lines and create a fractional township or section. Many surveyors found it difficult indeed to explain their creation in words alone; sketches and maps made discussions with farmers and congressmen more practical, especially when "section corrections" became the topic of conversation. Pickering's warning about converging meridians destroying the regularity and effectiveness of the grid was ignored until surveyors discovered that lines run over several hundred miles drifted far from their original courses. Congress debated the difficulty and determined that true north ought to be substituted for magnetic north in the surveyors' calculations; when the trouble persisted Congress reversed its decision. What evolved was the section correction, a common-design solution to a most vexing geometrical problem. Every few score miles, surveyors shifted the meridian lines a hundred yards farther west and continued platting. Hardly anyone on the ground noticed the irregularities scarcely visible as two right-angle turns separated by perhaps 300 or 400 yards, and readers of maps found them scarcely more obvious. In explaining section corrections, however, men learned that a quick sketch saved many words.

Congressmen repeatedly emphasized the need for accurate maps of the regions surveyed. They hoped, of course, to forestall title and boundary questions, and they felt that surveyors might record major topographical features as they worked and so explore the country. The quest for visual material had a more subtle source, however, although congressmen very rarely acknowledged it. Only the brightest minds understood the rationale for the grid form, and as Pickering's warning makes clear, even men like Jefferson did not entirely recognize the detailed ramifications of the grid. In speech after speech congressmen likened their land-planning work to painting, to the making of a visual image. In debating a reduction in section size, one congressman made the analogy of an artist painting a bat despite his client's instructions to paint a pheasant. It was unimportant how fine the painting of the bat turned out to be, remarked Representative Rutherford, if the client wanted a pheasant. Such visual analogies suggest that the Congress understood its work in visual as well as political terms, and that very often—as a rare Congressman was bold enough to remark—the visual implications of the amendments totally escaped them. At one point in the 1796 debates Representative Nicholas demanded to know how land could be surveyed in squares if it was not naturally square in the first place.[31] Such questions were best answered with maps and plans, not volleys of words.

For all its shortcomings, the grid proved reasonably effective in ordering the land for sale and settlement. People grew accustomed to it, so accustomed in fact that even had the federal government wished to alter it or to discard it for some better form, public opposition would have proved too strong. Phrases such as "a square deal" and "he's a four-square man" entered the national vocabulary as expressions of righteousness and fairness. By the 1860s the grid objectified national, not regional, order, and no one wondered at rural space marked by urban rectilinearity.

INTERNAL IMPROVEMENTS

The grid ordered the land to encourage common shaping, but it did nothing more. It was the individual farm families who settled the spaces defined by the rectilinear survey, who felled trees and broke sod, who created the distinct landscape Europeans wonder at today. Along with the Louisiana Purchase of 1803 the transformation of wilderness into farmland made all Americans suddenly conscious of their nationality, of their new identity as citizens of a political entity larger than the old parochial colonies. The consciousness found expression in a new flag, in Independence Day celebrations, and in a hearty enthusiasm for master-plan design. Americans hoped to create a national network of roads, canals, and other physical improvements.

Near the close of the seventeenth century one European nation after another discovered that good roads, safe harbors, and other facilities of communication strengthened political unity and military security. The physical expression and reinforcement of national government eventually concerned political theorists such as Emmerich de Vattel, a Frenchman who published *The Law of Nations, or Principles of the Law of Nature* at the end of the eighteenth century, when the political advantage of good roads and other improvements was proved. "The use of highways, bridges, canals, and, in a word, all the safe and commodious ways of communication, cannot be doubted," Vattel asserted. Like the self-evident truths of the United States Constitution, physical improvements were "naturally" good and ought to be built. Across the Atlantic, Federalists of every sort echoed Vattel's assertion so loudly that even their political opponents neglected to analyze his assumptions.

In *Federalist 14*, James Madison argued in 1787 that the United States was not so large a land that republican government would fail. Madison claimed that under the proposed new constitution "intercourse throughout the union will be daily facilitated by new improvements." Roads and canals would speed communication everywhere, along the seaboard and west into the backlands. The will of the people would travel quickly to Congress, undelayed by storms and swamps. Madison introduced only the political necessity for communications improvements, but he and other Federalists understood another, more compelling reason.[32] Tench Coxe explained it in 1788, in a speech before the Virginia Constitutional Convention, when he described the military reasons for good roads. The United States, he pointed out, lay surrounded by the colonies of Spain, England, and France, and its small army must be given every aid if the nation's independence was to remain secure. Like Madison, Coxe based his argument for republican national government and internal improvements on natural reasons. "The various parts of the North American continent are formed by nature for the most intimate union," he concluded, and the states will be drawn even closer together when the new roads and canals are finished. "The voice of nature therefore directs us to be affectionate associates in peace and firm supports in war."[33] Unlike the grid the nation's man-made communications network followed nature's hints. Where there were valleys, there ought to be roads; where there were rivers, there ought to be canals. Only then would the people and right government flourish.

Not until 1808 did Congress do anything substantial about building a national network of roads and canals. In that year Secretary of the Treasury Albert Gallatin produced his *Report on Roads and Canals* at the request of the Senate. Gallatin had lived in New England, the Piedmont South, and backcountry Pennsylvania since emigrating from Switzerland; he had worked as a college teacher of French, he kept a crossroads store, worked as a surveyor, and served in Congress during the 1796 grid debates. He understood the nation's different regions and spatial attitudes better than many native-born Americans, and he understood too the relation of European political philosophy to spatial development. His *Report* is a masterpiece of creative innovation.

Gallatin understood that the Louisiana Purchase had done more than double the nation's size; it had greatly magnified the difficulties of conducting government business. "The inconveniences, complaints, and perhaps dangers, which may result from a vast extent of territory, cannot otherwise be radically removed or prevented than by opening speedy and easy communications through all its parts. Good roads and canals will shorten distances, facilitate commercial and personal intercourse, and unite, by a still more intimate community of interests, the most remote quarters of the United States," he emphasized. "No other single operation within the power of Government, can more effectually tend to strengthen and perpetuate that Union which secures external independence, domestic peace, and internal liberty."[34] No American author has ever more clearly and deliberately examined the spatial implications of government, and none has ever provided a more comprehensive plan to strengthen government through spatial modification.

He suggested a massive building program financed by the sale of the backlands. He advocated the building of four coastal canals, one across

Cape Cod, another between the Delaware and Raitan rivers, a third between the Delaware and Chesapeake, and a fourth between the Chesapeake and Albemarle. From Philadelphia, Washington, Richmond, and Savannah (or Charleston) he proposed that canals run west to the Appalachians, connect with cross mountain roads, and run west from the farther side of the mountains. He wanted navigation improved on the Santee, Roanoke, James, Potomoc, Susquehanna, and Ohio rivers and hoped that several smaller canals could be built in Massachusetts, Virginia, South Carolina, and Louisiana. Finally, he proposed building turnpikes—he called them "artificial roads" because he intended that they be adequately graded and maintained—east to Detroit, Saint Louis, and New Orleans.[35] Not all the ideas were new (the Puritans had dreamed of the Cape Cod canal in the seventeenth century) but each reflected meticulous, large-scale thinking about spatial modification.

Gallatin suspected that his scheme would encounter two sorts of opposition. He explained that its great cost could be partially offset using revenue from the sale of public lands, and he suggested that the federal government provide financial support to private corporations intending to build toll roads and toll canals. He worried more about the second sort of opposition, sectionalism, and proposed that the improvements be undertaken simultaneously in all parts of the country. Despite his suggestions and solutions, very little came of his great plan. The quibblings about the word *establish* in Article One, Section Eight of the Constitution—some argued that Congress had the power to build roads and some retorted that it might only establish rights of way—masked a far deeper problem. Neither congressmen nor voters thought in national terms.[36] They understood their district or town or neighborhood or township intimately and perhaps felt some love for their region or state, but beyond that area they looked hesitantly, infrequently, and with disinterest.

LIGHTHOUSES

Congress did almost nothing about Gallatin's plans and the plans now and then submitted by others. It built the "National Road" from Cumberland, Maryland, to Zanesville, Ohio, but otherwise built only lighthouses. The towers however, marked more than dangerous shoals and narrow channels. They announced the end of the locally controlled complex of structures and man-altered spaces that most people recognized by the word *neighborhood*.

Early in the eighteenth century the colonies' more prosperous coastal cities began building lighthouses. Boston led the movement to improve commerce by improving safety; in 1680 the city reserved one of its harbor islands for "a general sea mark," and after a succession of studies and resolutions, erected a lighthouse on Little Brewster Island in 1716. Craftsmen modified the 60-foot-high tower almost as soon as they finished it. It suffered from fires and mortar difficulties, but mariners and merchants agreed that it made navigation easier and safer. Other lighthouses were soon erected, sometimes by coastal towns hoping to convert their harbors into commercial assets but usually by cities such as Newport, which carefully determined to maintain their commercial superiority. Lighthouses, as many committees charged with their funding and erection quickly discovered, required painstaking siting and careful construction.[37] The colonists learned that building a tall structure fully exposed to gales and surf demanded more than traditional techniques and guesswork. The lighthouse erected at Sandy Hook by the New York legislature in 1764 included all the improvements devised by lighthouse builders in other colonies. The New Yorkers built well; the lighthouse still stands in service, 103 feet high and 20 feet in diameter at the base. Such monumental buildings taxed colonial craftsmen, who chose to overbuild rather than risk collapse—the lower walls of Sandy Hook Light are at least 7 feet thick. Here and there towns chose to build wooden lighthouses (the double light at Gurnet Head outside Plymouth was wood) but the cheap solution proved impractical as long as the great lanterns burned oil; Gurnet Light burned thirty-four years after it was completed. Wood or stone, however, colonial lighthouses existed always as local projects intended to aid local commerce. Now and then a colony legislature funded the projects, but the lighthouses benefited the cities and towns whose harbors they marked. Their broader importance went unrecognized until after the Revolution.

By an act of the first Congress the new federal government assumed responsibility in 1789 for the twelve lighthouses built in colonial days and through the Lighthouse Service began building more. Congress insisted that federally built lighthouses be permanent structures; almost every one still stands today, thanks to materials and techniques like those specified in 1791 for the lighthouse at Cape Henry, Virginia. The tower's foundations, set 20 feet into the ground, support walls 11 feet thick and 72 feet high, along with a great lantern room. Except for the use of electricity, lighthouse technology has advanced very little from the days when the Lighthouse Service specified that the lantern-room windows "be covered with a network of strong brass wire so as to preserve the

glass in the lantern from injuries by hail or flights of birds in the night."
The service further specified that the oil supply be stored at a distance in
a vault and that a copper ventilator turned by the wind exhaust the
smoke from the lantern room. Everyone understood that a lighthouse
must function every night, through the severest storms, and that careful
design and meticulous regulation alone assured such constancy. "The
keepers of lighthouses should be dismissed for small degrees of remiss-
ness," declared President Jefferson, "because of the calamities which
even these produce."[38] Scarcely a year passed, therefore, when the new
nation did not erect another massive stone tower and wooden house for
a trustworthy keeper and his family. By 1817 fifty-five lighthouses
alerted mariners to danger.

Aside from the fortifications hastily thrown up during the Revolution,
lighthouses were the first structures over which local communities had
no control. Even tiny towns like Scituate in Massachusetts learned that
they deserved and received the finest in lighthouses but that the lighthouse itself was inviolate. Its builders and keepers answered to the new
national government, not the town elders. For the first time the old
notion of local community control no longer applied to a structure.
Community space suddenly included a man-made structure over which
the locality had no power whatsoever.

In ancient and medieval times the scepter and roland objectified established, legal government. Monarchs and elected officials carried the
scepter as a token roland; American bailiffs still carry one during court
processions, as when jurors are taken to the scene of a crime. The roland
or column is the scepter magnified to gigantic scale and permanently
fixed in the ground. Such columns still order the center of European
cities and recall the time when a city's greatest possession was its privilege
of self-government. The federal lighthouses are rolands too. They mark
the new strength of nationalism over localism, the new power of new
government. Officially at least, Congress built them well because of their
importance and precarious sites. But the federal government may well
have understood, if only vaguely, that the towers symbolized its strength
and that every man, woman, and child who saw their massiveness might
glimpse the permanency and strength of the infant republic.

TURNPIKES

Unlike lighthouses, canals and artificial roads appealed only to local
interests. Every Carolina seaman understood the importance of Sandy
Hook Light whether or not he was bound for New York; the light

warned of shoals and it marked the halfway point on the passage to Boston. But only a rare Georgia or North Carolina farmer understood the advantages of a turnpike from Massachusetts to Rhode Island, and if he did, he assumed that the citizens of those states ought to pay for it, not him. Internal communication improvements, then, remained essentially local in nature and usually locally funded and maintained. Not for many years did the nation possess the barest fragment of the network Gallatin proposed. Even today his great vision is incomplete.

A *turnpike* is not actually a road but a type of gate specially adapted to rapid opening and closing—today *turnstile* is more commonly used. A turnpike consists of four poles—*pikes*—mounted horizontally on a vertical axis, like spokes on a hub. The walker who pushes one pike ahead of him as he passes through the gateway unwittingly pulls one closed behind him. Perhaps no gate other than the draw-bar still used at customs checkpoints is more suited for pedestrian and mounted traffic, and builders of artificial roads in eighteenth-century England quickly recognized its utility for ensuring the collection of tolls. The gates became so common that they gave their name to any toll road.

A turnpike is a horizontal roland. It passes across many neighborhoods but its route and use are controlled by none. Only its makers and owners command its right-of-way and traffic; all others pay for the privilege of walking or riding upon it.

As Gallatin remarked, turnpikes are artificial roads. The term is puzzling only when the "natural" character of short-distance roads is unrecognized. Like the planners of Spanish settlements in northern Mexico, the New England author of "The Ordering of Towns," and the anonymous landshapers of the Southern and Middle colonies, almost all citizens of the new United States firmly believed that roads happened almost naturally. Design seemed only a matter of finding the best existing gradient—dairy farmers still swear that a cow can invariably discover the gentlest grades over a hill if given a summer in which to experiment—and clearing trees and other significant obstructions from the route. The resulting track constituted a road, even if it flooded, washed out, or devolved into a collection of rocks and holes. An artificial road was distinctly unnatural: politics, use, and economics determined its route, not casually found gradients, and its makers surfaced it with materials brought from a distance and carefully installed. Not surprisingly, artificial roads became popular first in the Southern and Middle states, where people understood the value of reliable roads and thought in spaces larger than the New England town.

Virginia opened the nation's first toll road in 1785 by appointing nine

Former turnpike, Worcester County, Massachusetts. (JRS)

commissioners "to erect, or cause to be set up and erected, one or more gates or turnpikes across the roads, or any of them, leading into the town of Alexandria." Pennsylvanians built the nation's first truly artificial highway, along the right-of-way of an old and decrepit natural road from Philadelphia to Lancaster they called "the king's highway."[39] The new road opened in 1794, and although work continued for two more years, travelers discovered that its more direct route (wherever possible its builders avoided the turns of the old highway) and solid surface of crushed stone justified the tolls collected at the nine gates. The Philadelphia and Lancaster Turnpike Company itself was an innovation, for corporations were little known in the new nation and attorneys and legislators long debated the states' capacity to charter them. Need rather than legal precedent encouraged states to charter turnpike corporations; such entities appeared as the only way individual investors might pool their resources and so gather the immense capital to build the roads. Of course the investors intended to make a profit, and with the consent of the legislatures they posted immensely complicated lists of toll. Turnpike corporations charged users according to two principles, value and damage. A pedestrian paid very little, and a horseback rider little more; herders of sheep and cattle paid by the size of their herds but they too paid modest sums. Carriages and wagons—and corporations distinguished among every sort of wheeled conveyance—paid proportionately more because of the value of the conveyance and its cargo. On the other hand, however, some great wagons passed free of toll altogether, as long as their iron tires were nine inches wide and their rear wheels followed a path different from the front.[40] Such cumbersome wagons were rare, but corporations prized them because their great wheels compacted and smoothed the highway surface. Tolls and regulations varied from turnpike to turnpike but the general character of the roads remained the same from Georgia to Maine.

Americans judged turnpikes according to standards of directness, evenness, and cheapness. "The straightest line is a straight one," asserted one turnpike promoter in 1806, "and cannot be rivalled, and as such, merits the first consideration." As Gallatin noted in his 1808 *Report,* most turnpike companies built directly and cheaply but unfortunately not always evenly. Gallatin could not gather detailed information about every turnpike in the nation, but his *Report* suggests that in New England and the Middle States centered the turnpike-building mania that marked the twenty years following the establishment of a strong national government. By 1808 Connecticut was crisscrossed by 770 miles of road and had hundreds more building, and New York, New Jersey, and Pennsylvania were building long-distance roads like those from Albany to Schenectady and Trenton to Brunswick, and most importantly, Philadelphia to Columbia.[41] A Philadelphia to Pittsburgh turnpike company had been chartered in Pennsylvania, and a "pike" from Baltimore to Boonsborough and from there to Cumberland was being built in Maryland. Turnpikes proved good investments, so good that politicians forgot the communication advantages cited by Vattel and Madison and hastened to conjure up real estate schemes and corporate profits. Unlike a federal lighthouse, a turnpike struck most Americans as a means of making money, and profit-making caused builders to lay out direct but hilly highways.

The typical turnpike of 1810 was about twenty feet wide and far straighter than even. Land cost so much to buy that most companies sacrificed gentle gradients for short distances. Since they had no competitors in their allotted region the corporations quickly forgot the exertions of their users' teams. Only a quick, safe, and cheap ride mattered to builders and patrons, not exhausted horses. State legislatures mandated secure surfaces, however, and the corporations embarked on a variety of surfacing experiments. English techniques of using broken stone on a gravel base proved the best but also the most expensive, and many companies chose to rely on gravel or corduroy (logs laid perpendicular to the road and wedged tightly together) rather than spend freely on stone.

Unlike the roads of England, then, American turnpikes required continual repair, not constant maintenance. Traveler after traveler remarked on gaping holes and deep ruts, and more than one experienced real fright as his coach tottered or overturned. Here and there a reformer proposed such curious improvements as guard posts at fords, each painted with a scale of figures to inform the unwary of the depth of the water, and guideposts. "A white board with legible black letters will answer," remarked one 1806 New Jersey promoter who had emigrated from England and longed for securely built turnpikes, "and if well battened on the back, will not be so apt to crack by the mischeivous pranks of boys throwing stones at it." Vandals caused only a tiny part of the problem. The real mischief-maker was profit maximization; the very farmers who cursed the holes and the flimsy bridges—outside Pennsylvania most turnpike bridges were wood, not stone—enthusiastically invested in turnpike stock and gloated over their dividends. Not until the good roads movement of the 1890s did highway surfacing and road design receive much detailed attention in America. Until then, most United States turnpike travelers experienced, if only occasionally, the sentiments expressed by one New York traveler: "It is anti-agreeable to post over a road which looks like a *river*, and where the course your conveyance is to take is indicated by stakes implanted in the solid part of that 'undiscovered country' over which you are rolling as it were in a ship."[42] Throughout the nineteenth century, European travelers rated American natural roads as the worst in the world and American turnpikes little better.

CANALS

The same travelers from Europe found fault with American canals but they did so incorrectly. Like the turnpikes, most canals resulted from the efforts of private corporations interested in short- and long-term profits. Investors in canals understood, however, that a canal was a very permanent modification of the countryside, and an expensive one too. The guesswork associated with so much turnpike siting, and the poor maintenance evident in the many holes and ruts on the undercapitalized projects found little parallel along the canals. American canal builders proved so innovative that their channels and locks perplexed all but the most open-minded Europeans who scrutinized them.

Americans immediately perceived canals as the "natural" competitors of turnpikes. Their chief promotor, Robert Fulton, argued constantly that water transport costs far less than hauling goods by wagon over turnpikes. In an open letter to the governor of Pennsylvania published in his 1796 *Treatise on the Improvement of Canal Navigation* Fulton explained the comparative building and capital costs of a canal between Philadelphia and Pittsburgh and a turnpike over the same route.[43] Unlike Gallatin and other government figures, however, Fulton advanced economic instead of political reasons for his scheme, asking "Would not the lands around Fort Pitt be as valuable as those around Lancaster, if the produce could be brought to market for the same sum?" Like subsequent canal promoters, Fulton knew that canal freight rates would undercut those offered by teamsters, even by those whose routes lay over turnpikes. He consequently envisioned canals as great stimulants to business of every variety. In a work of 1813 he asserted that everywhere in the United States "cheap and regional transport will draw forth the ponderous riches of the earth, and circulate our minerals for the benefit of the whole community. It will float the products of the forests of the western states to the sea coast, returning the necessaries and luxuries from foreign nations to our interior. It will encourage manufactures by a cheap conveyance of raw materials; promote and refine agriculture, increase population, and advance civilization throughout the whole range of our country." Only after enumerating the financial advantages of canals did he conclude that canal transportation, "by giving to our citizens an easy intercourse, will assimilate their customs, manners, and opinions, and bind them together as much by their habits as their interests." Fulton honored Adam Smith's *Wealth of Nations* and began his arguments by citing the conclusions of "the best writers on political economy." Economics, not political theory, dictated that the United States have a developed internal transportation network, and careful accounting clearly indicated, to Fulton and many others, that the network should consist of canals.

When David Stevenson visited the United States in 1838 he discovered 2,700 miles of canals already finished and many more under construction or proposed. The Scottish engineer became an acute observer of American building, and his book-length *Sketch of the Civil Engineering of North America* is a little-known but perceptive and exhaustive analysis of America's enthusiasm for canals and other engineering works. By 1838 two hundred lighthouses warned the ocean sailor that he approached the American coast, and thousands of miles of turnpikes linked towns with cities. Stevenson found Americans willing to try almost any project, once convinced of its profitability, and after several months he concluded that their boldness derived in large part from prior success. He traveled carefully throughout the whole nation, pausing to study any

View of a New England canal. From Barber, *Historical Collections.*

improvement that attracted his attention. Unlike the British tourists who complained about the poor food and wretched berths provided by canalboat owners, Stevenson examined what he soon discovered to be a wonder of engineering.

American canal builders confronted and surmounted obstacles far beyond anything encountered by Europeans. Distances between cities were greater—the longest European canal, he remarked, was 146 miles, slightly more than half the length of the Erie Canal—and gradients were steeper. American rivers sometimes flooded, especially in the winter and spring, and sent ice and trees crashing against canal dams. Traffic surprised even the most optimistic American designers. The Erie Canal was being widened from 40 to 70 feet when he passed along it, and he learned that many other canals were already too constricted for their traffic. Given the natural difficulties of canal construction and the spurting growth of traffic, Stevenson concluded, no one should wonder why Americans built in their peculiar "American" style.

Stevenson admired the very features that European pleasure travelers disliked. "One is struck with the temporary and apparently unfinished state of many of the American works, and is very apt, before inquiring into the subject, to impute to want of ability what turns out, on investigation, to be a judicious and ingenious arrangement to suit the circumstances of a new country, of which the climate is severe,—a country where stone is scarce and wood is plentiful, and where manual labor is very expensive."[44] Stevenson understood that travelers more interested in good food and a little privacy saw the wooden locks and low timber bridges as makeshift affairs, especially when compared with the great stone channels and arched bridges of European canals. He pointed out, however, that repairmen could easily and quickly rebuild a wooden lock after an ice flood, and that a stone lock was scarcely more likely to withstand the flood anyway. Beyond that, however, he also discerned something that escaped the notice of almost every other European observer. Corporations could easily replace a wooden lock or wharf or bridge when quickly increasing traffic demanded major modifications. After experiences like those of the Erie Canal builders, corporations learned that expense and difficulty accompanied any modification of massive stone structures.

The Erie Canal was begun in 1817 and completed eight years later; from Albany to Buffalo it stretched 363 miles, and its branch canals added another 180 miles to its aggregate length. In most respects the Erie Canal resembled most other American canals. It ran through generally level country (only eighty-four locks interrupted the main channel) and maintained its level wherever possible without the aid of locks. It crossed the Cayuga marsh as a channel dug down the center of a man-made embankment in some places more than 20 feet high, passed over the Genesee River on an aqueduct carried by nine 50-foot arches, traversed the "great levels" as a simple ditch, and terminated at Albany in a man-made basin surrounded by warehouses and drawbridges arranged after Dutch prototypes. The canal exemplified the American desire to build cheaply and directly, and it astonished everyone not familiar with the great canals of Europe.

Opening a canal sparked celebrations, confusion, and—above all—explanations. Onlookers puzzled over the level of the channel, the operation of the locks, and the mysterious stillness of the water. "The first admission of water into a canal is always attended with great solicitude," remarked a correspondent for the Utica *Patriot* in 1819. "It is the ultimate test of the accuracy of the levels, and affords most important inferences, as to the solidity and fidelity, with which the banks have been constructed, and the sufficiency of the feeders." He described the opening of the middle section of the Erie Canal as a great economic boon and something of a technological conundrum. "Considering the circumstances of our country, the great benefits sure to result to us from internal trade, the intelligence of our citizens to perceive and appreciate these benefits," he announced, "it is believed that the records of social life do not afford a scene more interesting." But what made the scene interesting? Surely not filling a ditch with water; every farmer had seen and done that. And surely not floating a boat on water. It was the extraordinary precision of it all that astonished and puzzled the crowd. "A navigable river opened through forests and morasses—over an extent of country so considerable, and in many places so uneven, and the whole completed in so short a period as to baffle the calculations, even of the most sanguine, is no ordinary event," concluded the journalist.[45] His readers agreed.

For all that it seemed a marvel, the Erie Canal lacked a portage railway like those that distinguished the Morris Canal in New Jersey and the Pennsylvania Main Line Canal. Builders recognized the difficulty and expense of building and operating locks, and when they confronted the Allegheny Mountains they determined that only a miracle would permit canal boats to cross them. Tunnels seemed impossible and a turnpike at best a poor solution; after all, it would raise freight and passenger tariffs dramatically. But the engineers solved the difficulty in typical common fashion; they built a railroad over the slopes and equipped it with wide cars attached by cables to winding gears at the crests. The cars rumbled into the ends of the canals, boats crept onto them, and the steam-powered winding apparatus, to the wonderment of all but the engineers, winched them over the summits of each mountain to the "level" beyond, where they were pulled by locomotives to the next winding station. Improbable as it sounds, the Allegheny Portage Railroad proved an immediate success; within a year after its opening in 1834, its owners added a second track to accommodate increased traffic.[46] Such railroads signaled the close of the canal era in the United States. They proved the power and reliability of railroads and steam power and hinted at speeds and economies impossible to achieve on water. Nevertheless, from about 1795 to 1840 canals enthralled the American imagination with wonders of increasingly professional engineering.

Far more than lighthouses and turnpikes, canals existed beyond the control of neighborhoods. Anyone could walk or ride on a turnpike as long as he or she paid toll, but corporations restricted usage on canals to those operating licensed boats and to those few adventurers like Thoreau who paid a toll for their rowboat. Restrictions were necessary indeed. Boats pulled by mules walking along narrow footpaths made converging and overtaking into acts of purely common-sense skill; with shouts and laughter men dropped towropes, mules brushed past each other, and helmsmen steered carefully away from boats, towlines, and the fragile banks. Locking proved even more complicated, especially when traffic was heavy or when rains had swollen water levels. For the first time, then, Americans discovered a wholly new sort of space, a space in which they not only paid a user's fee but were forbidden to do more than sit. It is understandable that so many European and American travelers complained about canal-boat food and accommodations; for the first time in their lives—unless they had been to sea—they were ordered about by experts who knew only too well that canal-boat passengers could not simply jump off after cursing the driver.

Those passengers who accepted the restrictions and inconveniences discovered a sort of magic in the ride Hawthorne described in "The Canal Boat," one of his little-known "Sketches from Memory." The boats moved so smoothly that all sensation of traveling vanished and passengers drifted into a remarkable illusion. The boat seemed stationary and the landscape struck them as a vast panorama slowly unrolling for their entertainment. Canal travel fostered the passengers' isolation; the boat moved too quickly to walk alongside and often the canal itself cut through swamp wildernesses inhabited by few people. Passengers read or talked politics or cursed the food; the land beyond the bank seemed only scenery casually composed for their entertainment.

Hawthorne and other careful observers discovered something remarkable in the scenery, something that Europeans usually missed. Like some turnpikes, canals cut through long stretches of unsettled country and brought prosperity to hopeless regions. Canals *created* towns. Canals were the dominant feature of towns such as Utica, where civic life focused on the docks. The most prestigious property was that along "the water," and old notions of city planning vanished in the haste to speculate. Wherever a lock interrupted navigation, as at Lockport, a hopeful business community immediately located, even in advance of farmers. "Surely the water of this canal must be the most fertilizing of all fluids," remarked Hawthorne after an 1830 Erie Canal trip, "for it causes towns with their masses of brick and stone, their churches and theaters, their business and hubbub, their luxury and refinement, their gay dames and polished citizens, to spring up, till in time the wondrous stream may flow between two continuous lines of buildings, through one thronged street, from Buffalo to Albany."[47] Had the Erie Canal, and the nation's other canals, not lost their traffic to railroads, Hawthorne's prediction might have been proved. He understood that canals did more than link places; they made places. They seemed almost places themselves.

Like towns and cities, most turnpikes and canals are remembered by proper names. Originally, however, people knew them by the places they linked and spoke easily of the "Newburyport Pike" or the Chesapeake and Ohio Canal. But by 1845 they called turnpikes and canals by names not intimately associated with their terminii. For teamsters and boatmen, turnpikes and canals were home—towns existed only as ends of the line of boats.

Most Americans adapted less easily to the new improvements, and as Gallatin feared, their elected representatives thought not in national or even regional terms but in the small-scale ways beloved and trusted by common builders, especially by those shaping the land for agriculture. War with England depleted the federal treasury while proving the military necessity of a quality national road system, but at war's end Congress hesitated to increase the national debt by funding great building projects. Quibbling about funding and constitutional powers beleaguered improvement proponents like Calhoun, who argued in 1817 that "if we look into the nature of wealth we shall find that nothing can be more favorable to its growth than good roads and canals," and that Americans were poor because they settled over a vast land so poorly knit together that it defeated attempts at political harmony and common defense as well as business. "Commercial intercourse is the true remedy to this weakness," Calhoun declared, "and the means by which this is to be effected, are roads, canals, and the coasting trade."[48] But as the debates paraphrased in the *American Register* make clear, many representatives and senators—and the president himself—shared visions less grand than those espoused by Gallatin and Calhoun. Voters worried about the loss of local control and the potential for federal tyranny of design and siting. Only the army, and the settlers in the emerging grid country, shared a national vision of large-scale improvements.

ENGINEERING

"Public spirit is alone wanting to make us the greatest nation on earth," claimed Thomas Pope in his 1811 *Treatise on Bridge Architecture*, "and there is nothing more essential to the establishment of that greatness than the building of bridges, the digging of canals, and the making of sound turnpikes."[49] Pope forgot (or deliberately ignored) the real difficulty confronting the Republic's national and local visionaries. Bridges, canals, and turnpikes, and aqueducts and viaducts too, required skilled builders, men trained in statics, surveying, and hydraulics, and the new nation possessed few such men. Colonial building had been a mixture of tradition and trial-and-error, and it proved ill-adapted to the projects undertaken so enthusiastically by state legislatures, the federal government, and corporations. Only an occasional farmer or craftsman understood at all clearly how to regulate water levels or submerge caissons; it was an even rarer individual who understood Pope's theories concerning "flying pendent lever bridges," even though Pope supplemented his graphs and sketches with a scale model. What was needed, Congress determined, was a corps of engineers.

By the time of the Revolution, military engineering had evolved from a craft to a research-oriented technology. Artillery made traditional fortifications obsolete in the fifteenth and sixteenth centuries, and seventeenth-century engineers like Stevin discovered that every innovation in battlements prompted an innovation in artillery or siege techniques. France led all Europe in emphasizing up-to-date military engineering; it employed an *intendant des fortifications* as early as 1662, and by 1690 a special group of sappers trained in erecting (and destroying) the finest of walls. Throughout the eighteenth century the engineers distinguished themselves in battle after battle, not only for bravery but for originality and skill. In 1732 the king rewarded them with distinctive uniforms and in 1776 with a royal edict making them the *corps royal du genie.*[50] Military engineers made possible more than victories in the field; they planted rows of trees to shade marching troops, laid out roads, and built bridges. They specialized in erecting fortifications, sometimes overnight, often over years. No one, not captains of cavalry and colonels of artillery, trifled with an officer of engineers. So essential was his art—and so mysteriously intricate—that he commanded instant respect not only as a soldier but also as an intellectual.

At Bunker Hill and elsewhere Americans learned that a simple ditch did little to repel a determined, disciplined charge. Knox and other officers understood the rudiments of engineering, but because they fought an offensive war their lack of skill caused little harm to the patriots' cause. When they could not overwhelm the garrisoned British forces, they surprised them by night or starved them into surrender. After the war, as the American officers well knew, the situation reversed. The army no longer attacked but waited inside its crude harbor and wilderness forts for Indians, the French, the Spanish, and the British.[51] As one diplomatic crisis followed another in the 1790s, Congress ordered that the nation's harbors be fortified. Benjamin Franklin convinced several prominent French engineers to undertake the task—no Americans knew enough.

In 1802 Congress created the present Corps of Engineers and ordered that it be garrisoned at West Point and function as a military academy in addition to building forts and batteries. Road building evoked constitutional questions but the threat of invasion led only to larger and larger appropriations. By 1808, as Gallatin presented his internal improvement plans to a cost-conscious Senate, the engineers' budget had been doubled to 1 million dollars a year. Education deteriorated as officers hastened to learn their calling from the French specialists; at West Point the few cadets received only the sketchiest information about their chosen profession. When war came in 1812, cadets from other branches joined them, and the academy at West Point desperately emphasized general training rather than military specialties. Not until 1816 did the corps and its school begin the rigorous training still respected today.

That year Albert Gallatin served as ambassador to France, and he dispatched one of Napoleon's finest engineers, Simon Bernard, to take charge of fortifications according to a new Act of Congress. Bernard's appointment as a brigadier general sparked heated controversy among American officers but it established permanently the French technique of military engineering. In 1815 two American officers had traveled to France to study fortifications at the École Polytechnique. They brought home almost a thousand books on engineering, a collection of maps, and a variety of instruments, but most importantly they returned determined to model West Point's curriculum and discipline after French prototypes. One of the officers, Major Sylvanus Thayer, became superintendent with the support of both Federalist and Republican leaders, and he quickly imported Claude Crozet to teach engineering just as he had in France—in French. That language, the "sole repository of military science" according to Thayer, became the official language of instruction, and French sketching and design became the standards by which instructors judged student work. By the 1820s army engineers worked at mapping (not surveying) the territories, planning canal routes, and designing bridges.[52] Wherever they worked they designed and built in the French manner.

By 1828 even Noah Webster found himself slightly puzzled about the meaning of *engineer*. He included two definitions of the word in his *Dictionary* of that year, noting that a military engineer is "a person skilled in mathematics and mechanics, who forms plans of works for offense and defense, and marks out the ground for fortifications." But, he added in a second definition, "engineers are also employed in delineating plans and superintending the construction of other public works, as aqueducts and canals. The latter are called civil engineers."[53] Webster's confusion derived from the curious role of army engineers; many worked only or chiefly on fortifications but others involved themselves, by order, in public or private projects like canals and, later, railroads. The officers quickly learned that civilian jobs paid higher salaries than military ones, and many resigned from the service. The resignations did not displease Congress because already the West Point academy had graduated more engineers than the army needed. By 1830 the military academy was indeed functioning as a technological college, and Congress was generally satisfied with its investment. Webster's uncertainty, then, is understandable. In the United States in the early nineteenth century most civil engineers had military training.

West Point engineers worked everywhere, on the Chesapeake and Ohio Canal, the Morris Canal, the Delaware and Raritan Canal, the canals of the Indiana Public Works, the Baltimore and Ohio Railroad, the Atlantic Railroad of Georgia, and the several railroads of Massachusetts. Engineers such as William Gibbs McNeill went from job to job even before they left the army. McNeill worked on the Chesapeake and Ohio Canal, the Kanawha, James, and Roanoke River Improvement Project, the Baltimore and Ohio Railroad, the Baltimore and Susquehanna Railroad, and a number of other projects before serving as examiner of North and South Carolina lighthouses and chief engineer of the naval dry dock in Brooklyn in 1844. Careers like his resulted from the crops' growing reputation for precision and accuracy. Corporations requested engineers only when difficult terrain clearly convinced them that traditional knowledge was insufficient. Monuments like McNeil's Canton Viaduct in Massachusetts are never found in gently rolling terrain but in the steepest ravines and gorges, places conquered by specialized skill.

West Point engineers trained the men who gathered about them at every worksite, men with some knowledge of surveying perhaps or of mathematics or stonecutting. The massive Erie Canal project—the Alaska Pipeline of the 1830s—attracted hundreds of eager young men like Herman Melville, who sought education along with paying work. By 1840 American students were being schooled by ex-West Point officers at Norwich Academy in Vermont and by civilians at the Institute in Rensselaer, New York, as well as by practicing engineers.[54] Young engineers, like their older colleagues, found employment everywhere in the Republic but particularly where the terrain was rough.

Of all the examples of early nineteenth-century American military engineering, the Starrucca Viaduct of the New York and Erie Railroad remains the most impressive. The immense structure towers 100 feet above Starrucca Creek at Susquehanna, Pennsylvania. Each of its seventeen arches is 50 feet across and each is faced with slabs of bluestone. When a corporation built it in 1848 to carry a double-track rail line across the valley, Americans knew it not only as the world's most expensive railroad bridge but as an engineering wonder. John P. Kirkwood designed it according to the rules of his teacher, the army-trained chief engineer of the Western Railroad of Massachusetts, George W. Whistler. Like his teacher, Kirkwood appreciated the sentiments of West Point's preeminent engineering instructor, Dennis Mahan, whose *Civil Engineering for the Use of Cadets* guided American builders for decades. A bridge or viaduct "should not only be secure, but to the apprehension appear so," remarked Mahan in a section on "style." "It should be equally removed from Egyptian massiveness and Corinthian lightness; while, at the same time, it should conform to the features of the surrounding locality, being more ornate and carefully wrought in its minor details in a city, and near buildings of a sumptuous style, than in more obscure quarters; and assuming every shade of conformity, from that which would be in keeping with the humblest hamlet and tamest landscape to the boldest features presented by Nature and Art."[55] Starrucca is Mahan's philosophy objectified. No moulding or other ornamentation softens the severity of the piers (such detail, Kirkwood knew, was superfluous in a wilderness location) and no real or apparent lightness of construction worries the awestruck back-roads travelers parked beneath it today. The viaduct, along with those at Canton and at Relay, Maryland, still carries freight trains. Kirkwood intended it to bear unforseen loads and to endure. It does.

Engineers introduced not only massiveness and great scale to American building, they introduced standardization too. Colonial governments had attempted to regulate building by promulgating construction codes. In 1679, for example, the Massachusetts General Court ordered all brickmakers to use only high quality, well-cured clay and to produce bricks capable of bearing up well under heavy loads and difficult weather. But bricklayers placed the standardized bricks according to the rules of common industry, and husbandmen built chimneys as always, although they used standardized bricks—when the brickmakers obeyed the court's wishes. By the early nineteenth century engineers had firmly implanted the economics of standardization in the minds of corporate directors.[56] The Chesapeake and Ohio Canal Corporation, for example, chose to build identical lock-keeper's houses at each lock and retained an engineer to design a single plan for all. He specified stone houses measuring eighteen by thirty feet, having two windows in each gable end, one above the other, having two doors of "one-and-one-quarter-inch heart pine not to exceed six inches in width, to be battened and fastened with wrought nails," and having a variety of other carefully defined features. Successful bidders contracted to follow the specifications exactly, to use "124 pearches of stone laid in clay, 4000 bricks of good quality laid in lime mortar," 4,000 shingles, and "sixty running feet of blue stone in steps, lintels, and sills." Standardized construction aided the corporation's ailing finances because it proved cost effective; the corporation knew precisely what the builders would produce when they finished, and precisely the cost.[57] Perhaps it aided the contractors who built the structures, perhaps not; they did know in advance what they had to produce and how much they would receive but their freedom to innovate was sharply restricted. Like Starrucca, however, the stone houses turned out to be massive if small, and they endure even now.

Standardization spread slowly, and then only along canals, turnpikes, and railroads. Identical structures, locks, and bridges objectified faith in engineering, of course—if the designer failed, the client had five or ten or twenty failures to contend with, rather than only one—but also the new American experiment with written design. Folk builders rarely make a model of the house or barn they intend to erect; even more rarely do they produce a detailed drawing. They know from example what is required. By the beginning of the nineteenth century builders no longer simply built. Farmers and "mechanics" were doodling on shingles, scraps of paper, even tavern walls, and devising structures of extreme complexity.

Not every project demanded a trained engineer, and not every corporate, public, or private client could afford the men from West Point or the men they trained. For every masonry viaduct carrying a canal or railroad, a hundred wooden bridges stood on timber piles or stone piers laid by amateur craftsmen who learned from one another what wood can and cannot do. They learned by visual example, by traveling 20 or 200 miles to see the latest common innovation, the most recent product of trial and error. They learned quickly and well.

Covered bridges are an American institution, the objectification of closefisted Vermont ingenuity determined to bridge a stream at the least possible cost. Roofs and sheathing mask the important facets of the bridges, the great trusses that rest on stone piers and bear enormous loads without difficulty. Rot and fire excepted, a wooden truss bridge knows no dangers and with proper, loving attention lasts almost indefinitely. The proof is in Vermont, along roads and railroads, elsewhere in New England, in Ohio, and in the Pacific Northwest, for wooden bridges designed for wagons filled with grain now carry automobiles and trucks.[58] Starrucca is a monument to trained technicians, to professional engineers. The nation's wooden bridges remember anonymous craftsmen who sketched plans on the ground or on shingles, if they sketched at all.

Ithiel Town conceived his famous truss design while sitting in a Connecticut tavern; the sketches he patented in 1820 he first sketched in charcoal on the tavern wall, and for years the landlord proudly showed them to men intimately familiar with "Town's Truss." Town only improved the trusses devised by scores of carpenters who understood that a truss can be replicated again and again, until the largest river is crossed, and that it can be assembled from small, easily handled balks of timber. Town devised an improved version, then, of a common, almost folk style of building. His bridges proved stronger—when floods lifted them from their piers, farmers towed them back upstream with yokes of oxen—and showed signs of distress long before they collapsed. With his plans any group of carpenters easily and quickly erected a long-lasting, perfectly secure bridge. Town priced his plans according to bridge length; the builders of a 20-foot-long Town truss bridge paid considerably less for the use of his design than the builders of the one across the James River, which ran 2,900 feet over eighteen granite piers. Most of his bridges carried roads but many eventually supported railroads. In 1900 the Boston and Maine Railroad had more than 100 of his bridges in regular mainline service and was only beginning to use the iron-reinforced bridges patented in 1840 by William Howe. As long as the shingles kept the rain from rotting the timbers (and as long as sparks stayed away from the wood) truss bridges satisfied railroads in all but exceptional locations. Wood and sometimes stone were the materials of common engineering—not metal.

Americans, Stevenson remarked over and over, lived completely at ease with wooden construction and seemed to him always ready to experiment. More than by any other product of American engineering, more than by wooden locks and truss bridges, he was amazed at the American ease of moving houses. He delayed his return to Scotland and stood outside a wood and brick house on Chatam Street in New York City, where he gaped at a sight he called "very extraordinary." By European standards, he quickly admitted, it seemed a wonder of skill and planning but New Yorkers only glanced at it, and walked on.[59]

Americans first moved only wooden houses, but their success, and the necessity for moving larger structures in the growing coastal cities, prompted them to experiment with jacking and rolling brick structures too. Stevenson watched a four-story brick house jacked up on screws and great wooden beams by a self-styled "house-mover" who had moved about one hundred houses during his fourteen-year career. Through drawings and lengthy explanations Stevenson described the process to his European audience, and he concluded his remarks by noting that New Yorkers customarily left their furniture inside the houses. The

structure he watched move housed a carver's and gilder's business, and
the craftsmen left their picture frames and mirrors stacked in an upstairs
room during the five-week operation. A few blocks away, Stevenson
remarked, stood a church capable of seating between 600 and 1,000 persons; it had been moved 1,100 feet from its old location with no damage
to its galleries and spire.[60] Such triumphs, Stevenson assured the professional engineers of Europe, resulted from the skill of self-taught
craftsmen who knew how to make hewn wood come alive.

Americans respected engineers wherever they worked but settlers in
the backlands particularly honored them. Without their expertise—
professional or common—the settlers well knew, canals and railroads
existed only as pipe dreams. Engineers, not farmers or architects, channeled the canal water across hills and made level the rights-of-way of
railroads. Indeed engineers made straight—made geometrical—the
paths of agriculture and artifice. Crops, ores, and manufactured goods
(and almost accidentally, the messages of government) flowed nearly as
smoothly as Fulton and Pope predicted.

Until the 1840s most Americans invariably respected and usually understood the creations of the engineers. Farmers listening patiently to
the instructions for assembling a truss bridge knew that the voice of
innovation had half-drowned the voice of tradition, but the new voice
promised new rewards. Even massive projects like canals seemed understandable with a little concentration, and everyone immediately recognized their immediate and long-term economic value. Neighborhoods
no longer controlled every man-made form within them; turnpikes, canals, and lighthouses existed beyond local government and beyond local
building techniques but common techniques built them and common
wisdom accepted them as integral to nationhood.

ROADS

Gallatin emphasized the artificiality of turnpikes because his countrymen accepted roads as natural, the result of prolonged travel over identical routes. In the colonies, roads usually appeared by chance, not intention. Although New England towns sometimes "established" the route of
a future road by marking trees and forbidding any husbandman to
encroach upon the public "right of way," most American roads in New
Spain, New England, and the South began as private footpaths. The
paths served husbandmen engaged in daily enterprises such as walking
from their houses to their farthest outlying fields or from their plantation or householding to the nearest estuary or river wharf. Routes,

gradients, and surface conditions derived from specific, local needs not from concern with the long-distance traveler condemned to meander from farmstead to woodlot to pasture to farmstead, forever detouring around or through swamps, bogs, and hills.

Colonists equated roads with ways. By informal definition a way gave access across a piece of land; depending on its ownership, the way existed for public, quasi-public, or private use. Often the way resembled what the French explorers called a *trace*, a simple line of footprints; in later decades the narrow footpath became two faint ruts made by cartwheels. New England town meetings now and then determined that a private way ought to be made public or that some husbandman had unjustly blocked a public way by "gating" it or planting it to wheat, but only rarely did they insist that the route or condition of the way be improved by public effort. As in New Spain and the southern colonies roads truly belonged to their abuttors and frequent users, to those expected to maintain them.

Such individual and local control of road siting and maintenance produced idiosyncratic routes of varying quality and made tiresome and dangerous any long journey. Colonists venturing far by foot or horseback (most roads made wagon and carriage travel nearly impossible) encountered mysteries and hazards unthinkingly accepted by those familiar with the path or road. Colonial legislatures and governors now and then attempted to declare some routes "post roads" or "royal roads" but little came of their efforts; the colonies had too little money to improve such roads and wise travelers moved by water whenever possible. By the late eighteenth century Europeans accustomed to high-quality highways and roads delighted in condemning the ill-kept roads they discovered in the colonies; travel narratives catalogue the obstructions that lamed horses and overturned carriages. Stumps, fallen trees, great rocks, enormous mudholes—such impediments annoyed travelers lost amid unmarked crossroads or benighted away from habitations. Since roads are of chief concern to any land traveler it is not surprising that visitors in the colonies devoted such great attention to them, but perhaps the descriptions exaggerate the poor quality of American roads.[61] On the one hand, travelers frequently wandered along roads local inhabitants avoided; with almost no way of ascertaining best routes other than casually asking directions, Europeans—and Americans from afar— blundered again and again. On the other, Europeans accustomed to decent roads and generally well-maintained royal highways fared badly when confronted by obstructions; they had little training in wilderness travel and so were unprepared for roads like wildernesses. And finally,

late eighteenth- and early nineteenth-century European visitors, especially those who wrote travel narratives as a profession, embellished their
accounts to convince their readers that they had indeed suffered to
acquire their information. Emigrant handbooks and advisories emphasize road conditions much less frequently than do travel narratives,
and local accounts such as those of Timothy Dwight suggest that by the
early nineteenth century poor roads lay off the main-traveled routes.
How then can the state of American roads be ascertained?

At least one Englishman arrived in the colonies charged with examining and describing the main roads used by postal couriers. Hugh Finlay's
Journal records his observations in 1773 and 1774, when he rode along
the Atlantic coast from Canada to South Carolina. Finlay had no need to
embellish his descriptions; the poor post roads and mail service derived
(in his opinion) from the lackadasical efforts of colonial assemblies and
malcontents like the dismissed postmaster general, Benjamin Franklin,
and he reported to officials interested only in factual accuracy.[62] So
Finlay rode carefully, scrutinizing the routes and condition of roads,
growing distrustful of the hatred of all things British, and acquiring
topographical provincialisms quickly, like the word *barrens*. Only a spy
might have paid closer attention to communication routes.

Almost never did Finlay find roads as good as those in England; usually he found poor tracks. "The road is one continued bed of rocks, and
very hilly," he wrote of one stretch in Connecticut. "It is impossible for a
Post to ride above four miles an hour on such road, and to do even that
he must have a good horse, one used to such a path." He encountered an
even worse stretch in South Carolina, however, and led his horse along it
rather than risk breaking its legs: "It is a tract of boggy land, the road
through it made of logs laid crossways, and covered over with the mud of
this bog; after rain it is a mere puddle." Finlay did not know the
Americanism designating the common wooden solution to paving a road
across a swamp; nowhere in the *Journal* does "corduroy road" appear.[63]
But Finlay recognized the danger of a rotting corduroy road and remarked that "the horse sank between the logs up to the belly." Such
description made clear the difficulties facing colonial mail riders, and
only rarely did Finlay feel obligated to desert his terse style. One road,
however, prompted a change in tone. "On the whole, the road from
Charleston to Wilmington is certainly the most tedious and disagreeable
of any on the continent of North America; it is through a poor, sandy,
barren, gloomy country without accommodations for travelers," he remarked of land he did not recognize as "butchered" by long-vanished
tobacco and cotton growers. "Death is painted in the countenances of
those you meet, and that indeed happens but seldom on the road.

Neither man nor beast can stand a long journey through so bad a country, where there is much fatigue and no refreshment; what must it be in their violent heats, when I found it so bad in the month of January!" Finlay encountered few travelers because almost all southerners traveled by water; only fools ventured from Charleston to New York by land.

Everywhere, however, Finlay found roads, even in the Tidewater. "I observe that there are many crossroads in the way between Charleston and Savannah, and no directions set up to guide a stranger," he lamented. "It is impossible that he should keep the road he wishes to follow."[64] Roads crisscrossed every New England town, every Pennsylvania and New Jersey neighborhood, every southern county, but invariably they existed to serve abuttors, not strangers like Finlay or royal couriers. Not even in New Spain did European edicts create the elevated, graded roads men called "highways."

Local control of road location, maintenance, and use endured until the early nineteenth century, when turnpike companies began building direct, long-distance, well-graded roads. Americans sharply circumscribed the road-building power of the new federal government and through Andrew Jackson's distrust of internal improvement plans limited it even further; postal riders continued to slog over badly marked, deeply rutted roads. The same fear of tyranny that forbade the keeping of a standing army retarded the building of "Federal highways"; even the success of the National Road scarcely lessened citizen fears that a government powerful enough to build roads everywhere might use its power to erode local rights. Turnpikes, therefore, along with canals and later railroads, struck Americans as a useful compromise between the evils of all-powerful, centralized government and the irritation of poorly routed, locally controlled roads.

Americans accepted privately built and privately controlled turnpikes, canals, and railroads partly because such creations proved less dangerous to freedom than government-built roads and highways.[65] But other considerations fostered support too. For one thing, turnpike tolls and canal fares taxed only users, not the generality of taxpayers; try as they might, Gallatin and other visionaries failed to convince most taxpayers that roads built at public expense created wealth. For another, such private routes of travel coexisted with old-style public routes; the penny-pinching traveler chose the "shunpike," the twisting, poorly maintained sequence of short-distance, locally controlled public roads on which he paid no toll but spent more time. And finally, as long as he controlled the road outside his door, every American traveled freely, secure from tolls and passports, two scourges of tyranny.

Some Americans attempted to mitigate the difficulties of land travel by sharpening people's perceptions of routes rather than by improving the roads. Christopher Colles published the first maps of his *Survey of the Roads of the United States of America* in 1789 in an attempt to quicken the political and economic communication of his adopted country. His maps, long strips illustrating important roads and roadsides, derive from the British and Irish road books of the middle eighteenth century and emphasize structures of importance to travelers. Colles located the hills, streams, rivers, and swamps, taverns and blacksmith shops, bridges and ferries, about which wise travelers wanted to know before undertaking their journeys, and he depicted too such landmarks as churches and mills, by which travelers could locate themselves. But Colles failed in his work, not only because most Americans trusted themselves to find their way along roads until the roads ended in wilderness, but because wealthier travelers, including Europeans, had learned the wisdom of traveling in uncomfortable stagecoaches driven by men who knew the shortest way between inns and towns. Not for several decades, in fact, did Americans begin to use road maps frequently.

As long as they traveled by turnpike, canal, and railroad, Americans felt little need for printed depictions of routes; such graphic aids as those created by Colles seemed extremely expensive and unnecessary. By the 1840s, however, vast numbers of Americans were traveling, especially to the western territories, and railroad travel along routes opened by professional and common engineers stimulated the national imagination. "Whatever else we may think, or hope, or fear, it is quite certain that this is an age of Roads," asserted Horace Bushnell in *The Day of Roads*. His 1846 pamphlet marks the new awareness of high-speed travel made possible by the railroad invention. "The Road is that physical sign, or symbol, by which you will best understand any age or people," he declared with enthusiasm. "If they have no roads, they are savages; for the road is a creation of man and a type of civilized society."[66] Not until the 1840s did the proponents of internal improvements win their fight, and then only through the success of the privately owned, privately operated railroads. Americans retained control of short-distance roads but they embraced the greatest improvement of the century: the rail-*road*.

Principles

Geometrical improvements from the land-ordering grid to the lighthouse and canal depended on a fertile mix of tradition and innovation. By 1845 a great skein of remarkably similar forms overlay the distinctly regional artifacts dating to colonial times. No one spoke of a Virginia-style turnpike or a New York-style truss bridge or a New Hampshire-style canal; such creations displayed a sameness like that emerging as the national character in government, economics, and the arts. The national forms presented themselves immediately to any long-distance traveler; the older, more traditional forms dominated the space of farmers and other stay-at-home citizens. The coexistence of traditional, local forms and the creations of innovative nationalism objectified several distinctly American principles of design.

Americans accepted the grid, especially the federal grid, not only because it was a useful invention tempered with such traditional attributes as the statute mile and the 640-acre allotment but because it directly encouraged common enterprise. Philadelphia proved that an urban grid allowed every sort of adaptation, and the ordering of Ohio proved that within a gridded wilderness industrious settlers could shape the land according to whatever techniques suited them best. Americans discarded principles like those objectified at Williamsburg, Annapolis, and Charleston because they conflicted with the supreme principle of late eighteenth-century American design, the simple principle that all land ordering ought to be immediately intelligible to ordinary citizens and supportive of traditional, common design. Americans found grids easy to know and easy to build within; they dismissed ciphers comprising initials and grids based on geographical miles. Government of, by, and for the people produced design of, by, and for the people.

Americans embraced a second principle too, that of replication. The grid of section lines reached across the backlands exactly as Kirkwood's massive arches and Town's wooden trusses reached across ravines. Common builders replicated squares, arches, and diamond-shaped trusses until they spanned chasms and rivers, accepting a standardization of building unknown to earlier generations of Americans. Men distrusted uniqueness. It mocked the proven American forms and suggested that what was good enough for the typical American was not good enough for its builder. Even as they praised innovation, they respected the old forms of tradition and the standards of the common man.

And finally, nineteenth-century Americans respected the colonial principle of local control. All the national improvements affected travelers and people with national business more than they affected people with limited horizons, people who thought of roads as the natural product of short-distance travel, for example. Congressmen unthinkingly accepted such views; after all, in the midst of heated, complicated debate about the federal grid survey, they neglected to mandate a system of "artificial" roads. For many Americans, perhaps the great majority, and for many of their elected representatives, turnpikes and canals, lighthouses and railroads lay beyond daily concerns. The space of daily activity, the house, barn, farmyard, and farm, the short-distance roads repaired one day each year by their abuttors, the town or county center, the schoolhouse and church building remained locally controlled and shaped chiefly by tradition. Engineers belonged at the site of future bridges and canals not on backroads, meddling in perfection.

Curious tensions characterized the 1840s. Traditional design contested with innovation, common building with professional engineering, regional identity with national form. Space divided into two sorts, that shaped and controlled by traditionalists accustomed to local practice, and that shaped and controlled by innovators with national outlooks. Great contradictions—like a vast rural grid based on an urban ordering of space—passed unnoticed, as the party of the future objectified in the federal grid, the truss bridges, viaducts, and canals and railroads confronted the party of tradition, the husbandmen-farmers who vetoed most government intervention in the shaping of space, who cherished the practices of their fathers.

AGRICULTURE

*My father left me three hundred and seventy-one
acres of land, forty-seven of which are good timothy
meadow, an excellent orchard, a good house, and a
substantial barn.*[1]

J. Hector St. John de Crèvecoeur
Letters from an American Farmer
1782

Connected farm buildings, ca. 1850, Norwell, Massachusetts. (JRS)

usbandry is not farming. Husbandry is noble in the eyes of others; it is the avocation of enlightened kings; it is the first work of God Himself. "It began with man and the world," preached an obscure English clergyman in 1652, "and has together with man and the world been perpetually continued throughout all ages without interruption." Sermons emphasized what husbandmen wanted to hear, that husbandry is sanctified by divine word and dignified by royal proclamation, and reinforced what every husbandman knew, that husbandry is necessary to the health of any nation. Without food there is no commerce, no building, no life.

Seventeenth-century English people understood husbandry is marital terms, in a gorgeously embroidered analogy. Without the husbandman the earth is sterile, as sterile as a woman without a lover or a wife without a spouse. "A husbandman is the master of the earth," wrote Gervase Markham in *The English Husbandman,* "turning sterility and barrenness into fruitfulness and increase" just as a husband begets children.[2] Earth itself is essentially feminine, then, something to be cajoled and shaped and impregnated into usefulness. "Mother Nature" is more than a casual contemporary catch-phrase. It recalls the furrow as womb and the host of planting customs that ensured fertility and large increase. It recalls the time when British husbandmen soaked bread in milk and holy water and placed the loaf in the first furrow they plowed, the time when husbandmen colonized the New World.[3]

Husbandry was even more exalted in the colonies, in large part because it was so immediately and obviously necessary but also because almost everyone turned up and planted the soil. It was the husbandman, clergy and historians never tired of repeating, who made the wilderness into a garden, who civilized a chaos and made it bear fruit and grain of every kind. It was the husbandman who fought wild animals and Indians, who raised meetinghouses along with barns, and who supported religion and right learning. And it was the husbandman who prospered, who insisted on more and more land, who became by the middle of the eighteenth century a *cultivator* or an *agriculturist,* and by 1820, a *farmer.*

Until well into the nineteenth century the American farmer enjoyed the honor and respect formerly reserved for the husbandman. Politicians joined clergymen in honoring the hardworking cultivators of the soil, the men who defeated the French and the Indians and who a few years later defeated the British too. But the word *husbandry* vanished from the paeans; by 1860 it appeared only fitfully in orations and poetry, and it scarcely affected common speech. It connoted a bygone era, when man lived at the mercy of the land, wilderness, and weather, when begetting a good crop required as much luck as skill. *Farming* bespoke the maturation of technical expertise, the first success of agricultural innovation. A farmer *farmed* the land, he *worked* it, he *made it pay*, he *mastered* it. He shaped it to his ideal and coerced it into fertility.[4]

The farmer, Emerson reassured the farmers gathered before him at an 1855 country fair, "knows every secret of labor." Emerson praised the farmers' expertise, their capacity to guide change and growth, to regulate harvests, to make even swamps and hills answer their wishes. His oration descends directly from the late seventeenth-century English and American sermons in praise of husbandry but its optimism dates only to the eighteenth century, to the years when Americans like Crèvecoeur asked Europeans "to examine how the world is gradually settled, how the howling swamp is converted into a pleasing meadow, the rough ridge into a fine field," to mark how American farmers lived no longer at the mercy of tradition but mastered the wilderness with skill. By Emerson's day the earth seemed no longer a wife, an equal partner, but a slave to the newly skilled farmer. "The earth works for him," Emerson told his audience, "the earth is a machine which yields almost gratuitous service to every application of intellect."[5] By 1860 the farmer envisioned himself not as a husbandman but as an engineer whose work seemed neither particularly mysterious nor particularly exalted, although it demanded new skills and rewarded modest innovation.

The shift from husbandry to farming found expression in the changing landscape. Nineteenth-century farms bore slight resemblance to the farms created by the first generations of colonists. They were larger, carefully ordered for specific rather than general ends, and shaped for efficiency. Behind the mask of white and red paint and larger fields, however, remained features of an earlier time. The first half of the nineteenth century was indeed "the farmer's age," but it was an age when tradition very slowly gave way to innovation.

LORE

"The best time to plant flowers and vegetables that bear crops above the ground is during the light of the moon; that is, between the day the moon is new to the day it is full," counsels the 1979 *Old Farmer's Almanac*. Its chief rival, the 1979 *Farmer's Almanac*, opens with a dissertation called "By the Light of the Moon," a defense of astrology in agriculture. "For many generations," the article begins, "up to and through the scientific age, the farmer believed that if the moon can control the tides of the oceans, it can influence the action of the soil." Even though "government agricultural forces have always scorned 'moon farming,'" the wisdom of the past is not "altogether unrealistic at a time when skepticism is growing against the omnipotence of science and its failure to explain many mysteries of life." The words might have been written three centuries ago, when almanacs began publishing what had previously been oral knowledge, folklore passed from one generation to the next; they are part of a great literary tradition in America. In 1979 the *Old Famer's Almanac* had been published for 187 consecutive years; its competitor for 162. And in every one of the years the almanacs provided astrological information for the use of wise farmers.[6]

Astrology appealed to sixteenth- and seventeenth-century husbandmen because it promised control through foresight. The wise husbandman agreed with the authors of *Maison Rustique, or the Countrie Farme*, a popular late sixteenth-century French handbook translated into English in 1600 that endured for decades as the epitome of right knowledge. In it the husbandman learned that garlic and radishes ought to be sown in March during the new moon, that in the same month during the old moon cabbage, onions, and melons should be planted, that artichoke seeds ought to be gathered in fair weather in the wane of the moon, that pigs and sheep slaughtered in the wane of the moon produced dry, tough meat, that horses born during the wane of the moon grow up and remain weak, that building timber should be cut in the evening during the wane of the moon, that herbs should be planted and meadows hayed during the new moon, and that grain should be harvested during the wane. This information is given the place of honor in the book; before the prose of the first chapter is a great geometrical table explaining in graphic format the right "season" of the moon for sowing and reaping any crop. Lunar interpretation alone, however, did not guarantee bountiful harvests. "It sometimes falls out," the authors explain in a chapter on kitchen gardens, "that notwithstanding your seed be fat, full, make a white flower, and be nothing corrupted or hurt, yet shall some evil constellation (which the gardeners do call the course of the heavens) hinders them that they profit not." So the husbandman—if he intended to prosper—paid attention not only to the moon and the sun, "the two organs and principal instruments of all the world," but to the stars and other signs as well.[7]

Signs were of all sorts, some simple to understand, some complex. If New Year's Day falls on Sunday, the authors explain, "winter will be mild and clear, the spring delightsome and windy and moist; there shall be peace; cattle shall be at a good price; all manner of good things shall abound." Every other day of the week carried a different meaning at New Year's. "If it fall upon a Tuesday, winter shall be windy, dark, and snowy; the spring cold, dry, and moist, the summer windy and moist; autumn very inconstant; women shall die, there will be grave danger to such as are upon the sea, uproars will happen between the people and their superiors, some fruits will be dear." The husbandman who wanted more precise information about the coming year resorted to prognostications suggested by the authors. He took twelve kernels of wheat, dropped each onto the hot hearth before his fire, and noted which "leaped" several times from heat, which leaped only once, and which lay still; the movements forecast the fluctuations or stability in grain prices during the twelve months following New Year's Day.[8] Husbandmen looked at such signs and watched the heavens; what they saw helped determine not only when they planted their crops and cut their wood but whether they planted some crops at all, built a new barn, or borrowed money to buy more land.

Folklorists know that agricultural astrology and other occult lore survive everywhere in the United States, not just in isolated mountain hollows in southern Illinois but in the suburbs of great cities where the almanacs are sold in shopping malls.[9] Many farmers and gardeners laugh at the planting tables as so much foolishness, but thousands of others read the columns with care and disguise their belief with laughter. Contemporary agricultural occultism recalls a time when agriculture existed not as the engineering endeavor praised by Emerson but as something much more traditional, as a craft wedded to such medieval ideas as the "four elements." It hints at less well-known beliefs that once governed where husbandmen located farms and how they shaped the land. It recalls an era when many farms objectified astrological belief, when field location reflected the four-element doctrine, and when men raised barns with a mixture of skill, prayer, and omen-seeking.

In *A Philosophical Discourse of the Earth* John Evelyn summarized and explicated the Old World lore of soils imported into North America. His treatise of 1678 reiterates the usefulness of four-element land classification and the value of astrological influence. Surface soil that is "black, fat, yet porous, light," he remarked in ordering soils according to fertility, "is the best, and sweetest, being enriched with all that the air, dews, showers, and celestial influences can contribute to it." While he accepted with reservation the Baconian doctrine that the best soil lies wherever rainbows touch the earth, he firmly believed that soil fertility could be ascertained according to the observations of past generations.

Vegetation, he asserted, is one key to understanding soil types and can instruct the husbandman inquiring after the most profitable crops for each sort of ground. Thyme, strawberries, and betony "direct to wood," but camomile marks "a mould disposed for corn." Burnet grows in soil useful as pasture, and mallows indicate soil favorable to root crops. Ground "so cold as naturally brings forth nothing but gorse and broom, holly, yew, juniper, ivy, and box" ought to be planted with pines and firs, for it is almost useless for field crops. Moss, rushes, wild tansy, sedge, flags, fern, yarrow, "and where plants appear withered or blasted, shrubbery and curled (which are the effects of immoderate wet, heat and cold interchangeably) are natural auguries of a cursed soil" that may with luck be successfully planted to forest trees.[10] Evelyn's information is remarkably well-ordered and complete, in part because of his prolonged studies of soils and vegetation but also because it descended from centuries of experimentation, casual observation, and accident.

After analysis of vegetation the surest tests of soil fertility involved the human senses. Evelyn explained that by tasting the soil a wise husbandman might discover the presence or absence of important salts, and that by carefully watching the soil he could see "exhalations from minerals and the heat of the sun" as well as its true color. But Evelyn insisted too on smelling the soil, especially after long droughts. "Upon the first rain, good and natural mould will emit a most agreeable scent; and in some places (as Alonso Barba, a considerable Spanish author testifies), approaching the most ravishing perfumes." Touch usually supplemented taste, smell, and sight, however; assessing soil fertility meant caressing the earth. "In a word," Evelyn concluded, "*that* is the best earth to all senses, which is blackish, cuts like butter, sticks not obstinately, but is short, light, breaking into small clods; is sweet, will be tempered without crusting or chopping in dry weather, or (as we say) becoming mortar when wet." Four-element philosophy infuses every part of Evelyn's book. His frequent references to degrees of moisture, airiness, warmth, and acidity (often couched in terms like "sweetness") and his faith in celestial influences reveal the power of medieval tradition in the early modern era. To "be well read in the alphabet of earth" required an understanding of the past.[11]

New World colonists sought fertile ground and avoided land poisoned by mineral deposits. Mines of gold and silver are "less innocent and useful" than fertile soil according to Evelyn because they seduce men into schemes for easy riches and lead only to greed and despair. Any mineral deposit is likely to poison the soil for crops, and Evelyn insisted that husbandmen smell the land carefully. "If the ground be disposed to any mineral, or other ill quality, sending forth arsenical, and very noxious steams," the wise husbandman ought to avoid it. The lore of husbandry, particularly that concerning land classification, clashed with the lore of artifice explicated by Alonzo Barba, the mining expert of seventeenth-century New Spain.[12] And because the mass of New World colonists came to plant crops, not mine the earth, it is not surprising that the lore of husbandry assumed great force. Husbandmen scrutinized colors and textures of soil, examined vegetation, and remembered the lore of old-country agriculture.

Seventeenth-century letters from North American colonists reveal the amazing complexity of soil analysis. "The soil I judge to be lusty and fat in many places, light and hot, in some places sandy-bottomed and in some loamy, reasonably good for all sorts of grain without manuring, but exceeding good with manure, some for wheat, some for rye, etc.," advised Edmund Browne of the Massachusetts Bay Colony. "The land is grovey and hilly in many places, the air clear and dry; the sun is seldom enerved by any cloudy interposition." But another writer, perhaps more experienced in New England husbandry, complained in 1637 that "the soil, it is, for the nature of it, mixed; the upland rather participates of sand than clay, yet our rye likes it not, an argument it is both cold and barren." The anonymous letter-writer worried that the Massachusetts soil "seems to have been fattened by the continual fall of leaves from the trees growing thereon" and determined that it must have a "natural coldness" because beans, millet, and other crops "which delight in a cold soil, prosper here alike."[13] Such differences in evaluation derived in part, of course, from differences in soils from one part of a colony to another but more so from the varied Old World experiences of the writers. Colonists carried to North America the soil lore of their fathers' fields and wrote always with old-country standards in mind.

Old World soil-color analysis worked almost perfectly in eastern America. Black soils proved rich, filled with humus and lime, bearing out Evelyn's assertions. Red soils produced smaller yields; wise colonists knew that the color derived from the weathering of iron indicated too much "dryness" or "warmth." White or "crayfish" soils quickly earned the scorn of any husbandmen ignorant enough to plant them. Colonization promoters advertised the universality of old-country soil classification systems. William Wood compared New England soils to those of Surrey and Middlesex in England, classifying the upland types into three sorts—clay, gravel, and red sand—and noting that a foot of black humus covered each type. Despite its cursory descriptions Wood's 1634 book emphasized the usefulness of Old World soil and land classification techniques. Almost everywhere in the colonies husbandmen discovered that the color of the soil faithfully indicated fertility or sterility. Despite occasional surprises (in parts of Virginia black soil turned out so fertile that wheat grew too tall to head or else proved so infertile that most crops failed) colonists quickly assumed that all old-country expertise would work perfectly in North America. Each national group discovered soils well known in traditional classification systems.

In New Netherlands, for example, Dutch husbandmen discovered with pleasure, in the words of one observer in 1656, that "the surface of the land generally is composed of a black soil intermixed with clay, about a foot or a foot and a half deep, in some places more, and in some less; below, the stratum is white, reddish, and yellow clay, which in some places is mixed with sand, and in others with gravel and stones." Not surprisingly, the Dutch quickly accepted the sandy or gravelly soils that Englishmen might have dismissed, for such they had left behind in Europe, and they were enthusiastic about the marshes that Evelyn would have scorned as hopelessly "cold." "These meadows resemble the low and outlands of the Netherlands," the New Netherlands observer continued. "Most of them could be dyked and cultivated. Where the meadows are boggy and wet, such failings are easily remedied by cutting and breaking the bogs in winter and letting off the water in the spring." Soils in New Netherlands passed the Dutch standards of color, texture, and temperature, and with a little improvement after clearing produced excellent crops. "They are wonderfully fertile," the observer declared, "which in short, is the general quality of such land, and of most of the places we have noticed."[14] But the wise found other proofs of soil fertility, like the gigantic trees growing almost everywhere and slowing the progress of Dutch husbandmen anxious to enlarge their fields. Any soil that bore such proofs of fertility made husbandmen eager to fell the trees and sow seed.

Seventeenth- and eighteenth-century colonists knew that trees had uses beyond building timber, shade, and firewood. Like the wheat grains hopping on the New Year's hearth, trees were signs waiting to be read. European tree beliefs dated to pagan times, when people credited trees with souls and knowledge and applied themselves to determining the secrets they hid from humankind. Christianity scotched many of the charms and other practices but husbandmen continued to examine trees as indicators of soil types. Every species indicated one or more peculiarities of soil fertility or sterility, and New World colonists quickly applied the traditional wisdom to America.

In 1759 Israel Acrelius described the trees of New Sweden (part of present-day Maryland and Pennsylvania) for old-country readers. He explained that each variety had specific uses and that among the uses was the indicating of soil types. The white oak, he remarked, indicated good soil but the hickory and sassafras marked the richest. Black oak indicated "any kind of soil," as did Spanish oak, poplar, and sweet gum. Where the locust grew very high, there the soil was dry and rich. Acrelius's adjectives, particularly the word *dry*, derive from the four-element philosophy.[15] Other writers noted with precision the "temperature" of the soil beneath the trees, referring to moist or cold ground and to dry or warm soil, Like Acrelius, they understood that by describing the trees, they described the soil's characteristics, for the evidence of tree cover seemed infallible. Every colony quickly produced lengthy descriptions of its trees; John Smith in Virginia, Thomas Morton in Massachusetts, David Pastorious in Pennsylvania, and other writers emphasized trees in their reports to Europe not to attract foresters but to give husbandmen the clearest possible statement about the land's worth for agriculture.

By the middle of the eighteenth century American colonists had combined the tree lore of several western European nations into one distinctively their own. It was the common property of all colonists, a sort of language in which the southern or New York dialects were no longer important. In 1799 appeared James Smith's account of his captivity with the Indians of the Northwest Territory. As Smith promised, his book is filled with "remarkable occurrences," but mingled with them is an account of the soil and timber of the Ohio Valley. In his wanderings with the Indians, Smith described four sorts of land. What he calls "first rate land" he knew by oak, hiskory, walnut, cherry, black ash, elm, beech, and several other trees. Second rate land he knew by the appearance of spicewood trees among the beech, and third-rate territory by the small size of all trees and preponderance of species like spicewood. Here and there Smith crossed land he called "worse than third-rate," expanses marked by "hurtle berry bushes" or prairie. His book explicates the intricacies of eighteenth-century tree lore.[16] Trees indicated soils of different types but always soil somewhat useful to the cultivator. Where no trees grew, but only scrub or grass, there, husbandmen knew, the soil *had* to be worthless. By the 1750s, when Smith was undergoing the trial he described years later, the inhabitants of the thirteen English colonies had already determined that only forested land had value. Scrub land was "barren" in their terminology even if it produced wild grasses several feet high. Men classified it as useful but temporary pasture and meadow, not as ground for prolonged planting. Colonists avoided the blueberry barrens of Maine and the pine barrens of New Jersey and Georgia and instead searched for land marked by trees like the hickory.

Where the hickory and a few other species grew tall, there they paused and inquired carefully into the soils.

Astute European visitors quickly understood American refinements of old-country belief. "The honey locust, which signifies fertile soil, perfumed the crest of the mountain with its flowers," wrote a Frenchman exploring Pennsylvania in 1791. "Hickories and stalwart oaks luxuriously extended their branches." Ferdinand Bayard caught a trace of the emerging synthesis of practicality and aesthetics. Americans found those trees most beautiful that indicated the most fertile soil. But most Europeans who inquired into the significance of trees usually learned only their practical importance. A husbandman "may know the quality of the land by the trees, with which it is entirely covered," asserted an English musician traveling through the backcountry in the first years of the United States. "The hickory and the walnut are an infallible sign of a rich, and every species of fir, of a barren, sandy, and unprofitable soil." Throughout the first half of the nineteenth century, Americans prized land covered with hickories and walnuts. "Since these trees only thrive where there is a very fertile warm soil which contains clay and sand and is neither too dry nor too wet," reported one German still familiar with the adjectives of four-element natural philosophy, "the kind of soil that is recognized in America to be excellent wheat land, their predominance in number and in large individual specimens is the most certain evidence of the vigor and the quality of the soil here."[17] J. G. Harker admired the certainty and systematic usefulness of the land classification technique devised by countless anonymous colonial and early national husbandmen. Along with the scattered church buildings, schoolhouses, and free-standing farms, it reflected a distinctively American approach to understanding and shaping the natural environment. "Occasionally the chestnut predominates, and this is an indication of soil containing gravel," he continued. "Less frequently and, usually, only in valleys where earth has piled up loosely, one finds the persimmon, the sycamore, the red elm, and the white beech." In East Tennessee and elsewhere he analyzed soils by ascertaining their tree cover. "As for conifers," he concluded proudly, "one finds the black pine in drier, sandier places—usually in single fine specimens—and on the banks of rivers the white pine and the cedar are found."[18] Eventually Americans associated the hickory, walnut, chestnut, and oak with more than soil adapted for husbandry. Such species represented dignity, strength, and courage, characteristics that won for Andrew Jackson the nickname "Old Hickory," and they epitomized national standards of arboreal beauty. Always, however, they first indicated soil rich enough to farm.

Farm location objectified more than traditional notions of soil fertility, of course. Husbandmen valued a dependable water supply as highly in New Mexico as they did in Maine, and after the first decades of English colonization, when commercial agriculture stimulated the fragmenting of nucleated settlements, husbandmen located near access to markets. Ready cash determined location possibilities too; wealthy immigrants bought better land than poor newcomers. Land-clearing difficulties prompted many husbandmen to locate on natural meadows or deserted Indian planting grounds. But traditional ideas of soil classification remained important despite the vagueness of all the evidence. In Pennsylvania, where almost all bottomland and gently sloping soil was remarkably fertile by any European standards, more immigrants settled on land underlain by limestone than on less fertile soil, and Germans may have chosen land according to standards not completely accepted by English and Scotch-Irish immigrants. Hickory, black walnut, and chestnut, along with black oak, seem to have attracted German immigrants, at least in the first years of colonization. Scotch-Irish newcomers, who arrived later than many Germans and found vast areas already purchased, distrusted what they called "dry limestone" and chose soils underlain by shales. Their choice proved profitable too because the soil was almost as fertile as that coveted by Germans, and within a few years Germans and Englishmen and Scotch-Irish recognized the worth of each other's land-classification techniques and began settling with no apparent old-country design. Becoming an American meant in part accepting different—but always traditional—theories of soil fertility.[19]

Early nineteenth-century popular agricultural knowledge embodied the ancient classification based on earth, air, fire, and water. An 1836 *Farmer's Cabinet* editorial, "On the Nature of Soils," echoed Evelyn's theories by asserting that sand, clay, gravel, chalk, loam, and marl have different "degrees of warmth, air, and moisture" and must be carefully identified so that corrective measures can be taken. "The best loams, and natural earths are of a bright brown, or hazely color," the editor noted. "Dark grey, and russet mould, are accounted the next best—the worst of all are the light and dark ash-colored." For the benefit of neophyte farmers unlearned in the ways of the past, he added that the best soil "emits a fresh pleasant scent on being dug or ploughed up, especially after rain; and being a just proportion of sand and clay intimately blended, will not stick much to the fingers on handling." Most soils never attained the perfect mix of sand and clay that constituted loam, and the editor concluded by urging his reader to "reduce his land to that state and temperment in which the extremes of hot and cold, wet and dry, are best corrected by each other, to give them every possible advantage

flowing from the benign influence of sun and air." Advances in agricultural chemistry scarcely affected the analysis and cultivation of American
soils; traditional knowledge appealed to farmers because it was obvious
and proven. A hand placed upon the earth, a clod held up to eyes and
nose, such simple examination guided settlement and planting and cultivation everywhere in the Republic.

For all that the rectilinear survey of the backlands objectified the new
doctrine of political equality, in no way did it homogenize the wilderness
soils into land uniformly fertile. Federal surveyors identified backcountry land as James Smith had, using terms such as "first rate" and "third
rate," and emigrants from Rhode Island, New Jersey, or South Carolina
interpreted official reports according to traditional local wisdom. Nothing more quickly precipitated a land rush from a settled eastern
neighborhood to a western valley than a trustworthy report that soils
were similar and fertile.[20] Enlightened men scorned the national reliance on astrology, but almanac publishers who condemned "superstition" printed lunar calendars and zodiacal signs, and agricultural reformers admitted the usefulness of the old lore of trees and soils. Farm
location objectified the American attachment to time-tested wisdom. Innovation, like dry red soil—and prairies—men approached with caution.

Only when settlers pushed west into the "oak openings" of western
Michigan and the small prairies of Illinois and Missouri in the 1790s did
the old lore clash with exasperating new experience. Grassland had long
indicated barrens like those that unnerved Timothy Dwight and
Thoreau even as the men explained the sterility of outer Cape Cod. "In
such ground no forest tree can grow either with rapidity or vigor," wrote
Dwight of the edge of the Cape grasslands. "On the driest and most
barren of these grounds grows a plant which I had never before seen,
known here by the name of beach grass." Fifty years later, as settlers took
up quarter sections on prairie, Thoreau slogged through the Cape's
"barren, heath-like plain," wondering at the poverty-grass "despised by
many on account of its being associated with barrenness" and inquiring,
as had Dwight, about the color of the soil. "'The yellow sand,' said he,"
remarked Thoreau in quoting a Cape Cod farmer, "'has some life in it,
but the white little or none.'"[21] Dwight and Thoreau classified Cape Cod
soil according to tradition, as James Smith had classified the soil of
unsettled Ohio a century before, but the New Englanders' technique was
obsolescent. Farmers in the western prairies had learned that some
grassland might be fertile.

Late eighteenth-century explorers of the far backlands determined
that despite the lack of tree cover, which they sometimes attributed to

great fires set by Indians chasing game, the soil was rich. "The quality of the land is excellent," wrote one traveler. "Its vegetable layer is about three feet in depth." In the first years of the next century husbandmen discarded most of the old tree lore, but careful observers continued to use the most traditional sort of soil analysis and old words too. "A large part is the finest quality of soil," counseled one student of the Illinois prairies in 1819, "being either a black vegetable mould, or a dark, sandy, loam, from fifteen inches to three feet deep; generally bedded on yellow clay, mixed with sand."[22] Such precise information convinced eastern farmers disheartened by stony, worn-out soil that the western dearth of trees meant nothing significant. Indian burning seemed a likely explanation for the prairies or *barrens,* and settlers soon learned that they had gambled well.

Old words endured, however, despite explanations like that offered in 1818 by Caleb Atwater of Ohio. In an article entitled "On the Prairies and Barrens of the West" he explained to readers of the *American Journal of Science* that a *prairie,* in backcountry language at least, denoted discrete patches of natural grassland up to about three by seven miles and covered with six- or seven-foot-high grass and "some weeds and plumbushes." *Barrens,* he took pains to explain, were vast, almost limitless areas covered with grass where low and moist and producing a few oaks and hickories where rising and dry. "From their appellation, 'barrens,' the person unacquainted with them is not to suppose them thus called from their sterility, because most of them are quite the reverse," he remarked in advising that most barrens needed only a little ditching. "This land lies so level that the waters stand on it too long for grain to thrive equally with grass, unless, indeed, the farmer should dig a long drain, which is easily effected by the plough, with a little assistance from the hoe and the spade." But for all his up-to-date arguments that standing water, not Indian burning, accounted for the vast prairies his neighbors called *barrens,* Atwater admitted that the land did not appeal to newcomers. "No pleasant variety of hill and dale, no rapidly running brook delights the eye, and no sound of woodland music strikes the ear; but, in their stead, a dull uniformity of prospect 'spread out immense.'"[23] Conservative settlers avoided the barrens and searched for hickory-covered, dry black soil.

Farmers maintained the complicated and sometimes contradictory traditions of astrologically determined planting, cultivating, and harvesting, of reading signs, of classifying land, and of farmstead siting inherited from Europe and from colonial husbandmen because like their forebears they had not mastered the land. In 1850—as in 1580—

agriculture still involved uncertainty, and every farmstead reflected the reluctance of farmers to abandon tradition.

FARMSTEADS

Once the husbandman ascertained the boundaries of his land, he set about choosing a site for his house, barn, outbuildings, and yard, the cluster of structures and spaces that comprise the farmstead. Astrology sometimes directed the alignment of the house. Even as late as the nineteenth century, settlers in the Ohio Valley sited farmhouses "right with the earth," parallel to vaguely understood lines of force that directed good health and prosperity to well-placed doors. Far more often, however, husbandmen located according to complex old-country advice, much of which contradicted itself. Gardens and orchards ought to be sited on the south side of the house, counseled Markham in *The English Husbandman* in 1635, "because your house will be a defense against the northern coldness, whereby your fruits will much better prosper." The kitchen should face west, he continued, toward the dairy, and north of the house should stand the stables, oxhouse, cow-house, and swine-house. Hay and corn barns ought to be placed south of the house, near the hen house and garden. Markham and other agricultural commentators produced such vague directives because their audience was little interested. European husbandmen worked centuries-old holdings. Away from rare places like the newly drained Dutch and German polders and the recently cleared forests of Bavaria, seventeenth-century agriculturalists inherited or purchased farmsteads designed in earlier times, and the new owners needed advice on maintenance and betterment, not information on pioneering. European commentators consequently provided only essential suggestions useful to the wealthy landowners opening previously untilled land and to men rebuilding after calamitous fires.[24] New World colonists were truly on their own, and while they clung to old-country lore, they hesitantly began to innovate.

Spanish husbandmen built casa-corral farmsteads well into the late eighteenth century, long after Chimayo and other plaza-oriented estensiónes north of the Rio Grande ceased to have any military purpose. Although it resembled a fort, the casa-corral derived from traditional Spanish and innovative central Mexican domestic design. A husbandman north of the Rio Grande located his casa-corral away from moist ground—dampness slowly eroded the dried-mud foundations, and moist land was too valuable to waste on farmstead-siting anyway—but invariably near an adequate and certain water supply, usually a clear

stream or an *acequia*. The house itself was usually only one story tall and
L-shaped, the interior angle facing south. Its north walls often lacked
windows and doors in order to conserve heat in winter; the entire structure focused on the sun, and on the four- to eight-foot-high adobe walls
that extended from the corners of the house to enclose a square sheltered from the wind. Along the inside of the walls the wise husbandman
located a number of buildings necessary in diversified agriculture, the
tasolera, the *caballerisa, barbacoca,* and the *dispensa* or *troja.* The tasolera
housed hay or forage in its upper story and sheltered dairy animals in its
lower. Horses were stabled in the caballerisa, along with harnesses and
other equipment. The barbacoca was a shed for storing corn and cornstalks; husbandmen piled shelled corn in its lower story and heaped
corn stalks to dry on its flat roof. The farmwife managed the dispensa,
the small structure housing the family's cookware and clothes. Scattered
about the yard stood other less important structures, a well house,
perhaps an outdoor oven, and on large holdings, a *cochera*, or wagon
house, all of which competed for room with a gateway area and a space
reserved for a dozen daily operations from milking to baking. Nowhere
inside the walls was there the slightest space for gardening, however,
even though the house, outbuildings, and high walls trapped the heat of
the sun and made the yard comfortable for men and animals even in
winter.[25] A casa-corral indeed defended its inhabitants but chiefly
against the wind and cold.

Casa-corral farmsteads still are built in Chihuahua Province, and
many survive in the United States, particularly in Arizona in the Pecos
Valley north of Santa Rosa, and in New Mexico, north of Taos along the
Rio Grande. They mark the usefulness of tradition in a new place where
economics and natural environment are similar to those left behind.
They mark too an old, almost ancient, understanding of the farmstead
as one house, a shelter for humans and for animals. As late as the
seventeenth century husbandmen and their families in Italy, the Netherlands, the German countries, and several provinces in France shared
their living quarters with farm animals. Cows, horses, and poultry occupied one end of a long, narrow building; at the other, separated sometimes by a low wall or hearth, lived the family. The casa-corral farmstead
is therefore a traditional *and* a transitional form because in it the animal
quarters are removed slightly from human habitation.

Casas-corral blended into the natural environment and objectified the
Spanish determination to utilize existing resources as fully as possible. In
spring the prickly pear planted to bind the packed-soil roofs blossomed
in a pale yellow that accented the tans and browns of the adobe walls,

and in autumn families strung the protruding *vigas* with bunches of bright red chili. Across northern New Spain the coloring of agricultural structures reflected a dying tradition of intervening gently and precisely in a familiar but fragile natural order. Unlike the high, angular houses and barns and outbuildings erected later along the Atlantic seaboard by English, Swedish, and German husbandmen, the casas-corral scarcely dominated the agricultural land about them. Their merging of family sleeping and working spaces with areas devoted to crop processing and livestock shelter epitomized the old agricultural accommodation to nature.

Away from the Spanish estensiónes, New World stead design derived much less from tradition and accommodation and far more from hesitant innovation. New Netherlands provided the clearest example of new thinking. For centuries before the settlement of the Hudson River valley, Dutch husbandmen frequently occupied structures called *loshoes*. At one end of the rectangular building was a great doorway through which horses pulled loaded haywagons in autumn and through which husbandmen drove livestock every day. Just within the door, on both sides of the long central aisle, stood two pigsties and slightly beyond them, again on both sides, stalls for horses, cows, sheep, and calves. Two-thirds of the *loshoe* sheltered animals and harvested crops; the remainder housed the husbandman and his family. The living accommodations were divided into several rooms beyond the aisle or threshing floor that ended in an open fireplace. Along one side were the enclosed "cupboard beds," each fitted with a door that shut off a sleeper from his neighbors. Between the beds and the weaving room was the "best room," a rarely used parlor fitted for ceremonial occasions. No wall divided animal from human space, but a cobblestone floor usually distinguished the living area; only hard-packed earth surfaced the aisle. Over both sections of the loshoe lay a loft filled with hay, in which children and servants sometimes slept.[26] Dutch settlers in the New World never built such structures although they knew them intimately and found all the necessary material.

Several very practical reasons prompted innovation. By the late sixteenth century Dutch husbandmen were outgrowing the loshoes and beginning to add a variety of outbuildings to the main structure. Bakehouses, storage sheds, and other small buildings straggled away from the "living" end and sometimes formed a sort of yard partly sheltered from the wind. The settlers of New Netherlands understood such old-country innovation and quickly discovered that Dutch forms did not easily adapt to the New World environment. The Dutch loshoe, for example, had no fireplace; families burned peat on an open hearth and allowed the smoke to drift upward through the hayloft to a hole in the thatched roof.[27] Settlers ignored the thatch grasses growing along the Hudson because they found little peat and knew that wood had to fuel the fires so necessary in New Netherlands winters. Dutch colonists determined very early that a loshoe created a very real fire hazard even if its roof had shingles; if it burned, the husbandman lost all his harvested produce, his livestock, and his domestic possessions. It seemed more practical to build houses like those erected by prosperous *poorters,* the city dwellers whose lifestyle all Dutchmen envied, and to site steeply roofed barns alongside the urban-like structures. A detached house represented not only fire insurance but wealth envied by Dutch husbandmen increasingly conscious of the town life—and town houses—of *poorters.*

Tradition guided the design of the New World Dutch barn but each husbandman innovated at will. The first shelters in the colony were underground hovels for families and rough sheds for livestock but within a few years more permanent structures appeared near the newly made fields. When a Dutch settler had the opportunity and funds to erect a permanent barn and house, he usually chose to retain such customary features as the great doorway in the gable end of the barn and the steeply pitched barn roof, but he abandoned the rectangular floor plan for one almost square. He placed a great door at each gable end of the barn to spare himself the cumbersome backing process that irritated old-country owners of loshoes and to provide better draft for the threshing process. With both doors open on a windy day the stiff breeze quickly separated wheat from chaff; if the wind blew too hard, he adjusted the doors and threshed on unhindered. Away from the barn he built a house modeled after those of Dutch towns, sometimes of wood but preferably of stone. Farmhouse types varied from northern New Jersey to the Albany area of the Hudson Valley, sometimes according to the region of Holland from which their builders came and sometimes according to the building materials available, but nowhere did their builders attach them to barns.

English and German settlers adapted to the New World environment as quickly as the Dutch. New England colonists immediately sheltered their livestock in sheds and as soon as possible built small barns, each with a single large door in one side. English settlers in Virginia and the other southern colonies built only crude shelters for horses and dairy cows, and only slightly more permanent structures to store curing tobacco and harvested corn. Germans in Pennsylvania abandoned the old-country equivalent of the loshoe and erected separate barns and farmhouses. Holdings determined barn size; in New England and other places where each family owned only a few score acres at most, men erected small barns but in Pennsylvania, where husbandmen worked large acreages, men built capacious barns. In single-crop areas, particularly in the Tidewater, barns tended to be specialized in ways unknown in Europe. Centuries of British agricultural tradition offered no guidance to the Virginian thinking about building a tobacco barn. He, like Germans in Pennsylvania and Dutchmen in New Netherlands, used the best of the techniques and forms he remembered, and invented the rest.

Pennsylvania Germans built the most imposing and innovative barns in the colonies. By the late eighteenth century they had replaced their small, New England-like pioneer barns with the bank barns that aroused the admiration of strangers like J. B. Bordley, a Maryland farmer. "On the ground floor are stalls in which their horses and oxen are fed with hay, and straw, and rye-meal; but not always the other beasts," he wrote in *Essays and Notes on Husbandry and Rural Affairs* in 1801. "The second floor with the roof contains the sheaves of grain, which are threshed on this floor. A part of their hay is also stored here. Loaded carts and wagons are driven in, on this second floor; with which the surface of the earth is then level; or else a bridge is built up to it, for supplying the want of height in the bank, the wall of one end of the barn being built close to the bank of a hill cut down." The bank or "Swisser" barn proved wonderfully efficient because of the upper-floor overhang, the *forschoos* in the dialect of the German settlers, that jutted over an enclosed yard designed to shelter livestock on warm winter days (bank barns almost invariably faced south or southwest) and collect manure.[28] Germans forked down hay to the animals in the basement and devoted little time to forking it up into lofts. Although the bank barn owes something to German tradition, most of its form derives from innovation, and British settlers eventually adopted the design too, convinced of its utility. Amish farmers still build bank barns, sometimes with the stone gable ends that appeared late in the eighteenth century, and still delight in their permanence and efficiency.

Innovation slowed during the first decades of the eighteenth century. Husbandmen in New England, the Middle Colonies, and the South determined that their fathers had discovered the best ways to build barns and farmhouses and the best way to organize a farmstead. Husbandmen championed local and regional peculiarities with growing fervor. New England husbandmen sometimes built barns on slopes too but they never stabled animals in the basement. Instead they placed a wagon

under a trapdoor and pushed manure directly into it, then pulled it to
the fields. Anyone who kept livestock in a damp basement, they claimed,
did not understand animal disease. Pennsylvania Germans, who
shoveled manure up into wagons, had the satisfaction of raking hay
down to their livestock. European visitors were quick to discern the
differences between regions but they rarely noticed the chief cause for
the dramatic decrease in innovation.

Until well into the nineteenth century Americans built barns and
houses using very heavy timbers. Brace-frame construction they thought
to be the most solid of all building techniques, and they respected its
reputation in Western Europe. Men squared whole trees for the main
supporting timbers and shaped lesser limbs for rafters and other load-
bearing beams; they notched each piece so that its ends interlocked
tightly with the notched ends of others. Many of the great timbers
weighed far more than even two or three husbandmen could lift. Men
hewed them on the ground from felled trees, dragged them with horses
or oxen to the building site, and assembled them—still flat on the
ground—into perfectly square subassemblies. Every builder understood
the folk "ground rules" of making perfectly square or rectangular subassemblies and cellar holes.[29] Using only a long rope and a peg, a builder
first inscribed a circle on the ground, using the peg as the center point
and the rope as a radius; then he stretched the rope at a tangent to the
circle drawn in the dirt, scratched a line following the rope, then pivoted
the rope about one of its ends until it again touched the circumference of
the circle, and making a perfect ninety-degree angle.[30] By knotting the
rope and varying its length, a man totally ignorant of mathematics could
produce a few rectilinear shapes as perfect as any grid line run by a
federal surveyor. On "raising day," when his neighbors assembled to
help lift the immense, awkward sections into place, he knew that traditional shapes would fit perfectly into a whole everyone understood.

Raisings ensnared everyone in adventures of luck and skill. Around
the square or rectangular floor of the barn-to-be men dragged the four
or more subassemblies of fitted beams, one each on a side. Slowly they
raised one of the sections, at first using only their bodies, then pushing
the assembly higher and higher with long poles. As quickly as possible
they raised a second section adjoining at right angles and immediately
fastened it to the first. Once two sections stood erect and locked at right
angles, the men proceeded to raise a third, and after all the side frames
stood secure, the most experienced of the amateur builders clambered
atop them and wrested the roof assemblies into position. The entire
raising operation crackled with danger because at any moment a lifting

Traditional barn frame, Norwell, Massachusetts. (JRS)

pole or poles might snap or a makeshift fastening break and an entire subassembly—or the whole half-finished structure—would crash down, crushing men and boys. Positioning the roof assemblies was the most exacting task, one that called forth shouts and curses and the screams of the women cooking the noon meal nearby. American English remembers the excitement in the old phrase "raising the roof." All day everyone's nerves tensed and frayed, but if all went well the evening meal celebrated common engineering. The husbandman and his family looked out at their new barn or house, or rather the frame of the structure, for the boarding over everyone dismissed as a one-man job best left to the owner.

Raisings already had a long history in Europe when colonists in the New World began erecting their first structures. In Germany a raising was an almost religious event, filled with ceremonies and rituals now nearly extinct. Once they locked the final roof beam into position, the tired carpenters began pounding on the frame. "Calling for wood" announced the start of the *Richtfest*. The master builder brought a freshly cut evergreen tree to the foot of the structure, where women and children decorated it with ribbons, gilded paper, and ornaments and paraded it three times around the finished frame. What followed varied from place to place and curiously wedded Old Religion paganism and Christianity. In some regions, after saying the Lord's Prayer three times, the master builder drove an iron spike into the largest oak beam in the frame. If the beam cracked the structure would burn someday; if it spurted water the frame would rot or an aged member of the owner's family would die soon. The omen was usually favorable since builders used only seasoned, close-grained timber in the frame, and the ceremony continued with another test of the future. The master builder, or his foreman or oldest craftsman, proposed a toast commemorating the celebration and flung his glass or bottle over the frame. Unless the vessel failed to shatter, which indicated the speedy death of the building's owner, the ceremony proceeded with a lay sermon followed by craft songs extolling the builders' exalted calling.[31] The harmony of builders, frame, and nature was assured, and the men raised the decorated conifer to the highest beam in the structure and temporarily fixed it. Thereafter the frame had the life of a living tree. "Keep all lightning and storms distant from this house," asked one recommended prayer, "keep it green and blossoming for all posterity." Songs over and prayers said, the builders, owner, and invited guests sat down to a glorious feast.

Everywhere in New England and in the Middle Colonies, and across parts of the South and the Middle West, husbandmen and their neighbors continued the raising tradition, although often in abbreviated or improvised form. Once they permanently secured the ridgepole, they christened the frame by smashing a bottle of rum against it and by attaching a small evergreen to the peak of the gable. Each frame, therefore, had a specific, given identity, and more than one was named in songs like one composed on the spot in the late eighteenth century.

> On the twentieth of April, in the year '99
> Our frame we got up in a suitable time.
> It's a very fine frame, the flower of the Plain,
> The timbers substantial and strong;
> The stories are high, it is forty feet wide,
> And forty-four feet it is long

> .   .   .

> The 'Flower of the Plain' is the name of the frame,
> We've had exceeding good luck in raising the frame;
> May God direct and instruct us in all that is right;
> It's the last day of the week, and late at night.[32]

Frames and farmsteads were named everywhere in the colonies in keeping with European tradition. Great Virginia plantations such as Westover and tiny Massachusetts farms such as Cedarcroft were significant places, as were houses called Belle House, and, as one seventeenth-century New England deed book records, "Musquashcutt Farm House, alias Conihassett Farm House." And, of course, as was the barn called "The Flower of the Plain."[33]

Raisings and ceremonies did more than provide a rural neighborhood with a day's hard work and excitement and a family with a newly framed house or barn. They retarded innovation and made work scarce for architects. Every husbandman laying out the subassemblies around the floor of his barn understood that his neighbors would devote one day to raising them into position. It was imperative, therefore, that he plan a barn immediately familiar to everyone because no one had time to discuss an unfamiliar construction. Builders frowned on novel designs not only because raising them took more time but because they proved dangerous. Raising subassemblies imperiled all helpers even when everyone, man and boy, understood them perfectly; raising a strange frame tempted fate. By the early eighteenth century, therefore, frames in each of the great colonial regions had been standardized, and builders kept them standardized until the middle of the nineteenth century, when wealthy farmers heeded the advice of reformers, hired architects and builders, and erected round, octagonal, and other strangely shaped barns and houses. But the standardized frames and the raising-day excitement and songs, and especially the christening, gave the builders, and particularly the owner, enormous satisfaction. Almost every American farmer had a personal stake in his farmstead. He and his neighbors built the structures themselves, without "foreign" help. If his house and barn were like his neighbors' structures, so much the better. His conformity displayed his solid position in the community, his willingness to abide by unspoken architectural—and social—ground rules. Architects were out of place in rural America. They worked in cities, where almost no one named structures.

Unlike houses and barns, small outbuildings required little if any neighborly help to erect and maintain. Between the farmhouse and the barn, surrounding the farmyard or barnyard, the husbandman located a smokehouse, a springhouse, a wagon shed, a woodshed, a corncrib, a pigsty, a dairy house, and sometimes one or more poultry houses. Not every colonial farmstead displayed each of the outbuildings; most lacked poultry houses because colonial farmers did not know that allowing chickens to roost in haylofts spread disease among the horses and cattle that ate hay soiled with manure. Colonial and early national agriculture was diversified, however, and farmers needed a variety of small structures because they engaged in a wide range of activities, some seasonal,

Four-foot-wide corncrib, Springboro, Pennsylvania. (JRS)

some year round. Woodsheds were important everywhere, not only to keep split firewood from rain but to provide a cold-weather chopping area. Springhouses, especially in the Middle Colonies, proved vital in dairying; the cool water flowing around pans of butter and milk and cheese allowed the farmwife to preserve products that otherwise spoiled. Corncribs too were common and important. Perhaps more than any other outbuilding, they proved the worth of traditional design.

Corncribs survive in many American farmsteads. As in colonial and early national times, some are thatched, some roofed with shingles, and some with boards; most are rectangular, opening through a door at the narrow end and slatted to allow moving air to dry the ears of corn. All are raised one or more feet from the ground and all are about four feet wide.[34] The four-foot width is mandatory; cribs wider than four feet produce rotten corn because the ears heaped in the middle fail to dry properly. When the "perfect" width was discovered is unknown but the most technical of contemporary structural plans retain the measurement.[35] From Maine to Florida corncribs were and are always raised off the ground to foil rats and other rodents, and invariably they are no more than four feet wide at the bottom. They recall an era when every husbandman built deliberately, according to tradition, not whim.

Alden house with outshot kitchen, ca. 1653, Duxbury, Massachusetts. (JRS)

FARMHOUSES

Farmers built farmhouses according to custom too, but the custom derived from the tradition of housewifery.[36] Almost every husbandman's guide included a section addressed to the husbandman's wife, to the "farmwife," because the woman's role in operating the holding had equal importance. Until well into the late nineteenth century American farm journals such as the *Cultivator*, the *Farmer's Cabinet*, and the *Wisconsin Farmer* discussed cheese- and butter-making, poultry-raising, woolcarding, and innumerable other activities with the clear understanding that such vital work was done by women—and managed by women. Until the 1880s the American farmhouse existed as a machine for working in.

Colonial and early national farmhouses had two identities, one public and one private. It is the public that attracts, as it should, the attention of traveling photographers and architectural historians. Wealthy farmers enjoyed adding Greek Revival and Gothic elements to existing structures and to houses being built in the prevailing style when they had the money to hire architects or carpenters versed in the latest fashion. It is these farmhouses that prompt the coffeetable books filled with full-color

photographs. They face the public highway across an interval of
meadow or pasture and announce the respectability of agriculture. Photographers are unwilling to wander up the lane and into the yard—gates
and barking dogs block the lanes—and rarely see the important part of
the houses they glorify.

Most American agriculturalists lived—and still do—in common houses
that lack most characteristics of architectural styles. Colonial husbandmen, like later farmers, were often too poor to build "fancy," but
they had other, more compelling reasons to ignore prevailing fashion.
Many settlers never intended their first dwellings to be permanent
houses. Instead the structures existed to shelter a family busily clearing
land and building a barn and other structures. Often families abandoned them when they had the time and funds to build a proper house;
sometimes they tore them down for firewood or building timber or
converted them into storage sheds. More frequently, however, husbandmen added to them and modified them again and again as families
grew, needs changed, and old timbers gave way. The typical American
farmhouse is not always one structure but is sometimes composed of
several substructures behind a stylish facade.

Colonists all along the seaboard abandoned their earliest dwellings as
soon as they could build permanent structures. They typically divided
colonial farmhouses into three sections: bedchambers, a parlor (called
"the hall" in seventeenth-century New England), and a kitchen or "keeping room." In the tiniest sort of house, of course, the family slept in the
parlor and in the loft, but the social necessity for a "best room" prompted most men to build a room for receiving and entertaining strangers
and for such semipublic ceremonies as funerals. The parlor, by whatever
name people called it, had no daily function in larger houses. It existed
chiefly as a symbol of status, a bit of conspicuous consumption. The
family with a parlor unusued on most days had money enough to
splurge on space.[37]

No family wasted kitchen space. Every processing activity except
threshing somehow involved the kitchen and the housewife. The husbandman's wife dried herbs, grains, and vegetables, smoked meats, and
processed dairy products; in her spare time she processed wool, cotton,
and flax, made soap from ashes, and slaughtered poultry. Cramped
space made such difficult work nearly impossible, and as larger holdings
produced greater harvests, families expanded their kitchens. At first
they built lean-to sheds, or "outshots," onto their houses; eventually they
built them as part of new houses, creating the unbalanced (two stories in
front, one in back) structures called saltboxes. In the southern colonies

Nineteenth-century kitchen ell, Clive, Iowa. (JRS)

families built free-standing kitchens. "All their drudgeries of cookery, washing, dairies, etc., are performed in offices detached from the dwelling-houses," Beverly remarked in 1705, "which by this means are kept more cool and sweet."[38] A moderate climate permitted outdoor kitchen work throughout much of the year, of course, but tobacco raisers refused to invest heavily in complicated dwellings that might be abandoned within a decade. The detached kitchen represented adaptation to climate and the transiency of tobacco culture. But away from the South, kitchens grew larger and larger, reaching out from the house to the farmyard and to the fields beyond, becoming the focus of family life.

By 1860 the kitchen wing, or "ell," was frequently larger than the house from which it extended. In it the farmwife spent most of her time and around its fringe worked her husband and children. Ell design preoccupied farm families, agricultural reformers, and even a few architects. Each month the nation's agricultural periodicals presented farmhouse plans that emphasized the kitchen ell above parlors and bedrooms. The model house was that described in 1859 by a writer in the Patent Office *Report*, "the rambling, capacious, and home-like residence, built with no object beyond the convenient, economical, and comfortable accommodation of the household."[39] Typically, the ell began with an outshot kitchen attached to the house, not incorporated into the main structure. An attached kitchen offered light and air on three sides and the possibility of easy expansion. Most extended to a wood room, a large storage shed filled with split logs for immediate use in the kitchen fireplace or stove. Opening off one side of the wood room and connecting directly to the kitchen stood a pantry, often one-third the size of the kitchen itself. Beyond the pantry and the wood room, sometimes along a hall, stood the washroom with its own stove and wash-boiler. The farmhouse washroom was a busy place, not only because many farmwives washed the clothes of their families and of their hired men but because there they soaked flax, washed wool, and sized and dyed new-made cloth. In the washroom too many farmwives boiled the garbage they fed to the family's prize pigs kept in an adjoining room. Swine-raising remained the farmer's responsibility, but caring for the two or three pigs selected for the family's private pork supply clearly required a woman's skill. Beyond the pigsty lay a small poultry room where the farmwife tended the family chickens and perhaps watched over the chicks her husband later cared for in the farm's main hen house. "A pig can always be kept, and fatted in three or four months, from the wash of the house, with a little grain, in any well-regulated farmer's family," remarked one writer in 1852. "A few fowls may also be kept in a convenient hen-house, if desired, without offence—all constituting a part of the *household* economy of the place." Somewhere in the ell, nearer the kitchen than the pigsty, stood the creamery or dairy, the room devoted to the making of cheese and butter and the storing of milk.[40] Some ells included a sort of carpentry shop where the farmer repaired his equipment on rainy days, but most contained only those rooms clearly understood as the farmwife's space.

Until well into the second half of the nineteenth century Americans worked diversified farms that produced a variety of crops and livestock for domestic consumption and for cash sale. Kitchen ells were consequently very large because farmwives managed a variety of complicated operations, most of which demanded specialized spaces. The few architects who involved themselves in farmhouse design rarely understood the complexity of the farmwife's tasks, and they designed houses totally unsuited for work. One New York farmer wrote the *Cultivator* in 1846 to complain that "there is something needed to meet the wants of the mechanic and farming community," and that "Mr. Downing's Designs and Plans are too expensive for general use among this class of persons; they will do for what are termed gentlemen farmers, and

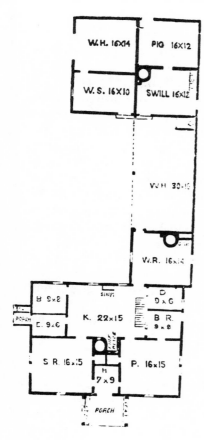

Floor plan for a practical farmhouse. From Allen, *Rural Architecture*.

mechanics who work, if at all, in gloves; but we want something for the industrious working man."[41] The anonymous farmer submitted his own sketches of a simple house with an ell almost as large as the main structure, an ell filled with a wood room, pantry, and other necessary spaces. Expense, it seems from his and the dozens of other letters published in agricultural journals, was not the chief failing of the designs included in Andrew Jackson Downing's *The Architecture of Country Houses,* John Riddell's *Architectural Designs for Model Country Residences,* and Alexander Jackson Davis's *Rural Residences.*[42] The lavishly rendered houses struck readers as expensive to build, but discriminating farmers instantly noted the absence of ells and the diminished size of kitchens. They dismissed the handsome structures as fit only for country gentlemen, not for men struggling to raise a variety of crops and livestock or for women burdened with a score of processing chores.

In 1852 a New York cattle breeder produced a book of plans based on his experience as a farmer. Lewis F. Allen's *Rural Architecture* includes designs for every imaginable farm structure but its thrust is hardly innovative. Instead it concentrates on traditional design, and particularly on well-ordered kitchen ells and farmyards. "On a farm proper," Allen remarks in a passage describing a farmhouse with an immense ell, "the whole establishment is a workshop," and every structure ought to facilitate organized industry, or "business." Allen's standard of farmhouse design is "the ease and facility of doing up house-work," and his standard of farmstead layout is labor-saving proximity and shelter from bad weather. Fire, he admits, is the chief drawback to building great ells rather than free-standing creameries, woodsheds, and family pigsties and hen houses, but he argues that "the additional cost of fire insurance is not a tithe of what the extra expense of time, labor, and exposure is caused to the family by having the out-buildings disconnected, and at a *fire-proof* distance from each other." Efficiency, not aesthetics, is of primary importance in each of his plans. His book is a key to deciphering the design of farmhouses and other farm structures and their relationships to one another because it is not inventive but rather only reflective of the best common design.

Allen explains many farmstead features that nowadays pass unnoticed or unexplained. He notes that beekeeping is traditionally the farmwife's responsibility and that the hives ought to be easily seen from a kitchen window. Clotheslines should be near the kitchen door but clearly visible through a kitchen window. Vegetable and herb gardens too ought to be near the kitchen, so that the farmwife or one of her children can quickly gather fresh vegetables and herbs.[43] The farmhouse environs, not only the house and other structures, ought to be planned for work not for aesthetic satisfaction. *Rural Architecture* is directed at the upwardly mobile farm family anxious to avoid the penalties of incorrect building and only secondarily interested in beauty.

As did most other nineteenth-century farmers, Allen rejected the aesthetic theories and details proposed by Downing and other designers. Agriculturalists cherished a venerable but strictly common aesthetic of ornamental planting and color. No American farmstead was complete without its honeysuckle or woodbine, rosebush or peonies, or—most especially—its lilacs. Many of the flowering plants were brought to the colonies by husbandmen—or their wives—who understood their usefulness in medicinal recipes. Caraway and chicory relieved eye irritation, mint counteracted poisonous bites and sped women in childbirth, concoctions made of peonies guarded against nightmare, thyme cured toothache and lovage settled stomachs, and anise was a useful aphrodisiac. Herbal and other lore involved the mystery of the four humors that informed traditional knowledge of soils, and like the soil knowledge, the beliefs about medicinal plants persist, particularly in the

Appalachian South. By mid-nineteenth century, however, much of the lore survived only in the memories of aged grandmothers who had learned in their girlhoods that medicinal plants were the responsibility of every farmwife. They understood that much ornamental planting was actually forgotten medicinal planting that farm families enjoyed for aesthetic reasons. Not all traditional lore disappeared, of course. Farmwives still planted tansy beside kitchen doors because it kept away ants, but other plants, especially herbs, remained near kitchen ells because they had always been near kitchen ells.

Not all plants were welcome near farmhouses. Farmers chopped down trees because they worried that they would fall and crush the houses beside them. Roofing maintenance also prompted tree felling. Cedar and other wooden shingles rot when shaded from the sun, and most farmers made certain of their roofs' durability by felling all nearby trees. Making farms almost invariably involved felling trees, and European observers remarked time and again that Americans seemed at war with trees. Had the European looked more carefully, they would have observed a curious phenomenon at odds with their assertion. From the seventeenth century on, many American farmhouses were graced by one or more trees as old as the houses they stood near.[44] The trees were markers planted to commemorate an auspicious event like the birth of a child, a marriage, the beginning of a dangerous enterprise, or the building of a house. In the spring of 1725, for example, a young Massachusetts clergyman went off to war as a militia chaplain. His last act before leaving was the planting of an elm in his parents' dooryard. He asked his friends to cherish the tree, for he somehow accepted the age-old belief that henceforth his life was intimately connected with its fortunes. Marker trees acted as barometers; when they withered, relatives knew that the distant adventurer was sick or shipwrecked or that evil was about to envelop the farm or house. No Puritan clergyman admitted to believing in the magic that invested the relationship, but Jonathan Frye at least thought that in caring for the elm his relatives cared for him. Frye died a few weeks after planting the tree, a clear defeat for vestigial Old Religion, but others practiced the custom, which survives to this day in rural places.[45] Marker trees were once quite common, announcing to every passerby that one or more events had occurred on a farm; often they indicated the number of children on a farm. Elms and oaks are often the identical age of the houses they stand before, and they have lived long because the fellers of trees lavished care on them when they stood as frail saplings unlikely to shade roofs.

Most farmers planted fruit trees in small orchards but they sometimes

planted an occasional apple or pear tree very near the kitchen ell. Old
farmsteads are often graced by several such trees planted in no obvious
order and of slightly different age. The fruit trees mark the former
location of the farmstead privy, which farmers moved from time to time
as the disposal hole filled. Most privies were crude structures located on
ground lower than the farmstead well and rarely shaded or ornamented
as the few surviving ones are now. Husbandmen located privies with
care, however, for even in the seventeenth century they understood the
connection between polluted drinking water and disease. And once he
moved the privy to a new location near the old, the wise farmer did not
resist the temptation to plant a fruit tree on the abandoned site. Unlike
urban architects, nineteenth-century farmers saw nothing improper
about prominently placed privies. Water-closets, remarked Allen scorn-
fully, "have no business *in* a *farmer's* house. They are an *effeminancy,*
only, and introduced by *city* life."[46] Allen suggested that they be attached
to the distant end of the kitchen ell if absolutely necessary but he clearly
agreed with most farmers, who dismissed indoor bathrooms as expensive, urban luxuries. After all, privies were cheap and easy to use, and to
farmers suspicious of miasma and disease, they seemed far more sani-
tary too.

Marker trees, doorway lilacs, and the fruit trees and vines that shaded
privies on hot summer days accented farmhouse color. After the early
eighteenth century, agricultural aesthetics involved house painting; as
early as 1710, papers in coastal towns advertised "painter's colors" to
colonists eager to paint their frame houses. Paint helps preserve wood,
of course, and many husbandmen applied it to prevent rotting and
splitting but it appeared earliest as a rich man's luxury. Colors like Indian red, olive green, pumpkin yellow, gray, and blue were applied to
houses owned by merchants able to import paint from Europe.
Gradually prices dropped and husbandmen devised homemade formulas; by 1750 many colonists painted their houses "Spanish brown," a
dull red color made by firing limonite and then grinding the residue into
skim milk. Spanish brown paint served wealthy householders only as a
primer but most Americans splashed it on houses, barns, and smaller
outbuildings.[47] It cost little once one procured the limonite because most
husbandmen sooner or later had extra milk on hand. As colonial commerce increased, merchants acquired a wider range of expensive European colors like vermilion, verdigris, chocolate brown, carmine, and
umber, along with costly "fancy" colors like Dutch pink, ultramarine,
Naples yellow, purple red, and rose-pink. Old World pigments sometimes required mixing with raw or boiled linseed oil or turpentine, and

had Parliament not passed the 1765 Stamp Act even poorer householders might have been able to afford them. The act so enraged the colonists that home manufacture of every taxed article (paint included) became a passion. In Philadelphia, for example, the American Society for the Promotion of Useful Knowledge published information about clays and minerals useful in paint-making, and in Boston one enterprising retailer advertised "very good red, black, and yellow paints, the produce and manufacture of North America."[48] By the onset of Revolution, American house coloring embroiled men in nationalism.

In earlier decades, when paint was still an expensive luxury beyond the means of many householders, only significant public buildings were painted. New Englanders devoted special attention to coloring the meetinghouses that marked the focus of religious and social life, and meetinghouse painting involved all citizens. Husbandmen took care to grow more flax than usual and save the seeds for linseed oil; sometimes the men mixed fish oil into the linseed oil, often in almost equal proportions. Many towns rejected white as a proper color for their most significant structure. In 1762 the Connecticut town of Pomfret voted "that the new meetinghouse should be colored on the outside of an orange color, the doors and bottom boards of a chocolate color, the windows, jets, corner boards and weather boards, colored white." Six neighboring towns so admired the brightly painted building that they too chose to paint their meetinghouses orange; Gilsum, in fact, voted to paint its structure "bright orange." Not every town chose orange, of course. At least thirty-eight chose one or another shade of yellow, eight chose green, eight chose red, and twenty-two selected white. When Dwight rode through New England he remarked on meetinghouse colors, and like another traveler, William Bentley of Massachusetts, he preferred white. Perhaps Dwight and Bentley understood the meaning of blue meetinghouses in the Connecticut Valley, where people called blue "sky-color." Breakaway religious denominations painted their meetinghouses blue and so set them off from the white-painted meetinghouses of conservative congregations; blue objectified the final destination of the worshipers and the decay of the one-hierophany town.[49] Any traveler in New England, even one unfamiliar with the nuances of theological doctrine and practice, could not have missed noticing the brightly painted meetinghouses that stood out against the colors of trees and fields. In 1796 the meetinghouse at Rindge, New Hampshire, was a yellow structure surmounted with a red roof, and as late as the War of 1812 the Cohasset, Massachusetts, meetinghouse was painted a bright pea-green and trimmed in white. New England meetinghouses symbolized the colonization of wilderness; they epitomized man's handiwork in the service of God. It is natural that their makers painted them in brilliant, artificial colors, even in the years after 1800, when white paint became less expensive and more easily obtained. Painting a meetinghouse involved skill, of course, and perhaps a reading of such paint-making manuals as Hezekiah Reynolds's 1812 *Directions for House and Ship Painting* but in the end it consisted chiefly of common evaluation.[50] In 1789 the town of Woodbury, Connecticut, determined that its meetinghouse would be "near the color of Mr. Timothy Tomlinson's house except it be a little more of a greenish as it." Woodbury might just as well have chosen orange or red or white; coloring a meetinghouse, like coloring a house, meant inventing or copying but not following the suggestions of architects enamored of brown.

Town dwellers and agriculturists used American colors long after independence but they imported ever larger quantities of European white lead paint. Until Samuel Wetherill established his white-lead works in Philadelphia in 1809, the most regarded and expensive house color in the Republic was foreign. After the Revolution, Americans produced turpentine and raw linseed oil in far greater quantities and discovered zinc oxides and other new pigments. White-lead epitomized the difficult making of late eighteenth-century paint; the substance could not be easily produced by husbandmen or other amateurs because it required a mixture of linseed oil and turpentine, and the colors with which it was sometimes tinted were mysterious pigments. Despite its expense, Americans quickly adopted it as the most proper house color and accented its brightness by painting window shutters a green made first from verdigris or verditer, and later from gamboge mixed with indigo. Wealthy householders painted their entire houses white, and less well-to-do owners painted at least the fronts of their houses. Poorer families, and those householders convinced that white lead did not preserve wood as thoroughly as older colors, continued to use pumpkin yellow or Spanish brown. Here and there, especially in New England, many husbandmen let cedar shingles and other exterior sheathing "weather" with no paint at all, or else only a coat or two of oil. By 1850 the cheap but high-quality Spanish brown was the most common color of barns, and no neighbor-conscious farmer used it on his house unless he coated his kitchen ell with it. Farmers slighted "fancy" European colors unless they painted a door Prussian blue or a best buggy Naples yellow.[51] White mattered most in the Republic—and green for shutters.

Nineteenth-century American architects argued that white was a glaring, hideous color. Downing and other professionals suggested that farmhouses and other houses be painted brown but farmers scarcely listened to them. White was more than a fashionable color. It was new, completely new, as new as a democratic government free from Parliament, and men and women embarking on the experiment in nationhood embraced it passionately. Along with a new flag, new currency, and new ordering of land, white lead paint announced a new country and a political philosophy grounded in liberalism.[52]

Every day farmers and farmwives worked with "natural" colors; pumpkins are indeed pumpkin yellow. White lead offered a dramatic change from the dull reds and browns and yellows of the colonial era. Against fields brown in spring, green in summer, and yellow in autumn, a white-painted dwelling acquired heightened significance. Only in winter, when snow covered the fields, did the house blend into the surrounding environment. Professional designers like Downing and Davis missed the political and psychological significance of white-painted houses that captured the eye of every passing traveler. In New England Timothy Dwight learned that townspeople painted their meetinghouses before painting their houses. Away from the vestiges of seventeenth-century ecclesiastical, civil, and spatial order, however, houses were as likely to be painted as meetinghouses. In backcountry Pennsylvania, New York, and Kentucky and in the backlands of the Mississippi Valley, men and women struggled to paint their farmhouses white to advertise their accomplishment of farmstead making, to focus the eyes of passersby on the real center of political and economic power. White emphasized the process of making agricultural land from wilderness. It announced the meaning of every farmhouse to the national polity.

Straggling kitchen ells and medicinal gardens objectified the marital spirit remarked in the beginning of *Letters from an American Farmer.* "I never do anything without consulting her," asserted Crèvecoeur of his wife in 1782. American agriculture, from the first years of colonization, prospered as husband-and-wife enterprise. Single men looked for knowledgeable women because they understood how much wives contributed to domestic economy. The kitchen ell that lengthened as farm operations prospered and diversified mirrored the farmwife's growing responsibilities and a growing nuclear family. A dozen children aided any farming couple. They provided cheap, easily instructed labor and inexpensive old-age insurance, but their first years added another burden to the farmwife. A farm focused, therefore, on the farmstead, and particularly on the straggling kitchen ell. To it returned the farmer and his sons, and near it worked the farmwife and her daughters. Lighthouses announced the presence of commanding national government;

farmhouses announced agricultural order.[53] No wonder families painted them white to set off fields and farming from wilderness.

FARMLAND

Long ago the word *land* meant something more distinct than firmament. It meant an open expanse surrounded by forest and covered with grass, what Europeans call a *glade* but what Americans call a *clearing*. The old meaning and the dialect variant *launde* are forgotten now but their spirit lives in the verb *launder*. To wash cloth means to make it free of dirt, to make it pure and useful again; the verb hints at the significance of the contemporary Saskatchewan colloquialism, *making land*. In western Canada land is not natural but artificial. It is that ground stripped of its trees and made ready for planting or grazing, for human advantage. Felling trees and grubbing up stumps epitomized the colonization enterprise of thousands of settlers along the Atlantic coast, just as they do that of pioneering homesteaders in Canada today. Clearing transformed American English as thoroughly as it transformed the seventeenth-century natural environment. Today *clearing* is a noun, a noun denoting a small grass-covered opening in a wooded region and connoting the hand of man. *Glade* is ignored by people whose ancestors laundered the earth, who created grassland in the midst of forest, and who labored to keep it free of brush and trees. Americans imagine glades with difficulty because the labor of clearing is continuous and constantly reinforces the struggle of the past.

As soon as the farmer ceases to plow and mow, wild grasses invade his clearings, scrub trees like juniper and sumac follow, and later white pine and the hardwoods. Robert Frost caught the relentlessness of succession in "Something for Hope":

> At the present rate it must come to pass
> And that right soon, that the meadowsweet
> And steeple bush, not good to eat
> Will have crowded out the edible grass.

> Than all there is to do is wait
> For maple, birch, and spruce to push
> Through meadowsweet and steeple bush
> And crowd them out at a similar rate.[54]

Meadows and pastures and planting fields are continuously cultivated—continuously cleared—because they *must* be, else they are overrun by the wildness gnawing at their edges. Colonists understood the tenuousness of open land because European fields succumbed to ecological succession too. But clearing virgin forest perplexed them.

Glades were scarce in the New World, and explorers and husbandmen sought them eagerly, for they offered relief from the unfamiliar drudgery of making land. While hardwood trees marked the richest soil, even the wisest land-hungry tobacco planter or New England husbandman recognized the worth of a few acres of wild grass. They nourished his horse and his milk cow and were easily turned up for a quickly planted crop or two. Colonization promoters advertised the open "champaign" ground in order to attract settlers, but although they argued as Adriaen Van der Donck in his 1656 *Description of New Netherlands* that there were meadows "so extensive that the eye cannot oversee the same," husbandmen discovered otherwise. In New Spain and New England natural grassland provided the only hay for winter fodder, and conquistadores and Puritans sought it as sites for estensións and towns. Today village names such as La Cienaga, Las Vegas, Fairfield, Bloomfield, Enfield, Brookfield, Plainfield, Marshfield, Northfield, Brimfield, Pittsfield, Springfield, Longmeadow, Topsfield, Hatfield, Deerfield, Lynnfield, Greenfield, Whitefield, and Newfields recall the immediate value of grass-covered land.[55] Spanish and New England law is filled with now-cryptic references concerning the managing of natural grassland for the good of entire communities. Land committees assigned grazing and haying rights eunomically and monitored carefully the size of individual herds because on the pastos comunes and "common hay grounds" depended the present and future well-being of struggling husbandmen. Until the men irrigated semiarid land and cleared the forest, livestock and community prosperity depended on wild grass, and despite the soothing advertisements of real estate promoters, colonists from the Rio Grande to the Piscataqua looked hard to find it.

Ignorance made clearing doubly difficult. Like farmstead siting and design, clearing meant very little to most Europeans. In the Weald of Sussex and Kent in England, in northwestern France, and especially in Scandinavia, husbandmen perfectly understood the felling of trees and the making of wild land suitable for plowing. But elsewhere husbandmen accepted arable fields as "natural," for not even their grandfathers remembered much about the great land-clearing operation that ended in the late sixteenth century. Europe's great age of clearing had almost closed before the colonization of North America. Only a rare Dutchman confronting the forests of the Hudson Valley recalled that "Holland" meant "land of forests."[56] He knew nothing but the fields and plains that replaced the oak forests centuries before his time, and like the Spanish and English settlers, he had scant idea how to make them. Clearing was reinvented in New Netherlands and in other colonies by transplanted Europeans who experimented with one technique after another, who injured themselves and their draft animals, and who made pitifully poor progress for decades. Until well into the nineteenth century, European observers scorned their efforts and misjudged their accomplishments. Indeed understanding the idea of clearing helped make a European an American because understanding came only with doing.

Clearing proceeded in fits and starts. Until the 1680s colonists in New England and New Netherlands felled every tree and grubbed up every stump immediately, making small fields perfectly suited to plowing. "I have also sent Daniel and two men, to set forward (what they can) my business there," wrote Samuel Symonds of his farm in New England in 1645. "They are raw planters as yet, they want experience, but I doubt not but you will be pleased to counsel and order them in their business," he remarked to John Winthrop, Jr. But Symonds himself was raw and ignorant of making land. "While the hard weather lasts," he continued, "I suppose that their work will be to deal in woodwork, as the stubbing of trees, clearing of grounds, and so on, and as soon as any open weather come, not to omit breaking up of grounds for Indian corn this year. It is indifferent to me whether they clear in the mowed plow ground, or in the other, only this I take it to be best, to begin where most ground may easiest and speediest be cleared." Haste in clearing outweighed any attempt to choose the most fertile soil. "I would get as much corn growing this year as I can, and then seed being gotten into the ground, we shall attend breaking up and tilling of ground for next year."[57] How young Winthrop interpreted Symonds's letter from England is unrecorded but surely Daniel and his two fellows understood the hopelessness of immediately clearing much ground. Symonds was one of "the men of great estate" provided for by the author of "Ordering of Towns," but great wealth made little headway against virgin forest. Perfect tillage ground derived from efforts greater than Englishmen like Symonds first imagined.

Everywhere in New England and New Netherlands men disregarded John Smith's pointed advice of 1625. "The best way we found in Virginia to spoil the woods," he counseled "unexperienced planters" in a guidebook written to encourage plantations by providing immediately useful technical information, "was first to cut a notch in the bark a hand broad round about the tree, which pull off and the tree will sprout no more and all the small boughs in a year or two will decay."[58] But "girdl-ing" proved unpopular among men used to open, easily plowed fields, and as late as 1650, when Cornelis Van Tienhoven published his *Infor-mation Relative to Taking Up Land in New Netherland,* immediate clearing remained common. "The trees are usually felled from the stump, cut up and burnt in the field," wrote the secretary of the colony, "unless such as are suitable for building, for palisades, posts, and rails, which must be prepared during winter, so as to be set up in the spring on the new made land which is intended to be sown, in order that the cattle may not injure the crops." Girdling became popular first in the Tidewater, where plan-ters constantly needed virgin soil to support tobacco, and gradually the technique spread through the northern colonies as well. Leafless trees allowed sunlight to reach the soil, which husbandmen spaded up as best they could and planted to Indian corn or tobacco, but they imperiled everyone. "The falling branches incommode us for years, covering our grain every winter and causing a great deal of labor in picking them up," complained one Pennsylvania settler. "The trees fall over fences and demolish them; sometimes they fall on horses and cattle, killing or maim-ing them, and not infrequently men and boys have been killed."[59] Hus-bandmen who decided that the inconvenience and danger of girdling offset its advantages continued to grub up stumps after burning off felled trees, but by the eighteenth century most men had abandoned the practice.

European visitors denounced the acres of girdled trees in terms even more strident than John Clayton and Johann David Schoepf reserved for tobacco-exhausted land in the Tidewater. Travelers watched Ameri-cans burning great heaps of felled trees or harrowing seeds thrown among stumps and scorned the stupidity of American husbandry. "The poor unenlightened inhabitant" first girdles the trees, noted William Strickland, an eighteenth-century English agricultural writer traveling in western New York, "and next attempts to plow, that is to say he tears the ground a little among the stumps and turns over with his plow the loose stones which almost everywhere cover it in this high country." The coun-tryside astonished Strickland. "The scene is truly savage," he continued. "Immense trees stripped of their foliage, and half consumed by fire extend their sprawling limbs, the parts of which untouched by the fire, now bleached by the weather, form a stronger contrast with the charring of the remainder; the ground is strewn with immense stones, many of them of a size far too large to be movable, interspersed with the stumps of the lesser trees which have been cut off about a yard from the ground."[60] He rode through the region in autumn, and perhaps the

lengthening shadows and the brilliant foliage of still-living trees account
for his chiaroscuro rendering of the scene, but a more likely explanation
is his own provincialism. The eighteenth-century English countryside
had few forests and supplied little wood. Husbandmen cared for their
few trees as tenderly as they cherished the small, friable fields they had
inherited or purchased. Waste of timber, or *spoil* in John Smith's terms,
was unthinkable, and sowing grain among stumps was unimaginable.
Clearing and planting like that described by Strickland and other European travelers in America must have seemed indeed follies of darkest
ignorance.

Husbandmen did waste trees, especially after the laws prohibiting the
"waste and stray of trees" out of an Old World regard for standing
timber had been as quickly forgotten as they had been enacted. Men
used timber for building and for fuel but otherwise considered it only an
encumbrance to be removed as expeditiously as possible. After a few
years' farming among stumps, boulders, and girlded trees, husbandmen
forgot the time-honored traditions of land-poor Europe and embraced
extensive agriculture, preferring moderate yields from many acres to
high yields from only a few.[61] Although tree-felling meant backbreaking
work, it proved easier than improving the virgin soil to old-country tilth
standards. European travelers were unnerved by acres of girdled trees
but they loathed the scraggly fields that eventually replaced them, for
the rough-plowed fields mocked the manicured lots of England, France,
and Germany. Their well-publicized accounts still condemn the American confronted by what even Strickland called unmovable boulders.

Had the travelers understood the economics of pioneering, they might
have discerned the spatial realities implicit in pioneer agriculture. A
husbandman needed not one but several fields, and he needed them
immediately. He needed one for corn or wheat, another for meadow,
and a third for pasture. He had no time to create one perfectly tilled
field free of stumps, roots, and rocks; he had little enough time to create
three filled with girdled trees, especially if he had located far from
natural grassland and needed hay for winter fodder. The savage-looking
space disdained by Strickland was actually an intelligent and innovative
response to a hazardous problem of providing food for family and livestock. Girdling was not the only invention. Husbandmen learned that
piling and burning all the felled trees in one spot caused real trouble.
The ashes so enriched the ground that grain grew as it did in the
Tidewater—all stalk and no ear. They learned to fell trees in parallel
lines to facilitate whatever crude plowing they intended, and to burn
felled trees against large stumps, both to spread ashes and to destroy

obstacles. Tall stumps resulted not from carelessness but from design; after a year or two, men chained an upright lever to them, yoked oxen to the upper end of the lever, and wrenched the weakened stumps out of the ground. Some husbandmen built stump pullers, great mallet-like rollers that they chained between stumps and yokes of oxen, and so produced the extraordinary leverage needed to yank a stump from the earth. Even the great rocks that disturbed Strickland sometimes succumbed to husbandmen using dry pegs and water to split and remove them, although such time-consuming operations began only after men had cleared several fields and assured their families of adequate harvests. The stone walls of New England and the Middle Colonies were built by men interested far more in land-clearing than in fencing. They piled the rocks not in heaps but in rows equidistant from the center of their rectangular fields, along each edge; rock clearing explains in part the small size of colonial fields. Men understood the great effort required to clear fields larger than one or two acres, and slowly—especially in New England—they learned how much longer they spent clearing one eight-acre field than eight one-acre ones. The great common fields were defeated perhaps by more than market agriculture and the urge to experiment with new crops and planting methods. The task of clearing them of rocks may have proved far too demanding, even for groups of husbandmen. European travelers disliked the stone walls because they seemed—and often were—poorly planned and poorly layed, liable to topple at the first frost, and certainly wasteful of space. As with so many other features of American farmland, the travelers misread the significance of the walls. American husbandmen looked not at ragged walls, or at stumps or girdled trees. Instead they focused on the emerging rock- and stump-free fields they called "arable."

Pennsylvanians, especially the Swedes and Finns who settled New Sweden along the Delaware River forty years before Penn's colonists arrived, cleared land far more efficiently than the English husbandmen of Virginia and New England. The Scandinavians were experienced in clearing forested land by *svedjebruket,* or burning, a method so wasteful of timber that the Swedish government passed ordinances against it in the seventeenth century and exiled some of the violators, especially Finns, to the New World colony, where they discovered forests perfect for svedjebruket. They felled deciduous trees in summer or autumn when the leaves were full; conifers they felled in winter. The foliage caused the wood to dry quickly, and after a year they chopped the limbs from the trunks and removed the largest for hewing into building timber. During the following summer the Finns spread the limbs and

Hillside after *svedjebruket*. From Retzius, *Finnland*.

remaining trunks evenly over the ground, read incantations to the tree spirits, and fired the wood, singeing the soil. A few weeks later they sowed rye, the favorite old-country crop, and after they harvested it in autumn, they heaped up any remaining logs and set them afire once again. After the second firing, they hoed or plowed up the ground more carefully than before and in the spring planted rye, oats, or wheat, but not maize. For five or six years thereafter Swedes and Finns planted the same grains again and again until the soil showed signs of exhaustion. Then they dragged branches and heavy limbs into the fields, heaped them up, and set them afire; in the spring they planted the newly enriched soil once more. Svedjebruket was an involved process, and one deeply embedded in Scandinavian folk culture.[62] It persisted into the nineteenth century and scandalized travelers used to well-tilled fields. "Between black, charred stumps—the remains of trees burned earlier— and innumerable boulders," commented a Finnish folklorist in 1881, "tower here and there a few stalks of rye, whose appearance surprises anyone not looking for them."[63] Gustaf Retzius tried to explain the usefulness of svedjebruket but his readers misunderstood the technique. Like travelers in America, they saw only the senseless waste of trees.

How decisively Scandinavians influenced later settlers in Pennsylvania is impossible to determine, but many Germans understood somewhat similar methods of clearing forested land. Germans knew at least four

words—*überlandbrennen, sengen, schoden,* and *brandrodung*—that described allied techniques and appearances. Perhaps the Swedes, Finns,
and Germans taught the English and Scotch-Irish how to clear land, for
although the British settlers retained their own lore of good soils, they
adapted quickly to clearing land according to the Scandinavian and
German custom. Not only were they quicker than New Englanders to
learn to girdle trees, they were also far more likely to chop them down
within a few years, heap them up, and burn them. But the "log rolling"
made Pennsylvanian land-clearing techniques distinctive. When the
neighbors invited to a rolling assembled on the appointed morning,
wrote one farmer early in the nineteenth century, "they generally divide
into two companies. A captain is chosen by acclamation for each company, and the captain chooses his men, each naming a man alternately.
When the whole is formed they set to work, provided with hand spikes,
and each company exerts itself to make more log heaps than the other.
Nothing is charged for the work and the only thing exceptional in these
frolics is the immoderate use of whiskey. In general, great hilarity pre-
vails."[64] At sundown, as bonfires lit the sky, the property owner looked
out over a holding almost "free and clear."

Swedes, Finns, and Germans introduced more than svedjebruket to
their English neighbors, but not for half a century did the English em-
brace the building of log houses. In the Tidewater, New England, and
New York settlers built frame houses like they had known in England
and Holland; they sawed trees into boards and timber, raised frames
jointly, and sheathed the frames with "cleftboards," or clapboards. Only
in Pennsylvania did Englishmen learn the wonderfully quick and simple
technique of log-house building, and they took it with them across the
Appalachians into the backcountry. Like frame-raisings and svedjebruket, log-house building was a community occasion. In some regions
neighbors held the prospective builder responsible for felling the necessary trees and cutting them to the proper lengths, for splitting several
immense trees into rough roof-slabs, and for hewing the lesser roof
timbers and chimney framing; in other places, neighbors assisted with
such tasks before or during the "raising." Unlike in communal land-
clearing teams, experienced "corner men" captained the raising teams;
such men best understood the difficult task of notching the ends of the
great logs lifted up to them. Two teams, each captained by two
specialists, raised the log houses, most of which measured about thirty by
twenty feet. Sometimes the men roughly squared the side and end logs
so that they fit more tightly; sometimes they scarcely squared them at all
and instead filled the slots between them with split saplings or mud.

Finnish log cabin. From Retzius, *Finnland*.

Speed, not quality of product, dictated techniques and form. Perhaps the corner men insisted on raising standardized structures, perhaps both teams agreed on a well-known style; in any event, "neighborhoods" quickly evolved a favorite construction method and standard house, and retained them; standardization of corner notchings and log lengths enabled the teams to raise a whole house in one day, albeit one lacking doors, windows, a finished fireplace and chimney, and the "chunking" or "daubing" of wood and clay between the logs.

Log houses displayed pronounced regional characteristics that defeated European efforts at description. Many took the dogtrot form; it was a simple matter to erect two square or rectangular "pens" of logs and join them with a common roof. The open-air corridor provided ventilation, and shelter for farming equipment, drying produce, children—and dogs. In southern hollows and clearings many houses were shaded by long porches supported by projecting gable logs and half a dozen upright posts. Like the arcades suggested by the Spanish town planners, the porches offered relief from the sun and sudden downpours. A log cabin "looks something like a bird-cage," remarked one English writer determined to explain its construction, its community significance, and its durability and to distinguish it from a log house. About the only difference between a log cabin and a log house, according to Thaddeus M. Harris, an American who published his *Journal of a Tour into the Territory*

American log cabin, 1850s ("Winter in the South").

Log cabin newly finished. From Hall, *Forty Etchings*. By permission of the Houghton Library, Harvard University.

Northwest of the Alleghany Mountains in 1805, was the degree of finish. Cabins "are built with unhewn logs, the interstices between which are stopped with rails, calked with moss or straw, and daubed with mud. The roof is covered with a sort of thin staves split out of oak or ash, about four feet long and five inches wide, fastened on by heavy poles being laid upon them." Log houses, however, are far less crude: "If the logs be hewed; if the interstices be stopped with stone, and neatly plastered; and the roof composed of shingles nicely laid on, it is called a log-house. A log-house has glass windows and a chimney; a cabin has commonly no window at all, and only a hole at the top for the smoke to escape." Harris was perhaps overly critical of the hastily erected dwellings that housed almost every pioneer family west of the Appalachians, but he understood that "after saw-mills are erected, and boards can be procured, the settlers provide themselves with more decent houses, with neat floors and ceilings."[65] But Harris completely failed to notice the ease with which owners of log dwellings covered the structures with sawed boards. Thousands of log houses masquerade to this day as frame structures, as houses.

Log construction extended beyond dwellings. All across the backlands, settlers built larger structures such as churches and courthouses of logs, and—sometimes—later covered them with clapboards. The Nodaway County Courthouse in Maryville, Missouri, for example, was built according to the most specific directions in 1846. Despite the bad grammar, the intentions of the county are clear. "Good hewed logs, of durable timber," the document begins. "House thirty-two feet long, and twenty feet wide." Whoever the county chose to build the courthouse was apparently expected to be intimately familiar with log construction, for the document repeatedly refers to "good" material without further describing it. But the county did insist that the walls be not left roughly finished; all were to be "covered with good shingles, good sheeting, etc.," and the whole house was "to be chinked, and well pointed with good lime mortar" and set on "six good strong pillows of stones one foot above the surface of the ground."[66] Certainly the courthouse exemplified a one-of-a-kind building project, most unlike the standardized Chesapeake and Ohio Canal lock-keepers' houses. But it objectified a common building technique, one every Missouri householder soon learned to understand. The staccato bursts of specification prose are the shorthand of clients and builders speaking a common language of standardized terms that instantly evoked clear visual concepts worked out one and a half centuries before in the Middle Colonies.

Innovation combined with old-country tradition to make clearing land in Pennsylvania a remarkably fast and thorough enterprise. Penn's colonists profited enormously from the hard-earned experience of southern planters who perfected girdling, from the New England or "Yankee" emphasis on small, easily tilled fields, and most of all from the Old World svedjebruket and other communal clearing techniques. The husbandmen assembled at a log rolling in Pennsylvania proved to be the most efficient makers of land in America, and perhaps in the world. By the middle of the eighteenth century the Pennsylvania landscape was far better cleared than that of the Tidewater and Piedmont, where girdling remained popular, and of New England, where men preferred to fell all trees almost immediately but leave stumps to rot for years. Despite the many nuances of clearing—for example, Dutch settlers devised special hoes to chop out a weed called red wortel that sent down tough, hardy roots among the stumps—discerning Europeans perceived the characteristics of the three regions.[67] They respected only those of Pennsylvania, and grudgingly so.

In every colony husbandmen made small fields, and each tried to make his fields equal in size so that when the soil in one wore out from repeated plantings of the same crop, he could pasture his cattle on it and plant a roughly equivalent sowing in the field formerly used as pasture. Few men knew of crop rotation, and those who did nevertheless preferred to clear new acreage rather than care for the old. For years, sometimes for decades, they cleared their holdings of virgin forest; depending on forest type and age, a man could clear from one to two or three acres a year, working part-time and using some of the felled timber for fuel. European observers almost invariably ignored the stark newness of everything, the necessity for doing all agricultural operations at once, in haste. No colonial or early national husbandman expected to live long enough to make one perfectly cleared farm. It seemed better to clear several fields slowly and poorly and to continually open new land for crops than to labor ceaselessly on one or two lots until they reached the tilth standards of Europe. All the innovations of old-country agricultural reformers—crop rotation, manuring, draining, and others—went unnoticed in the colonies because men labored at making one small field after another. They had no time for intensive agriculture. They were too busy making land.

American adjusted quickly to the scenery that so unsettled strangers, and they unconsciously acquired a new view of husbandry and cropland. Fields were at first gardens, opened and planted not with plows and harrows but with axes, mattocks, and spades. In New England and the Middle Colonies, where labor was scarce, the garden stage proved briefer than in the South but still it persisted for decades. Not until the 1670s were plows common anywhere away from New Netherlands (where the West India Company dispatched dozens of plowshares and harrows in the hopes of increasing its profits) and they remained oddities in the South into the eighteenth century. Slavery prolonged the garden husbandry of colonization, making it profitable until the Civil War. Tobacco and cotton did not adapt particularly well to plowing anyway but planters learned also the lesson of sabatoge.[68] Slaveowners agreed that blacks destroyed all but the simplest equipment, and blamed the destruction on inate stupidity, not passive resistance. Instead of using plows, they issued clumsy hoes modeled after West Indies prototypes and worked their fields with hordes of enslaved gardeners. Because planters continually opened new land for tobacco and cotton, gardening worked well. Slaves planted the crops among girdled trees and often abandoned the land before the dead trees decayed and fell. But away from the South, other techniques prevailed. Husbandmen gardened only while they readied their fields for plowing, although removing the plow-breaking stumps and stones took years and prolonged the gardening era.

GRASS

Accident, not innovative design, transformed the emerging landscape characterized by fields. Wild grass proved such bad fodder that cattle wintering on it sickened and died. As early as 1619 John Smith warned colonists that "there is grass aplenty, though very long and thick stalked, which being neither mown nor eaten, is very rank, yet all their cattle like and prosper well therewith, but indeed it is weeds, herbs, and grass growing together, which although they be good and sweet in the summer, they will deceive your cattle in winter."[69] Experience proved Smith correct. "Hay we have here of the lowlands, such as it is, which in my opinion is inferior in goodness to our reed and sedge in England, for it is so devoid of nutritive virtue that our beasts grow lousy with feeding upon it and are much out of heart and liking," despaired one New Englander in a 1637 letter to England. "Besides, it breeds among them sundry diseases which we know not how to cure." Once livestock cropped the annual grasses and so deprived them of all chance to reseed themselves, whole pastures turned to wastelands; burning the near-ripe grass in the hope of encouraging a more nutritious second growth proved equally calamitous. Desperate colonists groped for a solution. In the spring of 1647 Roger Williams responded from Rhode Island to an important question asked by John Winthrop of Massachusetts Bay. The governors wondered about the potential for sowing English grasses, and after polling his husbandmen, Williams determined that three bushels of seed sown just after a rain would successfully plant one cleared acre with perennial grass.[70] Haymaking had become an affair of state.

Even as Williams wrote, however, English grasses were already taking root, spreading from the seeds buried in the fodder and bedding shipped across the Atlantic with the colonists' cherished livestock. What the husbandmen called English hay thrived in New England and in the Middle Colonies, and it spread so quickly that settlers pushing west somehow mistook it for native and cheerfully christened it Herd's grass, after its chief popularizer. John Herd found it growing wild in New Hampshire around the year 1700 and immediately recognized its value even though he misunderstood its origin. It was perennial and extremely nutritious as forage and hay. Soon it was cultivated everywhere in New England by husbandmen eager to separate it from the wild grasses that competed with it. Timothy Hansen took its seed south to New York, Maryland, and the Piedmont, where it became so popular, especially among North Carolina cattlemen, that southerners still call it "timothy." No colonists remembered it as the lowly old-country catstail, and at least one Englishman newly settled in Delaware, "an old experienced farmer" according to the agriculturalist's handbook he published in 1793, failed to identify it. Timothy "is supposed to be a native here," noted John Spurrier in the *Practical Farmer*. "I cannot find any author who has given any account of it." English grass did poorly in the hot summers of the Tidewater but it prospered in the Piedmont, where another accidentally imported European species, *Poa pratensis*, naturalized and spread so quickly that westward-moving settlers called it Kentucky bluegrass, red-top, Indian bluegrass, goose-grass, and twenty-three other names, only one of which hinted at a European origin.[71] Tidewater settlers cared less for high-quality hay because they grazed their livestock year round, but accident provided them with marvelous forage grasses too.

Guinea grass and Bermuda grass arrived in Virginia and Maryland as bedding for slaves and quickly spread among indigenous grasses. Like molasses grass, an African variety that proved perfectly suited to West Indies soils and climate, Guinea and Bermuda grass were soon confused with native varieties. "Our grasses are Lucerne, St. Foin, Burnet, Timothy, rye, and orchard grass; red, white, and yellow clover, greens-ward, blue grass, and crab grass," remarked Jefferson in 1785 in his *Notes on the State of Virginia*.[72] Not one grew indigenously.

English grasses, especially north of Maryland where harsh winters killed the African imports, were perhaps the most visible sign of cultivation. Long after the first frost turned the native grasses brown and the leaves of trees red, orange, and yellow, the English grasses remained true to their old climate and stayed green, providing pasturage into December. Autumn signaled the fulfillment of clearing, for everywhere man shaped the land was green and everywhere he left it untouched it was brown. Herd's grass or Timothy announced the coming of civilization, of shaped land.

Imported grasses spelled the doom of the small New England town clustered about a natural meadow. Husbandmen moved away from the nucleated houses to widely scattered pastures and meadows. There they established herds of cattle and horses and experimented in market agriculture. Many forces conspired to shatter the early common-field husbandry of New England towns but the coming of English grass had the most significance.

Making hay remained a traditional craft, even as husbandry grew more innovative. Men argued about technique and, once free of common meadows, tested several curing methods but all agreed that hay could be stacked outdoors in America as it had in Europe. A haystack indicated more than a full loft. Many husbandmen chose to stack hay outdoors because they understood that lightning frequently strikes barns filled with drying hay. Before lightning rods became common, haystacks dotted meadows planted to English grass, and after Benjamin Franklin's invention was accepted by farmers who feared that lightning rods attracted only evil, haystacks objectified the unwillingness of men to risk their entire crop to fire.[73] Despite such inventions as the adjustable haystack cover perfected by Pennsylvania settlers, however, hay stacking was almost obsolete by the 1850s. English grass proved too precious to store outdoors, and the art of stacking vanished.

CROPS

Everywhere in Pennsylvania and in some parts of New Jersey and New York, husbandmen preferred wheat, barley, and rye to Indian corn. Maize was the favored field crop in New England and in the Southern Colonies because it grew well in poorly plowed, half-cleared fields. Soil fertility dictated the regional variation, however. Pennsylvanians found their soil too rich for wheat and sowed maize for a season or two to "season" the ground. "We have had the mark of good ground amongst us, from thirty to sixty fold of English corn [wheat]," reported Penn in 1685. "Upon trial we find that English corn and roots that grow in

England thrive very well here, as wheat, barley, rye, oats, buckwheat, peas, beans."[74] Perhaps the Proprietor embroidered the accounts of settlers in order to attract more colonists, but careful clearing methods combined with good soil and ready markets to make Pennsylvania and parts of New Jersey and New York the granary of the colonies throughout the eighteenth century.

Away from the rich limestone soils of the Middle Colonies, husbandmen determined that maize produced a greater yield than wheat, rye, and other old-country grains that by the late seventeenth century only traditionalists grew. Indian corn thrived among stumps and girdled trees, and its stalks proved useful as winter fodder in a land where good hay was scarce. Husbandmen planted the seeds in clumps or "hills" and after the corn sprouted sowed beans and pumpkins around the seedlings. Colonial cornfields in the Tidewater, Piedmont, and New England were actually large gardens; the cornstalks supported the climbing beans and shaded the pumpkin vines from the midday sun. "All kind of garden fruits grow very well," noted Edward Johnson of New England in 1654, "and let no man make a jest at pumpkins, for with this fruit the Lord was pleased to feed his people to their good content, till corn and cattle were increased."[75] Husbandry in New England and in the South began and remained garden husbandry, not field husbandry. Small fields, poorly cleared and roughly plowed, satisfied the settlers because agricultural technique could be adapted to them. But once the technique was adapted, settlers found it difficult to change, and while New Englanders and southerners hoed among maize and tobacco, Pennsylvanians built larger and better plows and harrows and adapted their fields to horse-drawn equipment.

In the year 1800 three distinctive field types characterized the regional landscapes. Across the South, particularly where slaves raised tobacco and cotton, fields became ever larger but were managed as gardens. Late eighteenth-century travelers in Virginia and North Carolina were as amazed by the lack of plows and other horse-drawn equipment as travelers a century earlier had been. In 1753 one observer rode 140 miles across eastern North Carolina without seeing a plow or even a wagon; two decades later another traveler remarked that twenty slaves did the work that elsewhere a man and boy and two horses accomplished.[76] Here and there, but especially in the backcountry, where men raised corn and wheat rather than tobacco and cotton, sharp-eyed travelers discovered a few plows and harrows although everywhere else the principal tool remained the hoe introduced from the West Indies. In New England, as in the South, men managed fields as gardens but the fields were smaller, sometimes only an acre or two in area. While they were cultivated in spring and autumn with plows and harrows, husbandmen tilled them in summer with hand-tools because horse-drawn equipment tore up the mixed growth of maize, beans, and pumpkins. Local belief (a result perhaps of small fields) helped convince farmers that fields ought to be kept small. "Cattle when turned into a pasture are uneasy—they will roam over the whole pasture, cropping here a little and there a little—treading and wasting as much as they can eat," cautioned a New Hampshireman in the *Farmer's Monthly Visitor* in 1852. "In a small lot they get over their roaming sooner, and go to eating in earnest."[77] Careful New Englanders who rotated crops followed such instructions not only out of like experience but because the guidelines slowly and anonymously developed in every town reinforced the farmers' strong desire to believe that small fields produced best. To believe otherwise meant beginning the backbreaking chore of removing stone walls and combining fields. Middle Colony farmers scoffed at the New Englanders' ideas when they heard of them, and contentedly worked far larger fields—from five to forty acres—with horse-drawn equipment. Their technique was unsuited to slavery or to rock-filled, hilly fields, and it moved westward, across Ohio and Indiana and Illinois, where no slaves impeded free labor and few rocks broke plowshares. Out of Pennsylvania came the midwesterners' love for large fields, perfectly trained teams, and heavy plows.

As the rich Pennsylvania soil began to wear out—and husbandmen near Philadelphia complained as early as 1730 that wheat yields had dropped from twenty or thirty bushes an acre to ten—men began casting about for remedies. Most simply rested their fields, abandoning them to all crops except English grass and pasturing livestock on them, to slightly enrich the soil with manure. Meanwhile they cleared nearby woodland, secure in the knowledge expressed by Thomas Jefferson. "We can buy an acre of new land cheaper than we can manure an old one," he remarked of Virginia soil. But by 1749, as the fallowing period increased from seven to fifteen years, a few Pennsylvanians abandoned Jefferson's thinking. The American Philosophical Society and the Philadelphia Society for Promoting Agriculture encouraged crop systems in which red clover and English grass alternated with corn and small grains such as wheat; by 1790 the technique was spreading across the state along with the use of gypsum and lime as fertilizer.[78] Farmers found the mineral fertilizers easier to transport than manure and discovered that they encouraged the growth of English grass, which in turn stimulated increases in livestock herds and in turn provided more manure. Some farmers were so troubled by immense heaps of manure that they invited their neighbors to whiskey-fueled "dung frolics," during which competing teams spread the manure across the fields. Almost everywhere in Pennsylvania, and in the newly settled western territories, folk traditions vanished in the face of successful experimentation. Southerners and New Englanders clung to methods invented in the early years of colonization. Pennsylvanians invested in experiment.

Between 1790 and 1830 Pennsylvanians produced one improved plow after another. Blacksmiths experimented with minor variations—a wrought-iron mouldboard, a cast-iron plowshare, a sharper coulter—that reduced the size of plow teams, turned the soil more deeply, and let men till more acres each day. Profit-seeking farmers and blacksmiths invented other devices as well, like drills that planted seeds in precisely separated rows and reapers pulled by horses. Cyrus McCormick invented his reaper in Virginia, but it was Pennsylvanians who slowly but surely popularized it. In 1830 local blacksmiths invented and manufactured improved plows and other tools; twenty years later factory owners had taken over.

Mass-produced farm machinery dramatically reshaped the size and topography of fields wherever farmers could afford to purchase the latest inventions. Unlike limestone or red clover seed, machinery was designed for typical fields, and progressive farmers quickly discovered that such fields were those of Pennsylvania and the new western states: large, flat, and rock-free. Hilly fields, rocky fields, any fields that could not be adapted to the delicate hay rakes and reapers and seed drills were worked in the traditional way until their owners learned the impossibility of profit. To farm competitively meant to farm with machinery, and by the 1840s New Englanders realized that machinery was not for them. Everywhere the hill farmers abandoned their land, selling their hard-won holdings for pittances and moving westward to lands advertised as "ripe for the plow." The wilderness returned.

"Save a potato field here and there, at long intervals, the whole country is either in wood or pasture," commented Herman Melville of northern New England in 1855. "As for farming as a regular vocation, there is not much of it here. At any rate, no man by that means accumulates a fortune from this thin and rocky soil, all whose arable parts have long since been nearly exhausted." Melville, like other observers, was disheartened by what he saw. "Some of those mountain townships present an aspect of singular abandonment. Though they have never known aught but peace and health, they, in one lesser aspect at least, look like countries depopulated by plague and war. Every mile or two a house is passed untenanted." What Melville found most striking was not the abandoned houses or the sod-covered roads but the countryside "intersected in all directions with walls of uncommon neatness and strength."[79] The walls had once enclosed fields. In 1855 they enclosed only trees, somehow mocking the function of fences.

FENCES

From the moment of colonization, fencing taxed the ingenuity of husbandmen. In New Spain men built walls of rock and adobe and charged the estensión herdsman to watch the livestock carefully, lest they forage among the crops. Elsewhere the colonists built wooden fences because wood was plentiful; at Jamestown the adventurers even fenced off the tip of the peninsula. The earliest fences were European in design, however, and from a tradition founded in conserving wood. Wattle fences were common in the first years of the Plymouth settlement because colonists wove them easily from split saplings. But in a very few years, perhaps within a decade, such fences gave way to experimental models. As happened frequently, a curious mix of material and economic practice united to produce regional variations.[80] By 1700 southerners cherished a fence type much different from that accepted by New Englanders.

Southerners fenced livestock out of arable fields. As long as the stock survived by feeding on acorns and other forest fodder, men refused to confine it. Instead, each husbandman erected a stout fence "hog tight and head high" around his few acres of Indian corn or tobacco. Soil exhaustion and the constant need to remove to virgin land prompted most men to erect the Virginia or worm fence, a zigzag line of split rails laid one on top of another. The worm fence was indeed easy to build and it served to protect crops from all but the most determined hogs. Its chief advantage lay in its construction. It required no postholes because it had no posts. "At first sight the worm fence appears very inefficient," remarked William Oliver in 1843, "but on closer inspection and more intimate acquaintance with its qualities it improves in one's estimation, and it would certainly be difficult for the pioneer settler to substitute anything so efficient and at the same time so easily to be got." Oliver explained to his English readers that a settler selected a large tree, felled it and logged it into ten-foot lengths, and split each section into thirty or forty rails. "In the bottoms where the timber is good," he noted, "many trees will make four or five cuts without a limb; affording from 150 to 200 heavy rails. It is reckoned a good day's work for a man to cut down,

Worm fence, South Carolina. (JRS)

log off, and split up such a tree into rails."[81] A typical worker built 200 yards of worm fence each day, according to Oliver's observations, and firmly believed that his fence would endure for twenty to thirty years. Most worm fences were simple stacks of eight or nine rails, and stood four-and-one-half or five feet high, but some carried additional "stakes and riders," eight-foot-long stakes wedged into the ground and locked over the topmost horizontal rail, and stood as high as six feet. The farmer who added stakes and riders added legal protection as well; the owner of any animal that broke down such a well-built defense paid all damages.[82]

Worm fences shared one real disadvantage that in the early years of colonization perturbed very few husbandmen. In order for the rails to balance, each section of fence joined the next at a 120 degree angle. The actual path of the fence, therefore, stretched almost ten feet wide, and the swath of ground occupied by the rails proved almost impossible to cultivate, even with a hoe. The one-and-two-tenths acres of land occupied by every mile of worm fence produced an abundance of weeds that harbored animal pests such as raccoons and woodchucks and continuously invaded the cultivated soil. Despite the scornful remarks of most Old World travelers—one Englishman dismissed the householders of Virginia and Maryland by noting that "their fences are extremely incomplete and kept in very bad order"—southerners persisted in building worm fences, as did pioneer husbandmen in western Pennsylvania and New York. Once overgrown with Virginia creeper and other weeds, the rough fences hid from even close examination, and all but the most discerning European travelers ignored them.

Worm fences were truly innovative. As decades passed and farmers away from the South experimented with intricate horse-drawn machinery, the fences proved to have a hidden quality. Men moved them easily. One or two men dismantled them quickly, loaded the rails onto a wagon, and rebuilt the fence a few hundred yards away or burned the timber as fireplace wood. New Englanders were far less fortunate.

Stone walls enclosed livestock everywhere in New England and in many parts of New York, Pennsylvania, and New Jersey. Circumstances almost forced colonists to build them; the ground lay strewn with small boulders New Englanders soon called "fieldstones." Plowing and harrowing proved impossible until the fieldstones were removed, and husbandmen fenced in their livestock with walls. Most walls stood four or four-and-one-half feet tall, and many were topped with one or two split rails. Wall building consumed vast quantities of time and human energy. An experienced man set between twenty-four and sixty-four feet of wall a day but only if the fieldstones were already heaped along the line the wall was to follow. Moving the stones to the site was far more arduous than lifting them into position; husbandmen experimented with carts, but most chose low sledges called "stoneboats," which were hard to drag uphill but were less likely to collapse under immense weight. Confirmed wall builders tried to convince southerners who prized slaves rather than carts and sledges that stone walls outlasted rail fences and consumed less space, but most southern and western husbandmen chose to replace their rail fences every fifteen to thirty years rather than build in stone. "About one hundred and eighty common-sized stones will build a rod of fence," counseled one farmer in an 1858 *Southern Planter* article reprinted approvingly in the *New England Farmer* a few months later. "Work nine hours in the day, and handle one stone the minute, and you will have made three rods of fence; and surely a man can do this."[83] Of course the correspondent neglected the time devoted to gathering the stones and transporting them to the site, and the time spent away from other vital chores. It was a rare southerner who took such New England-like advice, whether about wall building or the abolition of slavery.

Everywhere in the colonies husbandmen experimented with other fences. Perhaps the most common of the less popular types was the post-and-rail favored south of New England. It took many different forms. Post-and-rail fencing required more hours to erect than worm fencing but far less time than stone walls, and it wasted the least space of any variety. It was not simply moved but husbandmen learning to jerk stumps from the ground had little difficulty "yanking posts." Its chief drawback was rot. The posts set into the ground decayed very quickly. Even chestnut and cypress wood rotted within twenty years, and men using pine and other softwoods discovered that fences collapsed, especially in damp meadows, within five or ten years. By mid-nineteenth century a complex folklore guided the selection and preparation of fence posts. Some farmers cut trees for post wood only in winter; others cut post wood in summer during a full moon. Some farmers charred the posts before setting them, and others buried theirs reversed; that end of the post that faced skyward when a living bough they planted into the earth. Here and there a farmer departed from tradition (one Pennsylvanian dismayed at posts rotting in a wet meadow laboriously carved posts from slate and set them carefully into the mud) but most chose to follow the advice of neighbors and fathers, chopping trees at the proper time, setting the posts correctly, and frequently planting fruit trees alongside the fence for reinforcement and to save valuable field space.[84] Where wood grew plentifully, however, the worm fence predominated. Scarcely a traveler reported otherwise.

More than barns or arable fields or livestock, fences told the worth of their owners. "There is no feature in an agricultural district that is such a sure indication of finished husbandry as good fences of durable material," remarked the Boston *Cultivator* in 1851. "Among the permanent improvements on the farm, good fences are certainly first in necessity and importance. And while they are thus essential where a mixed husbandry is carried on, they are also unmistakably indicative of thrift and good order. Poor fences ever tell a sad story, and when we see a farm with fences all going to decay the conviction is irresistible that some shocking legend is connected with its history." Three years later a writer in *Soil of the South* confirmed the sentiment by noting that "nothing fixes our estimate of a planter sooner than the character of his enclosures."[85] What accounts for the emphasis on good fences? From Florida to Maine and across the developing western territories, men understood that fences maintained public order. Good citizens in the North and West confined their livestock; good citizens in the South protected their crops with a good defense—the worm fence. Not every fence separated one man's land from another's; many, of course, subdivided single holdings. But most fences did contribute to maintaining community order, and every community loathed the individual whose shoddy fences portended catastrophes caused by wandering livestock. Only New Englanders appointed fence viewers to regularly inspect all fencing but farmers everywhere away from the South informally scrutinized their neighbors' fences.

Colonial husbandmen and nineteenth-century farmers devoted many days' labor to building and repairing fences. They learned simple but subtle rules of geometry and much about the character of trees. A square 10-acre field requires 160 rods of fence to completely enclose it; a rectangular field of the same acreage requires 170 rods. Farmers puzzled over the 10-rod difference, and the more enlightened discovered that a triangular 10-acre field requires 182 rods of fence. A circular 10-acre field, however, requires only 141 rods of perimeter fencing. Square fields, therefore, became the simply surveyed national compromise, but still in the hilly country of New England, the Middle States, and the Piedmont, men layed out irregularly shaped fields—many almost triangular—and carefully fenced them despite the added effort and cost. Easily fenced land attracted many optimistic farmers to the western territories. Square fields were simply planned and quickly fenced, at least in the beginning, when standing trees provided ready lumber. Most 160-acre farms ("quarter-sections") were divided into 20- or 40-acre fields, many of which were square. But many more fields were rectangular; long, narrow fields were more easily plowed because the team and plow had to be turned less often. Men chose the best wood for rails and fenced the newly cleared land, unmindful of their descendants' trouble.

In 1860 a writer in the *Southern Cultivator* noted that locust rails last about fifty years but that second-growth pine rots within three or four. He pondered the growing difficulty of southern planters. Twenty acres of twenty-year-old locust trees, he claimed, produced enough rails to adequately fence about 200 acres. Woodlots filled with locust trees were rare by 1860, however, and in the South and in the Middle States farmers discovered that good fencing wood—indeed in some places any wood—could not be purchased.[86] Fencing and firewood needs had so depleted farm woodlots that timber shortages plagued farmers by the hundreds. Only in New England, where stone walls divided land, did men have wood for their urgent needs. But there farmers were moving west, abandoning their fields and woodlots alike.

COWPENS

New Englanders, southerners, and people from the Middle Colonies had begun settling west of the Appalachians in the middle of the eighteenth century, lured by the rich limestone-based soil of the Ohio

Valley. Until the first decade of the nineteenth century, settlers chose to locate on well-forested soil, away from the grass-covered openings they called "barrens." The trees indicated soil fertility, of course, and they provided much needed wood for house- and fence-building and for fuel; the vast grassy expanses called "prairies" by the few colonists who had learned something of French terminology at first offered little. Eastern traditions blended and contested in the Ohio Valley as agriculturists from different colonies chose and shaped the land hastily if clearly ordered by the federal surveyors.[87] Southerners, perhaps because they had less money to buy land from the speculators buying townships from the government, frequently settled on hillsides; Yankees, those people from Pennsylvania northward, sited their farms in the valleys, on "bottom land." Each immigrant group brought its own attitudes toward land use along with specific crops; southerners arrived with notions of flimsy dwellings and rough white "gourdseed" corn while Yankees arrived with ideas of building great barns to store their yellow "flint" corn. Everyone looked at glades of naturalized English grass, but until all the settlers determined to call it "bluegrass," southerners called it "Herd's grass" and Yankees called it "timothy," a perfect reversal of coastal custom. Everyone cleared the land, but in traditional ways, the southerners girdling trees and planting corn among them, the Yankees felling and burning them first. Soon easterners evaluated the developing landscape of the eastern Ohio Valley in terms Europeans once used to describe the newly made colonial fields of Virginia. "The manner of clearing land in this state is very slovenly," complained a New Yorker traveling in Ohio in 1816, "and from the great quantities of dead timber left standing through the fields, the farmer with his family and cattle, is not only in jeopardy, but the traveler, who approaches their borders, is necessarily compelled to partake." David Thomas took a charitable view, however, and concluded that "in a few years, the cause of these complaints will be removed." In the Ohio Valley every Yankee came to terms with southern agricultural practice because most Yankees adopted southern attitudes toward cattle raising. Southerners and Yankees alike built cowpens and raised cattle for eastern markets.[88]

Spanish settlers introduced cattle raising to New Spain in 1521, when they off-loaded a small herd in Mexico. In 1565 they landed a breeding herd in Florida and, by the late sixteenth century, had driven herds north across the Rio Grande to Santa Fe. Ninety years after the first herd arrived in western Florida, a second stocking herd was put ashore near present-day Tallahassee to take advantage of the natural grassland and to feed the garrison; within a few years settlers had arrived to raise cattle for profit. The spread of Spanish cattle paralleled the extension of Spanish settlement; viceroys and estensiónes elders knew the immense advantage of cattle as food and the ease with which Spanish cattle adapted to New World conditions. The *criollo*, the "cow of the country," was small, lean, and tough, capable of grazing on poor natural grass, of wintering outdoors on fallen leaves, and of taking on the less ferocious wild beasts that roamed the woods and glades. By 1701 the French settlers at the mouth of the Mississippi River had procured Spanish cattle from Santo Domingo; two years later they acquired another allotment from Cuba despite the best efforts of the Spanish viceroyalty, which feared the economic power of Frenchmen with large herds. The French bred their first cattle with enthusiasm and sent the offspring upriver; in 1800 settlers moving west from the southern states encountered the criollo for the first time and bred it with their stock of west European cattle.[89] One result was the mean-tempered, wide-foraging longhorn steer that provided the economic base for the post-Civil War settlement of the short-grass western plains. Another was the perfecting of Ohio Valley cattle raising by 1830.

Along with regional ideas about land clearing and land use, and along with local varieties of seed corn and building techniques, the settlers moving into the Ohio Valley late in the eighteenth century brought regional breeds of cattle. New Englanders arrived with Devons, large, yellowish cattle of Danish origin, and smaller red-and-white Dutch cattle. Settlers from New York brought other strains of Dutch cattle, particularly Hollands descended from cattle imported from Flanders, and West Indian cattle, an almost pure breed of criollo. Southerners, especially the Carolinians, arrived with Spanish cattle too, and with English breeds. Every group brought crossbreeds of every description, animals whose ancestry could only be guessed at by cattle buyers. The eastern cattle mingled almost at once with the Spanish cattle owned by French and Spanish settlers and with the few small herds of French cattle raised at several French agricultural outposts.[90] Yankees brought most of their cattle for dairy purposes but they quickly learned from their southern neighbors that cattle raising offered opportunities for profit-making, not just one means of subsistence farming.

All settlers of the Ohio Valley confronted a common problem of finding markets for their produce. Corn, for example, grew so well on the rich bottomland soil that settlers warned newcomers not to plant it near their houses; it grew so tall that it shaded roofs. But the corn could not be carted to market, at least profitably; the few roads were extremely poor, the rivers (including the Ohio) lacked bridges, and the Appalachians blocked the way to the East. Converting corn into whiskey seemed like an acceptable alternative, but the market for whiskey was quickly glutted and sending barrels of whiskey south to New Orleans and then shipping them around Florida to the coastal markets proved complicated and expensive. But the southerners in the valley convinced the other settlers that cattle raising might be profitable; after all, they argued, a fattened steer could walk to market even if the market was at Baltimore, Philadelphia, or New York.

Ohio Valley cattle raising—and swine raising too—depended on a number of environmental circumstances and on the livestock itself. Grassland was needed for summer pasture, and the valley had plenty of it in the barrens by-passed by its earliest settlers in favor of tree-covered land. Livestock raisers acquired the barrens at bargain prices and learned that they supported excellent English grass. The barrens of Ohio's Marion County, according to one report, comprised "a continuation of the most nutritious grasses from early spring until the setting in of hard winter," among them being "Blue grass, June grass, Timothy, Red and White Clover, Red top, etc., etc.," a combination that would have pleased Roger Williams and John Winthrop immensely.[91] Topsoil proved so rich that corn crops developed far beyond the settlers' dreams; the pastured cattle were assembled in the autumn and fed throughout the winter on corn and corn shocks, the former to add fat, the latter to aid in digestion. Finally, and perhaps most importantly, the valley climate was mild enough to obviate the need for barnbuilding. New Englanders puzzled about the southern habit of wintering livestock outdoors but they soon saw the sense in doing so. Large herds of cattle wintered in the cowpens, where combined body heat and the temperature raised by judiciously placed windbreaks allowed most of the animals to survive and even to add weight. Not all breeds of cattle prospered under such conditions but the breeds strengthened by criollo blood did. Spanish cattle added the necessary stamina to the breeds developed in New Hampshire and New Jersey.

Cattle drives began in late winter, usually in mid-February, and the droving season lasted until mid-August. Once George Renick proved in 1805 that a herd could be profitably driven from southern Ohio to Baltimore, farmers everywhere in Ohio, and later in Indiana and Illinois, either drove their cattle east themselves or hired a new professional, the drover, to take them. By the 1820s, six great cattle-driving roads ran eastward from Ohio and great herds of livestock passed the wagons rolling west with settlers. The roads, especially the Cumberland Pike, which later became the National Road, proved the worth of Gallatin's internal improvements schemes. A good road allowed livestock to travel several miles each day; herds of horses moved about twenty-two miles in a day, cattle about nine unless they were especially well fattened, in which case they moved about seven, and herds of cattle mixed with hogs about five miles. Most herds numbered between 100 and 120 head, although herds of 200 or even 1,000 head were not infrequent.[92] Droving depended, however, on reasonably well-maintained roads and particularly on bridges. The National Road became the most popular cattle-driving road chiefly because it had the most bridges; drovers understood the technique of ferrying a few steers across a river on a boat and so enticing the others to follow, but every fording took time, and time cost money. On good roads cattle and other livestock lost far less weight than on bad roads, and drovers used up far less nervous energy.

In the first decades of the nineteenth century Ohio and Indiana, and later Illinois, presented a puzzling aspect to visitors. Even in north Ohio and Illinois, barns were few until the years of pioneering passed and farmers had established their cattle herds. Arable fields, especially of corn, were fenced in, according to southern practice, and pastures were unfenced; livestock wandered everywhere. Fencing seemed crude—and southern—by Yankee standards; most of it was worm or post-and-rail fencing, like that later popularized by Abraham Lincoln, a northern candidate for president whose campaign nickname, "the rail-splitter," derived from building southern-style fences on the Illinois frontier. The valley really exhibited no specific regional characteristic; it was neither southern nor Yankee. It was surely not agricultural in the sense known to easterners who raised only a few head of cattle each year, and it was very strangely fenced, at least according to the standards of Pennsylvanians. But it prospered, chiefly because of cattle raising.

An Illinois farmer summed up the prosperity in 1837. "These bottoms, especially the American, are the best regions in the United States for raising stock, particularly horses, cattle, and swine," wrote J. M. Peck in *A New Guide for Emigrants to the West* of the bottomland that had once marked the limit of United States sovereignty and so earned the name *American*. "Seventy-five bushels of corn to the acre is an ordinary crop. The roots and worms of the soil, the acorns and other fruits from the trees, and the fish of the lakes, accelerate the growth of swine. Horses and cattle find exhaustless supplies of grass in the prairies."[93] New Englanders plowing rocky, eroded soil, southerners looking askance at tobacco-worn land, and newly arrived European immigrants read such words with hope and determined to move west, to land short of building timber but immensely fertile.

Until the 1830s the rush of immigrants into the Ohio Valley and into the Illinois Country boosted livestock prices and confirmed cattle raisers in their technique. Newcomers bought a few cattle or hogs to start their own herds and accepted existing standards of land use. Gradually, however, Ohio agriculture changed. As men cleared more land and finally ascertained the fertility of the barrens, they began buying young steers from Indiana and fattening them in pens; no longer did they graze their own livestock. Eventually the technique spread to Indiana, where farmers began buying young livestock from Illinois men who grazed them in their first year or two on the prairies. Although the transition from cattle raising to cattle fattening took four decades in Ohio, not everyone adjusted to it. Some farmers continued to graze cattle and chose to ignore the possibilities for fattening; whatever the facts, the farmers involved in fattening suspected that the men choosing to practice older techniques were southern. By 1840 the landscape reflected the diverging techniques; some farms were almost wholly planted to corn, had barns to shelter the draft horses needed for plowing and the dairy cattle neccessary for the cheese and butter so dear to Yankees, and large pens for fattening, but others were chiefly in pasture, without barns, and— lamented more and more farmers of northern extraction—without fences. Wandering cattle devoured any cornfield they entered, and such incidents provoked suspicion and bitterness. The opening of the Erie Canal began to alter agricultural practices in northern Ohio, and once it connected with other canals in that state and in Indiana, many farmers began to abandon cattle fattening for other forms of farming, particularly the growing of grain for export. Canals made easier the in-migration of more Yankees, people unaccustomed to any southern agricultural techniques at all and unwilling to accommodate insanities like fencing in crops rather than fencing in livestock.[94] In the Ohio Valley began the vague suspicions and prejudices that helped fuel the hatreds of the 1850s, when Yankees clashed verbally with the southerners about superior cultures. And in the Ohio Valley, for the first time on the continent, traditional agriculture clashed with a mutant offspring not yet called "ranching."

Hostility between farmer and rancher developed out of different land-use concepts. As the old meaning of *hacienda* indicates, a rancher's first allegiance is to his movable capital, his herd, and particularly to his pure-bred breeding stock; closely allied, but secondary, is his allegiance to his land, much of which he may rent or use without public authority. A farmer honors the old tradition of husbandry not out of nostalgia but out of necessity; his land is all he has, his present and future prosperity.

The differences about fencing that appeared in the Ohio Valley led to the battles between "sodbusters" and "cowboys" in the late nineteenth century, as farmers strung barbed wire over the open range.

WOODLOTS

Fence rails, firewood, and building timber originated in farm woodlots until late in the nineteenth century. Except in northern New Spain, where scarcities of useful timber prompted estensiónes elders to carefully administer *montes,* early colonists felled or girdled trees with no thought for succeeding generations of husbandmen, who might find the land as deforested as parts of England, the Netherlands, and the German principalities. New England communities awoke to timber shortages only in the late seventeenth century, and by the middle of the next century full-time loggers in Maine and New Hampshire regularly shipped firewood and building timber south to Boston and other seacoast towns learning the value of driftwood. Much of the enticing activity of coastal seaports derived from sloops and schooners off-loading firewood. Split logs were less intriguing than chests of spices and tea but coastal dwellers needed the former more and envied their shippers. A prosperous woodlot meant warmth and shelter.

Eighteenth-century Atlantic Coast husbandmen remembered little about forest management; neither they nor their fathers recalled the regulations and tricks used in Europe. Not until the late nineteenth century did farmers begin to agree on proper techniques. In the 1850s woodlot management combined error, tradition, common sense, and guesswork. Farmers agreed on the importance of woodlots but they agreed on little else. European travelers had once scorned the ragged appearance of just-cleared fields; by the nineteenth century they scorned the ravaged woodlots that marked almost every American farm.

Woodlots varied in size from region to region and from farm to farm. Men who purchased or inherited holdings with several dozen rocky acres were likelier to own larger woodlots than men with easily plowed acreage.[95] Fifteen acres was the approximate average area devoted to woodlots in the 1850s, an area slightly smaller than in previous decades because more farmers owned woodburning stoves. Stoves, as one editor of the *Farmer's Monthly Visitor* stressed in February 1852 (a good month to discuss fires and woodlots), consume much less wood than fireplaces, although how much he did not estimate. With proper care, the editor continued, "fifteen acres of wood and timber land will furnish a farmer his ordinary timber and wood for two fires. Ten cords of wood will

suffice for any man to keep two fires the year round, provided he has
tight rooms and good stoves." Proper woodlot care rather than draft-
free rooms and efficient stoves, however, comprised the center of the
editor's argument. "The farmer should commence on one side of his lot,
and cut the wood clean as he goes. In this manner the young shoots come
up alike, and they grow alike as they receive the sun alike," he emphasized in his defense of the "clear-cutting" method. "Now say there
are thirty cords of wood to an acre, if he cuts ten cords of wood a year, it
will take him three years to cut off the wood of a single acre—and it will
take him forty-five years to cut the wood off from his lot of fifteen acres.
At the end of forty-five years," he concluded triumphantly, "he may go
back to the first acre he cut, and cut thirty cords to an acre."[96] The editor
stressed that his figures derived from personal experience in tending a
woodlot filled with white, red, and yellow oak, chestnut, and maple trees,
and he, like other nineteenth-century writers, predicted that many of his
readers would obtain even better results.

Some did, but many did not. Clear-cutting suffered from several problems, not the least of which was fire. Slash left among the stumps caught
fire easily and burned the sprouts poking through it. Cattle and other
livestock browsed on the seedlings unless the harried farmer fenced off
the cleared area. American farmers preferred the technique to the selec-
tive cutting method urged on them by British observers because felling
the diseased and storm-damaged trees not only required much
additional labor but caused severe damage to nearby healthy trees. What
provoked them, and sometimes almost defeated them, was procuring
not firewood but fencing and building timber. Woodlots simply produced the wrong varieties of trees for the job at hand, or else not enough
of the species required. What did defeat farmers was the simultaneous
rotting away of hundreds of rods of fencing, all dating from the land's
clearing fifty or sixty years before. Sometimes whole woodlots could not
produce enough rails to correctly rebuild a farm's fences, and men
mortgaged their property to raise money for fence rails purchased from
more fortunate neighbors. Here and there men with rocky farms cropped their best trees and made a temporary profit, but away from the
frontier regions nineteenth-century farmers despaired of a solution to
the fencing problem. Pennsylvania and Ohio agricultural improvement
societies suggested that American farmers plant hedgerows, and in the
1830s and 40s many farmers did, planting osage-orange trees—a product of the Lewis and Clark Expedition—and hoping for the best.[97] Others piled uprooted stumps and heavy branches along worn fences and
used precious rails to repair only the worst gaps. By 1860, however, farm

woodlots were pitifully small, filled chiefly with saplings and brush too small for building timber and almost useless as firewood. New Englanders suffered almost as badly as farmers in the Middle States, and although pioneer farmers in Michigan and other western states still found adequate timber supplies in uncleared land, reformers knew that the crisis had just begun. Westward-moving farmers discovered that prairie land lacked trees and that wood had to be imported by wagon or railroad from the east or north. Arguments over slavery and secession masked the difficulties posed by deforested woodlots and treeless prairies, but almost everywhere farmers complained. Open and ordered as never before, the American landscape nevertheless objectified the new national awareness of diminishing natural resources. More and more farmers began felling diseased and storm-damaged orchard trees instead of pruning and otherwise treating them. Apple wood burned hot and long and stretched the capacity of devastated woodlots.

Fruit trees arrived in New England and in the Middle Colonies with the first colonists. Not all species did as well in the New World as in old-country orchards but many did better, spurred to greater yields by harder frosts and cooler, less humid summers. Whereas the techniques of woodlot management vanished in the race to learn the tricks of clearing, the niceties of grafting and other orchard skills improved in each decade. Farmwives served apples raw and used other varieties in baking and in cider making. Each farmer examined his apple trees with care, trying to discern which produced apples that were best for each of these purposes. Other fruits grew less well north of the zone marked by Pennsylvania and New York; pears, plums, and peaches required warmer winters than many varieties of apples but farmers grafted and grafted in the hope of producing a tree or two adapted to their peculiar soil and microclimate. Some farmers planted orchards on south-sloping hills, but others preferred shaded northern exposures in order that the trees would not bud before the last frost.[98] Eighteenth- and nineteenth-century orchard trees grew far larger than contemporary specimens and occupied greater acreage. Advice varied from farmer to farmer and from one agricultural periodical to another, but generally husbandmen planted the trees three or four rods apart so the roots of one rarely crossed those of another. Orchards consequently consumed much space, often occupying ten or fifteen acres of sandy or gravelly soil not particularly suited to field crops. After the trees matured, most farmers pastured cattle among them; the trees provided shade for the livestock, and the grass planted around them offered forage. Cattle browsed on the lowest branches of the trees and produced what farmers still call the "browse-line," the six-foot-high space empty of all limbs. Horticulturists and park superintendents unthinkingly adopted the browse-line standard for trees grown away from livestock—as in public parks—and carefully pruned trees, as they do today, so that the lowest branches just brush a man's head. American orchards outside rocky New England hill-farm areas were well tended by their owners and by their owners' cattle. It was a rare European traveler who discovered widespread carelessness in American orchard management.

Orchards—and field crops—require shelter from winter gales, and away from the hilly East farmers discovered that the winds whipping across the cleared land damaged unprotected trees. Siting an orchard required much care because the trees were permanent fixtures requiring some degree of shelter. Some farmers protected their orchards by locating them to the south of their houses and barns, and others placed them to the south of woodlots. By the nineteenth century many farmers were deliberately planting and maintaining windbreaks such as those proposed in an 1854 *Cultivator* article entitled "Shelter for Farms." Carefully designed windbreaks, the editor counseled, stop snow from drifting away from the winter wheat it ought to protect and into the barnyard, where it slows all human activity, protect grain crops from tempestuous summer storms, and shelter orchards from frost and wind damage. Farmers clearing land ought to leave belts of trees four rods wide and eighty rods long scattered here and there along streams or fence lines, and farmers struggling with already cleared holdings ought to plant rows of trees in similar shapes. Each row, the writer emphasized, "should be kept fenced on both sides, so as to allow the thick growth of young trees, which will render the screen more perfect, and afford a constant succession as the older trees are removed for fuel."[99]

As woodlots decreased in size, many farmers began planting windbreaks like those proposed in the *Cultivator;* they offered not only shelter but an accessible source of firewood and building timber. Eastern farmers were often provoked into planting windbreaks when their neighbors cleared woodlots which sheltered abutting crops, and like their contemporaries farther west, they learned that windbreaks grow slowly and are useless until they reach great heights. Men faced a difficult decision. If they planted locust trees in their windbreaks they could be almost certain to have fifty-foot-high screens within twenty-five years; the silver poplar, the chestnut, the elm, the European larch, the silver maple, and the Norway fir all grow extremely rapidly too, sometimes as much as thirty feet in ten years if the soil is rich. But the fastest growing trees are usually the worst for fuel or building timber, and farmers sometimes chose to plant slow-growing oaks in order that one day the windbreak would prove useful as a woodlot. In the face of acute shortages of firewood and building timber, the nation's farmers slowly relearned the lessons forgotten in the decades of clearing. By 1860 farming was no longer careless, except where economic and social conditions made it unprofitable. Reformers criticized slaveowners for ignoring the innovations inspired by wornout soil and woodlots, but even they slowly adopted or devised new techniques. East of the Mississippi, farmers focused on carefully maintaining resources. The age of clearing ended, except in Oregon.

Equilibrium

According to an eighteenth-century adage recalled with admiration by one nineteenth-century writer dedicated to agricultural improvement, every farm ought to be "suitably divided into woodland, pasture, and tillage." When Donald G. Mitchell wrote *Dream Life: A Fable of the Seasons* in 1851, he emphasized the importance of tradition, not innovation, in bettering the nation's farms. He remembered his grandfather's farm as a model of agricultural efficiency. "The farmhouse, a large irregularly-built mansion of wood, stands upon a shelf of the hills looking southward, and is shaded by century-old oaks. The barns and out-buildings are grouped in a brown phalanx, a little to the northward of the dwelling. Between them a high timber gate opens upon the scattered pasture lands of the hills," and between them too open other gates upon meadows, arable fields, an orchard, and a lane leading to the woodlot. Mitchell admired the old farm because its land provided for almost all its owner's needs, along with a small surplus for cash sale. Unlike the increasingly specialized farms surrounding New York City, it endured free from market irregularities and from the disasters of ecosystem imbalance.[100] Like other urban writers of the period, Mitchell despaired of correcting or countering price fluctuations but he was convinced that ecological difficulties might be solved and farms made even better.

Planning the perfect farm occupied the attention of many writers, particularly those employed by the many agricultural journals. Most of the plans, like one proposed in 1844 in the *Illustrated Annual Register of Rural Affairs,* incorporated traditional wisdom with new discoveries. The author of "Laying out and Dividing Farms" based his plans on the proven profitability of crop rotation and presented his readers with a meticulously detailed scheme for planning a 120-acre farm. Some facets of the plan are traditional—locating the farmhouse and outbuildings in the center of the farm to save walking, keeping the fields equal in size and square in shape to facilitate crop rotation and save fencing material—and others are innovative—leveling the farm lanes to make easier the labor of oxen and horses, using four- as well as three-course rotation, spreading the latest fertilizers, and even planting a few ornamental trees in the front pasture "to give it something of a park appearance."[101] On paper the plan is workable, and the illustrations are enticing. Nevertheless, experienced farmers undoubtedly would have noticed weaknesses in the *Register's* ideal farm plan for 1844.

Colonial husbandmen struggled to clear away forest and make the exposed ground suitable for plowing. In "making land" they forgot that stewardship is the essence of husbandry and that many natural resources, timber and topsoil in particular, are easily exhausted. Not until the middle of the eighteenth century, when *husbandman* was losing currency to the new word *farmer,* did men become aware that making land was not enough. Planted fields and meadows, like pastures and orchards, were frail; they succumbed quickly to a vast number of enemies and survived only by infusions of human energy. Clearing the land and building the farm were difficult tasks indeed. Maintaining the delicate equilibrium of artifice and nature proved even more challenging.

With English grass came English weeds, which thrived in the New World and spread so quickly that one, plantain, was called "Englishman's foot" by the Indians, who soon called the honey bee the "English fly." Along with native weeds, the imports invaded every newly made field and warred with precious crops such as English grass and wheat. Some weeds caused havoc. Stinkweed grew among English grass and produced abortions among pregnant mares, cows, and ewes. Saint-John's-wort grew among the grass too, and as in England its presence in hay so frightened livestock that they refused to eat. Couch grass strangled the sprouting Indian corn, and charlock proved so difficult to eradicate from fields that farmers nicknamed it "terrify." Some weeds, like the cockle that infested wheat fields, were easy enough to identify (cockle is pink and Saint-John's-wort flowers are yellow) but difficult to control. Pulling and hoeing seemed the only solutions, but approaching the weeds meant trampling grain. Hoeing often destroyed nearby seedlings, and pulling frequently uprooted mature crops. Adults sometimes delegated such monotonous, character-building tasks to children, but even industrious teenagers rarely succeeded in long controlling the infestations of wild plants that prospered best in newly cleared, freshly plowed soil. "To one unacquainted with new lands, it seems to him, after the removal of the wood, not a little astonishing to witness the numerous rank weeds which instantly spring up, where before scarce one was to be

seen; and we know of nothing which so strongly reminds us of the
primeval curse, 'thorns also and thistles shall it bring forth to thee,' as a
newly-cleared forest-field," complained one nineteenth-century colum-
nist. "The thrifty fire-weed shoots out like thick-sown wheat; the thistle
pushes up its head; and cockles, and briars, and burrs, come forth like
the fabled dragon's teeth."[102] Hoeing and pulling rarely sufficed to control such outbreaks of chaos, and although some farmers controlled
Saint-John's-wort by pasturing sheep on infested areas and others tried
burning over weed-choked fields, most resigned themselves to losing
part of every crop.

Blight was a far worse problem. As early as 1664 Puritans in Connecticut and Massachusetts believed that God had "blasted" their wheat
crops as punishment for community sinfulness. Prayer brought no relief, and the blight worsened each summer. In 1680 and 1685 they
reserved whole days for repentance and supplication. But black-stem
rust eventually destroyed New England's wheat-producing capacity and
stimulated the growing boom in Pennsylvania agriculture. Not until
1726 did men realize what French peasants had understood in the
1650s. Wheat rust is intimately connected with the barberry bush, a plant
imported from England because its berries are useful for jams and jel-
lies. The barberry is the secondary host to a fungal parasite whose chief
host is wheat. Once husbandmen perceived the issue, colony after colony
followed the example of Connecticut and ordered the plant eradicated.
But not everyone believed the theory—it was argued into the twentieth
century that barberry bushes have no relation to black-stem wheat
rust—and the blight continued.[103] Here and there, however, men
stormed into their kitchen gardens to uproot the barberry bushes, and
they patrolled their woodlot edges and fence lines to make certain that
no plants seeded themselves among less noxious weeds.

Farmers adapted to each new weed or blight or insect assault by rotat-
ing crops, eradicating host plants, and experimenting with resistant varieties of seed, pesticides, and fungicides.[104] Often they cooperated
against threats as they sometimes had in clearing forest and raising
frames. They organized shooting bees in which all men in a neighborhood gathered to hunt rats and other vermin, and they paid bounties to
young boys bringing in dead crows. Sometimes they assembled to rid a
particularly infested field of weeds or insects like the cotton worm and
the chinch bug. Most importantly, however, farmers chose to raise a
variety of crops because they knew that a new blight might strike at any
moment. American farms objectified the longevity of the Old World
terror of chaos. If the wheat crop failed, the corn in the adjacent field

fed its planters; if the corn failed the rye might thrive. Nineteenth-century farmers understood the profits possible in single-crop farming, but they understood too the example of southern planters battling the cotton worm. In 1783, 1804, 1825, and at twenty-one- and twenty-two-year intervals thereafter, the South American insect ravaged the cotton crop and convinced farmers in the north and west of southern stupidity. Variety was the best insurance against catastrophe even if it meant additional work.

In the years just before the Civil War the American landscape embodied the farmers' love of well-chosen variety. Almost every farmstead comprised nearly a dozen buildings devoted to specialized tasks like meat curing or cider making. Most structures were designed for storage of raw or processed produce or for shelter of livestock, but whatever the use, each existed *specifically* for it. Where agriculture was most diversified, especially in hill-country New England and in western Pennsylvania and New York, the complex of structures clustered about the kitchen ell was typically intricate. In the South, particularly in the Tidewater, many of the structures were lacking or were combined with others. The variety of structures perhaps confused European observers, who appear to have rated prosperity according to the condition, not the number, of structures and fields. A farmer with a dozen outbuildings and half a dozen crops often prospered when his neighbors' crops suffered from blight or unseasonable weather. He looked askance at the farms proposed in agricultural journals and continued to rely on traditional, proven variety.

Ideal farms did not capture the imagination of American farmers because their designers usually failed to allow for interruptions of chaos. Sketches of perfect farms almost never included information about abutting holdings, and experienced farmers well knew the dangers of farming next to slovenly fields and woodlots. If one farmer in a neighborhood refused to grub up weeds, burn caterpillars, chop down barberry bushes, or shoot rats, his hardworking neighbors suffered mightily. Innovation was respected by all but the most traditional (and perhaps pessimistic) farmers, but no farmer was free to innovate by abdicating his responsibility. Farming remained, therefore, a tradition-oriented occupation. Change seemed almost as likely to produce catastrophe as it was to produce great benefit, and men contented themselves with following the advice of the past. Agricultural periodicals circulated widely but their advice and plans and exquisite illustrations of ideal farms went largely unheeded. The equilibrium established over two centuries of making land and fending off one chaotic disruption after another was too fragile. Farmers chose to improve what they had and to experiment very slowly. They cherished equilibrium and rejected perfect, static design.

Land in equilibrium was beautiful. "The phrase 'beautiful country,'" remarked Timothy Dwight in 1822 of the magnificent New York agricultural region stretching 200 miles west from Utica, "as used here, means appropriately and almost only lands suited to the purposes of husbandry, and has scarcely a remote reference to beauty of landscape." By his traditional, almost landschaft-like standard of the exquisite conjunction of New England meetinghouse and clustered houses, the still-unfinished region was "dull and wearisome" despite the well-built farmhouses and carefully cultivated fields, and by the standards of poets and painters beloved by Dwight, it offered nothing "to behold under the influence of fascination, and to depict with enthusiasm and rapture."[105] Nevertheless, its inhabitants found it beautiful, and they liked it more and more as the last vestiges of wilderness became productive agricultural land. In 1822 Dwight's standard of spatial beauty was already provincial and old-fashioned; derived as it was from the New England attempt to replicate old-country spatial order and from reading English aesthetics, it failed to incorporate a new, national understanding of beauty in space. By 1840 Dwight's standard was forgotten, except in New England, and a new standard of spatial beauty—or visual quality—ruled the national imagination. Land in agricultural equilibrium—land cleared of wilderness and defended against the evils of weeds and blights and the return of wilderness—was land likely to remain fertile. A beautiful farm was a farm with a well-designed and well-built house and barn, tight fences, carefully tilled fields, pruned orchards, and even a well-managed woodlot, all crisply clear of any wilderness interruption. Such a farm endured from season to season, year to year, objectifying a comfortable if slightly static life-style and outlook, a certainty unknown in cities. It represented the continuity of its owners' independence and well-being, and a living inheritance for children. Mining, logging, and smelting, farmers quickly pointed out, are always in the end temporary enterprises; eventually the ore and the trees are exhausted and the artisans thrown out of work and forced to move. A farm, on the contrary, shelters and feeds its owners; indeed a family not only owns but inhabits a farm, free of external pressures and changes of fortune. In 1840 the national imagination accepted the farm as the perfect objectification of the perfect life and declared the most beautiful country to be that composed of beautiful farms and a few crossroads churches and schoolhouses, all in equilibrium with one another, with time, and with nature. Even the word *husbandry*, out of favor among farmers on most days, rang out during country fair orations, when speakers declared with Solomon that agriculturists are the most fortunate of men, the supporters of the nation, and the closest to divinity. Despite the fact that nineteenth-century farmers used machinery unknown to their grandfathers and contested against new blights and insects, they treasured the equilibrium of tradition and respected customs like planting a variety of crops. In resisting the proposals of agricultural reformers they often avoided serious catastrophe and always provided urban American with space out of an earlier time. A farm or collection of farms offered urban dwellers a vision of a traditional past free of industrialization and rapid change and reflective of times remembered as trouble-free. Currier and Ives, along with other illustrators, promoted the new standard of spatial beauty by producing one lithograph after another of farms in winter, barns filled with harvested crops, and other agricultural scenes designed for sale not only to farm families wanting to be certain that their lives and spaces were indeed worthy of artistic rendering but for sale to a quickly expanding urban population troubled by novel evils, disconcerted by new structures and spaces, and desperate for framed visions of the perfect spatial beauty a few score miles from their cities. Agricultural land characterized by equilibrium and variety was the standard by which almost all Americans judged all land, and the standard that impelled the first would-be suburbanites to live away from cities on two- or three-acre "cottage farms."

Land shaped by agriculture became the standard by which Americans condemned cityscape. Reformers such as Sylvester Judd insisted that urban form ought to be more open, more like landscape than cityscape. "No street should be less than four rods in width; no lane, or court, less than three," he argued in 1850. "Dwelling-houses should be blocked together in not more than twos. Why, alas! deem the 'corner-lot' the most eligible, when every house might look two ways?" Judd asserted that the land shaped by farmers provided the example for the perfect urban form. "Churches should be the most conspicuous buildings, and stand in lots of not less than ten rods square. Every school-house should have twenty-five square rods. Every dwelling-house should be removed two rods from the street, and not more than two families be permitted to reside under the same roof, and within the same walls."[106] His vision of the perfect urban form emphasizes openness and trees, the dominant features—along with single-family houses and barns—of the agriculture-shaped space that Americans loved. "There should be central, or contiguous, reserves of land, of twenty or fifty acres each, for public parks and promenades. There should be trees in every street, without exception,—trees about the markets, trees in front of the shops, and on the docks, and shading the manufactories." Unlike many mid-nineteenth-century reformers, Judd clearly understood the origin of his standard. "This would 'countrify' the city," he concluded of his plan, "and that is what we desire." He detested the fast-paced growth of East Coast cities, the "towns everywhere that are growing into cities, bunching together their houses, pinching their streets, stuffing skinny apartments with men, women, and children, as Bologna-meat" because he cherished the land shaped by agriculture.[107] Thousands of his contemporaries shared his views and supported "countrification" projects like the building of Central Park in New York City. But cities did not become more open, more tree-filled; instead they grew more choked, denser. Their residents often deserted them if they had the means to move to the land shaped by agriculture. Most Americans hoped to live in landscape, in communities they understood and liked.

*At distant intervals a line of fencing, some burnt
trees, a field of corn, some animals, a cabin made of
roughly shaped tree trunks put on top of one
another, indicated some denizen's isolated home.
One hardly sees any villages. The cultivators'
houses are scattered in the midst of the woods.* [1]

Alexis de Tocqueville
Notebook
1831

Crossroads church building, southern Oklahoma. (JRS)

ural America baffled Europeans searching for good land to settle or barbaric agricultural practices to describe in letters home. Farms looked so lonely in Pennsylvania, Kentucky, Ohio, Indiana, and Illinois that even the sharpest writers despaired of portraying a landscape with no obvious centers. "There ought to be five or six families living close together in these districts," complained Theophile Cazenove in a 1797 description of central Pennsylvania. "Then they would be very happy." Had the Frenchman stepped down from his two-horse carriage and ordered his manservant to wait while he talked with the farmers along the road, he might have learned that dispersed, seemingly haphazard settlement does not indicate loneliness. Like the pioneer farmers to the west, Pennsylvanians lived happily in indistinct neighborhoods.

Sensitive foreigners struggled to interpret the appearance and meaning of rural neighborhoods for readers accustomed to compact villages and converging roads. "What the New England people call towns and villages they call townships and towns," remarked Gershom Flagg of Illinois settlers in a letter dispatched to England in 1822. "I have asked many people what township they lived in and they could not tell. If you enquire for any place if it is a town they can sometimes tell, if a township you will get no information about it from one half the people." Flagg's terse language indicates his anger at mail going astray because settlers understood only their immediate neighborhood, and he blamed the general ignorance on the residents' southern heritage. "People who come from Connecticut," he was convinced, "are more enlightened."[2] New Englanders understood the meaning of words like *town* and *village,* and Europeans accustomed to the remnants of landschaften honored them for their accuracy of thought.

What astounded many travelers in the newly settled regions was the settlers' almost uncanny ability to name all the families within a wide area. "The new settler in the woods is soon as well known, among a wide circle of neighbors," noted a Scotsman in 1822, "that almost any person within ten miles of him can direct the stranger to his residence." Again and again Europeans discovered that neighborhood meant a very large area. Two settlers near Albion, Illinois, estimated the population of their neighborhood at 760 persons, even though one admitted that "we had only our own knowledge to guide us and most likely omitted several families."[3] Some neighborhoods covered almost 300 square miles, more than the area of eight of the 6-mile-square townships mandated by the 1785 Land Ordinance. Most neighborhoods were far smaller, of course, especially after farmers cleared and occupied all sections and subsections, but almost none focused on ecclesiastical-political centers. As in the Tidewater and in Pennsylvania, community was objectified in less manifest ways. By 1820 western Americans were perfectly accustomed to living without small, closely built villages on which to focus their public existence. Away from New England vast regions oriented themselves about a number of "occasional" centers serving religious, political, social, and economic needs. In every neighborhood evolved substitutes for the small-scale village life left behind in the states north of New York and in Europe.

Europeans vaguely distrusted the multicentered—or uncentered, in their terms—landscape west of the Appalachians. Plantation regions in the South they understood as an innovative, although increasingly hidebound objectification of a once inventive labor system. But elsewhere they kept to the well-traveled roads because they knew from bitter experience that roads in rural America converge not on villages but only on other roads.

LIBERALISM

As he rode through eastern Kentucky early in the 1790s, Gilbert Imlay looked down and noted and roadside vegetation. In 1792 English readers of *A Topographical Description of the Western Territory of North America* learned that he had crossed a region "covered with cane, rye-grass, and the native clover." Imlay took pains to accurately describe the reed-like cane plants that grew ten or twelve feet high and frequently towered even fifteen or sixteen feet above the ground, and he decided that although the rye and clover resembled European varieties, both must be indigenous. Beyond the fields of settlers, Imlay discovered few European imports.

Sixty years later a German traveler in the same region catalogued roadside vegetation too but discovered no cane or wild grass. "In the neighborhood of farms, where the ground has been worked, herbaceous plants predominate," he reported. "Familiar forms and ones closely related to those of our fatherland remind us of our native fields. Wild violets, strawberries, wild caraway, ragwort, burdock, thistles, plantain, ivy, mullein, numerous asters and ironweed are widely and numerously distributed."[4] A few years after J. G. Harker published his observations, another German traveler in the same region noted that camomile, mullein, and white clover flourished along the roadsides. Friedrich von Raumer shared Harker's ignorance of cane and wild grasses; such native plants had vanished decades before and been replaced by dozens of European species accidentally or deliberately imported and spread along roads, carried by livestock and wagons moving west.[5] Had the German observers thought to ask, old-timers might have told them of the change. Indeed the old settlers living in the middle of the nineteenth century might have told of many changes and in their telling decreased the European puzzlement concerning rural America.

Had Imlay, Harker, and von Raumer explored the backlands beyond the Appalachians in 1750 they would have found cane and native grass and dozens of other curious plants, much unbroken forest, and here and there fragile Old World territorial *landschaften* laboriously shaped and maintained by *habitants*, agriculturists from France or French Canada. Most Frenchmen in the Mississippi Valley hunted or else traded with Indians for skins; a handful prospected for precious metals, and a few worked mines of lead or silver. French Jesuits established and maintained a large number of small, widely scattered missions serving Indian tribes such as the Hurons and Iroquois, sometimes working with trappers and traders who made the mission settlements their headquarters and whose need for food eventually attracted agriculturists into the "Pays de Illinois," the region depicted with such enthusiasm in 1733 by Guillaume de l'Isle, a French cartographer. When English colonists—and later Americans—pushed into the vast territory west of the Appalachians at the close of the eighteenth century, geometrical surveying and liberalism clashed with outposts of custom.

In 1712 France defined its claims in western North America as extending "from the source of the Mississippi as far as the place where that river empties into the Gulf of Mexico." Royal counselors scarcely imagined how far the region described in Jesuit relations and cryptic reports from *coureurs de bois* actually extended. When l'Isle published maps such as "Carte de la Louisiane et du Cours du Mississippi" and "L'Amerique Septemtrionale" in his *Atlas Nouveau* he was forced to leave blank vast stretches west of the Mississippi and north of Taos. Illinois was chiefly wilderness in 1733, a vast chaos marked by widely scattered outposts of French spatial order, but west of it, beyond the vaguely known region l'Isle colored in pale yellow and called "Sioux de l'Ouest," lay only blankness.[6] No one, not cartographers, counselors, or coureurs de bois, knew where Louisiana ended.

Habitants arrived in the Illinois Country from eastern Canada and later from the Gulf of Mexico settlements at the mouth of the Mississippi River. Some came directly from Normandy and other French provinces, and almost all—even those from the *seigneurial* settlements along the

Saint Lawrence River—chose to live in clustered settlements and to manage in common arable and pasture land and such natural resources as forest. New World innovation only slightly modified the habitants' urge to build according to old-country standards. In the first years of the nineteenth century American surveyors platting the national grid encountered traditionally ordered French *villes* that had endured Indian assault, natural catastrophe, and—from 1762 to 1803—Spanish rule. Of the forty French settlements in the Illinois Country, perhaps the most representative of French common building was Sainte Genevieve in present-day Illinois.[8]

Sainte Genevieve began as an offshoot of Kaskaskia, a community that began as an Indian mission settlement on the eastern bank of the Mississippi in 1703. When the habitants of Kaskaskia required more arable land in the 1740s, a number moved across the river and established a new *ville*, and when a Spanish official examined it in 1769, Sainte Genevieve contained 600 people; thirty-one years later the population had grown to 1,163, partly because French subjects were abandoning the eastern shore threatened by the British. Between 1785 and 1794 the builders of Sainte Genevieve deserted their original location for another more secure from river erosion, but despite the three-mile move the ville prospered. Unlike the first settlement, however, the second was laid out according to the Laws of the Indies then applied to the whole of Louisiana. The first Sainte Genevieve objectified the force of French tradition; the second reflected that tradition as modified by Spanish law. And after 1803, when it passed into American jurisdiction, it slowly reflected the new spirits of geometrical order and liberalism.

Sainte Genevieve originally reflected the close-knit order of New France society. At its center stood the habitants' houses and other structures, including a church building; around the village lay the agricultural land worked in common, and around it lay the common woodlots. Beyond the woodlots lay "le domaine du roy," the wilderness domain belonging to the king from which further grants of land might be had when necessary.[8] Although not as regularly shaped as Chimayo, Sainte Genevieve displayed a more explicit over-all structure than most seventeenth-century New England towns.

Its center, marked by steads and church, objectified New France community ideals of neighborliness. Every stead nestled among its neighbors, and lanes between them were narrow and twisting, and shaded by the high pointed logs of cedar or oak that enclosed each houselot. Within the walls stood a house made of vertical logs placed on a stone foundation and chinked with clay, twigs, animal hair, and sometimes stone, often covered with planks or split saplings, and frequently surrounded by a porch on all four sides. Houses were single story and intimately related to the rest of the houselot. Sometimes the kitchen stood in a free-standing room, and sometimes habitants placed it in an enclosed part of the back porch, facing the barn, the poultry house, the slave cabin, and other structures. Among the buildings stood a vegetable garden and an orchard, and sometimes a flower garden too, all sheltered from winter winds by the palisade surrounding the lot.[9]

Away from the houselot cluster lay the common fields, at Sainte Genevieve stretching at right angles back from the river to the hill beyond the bottomland. Each householder possessed a strip in the great common field planted to wheat and was entitled to the produce from it, as long as he fulfilled his obligations to his neighbors. Little is known about the common fields of the first Sainte Genevieve settlement, but records concerning the "commons" at Kaskaskia across the river and at Cahokia and Prairie du Rocher suggest that each habitant held a strip one arpent (about one-and-one-half English acres) wide and perhaps fifteen to twenty arpents long, as well as the right to cut timber and gather building stone in the common woods. The husbandmen of Sainte Genevieve prospered, sending their wheat downstream to New Orleans or else milling it in small mills and selling the flour to hunters and traders, and to the miners at work in nearby lead mines. Had the Mississippi not eroded its banks, Sainte Genevieve might have grown even faster than it did.

Habitants long remembered 1785 as "l'annee des grandes eaux" because the Mississippi flooded so badly that many families lost almost all their possessions. "The waters have risen so greatly from their source that they have entirely submerged the village of Santa Genoveva," wrote the Spanish commandant in June. "All its inhabitants having been obliged to retire with great haste to the hillsides which are one league away from the said village. They abandoned their houses which were inundated, and their furniture and other possessions which they had in them."[10] Despite the destruction, however, some families tried to rebuild on the old site. Making a new Sainte Genevieve (or Santa Genoveva) required convincing the determined habitants that the flood was not wholly unusual.

Physical catastrophe helped shape the new town. Its founders located it away from the Mississippi on rising ground beyond the reach of even great floods. But its ordering was not the haphazard clustering cherished by the French. Instead, the Spanish officials insisted that it be layed out in a compact grid, about a plaza, and divided into blocks roughly 350 by 400 feet. Land was assigned eunomically, those higher in rank and wealth receiving entire blocks on which to build their houses and yards, and those families lower on the social ladder receiving scarcely enough land on which to erect a small house. Each *emplacement,* or building site, however, was palisaded with the 7-foot-high cedar or oak logs familiar to old-time Sainte Genevieve residents, and the larger houselots were soon jammed with barns, stables, sheds, poultry houses, slave cabins, outside kitchens and ovens, bakehouses, and *cabane a mahis,* or corn-storage sheds, all built not according to any Spanish practice but according to French common tradition.[11] The *Laws of the Indies* created the settlement framework but it did not dictate its structural details.

Nevertheless, the shift in location and the Spanish ordering fractured the old-country reliance on common fields. What remained of the *Grand Champs* continued in cultivation, but more and more frequently, innovative habitants eager to profit from the growing immigration of Americans moved their houses to isolated fields planted to whatever crops seemed most lucrative. In the 1790s, however, enough habitants practiced common-field husbandry to attract the interest of Americans. "Their agriculture was carried on in a field of several thousand acres, in the fertile river-bottom of the Mississippi, inclosed at the common expense and divided into lots separated by some natural or permanent boundary. Horses or cattle, depastured, were tethered with long ropes, or the grass was cut and carried to them in their stalls," recollected one American visitor many years later. "It was a pleasing sight, to mark the rural population going and returning, morning and evening, to and from the field, with their working cattle, carts, old-fashioned wheelplows, and other implements of husbandry."[12] For H. M. Brackenridge, the sight was a pleasant reminder of a spatial and social existence unknown in the new Republic. For the Spanish commandant of Sainte Genevieve the common fields and right-angle streets objectified right order, the order of conservatism.

Spanish counselors understood that Louisiana would perish unless more settlers arrived from Spain or anywhere else where men and women enthusiastically accepted Spanish rule and Catholic faith. Settlement regulations grew more enticing but remained rigorous; a headright system like that of the Tidewater rewarded newcomers with lots of varying acreage but required that every lot be located in a compact settlement and carefully improved. Revised Spanish land laws favored the *poblador,* the "populator," who arrived in Louisiana with a large family, servants, and hangers-on, by granting him high status and much land in the settlement he established. "The boundary and territory,

which are given under the contract to the *poblador,* shall be divided in the
following manner," the law ordered. "They shall first provide for the
residential sections of the town with sufficient commons and common
pasture, which shall provide an abundant pasture for the cattle of the
householders, and an equally sufficient amount for the private lands of
the town: the rest of the grant and boundary shall be divided into four
parts; one part of which shall go to the one responsible for founding the
settlement, he choosing it himself, and the remaining three parts shall be
divided into equal lots for the settlers." Settlers received tax exemptions
and sometimes financial subsidies, and on February 19, 1778, Governor
Galvez announced that every immigrant husbandman would receive two
hens, a rooster, a two-month-old pig, an allotment of corn according to
the size of his family, and an ax, hoe, spade, and a scythe or sickle.[13] Such
eighteenth-century inducements derived from long colonization experience and new problems. No longer did all newcomers consent to work
common fields; industrious settlers, and particularly *pobladors,* wanted
land that could be cultivated independently. Conservatism vied with
liberalism in the Spanish land laws of Louisiana, and in Louisiana itself.

Daniel Boone so coveted the wonderfully generous terms of Spanish
land law that he renounced American citizenship and received a grant of
1,000 arpents (roughly 1,000 acres) on the Missouri River. After he
urged a hundred Virginia and Kentucky families to move to Louisiana,
the Spanish crown awarded him an additional 10,000 arpents. Boone
was not the only American citizen willing to become a Spanish subject. In
1787 Bryan Bruin and several other heads of Virginian families
petitioned the Spanish governor for the privilege of settling along the
Mississippi River, claiming that Americans persecuted them for their
Catholic faith.[14] But Boone and other United States pioneers thought in
terms other than common land and clustered villages. Like the framers
of the 1785 Ordinance they understood scattered settlement and
cherished the free-standing farmstead; they rejoiced when the United
States acquired the Louisiana Territory in 1803.

Only a few Americans mourned the passing of the old French and
Spanish order. Brackenridge wondered about the change in Sainte
Genevieve habitants, remarking that "whatever they may have gained in
some respects, I question very much whether the change of government
has contributed to increase their happiness." But Brackenridge said
nothing more. Common-field husbandry seemed an anachronism beneath the attention of American pioneers, and corporate land planning
struck them as a vestige of tyranny.

Like   northern   New   England,   the   southern   trans-Appalachian

Mountain region, and the Ohio Valley, the Illinois Country and the rest of Louisiana meant "backlands" to late eighteenth- and early nineteenth-century Americans considering a move west. "Frontier" identified a state of Indian trouble, land speculation, intermittent lawlessness, transient hunting, federal surveying, military movements, and high prices more than it denoted a particular place or places. In the backlands of Vermont or Kentucky the frontier condition passed quickly west, and the residents of the former wilderness cherished the half-shaped land they called—if they called it by a generic term at all—"rural America." Away from the long-shaped coastal regions, rural America was remarkable for its basic sameness. Over a standard structure, over the ubiquitous grid, men sculpted a form that evidenced regional peculiarities accenting a national style. Americans and foreign visitors did not usually notice the style; it extended unbroken over thousands of square miles. But when that style abutted one totally different, a French ville or Spanish estensión, even casual observers understood the objectification of liberalism.

Implicit in the new federal Constitution and objectified everywhere in late eighteenth- and early nineteenth-century rural America, classical liberalism derived from the realities of market economy and continuous change. Life, liberty, and the pursuit of happiness, the "unalienable rights" cited by Jefferson in the Declaration of Independence in 1776, are the reason—according to the Continental Congress—why men create government. Indeed government exists to protect the lives and freedoms, and pursuits of happiness, of its makers. Men therefore do not live to serve a political entity; they hope to live unencumbered by public obligation, at liberty to pursue happiness—or property—as they best can.

Liberalism defeated the old social, economic, and political order of the seventeenth-century New England town.[15] New Englanders wanted liberty from the unity of government and church that directed their daily lives, a liberty like that discovered by southern colonists and later by Pennsylvanians. By the late eighteenth century they had accomplished the transformation; Americans inhabited different spheres at will, on the Sabbath embracing an ecclesiastical order, on training day a military one, on town-meeting or court day a political one. Government worked best when it governed least, like religion that impinged only when desired. Europeans accustomed to a fractured but still coherent single sphere of established national churches, nondemocratic governments, and more or less rigidly manipulated economic systems wondered at the seeming fragmentation of United States public life and worried about its implication for European order. In the revolution year of 1848 Alexis de Tocqueville summed up the worry in a new preface to an analysis of American institutions he had published thirteen years earlier. "This whole book," he asserted of *Democracy in America*, "has been written under the impulse of a kind of religious dread inspired by contemplation of this irresistible revolution advancing century by century over every obstacle and even now going forward amid the ruins it has itself created." As the *ancien régime* crumbled across Europe, Tocqueville had good reason to ponder the destroying force of liberalism. So many institutions seemed to crumble so utterly. In the midst of change Tocqueville saw mostly ruin.[16] Across the Atlantic, especially in the backlands he had once visited, only a few villes temporarily resisted the force. Liberalism shaped institutions, and it shaped space too.

Rural America lacked intersections of combined economic, ecclesiastical, political, and social order. European travelers reared in lands where markets and shops, churches and convents, *ratshauser* and guildhalls, and inns and taverns clustered at irregular intervals puzzled at the scattered public buildings and spaces in the United States. Benighted travelers sought church spires in expectation of nearby inns, and found only churches; they encountered graveyards far removed from churches, and schoolhouses sited at quiet crossroads. The countryside seemed very like the plants described by Imlay, similar to but not identical to European shaped space. And, like the roadside ecosystem, the countryside evolved continuously.

Imlay wondered about the meaning of American institutions and tried to compare them to American plants. "It naturally struck me that there must be something in climate that debased or elevated the human soul," he suggested. What Imlay and other Europeans put down to climate or fertile soil, however, Americans ascribed to "democratic institutions," to the complex of beliefs and practices manifested in a variety of spaces and structures and now understood as classical liberalism.[17] Many of the spaces and buildings were innovative and distinct parts of an American "national style"; a few (like graveyards) objectified old-country tradition only slightly modified.

GRAVEYARDS

Much rural socializing occurred at bees like one cited by Frederick Law Olmsted in 1860, in a narrative he called *A Journey in the Back Country*. He carefully noted that twenty neighbors, "residing within a distance of three miles" of a Tennessee farmhouse, had gathered one day during the previous winter to shuck corn and exchange information about the bears, wolves, panthers, and wildcats killing their free-ranging livestock. The cornhusking was a social event as much as it was a collective enterprise. Like frame raisings and log rollings, huskings and other bees brought neighbors together frequently. In 1821 one Illinois newcomer hosted two "rail maulings" in which his neighbors gathered to split trees he had felled. Neither was an unqualified success. Rain made the wood bind and the men slow, but each time the fifteen volunteers split between 600 and 700 rails, about 300 fewer than customary on a dry day. The same settler turned out to help raise a neighbor's barn frame, returning the assistance given him and enjoying a Friday's excitement.[18] For all that the American countryside appeared the epitome of independence and loneliness, its inhabitants regularly practiced cooperative building and processing. Farmers were notoriously unwilling to give or lend cash but they gladly offered their voluntary labor. Winter passed in a succession of huskings and logrollings and rail maulings, and spring was a time of frame raisings. Neighborliness shaped the land.

Not every gathering was cheerful. Unlike dung frolics and quilting bees, burials were solemn occasions. Neighbors assembled for a brief service in the burying ground and devoted the remaining hours to conversation, usually at the deceased person's former home. Birth was a semiprivate affair that attracted only one or two women especially friendly with the expectant mother. Burial was public and attracted every neighbor healthy enough to reach the gravesite.[19]

Well into the nineteenth century, American graveyards reflected ambivalent attitudes toward death, afterlife, and the invisible world of souls and demons. Funerals were family and community rituals enacted on hallowed ground by people deeply cognizant of age-old traditions. Burial is always an imaginative moment, and throughout the seventeenth and eighteenth centuries shades of pagan fear tormented neighbors gathered around the pit. In the common imagination, graveyards were one step removed from Heaven, and half a step from Hell.

The first colonists brought with them a half-pagan, half-Christian heritage of burial and graveyard design that only the foolhardy questioned. Europe's priests had long struggled to convince parishioners that consecrated ground was safe from Satanic inroads, even after nightfall, and that old beliefs about protective trees and stones were sinful failings of faith. By day people believed that graveyards were hierophanies, vortexes where the world of God touched the world of humans.[20] At night, however, the old fears rushed back.

The underworld, the perpetually sunless place of Hell, demons, and putrefaction, quivered beneath the graveyard grass. Since humans consecrated the graveyard to the God of Light, it seemed only natural that the Prince of Darkness wished all the more to violate the corpses interred within it. People looked on burial and graveyards with hope and horror, and watched uncertainly as they filled the hole and mourners deserted the consecrated ground. Christianity might triumph in the end but as dusk fell the powers of darkness gained temporary advantage. So strong was the uncertainty in the northeastern counties of Scotland that many farmers and villagers set aside plots of ground sacred to the Devil. "Clootie's Croft," "Black Faulie," "Devil's Croft," and the "Goodman's Field" were pieces of the best land, sometimes as large as four acres and occasionally walled off from surrounding parcels, that no one planted, and where men hoped the Devil might be satisfied to remain. The older crofts, some with ruined cists of ashes and heaps of stones, dated to pagan days and were remembered as places where priests blessed livestock and seed or sacrificed to harvest gods. Medieval Scots dedicated crofts when they brought wild land into cultivation, despite the clergy's prohibition of such blasphemy and strict punishment of offenders. Early modern Scots believed that souls tarried in the crofts or "faerie hills," frequenting especially those near graveyards, and wise folk left such places strictly alone, as the folksongs recommended.

> The moss is soft on Clootie's croft,
> And bonny's the sod o' the Goodman's toft;
> But if ye bide there till the sun is set,
> The Goodman will catch you in his net.

Greedy husbandmen who disregarded such warnings and cultivated the crofts learned of Satan's wrath. One woman spaded up a croft near Unst and her best cow died shortly afterward; she entered the field again, planted grain in the loosened soil, and the Devil struck her husband dead.[21] Nineteenth-century Scotland was still dotted with the small, secretly unworked plots about which people gossiped, but by then far fewer Scots believed that the Devil must have a physical place in every community lest he wander about doing evil. Eighteenth-century Scottish immigrants may have carried the belief to America, but if they did, it withered before they dedicated crofts to Satan. Like most other colonists, Scots believed that Satan was most likely to frequent the graveyards laid out near meetinghouses or near crossroads. And they took precautions.

European laymen determined in the Middle Ages that the safest spot in any churchyard burying place was the ground next to the east wall of the church. There, nearest the altar, corpses were most secure. Nobles and wealthy commoners often were buried beneath the church floor or within the structure's walls as an added precaution, but lesser folk contented themselves with the uncertain outdoors. The north side of the churchyard was thought most vulnerable to evil spirits, for every earthly trouble from winter gales to Vikings came from that direction. The west was scarcely better, but the south was almost as safe as the east. It is no accident that the gargoyles and other monsters of twelfth-century churches adorn facades and not interiors.[22] The carved figures warned all passersby that only the covered sanctuary was safe; even the yard was subject to Satanic depredations. Try as they might, parish priests failed to eradicate such lay beliefs. Everywhere grave alignment and location mainfested the folk fear of the supernatural and the confusion of pagan and Christian theology.

Christianity was only a veneer overlaying pagan belief and ritual. Iron Age corpses were interred with their feet to the east, facing the first glimmer of light. Christian missionaries countenanced the practice by burying the newly baptized alongside the eastward-facing heathen. In time the Second Coming was confused with the dawn. Christ would come again, but only from the east, with the sun. It was easy to conflate the Son of God with the sun because Christian holy days often coincided with older, astrologically determined festivals. Across Europe, builders sited churches with their altars to the east, many facing the exact point where the sun rises on the feast days of their patron saints. In Wales, where to this day the east wind is called "the wind of the dead men's feet," and elsewhere in Europe, every burying ground somehow recalled the Old Religion.

Graveyards were exclusive places. Suicides were almost never buried in hallowed ground. The earthly punishment for the sin of self-murder was severe; the suicide's property was forfeited to the crown, and his body buried without benefit of clergy at some remote, unmarked waste space, frequently a crossroad. Frightened relatives hoped that crossroads burial would so confuse the troubled spirit that it would never find its way home to haunt them and would instead wander aimlessly from one landschaft to another. Sometimes cautious men solved the problem of wandering spirits more directly by driving a stake through the suicide's body before filling the grave. Lunatics too were buried beyond the graveyard perimeter because neighbors attributed their madness to demonic possession. Unbaptized children and the excommunicated were likewise buried away from the graves of honest people.

Some sinners received different treatment. Murderers and other felons, particularly in German principalities, sometimes were buried at crossroads after dark so their memories might be lost and their wandering souls forever disoriented. Not until 1823 did an act of Parliament permit the English to bury murderers in churchyard burying grounds, and then only at night, between nine o'clock and midnight. Lesser sinners, and suicides and stillborn infants in more charitable parishes were buried inside churchyard walls. They lay north of the church, their perpetual penance marked by reversed headstones surmounting graves aligned north to south. Witches were buried face down, usually outside hallowed ground, in the fervent hope that they would not return to torment their former neighbors who had condemned them to death. Priests alone of honest Christians were buried out of eastern alignment; their parishioners interred them facing west, so they might watch over their congregations in death as they had in life.

At the close of the sixteenth century, burial customs and grave arrangements were well established, although still flexible. The gravediggers in *Hamlet* dispute Ophelia's right to churchyard burial and conclude that her rank will obtain for her other than a suicide's lonely, unmarked grave. But Shakespeare himself would have been denied churchyard burial had he died in France. Not until the early nineteenth century were actors allowed such a favor there. Well into the modern era, therefore, immigrants arriving in America brought with them a complex folklore of death and burial. Each new ethnic group added more beliefs and practices to the American way of death.

European graveyards were Christian by consecration but pagan by planting. Such favorites as yew trees and holly symbolized in their constant greenness the resurrection of spring long before the first missionaries reached Western Europe. A great folklore of plants thrived in graveyards, where almost every plant carried special meaning.[23] German peasants considered rosemary particularly potent; a garland put about a corpse's neck kept away witches and the Devil. A dream of rosemary warned of impending death, according to at least one folksong, however, and graveyard visitors plucked it and other flowers with utmost care. In some parts of Europe the laity believed that a soul left its corpse only in spring, as flowers blossomed above graves. Perhaps for that reason trees thought to ward off evil spirits—evergreens and beeches were most respected in that regard—were planted among the stones to protect captive spirits during the winter. The willow acquired symbolic significance by default; it was first planted to drain low-lying graveyards and was eventually associated with death and weeping. Even the grass, however, had magical powers. A clump of sod from the grave of a wandering spirit placed for four days beneath the church altar was certain to end nighttime straying. Love potions and folk remedies often incorporated some bit of graveyard flora, sometimes clipped on a moonless night, as an essence of divine—or infernal—power. Such charms often worked; it was a rare maiden who doubted the intensity of a youth's love when she learned that he had entered a graveyard after dark to obtain the flowers needed for his spell.

Stones more than plants epitomized constancy. Peasants were often buried in unmarked graves or in a common crypt beneath the church building until the end of the Middle Ages. As the old social order decayed, more and more people hoped to lie under marked graves, and stonecutters and ironworkers fashioned markers to suit far-sighted buyers or bereaved descendants. Substantial people too poor to request burial inside church walls settled for rudely chiseled stones set over outdoor graves east of the church. Even an unworked gravestone commemorated a dead person's position in the landschaft social order as it marked his or her place of burial, for in small, closely knit communities the biography of the deceased was cherished by relatives and neighbors who understood the person's life history as intimately as they knew his or her final place in the graveyard.

The pre-Reformation churchyard burying ground was a place of intense design, a place simultaneously in and beyond the everyday world. Every element from plants to stones to orientation of graves carried traditional meaning. Funerals of honest people involved every member of the landschaft. The priest met corpse, pall bearers, and mourners at or near the lych-gate (from the German *leiche*, a corpse) and ushered them through the churchyard into the church. At the close of the service someone tolled the bell in keeping with the custom of frightening away the powers of the air, and the corpse was borne to a grave aligned with the rising sun and soon to be marked with a simple stone. After the burial the mourners left the sacred enclosure by another gate lest a lingering spirit follow them home. Folk burial involved an actual passage into another world, into a zone where souls hovered between Heaven and Hell. In the churchyard burying ground all dead were eternally present, eternally in the thoughts of the living, because for most medieval believers the dead were never wholly absent from the ground in which they lay, and they were always interested in the affairs of the living. Courts of law met intermittently in English churchyards, and fairs and markets and of course afterservice socializing were common churchyard activities, largely because churchyards were conveniently located open spaces. Within the walls but away from the stones, men and boys played sports as well, and until the Reformation ecclesiastical authorities condoned such worldly uses of sacred space. After all, such events made people mindful of last things and were easily monitored by the clergy. Businessmen favored graveyards for intermittent markets because crime was less likely in hallowed space, and sports (unless the players used a skull for a ball) seemed harmless. By the time of Edward I of England, however, bishops and priests distrusted the activities they by then called profane, and laymen learned to shop, sell, and play outside churchyard walls. The Reformation, and later Puritanism, destroyed the old friendship between the quick and the honorably dead. The religious zealots who smashed altar rails, organs, and stained glass in the name of purity left graveyards untouched but raised about them a wall of prohibitions. Hallowed ground was entered less and less frequently, and then only for specific reasons.

With the termination of fairs and games began a century of neglect. Despite royal proclamations to the contrary, husbandmen frequently used graveyards as livestock pasture, and the tale of the bumpkin frightened by grazing sheep became common. Vestries debated the ownership of graveyard trees with rectors determined on a winter's supply of firewood or timber for parsonage repairs, and some clergymen planted turnips and other crops among the stones. Not only the yew was said to thrive on human remains; for generations the richest grass was believed to be graveyard grass, and seventeenth- and eighteenth-century husbandmen learned to covet it as hay or forage. Villages began leasing graveyards as meadows, and leaseholders cut grass not out of respect for the dead but for fodder. The Puritan assault on superstition and on vestigial Catholicism fragmented the old perception of the graveyard as sacred place. Bits and pieces of the former view survived the crossing to the New World but they contested with the half-pagan lore that arrived almost intact. American graveyards away from New Spain were sacred and chthonic simultaneously, as they had been for centuries in Europe.

Spanish settlers remained secure in Catholic tradition, and they expressed their faith in dozens of estensión graveyards. Most burying grounds in New Spain abutted church buildings, but here and there graveyards were removed from churchyards as a result of eighteenth-century fragmentation of estensíones. Today the best surviving examples of colonial Spanish burying grounds are concentrated in the Sangre de Cristo Mountains. Originally most were fenced to keep out cattle and other livestock but now many are neglected. Tumbleweed, sagebrush, and rabbit bush grow among the markers. Close examination reveals an extraordinary presence of folk art, part relatively recent, part very old. Stone and wooden markers are carved with all the traditional symbols of

Catholic faith: the cross, dove, sheep, angel, tree of life, and human heart. Moreover, the markers are arranged according to Old World pre-Reformation practice; almost all face east and are surmounted by a great cross six to ten feet in height. As in the late sixteenth century, the cross announces the presence of Catholic mysteries, the making of holy ground.[24] Priests emphasized the consecration of churchyards in New Spain, and husbandmen adorned them as best they could. Certainly the Devil roamed over New Spain but he did not overly frequent graveyards.

Away from New Spain, yards and artwork were different, in part by intent and in part by accident. A Spanish churchyard was part of a hierophany that focused on Heaven; elsewhere graveyards opened as much on Hell as on regions above. Eastern North America was settled by immigrants from many nations who earnestly desired religious freedom. Not surprisingly, they differed about matters of graveyard design, and graveyards quickly reflected sectarian argument.

For the Puritans who settled New England the graveyard was simply a place of burial, and almost every tradition associated with it they suspected of pagan or papist roots.[25] New England divines determined that the best way to excise old beliefs was to replace them with new, eminently logical ones. At first, therefore, they aligned graves randomly and for decades interred bodies with no graveside prayer at all. After all, the clergymen argued, what was important was the soul, not the carcass. In sermon after sermon Puritan clerics emphasized the way to salvation and the dangers of popery. They stripped away the few remnants of Catholic practice and tried to substitute reasonable doctrine. And they failed.

Every New England town owned a burying ground, and the location of the town meetinghouse determined its site. Typically, the meetinghouse stood at the approximate geographical center of town, and the graveyard lay on one side of it. Settlers were not particular about which side, but they did attempt to recreate something of the old-country churchyard because death and Satan were frighteningly palpable, and the nearby meetinghouse offered some slight protection from the evils so vividly described by Puritan preachers.

New Englanders personified death. In 1728, for example, the Massachusetts clergyman Thomas Prince preached a funeral sermon for his father. He described Death in terms like those used by the Austrian writer Johann von Saaz in 1500. "Some He on sudden pierces with gashfull wounds and intollerable torments: some He kills as quick as lightning: some He strangles, and some He crushes all to pieces," announced Prince. "He drinks up their spirits, and works like poison, like the gall of asps within them."[26] When von Saaz wrote *A Beautiful Discus-*

sion Between a Husbandman and Death such personification was common; when Prince published his sermon it was the only way of describing death. New Englanders lived each day in preparation for death and judgment and educated their children to do likewise by resorting to medieval imagery and spatial design.

Puritans designed their graveyards as teaching devices, as unmistakable reminders of the coming of Death. Very few graveyards were carefully tended, and because meetinghouses and adjacent burying grounds were deliberately sited on infertile soil, vegetation was frequently scraggly. No ornamental planting was attempted but here and there a graveyard was encircled with a stone wall. In 1648, for example, the Massachusetts Bay Colony town of Roxbury employed one of its husbandmen in walling off its burying ground. It ordered John Woody to build a strong stone wall and a double gate six or eight feet wide, and to complete the task within six months. Until the end of the eighteenth century such consideration usually derived from town meeting wishes to lease graveyards as pasture. But once walled, the typical graveyard was not otherwise maintained. Joshua Lamb donated a quarter of an acre in 1725 to enlarge it but he noted that he was "reserving to himself the herbage thereof." Graveyard grass was indeed the richest grass, but only after a century of burials.[27]

The Roxbury graveyard was a wilderness in the midst of shaped space and structure, a chaos that gave every passerby a terrible reminder of death. Weeds and English grass obscured the stones except where paths were worn, and many markers leaned half-toppled by frost. A graveyard such as that so carelessly abandoned in Roxbury was more than a memento mori. It was a carefully articulated emblem of the wildness of personified death. To the Puritan, life was represented by the town, by the cleared and cultivated land; death was represented by the wilderness. Every graveyard, then, was intentionally chaotic, intentionally representative of sudden pierces, stranglings, great disorders, darkness, and horror.

Puritan gravestones deliberately complemented the chaos. Each stone marked the grave of an honest man or woman, for New Englanders denied suicides and other criminals graveyard burial.[28] More importantly, however, each stone reinforced the meaning of graveyard disorder in a carefully selected epitaph that accompanied the chiseled name and dates. Townspeople were expected to pass by the graveyard every day to note its tangle of weeds and leaning stones and to ponder the epitaphs that whispered from what Cotton Mather called the "invisible world."

Puritan gravestones are portal-shaped, and the shape is significant. Each stone represents the portal through which every dying Puritan passed. On one side of the portal everything was bright and cultivated but on the other things were mysterious indeed. Many Puritans died convinced that they were predestined for eternal bliss; for them death's portal opened on light alone. Others died loathing their own sinfulness, fearing the Hell so skillfully pictured in Sabbath-day sermons. Most died uncertain, and in their uncertainty conceived only wildness. To stand in a Puritan graveyard was to stand alone between Heaven and the pit, to read the meaning of the epitaphs and the portal-shaped stones. Indeed the graveyard was the stopper of Hell.

It remained so until the late eighteenth century, when Unitarianism replaced Puritan dogma and New Englanders abandoned the old dread of death. New Haven's New Burying Ground, designed in 1796 by James Hillhouse when the Old Burying Ground proved so crowded with coffins and gravestones that the townspeople determined upon a wholly new graveyard, was the first to represent the change in philosophy. A ten-acre field was leveled and enclosed, remarked one observer in 1821, and "then divided into parallelograms, handsomely railed, and separated by alleys of sufficient breadth to permit carriages to pass each other." Each parallelogram was purchased by an individual family (except several reserved for religious congregations, Yale College, and the poor) and ornamented with trees and marble stones. New Haven's New Burying Ground objectified more than the geometrical spirit that swept the new nation; it manifested a far less fearful attitude toward the afterlife. Urns and willows and the simple phrase "sacred to the memory of" replaced the skulls, hourglasses, and lengthy epitaphs of Puritan headstones. The New Burying Ground epitomized rational order in this world—and the next.

Europeans were immediately impressed with its layout, as Edward A. Kendall proved in an 1809 description. The ground "is a square plot of large extent, divided by smooth walks into small squares. These squares are again divided into squares so minute as to be reasonably occupied by families." New Haven's fascination with squares (or parallelograms) fascinated Kendall, who noted that "the squares are bordered by trees which unfortunately are not square also, but which, being Lombardy poplars, have promised to grow with the least irregularity possible."[29] In 1796 the New Burying Ground was unique; by the 1850s its form was common throughout New England, wherever large towns outgrew their old graveyards and men outgrew seventeenth-century dogma.

Tidewater settlers confronted death and burial too but in a manner different from New Englanders.[30] Many southerners, at least in the early seventeenth century, were Anglican, and were convinced like Catholics that dying was mitigated by the church. A Puritan who left his town entered a dark, thick forest filled with unknown evils; clergymen used the wilderness through which men traveled alone as an image of death. Southerners, however, approached death as they did their forests, secure in their own worth and heartened by a staunch belief that the Church of England consigned few men and women to Hell. Tidewater and Piedmont graveyards never existed as contrived wildernesses or as reminders of demise. Instead they objectified two beliefs dear to southerners: family and indiscriminate location.

Southern colonists buried their loved ones in private plots consecrated sometimes by clergymen but more often by lay prayer. Behind most houses lay a burying ground carefully tended by relatives or by slaves. Unlike New Englanders, southerners took care to maintain the surface of the plot; in many regions the living scraped the surface of the burying ground once or twice each year.[31] Husbandmen worked hard to keep grass out of their cotton fields, and more than one hoped to rest under open ground after a lifetime of hoeing. As in New England, the earliest markers were wooden, but within several decades southerners carved markers from sandstone or iron rock or some other locally available stone. Unlike Puritan markers, the gravestones were carefully maintained by family descendants. Traditionally, southern family and community burying grounds were planted with cedars, gardenias, mimosas, and crepe myrtle. Near almost every southern house lay a plot of contrived beauty.

Family graveyards remained beautiful only through continuous maintenance, particularly "scraping." Many returned to wilderness when families chose to move on to fertile, virgin soil, and by the early nineteenth century southerners were familiar with abandoned graveyards everywhere. In many the few small stones were submerged in leaves or humus, and only a low wall or stand of cedars or mimosas announced the land's former use. Hunters wandering in the grown-over cotton fields learned to jump backward over any grave they accidentally crossed; to fail to do so was to ensure the death of a kinsman. Southern burial was always uncertain because the caretakers were likely to move away but graveyards were carefully respected whether cared for or not.

In the backcountry of Virginia and the Carolinas and everywhere in New York and the other Middle Colonies, family plots outnumbered community graveyards.[32] Like the Catholic estensiónes of New Spain, the inwardly focused New England towns were religiously pure; no one hesitated to bury a relative in the community graveyard because everyone in the graveyard was there by right. In New York, Pennsylvania, and the southern backcountry, people of many denominations lived in perfect harmony but were unwilling to be buried side by side. Quakers, Dutch Reformed, Methodists, Baptists, and Anglicans might have solved their difficulties by making denominational graveyards in every neighborhood but the family plot was a simpler solution. South and west of New England, community graveyards remained rare until like-minded settlers grew numerous enough to make and maintain them.

Funerals were neighborhood affairs in New Spain, New England, the South, and the West. Mourners gathered at the estensión, or town graveyard, and at the family plots behind houses. Even New Englanders recognized the social meaning of burial and by the 1650s spent large sums to provide rum, cider, and sugared water to mourners assembled after the interment. In 1712, for example, the estate of John Richard of Plymouth paid for thirty-three gallons of rum and a "hundred of sugar." Such an amount of rum was far greater than that provided by the public treasury at the raising of a meetinghouse or other public building. If drunkenness resulted, at least the occasion was safer than raisings, and the rum encouraged people to drown their fear of death along with their sorrow. Conversation flowed as freely as rum, however, and perhaps folk remembered the deceased with kindness. Almost no one described common rural funerals; participants thought them unworthy of comment, and even discerning travelers rarely discovered one in progress or else had the good grace to ride on and not intrude. "Americans most commonly bury their dead near the place where they die," remarked John Woods in an 1822 description of "the Illinois country," and "erect a small pale fence around the grave, to prevent its being disturbed."[33] Perhaps Woods failed to note the social significance of burial even though he understood the ease with which Americans accepted religious pluralism. "I have had much conversation with Baptists, Methodists, and Quakers," he commented in a passage on religious harmony. "They all expressed much charity for those of other sects, although most of them seemed to have a high opinion of their own."[34] Private burying grounds derived from high opinion but the funerals held in them derived from open-minded charity—and perhaps a need for sociability.

Burying grounds accomplished in the southern and Middle States and in the grid-country what the hierophanies of church and meetinghouse accomplished in New Spain estensiónes and New England towns. Graveyards gave sacred meaning to land platted according to civil law and sold according to economic demand. Every rural neighborhood was eventually marked by dozens of tiny eruptions of holiness, places where the world of farms and canals and section lines intersected the world of angels and infernal spirits. The graveyards did not order the land; no roads converged on them and no villages grew about them. But they ordered residents' perception of the land and gave identity to every neighborhood.

CAMP MEETINGS

"At first appearance," Richard M'Nemar remarked in 1808, "those meetings exhibited nothing to the spectator but a scene of confusion that could scarce be put into human language." Throughout the first half of the nineteenth century, clergymen, foreign observers, and born-again Christians struggled to describe the confusion and wonder of the great religious revival meetings held across the South and the Midwest. Believers saw New World models of New Testament prototypes; again and again they described the vast crowds gathered in Kentucky and Indiana groves in terms formerly reserved for multitudes gathered in Galilee. Scoffers witnessed only hysteria, immorality, and the illusion of divine grace. No observer, however, dismissed the great convocations. One thousand, 10,000, or 20,000 people temporarily assembled for worship deserved attention.

M'Nemar described the earliest camp meetings, informal and unplanned convocations that attracted the farmers of the upland South.[35] Little is known about the Kentucky meetings that set Bourbon and Harrison counties ablaze with the Holy Spirit or with mass hysteria and that sparked hundreds more to the east and north. Determined preachers discovered thousands of frontier families living beyond the range of the moribund and suspect Anglican Church and thirsting—more or less—for organized religion. Presbyterian, Baptist, and especially Methodist clergymen offered an attractive alternative to the formal, read service of the Anglicans and advertised their alternative in every mountain valley. Itinerant preachers conducted services in barns, cabins, and under trees; they emphasized sermons and hymns, not prayer books. Many were not particularly well educated but felt "the call to preach" and understood the half-literate, rough-living men and women who comprised their congregations far better than the seminary-trained clergymen who quickly retreated to the Tidewater. Throughout the Revolutionary War and the decades following, southern frontier religion acquired the characteristics that infuriated New Englanders and mystified foreigners.

In 1800 and 1801 several itinerant preachers, chiefly Methodists, wondered at the larger and larger crowds enthusiastically attending their
occasional services. Buildings proved too small to hold the congregations, and the preachers decided to advertise a series of outdoor meetings. Attendance grew with religious feeling.[36] People feared the end of
the world, the judgment of sinners, the last offer of God's grace. On
August 6, 1801, twenty thousand people converged on an obscure woodlot in Bourbon County and worshiped for six days. The meeting at Cane
Ridge sparked hundreds more, but none ever surpassed it for excitement and meaning.

"At night, the whole scene was awfully sublime," wrote one contemporary. "The ranges of tents, the fires, reflecting light amidst the branches
of the towering trees; the candles and lamps illuminating the encampment; hundreds moving to and fro, with lights or torches, like Gideon's
army; the preaching, praying, singing and shouting, all heard at once,
rushing from different parts of the ground, like the sound of many
waters, was enough to swallow up all the powers of contemplation."
More than any other word, *awe* informs the descriptions of Cane
Ridge.[37] The meeting was indeed awe-inspiring. In a land without cities,
without even large towns, where towns of any size were few and villages
were fewer, the crowd itself was extraordinary. Eighteen Presbyterian
ministers and unknown numbers of Baptist and Methodist preachers
stood shouting above the din of reforming sinners, saved sinners, and
hopeless sinners, above the din of crying infants, braying horses, and
hymn-singing or praying believers. It was perhaps America's first mul-
timedia experience. Firelight reflected from the trees above and from
the faces of the multitude milling about, and the thunder of voices
carried for miles. "The noise was like the roar of Niagara," wrote one
self-confessed scoffer. "The vast sea of human beings seemed to be
agitated as if by a storm. I counted seven ministers, all preaching at one
time, some on stumps, others in wagons, and one standing on a tree
which had, in falling, lodged against another." James B. Finley arrived to
scoff, but he soon experienced "a peculiarly-strange sensation" that
afflicted his heart and his knees and prompted him to walk far into the
woods to recover his original calm. Finley was not alone in his terrified
observations; one clergyman counted the fallen and arrived at the
number: 3,000.[38] Eventually the spirit, divine or otherwise, overmas-
tered Finley although he had retreated to the surrounding woods a
second time. The scoffer was converted and became an itinerant clergyman himself.

Cane Ridge was not the largest camp meeting; at least one other, at

Camp meeting in progress. From Gorham, *Camp Meeting Manual.*

Cabin Creek, attracted 20,000 people. But Cane Ridge proved the worth of the revival meeting technique. Thousands of sinners were born again, and many others were awakened to their impending doom. Clergymen, particularly circuit-riding Methodists, planned additional meetings and eventually regularized them across the upland South and in the western states. Most convened in late September, when families finished summer farmwork and the summer heat lessened, and although few attracted more than several thousand individuals, almost all developed loyal followings. Camp meetings offered all the delights of cities and required few urban responsibilities.

Much of the excitement of camp-meeting convocations derived from the pure pleasure of group activity. For families accustomed to week-long isolation and hard work, meetings offered a social release unlike that of raisings, bees, and funerals. Neighborhood gatherings attracted only neighbors, but camp meetings attracted strangers, and strangers among strangers lost their inhibitions.[39] Born-again sinners expressed the power of the Holy Spirit by leaping over tree stumps, by barking, and by jerking and rolling in the dust. One German observer noted that the hearers' "sighing, groaning, howling, quaking, clapping, rubbing, and wringing their hands, barking like dogs, and making a noise like the rushing of several streams" was once regarded as the Devil's work. Frederik von Raumer witnessed none of the violent nonverbal exercises that scandalized other camp-meeting visitors such as Finley, but such gymnastics were commonplace. Women ripped open their dresses, men danced wildly, and both sexes rolled head over heels through the crowd. Anonymity encouraged such outbursts and attracted hordes of staid but curious individuals intrigued by them. Novelty and mystery suffused every camp meeting as they did stories of every far-off city.

Not everyone came to pray. Many believers discovered the financial rewards of establishing temporary horse-pounds, boarding tents, bread-stalls, and tobacco shops, and countless others bought and sold horses and land between and during services. One writer reported that politicians gathered at camp meetings along with constables and bill collectors. Hucksters arrived to sell boot polish, newspapers, books, and liquor (more than one observer noted the thirst worked up by praying and shouting) and to hawk services such as barbering, physic, and "pulling teeth." Dandies and beaus arrived to woo "the numbers of young, beautiful, and accomplished ladies, who, arrayed in rich and costly attire, spend their golden moments in thoughtless levity."[40] Criminals congregated to rob and cheat, and prostitutes arrived to tempt. Immorality troubled every clergyman and alarmed the righteous—after the Saturday evening service at Cane Ridge, for example, a woman of easy virtue was discovered entertaining six men beneath a preaching platform. All manner of sin was possible according to the preachers; adultery was forever suspected and sometimes proved, and young people fell into every vice from gambling to inchastity. Brawlers and scoffers assembled to heckle the preachers and to fight with the righteous dispatched to silence them.[41] Camp-meeting days crackled with potential excitement, with the electric confrontation of saints and sinners.

Camp-meeting grounds quickly reflected the religious and social needs of the vast but temporary congregations. Siting the ground was a complex exercise worked out over three decades and formalized in an 1857 manual that enumerates eleven essential characteristics of a good location. Since "a congregation of several thousands will consume an amount of water entirely incredible to persons not experienced in such matters," of first importance is "a bountiful supply of good water." Everything else, adequate nearby pasture, ease of access from principal roads, a nearly complete "canopy of shade," a level central place, windbreaks, and a central location in the region, is secondary to the supply of drinking water.[42] Not every participant left a camp meeting invigorated by the Holy Spirit and fresh air; dysentery and other diseases spread through some meetings and caused an immense concern with sanitation. Discovering a perfect site taxed local talent but because groups purchased or received as gifts the best locations, site-hunting troubled few regions for long.

Improving the site involved a week's work by selfless men who cleared away brush, stumps, and roots and trimmed branches to a height of twelve feet. One or two experienced clearers of land inspected the site for diseased limbs that might fall on the worshipers and chopped away any they discovered. The same crew graded the central ground and built one or more preaching stands of varying complexity. Sometimes the stands were simple platforms, but sometimes too they were roofed and equipped with doors and stairs; almost always they stood at the north end of the ground so that congregations never faced the sun. After they finished the stands, the builders laid out log seats and built an "altar," a kind of enclosure (sometimes called a "pen" by preachers) near the stands. Within the pen they fashioned a number of seats for the "mourners," those people afflicted with particularly grievous feelings of sinfulness and anxious that the entire multitude pray for them. Since mourners were likely to pass out or engage in the jerks or rollings, penning them in was a sound idea. Not only did the enclosure protect the fallen from being trampled, but it focused the multitude's attention on the prime reason for the revival: saving souls. Around the circular or oblong ground were arranged rows and rows of tents, but only after the righteous—and the doubters and the confirmed sinners—arrived.

Order vanished as the canvas or sailcloth tents sprang up among the trees. Families located their tents wherever they liked, and most crowded around the perimeter of the open worship area. Until the 1820s many people slept in sexually segregated communal tents, but as camp-meetings were regularized more and more families abandoned the fifty-foot-long "society" tents for much smaller private tents divided into two sections. The front "room" served as a kitchen and parlor, and the back functioned as a sleeping compartment.[43] Clergymen disliked "family tents" because they reinforced the urge to gossip and cook, but they understood that nearly everyone preferred them. "Board tents," hovels built of split or sawed lumber, were disapproved of by almost every experienced camper. Wooden structures leaked, "produced low and ludicrous ideas," blocked sunlight, and mocked "the goodly tents of Jacob" mentioned in Numbers. Snowy white tents alone did not ensure order, however, even though experts preferred them to wooden dwellings.

The narrow footpaths that separated the tents quickly acquired the character and reputation of urban alleys. At mealtime they were blocked by women and girls cooking over open fires that constantly threatened to

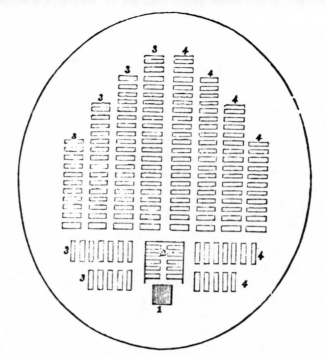

Ground plan of Camp Ground, **14** *by* **16** ***rods.*** **Scale,; 5**
rods to the inch.

REFERENCES:

1. Stand, or speakers' platform.
2. Altar.
3. Seats — ladies' side.
4. Seats — gentlemen's side.
C. Circle on the outside of which the tents are to be built.

Plan of camp-meeting ground. From Gorham, *Camp Meeting Manual.*

ignite the entire complex, and late in the evening they were packed with men and boys exchanging stories. During services and late at night they were frequented by backsliders, the irreligious, and people seeking sin. Such characters lurked half-hidden by the many acute angles produced by the haphazardly arranged tents and by the height of the tents themselves. Adulterers and other sinners skulked about, relatively secure in their anonymity and usually unseen. Rules of order were printed and prominently posted at many campgrounds, and civil law enforcement officers were sometimes hired to patrol the tent areas.[44] Despite rules and patrolmen and the firm orders of clergymen, the footpaths offered easy access to vice.

Southern camp meetings attracted hill farmers and artisans, not the owners of large plantations. Until the 1840s most wealthy owners of slaves were Anglicans who only sneered at camp-meeting sects. Attendance at camp meetings was not predominantly white, however, because many farmers owned one or two slaves and realized that the slaves had to be brought to meeting lest they run away in their masters' absence. Most southern camp-meeting grounds were racially integrated, although slaves preached, mourned, prayed, sang, danced, jerked, sinned, and camped in one part of the grove. Black preachers enjoyed the opportunity to gather large audiences, and family members relished the opportunity to visit members sold to distant masters. Blacks partook too of the extraordinary emotional power of the gathering—they sang, groaned, rolled, and jerked with as much abandon as the whites a few yards away. At many meetings the last service was interracial—masters and slaves joined together to pray over the most recalcitrant sinners, to glorify God in song, and to march in a great torchlight procession.[45]

Camp-meeting theology reinforced the fleeting nature of the gathering. Unlike the doctrines of New England Puritanism and subsequent Congregationalism and Unitarianism, and unlike Quakerism and Lutheranism, the theology developed in frontier revival meetings emphasized the individuality of salvation. Not only did the individual initiate redemption by requesting divine aid, but the individual alone received grace. Certainly the friends and strangers praying for his or her salvation were important but the battle and the victory (or defeat) were personal.[46] Puritan, Anglican, and Quaker divines emphasized to one extent or another the immense importance of God's initiation of the salvation process and the significance of the church; Mather's sermon on neighborliness derived from a theology that balanced individual salvation against group responsibility. The sermons thundering about camp-meeting grounds stressed the uniqueness of individual sin and the uniqueness of individual grace. Hymns, not biblical explication or intricate polemics, revealed the individuality of salvation. Camp-meeting participants saw salvation and the entire camp-meeting experience in personal, private terms: sinner and God are on intimate private terms in many hymns that were sung by thousands assembled for private benefit. The camp-meeting community was comprised of self-interested individuals. Only the preachers and the selfless saints in the throng prayed for the mass of unconverted, cold-hearted sinners. Most participants prayed chiefly for themselves.

In January the camp-meeting ground was empty; from the roadside it looked like a well-kept woodlot although from the garbage he saw at one deserted grove Thoreau determined that "a camp-meeting must be a singular combination of a prayer-meeting and a picnic." Travelers, particularly Europeans, endeavored to visit at least one camp meeting but they cared nothing for the camp-meeting ground itself. For fifty-one weeks in the year it scarcely existed in anyone's imagination; unlike a crossroads store it sat at no intersection, and unlike any of the thousands of family graveyards it attracted no one except at a previously designated time. Late in September, however, it became a city, with all the city's delights and vexations. It depended for its existence upon an almost crime-free countryside—even its ardent supporters realized that farmers felt uneasy when abandoning their farms for three or four days— and upon a crop-based agriculture. Not every agriculturist could leave his farm even if he cared for camp-meeting theology; cows had to be milked at morning and evening, penned-up chickens had to be fed twice daily, and coutless other chores needed daily attention. Nonetheless, southerners could leave corn and tobacco, and they did; they hitched their milk cows to their wagons and brought them to meeting and they turned their other livestock into the forest. Wherever southerners and southern agricultural practice moved, the camp meeting followed, deep into Tennessee, Texas, Indiana, Illinois, and Arkansas. It gave families a yearly glimpse of city life, and a yearly dose of urban problems. Its theology encouraged individualism, not the communitarianism necessary for urban life.

RURAL CHURCHES

As the frontier grew more settled, the range of camp meetings extended and contracted. Westerners adopted the practice of yearly revival meetings but each meeting attracted families from smaller regions. In the early decades of the nineteenth century a revival meeting drew families from a circle 100 miles in diameter; by the 1840s the circle had shrunk by half but the number of participants remained the same, or else grew. Many groves developed into year-round religious centers; a small church building replaced the trees or else stood to one side of the grove still used, for old time's sake, once each summer.[47] A few of the groves developed into prosperous towns (names such as Pleasant Grove, Holly Grove, Prairie Grove, Fox River Grove, Buffalo Grove, Franklin Grove, Beech Grove, Pilot Grove, and Mountain Grove today identify towns in the Old Southwest and Old Northwest regions that began as camp-meeting grounds) but most groves, even those eventually dignified by a simple church building used every Sunday, served rural neighborhoods that lacked clustered-village centers.

Like Lewis F. Allen's *Rural Architecture*, the Reverend Mr. Gorham's *Camp Meeting Manual* presented the best of traditional designs, and like farmhouses and camp-meeting grounds, most rural church buildings away from New England (where locals called them "meetinghouses") derived from tradition.[48] Few attracted the attention of foreign travelers, partly because they were undistinguished by the architectural standards of Europe and partly because they were frequently located far from main-traveled roads. Unlike the exquisite white meetinghouse that marked the geographical center of almost every New England town and charmed observant passersby like Timothy Dwight, backcountry church buildings were erected by farmers and carpenters who understood almost nothing of intricate architectural ornamentation and who relied on voluntary contributions from small congregations, not sums raised (as in New England towns) through government-collected taxes. Rural churches displayed nothing complicated and nothing expensive. Spires, for example, were lacking, as were belfries—and sometimes bells—and large windows, porches, and windvanes. Backcountry church buildings resembled houses or barns and caused few travelers to remark their simple beauty.

Old Rehoboth Methodist Church in Monroe County, West Virginia, objectifies backcountry religion and ecclesiastical architecture. Services were first held in the poplar grove that abuts the church and later in settlers' houses and a schoolhouse. In 1785, one farmer donated a small lot of land for a church building and an additional five acres for a burying ground. In June 1786 the structure was completed, made of logs like all other nearby buildings and roofed with slabs held down by heavy poles. At one end and along both sides the farmers erected a solid gallery so that more worshipers might crowd into it.[49] Near its door was a heap of rocks to support a bonfire that warmed the parishioners before they entered the structure; once inside, they expected to be warmed by the preaching. A traveler passing along the nearby road that eventually became the Union-Sweets Turnpike easily might have mistaken the church building for a large house, especially if evening was approaching and he was tired.

Church buildings such as Old Rehoboth Methodist Church helped organize the landscape but only for people intimately familiar with the landscape. Strangers understood the landmark significance of the white spires thrusting above New England woods. Sooner or later, New England town roads converged on the meetinghouse, and near the house of God was usually an inn for travelers. Elsewhere in the United States backcountry church buildings stood along roads, not always at crossroads and often alone; their ministers lived a mile or two away, and only on Sunday was a traveler likely to discover anyone near them.

Denominational pluralism explains the siting of many backcountry church buildings. After the late eighteenth- and early nineteenth-century wave of religious awakening and ecumenicalism, rural populations divided and divided again into a bewildering array of denominations and sects, the members of each building their own structure for worship. Methodist, Presbyterian, and Baptist church buildings dotted the backcountry, along with edifices erected by Disciples of Christ, Assemblies of God, Universalists, and dozens of other, far smaller denominations.[50] Many congregations accepted no larger denominational affiliation at all and called themselves churches of God. In New Spain and New England such pluralism was unthinkable; civil government maintained the established denomination, Catholic or Puritan. As late as the 1830s Massachusetts towns collected taxes to support Congregational clergymen; dissenters, Baptists in particular, fought long and hard against supporting their own and the "established" clergy, along with two meetinghouses, their own and "the town's." Estensiónes and New England towns focused on single ecclesiastical structures because their residents either forbade or only slightly encouraged the building of others.[51] It was a relatively simple matter to determine the geographic center of town and to site the meetinghouse—many New England town meetings drew lines from each boundary corner and located the meetinghouse at the intersection—and to direct the roads to the meetinghouse. Almost everywhere in New England meetinghouse location was synonymous with civil center; town meetings were held in the town's meetinghouse, often after Sabbath-day services, and throughout the nineteenth century town halls and sometimes schools stood on the "town field" aubtting the structure. Elsewhere in the nation denominational pluralism ensured a multitude of ecclesiastical structures in every civil jurisdiction, most located near the center of their supporters on any lot of land that was free or inexpensive.

In time the bewildering locations of backcountry church buildings were memorized by families "in the neighborhood," and children and adults directed lost travelers to turn right or left at or a mile past a specific building. Sometimes the travelers recognized the church building for what it was but occasionally they did not. Almost invariably, however, they missed the cultural significance of the small, simple structures located in no apparent pattern.[52] Backcountry houses of worship made sacred the grid-ordered countryside devised by Enlightenment deists. Along back roads across the emerging West were countless irruptions of the sacred, hierophanies where Heaven intersected earth. The number of church buildings in a particular valley, county, or neighborhood indicated the godliness of its residents, and by many accounts, backcountry Americans (after the camp meeting years anyway) were especially godly, if not theologically precise. Church buildings did not dominate the landscape but they marked neighborhood and denominational affiliations clearly recognized by residents.

SCHOOLHOUSES

Formal education came late to many colonies away from New England and Pennsylvania, and it spread slowly through the Republic. As late as 1834 B. F. Morris lamented in the *Schoolmaster and Academic Journal* that more than 4 million free white children were "without even a common school." Other editors, columnists, and reformers shared his belief that education alone preserved democratic government, and his alarm at the ignorance believed to prevail across the South and in the states and territories west of the Appalachians. Like most other Yankee schoolmasters and reformers, Morris understood public education in small-scale neighborhood terms; he envisioned school "districts" and helped convince the nation to educate its children according to the New England way—in schoolhouses.[53]

America was explored and settled during the two centuries following Gutenberg's invention of movable type. Away from New Spain, colonists thought in two traditions, one old—almost ancient—and oral, and one far newer and written. Oral tradition guided the choosing of soil, the felling of trees, the planting of crops; it shaped graveyards and persecuted witches. While far less venerable, the tradition of literacy influenced concepts of government, law, and the celestial spheres, the practice of medicine and surveying, and the accounting of business, particularly commerce. Above all, it fueled the fires of religious discord and discovery; the Bible was easily available to anyone along with innumerable tracts, diatribes, and explications. Puritanism and all the other Protestant denominations derived from accessible Scripture and impassioned written argument. And education was transformed even as the American wilderness was transformed into landscapes—sometimes deliberately, often accidentally.

Seventeenth-century education meant domestic education except in a few New England towns. Parents explained the intricacies of husbandry and housewifery to sons and daughters eager to know about planting times, natural dyes, and kitchen gardens. Craftsmen instructed their sons, and the apprenticed sons of neighbors, in crafts such as milling and shipbuilding, smithing and carpentry. Almost all such teaching was oral and spiced with countless examples; little of it related directly to the reading and writing taught in the morning and evening by parents and older siblings.[54] Learning to read was made easier by well-chosen texts; children knew by heart the Lord's Prayer and such classics as Michael Wigglesworth's 224-stanza-long "Day of Doom" before they spelled out the words. Daily Bible readings, communal readings, and responsive readings occupied many colonial families too; reading was one path to salvation, and by 1700 most New Englanders and many other colonists knew that it was a likely route to earthly wealth as well.

In 1647 the Massachusetts Bay Colony, aware that "it being one chief project of that old deluder, Satan, to keep men from the knowledge of the Scriptures," provided for formal public schooling. "It is therefore ordered," the General Court agreed, "that every township in this juris-diction, after the Lord hath increased them to the number of fifty householders, shall then forthwith appoint one within their town to teach all such children as shall resort to him to write and read."[55] Not every town obeyed the order but since each ordinarily employed a learned clergyman, formal instruction even in the classics was usually possible. A knowledge of Latin fitted a boy for a chance at the new Harvard College and a career as a clergyman, and many parents insisted that their sons master the rudiments of the liberal arts. Other parents encouraged their sons, and sometimes their daughters, to progress be-yond the limits of domestic education if not to the fringe of the classics.

Matters differed in Virginia. In 1671 the colony governor reported to the Commissioners of Trade and Plantations that education languished. "But, I thank God, there are no free schools nor printing, and I hope we shall not have these for a hundred years," Berkeley wrote, "for learning has brought disobedience and heresy, and sects into the world, and printing has divulged them, and libels against the best government. God keep us from both!"[56] Not all Virginians agreed with their governor; most in fact disagreed with Berkeley about everything. But many simply did not care. By 1671 the indiscriminate settlement pattern built on estuaries, tobacco-exhausted land, and increasing skill at pioneering—and slavery—was already making preaching difficult. It was almost im-possible to assemble children in a schoolroom if they lived so far apart that their parents could not assemble in church. Here and there a weal-thy planter family hired an English or a Yankee tutor for its own chil-dren or bequeathed money or land to support a "free school," but most southerners learned to write and read at home, if they learned at all.

Every colony emphasized different approaches to public education but none coped successfully with the scattered settlement patterns so evident south of New England. Even as the Revolution increased men's desire for written information and for firsthand participation in government, more and more families lived too far, often hundreds of miles too far, for their children to walk to school in the early morning and walk home at dusk. Lamentations like those of Morris struck at national pride and common-sense concern, and gradually parents and politicians devised a way to educate the unschooled millions.

Localized education, or "the district system" as it was popularly known at the close of the eighteenth century, was a purely common innovation. New England town meetings gradually divided their towns into educational districts and charged each with building a schoolhouse, employing a teacher, and buying supplies. In 1789 the Massachusetts legislature formalized the practice, and eleven years later ordered the inhabitants of every district to determine sites for new schoolhouses and to tax themselves for school purposes; in 1827 the legislature permitted each district to elect a committee to oversee its building and teaching. The district system spread quickly throughout western and northern New England, across New York, and into Ohio, Michigan, Indiana, and Illinois; it moved southward more slowly, in part (as southerners admitted) because of scattered settlement patterns but also because of lack of interest.[57] And everywhere it was objectified by one-room, simply-constructed schoolhouses located in the oddest possible places.

Unlike farm and farmstead siting, and unlike the locating of crossroads stores and rural church buildings, schoolhouse siting involved entire neighborhoods and frequently revealed the petty mediocrity of rural democracy. Squabbling began when towns, townships, and counties determined the rough boundaries of their several school districts. In much of New England and the eastern parts of the Middle States neighborhoods were well understood by their residents and by the residents of the contiguous neighborhoods that comprised towns and townships. Defining school districts in neighborhood terms was sometimes ticklish but usually possible, and New Englanders prided themselves on clearly defined districts. Across the South and in the newly admitted western states, however, determining school districts was an infernally intricate matter involving not only perceived neighborhood boundaries but ratios of school-age children to area and expected population shifts.[58] Rectilinear lots and section roads exacerbated the problems already plaguing the South, western Pennsylvania, New York, and northern New England. In the grid country many farms were so large that spatial neighborhood was a dimly understood concept, especially if the land was newly or partially settled. Section sixteen failed as a location for township schools; it was too distant from township corners. It failed too as a source of income to support district schools; neither its sale nor its lease produced the funds necessary to pay several teachers.[59] When school districts were immediately perceived as congruent with neighborhoods, parents set about building a schoolhouse; when they were not easily identified, when parents argued about the inclusion of a single-child family that lived on the fringe of what everyone else called a neighborhood, argument persisted for months.

Once districts were determined to the satisfaction of all or most of the residents of the larger town or township, the inhabitants of each district set about siting a schoolhouse. Almost invariably they dismissed demographics. One part of the neighborhood might have more children than the others combined but there was usually little desire, even among its residents, to locate the schoolhouse in it. It was all too likely that the center of school-age children would shift within a year or so, and the schoolhouse seemed an almost immovable object. Instead, most districts sited their schoolhouses according to cheapness of land and geographic centrality. Only rarely did the simple compromise satisfy all parties. Almost never did it satisfy the children.

Critics scorned the compromise locations and by the 1830s their barbed remarks were venomous. "Many schoolhouses, because they must be in the center, are placed in such low swampy, and uninhabitable situations," wrote the directors of one New England county teachers' association, "that we are persuaded, not one of all concerned in erecting them, would with the gift of the land for a considerable distance around, have placed his own dwelling there, on account of the inconvenience, if not danger, he would apprehend from mire and water around it." Little hyperbole biased such denunciations. School siting according to geographic centers caused buildings to stand in ridiculous places. "A few years since one of these buildings was noticed," the directors continued, "situated in the midst of a wood, nearly half a mile from any house, and where from the little passing, there would be great difficulty in children's getting to school at all in the season, when schools are generally in operation, while with a little of the spirit of accommodation, this building might have stood on a very pleasant public road, on which most of the district lived."[60] Isolated schoolhouses marked every rural neighborhood interested in education; the buildings objectified the American commitment to education for democracy but their locations objectified democratic difficulties. Until the 1850s few farmers listened to the critics, and still fewer responded by relocating schoolhouses to healthful if off-center sites. In the first decades of the Republic and in the first decades of western settlement a schoolhouse itself seemed accomplishment enough.

Amish farmers "raising" a schoolhouse, 1980, central Pennsylvania. Photo courtesy of Christopher MacNeal.

Very often a public-spirited or tenderhearted if slightly selfish farmer donated a quarter-acre parcel as a schoolhouse site, and often it was accepted by a district determined to spare itself the cost of purchasing more centrally located land. Donating a "school lot" produced few tangible results. A few fathers worried about the effects of long winter walks on a sickly son or daughter, and others prized the labor time saved from hour-long walks to a distant schoolhouse. Not every donor was pleased with his decision, however, for most learned quickly about the dangers of recess. Every donor "knows that his own cultivated fields must and will be made the place of the scholars' recreation," remarked the authors of a *Report on School Houses* in defense of schoolhouse lots "large enough for the rational exercise which the children ought to have, and will take."[61] Isolated schoolhouses were consequently isolated for a very pragmatic reason. No farmer wanted his young oats trampled by a game of crack-the-whip or his mature English grass broken by youngsters playing hide-and-seek. No farmer wanted a horde of children balancing on his walls or fences or taking shortcuts through his fields. And no farmer wanted to host the pack of dogs that arrived lamb-like at school each day and tormented nearby livestock. By finding the geographic center of the neighborhood, many district committees placated farmers who wanted a schoolhouse as far as possible from their fields and riled only one or two who could hardly complain at geographic chance.

Like rural church buildings, most schoolhouses were erected by the

men of the district. Not every schoolhouse was carefully built, and many
that were not quickly deteriorated. "Do not imagine, in choosing a Building Committee," the editor of the *Farmer's Monthly Visitor* counseled his
readers in 1853, "that a man, because he has built a barn once upon a
time, that was capable of protecting cattle and their food from the
weather, is qualified for building a school house that shall best answer
the purpose of instruction."[62] Farmers simply did not understand the
necessities of schoolhouse design, the editor continued, and "hence we
have the most uncouth, ill-constructed specimens of schoolhouse architecture throughout the country." What perplexed farmers most about
building schoolhouses? Reformers differed, but many chose lighting as
the chief weakness in schoolhouse design. Windows were either too high
or too few or were symmetrically placed along both sidewalls. On cloudy
days children struggled to see their lesson books; on sunny days the glare
almost blinded those sitting next to the windows while shadows irritated
those seated near the center of the building. Part of the difficulty lay in
positioning the schoolhouse on its site. Aligning the structure on an
east–west axis troubled those students forced to sit in the glare from
south-facing windows. Aligning it at right angles to that axis meant opening doors into north winds or else—if the door or doors in the gable end
faced south—orienting the blackboard end of the structure to the north
and ensuring that morning sunlight fell across desks but not the
blackboard.[63] Farmers were not always aware of such problems, and
even when they were they discovered no easy solution. Other matters
such as the proper height of benches and desks, the distance from
blackboard to the rearmost benches, and the usefulness of any particular
sort of stove in evenly heating one large room confused them further.
Sometimes a carpenter or two gave good advice and sometimes a well-
built prototype prompted several copies, but most often the district inhabitants assembled on raising day and built a strcuture remarkably like
a house or small church building.

Like lighthouses, schoolhouses were invented. No tradition of design
and material guided the farmers who built them; some structures were
almost square while others were rectangular, some in the North were
heavily framed, some in the South were built of logs. Reformers claimed
that most were built poorly, using the cheapest materials, and often the
reformers were correct. Children were expected to bear discomfort because discomfort built character; straight-back benches and overheated
stoves were part of the educational experience. It was more than the
poorly constructed buildings that prompted so many critics, like one
quoted approvingly in an 1856 issue of the *Wisconsin Farmer,* to remark

that they "could at once tell a district school house from any other build-ing, by its being the *worst-looking* house in the neighborhood."[64] Unfamil-iarity with purpose or difficulty in planning cannot fully explain "broken windows and broken walls, and a general air of desolation." The poorly sited structures cannot be laid to compromise alone.

Contrary to the orations of the period, Americans—and farmers especially—viewed education with mixed feelings. Until the beginning of the nineteenth century education was chiefly experiential; sons learned farming from fathers, who showed them the techniques of their fathers. Reading was necessary for salvation and to interpret the almanac at planting time but was otherwise secondary to the enormously rich oral tradition that explained husbandry, housewifery, and well nigh every-thing else. Settlers erected church buildings before schoolhouses, there-fore, because they considered salvation vastly more important than the techniques and knowledge acquired in formal schooling. Schoolhouses reflected people's assessment of formal education: necessary but neither immensely important nor immediately useful. Only in cities, where ex-panding commerce made clear the growing usefulness of wide learning, were schoolmasters respected and schoolhouses carefully built. Else-where, especially in the southern and western backcountry, schoolmas-ters were as funny as Washington Irving's Ichabod Crane and schoolhouses as primitive as Sleepy Hollow's citadel of learning.[65] Editors and other writers understandably supported the growing power of written knowledge, particularly that knowledge they published, and labored to convince farmers that schooling was far more necessary than it had been in the late eighteenth and early nineteenth centuries.

"There is no better index to the character of a people than their schoolhouses," asserted one *Wisconsin Farmer* letter writer. In 1856 many farmers still judged the character of a neighborhood by the quality of its fences, but more and more had recognized that much traditional knowl-edge like the influence of the moon on planting and harvest times was indeed little more than superstition and ignorance. "What is book farm-ing?" asked J. M. Merrick in a three-part *Farmer's Monthly Visitor* article entitled "Claims of Common Schools Upon the Farmer" in 1852. "Not theory or guesswork, but the result of profound and skilful enquiry, of an accurate analysis of the soil, of its products and of their relations to each other."[66] But book farming, he noted, is available only to those farmers well enough schooled to understand its complexities, and to sons studying in well-regulated district schools. "Go through our country towns and how small a number of young men will you find able to survey a farm accurately?"[67] Merrick did not doubt the dismal answer, but many farmers did. Few wanted to accept the overwhelming evidence that they and their sons were no more able to calculate the area of an irregularly shaped field than their seventeenth-century ancestors had been, and few wanted to admit that agricultural innovation confused and disheartened them because they could not understand it. Not until the last years of the nineteenth century, when state legislatures mandated school superintendents, normal-school-trained teachers, and standardized, sometimes consolidated school buildings, did rural schooling dramatically improve. Until then the one-room district schoolhouse objectified the final battle between oral and written traditions.

Lucky children received solid general educations in well-built, well-fitted, well-taught schools, and when they grew old recalled their school days with pleasure. Late nineteenth- and early twentieth-century American literature abounds with poems and short stories extolling the virtues of one-room schoolhouses surrounded by sumacs and creeping blackberry vines. Some of the visions are undoubtedly true, or only partly colored by time and wishful thinking; after all, the schools did produce the writers. Few writers paused to recall the "square pine box painted a glaring white on the outside and a desolate drab within" described by Hamlin Garland in *A Son of the Middle Border,* or to mention the millions of half-educated Americans who trusted old ways because their common-school learning proved so inadequate that they could not understand the new.[68]

Schoolhouses served purposes other than education, however, and in many neighborhoods the other purposes helped ensure well-built structures equipped with efficient stoves. At Christmas, for example, neighbors celebrated in the only nondenominational heated structure large enough to hold a hundred or more people; benches and tables were pushed to the walls, and people jammed against the blackboard and coatrack. Holding such ecumenical celebrations in the schoolhouse spared the neighbors the difficulty of honoring any particular rural church at the expense of another. By holding square dances in the schoolhouse, the same neighbors placated those who felt that dancing dishonored a church building. Perhaps politicians were invited to speak at schoolhouses for that reason too, or else they preferred a civil rather than a denominational forum. Occasional traveling lecturers invited the public into schoolhouses for discourses on "elevating and educational" topics, and now and then a tiny acting troupe performed on the teacher's dais. Such performances were rare, of course, because most schoolhouses were too small to shelter large audiences and too distant from population centers. Nevertheless, the buildings served well-defined social purposes as well as educational ones.

Despite their poor condition and intermittent use as social centers, schoolhouses exemplified the growing interest in printed wisdom. Within their walls oral tradition dictated almost nothing. To the schoolmaster proud of his rudimentary book learning, tradition was already superstition; to his scholars huddled about the stove or crowding the opened windows, it was what governed planting, harvest, and almost every shaping of land and structure. Tradition was manifest in the arrangement of fields and kitchen ells, in the alignment of graves, and in the style of corncribs, fences, and barns. Tradition clashed with innovation everywhere, but within schoolhouse walls the clash was loudest. A ticking pendulum clock regulated the passing hours; time was not marked by a "moving" sun or the lowing of cows. Printed maps contested with mental images of neighborhoods, counties, states, and nations; in 1789 Jedidiah Morse published *The American Geography* for adults and an abridged schoolroom edition "calculated early to impress the minds of American Youth with an idea of the superior importance of their own country, as well as to attach them to its interests."[69]

Topographical knowledge no longer derived only from topographical experience; Morse filled his book with maps, charts, and lengthy prose descriptions of states, regions, rivers, territories, forests, soils, and agricultural and mineral riches. *The American Geography* presented standards by which every neighborhood and its residents might be judged. "The good land in the southern counties lies principally on the banks of the rivers and creeks," wrote Morse of New Jersey. "The soil, on these banks, is generally a stiff clay; and while in a state of nature, produces various species of oak, hickory, poplar, chestnut, ash, gum, etc. The barrens produce little else but shrub oaks and white and yellow pines." Tradition only tinged such description; Morse emphasized that his information was scientific and reliable, and schoolmasters commanded students to memorize it. Scholars learned that New Hampshire was filled with mountains and cascades, that North Carolina "abounds with medicinal plants and roots" like ginseng, Virginia snakeroot, Seneca snakeroot, and lion's heart, and that the Spanish Dominions truly needed American improvement: "The characteristics of the Californians are stupidity and insensibility; want of knowledge and reflection; inconstancy, impetuosity, and blindness of appetite; an excessive sloth and abhorrence of all labour and fatigue; an excessive love of pleasure and amusement of every kind, however trifling or brutal; pusillanimity; and, in fine, a most wretched want of every thing which constitutes the real man, and renders him rational, inventive, tractable, and useful to himself and society."[70] Californians neglected rich soil, a productive climate, a valuable pearl fishery, and mines of gold of "very promising appearance" to sleep in the sun. Morse prepared thousands of American schoolchildren for the gold rush of 1849, for the great rush to the land where "there falls in the morning a great quantity of dew, which, settling on the rose leaves, candies, and becomes hard like manna, having all the sweetness of refined sugar, without its whiteness," for the great rush away from well-known neighborhoods and farms to lands imagined first in books, not oral tales.[71] Inside every schoolhouse tradition clashed with invention and imagination; almost always tradition lost to the invention and imagination recounted and inspired in books.

Across rural America, even in the South and along the southern frontier, alert people sought out books and found them at crossroads stores. All sorts of books lined one or two shelves in most "mercantile establishments," and storekeepers' ledgers reveal which sold faster than others. In Kentucky, southern Indiana, and southern Illinois schoolbooks outsold novels and biographies. Parents purchased grammars, spellers, and readers for children attending schools that did not supply them, or else purchased them and taught directly from them until they built a one-room schoolhouse and installed a teacher. Adults bought books for themselves too, particularly Bibles and other religious works such as hymnals, and they and precocious children browsed among the almanacs, dictionaries, histories, and other volumes offered for sale. Within a year after the settlement of Princeton in southern Indiana, for example, Robert Stockwell opened a general store and stocked it in part with books calculated to appeal to adults searching for relaxing fiction and inspiring history. Among the schoolbooks stood Brackenridge's picaresque novel *Modern Chivalry* and the anonymous *History of the War in America between Great Britain and the Colonies,* and a variety of almanacs.[72] Every crossroads store nurtured the evolving habit of reading, of testing tradition.

Every schoolhouse—and every store—represented an irruption of printed knowledge in an otherwise tradition-oriented neighborhood; like graveyards, Puritan meetinghouses, and crossroads church buildings, schoolhouses opened on another world, one not entirely trusted by farmers eager to keep sons and daughters sober and pure. Unlike canals, viaducts, and lighthouses, schoolhouses were locally controlled, but they represented the new age of written information and professional design as clearly as any structure erected by army-trained engineers. Book learning forever threatened to shake off the reins tightly held by district-school committees, overseers, and parents worried about sinful innovation and destructive invention. A good schoolteacher, they determined, was not necessarily one well read and well prepared; a young neighborhood lad or girl with a little learning was more easily trusted and more easily controlled than an outsider armed with new books and new maps and even newer ideas. Low salaries and occasional ridicule demeaned the schoolhouse educators, as did the custom of "boarding around." Uncertain young men and women condemned to eat and sleep with a different farm family each week or month were not always welcomed by men and women struggling to understand the intricacies of local soil and crops. *The American Geography,* like formal education, opened on a complex world not wholly desirable but not actually evil, a world entered through the schoolhouse door.

Schoolhouse location and design represented the mixed feelings almost perfectly; it was a rare nineteenth-century farmer who denied the advantages of some book learning, especially if the learning concerned agricultural chemistry, but not many advocated extensive educations for their sons, and still fewer suggested that girls receive lengthy formal training. Nowhere were the feelings more clearly reflected than in the South, where schoolhouses were few and laws forbade the teaching of slaves. Schoolhouses objectified the open door to experiment and social mobility that slaveholders denied, and schoolhouses were conspicuously absent in slaveowning regions. Wealthy planters employed family tutors and sidestepped harsh realities about neighboring poor white children no better educated than slaves. Olmsted learned the realities of ante bellum southern education during his long rides from crossroads store to plantation to poor-white hill cabin. "Nor is it possible for so small a number of whites to maintain a church or a newspaper," he remarked of the twenty or so poor white families living in a neighborhood dominated by a few wealthy owners of many slaves, "nor yet a school, unless it is one established by a planter, or two or three planters, and really of a private and very expensive character."[73] Throughout the first half of the nineteenth century southern formal education, especially rural southern formal education, languished as Governor Berkeley had hoped it would languish. Elsewhere district education existed with varying support from farmers more or less willing to accept printed rather than orally transmitted ideas. Here and there, where farmers embraced the values of "book farming," district education thrived. It thrived, in fact, as agricultural fairs thrived.

FAIRS

Elkanah Watson invented the American agricultural fair in 1809, in the small Massachusetts town of Pittsfield. His aim was simple. Farmers in the New England hill country were unacquainted with the fabulous Merino sheep smuggled out of Spain into the new republic. Periodicals like newspapers and agricultural magazines did not convince the Yankees to experiment with the new breed; Watson's extensive conversation also failed. So Watson hit upon the idea of tying two prize sheep to a tree on the town common and urging farmers to inspect them. "Many farmers, and even women, were excited by curiosity to attend this first novel, and humble exhibition," he recalled in 1820. "It was by this lucky accident, I reasoned thus,—If two animals are capable of exciting so much attention, what would be the effect on a larger scale, with larger animals? The farmers present responded to my remarks with approbation.—We became acquainted, by this little incident; and from that moment, to the present, agricultural societies, cattle shows, and all in connexion therewith, have predominated in my mind, greatly to the injury of my private affairs."[74] In the years immediately following his 1809 experiment Watson encouraged his neighbors to display their best livestock, to form an association to sponsor an annual exhibit at which livestock was judged and prizes were awarded and at which a distinguished orator spoke on the glory of farming. Watson invented an "agricultural ball" to entice farmwives and farmgirls, and discovered that the women wished to enter prize examples of domestic manufactures. His invention succeeded where several agricultural improvement societies had failed. Farmers did not adopt book farming exactly, but they came to the exhibits and looked and talked and learned about the latest techniques and seeds and breeds—and had a good time too. Agricultural fairs swept across the northern and northwestern states, educating farm families in agricultural invention and urban delights.

European fairs catered to merchants and craftsmen, not agriculturalists, and their tradition failed to cross the Atlantic. Still, Old World fairs such as the Sturbridge Fair described in 1753 by Daniel Defoe illustrate the essential attractiveness that led Simple Simon to walk the same road as the pieman. "It is impossible to describe all the parts and circumstances of this fair exactly," wrote Defoe in *A Tour Through the Whole Island of Great Britain.* "The shops are placed in rows like streets, whereof one is called Cheapside; and here, as in several other streets, are all sorts of traders, who sell by retail, and come chiefly from London. Here may be seen goldsmiths, toymen, brasiers, turners, milaners, haberdashers, hatters, mercers, drapers, pewterers, China-ware-houses, and, in a word, all trades that can be found in London; with coffeehouses, taverns, and eating houses, in great numbers; and all kept in tents and booths." Defoe marveled at the exotic merchandise, the crowds, and the pulsating excitement. "In a word," he concluded in wonderment, "the Fair is like a well-governed city, and there is the least disorder and confusion (I believe) that can be seen anywhere, with so great a concourse of people."[75] Certainly much of the order resulted from the holiday attitude of the people—most visitors came only to marvel and feast, not trade with the wholesalers and retailers—and from the Fair's rural location. Orderly streets and squares encouraged order too, perhaps, as did a conveniently located temporary court of justice. Most importantly, however, everything was new and intriguing and ephemeral; the fair opened in August and closed in September. For husbandmen and their families, and perhaps for petty merchants too, it provided a fantasy world in which people behaved well out of enchantment with their surroundings and with one another.

American agricultural fairs convened in September usually for one or two days, but they struck farm families almost as sharply as Sturbridge Fair struck Defoe. Within the enclosure made by fences and by tethered horses and buggies and farm wagons was an almost magic space, one devoted to the honor of husbandry, self-improvement by example, and sheer fun.

Orators such as Emerson, Thoreau, Whittier, Daniel Webster, Henry Clay, Stephen Douglas, and Martin Van Buren emphasized that farming supported the Republic, had always supported liberty, justice, and freeholding, and would conquer the forests—and prairies too, given time and luck—of the West. They spoke of farmers making land, of farmers defending cherished rights against British and French opponents, of farmers raising independent, intelligent (and hopefully well-churched and well-schooled) children to carry on the farming tradition. Like Watson, who by 1819 was a sought-after fair orator, the speakers told farmers what they wanted to hear: "You, who are so fortunate as to rest, and rise from your pillows, conscious you are freemen in all respects—that you are indebted to no man—that you fear the face of no man—and can step over your fields, the proud monarchs of the soil you cultivate in the sweat of your brows. You who are thus fortunate are doubly blessed—blessed beyond all other farmers in every other country—blessed beyond every other class of the community, in your own country."[76] Their addresses were reprinted entire or in excerpts in agricultural publications such as *The Plough Boy*. Editors knew that readers wanted to savor the memories of orations tailored to evoke cheers and instill self-confidence.

Confidence led to self-improvement. Farmers wandered about the fairgrounds impressed with themselves and with their calling, and evidenced an openness to experiment that amazed well-educated agricultural reformers accustomed to ridicule and rejection. Fairgoers confronted the latest agricultural contrivances and watched similar machines compete against one another for blue ribbons and other awards. Cyrus McCormick began his climb to fame and success when his reaper received a certificate of merit at the Hamilton County Fair in Ohio in 1844. Such prizes were powerful promotional material; they attested not only to quality, but quality in competition.

Every fairground provided arenas for bulls to compete with bulls, pies with pies, wheat with wheat, reapers with reapers. Many arenas were simple sheds or else pitched-roofed, wall-less structures designed to shelter prize stock and produce from sun and showers. Others were large corrals in which sheep and other animals were displayed by their owners during public judging. Open arenas attracted crowds of interested on-lookers delighted to learn about the best specimens of the best breeds, and delighted too by the suspense of the judging. Very often such judging ceremonies attracted farmers intrigued by breeds or strains mentioned in agricultural periodicals and eager to see how Short Horns compared in the flesh with Devons.

Not every contest was dignified and orderly. Plowing and drawing contests generated excitement, gambling, and all manner of noise. "The working oxen were tested with a loaded wagon weighing 3,600 lbs., on a well-selected piece of ground, where there was a short steep hill that severely tested their honesty, patience, strength, and excellent training," an anonymous letter-writer informed the readers of the *Cultivator* in 1840. "The three-year-old steers managed this load surprisingly; and Mr. E. Parker and his steers walked off with load and the first premium, greatly to their credit." Like any winner of such a contest, Parker could count on offers for his steers and for his breeding stock; he reaped more than shouts of approval. The anonymous correspondent described the Butternuts Fair in Otsego County, New York, at length, but he plainly enjoyed the drawing and plowing contests best. "There was on the ground, a committee to keep the time, and maintain order, and enforce the rules of the Society," he wrote of the plowing contest. "The time bill was then given to the judges of the work, who came on after it was finished and number; and they awarded the premiums to the respective numbers without knowing to whom they belonged; in this way all jealousy was laid to rest."[77] Contests emphasized the essential equality of the contestants; like the sections of the grid, one man was as good as the next, and any might try his skill. Not surprisingly, many did, to the edification and amusement of all.

Fairs, and especially contests, were theatrical exercises. Rural people flocked to them for a glimpse of another world, a world of patent medicine, shiny machines, household gadgets, and—above all—crowds. No experienced designer proposed ideal or even time-tested models of fairgrounds; most grounds were simple groves or fields given over to one or two days' excitement. Their most common feature was a great gateway arch through which fairgoers passed into the grounds. Not every fairgoer entered through the arch, especially if the fairgrounds were unfenced, but many did; it was a portal opening on knowledge— chiefly orally transmitted knowledge and knowledge transmitted through example—excitement, and urban adventure. Entire county populations emptied into the county fairground; for one day each year, perhaps for two consecutive days, Methodist comported with Episcopalian, Republican befriended Democrat, wheat farmer embraced dairyman in a thronged arena of competition. Here and there fairs blossomed on the outskirts of growing cities but most were chiefly rural and attracted rural people, to whom great crowds were unknown. Frances D. Gage caught the spirit of fair-going in an 1857 *Ohio Cultivator* poem structured around a farmer debating fair-going with his wife. Enthusiasm, and husbandly rule carried the argument:

> Kate looked up with a smile, and said, 'Ben, we'll go;
>   There may be better oxen than ours,
> Horses swifter on foot, and finer by far,
>   Better butter and cheese, fruit and flowers,
> But there's one thing I claim I know can't be beat
>   In the whole Yankee nation today,
> I'd not swap him, I know, for a kingdom to boot—
>   That's my good man,' and Kate ran away.[78]

Kate determines to go to the fair because, in the end, she intends to exhibit her husband. In her eyes at least, Ben is a prime specimen of man. Together they will promenade, be seen and see. They will engage in an essentially urban experience: they will be anonymous among strangers and confronted with novelty. They will enjoy what the Spanish call the *corso*, the cruising walk that leads from encounter to encounter for the joy of encountering.

Like the camp meeting, the country fair served rural families as an occasional city, providing most of the urban delights and almost none of the urban responsibilities. One day after its closing, the fair had vanished; only a few sheds and perhaps a fence marked the fairgrounds thronged with people and packed with exhibits only a few hours earlier. Country people eventually believed that they lived very well without cities; after all, the latest mechanical aids were displayed in the booths alongside the latest seeds and breeds, the most prominent orators spoke, and strangers of every sort arrived to sell notions and pamphlets or perform tricks. Fairs confirmed the smugness of agricultural families secure in social self-sufficiency and slowed the growth of villages, the collections of structures southerners called towns.

ARMATURE

Village life, space, and culture reached a zenith after the Civil War, but by the beginning of the nineteenth century astute observers of the surveyor-ordered and farmer-shaped countryside west of Pennsylvania understood that Americans were creating villages unlike the nucleated towns of New England, the seaboard mercantile cities, or even the Middle States hamlets.[79] No farmers lived in the villages, only the storekeepers, blacksmiths, grain dealers, barbers, physicians, attorneys, hardware salesmen, newspaper publishers, tavern keepers, and other businessmen who depended on the neighboring farmers for their livelihood, and who grouped their "mercantile establishments" along the armature that in town after town came to be called Main Street.

How did such villages develop? Crossroads stores answered many retail needs for decades, and farmwives cut men's hair, made clothes, and "doctored" the sick. Traveling buyers acquired tobacco and other crops ready for market, and drovers purchased what livestock farmers did not drive to coastal cities or to the few western cities such as Pittsburgh. Neither religious nor educational endeavors depended in the slightest upon urban resources, and preachers, schoolteachers, and country-fair orators frequently denounced the evils of urbanism. Although not self-sufficient, farm families far from crossroads stores discovered peddlers knocking frequently at their doors and unwrapping packs filled with eastern "fancy goods" like ribbon and spices. No eighteenth-century southerner, including Jefferson, assumed that villages were necessary, and certainly no eighteenth-century New Englander intended to recreate in the West the obsolete housing and field pattern of Puritan towns. Village making slipped the minds of the grid designers too; nowhere does the 1785 Ordinance describe how villages are to be incorporated into the larger national grid. But by 1800, main-street villages appeared often enough in the land shaped by agriculture to attract the attention of discerning travelers.

Few travelers explained the origin of the villages, but one British observer guessed correctly at part of the cause. When farmers had made land and produced enough good harvests to pay off debts and erect satisfactory houses, barns, and fences, they began to desire goods and services beyond the capacity of their neighbors. "The prosperous circumstances of almost every family," wrote Morris Birkbeck in 1817 of the farm people he encountered in Ohio, Indiana, and Illinois, "are daily creating new wants, and awakening fresh necessities."[80] Birkbeck never explicitly noted the connection between agricultural prosperity and village making, but the chronology of development in the Ohio and Mississippi valleys suggests that village retailers and professionals followed farmers.

Speculation also fostered the building of villages. Owners of farmland near a mill or along a frequently traveled road and surrounded by prosperous farms sometimes determined to survey or "plat" a village site of two or three streets crossing at right angles and bordered by square or rectangular lots. "Hundreds of these speculations may have failed, but hundreds prosper," Birkbeck noted, "and thus trade begins and thrives, as population grows around these lucky spots; imports and exports maintaining their just proportion." In 1817 townsite speculation was just beginning to grip the imagination of Americans with a little spare cash to invest. By the 1830s buying and selling village lots ensnared thousands of Americans in a real estate frenzy that culminated in the panic of 1837.

Not all speculators were honest farmers intent on making a small profit by selling lots in a town at the fringe of their farms. Many practiced the most devious deceptions, buying hilly land, crudely surveying it, and then printing elaborate maps of the places, advertising them as potential or existing villages likely to become cities, and informing no buyer of such problems as periodic flooding, poor drainage, and heavy forest cover, conditions like those Charles Dickens depicted in 1844 in *The Life and Adventures of Martin Chuzzlewit.*[81] But English immigrants were not the only buyers cheated by unscrupulous speculators; Americans succumbed to temptation too, often buying lots without visiting them or buying lots in proposed villages located too near other proposed villages. "You were not old enough to appreciate the different phases of the inflation," remarked one speculator in the proposed village of Allegan, Michigan, to a younger man inquiring about the panic, "beginning with a gentle breeze in 1834, increasing to a gale in 1835, to a storm in 1836, to a change of wind and an adverse tornado in 1837, leaving wrecks on every hand, succeeded by a dead calm which lasted up to 1844." Detroit hotel lobby walls were papered with village plats throughout the early 1830s, and small-time financiers sold and bought and sold. "Nearly everybody became wild and extravagant on the strength of fancied wealth," one participant recalled and "at the hotels champagne took the place of water, and bottles popped and cracked like pistols in California."[82] When the crash came, many speculators lost everything, and many proposed towns remained cornfields or half-cleared forest.

While the panic of 1837 had several causes, two spatial factors contributed to the collapse of village land values. Certainly the farmers had become prosperous and required the goods and services available most conveniently in villages. But by 1837 a sizable number of main-street villages had taken shape and were prospering; their presence made it difficult to establish newer villages near them. A population of prosperous farmers can support only so many villages; although farm families usually shopped within a six- to twelve-mile radius of their houses and certainly preferred having a choice of retail establishments, they had so little discretionary spending money at some seasons of the year that retailers competed fiercely to stay in business. Secondly, many fledgling villages proved so poorly located that their residents lost business to more accessible competitors. Travelers sometimes discovered that a "city" located on state or territorial maps and advertised as prosperous and bustling turned out to be a crossroads store owned by an ambitious promoter oblivious to his swampy site or else, in the words of one old-timer, a lake "where a seventy-four-gun ship could ride at anchor over the chimneys of the hypothetical houses." A stable main-street village objectified many things in 1838, but if it endured, it objectified survival in a whirlwind of speculative planning, rapid inflation, and catastrophic collapse.

Birkbeck offers what is perhaps the simplest description of a typical village evolving from a piece of land roughly surveyed in a miniature grid and sold at auction or by agents. "The new town then assumes the name of its founder: a storekeeper builds a little framed store and sends for a few cases of goods; and then a tavern starts up, which becomes the residence of a doctor and a lawyer, and the boarding-house of the storekeeper, as well as the resort of the weary traveler: soon follow a blacksmith and other handicraftsmen in useful succession," and the village grows. "Thus the town proceeds, if it proceeds at all, with accumulating force, until it becomes the metropolis of the neighborhood."[83] By "metropolis," however, Birkbeck means something very different from the coastal mercantile cities, for in 1817 land shaped for agriculture dominated main-street villages.

Philadelphia and other coastal cities, although they too were surrounded by agricultural land and interrupted throughout by vegetable gardens and other remnants of agricultural origin, presented the vaguest edge to entering travelers. The twisting road became a straight street, houses appeared in rows, and near the waterfront almost every foot of ground was dominated by man-made structures or else paved with stone or trampled to mud. At the beginning of the nineteenth century certain intersections and open spaces in the coastal cities reflected the final domination of man. However he turned and stared, the visitor suddenly lonely for trees and grass and an equilibrium of natural and agricultural space discovered only man-made form. A few minutes' walk, of course, brought him to houses surrounded by shade and fruit trees and backing on gardens, and another minute or so brought him to the fringe of agricultural space. Nevertheless, his momentary glimpse of cityscape was impossible in the main-street village because in almost every instance Main Street ran straight between two rows of shops and houses and opened in two directions on farmland.

Many villages consisted of only one short street, and the gardens and small pastures behind the houses abutted the fields of farmers. Poultry coops, cow barns, smokehouses, pigpens, and small stables stood behind most of the houses, not only because many residents understood the value of raising at least some of their own food but also because few businessmen earned enough to free their wives from productive work. In the grid country, therefore, few farmers or villagers could accurately designate the "edge of town" because the village retained agricultural spaces.[84] Even on Main Street the distinction remained unclear; all roads were straight in the region ordered by the grid. Usually villagers agreed with farmers that the village ended with the last structure not used wholly for agriculture. Try as they might, villagers found it difficult to convince themselves that they lived in urban space.

Main street did illustrate the separation of men and women, however, and farm families arriving on Saturday to pick up mail at the general store (or post office if the village had grown enough to warrant one) recognized the spatial reinforcement of life-style differences. Certain structures catered only to men, and women and girls avoided them. Saloons, of course, attracted men but perhaps the most male-dominated structures of all were the livery stables, where strangers rented horses and wagons and where farmers "put up" their teams on market day. The livery stable, like the saloon, provided a place to conduct business and discuss politics free of feminine restrictions on ethics and language. Because their owners respected and worked with animals, livery stables seemed to farmers more comfortable than such other men-only establishments as barbershops and blacksmith shops. Usually the livery stable stood at the outer fringe of the village because it backed upon a paddock and perhaps a small pasture, and it served farmers as a place built upon

agriculture but located in a village emphasizing other than strictly agricultural pursuits.

Women recognized that many village establishments catered only to
them or at least emphasized the role of women consumers. General
stores stocked merchandise used by both sexes but women delighted in
browsing among bolts of cloth, thread, buttons, and other notions, and
household appliances such as stoves. In more prosperous villages, Main
Street boasted a dressmaker's shop and perhaps even a dry-goods store
specializing in cloth.[85] Women shopped with the understanding that
shopping emphasized social intercourse; in the stores and along the
street, they encountered friends from other farms or friends resident in
the houses that stood on the street or two that paralleled Main Street or
else intersected it.

Not every business catered to a sexually segregated clientele. Newspaper offices, real estate offices, shoemaker shops, attorney and physi-
cian offices attracted men and women. But the village was nevertheless
an arrangement of structures exemplifying the separate if equally important roles of farm men and farm women, and few villages provided
establishments welcoming both sexes equally.

Until well into the nineteenth century village businessmen depended
solely upon the trade of neighboring farm families and knew that a poor
harvest meant little money spent in their stores and shops. Because they
had invested heavily to buy their small Main Street lots, to erect a store
and perhaps a separate house for their families, and to purchase their
merchandise or stock, the villagers built cheaply and modestly at first
and tried to increase their income not only by keeping a cow, pigs, and
chickens behind their shop or house but also by building two-story establishments. Main street verticality resulted from businessmen's desires to
imitate the dynamic enclosure of city streets, of course, and many entrepeneurs built two-story facades on one-story shops in order to make
their places of business seem significant.[86] But verticality resulted too
from property owners' understanding that land costs decreased according to the income produced on each lot. In village after village, men built
two-story structures; in the first years businessmen lived with their
families above or perhaps behind their stores, but as business increased,
they hired carpenters to build houses according to directions published
in periodicals aimed at the nonfarming public. The vacant upper stories
they rented to physicians or groups in search of a meeting room or even
to religious congregations as yet too poor to build a church.

As the town prospered and the Main Street businessmen paid off their
original debts and accumulated capital, the simple wooden stores gave

Main Street verticality, Gunnison, Colorado. (JRS)

way to brick edifices, some large enough to be known as "blocks." The block of two or three stores standing two or perhaps even three stories tall rarely occupied an entire "block" of land, that area along Main Street between two intersecting streets. But brick-built structures announced the end of village pioneering and the official beginning of long-term growth. Owners emphasized the meaning of the blocks by setting their names and dates in stone markers prominently located on the facades. The well-built main-street village objectified prosperity to its builders, but by 1840, at least in the eastern part of the country long enough settled for the business-building process to mature, the main-street facade represented in the eyes of farmers the persecution of agriculture for the good of retail business. Villagers divided their loyalty between their farmer customers and their urban wholesalers and financial backers. While camp-meeting preachers railed against urban sinfulness, and one-room schoolhouses echoed with recitations of country-fair orations honoring agriculture, villagers struggled to make their main street more and more urban. They built sidewalks, erected streetlights, and displayed the very latest "eastern" or fancy merchandise, not only in their shops but on their persons. But when city wholesalers refused credit or raised prices, or when produce prices dropped because of eastern market manipulations, village businessmen championed the cause of agriculture and extolled the purity of village life. Divided loyalties did not

escape the notice of farmers, their wives, and their children; as Main
Street grew more dignified and prosperous, its businessmen began lend-
ing money, perhaps even establishing banks, and gradually farmers discovered the financial power that produced brick blocks and foreclosed
farm mortgages. No longer did farmers and villagers dress identically;
every year that passed saw farm families dressed more simply than the
villagers and less and less able to purchase the more expensive goods
displayed in stores. Main Street developed into a place half-consciously
designed to manipulate farm families into a feeling of inferiority, and
the farm families countered the manipulation by strengthening institutions such as the camp-meeting revival, the one-room school, the crossroads church, and the agricultural fair. And they all went to "town" on
the same day, for safety in numbers. Saturday was business day in main-
street villages everywhere west of land shaped in colonial time.

From a distance, however, the main-street village seemed over-
whelmed by farmland, and even up close, travelers found it difficult to
distinguish where farmland ended and the village began. Despite their
longing for urban glories—and urban prosperity—main-street businessmen knew that their livelihoods depended on farm income and
spending, and Main Street long reflected the agricultural basis of village
life, not only in the vegetable gardens wedged behind stores and houses
but in the goods displayed for sale and the services offered. Main Street
never objectified and reinforced a closed-world society like that evident
in the New Spain estensión or the New England town. Always it objectified the openness of an armature; villagers lived in daily contact with
one another but depended for their livelihood on farm families beyond
the "ends" of the main-street axis, where the street became a road.
Philadephia, as Christopher Colles clearly depicted in his maps of roads,
ended where its straight streets suddenly contorted.[87] Main streets east
of the grid-ordered country ended more subtly perhaps because eastern
main streets rarely ran straight for any distance, but the main streets of
the grid country ended more subtly than any, at a vague edge marked
only by increasing space between houses and the larger size of barns.
Nineteenth-century villagers spoke easily of "edges," but few precisely
located the scarcely visible boundaries that linked rather than separated
their space from that of farmers.

Agrarianism

Although the American countryside objectified home-grown political
and economic liberalism in that settlers first shaped the wilderness according to individual conceptions of private enterprise and prosperity

and only later established community institutions (and those designed chiefly to further individual progress, either in this world or the next), its inhabitants grew increasingly wary of change as the nineteenth century progressed. Sometimes their resistance took physical form, as in the badly maintained, simple structures that housed students learning from outdated texts or in traditionally ordered graveyards or barns built in the "customary" style. More often it surfaced in ephemeral documents such as Conrad Zentler's Pennsylvania almanacs, used by rural people to determine the astrologically favorable planting and harvest dates and reflecting a growing unease.

In the 1840s American agriculturists confronted several intricate and tormenting national problems, particularly the war with Mexico and the looming terror of disunion and civil war. Some of their nervousness surfaced in disguise, however, in tracts and sermons explaining how Satan once again walked the land. Zentler's almanacs frequently included engravings of demonic, bonfire-lit revels, walking skeletons, and sorcerers, almost all depicted in seventeenth-century starkness. William B. Raber summed up the early nineteenth-century rural fascination with Satanism in 1855, in a book entitled *The Devil and Some of His Doings*. Amid long descriptions and denunciations of astrology, witchcraft, omens, and other demonic practices and manifestations, however, pulsates an intense dread of cities. "It is evident, if the Devil cannot make his dupes happy, he does his utmost to make them foolish, and brings about something ludicrous to gratify their depraved hearts," he remarks as a preface to a denunciation of such urban recreations as theater-going and oyster-cellar-visiting. "There has been, and still is, a system of popular foolery, generally originating in cities and large towns, then gradually making its way into villages and country places."[88] In the early nineteenth-century rural imagination cities such as Boston and Baltimore and especially New York began to acquire images like those previously accorded to wilderness areas. In Zentler's illustrations, evil is as likely to flourish in an urban drawing room as in the wildest forest.

Tirades against urban evil took many forms in rural churches and at camp meetings, in one-room schoolhouses and at country fairs, but most shared a commitment to husbandry as the only proper way of life and a dread of too much novelty. Because rural people depended not on cities for their education and amusement but on their own well-organized, permanent institutions, such tirades grew in force, fueling the fires of nativist and anti-Catholic movements before the Civil War, just as they supported temperance, Social Gospel, and fundamentalist crusades later in the century. American farm families, especially those living beyond the Appalachian Mountains, inhabited a world shaped to reinforce individual and family freedom, the freedom objectified everywhere in farms built according to their makers' wishes not according to any community design. Imlay, Tocqueville, and other observers had cause to wonder about the tension between liberalism and agrarian reaction; everything in the grid country emphasized individual discretion and individual enterprise. Even the community institutions existed to educate individual minds or save individual souls; joint or corporate responsibility attracted very little attention, and as familiarity with it diminished, rural people ceased to understand the commitment to others required in urban living. Evil came to bucolic regions from cities teeming with immigrants, artisans, and scoundrels, people who stole or cheated for their living and whose dirty lives were reflected in filthy streets and overcrowded dwellings. City life might fascinate the rural young but only if the children learned of it; in schoolhouses and crossroads church buildings, however, teachers and clergymen said little of it, and what they said of it was prejudicial, almost as prejudicial as what they said of artifice. Landscape, not urban form, objectified the only proper life.

ARTIFICE

*Within was seen the forge, now blazing up and
illuminating the high and dusky roof, and now
confining its lustre to a narrow precinct of the
coal-strewn floor, according as the breath of the
bellows was puffed forth or again inhaled into its
vast leathern lungs. In the intervals of brightness it
was easy to distinguish objects in remote corners of
the shop and the horseshoes that hung upon the
wall; in the momentary gloom the fire seemed to be
glimmering amidst the vagueness of unenclosed
space.*[1]

Nathaniel Hawthorne
"The Artist of the Beautiful"
1854

The Cornwall Furnace smelter. (JRS)

usbandry caresses the soil, urging it to bear fruit in its own time, at the proper season; husbandry is cyclical and illuminated by the sun. Artifice embodies rape, and abortion and transmutation too. Artifice thrusts into the very womb of mother earth, into infernal dark, and wrenches living rock from living rock. Smelting, forging, and casting torment the aborted fetuses with fire. Earth, air, fire, and water combine in an unholy alchemical alliance from which husbandmen stand away, shielding their eyes. Embryo becomes artifact. In the mine and at the furnace, at the mill and inside the smithy, the artificers stand and sweat and wrestle with powers beyond the comprehension of husbandmen accustomed to oxen and horses. All the mystery of making obscures the places of artifice. Only the artificers understand. Onlookers stand back and hope for success, and are afraid.

"It was a rude, round, tower-like structure about twenty feet high, heavily built of rough stones, and with a hillock of earth heaped about the larger part of its circumference," wrote Nathaniel Hawthorne in 1851 of a New England limekiln. "There was an opening at the bottom of the tower, like an oven-mouth but large enough to admit a man in a stooping posture, and provided with a massive iron door. With the smoke and jets of flame issuing from the chinks and crevices of this door, which seemed to give admittance into the hillside, it resembled nothing so much as the private entrance to the infernal regions, which the shepherds of the Delectable Mountains were accustomed to show to pilgrims."[2] Hawthorne knew the old, almost ancient significance of mining and smelting, the eerie lore of mountains and Hell. The Delectable Mountains of John Bunyan's *Pilgrim's Progress* are no seventeenth-century invention, nor is their sinister kiln-like door in the hill. Mountains, subterreanean fire, and writhing minerals repelled and fascinated classical and medieval inquirers long before Bunyan conceived his topographical allegory. Hawthorne and other nineteenth-century American writers felt the same essential strangeness of the subsoil world, the attraction of buried riches and the calamities of accidental interment. Like other residents of the United States, they saw the odd structures associated with artifice, and like many they realized them in Old World, traditional terms. They knew the smell of brimstone.

Brimstone is a venerable word, and not Latinate. It derives from the Old Norse for "burning stone," and it connotes more than sulfur. Before it announced the presence of Satan it announced the writhing of chaos, the splitting of rock, and the upheaval of marshes. Brimstone is the smell of earthquake. The word itself descends from a chthonic vocabulary that incorporated such terms as *dwarf* and *Wichtlein* and *trow* and *duergar,* all names for humanoid creatures native to caves and mines, afraid of the sun, and smelling not like moist warm soil ready for sowing but like the flames of Hell.[3] Old words and old beliefs endured well into the nineteenth century, even in the United States, because they helped satisfy the urge to define *artifice*. Many thrive today. Miners follow *veins*, seeking *mother lodes;* steelworkers glimpse the maiden of the open hearth, the woman outlined in cascading liquid steel. Farming is almost as gentle as husbandry; artifice is no more pacific now than in the 1580s, when Spanish conquistadores sought *criaderos* north of the Rio Grande.

ELEMENTS

"What is the center of the earth? is it pure element only, as Aristotle decrees, inhabited (as Paracelsus thinks) with creatures whose chaos is the earth, or with fairies, as the woods and waters (according to him) are with nymphs, or as the air with spirits?" asked Robert Burton in 1621. "Or is it the place of Hell, as Virgil in his *Aeneid,* Plato, Lucian, Dante, and others, poetically describe it, and as many of our divines think?"[4] Burton addressed such questions because *The Anatomy of Melancholy* depended upon a perfect understanding of the four elements, not only as they occurred in the human body but in the physical universe as well. Blood, phlegm, yellow bile, and black bile corresponded to fire, water, air, and earth. To understand the constituent elements of the universe was to understand the elements comprising human life—and of course to understand such imbalances as that causing melancholy. Unfortunately for Burton and for many other thinkers of the era, interpreting the evidence of creation was no easy matter. At the center of the difficulties lay the center of the earth.

Was the center of the earth inert, enlivened by the sun, or did it burn and writhe? Almost every alchemist, theologian, and miner confronted the question, turned to the Bible for aid, and discovered only confusion. Everyone agreed that metals were created on the third day, either directly by the will of God or indirectly, by sunlight perhaps, or by subterranean heat. But Genesis is vague on the subject, and too much evidence suggested that stones and ores developed gradually out of third-day firmament, from scattered seed-beds stimulated by sunlight, or else from some central womb-like molten core. Formations like stalagmites and stalactites encouraged those who believed in gestation; the discovery of coral confirmed their view that minerals mature. But what force sustained the growth? Celestial or infernal heat?

Aristotle suggested that sunlight causes the earth to give off two exhalations, one light and consisting of water vapor, and one dark, consisting of fumes emanating from rocky outcrops. From the light exhalation come white clouds; from the dark come haze, black clouds, thunder, earthquakes, lightning—and stones. Aristotle explained that the dark exhalation condenses on the earth and leaves behind each night a tiny portion of its solid nature. His theory survived into the eighteenth century because it explained a variety of meteorological phenomena and the presence of stones lying in fields above soil. Obviously the stones congealed out of dark exhalations. More than a trace of his thinking infuses Morse's *American Geography*; the candy-like manna of California is the residue of evaporated dew.[5] Schoolchildren poring over his book absorbed a trace of the old beliefs about the celestial-incubated growth of ores and rocks. Outside the schoolhouse door they absorbed more.

Folk Christianity confused the sun and the Son of God, and confusion persisted into the eighteenth century. Thomas Browne argued in *Religio Medici* that "the Spirit of God, the fire and scintillation of that noble and mighty essence," is not infernal, but "a fire quite contrary to the fire of Hell." Divine fire shaped and incubated the universe: "This is that gentle heat that brooded on the waters, and in six days hatched the world; this is that irradiation that dispels the mists of Hell, the clouds of horror, fear, sorrow, despair, and preserves the region of the mind in serenity." Browne's thinking is that of every seventeenth-century digger of graves; the sun is light, God is light, light is God, darkness is terror and death. But Browne did not explain the actual presence of metals, and he did not address their curious growth. Matthew Hale did, in *The Primitive Origination of Mankind Considered and Examined According to the Light of Nature,* a carefully reasoned tome that appeared in 1677, forty-two years after Browne wrote *Religio Medici*. "It is evident that divers minerals are bred in the earth from an earthly consistence, by the heat of the sun and other concurrent causes successively, as may appear to any man's observations touching coals, rocks, especially of stones, which from a sandy kind of earth gradually concoct into free-stone," Hale argued, "as may be seen in many quarries by those pieces of unconcocted earth not yet perfectly digested into stone." Minerals, he continued in a meticulous explication of the great chain of being, "are a degree below vegetables yet they seem to have some shadow of the vegetable life in their growth, increase, and specific configurations."[6] Browne, Hale, and other proponents of the gestation theory bickered with devotees of infernal fire, and their controversy crossed the Atlantic with the Spanish and English colonists.

Ores "were at first made in the earth," counseled Samuel Willard in *A Compleat Body of Divinity,* published at Boston in 1726, "and its womb was then impregnated, and made fruitful of them, which are continually generated by the influence of the sun, at the places naturally adapted for them."[7] Theories of solar influence depended in part on the proven and widely known traditions of husbandry. Clearly the sun helped plants mature; it seemed logical that sunlight assisted ores to mature into metal. Here, however, the colonists discovered the problems that plagued the ancients. Did the planets influence ores as they did plants? Many seventeenth- and eighteenth-century writers agreed with their learned forebears; each of the seven useful metals responds to the influence of one of the seven planets. Iron, for example, responds to the light of Mars, and lead responds to the dull gleam of Saturn; alchemists had long used planetary symbols to identify metals and knew that gold responds to the influence of the sun, and silver to the moon. Centuries of observation, experimentation, and debate culminated in an eighteenth-century conviction that gold is the perfect, most mature metal. All its impurities were long ago burned away by the sun. Silver is less pure but more common, and proves the point. Again and again miners found tiny veins of silver twisting through far larger veins of lead. Quite apparently not all the lead had matured. When it did, the vein would be pure silver. Willard, like most learned colonists, accepted the divine—or almost divine—power of the sun.

Could a man capture the power of sunlight and change lesser metals into gold? Paracelsus argued that he could, explaining in his *Short Catechism of Alchemy* that the "living gold of the philosophers" is the essence of gold, mercury, and sulfur, a sort of elixir of growth: "It is exclusively the fire of Mercury, or that igneous virtue, contained in the radical moisture, to which it has already communicated the fixity and the nature of the sulphur, whence it has emanated, the mercurial character of the whole substance of philosophical sulphur permitting it to be alternatively termed mercury."[8] Men like Jonathan Brewster and Governor John Winthrop Jr. pondered such passages before beginning their alchemical experiments in isolated Connecticut towns early in the seventeenth century. The younger Winthrop assembled one of the world's most substantial libraries on alchemy and persevered year after year in his trials of various ores. Such activities later were sanctioned by Harvard College; the school's official scientific text, Charles Morton's *Compendium Physicae* adopted in 1687, emphasized the occasional successes of alchemists such as Paracelsus, who knew that metals were "generated in the veins of the earth out of sulphur and mercury or quicksilver by virtue of the heavens." Morton's manuscript text convinced a generation of students that alchemy was practical; throughout the eighteenth century educated New Englanders inquired after the philosopher's stone. Even the president of Yale College performed experiments. In the summer of 1787 Ezra Stiles recorded in his journal that a friend had purchased "the Governor's Ring, as it is called, or a mountain in the northwest corner of East Haddam, comprehending about eight hundred acres or above a square mile area." Stiles knew that it "was the place to which Governor Winthrop of New London used to resort with his servant; and after spending three weeks in the woods of this mountain in roasting ores and assaying metals and casting gold rings, he used to return home to New London with plenty of gold."[9] Like Winthrop, Stiles was both alchemist and astronomer; he discerned the curious relation of metals and heavenly bodies, the double definition of *mercury* as quicksilver and planet.[10] The essential oneness of sulfur, mercury, and gold was lost on most husbandmen, however, who missed the connection between sunlight and ores. Celestial gestation theories and alchemy lured only college students and learned investigators. They repelled husbandmen, who equated mining and experiments with brimstone and the fires of Hell.

Mountains, volcanoes, and earthquakes convinced many uneducated observers that some force lurked within the Earth, incubating ores into metals and now and then erupting with terrible fury. Learned men offered several explanations for mountains. Pythagoras suggested that within the Earth great winds pushed and tore at the Earth's crust; Albertus Magnus agreed but suggested that the winds now and then ignited coal and sulfur, which in turn produced earthquakes and volcanoes; other philosophers speculated that sunlight or starlight had ignited the center of the Earth and that intense heat forced up mountain ranges from below; Dante and other thinkers argued that mountains somehow derived from the Deluge, and proved their point by identifying marine fossils cemented in mountaintops. By the late sixteenth century the learned opponents of celestial incubation had produced several different theories to explain phenomena that unnerved the common folk who could not read their treatises but remained convinced that somewhere beneath the sunlit earth, somewhere far below the graveyard sod, burned a great demonic fire known by its brimstone stench, incubated metals, and periodic writhings.

Earthquakes mystified Europeans long before Milton offered his own explanations in *Paradise Lost.* In keeping with seventeenth-century practice he presents two explanations, one drawn from learned sources and one from folk tradition. He notes first how "the force of subterranean wind transports a hill," but then refers to "thundering Etna, whose combustible / And fuelled entrails, thence conceiving fire, / Sublimed with mineral fury" create "stench and smoke." Some of Milton's better-read contemporaries agreed with the Roman philosopher Lucretius that terrible winds or vapors course through the bowels of the earth, in "antres vast, immense recesses, and vast spaces," but only a few believed the Roman's corollary assertion that "animals are also produced in them, but they are slow-paced and stupid."[11] But common folk did, even though they had never heard of Lucretius. "It often happens in one place or another that the earth shakes so violently that cities are thrown down and even that one mountain is hurled against another mountain," wrote Conrad von Megenberg in his *Buch der Natur* as early as 1374. "The common people do not understand why this happens and so a lot of old women who claim to be very wise, say that the earth rests on a great fish called Celebrant, which grasps its tail in its mouth. When this fish moves or turns the earth trembles. This is a ridiculous fable and of course not true but reminds us of the Jewish story of the Behemoth."[12] Von Megenberg might well have added that it savors of countless other European tales involving dragons and other chthonic beasts, most of which inhabit a smoldering realm of uncertain heat, the fueled entrails of mother earth.

Anthanasius Kircher explored the entrails in *Mundus Subterraneus,* a massive, profusely illustrated folio that appeared at Amsterdam in 1664. Kircher understood alchemy, subterranean fire, dwarfs, astrological affinities, and dragons and presented them in an intricate web of learned and folk beliefs. He described three loathesome dragons that inhabited deep caves; two were winged, and one breathed fire. *Mundus Subterraneus* appealed only to the very learned but it analyzed many opinions popularly held by the common people. Dragons have long populated the deeper caves of Europe, and they have long breathed fire, like the seven-headed mountain dragon described in "The Two Brothers," a tale recorded by the Grimms in the 1850s. Folk Christianity portrayed such reptiles as monstrous relatives of the primeval serpent, and the Catholic Church canonized those intrepid souls who slew them. Dragons (and dwarfs, trolls, kobolds, and other humanoids) were associated by the common people with Satan, Hell, and the sea of fire awaiting sinners condemned to burn within the Earth.[13] And well into the eighteenth century they were associated with earthquakes, and with metals too.

God cared very little about metals, argued the opponents of the celestial incubation theory, or else Genesis would specifically record their creation. Since Scripture is almost mute, Samuel Willard affirmed in 1726, New Englanders ought to realize that metals, and particularly gold and silver, are tainted. "God laid them low, placed them in the bowels of the earth, to be trodden upon," he argued in a passage directed against "greedy desire" and idolatry, "but man adores them, sets them up in his heart, and worships these, advancing them as high as God, and setting them in His throne." Gold and silver, he asserted in the long tradition of pious Old World clerics, "are two adored metals with which the god of this world seduces men into idolatry." Earthly riches are a chief weapon of Satan, the Lord of the Underworld, and Scripture recounts temptations of gold and silver. European folklore is likewise spiced with tales of children and husbandmen lured from righteousness and landschaft with promises of gold and silver in heaps. Almost invariably such riches work only evil and cost the souls of the tempted; gold turns out to be ashes, and silver is discovered to be rocks. Eldritch gold lies beyond the landschaft edge, in forests and mountains, and wise husbandmen refuse the seductions of Satan and dwarfs. Gold is only bait above the brimstone pit.

Brimstone consequently scented the activities of every alchemist, and of their scarcely less sinister colleagues in artifice, since everything underground is evil. Husbandmen and other common people suspected artificers of trading souls for knowledge, of experimenting at the edge of Hell, of devoting time and spiritual energy to things thought little of by God.[14] Everywhere in Europe artifice was suspect, abhorred by people of good will, by husbandmen eager to caress and nurture the soil of every landschaft. Mining, smelting, forging, and alchemy remained tainted with the black art of artifice, and fearful men assigned them to proscribed places beyond landschaften and decent industry.

When the conquistadores discovered gold and silver in Mexico and Peru, however, debates about sunlight and quicksilver, mountains and brimstone, alchemy and infernal heat suddenly involved not only alchemists and theologians but merchants, kings' counselors, explorers, and colonists. What had formerly attracted little attention was no longer esoteric but immediately useful; information about the gestation, location, and transmutation of ores and metals inspired books, pamphlets, sermons, and addresses of every sort. Much of the printed knowledge was scholastic or new but a vast amount was not. Tales concerning dragons and trolls merged with descriptions of celestial and infernal gestation; miners and blacksmiths were consulted by inquirers confused by natural philosophers, alchemists, and lapidaries. The sixteenth-century explosion of interest in the subterranean world incorporated the old debate about celestial versus infernal heat, and, colonists newly arrived in New Spain, Virginia, New England, and Pennsylvania confronted, along with ancient and conflicting beliefs about the four elements and dragons and mountains, the old dread of artifice. By the close of the eighteenth century most husbandmen had determined that artifice, although useful, was usually ignoble, sometimes dangerous, and occasionally downright Satanic.

CRIADEROS

Late in the autumn of 1582 Antonio De Espejo, with fourteen soldiers, a Franciscan friar, and some servants, rode north from the mines of Santa Barbara in Durango to rescue two missionary friars at Purray Pueblo in New Mexico and to explore the land so hastily reconnoitered by Coronado years before. At Purray he learned that the friars had been murdered and, after wondering about turning back, consulted his men and decided to push on, into a half-arid country dotted with large pueblos. "There are indications of mining possibilities in the mountains of this province, for I saw the signs while traveling through it," he reported of the Rio San Jose region. "We noticed much antimony along the way, and ordinarily one finds rich silver ore wherever there is antimony. Moreover, in this province we found metals in the houses of the Indians." At Zia Pueblo he learned that there "were mines near by, in the sierra," and the inhabitants showed him rich ores. Near Acoma Pueblo he found further signs and remarked that "in the adjacent mountains there are indications of mines and other riches." And at Zuñi Pueblo, he remarked with pride, "I found the mines, and took from them with my own hands ores which, according to experts on the matter, are very rich and contain a great deal of silver. Most of the area around the mines is mountainous, as is the route leading to them."[15] Espejo returned to Santa Barbara well pleased. He had found criaderos, the places where minerals grow. He had read the signs.

Geological investigation troubled the first generations of Spanish, French, and English explorers because it was unfamiliar and confusing. European mining experts were rude men, inhabitants of Saxony, north Italy, and parts of Austria and Hungary. A few mines existed in Spain and in France, but like the lead mines of Cornwall and Devonshire in England they were ancient operations. Spain invited German miners into New Spain in the first decades of colonization, and a few arrived to work the diggings opened by Indians long before.[16] Western Europeans looked to the Alps for expert advice about prospecting techniques, and by mid-sixteenth century instructions appeared in many languages. Every adventurer hoped to master the new knowledge and find great treasure.

Richard Eden translated part of Vannuccio Biringuccio's *Pyrotechnia* into English in 1555, only fifteen years after the work appeared in Italian. The age when "men thought it cruelty by breaking the bones of our mother the earth, to open a way to the court of infernal Pluto from thence to get gold and silver" is gone, announced Eden in his preface, and Englishmen should no longer be ignorant of the metal-finding art. Biringuccio's advice was not especially complex but it depended on a clear understanding of the four elements. Metals, counseled the Italian expert, are likely to exist in any mountain, "by reason of the great barrenness and roughness thereof," but only wise men understand how to locate the veins. They know that spring water tastes metallic near veins, that mountains "rough, sharp, and savage, without earth or trees" are likely prospecting sites, and that wherever mountain herbs or grass appear faint in color "and in manner withered and dried," ores most probably lurk just beneath the surface. Gold "is engendered in divers kinds of stones in great and rough mountains, and such as are utterly bare of earth, trees, grass, or herbs," and often its presence is announced by specific sorts of surface rock. Neither Biringuccio nor his translator cared much for theory; they admitted that gold and other metals grew for one reason or several, and "that in some places in Hungary at certain times of the year, pure gold springs out of the earth in the likeness of small herbs."[17] Only location concerned Biringuccio and Eden—not astrology, alchemy, or religion.

Eden appended his translation to a much larger work outlining navigation to the New World, and for years it and other tracts, some original and many reprinted or translated, offered English dreamers their only view of Spanish gold. By the seventeenth century people demanded better works based on New World experience, not Alpine tradition. Alvaro Alonso Barba published *The Art of Metals* in 1637 while supervising exceedingly profitable mines at Potosí in Bolivia, and it soon appeared in English, French, and German. Europeans devoured it eagerly, for Barba described not only prospecting techniques but methods of assaying, extracting, and refining precious ores. He explained how to follow streams and scrutinize eroded rock, how to use the *cateador*, or prospector's pick, and how to identify the lines of plants half-sickened be metallic exhalations from ore veins beneath their roots.[18] Much of his book derives from European tracts and experience, and its background made it more immediately intelligible. Spanish readers no longer required such detailed instruction books, however, because they had acquired several decades of valuable experience. When Espejo rode north from the mines of Santa Barbara he took with him an orally transmitted tradition of land classification.

The English slowly acquired such knowledge, but only secondhand, through such works as Gabriel Plattes's 1639 masterpiece, *A Discovery of Subterraneall Treasure*. Plattes asserted that metals mature because of sunlight and that gold and silver are common in the "burning zone" along the equator. After dismissing valleys and grassland as unlikely locations for ores because "the womb of such earth is not apt for such a generation," he proved that mountains are the best sites for discovery. "When we come to the rocky and craggy mountains, the first thing we are to observe, is the barrenness of them, for the more barren they are, the greater probability there is that they contain rich mines and minerals," he explained in an introductory chapter.[19] After distilling any nearby spring water and noting the residue (a greenish cast, for example, indicates nearby copper deposits), he continued, "the next work is to go to the bare rocks, and there to find out the clefts, crooks, and crannies . . . till you find some grass growing right upon the top of said crannies, and then to observe diligently the kind of that grass, and how it differs from other grass ordinarily growing in the same mountain." Plattes undoubtedly derived much of his information from Old and New World experts, but some of it, according to him, derived from experimentation.[20] "About midsummer, in a calm morning," he wrote of a successful attempt to discover a vein of lead, "I cut up a rod of hazel, all of the same spring's growth, about a yard long," and he wandered about likely sites until the wand bent down and indicated the exact location of the ore. Divining for metals proved a complicated art; hazel twigs sought out silver but the wise prospector knew that ash twigs responded best to copper deposits, pitch pine to lead and especially to tin, and rods made of iron and steel to gold. Plattes was a practical man, dedicated to making the English adept at prospecting, panning for gold flakes in rivers, and assaying discovered ore. He focused on England's New World possessions, for only they had heat enough to breed much precious metal. "Now in the new plantations, as New England, Virginia, Bermudas," he concluded at the end of his guide to prospecting, "where it is likely that few or none have ever tried, that had any skill in these affairs, it is very probable that the orifice of divers mines may be discerned with the eye in the clefts of the rocks, . . . and yield more gain in one year than their tobacco and such trifles would yield in their whole lives."[21] *A Discovery of Subterraneall Treasure* synthesized the old and new information that the

English carried to the New World and applied in a frenzied attempt to recreate Spain's wonderful discoveries.

A mad mix of superstition, tradition, and experimental technique caused near chaos at Jamestown, as one anonymous participant recalled in 1612. "Gilded refiners, with their golden promises, made all men their slaves in hope of recompence," he wrote of the episode. "There was no talk, no hope, nor work, but dig gold, wash gold, refine gold, load gold." One settler was so convinced of the golden magic of Virginia soil that he demanded to be buried in the sand, so that his bones might become gold. Only mica was shipped to England, but the derision of old-country goldsmiths and the colonists' continuing mistakes did not at once shake the faith of the English in subterranean treasure. Even a Spanish spy put ashore in Virginia in 1611 saw signs of gold and silver; Don Diego De Molina urged his king to conquer the colony at once.[22] In Virginia, gold seemed to be everywhere.

By the time Virginians realized that gold was not everywhere, certainly by the time Plattes published his comprehensive guidebook, Spanish adventurers had learned that discovering criaderos did not lead at once to riches. Even veins such as those found in 1599 in the Aquarius Mountains of present-day western Arizona by Don Juan De Oñate, veins "so long and wide that half of the people of New Spain can have mines there," in the words of their discoverer, required vast efforts to exploit. Oñate took possession of the veins partly because the Indian owners had already sunk a shaft three *estados* deep into the multicolored ore, and partly because nearby were running water to power machinery and good timber for framing cribwork. Like other late sixteenth-century conquistadores, Oñate understood the ways of mining. He knew, for example, the word *estado* and its meaning as a mining measurement derived from the height of a man and equivalent to approximately six-and-one-half English feet. Diego De Luxan, one of Espejo's companions in criadero-seeking, likewise thought in terms of mining and carefully recorded the presence or absence of trees near every mineral outcrop. "All the ranges and gorges are covered with juniper trees, and, in some part, oak groves, a fine asset for the exploitation of silver," he remarked of a ridge near San Felipe Pueblo that contained a twelve-mile-long indication of silver. Shortly before that happy discovery, however, Luxan noted that in another location the expedition found "large numbers of promising mines" but chose not to claim them "because there were no woodlands in the neighborhood."[23] Without nearby forest, mining was practically impossible, a fact overlooked by Plattes and other counselors accustomed to moist climates and forested hillsides. Cribwork required heavy beams, of

course, but smelting operations consumed vast quantities of charcoal.
Precious metals mature best in barren mountains, and barren mountains
produce few trees. Northern New Spain was rich in ore but poor in
useful timber; the English Atlantic colonies were well forested but almost
wholly lacking in gold and silver. In both regions prudent men devoted
themselves to the small but reasonably certain rewards of agriculture.
Only the bold—or foolhardy—dug mines.

REAL DE MINAS

Miners camp. Unlike the makers and sustainers of landschaften, men
who clamber about in the womb of the earth care little for surface development. Medieval miners concerned themselves only with finding
and extracting ore, not with erecting houses and steads and defending
arable land against the inroads of weeds and brush. In Saxony, Bohemia,
Silesia, the Harz, Hungary, the Schwarzwald, throughout Austria, and
elsewhere in central Europe permanent settlements did evolve around
the richest mines. Freiberg in Saxony, Iglau in Moravia, and Schemnitz
in Hungary developed from orderless mining encampments into prosperous towns, and some like Goslar in the Harz produced model municipal codes. But such permanent, well-ordered settlements were exceptional. Mining operations lasted only as long as the ore could be worked.
When the vein "ran out" or when water flooded the workings, miners
left for other regions, leaving behind piles of tailings, gaping shafts, and
collapsing huts. Uncertainty of residence reinforced the miners' reluctance to learn above-ground building skills. As long as they dug out the
ore, the miners could buy food, and so had no use for cultivated fields
and husbandry; as long as they worked long days underground, they
had little need for houses—as Parliament recognized in its 1589 act
permiting landlords to erect cottages without yards for mining families.
Wives and children lived as best they could in temporary hovels built by
indifferent husbands or thrown up by the *Grundherren,* the landlords
who owned the ground the miners worked.[24]

Sixteenth-century European mining settlements superficially resembled traditional agricultural landschaften. The landschaft focused inward on a circle of houses and yards surrounded by fields; the mining
settlement focused inward too, on *dwellings* and one or more mineshafts.
A roland objectified the communal spirit that shaped and sustained the
landschaft; it objectified too joint decision-making and joint landholding, although the land itself might be owned by a noble. No such form,
except perhaps the shaft itself, ordered the mining settlement because

the settlement was not a community. Only nobles and companies of wealthy merchants possessed the capital needed to support exploratory digging, to build roads and furnaces, and to pay specialists during the long months when new mines produced no income. The miners of early modern Europe were an independent lot because they were highly skilled in a dangerous and much needed occupation, not because they controlled the ground they worked. Landlords treated them with respect but paid them wages rather than sharing profits. A good landlord provided for his miners as he might provide for valuable horses. Miners did not provide for themselves.

Biringuccio described the relationship in *Pyrotechnia* and explained the landlord's duty in laying out mining camps. After outlining the preferred way to locate a mine shift, he noted:

> Also beside that place where you have determined to make the entrance and beginning of the cave, you must make choice of another place, either on the front of the mountain or on the side that it may be near and commodious to make one or two or more cottages for the commodity and necessity of the workmen. One of these must be appointed for their dormitory where some may rest and sleep while others work, and that you may the more commodiously be present and assistant to their doings, diligently to behold all things and to comfort them in their labors, also to dispense and bestow their vittals as shall be needful, and to reserve the same in safe custody, with daily provision of all things appertaining. The other must be as it were a smith's forge wherein their worn and broken tools must be renewed, and others new made, to the intent that the work be not hindered for lack of necessary instruments.

Like other commentators of his time, Biringuccio stressed that such steps must be taken to ensure the miners' good humor and the prosperity of the mine. Almost nothing of stewardship, Christian duty, or even neighborliness informs the suggestions about building mining camps. All is oriented toward profit.

Not every sixteenth-century mining expert accepted the profit-maximization theme, but the few who insisted on the inherent worth of mining as an occupation and the nobility of grimy miners were few indeed. Georgius Agricola, whose *De Re Metallica* of 1556 remained the standard reference work on mining for two centuries, argued that "not even the common worker in the mines is vile and abject. For, trained to vigilance and work by night and day, he has great powers of endurance when occasion demands, and easily sustains the fatigues and duties of a soldier, for he is accustomed to keep long vigils at night, to wield iron tools, to dig trenches, to drive tunnels, to make machines, and to carry burdens."[25] Agricola's comparison of miner and honored soldier had little impact, however, for most Europeans scorned the men of the mines.[26] Landlords exploited them although they knew that they were likely to leave for other diggings at the slightest insult. Peasants distrusted them, for their chthonic operations consumed forests and polluted waterways. Miners were grimy and mysterious, and when they walked from landschaft through landschaft in search of work, or wandered about a landschaft in search of veins of ore, husbandmen stared with suspicion and fear at their peculiar hooded outfits and strange tools. High up on mountains, far from the good land beloved by husbandmen, miners chopped into the womb of the earth and sent forth riches and pollution. Like barbarians, they lived in crude, temporary settlements focused on the maw of Hell.

Old World suspicion and exploitation appeared as quickly as mining camps in New Spain, and viceroys and other officials struggled with perplexing problems for which Spanish law offered few solutions. Criadero-seeking culminated often enough in discovery, and discovery produced social chaos as would-be miners descended on the find. According to a legal definition of 1584, a mine was a marked rectangle 120 by 60 yards; by another definition a mine was any shaft opened to a depth of three estados. The confusion derived from Spanish ignorance; throughout the fifteenth century few Spaniards concerned themselves with the nation's unimportant mines. Until 1584, in fact, codes adopted in 1255, 1348, and 1505 formed the nucleus of Spanish mining law; additions such as the 1548 code based on German law altered few old practices. New World conditions proved so extraordinary that a series of laws begun by Viceroy Mendoza in 1536 and codified in 1550 served the miners of New Spain only until 1577, when mining laws were collected and modified in the *Recopilación*. In 1680 and again in 1783 new variations appeared as viceroys struggled to order an almost chaotic situation.

In New Spain mining law a mining settlement was more than a band of miners temporarily encamped about a shaft.[27] The *real de minas* resembled an estensión. At its center was a mine, or perhaps several, and near the shafts stood the dwellings of the miners and the casas-corral of the husbandmen cultivating the *real* fields. From the fields and any nearby stock ranches came the miners' food, and from the *montes* came building timber for cribwork. Any nearby salt flats were incorporated into the *real* because salt was useful in smelting ore. A real de minas, however, was neither self-sufficient nor cooperatively managed.

Mining consumed vast quantities of timber, of course, and the miners consumed large amounts of food. But the mines consumed all sorts of foreign equipment, particularly iron tools that New Spain failed to produce as long as the colony's incipient capitalists insisted on mining only gold and silver. Wedges, sledgehammers, axes, picks, and great thirty- to forty-pound crowbars were imported from Spain, along with lighter but even more expensive items such as blasting powder.[28] Extensiónes developed and prospered chiefly through hard work; little outside capital was needed to maintain them. A real de minas depended on continuing infusions of capital and on a steady supply of miners.

Experienced Indian miners were enslaved almost at once by greedy conquistadores and condemned to labor in mines of their own making. Slaves lugged ore in fiber baskets, carrying it along horizontal galleries and up ladders that stretched hundreds of feet. Each basket held up to 350 pounds of ore, and every ounce was precious. Miners were stripped and searched after every shift three centuries after their official emancipation in 1550. Indian miners suffered while they worked, and their Spanish foremen fared little better. Life in the *reals de minas* was bitter.

Not one real de minas was established north of the Rio Grande despite proven reports of ore. Circumstances such as the continuing profitability of mines in lower New Spain and the incessant attacks of Apaches and other tribes combined to keep most miners away from the northern frontier. *Gambucinos,* independent men who drifted from one criadero to another, dug ore throughout the eighteenth century but large-scale mining began later, in the first years of the nineteenth century, when Indians were less of a menace and roads were reasonably passable. Spanish and Anglo prospectors knew a vague mix of history and wishful thinking and searched for mines they believed the Jesuits worked in the late seventeenth century. According to tradition, Indian tribes camouflaged the mines after the temporary success of the Pueblo revolt of 1680, and gambucinos listened to tales of lost mines as eagerly as they read the signs identified in the sixteenth century.[29] "In every quarter of the territory," wrote Josiah Gregg in 1844 of New Mexico, "there are still to be seen vestiges of ancient excavations, and in some places, ruins of considerable towns evidently reared for mining purposes."[30] Gregg was not wholly taken in by tall tales. Two or three old workings, like the mines of Cerrillos, a tiny settlement twenty miles south of Santa Fe, had once produced great quantities of gold, silver, and lead. Like other nineteenth-century Anglos, however, Gregg uncritically accepted the Spanish conviction that veins deep beneath the ground are wider and richer than those near the surface. The conviction derived, of course, from the medieval conception of veins as maturing branches of some central tree or mother lode at the center of the underworld. It survives in the half-abandoned mining towns of Colorado and New Mexico to this day, where old-timers tell inquiring travelers that the mines are not worked out, that somewhere is the great vein the miners missed. Gregg and other pioneer Anglos in New Spain accepted the Spanish thinking because their own tradition derived from Spanish experience. Miners digging in colonial Virginia, Maryland, Pennsylvania, and New England understood the medieval tradition of the four elements and the old techniques of prospecting, but they understood too the Spanish land classification system translated by innovators like Plattes. In 1784, almost one-and-one-half centuries after its first appearance in London, *A Discovery of Subterraneall Treasure* was reprinted in Philadelphia.[31] Despite a complex heritage of Atlantic-coast iron mining, the citizens of the new republic hungered for Spanish knowledge, for insights into criadero-seeking and into the establishment of reals de minas.

As early as 1497 Sebastian Cabot discovered precious metal along the Atlantic coast of the New World; he eyed the ornaments of the Indians carefully and determined that nearby must be veins of pure copper. Twenty-seven years later Giovanni Verazzano found copper on Nantucket Island; another explorer found iron ore in present-day North Carolina in 1585. More discoveries followed, and King James I ordered that one-fifth of any gold discovered—for surely it seemed about to be discovered—revert at once to his own purse. His 1606 proclamation seemed wise enough three years later, when thirty-five tons of Virginia iron arrived at Bristol for smelting. No one doubted that gold was growing somewhere near such high quality iron ore, perhaps in the sun-warmed hill country of Virginia. By 1650, however, such dreams were finished. Most colonists thought only of clearing and planting the land, and only a handful of farsighted and well-read men looked to Europe for experienced miners and workers, for adventurous, out-of-work artificers willing to fight Indians while they found and dug iron ore. Miners from Cornwall, Wales, and German principalities transplanted the medieval traditions of their craft along with their wives and children and began shaping the land for artifice. In New England they worked in corners, or "neighborhoods," of towns settled by husbandmen, but in Pennsylvania, Maryland, and especially in Virginia they settled where the iron grew and created their own version of the real de minas, the eighteenth-century iron plantation.

As early as 1619 the London Company dispatched professional miners and ironworkers to Virginia. One hundred and fifty artificers arrived and settled on Falling Creek in present-day Chesterfield County. From the start the men were optimistic and planned on shipping refined iron within a year. "The iron proved reasonably good," remarked Robert Beverly in 1705, "but before they got into the body of the mine, the people were cut off in that fatal massacre, and the project has never been set on foot since."[32] Only two small children survived the massacre of 1622, when Indian bands fell upon the settlement and demolished the structures and equipment, and throughout the seventeenth century Virginians relied on imported iron to support their agricultural and military activities. An "iron work erected would be as much worth as a silver mine, all things considered," argued the anonymous author of *A Perfect Description of Virginia* in 1649, "not only to make all instruments of iron for the plantation uses, but for building and shipping."[33] Tobacco raising seduced every immigrant into agriculture, however, because it promised immediate return on very little capital, indeed on nothing but the labor of clearing land. Ironworking languished; in 1662 and again twenty years later the Virginia assembly prohibited the export of any iron equipment from the colony. Iron was almost as precious as silver, for without it clearing land and raising tobacco, the whole labor of planting, were impossible.

No miners arrived to exploit the ready market. Mining required large capital investment and exquisite organization along with expert miners. Individual miners alone made little impact on a region, as the Spanish in northern New Spain learned from watching the pitiful attempts of gambucinos hacking away at rich criaderos. A real de minas succeeded only when its backers hired a large number of good miners and supplied them with shelter, equipment, and food during months of exploratory digging. Not until 1714, when Governor Spotswood arranged the immigration of forty men, women, and children from the iron-mining Sieg Valley in Westphalia, was Virginian iron explored and exploited.

Spotswood settled the Westphalians thirty miles west of the nearest plantation, beyond the falls of the Rappahannock near its confluence with the Rapidanna. He built a small fort, armed it with two cannon, and called the outpost Germanna. For two years, while he waited for royal permission to begin silver-mining operations, the Westphalians did very little but look about themselves. They read the signs and found iron ore; by 1716 Spotswood had acquired title to Germanna and begun a fledgling iron industry. His use of colony funds to support what seemed to his opponents a strictly private venture caused him difficulty, however, and even the miners moved on, to a place in Stafford County that they called first Germantown, then Prince William. But Spotswood was undismayed. He had learned of an inexpensive, extremely efficient way of iron mining. Like the Spanish before him, Spotswood organized his iron plantation like a real de minas and employed slaves below and above the ground.[34] His example spread across Virginia into Maryland, and from there into Pennsylvania. His venture at Germanna attracted the curious, even successful tobacco planters like William Byrd of Westover Plantation.

Byrd recorded his impressions of Virginia iron mining in a diary called *A Progress to the Mines in the Year 1732,* an account of a trip he made to "spy the land" and learn something of "the mystery of making iron." He visited the iron plantation owned by Spotswood and another, smaller mining and smelting operation owned by Augustine Washington. At both places he asked how to read the signs of subterranean ore, how to extract ore from the ground and prepare it for smelting and founding, and how to engage experienced artificers. A little iron ore, "very spongy and poor," prompted his long ride through the backcountry.[35] He had discovered a vein on his plantation and needed more information than books could supply. He needed to speak with artificers.

Charles Chiswell, the manager of Spotswood's enterprises, explained that Byrd must first explore the quality and quantity of his new-found vein and "keep a good pickax man at work a whole year to search if there be a sufficient quantity." Assaying was a task best left to experts because rich ore yields brittle iron, which is almost as useless as poor quality ore. Chiswell taught according to the oral tradition, by example and reference to the four elements. "He showed me a sample of the richest ore they have in England, which yields a full moiety of iron," Byrd recorded. "It was of a pale red color, smooth and greasy, and not exceedingly heavy; but it produced so brittle a metal that they were obliged to melt a poorer ore along with it." Byrd, and Chiswell too it seems from the record kept by his industrious student, thought sometimes in medieval terms and used words like *brimstone* in the midst of technical sentences. Certainly some remnants of the four elements philosophy outlined in Burton's *Anatomy of Melancholy* survived in eighteenth-century Virginia. One of Chiswell's indentured servants stole Byrd's medicinal brandy and caused Byrd to inquire into her character. "This unhappy girl, it seems, is a baronet's daughter," he determined, "but her complexion, being red-haired, inclined her so much to lewdness that her father sent her, under the care of the virtuous Mr. Cheep, to seek her fortune on this side of the globe."[36] Byrd thought in wholistic terms about the nature of reddish iron ore and red-haired women; a trace of his philosophy informs Morse's 1789 *American Geography* description of Californians sun-

ning themselves atop criaderos. Byrd requested the latest technical information; Chiswell replied in centuries-old terms and philosophies.

But Chiswell and Spotswood understood only modern economics.[37]
Both men convinced Byrd that small-scale mining enterprises made little
profit, and that an iron plantation succeeded only if it was properly laid
out, according to tradition. Spotswood thought that at least 100 slaves
were needed to support the work of trained European artificers; Chiswell suggested 120, "and the more Virginians amongst them the better,"
because newly arrived Africans rebelled against their hard lot.
Spotswood expected "that those upon good land would make corn and
raise provisions enough to support themselves and the cattle and do
every other part of the business." Slave labor, according to Spotswood,
depressed the wages of high-priced European artificers. He and Chiswell ran their operation with only eight white craftsmen, and only the
miner, founder, and "collier" were particularly well skilled. Slaves did
almost all the heavy digging and loading, but blasting remained a complex art delegated to a white "engineer." High wages disturbed
Spotswood. His Westphalian miners moved ten miles west from Germanna and went into business for themselves, and newly arrived artificers proved independent as well as expensive. Spotswood's iron founder,
"one Godfrey of the kingdom of Ireland," was paid by the ton of melted
iron and given free board; the mason who erected Washington's furnace
and Spotswood's at Fredericksville was paid "from the time he left his
house in Gloucestershire to the time he returned thither again, unless he
chose rather to remain in Virginia after he had done his work."[38] Miners
and metalworkers were highly skilled and highly paid men but they were
not always literate. Washington's ironmaster, who served as master of
the mines and furnace at Principia in Maryland too, was totally illiterate
but wonderfully learned in the mystery of iron making. Such mystery-
knowing men fulfilled the dreams and emptied the pocketbooks of
profit-seeking governors and planters. An iron plantation depended on
up-to-date financial management but its makers shaped it according to
traditional dictates.

Spotswood's iron plantation superficially resembled the tobacco plantations established farther east by wealthy colonists. It focused on a big
house and dwellings for the overseers and skilled artificers, and on slave
quarters too. It was surrounded by arable fields planted to grains and
other food crops. But it was not intimately associated with the Tidewater,
and it fronted on a flowing stream, not an estuary. The stream powered
the bellows that blasted the furnace fire into white heat, and it was of no
use in transportation. Slaves carted ore one mile from mine to furnace,

and sow and pig iron was carted fifteen miles to waiting ships. When
Byrd visited it, the plantation was not yet self-sufficient; Spotswood
bought provisions to feed the slaves at work in the mines and at the
furnace.[39] Indeed the plantation was not an agricultural shaping of
space but something wholly different. "All the land hereabouts seems
paved with iron ore," wrote Byrd of the land near Spotswood's mine, "so
that there seems to be enough to feed a furnace for many ages." Artifice,
not agriculture, shaped the wilderness.

Spanish technique inspired Spotswood, Byrd, and men like them who
dreamed of subterranean wealth. Near the end of his visit with
Spotswood, Byrd spoke with him about the *flota*, the treasure fleet that
sailed yearly from La Vera Cruz to Spain, carrying the riches of the
Philippines, Peru, Mexico, and New Spain. Spotswood explained the
intricacies of the operation, and the significance of the *azogue* ships "that
carry quicksilver to Portobelo and La Vera Cruz to refine the silver."
New Spain was much on the minds of the two men; by the 1713 Treaty
of Utrecht, Great Britain acquired a thirty-three-year monopoly of selling African slaves everywhere in New Spain as well as the prized right to
send one trading ship each year. Relations between Spain and England
were often strained, sometimes even by war, but in 1732 interested Englishmen knew a great deal about the fabulous riches the Spanish attempted to hide, and in particular they knew about the reals de minas.
Mining and refining technology flowed fitfully from New Spain to
Europe, and to the English colonies, carried by the flota, by English
slavers, and by exchanged prisoners, adventurers, and fortune-seeking
runaways. Enslaved miners were only the most obvious similarity between the reals de minas and the iron plantations.

Africans made unruly slaves but they seemed to learn ironmaking very
quickly, so quickly in fact that Spotswood was convinced his slaves could
be taught the mysteries of mining and iron founding and so relieve him
of exorbitant wages. He and Byrd were unaware of the mining and
founding heritage of the young Africans, many of whom were wrenched
from sophisticated mining and iron- and steelmaking West African
tribes who shipped their products hundreds of miles from their Niger
River villages.[40] Arabs and Europeans had long known that certain tribes
were particularly well skilled in ironwork, but slavers cared only for
healthy young men and women and so missed the opportunity of importing iron founders. Nevertheless, the iron plantations of Virginia,
Maryland, and Pennsylvania exploited men at least vaguely familiar with
their tasks. Indeed slavery made the iron plantations successful because
slavery ensured a steady supply of laborers. White immigrants wanted

high wages to slave in a pit or at a furnace, and most chose to plant tobacco rather than work for wages.

Iron plantations mystified all but their creators, however, no matter how diligently men such as Byrd and the African slaves struggled to understand them. Each plantation was a traditional ordering of space but one that made little sense either to well-read owners and visitors or to imported slaves. It was the miner who knew how to follow the veins of iron ore, how to shore up pitheads and shafts, how to blast free the solid rock, and it was the iron founder who knew the mystery of heaping charcoal and ore into a furnace blasted by bellows worked by a waterwheel, and built by a specially skilled mason. Outsiders saw order, of course, and owners like Spotswood were pleased to guide visitors on intricate tours. But the order was understood by the artificers alone, and only they—and their landlord—profited at all from the enterprise. And even then, the artificers earned only wages or else shared in some elaborate piecework scheme. An estensión, a New England town, a Pennsylvania or backcountry neighborhood belonged to its makers and sustainers and was intimately understood by all. An iron plantation was understood by only a handful of specialists, and it belonged to its landlord and no one else. In Virginia, as in Durango, the real de minas was traditional but very different from communities devised for husbandry.

Artifice and husbandry coexisted fitfully in colonial New England towns administered by husbandmen devoted to caressing, not raping, the earth. Mining worried the men who shaped the forested wilderness into planting fields, meadows, pastures, and houselots. Husbandmen feared the poisoning of water and soil, and they loathed the scent of brimstone.

In 1705, for example, the husbandmen of Simsbury, Connecticut, assembled to investigate a report "that there was a mine, either of silver or copper, in the town." Someone had read the signs and found what proved to be veins of copper in an unsettled corner of the town. Two years later a company of husbandmen hired contractors to dig out the ore and three college-educated clergymen to direct its smelting. But book learning turned out to be no substitute for experience, and by 1721 German miners were digging the ore and German foundrymen were smelting it. Artifice quickly drained the husbandmen's limited resources, and soon men in Boston, New York, London, and even Holland had combined to assume the costs.[41] As in Virginia, experienced miners were eventually assisted by slaves and later by convicts. Only profit mattered to the absentee landlords.

By 1750 Copper Hill was riddled with exploratory shafts and producing mines. Names such as Sydervelt, Hoofman, and Müller entered the town records, and the small smelter built by the inexperienced clergymen was rechristened Hanover by Hanoverian artificers. Shafts forty-five to eighty feet deep opened on horizontal galleries that followed the veins several hundred feet in all directions. It was easy enough to identify the copper-bearing ore; it was yellowish-gray in color and mixed with blue-colored sulfuret and yellow pyrites. When British mercantile laws prohibited colonial smelting and casting of metal, the landlords continued their operations in secret and satisfied the crown by shipping occasional cargoes of raw ore to England.[42] From 1707 to the middle of the nineteenth century the mysteries of artifice puzzled the husbandmen of Simsbury.

Only rarely did husbandmen work in the mines or at the smelter. When the German miners followed the veins beneath the water table and required twenty-four-hour-a-day pumping to clear the galleries, between twenty-five and thirty husbandmen were recruited to work surface pumps, but few worked willingly with spade and pick far beneath the surface. Perhaps the husbandmen feared the "damps" described by John Woodward in *An Essay toward a Natural History of the Earth* in 1695, the "suffocating damp" that chokes miners and the "fulminating damp" that now and then causes explosions "so forcible as sometimes to kill the miners, break their limbs, shake the earth, and force coals, stones, and other bodies, even though they be of very great weight and bulk, from the bottom of the pit or mine, up through the shaft, discharging them out at the top or mouth of it." Explosions of sulfurets and pyrites worried cautious men but silent pollution concerned them too. Copper ore poisons plant life, as the Simsbury husbandmen learned when yellowish heaps of it were piled along roads, awaiting carting to docks. As late as 1876 a great circle marked by "an entire dearth of vegetation" reminded men where ore had been heaped prior to shipment to England more than a century before. Artifice poisoned the land, perhaps for eternity, and husbandmen feared the greenish soil and water that lay about mines and furnaces as much as they feared the dark pits and shafts from which fire sprang.

In 1751 a flame "as large as a common-sized man" burst out of a field near East Brunswick, New Jersey.[43] For three years great lumps of virgin copper had been turned up by plowmen tilling the field, and the flare (perhaps a result of pyrites exploding, perhaps a more mysterious "damp" or exhalation) convinced a company of Philadelphians to buy the field and sink a shaft by the stake driven to mark the sign. At fifteen feet, according to an account published in 1793, the miners "came on a vein of bluish stone, about two feet thick, between two perpendicular loose bodies of red rock, covered with a sheet of pure virgin copper, a little thicker than gold leaf." Farther down the men found more bluish stone "filled with sparks of virgin copper" and great lumps of pure metal. When water flooded the mine, the first company abandoned the enterprise to another that built pumps and a stamp mill. The pumps cleared the shaft and the mill pulverized the ore-bearing stone and washed free the pure copper, which the owners shipped to England. As at Simsbury, the mines were abandoned when the copper market collapsed, "although the vein when left was richer than it ever had been." And as in Connecticut, the tailings loomed above the fertile earth.

Words like *sparks* and *virgin* recall the old beliefs about mining that endured into the nineteenth century, as John Grammer's "Account of the Coal Mines in the Vicinity of Richmond, Virginia" of 1818 makes clear. The *pits,* as the local people called the mines, had been opened in the 1780s, abandoned when the coal seam caught fire, and reopened by two Scotch miners and a number of slaves. A steam engine pumped water from the three shafts, each of which reached at least 300 feet into the ground, and from the 1,350-foot-long gallery that followed the seam. But Grammer paid scant attention to the precious steam engine imported from England; his imagination reeled as he descended the shafts. "The gloomy blackness, however, of most of the galleries, and the strange dress and appearance of the black miners, would furnish sufficient data to the conception of a poet, for a description of Pluto's kingdom," he wrote. "A strong sulphurous acid ran down the walls of many of the galleries; and I observed one of the drains was filled with a yellowish gelatinous substance, which I ascertained, on a subsequent examination, was a yellow, or rather a reddish, oxide of iron, mechanically suspended in water." At the coal mines Grammer discovered all the chthonic phenomena and perils described centuries earlier by Kircher and Plattes. Not only was coal in a contiguous seam on fire, but "a strong sulphurous fume" shot steadily "from an irregular hole in the side of the hill of about two feet in diameter," encrusting the nearby soil with crystals of pure sulfur.[44] Explosions of some sort of damp, probably "carburetted hydrogen gas," had killed some of the miners, and Grammer appears to have quit the mines with relief.

Patriots converted the unworked Simsbury Copper Hill mines into a prison for Loyalists and other criminals, and "the Newgate of Connecticut" served until 1827, although convict mining was abolished when prisoners used their tools to dig escape tunnels and attack guards. The prison was economical; only a few keepers were needed for the top of the shafts. But more than penny-pinching explains the subterranean imprisonment. To be buried alive was to be cut off not only from the world of men—any prison might do that effectively enough—but to be severed from the world of sunlight, fresh air, and vegetation, a just punishment for felons. Living burial fascinated Americans throughout the early nineteenth century and prompted popular tales like Poe's "The Cask of Amontillado" and George Lippard's *The Quaker City*. Such Gothic fiction appeared as the old dread of graveyards ebbed and the old fear of artifice grew stronger. Americans who no longer worried (at least publicly) about crossing graveyards after dark still dreaded a visit to a working or disused mine. After their abandonment as mines and prison, the shafts and galleries at Copper Hill frightened the tourists who came to be thrilled. But most visitors contented themselves with a long glance over pitheads into blackness and chose not to explore the reeking, dripping tunnels. Women shivered and men warned of earthquakes and bad air but all knew that the world below was a world apart. Mines, like the smelters, furnaces, and forges multiplying everywhere in northern Virginia, Maryland, and especially in Pennsylvania, were as mysterious and as suspect as ever.[45] Artificers knew of things beyond the light of day and wrought things beyond the knowledge of farmers and other people of sunlight. As Grammer said, they were of Pluto's kingdom. They raised the Devil out of the ground, or released him in fire from ore.

FURNACES

Iron ore is not iron. Before it can be cast or forged into useful shapes it must be smelted; all its impurities must be burned or melted away in a fiercely hot fire. "It is no work to be done in the chimney corner," asserted Gabriel Plattes, who understood the scale and implications of smelting.[46] A furnace dominated its site, dwarfing nearby buildings and consuming prodigious quantities of charcoal. It squatted at the center of a vast, every-broadening circle of cleared land devoted to no use whatsoever. By day its smoke blanketed the dwellings of the ironmaster and laborers or else drifted to distant farms and plantations. By night the glare from the top of the stack illuminated clouds, dwellings, and the fallow land in a dull, pulsating reddish light. Around the clock the furnace objectified what Byrd and others called the "mystery" of making iron.

At the outbreak of the Revolution at least eighty-two charcoal blast furnaces provided the iron used to manufacture the tools demanded by husbandmen, seamen, craftsmen, and merchants. Pennsylvania had twenty such furnaces, and Maryland seventeen; Massachusetts and Virginia had fourteen each, and most other colonies from one to eight. Colonial iron making threatened the iron industry of England, and as early as 1719 the mother country interfered in American operations, seeking to limit the production of small furnaces. Like the copper smelters of Simsbury, however, American ironmasters worked illegally when they were forbidden to make iron, and much of the time the increasingly complex English regulations proved unenforceable anyway. As early as 1646, when John Winthrop, Jr. established a furnace at Lynn, Massachusetts, the colonists recognized their growing need for cheap iron and they happily circumvented English law to satisfy it. By 1719 every smoking furnace objectified colonial self-determination.[47]

Traditional technology dictated the position and form of every furnace. Each stood as near as possible to a proved deposit of iron ore, next to a stream that turned the great wheel that powered the bellows so necessary in producing the blast of air that superheated the charcoal. Each stood on the side of a hill so that the charge of charcoal and ore was easily carted on a ramp to the top of the furnace and dumped onto the half-molten mass at the base. And finally, each furnace stood near a supply of firewood. Everything else, dwellings included, counted very little. Structures were erected wherever there was room, and vegetable gardens occupied fertile spots among the slag heaps. What mattered were the ore, the furnace, and the wood.

Byrd was astonished by the firewood needed to make charcoal. "When we approached the mines there opened to our view a large space of cleared ground," he wrote of his journey to Fredericksville, "whose wood had been cut down for coaling." Clear-cut fields surprised Byrd. He was accustomed to girdled trees towering above fields planted to tobacco, not acres upon acres of treeless fields abandoned to weeds. One ironmaster told him that the best timber for charcoal making was pine, walnut, hickory, oak, "and in short all that yields cones, nuts, or acorns." But what surprised Byrd was the amount of timber required for the coaling operation; his informant told him that two square miles of trees would supply a "moderate furnace" but only if the cleared acres grew up immediately after cutting.[48] Iron making, like all metallurgy, demanded wood, and most colonial furnaces devoured more than two square miles of forest.

Wood was scarce almost everywhere in New Spain, and criadero-seeking explorers quickly understood that large-scale mining and smelting might prove impossible north of the Rio Grande. One adventurer reported that he abandoned mines south of the river because "they did not contain enough silver to pay even for the charcoal used in smelting."[49] Despite innovations of artificers like Alvaro Barba, who found the *yareta* tree to burn better than other species because of its resinous sap, conquistadores in northern New Spain passed up rich criaderos when contiguous land produced few trees.

English colonists discovered massive stands of timber near almost every mining site, and newly arrived artificers started the felling of trees even as they began building their furnaces. Charcoal making required "colliers," men skilled in stacking and burning cordwood. Obtaining the wood presented few difficulties; colliers felled and split nearby trees and received cordwood sledged to them by husbandmen eager to earn wages during the winter. From late spring to early autumn, the colliers meticulously stacked the four-foot-long balks of wood in shallow pits some thirty to forty feet in diameter and covered each pit with earth and leaves. After igniting the wood through a hole at the top, the colliers tended the smoldering heaps for one or two weeks, until the combustion ended and all that remained was charcoal. While they watched the great stacks and made certain that the buried wood never burst into flame, the colliers and their helpers lived in hastily erected huts called "float cabins" and received their food from children who walked to the outposts from the dwellings near the furnace. A good collier made thirty-five to forty bushels of charcoal from each cord of wood but he did so at the cost of companionship. A visit to the furnace dwellings meant risking a flare-up and the certain destruction of an entire stack. Not surprisingly, colliers stank of smoke and dirt and quickly gave up keeping their cabins clean. Iron companies paid them according to the amount and quality of the charcoal they produced, and many colliers abandoned the work for better paying occupations. At Hopewell Furnace in Pennsylvania, and at other furnaces in that colony and in western Maryland, many of the colliers were newly arrived Irishmen who understood their skill but realized quickly that husbandry offered far more prestige, and a larger income.[50] They knew too that husbandmen disliked colliers.

Experts constantly debated which species of trees made the best charcoal. Many agreed with Byrd's informants: hardwoods like hickory made the heaviest charcoal. One bushel of charcoal weighed about ten pounds if made from white pine, but almost nineteen pounds if made from sugar maple. Artificers knew a traditional ranking of trees but one that ordered trees according to their value as fuel, not as indicators of fertile soil. "Charcoal from the hickory is used as the best," wrote Israel Acrelius in 1759 after visiting several Pennsylvania iron-making enterprises, "next to this that of ash and white oak, but still more of black oak, as that is most abundant and can best be spared." Like husbandmen, colliers sought out land covered with stands of hickory and white oak; husbandman and artificer understood the same hierarchy of trees and knew the meaning of the four elements. Hickory made the best charcoal but it indicated the richest, "warmest" soil; white oak made second-best charcoal and indicated soil only slightly inferior to that covered with hickory; white pine made poor charcoal and indicated almost worthless, "barren" ground.[51] Charcoal making clashed with husbandry, however, because iron-making companies intended to reforest whatever land they cleared. Husbandmen avoided iron plantations and pursued land covered with hickory and evidencing not the slightest indication of ore.

A typical New Jersey iron plantation incorporated about 20,000 acres of good forest. Each year the colliers felled about 1,000 acres of trees and converted the logs into charcoal. When they cleared the final thousand acres, the first thousand acres had grown up in trees about seven to twelve inches in diameter, the thickness preferred by European colliers long accustomed to scanty forest resources. Second-growth timber usually proved poorer in quality, but without it furnaces failed. Eighteenth- and early nineteenth-century forest management was born in the anxiety of iron-making companies. Colliers struggled to ensure an adequate harvest of cordwood and to prevent erosion.

Clear-cutting destroyed the forest ground cover, and the network of roads hastily devised by iron-plantation carters channeled heavy rainfall down slopes and into mud-choked streams. Medieval peasants complained about erosion and pollution caused by mining and metallurgical enterprises on the slopes above their fields; they declared that drainage so poisoned clear streams that fish died and that once-quiet landschaften had become nightmarish confusions.[52] Husbandmen in Pennsylvania and other colonies confronted identical problems. For all that they prospered by supplying food and livestock to the iron-making workers, husbandmen knew the causes and effects of deforestation and pollution from half-toxic slag heaps. At the close of the eighteenth century the typical iron plantation was isolated not only by its vast surrounding acreage of standing forest and clear-cut fields but also by the unwillingness of husbandmen to live near artifice.

Within the ring of cleared land stood the furnace and perhaps a forge and a trip-hammer. Clustered about the furnace were an open-sided shed filled with about 30,000 bushels of charcoal, stables for the company's cart horses, and storehouses filled with everything from lime for flux to new tools. Nearby were the "big house" of the ironmaster and his family and a number of dwellings housing the artificers and their families.[53] When the furnace was "in blast" men tended it continuously; everyone lived with the smoke by day and the glare by night. For 80 to 300 or 400 days at a time the intermittent forced-draft roar echoed from the surrounding hills. And from the base of the furnace issued forth molten slag and molten iron.

A typical eighteenth-century furnace tapered from about twenty-two feet square at its base to eleven feet square at its top; it stood about thirty feet high, set against a hillside and connected to it by a "bridge house" or "casting house" from which the charge was dumped. Furnace making was a skilled occupation because the furnace withstood immense heat; most were built of stone and brick and lined with clay. At one side of the furnace was the bellows operated by a waterwheel; water was usually channeled to the wheel along a sunken or elevated race linked to the nearby stream and storage ponds. One bellows produced consecutive blasts; a pair operating alternately created a continuous roar and even hotter temperatures. A smoking, roaring furnace betokened prosperity, and ironworkers admired it. It objectified their mastery of nature.

"Excellent smelters," commented Georg Agricola in 1556, "know how to govern the four elements." He explained that "they combine in right proportion the ores, which are part earth, placing no more than is suitable in the furnaces; they pour in the needful quantity of water; they moderate with skill the air from the bellows; they throw the ore into that part of the fire which burns fiercely."[54] Furnace operation changed little between the mid-sixteenth century and the prosperous years of the eighteenth century, as did men's feelings about it. While American ironworkers sometimes spoke in medieval terms, they almost invariably practiced customs derived from the ancient concern that metallurgy torments the embryos ripped from the womb of mother earth. Colonial American furnaces had personalities; they were named and very often had dates and mottoes chiseled into their stones. Sometimes, as at Cornwall Furnace in central Pennsylvania, the mottoes were German, the work of immigrant experts continuing Old World practice. But an even clearer link with age-old belief involved the women of the plantations. Very often furnaces were called by women's names, and the fires within them, whenever possible, were kindled by women and then tended by men. When a bride visited a furnace, the artificers pulled off one of her shoes and held it until she promised them a "treat," perhaps a kiss or fancy baked goods.[55] The web of custom indicates a half-conscious wish to make the furnace fertile and to keep it so. Like a mine, a furnace was somehow a womb, and excellent smelters found satisfaction in age-old tradition.

Husbandmen disliked the furnace. Although few recorded their impressions, oral folklore suggests that artificers and their infernal wombs attracted suspicion. Tales like one that survives near Cornwall Furnace to this day explain less about their subject than they do about their narrators. That the ironmaster of that furnace had bad luck while hunting and deliberately flung each of his dogs into the roaring furnace—including his prize hound, which stared at him pitifully before he picked it up and heaved it through the door—is terrible enough. That the tale lived on and on, and was embroidered with details such as the everlasting wail that echoes in the furnace roar, hints at the husbandmen's feeling for the ironmaster and for his awesome, alchemical womb that devoured earth and trees and spewed forth poisonous slag and molten metal.

Women had no real position in the iron plantation. Their housework was quickly accomplished and they rarely worked outdoors, except in vegetable gardens. Unlike the farmwife busy all day in her kitchen ell and sharing a variety of tasks with her husbandman-husband, iron-plantation women baked and made cheese and milked a single cow not for income but for family use. Here and there, as at Hopewell Furnace, one or two cooked for the unmarried workers, sewed clothes to be sold at the company store, and even cleaned castings near the furnace. But most, and most young children, did little farmwork because there was little to be done; they were separated from the world of their husbands, the world of men, and they inhabited rented dwellings.[56] Sometimes they cooked in kitchens designed for four families, and sometimes they packed their few belongings and moved to another plantation when their husbands' employers went bankrupt. It is no wonder that husbandmen and their wives distrusted the artifice and life-style so evident on every iron plantation. The mystery of iron making disrupted and sometimes destroyed traditional agricultural space. Somehow furnace smoke mocked age-old agricultural notions of fertility and marriage.

Husbandmen and their wives distrusted the artifice so evident in every iron plantation, but they cheerfully purchased the products of artifice, the stoves, skillets, shovels, hoes, nails, and—above all—plows and mouldboards that made possible the transition from husbandry to farming. Charcoal iron was well suited to agricultural uses; it was not so strong as nineteenth-century anthracite iron but it was rugged enough to support the massive experiment in land manipulation that swept the North and West. By the 1820s Hopewell Furnace was producing chiefly for the expanding agricultural market, the company clerk recording castings such as coulter lays, "corn-plow machines," small wheels, "shear wings," "land sides," and "wagon irons." Within ten years the list in-

cluded "plow castings," "threshing machines," "shelling machines," and
"wagon boxes."[57] Farmers who scorned wage earning and believed every
rumor about hardhearted ironmasters insisted on purchasing whatever
new tool or machine county-fair competitions proved to increase harvests or lighten work. Until the 1840s artificers produced chiefly for
husbandmen-farmers who distrusted the very processes that created the
tools used in a supposedly purer calling. Not until the first experiments
in railroad building did iron plantations begin producing for other artificers.

Ironmasters exploited larger and larger acreages of forest as they
struggled to meet the growing demands of experimenting farmers.
Their companies backed turnpikes and canals because charcoal was
shipped from ever more distant locations, and rough roads raised its
price enormously. Four-horse charcoal wagons carried only 100- to
300-bushel loads, and an operating furnace demanded a constant stream
of deliveries. Shipping charcoal by canal proved profitable to the
Hopewell Furnace owners, who quickly abandoned many of their wagons. Iron ore began to move along canals too, precisely as Fulton had
predicted; in Pennsylvania especially, ore began to move over much
longer distances than horses could profitably manage. Ore dug at
Cornwall Furnace arrived at Hopewell Furnace in the 1850s at two-
thirds the cost of wagon transportation.[58] But the owners of iron plantations supported turnpikes and canals not only because the age of
charcoal-fueled furnaces was giving way to a new era of coal-fired furnaces, steam-powered bellows, and higher quality iron.

Every furnace produced heavy, bulky products that tormented horses
and teamsters alike. Stoves, plows, and especially "blacksmith iron," or
bar iron, were difficult to cart over smooth, level roads. On rutted,
washed-out tracks, especially in the hilly regions where furnaces were
located, such cargoes proved almost impossible to move. Experienced
teamsters lost wagons down ravines or watched helplessly as wheels
mired in mud. Iron-making companies consequently purchased shares
in turnpike and canal companies because good roads and water transport
offered secure, inexpensive access to markets. So close was the relationship between iron plantations and canals that markets were determined
by canal access; if a canal served an area, iron products moved into it
quickly, but if it was hilly and without canal routes, iron-making companies sometimes ignored it completely. It was such calculated decisions
that underlay the farmers' enthusiasm for canal openings. Canals not
only offered cheap outlets for agricultural produce, they permitted the
inexpensive import of cumbersome farming tools produced hundreds

of miles away.[59] By the 1850s most iron plantations were linked by turnpikes or canals to the major agricultural regions of the North. Pittsburgh,
a city growing up around a dozen furnaces, was linked by the Ohio to
the entire Mississippi Valley.

Until the early 1840s most iron plantations retained their isolation.
The northern rage for railroad building quickly transformed the
metal-making industry; by 1860 most plantations were connected by
roads and railroads with population centers, and almost all had
exhausted their stands of hardwood forest. Smaller enterprises remained in business, relying on second-growth pine and other softwoods
for the charcoal to produce agricultural implements and blacksmith
iron. But newer furnaces in Pennsylvania, Maryland, and Vermont required coal to produce the high quality iron and steel castings needed by
railroad builders and other new-generation industrialists, and their
owners incorporated themselves in order to attract enough capital to
support the large-scale operations. Anthracite furnaces destroyed little
forest but consumed vast quantities of coal; they represented, along with
the great coal mines being opened in Pennsylvania, the triumph of corporate artifice. Valley Forge became a nonsense term in the 1860s; children knew its connection with Washington's winter encampment but
scarcely understood its meaning. Small furnaces were passing into obliv-
ion. In every agricultural community, however, one remnant of
charcoal-fueled artifice endured.

Longfellow wrote "The Village Blacksmith" in 1839 as the United
States entered the new era of capital-intensive, coal-fired artifice. His
poem is as restful as Vautin's 1845 watercolor sketch of the Cambridge,
Massachusetts, smithy that inspired Longfellow to depict a bastion of
artifice in terms usually reserved for agricultural spaces, structures, and
life-styles.[60] When Longfellow compared the measured beat of the
blacksmith's hammer with the ringing of a church bell and Vautin surrounded the smithy with clear air and colorful trees, art forever camo-
flauged the significance of smithies. By the 1840s the blacksmith no
longer commanded the respect of his agriculturist neighbors or millers
and other artificers. In many communities he was reduced to shoeing
horses and fixing wheel-rims, and often his forge stood cold.

Late in the eighteenth century eastern blacksmiths learned that inventors required complicated devices to further their schemes for mine
pumps, textile looms, and other contrivances, and many smiths, like
Oziel Wilkinson of Pawtucket, Rhode Island, began experimenting with
new casting and fabrication techniques. In February 1790 Wilkinson
advertised his new skills. "The subscriber has lately erected, at Pawtucket

Falls, a steel manufactory; where he has for sale for cash or bar-iron, steel in the blister or drawn into bars," ran his advertisement in the *United States Chronicle*. "He also makes paper-mill, clothiers', and print-ers' screws, machines for cutting cold nails by water or hand, irons for carding-machines and spinning jennies, mill irons, anchors, etc."[61] Not all Wilkinson's castings and machinery proved successful, but his ability—and the ability of men like him—to fabricate metal according to specification ensured the prosperity of the fledgling cotton-spinning en-terprises and earned him the title of "machinist." Machine tools, of course, are machines that make machines, and that announce the end of the first era of artifice. By the 1840s blacksmith work seemed crude alongside precision machines made by machinists using other machines. It was comforting for Longfellow and Vautin to gaze at a quiet smithy and recall the less complicated artifice of bygone days. In their nostalgia they forgot or deliberately ignored the once-powerful symbolic force that inhabited every blacksmith shop.

Every blacksmith operation displayed in reduced scale the mysteries of furnaces, and every smith inhabited a tiny microcosm of artifice sur-rounded by dominant agriculture. Husbandmen needed his services and his products but they distrusted his work almost as thoroughly as they distrusted the work of miners and furnace operators. A blacksmith con-sumed vast quantities of wood in order to make the charcoal essential to his metal processing, and he did business with iron plantations.[62] All day he polluted the air, not only with smoke but with noise; his constant beating of red-hot iron against an iron anvil echoed from within his deliberately darkened shop (only in gloom can a smith accurately discern the colors of iron glowing at different temperatures), reminding hus-bandmen beyond the range of smoke that in their midst labored some-one different from themselves, one linked to the darkness of the mine and the furnace. More than miners and foundrymen, smiths are re-membered in countless folktales as possessing strange powers or pos-sessed by sinister forces; no husbandman fully understood their craft, and almost everyone feared their fire.

An agriculturist's fire produces warmth and well-cooked food, and while a man chops and splits and stacks its fuel, its maintenance is part of housewifery. In the popular imagination of the seventeenth, eighteenth, and early nineteenth centuries a smoking farmhouse chimney connotes the warmth implicit in a close-knit, loving family because its smoke is an indirect product of the gracious light of the sun. "The properties of the divine fire that is above, are heat, making all things fruitful, and light, giving life to all things," wrote the sorcerer Henry Cornelius Agrippa in

1533 in a book translated and quoted approvingly into the nineteenth century. "The celestial and bright fire drives away spirits of darkness; also this, our fire made with wood, drives away the same." At night, particularly during winter storms, the entire farm family arranges itself about the hearth, tells tales, perhaps seeks omens in leaping kernels of wheat, and locked in reverie gazes at the flames dancing half-confined above the wood.

But fire, especially constricted blazes fueled with charcoal or coal, connoted the torments of Hell. "The properties of the infernal fire," Agrippa warned, "are a parching heat, consuming all things, and darkness, making all things barren.[63] Puritan clerics, eighteenth-century ecclesiastics, and nineteenth-century camp-meeting revivalists and almanac editors often explained infernal fire by analyzing the blacksmith's glowing forge. When Michael Wigglesworth published his *Day of Doom* in 1662 he little knew that it would become so popular that one in every thirty-five New Englanders would own a copy and that children would be made to memorize all 224 of its stanzas; a century later New Englanders could still recite its versified depiction of the Last Day, including stanzas detailing the fire of Hell. Wigglesworth knew the fascinating power of fire imagery and filled his long poem with references to the lake "where fire and brimstone flameth," to the divine vengeance that "feeds the flame/With piles of wood, and brimstone flood," and to the wretches bound with iron bands and flung into eternal conflagration before concluding that no human can accurately imagine the "plagues of Hell, and torments exquisite."[64] In colonial theology the fire of artifice connoted future punishment for earthly sin and confirmed folk beliefs in subterranean explosions, demons, and exhalations.

Now and then a particularly astute cleric recognized the power of fire imagery and refined it for spiritual ends. Jonathan Edwards, for example, knew that all his parishioners had at one time or another been burned by an ember in a fireplace, and in 1740 he preached a sermon enlivened by fire symbolism and by references to the furnaces of eighteenth-century artifice. "But to help your conception, imagine yourself to be cast into a fiery oven, all of a glowing heat, or into the midst of a glowing brick-kiln, or of a great furnace, where your pain would be as much greater than that occasioned by accidentally touching a coal of fire, as the heat is greater," he noted in "The Future Punishment of the Wicked Unavoidable and Intolerable." His sermon is filled with references to the "deluge of fire and brimstone," to houses on fire, and to comparisons of humans in hellfire with insects: "You have often seen a spider, or some other noisome insect, when thrown into the midst of a fierce fire, and have observed how immediately it yields to the force of the flames." In the sermons of Edwards and many other eighteenth-century clergymen, fire is the fire of artifice, the fire half-contained in furnaces and scented with brimstone, not the odor of dried wood. The molten lake described in Revelation seemed perfectly embodied in the flowing metal familiar to any visitor to an iron plantation—or to anyone who stopped to gaze at the white-hot, writhing metal pulsing in the blacksmith's forge. In an age of open fire, everyone knew the instantaneous pain of contacting glowing coals, and clergymen repeated the lesson for the sake of souls wandering in sin. Hellfire burns everywhere in American popular tradition, just as it informs the finest national literature. When Hawthorne described the flaming lime-kiln in Old Testament terms and Melville described the hideous appearance of the Galapagos ("in many places the coast is rock-bound, or more properly, clinker-bound; tumbled masses of blackish or greenish stuff like the dross of an iron-furnace"), their audience had been conditioned for generations to regard the furnaces and smithies in which unnatural fire twisted and leaped as the very emblems of Hell itself.[65] Not even mills could be more sinister.

MILLS

"No miller goes to Heaven." Husbandmen everywhere in early modern Europe vented their distrust of millers and mills in sayings like the old Norman one. "Beside ever mill stands a mountain of sand" reflects what every German peasant suspected to be true. Millers adulterated meal and finely ground flour with powdered bark and roots, with ground limestone, and with sand, returning to hapless peasants not the wholesome fruit of agricultural labor but an artificial mixture fit for no man. Millers carefully filled sacks first with coarse black meal, then topped them off with a few inches of fine white flour, and sold them to unsuspecting husbandmen. When peasants brought grain to be ground, millers diverted some of it down the "thief's hole" before weighing and grinding the remainder.[66] By law, every miller could keep no more than about one-fourteenth of any peasant's grain as a fee for grinding, but no peasant peering about at the chutes, scales, revolving gears, and dusty gloom trusted himself to watch the miller closely enough. "Every honest miller has a tuft of hair in the palm of each hand" went the English saying. Children learned early that such millers were rare indeed.

Unlike smithies, water mills and windmills are relatively recent inventions. A few were known to the classical Greeks and Romans but the improved versions were invented in northern Europe. As a substitute for ancient hand mills they spread slowly, and not until the twelfth century did Germans begin to improve upon earlier primitive designs. Millers were consequently suspected not only of dishonesty but also of controlling a new and dangerous force, or combination of forces. For one thing, water-driven mills ensnared free-flowing water in a prison of wheels and sluices, prompting many peasants to worry about the anger of water sprites. Early modern Europe remained dotted with countless springs and streams of supernatural potency to which barren wives and other stricken people resorted for help. Pagan respect for certain bodies of water increased when Christian missionaries explained baptism, and endured into the nineteenth century across Western Europe; in the "utmost skirts of the north" of Scotland it survives today despite prohibitions enacted in 1579, 1629, and 1656.[67] Seventeenth-century Scots believed that south-flowing water and water from certain springs brought fertility and cured illness, and on May Day they drank the water and hoped, if they did not pray. Such half-pagan, half-Christian beliefs clashed with the miller's desire to ensnare the water, to "enslave" it forever. Of course the flowing water occasionally rebelled, sometimes successfully as one German proverb still announces: "Whoever lives in a mill always fears the revenge of mishandled elements."[68] The saying encompasses windmills too, whose sails entangle the wind as wheels entangle water, and rightly so, for windmills, like water mills, are frequently damaged or destroyed in storms. Peasants misunderstood the mill long after they learned to rely on it. Unlike Don Quixote, who jousted with the windmills he mistook for giants, husbandmen made no war on mills. Along with flowing water and the wind, they were ensnared by the millers' technical expertise and account books. Agriculturists hated mills not only because they enslaved the elements; mills controlled the fortunes of husbandry too.

Not surprisingly, agriculturists associated mills with tales of devils and eldritch humanoids who ground up humans and livestock late at night. But the tales derived from more than vestiges of the Old Religion and financial misery. Mill sites rarely coincide with land suitable for agriculture. Millers in early modern Europe sought out natural mill seats, places near waterfalls or atop cliffs or near beaches, anywhere near adequate, dependable water or wind power. Such locations almost invariably lay beyond the outermost fields in any landschaft, and certainly away from the clustered steads. But mills nevertheless had great value and demanded continuous protection, so millers with their families lived in or beside them and eventually by virtue of their lonely and mysterious lives acquired the status given to other inhabitants of the landschaft fringe (woodcutters and huntsmen) and aroused the suspicions of men and women at the landschaft center. Histories of devils, robbers, and sorcerers frequently cite millers as accomplices. Honest people suspected the lonely millers almost automatically. While peasants slept unsoundly on windy nights, millers ground grain by candlelight; the flickering light attracted robbers, murderers, and every other criminal, along with bewildered young women.[69] Agriculturists popularly imagined millers to be seductive and adulterous; it is this belief that makes Chaucer's fourteenth-century "Miller's Tale" so hilarious—the miller is cuckholded for a change. Even now, streets of ill-repute in German cities are called "Mill Street," for German popular culture recalls the isolated locations that led millers to join robbers, rapists, and Satan himself.

Landschaft elders did not happily locate a mill among their houses. Although the location simplified social control and lessened the likelihood of nighttime evil, it increased the danger of fire. Occasional explosions of grain dust terrified peasants and millers alike, who understood nothing of their cause. On mills—and millers—focused the early modern understanding of artifice as danger. Whether it was better to have a mill beyond the edge of a landschaft or at its center few would say. In 1671, however, some Baltic peasants made the decision soon after the completion of a water mill. Once the waters of the stream were damned, channeled, and twisted, the peasants observed, their landschaft suffered a year-long drought. To propitiate the water spirits or God, or for some other reason known only to themselves, the peasants burned the mill to break the drought. At least they spared their landschaft the horror of an unannounced grain-dust explosion.

When in the fourteenth century Dante likened a windmill to Satan threshing his arms, novelty sharpened the simile.[70] Even as late as the early seventeenth century, when Cervantes wrote *Don Quixote,* windmills were still uncommon in some parts of the Iberian peninsula; the misguided nobleman jousts not only out of error but out of a vague awareness that windmills epitomize the new economic order in La Mancha. Along the coasts of seventeenth-century England, Holland, France, and the German nations, however, windmills turned everywhere. And like the inland water mills and a few tidal mills, the wind-driven machines were intricately placed in a developing market economy that sapped the old self-reliance of landschaften.

Siege engines excepted, mills were the first machines so big that men entered them. Windmills and water mills thundered and vibrated as they "worked," and visiting husbandmen found few stanchions and bars secure enough to grab. Ropes, levers, wooden blocks moved at the discretion of the miller, but the gyrations of shafts and cogwheels and gears sometimes suggested a half-wild living being writhing free of restraint. On quiet days millers enjoyed peaceful hours of tending their wooden apparatus, but when the wind suddenly freshened or a sluice gate broke open or a floating log drifted into the waterwheel, the men scurried about, disengaging drive trains, furling sails, and diverting water. At such moments mills teetered at the brink of destruction; if the wooden gears revolved too quickly and the animal-fat lubrication dried, friction set ablaze the places of close contact.[71] Flames reached other parts quickly and, unless the miller reacted faster, engulfed the entire mill. Children assisted their fathers at all times in the mill but especially during moments of intense activity and crisis. They learned the craft of milling and learned to scorn peasants afraid of machinery.

Mills varied in size and form. Windmills, particularly those used in the Netherlands after the early fifteenth century to pump seawater from reclaimed polder, towered seventy feet or more; many were conical or almost cylindrical and in some way moved to face the wind. Post mills dated to the late twelfth century; they were small, box-like structures mounted several feet above the earth on an immense beam dug into the ground; the entire mill, housing and vanes, pivoted about the vertical axis. Tower or cap mills appeared about two centuries later in France, and although they never supplanted post mills, their large bulk attracted the attention of peasants everywhere. Only the very top or cap of the larger mills swiveled to direct the placement of the vanes; the lower part of the tower remained stationary, housing the millstones, machinery, and sometimes the miller's family. In flat country the windmills served as landmarks to the wayfarers searching for landschaften; travelers knew that church spires marked the focus of landschaften but the mills became useful guides too.[72] Water mills, of course, were far less obvious. Often they nestled in twisting, rocky ravines beyond the casual gaze of travelers, and many adventurers came upon them suddenly and stopped to ask directions. European water mills, unlike windmills, were often built of stone to help ensure permanency but just as often they were wood. Early modern European mills were compact, and many in poorer regions were very simple, as simple as the first colonial mills.

Settlers in northern New Spain found the local Indians using hand-powered grinding stones like those used in sixteenth-century Spain, and for decades many estensiónes relied on the crude but effective devices. Neither wind nor water was plentiful north of the Rio Grande, and settlers struggled to apportion water between husbandmen desperate for irrigation and millers dependent on power. Some Spanish millers used the most primitive waterwheels, the horizontal, "Greek," or "Norse"—the names reflect the continuing controversy over origins—wheel. At the San Jose Mission near San Antonio, Texas, is a Spanish horizontal wheel, a small, not particularly powerful device that has the advantage of using very little water. Elsewhere in northern New Spain colonial millers built larger structures out of adobe and erected undershot or overshot wheels such as the one at La Cueva in northern New Mexico. La Cueva mill is mostly adobe and straggles along the millrace; over the centuries it has been modified again and again but its location remains the same. At La Cueva the mill is beyond the fields of the settlers, at the fringe of the estensión, at a naturally advantageous site, a mill seat.[73] But although the mill was at the edge of the estensión it was integral to the prosperity of the community. In New Spain and in the English colonies husbandmen regulated mills and millers for the public good.

Regulation proved difficult to establish and even harder to maintain, as the Plymouth Colony town of Scituate learned as early as 1636. Like other New Englanders, the husbandmen of Scituate immediately recognized their need of a gristmill, and they offered their fellow colonist William Gillson a few acres of prime agricultural land on which to build a windmill. Gillson received his excellent acreage only because it happened to lie along the edge of Third Cliff, overlooking the Atlantic and subject to continuous breezes. In 1636 the Scituate husbandmen had been three years without a mill; since their arrival in the New World in 1633 they had ground grain in hand mills. But Gillson soon fell ill, and died in 1639, leaving his mill (perhaps unfinished) to a nephew. The townspeople determined that a miller from outside Scituate might be encouraged to settle if offered a monopoly and other benefits. Isaac Stedman accepted their offer and by 1640 had erected a small water mill about one mile from the cluster of houses that marked the focus of Scituate existence.[74]

Scituate's difficulties with Gillson's windmill and with attracting a qualified miller were typical. Just as any man might learn how to clear land according to svedjebruket or build a log house, any intelligent man might learn how to build and operate a simple gristmill merely by observing one for several months, perhaps as a part-time apprentice. Nevertheless, many millers preferred to keep their craft secret, and husbandmen trying to build mills in the New World committed a variety of blunders. They located mills incorrectly, at sites where spring freshets destroyed them or on brooks that dried up in summer and remained so until late autumn, and sometimes they built machinery incorrectly. Obtaining millstones taxed the resources of every would-be miller because most New England rock, even the hardest granite, pulverized itself faster than it pulverized grain. If stones were ordered from England or from the Continent (the best millstones in England came from the Peak District of southwest Yorkshire and the northeastern part of Derbyshire and the best from the Continent from Mayen and Nieder Menting, the regions near Cologne), the miller had to pay cash or else establish credit, along with paying shipping. But until experienced stonecutters discovered the quartz-shot sandstone on Mount Tom in Connecticut and other equally useful varieties at Westerly, Rhode Island, in Ulster County in New York, in Rowan County in North Carolina, and in Lancaster, Berkshire, and Carbon counties in Pennsylvania, colonists ordered stones from Europe and paid the price.[75] Attracting an experienced miller, therefore, was a difficult operation. Not only did a town have to assure him of a permanent income but it had to subsidize his initial investment. Most towns did as Scituate. They offered interested millers a monopoly for a specific length of time and permanent right to a mill seat, arable land, and woodland, along with the right to keep a proportion of all flour. Many towns agreed that one-fourteenth of all flour was fair but Scituate bargained less well; Stedman agreed to keep one-twelfth of all flour in exchange for settling in the town. Scituate received his services and his promise to grind townspeople's grain before milling the grain of outsiders. After all, in a drought not all grain might be milled, and the Scituate husbandmen were determined that their miller would serve them first. In the hierarchical order of town society Stedman stood very near the top, with most New England millers.

Throughout the seventeenth century, New England towns tried to attract millers by offering them land and privileges. In 1673 Scituate attempted to establish a second mill to accommodate a new generation of successful husbandmen committed to market agriculture. That year the town meeting offered a valuable reward, "thirty acres of upland" to anyone who "will within six months engage to build a corn mill or gristmill upon the Third Herring Brook in Scituate within seven years next after the date of these presents and set hard to work and also engage to keep and tend the said mill for the term of fourteen years after she is set to work."[76] The contract implies that erecting a mill takes time but the seven-year period is more significant. Scituate husbandmen realized that it might take years for one of them to learn not only the craft of milling but enough about mill construction to know where to site one and how to build it, and perhaps even seven years to obtain the capital to order the stones from Europe. Perhaps the men were overly cautious; by 1676 Charles Stockbridge had established a mill but his feat compared poorly with Stedman's adventure forty years before. By the 1670s New England's artisans included a small, elite group of specialized craftsmen called millwrights, men who traveled from town to town building mills for half-skilled millers to tend. At the beginning of the eighteenth century, mill-building had become part of the emerging American tradition of common engineering.[77] But despite the presence of millwrights, establishing a mill remained an expensive task, as the husbandmen of Scituate—and of many other New England towns— knew. It required a taste for adventure and innovation, and townsmen found only a few men willing to abandon husbandry for the uncertain rewards of artifice.

Milling was uncertain for several reasons. Regulation restricted millers until well into the eighteenth century; a mill was something like a public utility, and millers found scarce encouragement to raise rates. Climate proved an impediment too. Every winter threatened a miller's livelihood because most streams and many rivers froze quite solidly and denied the miller his source of power. Summer droughts also stopped his mill, sometimes into the autumn. And spring freshets and winter storms ripped away his dams, sluices, and wheels and now and then (as the old German proverb insisted) destroyed his mill too. Windmills worked in all seasons, of course, and many New England and Long Island towns favored them over waterpowered mills, not only for security but also because when water-millers compensated for the whims of climate, their adaptations angered the men who depended on the mills. Dams, for example, lessened dangers from drought and even from flood; low dams of stone, logs, and packed earth stood upstream from many seventeenth- and eighteenth-century mills. But the dams impounded acres of water that killed standing timber, flooded waterside meadows, and—in the summer, when water levels dropped—turned whole stretches of ground into mud. In 1673 the Scituate town meeting worried about a leaking milldam, noting that "when it is down the mill pond will be the occasion of miring of many cattle."[78] The husbandmen agreed to fence in the mire and—since the mill was to be relocated upstream—use it for pasture once it had dried. Water rights and impoundments puzzled town meetings because they pitted agricultural needs against the requirements of artifice, and wise millers suspected that husbandmen angered by milling costs might turn against them by regulating the source of power. Beneath the accords reached in town after town lay always a tenseness that familiarity never wholly vanquished. Always the mill was necessary, and always the miller kept some part of the husbandmen's harvest; sometimes he inundated their land as well or decreased the flow of streams on which they depended. Now and again he inadvertently mired or drowned their livestock.

In the Tidewater and Piedmont, mills were far scarcer and far less regulated than in New England. Southerners imported much of their grain, either unground or as flour, and concentrated on raising and exporting tobacco. As the rich land wore out and more and more planters and householders began raising corn and other grains, however, men learned the need for waterpowered mills. Previously slaves had pounded grain in stone handmills as they had in Africa or else ground their masters' crops with horsepowered mills. Householders brought their grain to the nearest plantation and watched the planter keep some of it as fee for grinding the rest. In the mid-eighteenth century such casual enterprises were refined by men like William Allason, a Virginia planter who selected one of his holdings as the site for a waterpowered gristmill.[79] North Wales Plantation in Fauquier County comprised only 565 acres but it was crossed by a trustworthy stream called Great Run and stood in a neighborhood of householders. By August 1775 he had selected a millwright named John Ball to design and build his mill; Ball came with good qualifications, among them perhaps a hand in building the mill on George Washington's Mount Vernon Plantation, and certainly an expertise in a difficult craft. When Allason visited his completed mill he found it built of thick stone walls that reached up almost twenty feet and sheltered a thirteen-foot overshot waterwheel powered by water brought from Great Run through a headrace half a mile long and turning two pairs of grindstones. The mill used iron hardware purchased from a Frederick County forge, timber brought from other counties as well as from parts of Fauquier, and twenty-four hogsheads of shells carted from the seashore to be used as mortar. Like most common engineers, Ball deviated constantly from his plans, innovating and improving as he worked. Twenty-three men worked on the mill between August 1775 and July 1777; thirteen were slaves, including two carpenters. In a letter written at the beginning of the enterprise Allason noted that the millseat was on a good road and so ought to attract a variety of customers. By the summer of 1777 Allason was well pleased. Despite the war his mill showed promise.[80] It served his plantation, neighboring plantations, and smallholdings; he hoped it would profit.

Allason was not alone in his entrepeneurial enterprise. In every colony outside New England adventurous men erected mills wherever it seemed profitable and wherever they could obtain colony permission, if

such permission was needed. In New Amsterdam, for example, a patroon named Frederick Philipse erected a gristmill at the confluence of
the Pocantico and Hudson rivers, at the edge of the Patroonship of
Philipsborough. Sometime between 1680 and 1684 Philipse ordered that
a wooden mill built on stone foundations be constructed to serve the
needs of his tenants and to provide him with flour for export. At Upper
Mills, as the millseat became known, developed an entire community
under Philipse's careful direction. The patroon built a church for his
tenants, a cooperage to produce barrels in which to freight his flour to
New Amsterdam, and even a bakehouse to produce ship's biscuit for sale
in New Amsterdam to shipowners. By 1750, eleven hundred people
lived in the neighborhood of the mill and looked to the miller—and
beyond him to the third-generation patroon—as the leading figure in
local trade.[81]

Everywhere, even in New England, where old restrictions endured for
decades, millers acquired economic power beyond their milling fees.
Joshua Jacobs made the discovery for himself in the middle of the
eighteenth century after Scituate had discarded its seventeenth-century
regulations. He built a mill in the west end of town and gradually began
accepting payment in vegetables, labor, and goods. Tentatively at first,
then decisively, he began retailing such articles as molasses, and his little
mill below the shallow twenty-acre millpond and small wooden dam
became a store.[82] No longer did Scituate have a single ecclesiastical and
commercial center; by 1750 it had several, each ordered about a miller,
one of whom sold molasses and other non-native goods. Jacobs Mill
scarcely reordered the countryside of Scituate but the crossroads near
which it stood became an increasingly important landmark for travelers.
The important spatial significance of the mill store developed in the
backlands under frontier conditions.

In western New York and Pennsylvania, and everywhere in the Old
Southwest, in fact everywhere where New Englanders did not choose to
replicate the clustered towns of home, mills served as economic and
social centers. Very often millers kept general stores and often they
advanced credit to farmers anxious for cash. They combined small
shipments of grain into quantities worth shipping to the coast or later
down the Mississippi to New Orleans. Even in land ordered by the federal grid, mill locations served as centers, especially in the autumn, when
farmers brought grain to be ground. Each mill served an area of varying
size; typically in the Ohio Valley at least, mills extended their influence
perhaps ten miles in any direction. Within that twenty-mile diameter,
farmers knew that their grain would eventually be ground at an estab-

lishment useful for other matters. At a mill a farmer might obtain a cash loan against a coming crop or cash for delivered grain; either way, the farmer escaped from a subsistence level of agriculture to one intricately bound to a market economy. He might purchase manufactured items if the miller conducted a store, and of course he found a social center where he could visit with other farmers from different locations within the miller's sphere of influence.

Therefore, westward-moving agriculturists appreciated the coming of millers because milling, along with decent road or water transportation, introduced market farming. Millers seeking likely locations understood that farmers would support their enterprises, not only by providing grain but also by petitioning legislatures for rights to dam streams and rivers. Like the blacksmith shop, the gristmill objectified the joining of agriculture and artifice.[83] Notwithstanding that agriculturists disliked and wondered about the forge and the grindstones, they tolerated them as necessary adjuncts to plows and scythes.

S A W M I L L S

No such toleration lightened the burden of sawmill operators. Certainly husbandmen appreciated the ease with which logs were sawn into beams and boards useful in building houses and barns, but after the initial enterprise of colonizing the forest passed, they scorned sawmills as greedy devourers of useful timber. Now and then a husbandman prospered by felling woodlot trees and sledging them to a nearby sawmill; such wintertime operations filled idle days with hard work and profit. But as early as the mid-seventeenth century, at least in New England and in Virginia, husbandmen and planters worried about "waste and stray of timber." On the one hand, they heartily agreed with the sentiments expressed in 1662 by the Reverend Mr. Michael Wigglesworth, who poetized about

> A waste and howling wilderness,
>   Where none inhabited
> But hellish fiends, and brutish men
>   That Devils worshipped,[84]

and looked with mixed loathing and fear upon the forest encircling their fragile fields. On the other, they recalled the terrible shortages of timber that afflicted England in the 1620s, shortages that helped prompt the Atlantic migration. Across England the poor resorted to destroying saplings, posts, rails, hedges, and gates and bridges to obtain firewood; their desperate robberies began in the early sixteenth century. Between the 1540s and the 1570s the price of firewood doubled; by the 1630s it had tripled, and shortages afflicted artisans like coopers and shipwrights. Copper and iron smelting languished due to a shortage of charcoal, and even the navy was threatened. "If our timber be consumed and spent it will require the age of three or four generations before it can grow again for use," cautioned Admiral Sir William Monson in 1615. Fuel seemed less of a problem than building timber; during the reign of Henry VIII English miners produced some 200,000 tons of coal annually, and under Elizabeth the tonnage increased. But miners required more and more timber to support their shafts and to build their carts, and shipwrights demanded high quality timber to build the coasters that transported the coal to markets like London. By the middle of the seventeenth century English builders were fully accustomed to importing fir and oak boards and fir masts from northern Europe, particularly from Norway and Russia. Husbandmen learned that any timber, especially standing timber useful for building, was extremely valuable.[85] North America seemed to its earliest English settlers decidedly overblessed with forested land, but within several decades the rapacious appetites of sawmills cutting boards for Europe began to worry colonists still mindful of Old World scarcity.

Sawmilling came earlier to the colonies than to England, and the first sawmill builders and operators, particularly in Virginia, may have been hired directly from Holland. In 1621 the Virginia Company directed its colonial governor "to take care of the Dutch sent to build sawmills, and seat them at the Falls, that they may bring their timber by the current of the water." A few years later the management officials in Virginia declared that "with great care and cost there were procured men skillful in sawing mills from Hamburg." Late in the sixteenth century the Dutch had begun perfecting "paltrok" windmills designed to saw logs into boards but fifty years later such mills were novelties in England. What accounts for the English lack of interest in such a useful, proven invention? English merchants knew of such wind- and water-driven sawmills; many had visited them in Holland or along the Baltic coast, and one suggested as early as 1623 that sawmills ought to be built in England.[86] Social and economic crisis, not technological inability, stymied proponents of sawmills; into the eighteenth century the English guilds of sawyers insisted that logs be sawed by hand, by pairs of men working single-bladed saws. For centuries one sawyer had stood beneath the log or beam to be sawed into planks; his partner stood above him, on the beam itself. Hour after hour, the sawyers pumped their great saw up and down, producing at the close of day perhaps five or six 10- to 15-foot-long boards an inch or two in thickness. Pit-sawing employed thousands of Englishmen, many the sons of sawyers, and many former laborers exiled from their rural occupations by enclosure but strong and accustomed to hard work. Sawyers detested the newfangled paltrok mills and water-driven sawmills, and their guilds convinced innovative millers to ignore such inventions. Now and then millers persisted in erecting sawmills against the wishes of the guilds, and the guilds acted at once. In 1663, and in fact as late as 1767 or 1768, English pit-sawyers pulled sawmills to pieces.[87] It is no wonder that in 1624 the only men able to build sawmills were Dutch, German, and Polish specialists. Nowhere in England lived men expert enough to build them.

Conditions in the English colonies prompted thoughtful men to dream of sawmills immediately. Able-bodied men were of course making land and practicing husbandry; the few carpenters discovered such a great demand for their services that they drastically increased their fees to twice or three times those of their English counterparts. Sawmills seemed a perfect answer to the combined difficulties of building houses and ships, of producing a valuable commodity for export, and of circumventing the severe labor shortage. Quickly the colonists understood the concept later expressed by the English pamphleteer; a sawmill was necessary in a great city because great cities demanded vast quantities of lumber, and a sawmill was equally necessary in a great forest because only a sawmill sawed felled timber quickly enough to subdue and "improve" the forest for human use.

By 1632 Virginians were sawing logs by waterpower. Despite the death of several millwrights in the 1622 massacre, the colony's program of building mills was succeeding, although slowly, and by the middle of the century Virginians were busily building shallops and small ships to transport tobacco to England. But the building of sawmills remained a continental art. As late as 1685 William Byrd discovered that in order to build a sawmill, a saw with its crank, rack, and nut had to be ordered from beyond England. "I am told that it may be best and cheapest had out of Holland," he told his London merchants, and he worried that such items might not be eligible for export.[88] Sawmill equipment proved so difficult to obtain that mill building slowed, especially in the Tidewater. The building of the College of William and Mary in the three years after 1695 meant including substantial wages for hand sawyers in the construction budget. Eventually, however, Byrd and other determined men built their sawmills and enjoyed watching the machinery perform wonders. In November 1709 Byrd watched a two-saw mill cut 1,000 feet of plank in six hours, "to the confusion of Webb and Woodson," two planters who had wagered that the job could not be done in ten. Woodson proved hard to convince; within a year he bet Byrd forty pounds that the sawmill could not do better, and the two planters and their friends gathered at the mill to see.[89] In five hours the mill cut 2,000 feet of plank, and another 1,000 in four hours more. Woodson left convinced.

Eighteenth-century Virginians, according to one observer, were definitely "persuaded" of the utility of sawmills, perhaps by informal stunts like those arranged by Byrd. Planters understood that slaves ought to be employed at tasks requiring some degree of difficulty; only fools set them to work hand-sawing when milled planks were available cheap. The English, however, hoped that Virginians would build even more mills and thus lower the price of lumber shipped to London. Hugh Jones knew the significance of Admiral Monson's earlier thinking; American lumber—and mast trees—were essential to English economic and military survival, and sawmills ought to be encouraged.

New Englanders needed no such encouragement. By 1700 almost every town in Massachusetts enjoyed the advantages of at least one sawmill, and sawmills were generously distributed across the other New England colonies as well. At first New Englanders coveted sawmills for their own, essentially local uses, just as they desired gristmills. In 1656, for example, the residents of Ipswich in the Massachusetts Bay Colony "voted that there be a sawmill on Chebaggo River, with liberty to cut timber, if one-fifteenth of what is sawed there be allowed to the town, and that no timber be cut within three miles and a half of the meetinghouse, and the inhabitants be charged no more than four per cent for sawing."[90] Implicit in the contract, of course, is a clear understanding of the space of the town: at its center is a meetinghouse, and around that center is agricultural land. Implicit too is an awareness that the mill exists to further the town's economy, not only by producing as a sort of licensing fee one-fifteenth of the lumber for such community projects as bridge- and meetinghouse-building or for sale to raise specie and so lower taxes, but by sawing wood for inhabitants at a low cost. Also implicit is a vague awareness that the trees to be felled and cut are those beyond the circle of fields; the sawmill is a powerful weapon against the wilderness described in "The Ordering of Towns." Town after town contracted with sawmillers to build and operate sawmills, and in almost every instance the townsmen insisted that millers provide permanent service to the towns by offering reduced rates, by donating some proportion of the timber, even by employing out-of-work townsmen. Terms could not be overly restrictive, however, because building sawmills

Rural sawmill, ca. 1880, Norwell, Massachusetts. (private collection)

turned out to be difficult and expensive; after all, few colonists had ever seen one in England, and no one town could offer a German or Polish millwright the inducements promised by the London Company eager to establish sawmills in Virginia.

Most of the small-scale, locally chartered New England sawmills were jointly owned by several townsmen, who pooled their resources to buy the saw, crank, and ratchet so necessary to mechanical operation. In the early years of the seventeenth century, millwrights perhaps worked from sketches; Byrd sent a "pattern" to his London merchants, and several Europeans printed plans of simple sawmills. In time local ingenuity supplemented and then replaced pictorial aids, and New Englanders soon invented a number of improvements and borrowed them from one another. As in Virginia and elsewhere in the Tidewater, New England sawmills were small, mostly open structures situated near a fall of water that drove the wheel.[91] Beneath the roof was a chiefly wooden mechanism that simultaneously operated the up-and-down saw and thrust the log carriage and log against the blade. Within a few decades New Englanders no longer needed imported iron machinery; local mines and furnaces produced the necessary material and blacksmiths simply duplicated imported European prototypes. Every sawmill was intimately linked with the products of mines, furnaces, and smithies, and in turn it supplied miners, foundrymen, and smiths with inexpensive lumber. Like the small blacksmith shop, the diminutive New England sawmill offered husbandmen a clear glimpse of the world of artifice.

North of Massachusetts sawmills produced lumber for export too, not only for local consumption. Boston provided a ready market for lumber, and seventeenth-century diarists recorded ship after ship off-loading boards and beams at Town Cove wharves. Much of the lumber moved farther south too, not only to the Middle Colonies and to the Tidewater but to the West Indies as well.[92] The northern mills profited the English and colonial investors who erected them and who sought markets for their lumber; the investors emphasized efficiency, and their mills worked free of the restrictions applied to smaller mills serving town needs. In 1682, twenty-four mills operated regularly in Maine, and six were equipped with four-blade saws. According to an expert witness testifying in a seventeenth-century lawsuit trial, a mill at Exeter, New Hampshire, between 1650 and 1651 "produced about four score thousand . . . boards and some planks . . . and about 60,000 in 1652 and 1653." Clearly the Exeter mill, which may have been a multisaw or "gang" mill, far surpassed sawmills like those operated by Byrd or millers in New England towns. In New Hampshire and Maine, sawmills dominated man-shaped space.

Francis Small, a "planter" of the New Hampshire town of Piscattaway, explained in 1685 how an English merchant established sawmills at a place called Newichwannock in the 1630s, when Small was a teenager newly arrived in the plantations. He testified that he did "very well remember that Captain Mason sent into this country eight Danes to build mills, to saw timber, and tend them, and to make potash." Mason, like Ferdinando Gorges, who at one time claimed patents to vast areas of present-day New Hampshire and Maine and who financed sawmills at Pascataquack and Aguamenticus, hoped to rival the Scandinavian suppliers of timber and build a tiny fiefdom on his profits.[93] But the English entrepreneurs faced two almost insurmountable problems: experienced millwrights proved difficult to find (one was sued in 1653 for building an "insufficient" mill in New Hampshire) and sawmill plantations proved difficult to supervise. As early as 1623 Gorges sent his nephew to watch over the craftsmen hired "for the building of houses, and erecting of sawmills." Small-scale sawmilling succeeded well enough in agricultural plantations like Exeter in New Hampshire—whose husbandmen restricted sawmillers with such regulations as that passed in 1640, "whosoever shall dig a sawpit and shall not fill it or cover it, shall be liable to pay the damages that shall come to man or beast thereby," even as the sawmillers were building mills—but sometimes failed in the lumber plantations owned and controlled not by husbandmen but by absentee landlords whose quest for profit bypassed commonsense concerns. The early settlers of the Piscataqua River valley lumber plantations imported ground flour from England and Virginia; not only did they lack a gristmill, they lacked the time to grow their own grain. Slowly the English gave up their dreams of instant wealth, and eventually Massachusetts merchants began buying and improving the English operations. By the middle of the seventeenth century at least fifteen sawmills operated in the Piscataqua River valley alone, and by 1700 more than sixty between present-day Hampton, New Hampshire, and Casco, Maine.[94] Millwrights and investors evaluated land not according to soil fertility or the presence of glades but by assessing its forest cover, proximity to waterfalls, and nearness to estuaries. Sawmillers selected sites covered with oak, pine, or hemlock and threw up crude dams and flumes at the nearest waterfall; great mast trees destined for English shipyards and sawed boards floated down the rivers to coastal loading docks, unless the mill stood at the confluence of a powerful falling stream and a navigable estuary. Sawmillers and loggers quickly mastered the craft of floating logs to mills, of sawing them with gang saws numbering up to twelve up-and-down blades, and of floating them or carting them to loading docks. Small's lifetime spanned the years of hesitant experimentation to the era of skilled forest exploitation.

Husbandmen in southern New Hampshire and in Massachusetts, Connecticut, and Rhode Island shipped flour and other produce to the lumber plantations. In many instances one or two Boston merchants controlled the imports and exports of one or more lumber plantations. They owned the ships that carried food and supplies to the camps and carried sawed lumber to the West Indies or England, just as they owned the sawmills and forests. Unlike the ordered towns of southern New England, the lumber plantations objectified neither religious order nor agricultural expertise, and Puritan clergymen and Massachusetts officials worried about the religious and social state of the sawmillers and loggers so busily clearing the forest. Despite powerful efforts to absorb New Hampshire into Massachusetts and to closely control the founding of towns in Maine, the lumbermen persisted in irreligion and in building flimsy dwellings, few barns, and sometimes no meetinghouses. Decade after decade the woods retreated faster before ever more numerous sawmills surrounded by the dwellings of millers and loggers. Maine towns such as Bucksport, founded in 1764 by a small group of men "who removed thither with their families, and built a sawmill and two dwelling houses the same year" according to one early nineteenth-century historian, eventually became agricultural settlements by default.[95] When the last of the accessible trees were felled and sawed into boards, the stump-filled open land was already being planted by husbandmen braving a difficult climate and infertile soil. Yet in the south of New England, husbandmen, clergymen, and government officials long distrusted the occupation and behavior of the woodcutting northerners.[96] Until the nineteenth century Maine remained a "district" of Massachusetts, an isolated, distinctly second-class place half-alien to agriculturists suspicious of its inhabitants and their capacity for orderly self-government.

But sawmilling civilized the land. "There are still vast numbers of frogs, toads, owls, bats, and other vermin upon the borders of the un-cleared part of the country," remarked one New England historian in 1720, "which make such a hideous noise on summer evenings, as would terrify those that are not used to it."[97] Wolves and panthers, however, retreated with the forest, and so husbandmen south of New Hampshire, as far south as the Carolinas, grudgingly approved of the large-scale lumbering enterprises in the North. Anything that repelled wild beasts—and Indians and French soldiers too—deserved at least some respect, even if its directors honored a land-use ethic different only in degree from that of miners. Lumber exported to the West Indies and to Europe helped produce a sensible balance of payments too while providing husbandmen and craftsmen with cheap building material. Every local sawmill cutting up a few dozen trees each day hinted at the great subjugation of forest in northern New England, at the end of wilderness.

Despite the financial success of the New Hampshire and Maine saw-mill corporations, most colonial sawmills remained tiny and owned by two or three men, one of whom operated the mill. By the early eighteenth century sawmills functioned more or less successfully in every English colony, and by the middle of the century sawing techniques had improved quite dramatically. Gang saws supplanted single saws, particularly in well-wooded places such as North Carolina and New York. Governor Tryon of North Carolina reported in 1767 that about fifty saw-mills "and more constructing" operated on the Cape Fear River and its tributaries alone, most equipped with two saws and each able to cut about 150,000 feet of lumber annually, each board measuring roughly 25 to 30 feet in length. Tryon thought that the mills ought to be made larger to accommodate logs 50 feet long, and he assured the board of trade that North Carolina could supply the best ship timber and masts. A few years earlier a traveler in the Middle Colonies remarked on the many sawmills and noted that Albany merchants bought forest land as an investment. "If their estates have a little brook," he remarked, "they do not fail to erect a sawmill upon it for sawing boards and planks, which many boats take during the summer to New York, having scarcely any other cargo."[98] But Peter Kalm, perhaps because of his agricultural training and his Swedish familiarity with sawmills, discerned what observant colonists had noted a century before. Sawmills were destroying the colonial forests and creating ecological havoc.

In the Tidewater and in much of the Piedmont the damage was slight. Tobacco raising seemed more profitable than sawmilling, and the gentle flow of water, particularly in the coastal flatlands, made large-scale milling almost impossible. In New England, however, trouble began early and it spread slowly through New Jersey, New York, and Pennsylvania before reaching into the territories west of the Appalachians. Perhaps the Indians of Maine were the first to formally notice the crisis; in 1691 Governor John Easton of Rhode Island noted that English colonists in Maine "say that the Indians had some just cause of offense that corn was promised them for harm they received by sawmills soiling their fishing." Easton concluded that "this could not be cold truth," but his very mention of the matter suggests that gang saws did pollute streams.[99] The up-and-down saw used in sawmills until the invention of the circular saw in the middle of the nineteenth century produced extraordinary quantities of sawdust. Most millers simply shoveled the sawdust into the water beyond the mill wheel or else allowed it to fall directly into the stream beneath the mill. Even small, single-saw mills produced great quantities that "soiled" streams and drove away fish almost as quickly as pollution from mines and furnaces. But the problem of sawdust was (except to Indians who lived by fishing) slight compared to others.

Deforestation precipitated ecological catastrophe. Until the middle of the seventeenth century, few husbandmen understood the large-scale damage wrought by New Hampshire and Maine loggers and sawmillers because few husbandmen worked land near the acres of felled trees. By 1700 even the small, locally oriented sawmills of southern New England disturbed husbandmen, however, and by 1750 agriculturists in several colonies learned that dreaded wildernesses tormented people long after their trees were felled and sawed. Soil erosion troubled husbandmen planting land cleared by loggers, and it angered other colonists who depended, like several Indian tribes, on seasonal migrations of herring and other fish. Streams that once swarmed with fish turned muddy as silt and sawdust drifted downstream, and soon the fish vanished.[100] Operators of sawmills and gristmills learned that deforestation meant low water, sometimes year-round, and occasional periods of no water at all. Millwrights began building larger impoundment dams that trapped silt and blocked fish and did very little to ensure adequate supplies of water, although they sometimes flooded the low-lying fields of husbandmen. No colony adequately addressed the intricacies of deforestation, but town after town forbade the indiscriminate cutting of trees on the common land and the setting of fires in fields and woods. When farmers confronted the firewood and building-timber shortages of the early nineteenth century they often blamed their own wastefulness. By then sawmills—and great forests and running streams—had disappeared, or else the mills worked short hours and reminded few young men of the damages wrought decades before.

Farmers, carpenters, shipwrights, box makers, cabinetmakers, even coffin builders demanded lumber, however, and across western New York and Pennsylvania eighteenth- and early nineteenth-century loggers, sawmillers, and speculators sought out healthy stands of hardwoods and conifers near waterfalls and half-navigable rivers. Trees were felled and floated or sledged to the mills, and sawed timber was rafted downstream to aspiring towns like Pittsburgh. From the year 1790 on, the little Massachusetts town of Canton built between 150 and 200 prefabricated sawmills annually and shipped most of them to the north and west.[101] Such mills were simple and small but they were carted—or shipped on canals—into forests beyond the frontier of agriculturists, assembled quickly, and set to work. When farmers and craftsmen arrived, needing housing for themselves and their animals and tools, the sawmillers were ready.

In 1815, for example, the Chautauqua County, New York town of Jamestown consisted chiefly of a gristmill, a store, two blacksmith shops, and three sawmills, two with single blades and one with a gang saw. Despite the presence of the gristmill, farming was not yet established. "Almost the entire business of the place, then called 'The Rapids,' was cutting some *three million feet of boards* a year," one ex-logger later recalled, "mostly run down the river; and most of the provisions and groceries used by the people were brought from Pittsburgh in keel boats; as flour, bacon, dried apples and peaches, tobacco and whisky; also nails, glass, and castings." All three sawmills ran all day and all night, except on Sunday; operators worked in two shifts, one beginning at noon and working until midnight, the other working from midnight until noon. The place stood at the center of a widening circle of deforested land, and soon the consequences of large-scale logging and sawing struck the inhabitants. "The quantity of saw-dust shoved into the outlet from these mills in a year was enormous," the ex-logger remarked in 1858. "The mill ponds below, and the willow bars, eddies, etc., received these deposits; and the accumulation of years is still to be seen along the outlet, in bends and other places." The result of such deforestation and pollution soon grew apparent; the flow of water decreased. But Jamestown's sawmills dominated the land, even from afar. Day and night a vast heap of 'slabs, butts, and edgings of boards" smouldered a short distance from the mills in a great common heap, "which was kept almost constantly burning, winter and summer."[102] Unlike the smoke of farmhouse chimneys, the sawmill smoke and glare, like the smoke and glare of Pennsylvania furnaces, announced the workings of artifice. Jamestown objectified the same ethic objectified by the Simsbury copper mines and Cornwall Furnace, an ethic based on the temporary exploitation of finite natural resources.

That ethic drew men westward to the great forests of Michigan, Ohio, and Arkansas; the loggers and sawmillers arrived years before farmers. Around 1835 one ambitious man purchased section twenty-nine of a nameless Michigan township surveyed only a few years before by federal land officers. The 640-acre lot seemed perfectly suited for a sawmilling enterprise; it was thickly forested and crossed by a powerful, falling stream. Within a few years the sawmill became the unofficial center of a tiny community called by its inhabitants "Sharon Hollow" and within a few years more provided farmers with lumber. The farmers arrived to cultivate fertile soil but the prospect of deforested land attracted them too. By 1850 the sawmill was surrounded by farms whose owners cheerfully sledged logs to it in winter.[103] But always it was alien to the emerging countryside of husbandry. One day a sixteen-year-old boy drowned in the snarling waters of its sluice; on another a child discovered among the gears a tiny friction fire that threatened to engulf the mill and—in the imagination of farmers—the nearby structures too. Like the mills at Jamestown, the Sharon Hollow sawmill announced the first tentative attempts to exploit the forests of Michigan.[104] It heralded the deforestation of prime land, not for the sake of agriculture but for the glory of artifice.

Near every sawmill village stood one or more logging camps, like those described by a Maine writer in 1837. "The camps are built of logs, being a kind of log houses. They are made about three feet high on one side and eight or nine on the other, with a roof slanting one way. The roof is made of shingles, split out of green wood, and laid upon rafters." While such structures reflected the skill of American axmen in hewing out doors and chimneys, the expert continued, they proved drafty and dangerous. "It is obvious, from the construction, that nothing but the greenness of the timber prevents the camp from being burnt up immediately." In comparison with the log cabins and log houses erected by cooperating agriculturists in the course of making land, the logging habitations seemed little more than hovels; indeed the Maine observer noted that oxen enjoyed shelters "very similar" to those of the loggers. Away from southern New England, where memories of English timber shortages and early deforestation combined to restrain them, sawmillers and loggers worked with impunity, erecting the flimsy, clearly temporary mills and camps first built in New Hampshire, Maine, and North Carolina and living for a short time at the very center of artifice. When they felled and sawed the best trees, the artificers moved, leaving despoiled land to those farmers willing to chance erosion and flooding in exchange for freedom from having to make land from pure wilderness. The farmers repaired or rebuilt—or demolished—the crude shelters abandoned by the lumbermen, and shaped the land for planting.

Sawmilling dramatically aided American common engineering by making boards, planks, and beams easily and cheaply available to inventors such as Ithiel Town, whose strong and quickly erected truss bridges depended on pre-cut beams of standardized size. By the end of the eighteenth century American builders knew the peculiar strengths and weaknesses of trees, and they selected lumber carefully for each project. Workmen used hemlock, yellow poplar, tupelo, and oak to floor warehouses, stables, and bridges, sycamore to build windlasses, and white elm to make wheel naves. In New Orleans they used cypress logs for water mains, in Connecticut they chose oak, cherry, and laurel for clocks, in Virginia, New York, and Pennsylvania they used white oak for wagon and coach frames, and the shipwrights who built the *Constitution* in 1797 used New Jersey white oak for the keel, Maine white pine for the masts, and Georgia live oak and red cedar for the frames.[105] Shipwrights consumed vast quantities of naturally curved timbers but they required thousands of beams and boards too, cut at sawmills far inland. Usually they cut the lumber by hand but in 1806 the Anacostia Naval Shipyard in the District of Columbia began using a great waterpowered gang saw. Building warships, like flooring bridges, required great beams and heavy planks, but merchant ships were lightly built, designed for rough, short lives and—like Erie Canal locks—for replacement by bigger and better successors. Shipwrights building one merchant ship after another learned the lesson of light construction, and eventually their understanding changed American building techniques.

Balloon framing appeared in the early nineteenth century as a new way of erecting structures, particularly houses. It depended on mass-produced, cheap iron nails—the product of advancing mining and smelting enterprise and of several inventions by ingenious New Englanders—and on cheap, standardized lumber, the product of sawmills located not only in the old colonies but in Michigan, Ohio, and other newly settled places. It epitomized common building in wood. "The method of construction with wood, known as 'balloon framing,' is also the most important contribution to our domestic architecture which the spirit of economy, and a scientific adaptation of means to ends, have given the modern world," remarked the authors of *The Great Industries of the United States* in 1872. "The heavy beams, the laborious framing, the use of mortises and tenons, have all been replaced by lightness and constructive skill, so that a single man and a boy can put up a house, such as formerly, for its 'raising,' required the combined force of a village."[106] Despite being "eminent writers upon political and social economy, mechanical and social economy, mechanics, manufactures" and other fields, however, the authors were unable to learn the origin of the technique: "When it was first used is not known with any definiteness, but it has, within the last fifty years, entirely replaced the old method of construction." George Washington Snow, a New Hampshire settler of Chicago, is most likely the inventor; he bought a lumber yard and went into the contracting business, and perhaps erected St. Mary's Church in 1833, the first known balloon-frame structure.[107] The invention, not the inventor, is of importance, and builders everywhere in nineteenth-century America understood it; they adopted the balloon frame with alacrity.

Essentially, a balloon frame is built of extremely light timbers two inches wide and four inches deep; in the early years such timbers stretched as long as the house stood high. The upright studs were nailed to sills and cross-braced: one man (perhaps with the aid of a boy) easily lifted the largest of the timbers and set it in place. Nothing interlocked; the builder nailed in place every stud and nailed a skin of boards over the studs. No longer did a house frame appear massive; instead it seemed frail, as fragile as a balloon. In reality, however, it was stronger than the brace-frames erected by Americans since colonial times.

Although the balloon frame objectified the intimate relation of sawmills and nineteenth-century builders, it encouraged individualism and innovation. No longer did a farmer worry that his neighbors might assemble on raising day and not understand some change he had made in traditional forms. Instead he built his house alone or hired a carpenter or two, and he built however he liked. Balloon framing prompted a variety of idiosyncratic houses, as well as much aping of mansions and European styles; it encouraged the Greek Revival style of housebuilding, and it encouraged writers such as Downing, who knew that farmers were free of traditional building restraints and were—perhaps—open to suggestion. Certainly the plans of architects turned out to be expensive and often impractical but they derived from a new capacity for experimentation that sparked whimsical adventures in design. When Lewis Allen counseled farmers to build practical, useful houses, he did so out an understanding of the seductive power of balloon-frame construction. Wherever sawmill lumber was available, builders rushed to build new sorts of houses, to add dormers and bays and wings and strangely shaped front porches. They abandoned the traditional lore of house-building.

No longer, for example, did a family choose to raise a complete house frame in one day. Instead it accepted the advice of innovators like Solon Robinson, who argued for balloon-frame houses and published simple house plans. "It is particularly intended for the *new settler,* and to be built on the *balloon plan,* which has not a single tennon or mortise in the frame, except the sills," wrote Robinson of a plan he published in the *American Agriculturist* in 1846, "all the upright timber being very light, and held together by nails, it being sheeted upon the studs under the clapboards, is very stiff, and just as good and far cheaper than ordinary frames." Robinson designed a house as practical as any envisioned by Allen; his plan focuses on a great central kitchen that opens on a wood room, a washroom, a pantry, and a storeroom. But Robinson emphasized that the house frame ought to be erected in stages, as the farmer stole time from the difficulties of making land and building fences. "Now, suppose a family just arrived at the 'new location,' and designing to build a house upon the above plan," he continued. "First, they need some immediate shelter. Two hands in two days can put up the room thirteen by thirteen, marked wash room in the plan, with a lean-to roof."[108] In later months, if all goes well and the light lumber is delivered to the site, the farmer and his family can build the additional rooms. No longer do they require the help of neighbors, and no longer must they accept traditional house styles.

Not every prospective householder chose between the time-tested plans of Allen and Robinson (even though they were devised for balloon framing) and the more elaborate designs of Downing. Several hundred determined to build eight-sided houses, having been convinced by Orson Squire Fowler in 1848 that rectilinear houses and kitchen ells create unnecessary expense. Fowler insisted in *A Home for All* that his eight-sided house enclosed more space at less cost than any other form of house, that it made heating and lighting simple, and that it provided

A Fowler octagon, western Massachusetts. (JRS)

practical, spacious rooms while dispensing with dark, useless corridors. "Wings on houses are not in quite as good taste as on birds," he remarked in his carefully reasoned book. "How would a little apple or peach look stuck onto each side of a large one?" Between 1848 and 1857 his slim volume went through at least seven editions, and scores of "octagons" appeared in the northeastern states, erected by men willing to abandon not only brace-frame construction but any framing technique. The key to Fowler's technique was sawed lumber. "I liked the plan so well," he wrote of several houses he discovered in central New York, "that I immediately ordered boards sawed as required by this plan, and drew a plan after which to build it."[109] His octagon plan did not truly originate with him, but he cleverly adapted the design of a few roundish, strictly common houses, and created a house form that swept away brace-frame nostalgia. By 1850 innovation triumphed over tradition; housebuilding no longer involved neighbors and custom, but carpenter's drawings, building supply catalogs, and—of course—sawmills. Milled lumber spawned the balloon frame and the octagon just as sawmills destroyed forests and traditional housebuilding.

Tradition endured only in the building of barns. Farmers convinced of the worth of balloon-framed houses distrusted the seeming weakness of light timbers and continued to erect heavily framed barns in the customary way. Their conservatism hinted at the growing conservatism of farm life everywhere in the nation. Farmers built larger and larger barns but the regional forms went essentially unchanged. Artificers experimented with new frames and soon accepted them; agriculturists embraced the past.

Cheap, easily accessible small-cut lumber remade the American scene from 1850 onward. The same spirit of common engineering that produced the lightly framed clipper ships and covered truss bridges produced the resilient balloon-framed houses, but only with the assistance of sawmills. No longer were the houses of a particular Maryland county or New Jersey village similiar; they were interrupted here and there by innovative structures born of a powerful spirit of originality. "To find an original man living in an original house," mused Andrew Jackson Downing near the middle of the century, "is as satisfactory as to find an eagle's nest built on the top of a mountain crag."[110] What the architect thought of the standardized habitations under construction in dozens of cotton- and wool-milling towns is not recorded. But artifice was fueling the erection of a new sort of *dwelling*, one scarcely anticipated by the builders of 1800.

FACTORIES

Herman Melville distrusted factories as thoroughly as Hawthorne suspected mines and furnaces; in Melville's view, water ensnared in wheels and sluices writhed as fiercely and Satanically as any fire bursting from the earth. "It lies not far from Woedolor Mountain in New England," he wrote of a paper manufactory. "Turning to the east, right out from among bright farms and sunny meadows, nodding in early June with odorous grasses, you enter ascendingly among bleak hills. These gradually close in upon a dusky pass, which, from the violent Gulf Stream of air unceasingly driving between its cloven walls of haggard rock, as well as from the tradition of a crazy spinster's hut having long ago stood somewhere hereabouts, is called the Mad Maid's Bellow-pipe." Melville leads his reader farther among the hills to Black Notch, where "the ravine now expandingly descends into a great, purple, hopper-shaped hollow, far sunk among many Plutonian, shaggy-wooded mountains," through which Blood River flows past a long-abandoned sawmill and worthless, second-growth timber. "By the country people this hollow is called Devil's Dungeon," he continues, and near its bottom is the paper manufactory, "a large whitewashed building, relieved, like some great white sepulchre, against the sullen background of mountain-side firs." Surrounding the great structure are "other and smaller buildings, some of which, from their cheap, blank air, great length, gregarious windows, and comfortless expression, no doubt were boarding-houses of the operatives," clustered in "various rude, irregular squares and courts." Everywhere is a strange, "whirring, humming sound" emanating from the manufactory, conquering even the roar of Blood River. "A snow-white hamlet amidst the snows," Melville concludes, a hamlet damned in ice instead of fire.[111]

Melville's description of a fictional factory village owes much to the romantic school of writing but his Poe-like intensity derives too from first-hand observation. By the middle of the nineteenth century, no one called New England a prosperous agricultural region. Wilderness had regained its hold on fields abandoned by families heading west to farm or raise cattle, and near the larger falls of rivers, entrepeneurs had erected factories on the sites of abandoned gristmills and sawmills. Sensitive partisans of husbandry, men like Melville and Hawthorne, distrusted the new sort of spaces not because they unthinkingly accepted the "dark, Satanic mills" philosophy of Blake and Wordsworth, but because the factory village objectified the twitching end of agricultural order and the beloved values Americans thought it objictified. For all its half-Gothic tone, Melville's description accurately portrays the essence of a factory-dominated space.

Textile milling began early in the American colonies, at least as early as the 1650s in Massachusetts, but its growth remained slow. Not until the eighteenth century did English inventors begin perfecting waterpowered spinning, and the expansion of mechanical spinning on a large scale began as late as 1771, when Richard Arkwright erected a large manufactory on the Derwent River in Derbyshire to spin cotton imported from the American colonies. Factory after factory rose along the Derwent in tiny hamlets like Milford and Belper, each transforming space and life-style. Around each spread identical cottages for the families (men, women, and children) retained to operate the spinning machinery, and the machine shops to build the improved equipment invented ever more frequently.[112] Few Americans visited the growing fiefdoms of artifice presided over by men such as Arkwright but perceptive colonial merchants determined to wrest the spinning industry from England. They schemed to violate Parliament's injunction against exporting spinning machines or drawings, and after the War of Independence they succeeded.

In December 1790 waterpower spun cotton thread for the first time in North America in a small, house-like structure on the Blackstone River in Pawtucket, Rhode Island. Moses Brown of Providence had determined to diversify his commercial interests a year or two before and after much difficulty had succeeded in hiring a young expatriate Englishman familiar with Derbyshire technology. Samuel Slater did more than convert the small mill and build new machines; he introduced the whole "Arkwright system" of spatial planning and business management. Brown's capital and Slater's skill sparked duplicate enterprises across Rhode Island; by 1804 the hesitancy had ended and four or five new spinning establishments opened each year.[113] Jefferson's Embargo Act of 1808 and the subsequent War of 1812 freed the Rhode Islanders from English competition, and the factory companies enjoyed several years of extraordinary profits, most of which they invested in further technological improvements. Between 1810 and 1812 the price of shares in the Lippitt Mill jumped by over 33 percent, and merchants looked from their ships to the factories in the backcountry.

Rhode Island proved ideal for mechanized spinning. Brisk, full streams and rivers laced much of the state, and their valleys were easily modified by dams to increase falls and build holding ponds. In most years enough rain fell to keep streams high even in summer, and the groundwater was soft enough that it required no treatment before bleaching and dyeing operations were begun. Frequent rains and fogs from the Atlantic kept the air humid enough so that thin strands of yarn remained whole throughout the spinning operation. Social circumstances also supported the new enterprises. Merchants like Brown had prospered in the years immediately following the Revolution and had capital to invest in risky ventures.[114] Many farmers had not prospered on the rocky, infertile soil of the north and west of the state and were leaving for the Ohio Valley or else looking for other employment. Merchant shipping employed not only seamen but also large numbers of craftsmen capable of building in wood and especially in metal. Indeed Rhode Island blacksmiths contributed to the developing spinning industry their proven expertise and unsuspected inventiveness. When Slater described his needs, the smiths and machinists understood him at once.

Finally, and perhaps most significantly, visionaries like Brown and Slater inherited the Rhode Island custom of noninterference with millers. In the seventeenth century, when towns desperately needed mills to grind grain and saw logs, the colonial legislature determined that millers might impound water with impunity. If their millponds flooded the land of other property owners, even the best arable land owned by husbandmen, the courts might determine yearly compensation for the victims of the flooding, but no miller had to request permission to flood so long as his impoundment did not interfere with an upstream mill dam or a downstream mill. Millers essentially exercised the right of eminent domain and the eighteenth- and early nineteenth-century textile entrepeneurs assumed the right too; when the General Assembly finally agreed in 1837 to hear the complaints of farmers flooded out by the new and far more massive dams, it failed to act.[115] Agriculture was no longer greatly significant in Rhode Island, and the flooded fields of good bottomland announced the new political power of artifice. The old tradition of regulation fragmented when confronted by large-scale economic and technological power. More and more farms were abandoned and the factory villages grew larger.

At first, textile enterprises combined innovation with tradition. Cotton spun by machines was taken to individual houses, where women—and men—wove it on hand-operated looms. As more spinning factories were built, however, the hand-weavers fell behind and by 1810 raw yarn was sold as far west as the Ohio Valley. But Americans wanted cloth, not only spun yarn, and manufacturers began installing hand looms in their factories, where weavers and quality were more easily supervised. After 1812, when the power loom supplanted the home, or "cottage," weavers, factories and factory villages grew in size and importance as farm families who had eked out a living by farming and weaving moved from their farms into the residences erected for them by the manufacturers. They went to places such as Lippitt and Harris in Rhode Island, Harrisville in New Hampshire, and Rockdale and Crozerville in Pennsylvania. Nothing emphasizes more the curious mix of innovation and tradition than the names selected for so many of the villages; to the name of the entrepeneur was added the suffix *ville*, the Old English equivalent of landschaft. Factory villages combined the futuristic technology of their founders with the spatial organization of the distant colonial past.

Lippitt in Rhode Island exemplifies the early textile industry attempt to order work and dwelling space. Like most spinning and weaving enterprises, the complex of factory, support structures, and dwellings nestles against a natural waterfall on the Pawtuxet River, where the valley narrows into a "notch." The four-story, rectangular mill stands with its back to the river and the dam that improves the fall of water; it faces a cluster of small, vaguely European dwellings that exhibit a striking similarity of design and construction. A few yards north of the mill are several outbuildings, and beyond the twentieth-century stores, more standardized but two-family dwellings. At night the village appears like many New England town centers, a clump of houses with a church. Only if the motorist slows and peers up at the structure that crowds the road and dominates the dwellings does he see that it is not a meetinghouse that structures space but a great wooden mill topped by a steeple and belfry, and that the yard-less dwellings are not houses.

Lippitt Mill represents the second stage of mechanical spinning. As soon as Slater proved the worth of his experimental machinery, his partners determined to build a new mill; the English artificer designed it according to his experience in Derbyshire. It measured only twenty-nine by forty-seven feet and stood two-and-a-half stories high, less than half the size of other experimental textile factories in New Haven, Connecticut, and Paterson, New Jersey. Smallness reflected Slater's experience, not backwardness; he understood the danger of tying up capital in over-large structures filled with cumbersome machinery, and he scaled the new mill to the needs of his market and the power of the Blackstone River. Time quickly proved him correct; in 1801 he added a fifty-foot-long wing, and shortly after 1812 added another of the same size. No longer did his factory resemble a large house surmounted by a belfry. It resembled, as far as it resembled anything, a New England meeting-house, or the mill at Lippitt, although its heavy framing was clearly similar to that employed in barns everywhere.[116] Nevertheless, by 1809 entrepeneurs no longer thought in terms of domestic scale; when Lippitt Mill was built it was almost the size of the enlarged Slater Mill. Its build-ers knew of no other model for such a structure than the meeting-houses of the region, and the mill reflects their choice, coupled with English technical innovation.

Certainly the mill resembles a meetinghouse. Its 30- by 104-foot shape reflects the rectangular form so common in New England, and the cupola crowning a square tower-like base over one gable end encloses a belfry and is topped with an ornate wind-vane, again in the manner of New England common building. Beyond the more obvious shape and features are ornamental details similar to those beautifying meeting-houses, mouldings that frame windows and doors, cornices carefully carved, and delicate supports carrying the belfry roof. But the fourth story derives from a clerestory roof that admits light into the attic, a device imported from Derbyshire mills; indeed the similarity between Lippitt Mill and Arkwright's Lower Mill at Cromford is astonishing, and perhaps the result of intent, not accident.[117] By 1812 ecclesiastical re-semblances were less pronounced, for by then investors built in stone; structures like the Nightingale Factory in Georgiaville reveal that Rhode Island craftsmen were still unfamiliar with stoneworking even though investors eager to profit from the lack of competition demanded strong buildings. The Georgiaville edifice resembles English factories more than it does meetinghouses, but its belfry still echoes common ecclesiasti-cal design.

Lippitt Mill. (JRS)

Such echoes seemed very real in New England because the factories and the factory villages ran according to the Arkwright system. Essentially, the Arkwright system assumed that families made the best factory work force and that the factory owner must oversee every facet of family life in order to ensure stability and industry. Fathers did heavy lifting or else learned to spin alongside women; later they learned to weave. Children tended the machinery too, often crawling or sitting beneath spinning mules and looms to tie together broken threads, pick lint from the lines, or clean the ginned cotton as it was unbaled. Nuclear families seemed best suited to textile manufacturing; since every member worked in the factory, it was easy to control everyone. "Three or four families with children will meet with constant employment and good wages at the Hope Cotton Factory" read an advertisement in the July 14, 1810 issue of the Providence *Gazette*, and like many others, it was quickly answered.[118]

Employing families at the bottom of rocky ravines produced a need for housing slightly different from that experienced by owners of mines and furnaces who employed a largely male work force. Boarding houses were inappropriate, the manufacturers decided, and they determined to erect the detached, single-family cottages favored by Arkwright and other English factory owners. In the first years of mechanized spinning, the dwellings resembled English prototypes because English spinners were imported to operate the equipment and the old-country style appealed to them. Immigrant spinners and weavers knew their worth and expected good wages and adequate living accommodation in exchange for practicing their skill; even American weavers at first scorned work other than their own, and Slater himself spent two or three hours each winter morning hacking ice from the mill wheel because none of his employees would demean himself to do it. More importantly, however, the manufacturers knew that most Americans viewed repetitive factory work with suspicion almost as strong as Jefferson's. "I consider the class of artificers as the panders of vice and the instruments by which the liberties of a country are generally overturned," he wrote in 1785 as the first federal surveyors began ordering the Ohio Valley lands, and not until after the War of 1812 did he conclude that "we must now place the manufacturer by the side of the agriculturist" because national industry was integral to national independence. But Rhode Island farmers often preferred to move west and continue the noble tradition of husbandry rather than rent a small dwelling and spin or weave. So the manufacturers built solid, comfortable cottages to attract sober, hardworking families; although small, the dwellings exhibited careful design and construction.

Factory housing typically reflected the manufacturers' urge to supervise their work forces and to prevent dissension. Partly to lower costs and partly to quell any cause of disagreement, they erected identical dwellings. At Lippitt the dwellings are extremely small and close together, and while they are all brace-framed and tightly made, they were erected almost simultaneously, by carpenters. As elsewhere, the dwellings face the mill, the hub of daily life, but in some factory villages, as in Harris, for example, the dwellings stand in courts, about open yards once marked by jointly used wells and family privies. The story-and-a-half dwellings are small and originally contained only two or three rooms—kitchen-parlor and bedroom or kitchen, parlor, and bedroom—with children's sleeping quarters in the attic above.[119] The inward-facing arrangement of dwellings objectifies the focus of life in the factory villages; every manufacturer attempted to keep evils away from his worker by prohibiting liquor and gambling and other vices likely to destroy the souls and working capacities of his employees. Dwellings were small because mill families had little kitchenwork or free time; except on Sunday they worked in the factory for at least twelve hours each day, and even at night they heard the groaning of the waterwheel, which could never be stopped lest it unbalance itself. The noise of the wheel intruded upon the workers' domestic life exactly as the factory owner's authority did; it was ever-present, ever-noticeable. "The usual working hours, being twelve, exclusive of meals, six days in the week, the workmen and children being thus employed, have no time to spend in idleness or vicious amusements," reported one Connecticut manufacturer in 1835. "In our village there is not a public house or grog-shop, nor is gaming allowed in any private house, if known by the agent, and very few instances have occurred in twenty-nine years, to my knowledge."[120] The Connecticut manufacturer responded to a persistent criticism of factory life, one that prompted continuous alteration of working conditions and the constant manipulation of domestic arrangements. Work in textile factories and life in factory villages, said the partisans of agriculture, made people—especially children—immoral.

Manufacturers responded to the criticism by retaining some vestiges of ecclesiastical architecture in their factory buildings, by building sound dwellings carefully placed in relation to factories and to one another, and by regulating with bells and ordinances the daily lives of their employees. As long as the manufacturer owned all the dwellings and all the land abutting his village, he could summarily evict evildoers and keep grog-sellers and other undesirables from locating near his employees. Now and then an astute factory owner admitted that obtaining honest, industrious workers was more difficult than keeping employees from sin and sloth. Factory workers lived in an objectified order so clear and evident and powerful that it supposedly converted wastrels and other evildoers into responsible, industrious operatives.[121]

Slater and his Arkwright factory, factory village, and management system succeeded, and within twenty years similiar operations prospered along the Pawtuxet and Blackstone rivers, including one village crisply called Arkwright. Soon the native American operatives made unnecessary the importation of British craftsmen and the building of cottages patterned after those in Derbyshire, but the essence of the Arkwright system survived unchanged. At the focus of every village stood a factory, and the village reflected and reinforced the industrial order vital to the factory operation.

Common innovation succeeded splendidly in hundreds of tiny factory villages huddled about waterfalls at the bottoms of ravines. Despite the resumption of English competition and several serious financial panics, American factory owners prospered, and thousands of families found work in their well-regulated establishments.[122] But public criticism, if not condemnation, continued; somehow the villages annoyed the farmers of the country. By 1840 almost no one spoke of ensnared water spirits, and certainly no one accused the factory owners of building flimsy dwellings; unlike the furnace and sawmill owners, manufacturers of textiles and paper expected their enterprises and buildings to endure for decades, perhaps for centuries. Two things, it seems, worried those Americans who passed through the growing number of factory villages and wondered at the activity and the order. On the one hand, the villages objectified the very opposite of agricultural liberalism; daily economic and social life was rigidly circumscribed and beyond the control of the operatives. Factory owners controlled working hours, amusements, and almost all other activities from planting gardens to repairing roads.[123] Operatives inhabited eunomic space that reinforced hierarchical social order; senior employees with responsible positions, mechanics and foremen for example, inhabited larger dwellings than more lowly operatives. Isonomy was foreign to factory village life despite its rule over the grid country beyond the Appalachians. On the other, operatives rented their housing and understood the temporary nature not of the structures themselves but of their right to inhabit them. By 1840 the notion of house ownership was deeply seated in the national imagination; only a small percentage of farm families rented their farms, and those hoped to own farms someday. To live in a factory village almost invariably meant living in housing not one's own—it meant living in dwellings. Families exiled from factory villages were not exactly "broken" (no manufacturer pulled down one of his perfectly sound residences after expelling a lazy or criminal family) but they were sometimes blacklisted and so forced to wander far from their original place of employment or else seek agricultural work. A factory village objectified newer evils than the very old ones evident in mining, smelting, or logging settlements, evils some Americans had begun to associate with cities, rented lodging, and coercion.[124] No matter how well established the firms, how safe, regular, and well-paying the work, how solidly and comfortably built the dwellings, how free from crime and vice the communities, factory villages irritated and troubled most Americans, who judged them according to agricultural spaces and structures and who evaluated their life-style against the standard of agricultural liberalism and proven tradition. Well-meaning manufacturers found it difficult to attract farm families to places criticized by slaveowners as less safe and less healthful than plantations, to factories characterized by boring, monotonous, indescribably noisy work regulated by bells. All the old mystery of artifice lived on in the humming and roaring and groaning of the factory machinery. "Always, more or less, machinery of this ponderous, elaborate sort strikes, in some moods, strange dread into the human heart, as some living, panting Behemoth might," mused one observer concerned with power perhaps surpassing human control. The rumbling of factory machinery worried passersby, who wondered what force it was that writhed half-leashed behind the windows nailed shut to retain humidity. Like the imaginary dragon of the deep mine that extended almost to Hell, the dragon of machinery terrified agriculturists who knew that factory dams impounded water that overflowed valuable fields upstream, and who suspected that more insidious evils lurked within the walls of factories squatting at the center of factory villages. In the popular imagination, factories and factory villages pulsed with alien, quasi-Satanic forces. Perhaps no men belonged near them; certainly no women.[125]

Technique

Artifice created wealth faster than did husbandry. Even Emerson, praising husbandry at a country fair, admitted that the farmer "represents continuous hard labor, year in, and year out, and small gains" notwithstanding that his occupation changes the face of the earth and feeds all mankind.[126] Mines, furnaces, sawmills, and factory villages clearly reflected a changing attitude toward earthly riches; invention and technology made money and did it far more quickly than traditional husbandry. Artifice represented big gains, the mountains of gold and silver hinted at in folktales told and retold long before the 1840s perfection of steam-powered technology. Men and women knew that gold and silver no longer bought only clear title to farms and security in old age; they purchased cast-iron stoves, haying machines, and all the other glistening products of artifice that made home-built objects look crude and ugly. Artifice produced countless new things whose possession meant— or was thought to mean—bliss.

Bliss has not always identified happiness. In 1634, for example, William Wood found another meaning. "For such commodities as lie underground, I cannot out of mine own experience or knowledge say much, having taken no great notice of such things," he noted carefully in *New England's Prospect,* "but it is certainly reported that there is ironstone, and the Indians inform us that they can lead us to mountains of black lead, and have shown us lead ore, if our small judgement in such things does not deceive us, and though nobody dare confidently conclude, yet dare they not utterly deny, but that the Spaniards' bliss may lie hid in the barren mountains." Spanish bliss is, of course, gold ore, the substance by which immediate wealth is obtained, and all the things and powers it can purchase. Wood knew the mineralogical land classification system, the significance of barren mountains, and the portentous importance of lead deposits. And he glimpsed the seductive glimmering of instant wealth.

That glimmering endured across centuries, finding a niche in traditional knowledge and always ever so slightly biasing every husbandman's vision of his life's work. "The settlers in Maine, like all the other settlers in New England, indulge an unconquerable expectation of finding money buried in the earth," marveled Edward Kendall in 1809. "The money is supposed to have been buried by pirates; but the discovery of its burial-place is hoped for only from dreams. Where dreams have conveyed some general information of the place, then mineral-rods are resorted to, for ascertaining the precise spot at which to put the spade and pick-axe into the ground; and then charms and various observances, to defeat the watchfulness of the spirits that have the treasure in charge."[127] Kendall dismissed such matters as superstition having no more than entertainment value for his English audience and ignored the national love and quest for buried treasure. But by the middle of the nineteenth century American authors had realized mine- and treasure-seeking as a peculiar facet of United States culture. Melville, Hawthorne, Poe, and others pondered the trait and wove out of it a number of tales, the best known being perhaps Poe's "The Gold Bug." For gold ore Poe substituted Captain Kidd's already legendary buried treasure but even in 1843 he retained the colonial notion of Spanish bliss and Spanish land classification.

Although the treasure is eventually discovered on the mainland, on the crest of a hill topped with large trees, Poe begins the tale by describing the small sandy island covered with scant and dwarfish vegetation on which the clues to the treasure are first discovered. Much of the tale, while imbued with what Poe calls "some of the innumerable southern superstitions about money buried," concerns the working out of secret codes written in invisible ink and the relating of the cryptic message to the land.[128] Enamored as he was of scenery description and of the new profession of landscape architecture in particular, it is not surprising that Poe devotes careful attention to the setting of the tale. But his point, aside from creating a half-gothic entertainment, concerns the extraordinary power of technique applied to the problem of getting wealth. "The Gold Bug" reveals Poe's perception of the power of technology to make immediate use of land scorned by agriculturists, to make it pay. When the hero unearths the chest filled with Spanish gold and jewels he fulfills the fantasies of tradition-bound Maine farmers by using modern technique to get wealth, not the casually accepted tradition of the past.

Poe discerned the essential spatial importance of almost every form of seventeenth- to early nineteenth-century artifice. Mines, furnaces, and mills of every sort almost invariably lay near but not on land suited to agriculture; even sawmills lay within forest. Artificers made money out of land ignored by agriculturists, and whereas pollution and other products spread across the fertile land, the place of artifice usually remained separate, an eruption of technique in space ordered by custom.

And as long as the enterprises of artificers remained modest, they coexisted with farms and poisoned few agriculturists against them. Their growth, however, caused men to worry about their attendant evils and to think in terms as old as Milton's 1667 description of Hell, that place

> where peace
> And rest can never dwell, hope never comes
> That comes to all, but torture without end
> Still urges, and a fiery deluge, fed
> With ever-burning sulphur unconsumed.[129]

It is no accident that the nation's authors found artifice a fit subject for fiction and essays in the 1840s or that they scrutinized it in traditional terminology. When Hawthorne described the flames from the lime-kiln in Old Testament terms and Melville shuddered at the icebound Devil's Dungeon factory village, less articulate men and women had already experienced the wrenching tension implicit in large-scale artifice.

Behind every blessing of artifice, every new tool or lightened task, lurked some shadowy curse like occupational disease or injury or air or water pollution or fire or—most importantly—the collapse of beloved ways of life based on agriculture. The tension helped spark a reawakening of interest in the demonic, mysterious forces long thought to accompany artifice. As early as the fourteenth century Chaucer wondered about the tension implicit in artifice, and in alchemy in particular. His distrust surfaces in "Cannon's Yeoman's Tale," a poem that begins with a recounting of alchemical disaster:

> Although the devil didn't show his face
> I'm pretty sure he was about the place.
> In Hell itself where he is lord and master
> There couldn't be more rancour in disaster
> Than when our pots exploded as I've told you.[130]

Chaucer's interpretation reemerged in the early nineteenth century not only in works by American romantics who knew his poetry but also in almanacs and other inexpensive publications aimed at general readers. Witches, demons, and sorcerers at work in caverns appeared in almanacs such as those published by Conrad Zentler in Philadelphia; engravings of witches' sabbaths and subterranean conjurings accompanied the detailed explications of Satan's sudden interest in the United States. Monographs such as William B. Raber's 1855 *The Devil and Some of His Doings* and Joseph F. Berg's *Abbadon and Mahanaim; or, Daemons and Guardian Angels* of 1856 played upon the fears of rural people increasingly threatened by industrial processes, corporate economics, and urban culture. Again and again, writers drove home a simple message: return to the pure ways of agriculture lest Satan envelop the nation in his smoke-black wings. All the half-forgotten fears of artifice reared up in sermons, cheap tracts, and the terrible tales related by men and women formerly employed in furnaces, factories, and mines.

Here and there artifice found articulate defenders like Jacob Bigelow, who created a new word in 1829 to simplify the title of *Elements of Technology*, but most Americans agreed with Melville, Hawthorne, and Raber—and with Chaucer—that artifice involved something sinister.[131] To be sure, the looming of civil war cast shadows over all activities, but in the middle of the nineteenth century its blackness acquired depth from the pall spreading over the agricultural Republic. No longer did agriculture shape and dominate the land. In the East artifice became industry and dominated space. It destroyed the old equilibrium of wilderness, husbandry, and artifice, the equilibrium objectified in landscape.

CONCLUSION

The Americans love their country, not, indeed, as it is, but as it will be. They do not love the land of their fathers; but they are sincerely attached to that which their children are destined to inherit. They live in the future, and make their country as they go on. [1]

Francis J. Grund
The Americans
1837

Contemporary *landschaft*, Albuquerque, New Mexico. Photo courtesy of John Brinckerhoff Jackson.

enry James returned to the United States in 1904 after a twenty-four-year sojourn in Europe. Twelve months later he left for England, badly shaken by the social and spatial change that figures so prominently in *The American Scene*. His 1907 travelogue is cryptic, filled with misadventure, disappointment, and disgust and twisted by an almost desperate confusion.

James arrived in the United States near the end of a half-century-long transformation. His prolonged absence sharpened his perception but his boyhood love of traditional landscape endured to bias his understanding of urbanization, industry, and linearity. James oscillated between backward areas and the most up-to-date cities, between Berkshire farmhouses and Manhattan hotels. He landed in New York City already astonished by its skyline, and fled after several days to the quiet of rural New Hampshire and Cape Cod. From there, his wits collected, he returned to New York City and plunged into the Bowery, the Lower East Side, and the rest of Manhattan, striving to experience and know a city almost wholly reshaped. After several exhausting weeks he retreated to the unchanged stillness of Newport and after a second rest set out for Boston. Oscillation between industrial, vehicular-oriented cities and little-changed, almost backward rural areas structured his book. His last exploratory thrust, into the booming resorts of Florida, forced him home to England for a final recuperation. New spatial elements taxed and overtaxed his powers of observation and composition. In the end description and analysis proved impossible; James never completed the second volume of the book.

James felt secure in traditional landscape: the agricultural regions of New Hampshire, the fishing villages of Cape Cod, the small towns of the Berkshires, each with its elm-lined street, white-painted houses, and quiet. In such places, he remarked, "The scene is everywhere the same; whereby tribute is always ready and easy, and you are spared all shocks of surprise and saved any extravagance of discrimination." Cambridge drowsing in the early September sunlight, Newport deserted in off-season, George Washington's monumental Mount Vernon, and "the old Spanish Fort, the empty, sunny, grassy shell by the low pale shore" in Saint Augustine were all fragments of the remembered landscape of boyhood. James walked through them, restoring his spirit for adventures in new sorts of man-made environment. Such places were, in James's phrase, "finished" and acquiring a thin patina of time.[2]

No such patina softened the roughness of new urban and suburban form, and most of *The American Scene* documents James's excursions in understanding it. New York resembled a pincushion, he noted after his return from New England, studded with skyscrapers "grossly tall and grossly ugly" that overpowered church spires and funneled winter gales along streets jammed with electric cars. The trolleys, "cars of Juggernaut in their power to squash," terrified him, and in a moment of desperation he determined that they were "all there measurably *is* of the American scene." They prevented his crossing streets, surrounded monuments, destroyed any hope of quiet, and at times kept him from entering his hotel. New Yorkers skirted death at their fenders and fought for life at their doors as frantically as they did at elevators. Wherever he stopped, James was jostled and shoved or warned by gongs and by shouts to get out of the way. In New York he took refuge in Central Park, in Boston he rediscovered the twisting, peaceful residential streets built up in the eighteenth century, and in Baltimore he explored the halls and courts of Johns Hopkins University, searching constantly for pedestrian islands in vehicular space.[3] Bridges, especially New York City bridges, "the horizontal sheaths of pistons working at high pressure day and night, and subject, one apprehends with perhaps inconsistent gloom, to certain, to fantastic, to merciless multiplication," became his symbol of urban form and frenzy. He could not walk in the way of pistons and view space at his leisure.

So he began "touring" on wheels. Much of New York City he saw from within trolleys; elsewhere he traveled by automobile, at first fascinated by "the great loops thrown out by the lasso of observation from the wonder-working motor car." Most of the time he traveled by train, "the heavy, dominant American train," which he said made the countryside exist for it and whose great terminals made the cities' only portals. Railroad schedules determined his itinerary and on one occasion allowed him only fifteen minutes in which to glimpse Savannah. In the small hours of the morning, during a two-hour layover in a deserted Charleston station, James set out to examine the workings and meaning of the great junction, to learn the true significance of mechanized linearity. He turned back, convinced in the gloom lit only by signal lamps and flaring fireboxes that the wisest course was "to stand huddled just where one was."[4] Later, as he raced south in a well-upholstered Pullman fitted with plate-glass observation windows, he suddenly knew that he could not discern the Florida border, that the plate glass and tremendous speed insulated him from the land beyond the right-of-way.

Cities, industrial districts, and high-speed railroads meant a great deal to James. He loved London in all its gas-lit imperial splendor and squalor and knew the fast pace of European trains. What disturbed him so deeply about the United States "scene" was its rapid transformation from landscape to a complex—and confusing—amalgamation of landscape, cityscape, and interface areas. James cherished the landscape he remembered, and used his memories as the standards by which he condemned the new scene and the social and economic forces it objectified. But the changes that took such stark and sometimes sinister form at the close of the nineteenth century began in James's boyhood, or even earlier.

Around 1845 the stability that characterized the synthesis of agricultural and artificial spaces and structures called *landscape* began to erode. Technology, especially the technology of steam production and power, made practical the riverboat and railroad locomotive.[5] Steam-powered transport expanded the scale of commercial enterprise and prompted investors to organize corporations to fund ventures in land development and industrial invention. Corporations employed specialists trained not according to tradition transmitted orally and by example but by mathematical theory. A cash-based economy conquered all but a few remnants of the older agricultural economy, partly by moving crop processing from kitchen ells to distant mills and partly by selling to farmers an ever wider range of machinery. Railroads and centralized capital investment encouraged the growth of cities; steam power enabled factory owners to locate near population centers rather than at isolated waterfalls, and masonry and iron-frame construction permitted the building of ever-larger industrial structures. Slowly the machine-tool industry made blacksmithing obsolescent, and the traditional house gave way to the structure built of premanufactured components. By the time of the Civil War, a few astute observers discerned the changes and lashed out at what they saw as evil artifice; after the war and its proof that great numbers of men could work in groups and that heavy industry did make profits, the trends became even more pronounced.

In the West, eastern industry shaped the land before settlers arrived; the railroad ran into the almost treeless wilderness that disproved the claims of tradition by producing excellent crops. Tracks crossed the High Plains and structured small towns; barbed wire and windmills made new-style farming pay. Regional peculiarities almost vanished west of the ninety-ninth meridian, in the land James crossed by train but chose not to describe.

The infant changes of 1845 wrought immeasurably significant spatial change, the change that defeated James's nostalgic visions. But vestiges of landscape, and vestiges of attitudes intimately associated with traditional landscape, endured as the standards by which Americans judged the new-style man-made environment.

Keepsakes

Rail fences, estensiónes, Pennsylvania bank barns, small-town main streets, covered bridges, graveyards, crossroads stores, kitchen ells, blacksmith shops, orchards, gristmills, camp-meeting grounds, one-room schoolhouses, and meetinghouse-centered New England towns all survive as reminders of the now fractured traditional landscape. Among them stand lighthouses, army-engineer-designed viaducts, factory villages, furnaces, canals, turnpikes, and section lines marked by fences and roads, the early heralds of a new, translocal, innovative way of building. Many keepsakes lie in ruins; canals are silted up, and small schoolhouses shelter only phoebes and other birds. Thousands more have vanished, leaving behind only cellar holes or ornamental shrubbery (lilacs, most often) to guide the searcher. But vast numbers of keepsakes endure, serving not only the everyday purposes for which Americans built them but modern uses too. The surviving keepsakes together constitute the vestiges of landscape that still serve Americans as the standard by which new form is judged. Amateur and professional designers alike continue to recreate the keepsakes of the past.

More than any other constituent of the pre-1845 landscape, the detached house surrounded by land kept in equilibrium remains the spatial epitome of the "good life." A typical suburban house lot recreates in miniature the farm of the past. The front lawn, frequently fenced and always carefully mowed, assumes the role of the meadow, although the householder often destroys the grass clippings rather than curing them into hay.[6] Behind the house lies the yard, again often enclosed, but serving as both farmyard and pasture. The backyard provides privacy, of course, and shelter from rough winds but most importantly offers an outdoor workplace. Chores from burning trash to changing automobile-engine oil to splitting firewood require private space; the backyard and the descendant of the barn known as the garage or toolshed encourage the manipulation of objects. Interrupting the front and back yards are the ornamental trees, sometimes exotic but more frequently selected from the range of species that indicates fertile soil, and ranging among them are the substitute livestock, the family dogs and cats still fenced out of the substitute arable field, the vegetable garden. Lawns and yards may indeed exist to fulfill some innate human love and need for beauty but more likely they still announce the dignity and responsibility of their owners. Proper householders keep their live-stock from their neighbors' land and eradicate crabgrass before it over-runs abutting lawns. But more importantly, the detached house and surrounding land provide their owners with the opportunity for creative manipulation, an opportunity usually denied them if they work in a factory or an office. Manipulation produces many spatial effects; ar-rangements of plaster gnomes, carpet-like lawns, geometrically ordered organic vegetable gardens all objectify manipulation strongly charac-terized by tradition, example, and hesitant innovation, although now strongly affected by semiprofessional do-it-yourself guidebooks and in-frequent professional advice. The same neighborhood standards and assistance that retarded innovation in barn- and housebuilding in 1750 continue to guide amateur building. Neighborly advice and electric power tools enable the American householder to manipulate his stead, to experiment with homemade solar panels and wood-burning stoves, to keep in perfect equilibrium the objective correlative of his status of re-sponsible citizen-taxpayer. *Cottage* connotes a landless, rather frivolous dwelling in beachland or recreational forest; as Parliament understood in 1589, a house is vastly more significant than a cottage. It has land and permanence.

Professional designers and builders recognize the enduring strengths of landscape vestiges too. Most recently, they translated the small-town main street armature into the shopping mall concourse.[7] A great shop-ping mall axis resembles an early nineteenth-century main street because its designers intend it to evoke memories of gentle-paced, small-scale community. Stores open on pedestrian space interrupted by benches and small, sometimes plastic trees, and the mall is free of automobiles. The stores alternate, every other one serving men, the ones in between catering to women shoppers or to clienteles of both sexes. At the ends of the concourse are department stores, not houses, but future malls will likely have condominia or apartment complexes attached to them. Care-ful designers subtly copy the smallness of the old main streets and strive to recreate the unhurried atmosphere Americans associate with dry-goods and hardware stores, and with livery stables.

Suburban houses and houselots, like shopping mall concourses, attract critics certain that the late twentieth century caricatures rather than imitates the best of the past. The quarter-acre lot is too small for a proper garden or lawn, they claim, and the shopping mall concourse lacks the business and social diversity of main street. Many Americans share their misgivings and choose to live on larger acreages beyond suburban developments or determine to revitalize and restore main street businesses and buildings. But always the memory of landscape, the memory kept vivid by the enduring keepsakes, shapes present building and design.

Values

The memory of landscape heightened by the enduring keepsakes shapes attitudes as well as space and structure. Much of the contemporary American love of landscape derives, of course, from the Christmas-card-like advertisements repeatedly presented on television and in magazines. But the advertisements succeed in selling products partly because viewers and readers react favorably to the landscape vestiges that decorate them. Gristmills, orchards and meadows, main streets, and especially barns still connote the "good life" that once created landscape. Surviving vestiges of landscape, and repeated attention directed at them, reinforce old, traditional American values concerning the man-made environment.

Plastic space and structure enjoy tremendous favor among most Americans. Almost every household owns a hammer, saw, and other tools useful in building and shaping structure, but only structure made of wood. Timber remains the favorite building material in the United States not only because it is enduring and inexpensive but because it is easily modified. American men, and increasingly women too, of every economic class enjoy hobbies that involve reshaping domestic structure. For blue-collar families, shaping and reshaping furniture, rooms, and whole houses—along with garages, carports, and other outbuildings— save hiring professionals. Farm families also shape much structure because they cannot afford to employ craftsmen or else cannot find craftsmen who understand the proposed projects. But among blue-collar and farm families, as among upper-class families, cutting a window in a wall or building a garage or toolhouse or adding an outshot kitchen or dining room provides an even more powerful creative manipulation than making and mowing a lawn. After all, a new porch or dormer is reasonably permanent, a gift to one's family and to the ages. Not surprisingly, many Americans dislike living in structures that somehow resist such modification. Metal trailers, stone and cement houses, and rigidly controlled apartments stifle what many Americans assume is an almost natural right, the right to make small-scale changes in wooden structures. Where building codes and fire-prevention ordinances prevent such modification, residents either hire experts skilled in masonry construction or else grudgingly learn how to set bricks and pour concrete. The American tradition of common engineering in wood endures in the minds of millions of householders, sparking the renovation of old houses and the building of outshots. It endures too in the minds of trailer and apartment dwellers, sparking discontent with the high mortgage rates and real estate prices that confine people to housing in which modification is difficult or forbidden.

Vestiges of landscape reinforce another common value, that of pedestrian-scaled space and structure. The high-speed railroad view perfected in the 1840s distorts individual perception of the space and structure beyond the railroad car. As the express train begins to move, passengers look through windows at the station platform, the fences and houses abutting the right of way; but as the train reaches perhaps twenty-five miles an hour, the trackside blurs and passengers direct their gaze at newspapers and books. Of course, the built environment alongside a railroad is confusing in its own right but the very speed makes analysis difficult, or worse, boring. Landscape evolved in an age of slower travel, and the lucky American who wanders into "unspoiled" areas discovers—if he is perceptive enough—that walking is every bit as pleasant and intriguing as Thoreau asserted long ago. Space and structure are knowable; no field is so vast as to preclude visual bounding, no barn too high to distort close scrutiny. Nothing dwarfs the observer fortunate enough to find assembled vestiges of landscape, and nothing stuns his capacity to see.

Of all values, however, landscape most forcefully reinforces the traditional love of agriculture and distrust of artifice. Certainly landscape vestiges even now are usually immediately understood; a city dweller recognizes a barn and guesses (usually correctly) at its general use, and even a child of the suburbs recognizes the use of an abandoned one-room schoolhouse. But landscape vestiges strike contemporary Americans as safe and placid, unlikely to hurt or disturb. So deeply seated is the traditional antipathy to artifice—now industry—that advertisers and journalists exploit it at will. News reporters juxtaposed the striken atomic power plant at Three Mile Island with the Amish farms just miles away, blatantly implying the evil of one and the good of the other. Only a rare American murmurs "pretty country" as the express train races among chemical plants and oil refineries, through smelting complexes and mining regions; but if the train slows down, most passengers enjoy the young calves and colts frolicking away from the locomotive whistle and wave at the farm families at work in the fields and farmyards. Passengers may not recognize the crop in the ground but traveling through "farm country" delights them as much as a bright-painted meetinghouse delighted Timothy Dwight.

A value system that honors plastic space and structure, a slow-paced pedestrian scale, and land shaped for agriculture and agriculture-related industry might well coexist with a parallel, urban-oriented system. But Americans remain faithful to the spatial values of their ancestors and apply them to spaces and structures objectifying totally different systems accepted by minorities. No city park or plaza can compare well with landscape recreation spaces, just as no industrial district compares well with a single gristmill surrounded by fields or a small sawmill nestled among second-growth timber. The landscape value system, and particularly the aesthetic it produces, unfairly condemns whole areas of industrial cityscape, of non-landscape. And as long as the vestiges of landscape endure, partisans of cityscape and great industry must fight a lonely fight, one contrary to the common wisdom of Americans descended from the makers of landscape.

NOTES

PREFACE

1. The best introduction to landscape studies is the work of John Brinckerhoff Jackson and W. G. Hoskins. See Jackson, *American Space, Landscapes,* and *The Necessity for Ruins.* Jackson founded and edited for many years the journal *Landscape;* some of his many articles are collected in *Changing Rural Landscapes.* See also Hoskins, *The Making of the English Landscape, English Landscapes,* and *One Man's England.* The theoretical writings of Tuan are especially insightful; see his *Topophilia, Space and Place,* and *Landscapes of Fear.* Perhaps the best introduction to the methodologies of landscape history and analysis is Maurice Beresford, *History on the Ground.* See also Lewis, "Axioms of the Landscape: Some Guides to the American Scene"; Zelinsky, *The Cultural Geography of the United States;* and Hart, *The Look of the Land.* All these works concern the larger landscape, not formal gardens or scenery painting. One of the strongest anthologies of studies of the contemporary man-made American environment is *The Interpretation of Ordinary Landscapes,* ed. D. W. Meinig.

LANDSCAPE

1. Emerson, *Journals and Miscellaneous Notebooks,* III, 137–38. For this quotation I am grateful to Miss Nancy I. Kalow, Harvard College, 1981.
2. For other definitions of *landscape,* see Dickinson, "Landscape and Society"; Jackson, "The Meaning of 'Landscape'"; Schmithüsen, "Was ist eine Landschaft?"; Schwarz, *Allgemeine Siedlungsgeographie,* pp. 162–220; Ruskin, "The Cor de la Faucille," *Praeterita* [1889], pp. 143–58; Hamerton, *Landscape,* pp. 9–12: Fischer, "Landscape as Symbol," *Landscape;* and Cayrol, *De l'espace humain.*
3. On common knowledge, see Burke, *Popular Culture,* esp. pp. 23–64, and Quinby, *Material Culture and the Study of American Life.*
4. Thoreau, *A Week on the Concord and Merrimack Rivers,* pp. 42–43.
5. *German Folk Tales,* pp. 192–200. For an introduction to the meaning of wilderness, see Williams, *Wilderness and Paradise in Christian Thought;* Mannhardt, *Wald- und Feldkulte;* Baasen, *Wald und Bauertum;* Glacken, *Traces on the Rhodian Shore,* pp. 318–45; Hermes, *Handbuch . . . Forst- Jagd- und Fischerei Gesetzgebung;* Stenton, *English Society in the Early Middle Ages,* pp. 97–119; Leyen and Spamer, *Die Altdeutschen Wandteppiche in Regensburger Rathaus,* pp. 16–18; Baumgart, *Der Wald in der deutschen Dichtung,* esp. pp. 33–47; Benros, *Aus dem Walde;* Darthelmess, *Wald Umwelt des Menschen;* Köstler, *Wald-Mensch-Kultur;* Deveze, *La Vie de la forêt française au XVIᵉ siècle;*

Hilf and Röhrig, *Wald und Weidwerk;* and Seidenstickes, *Waldgeschichte des Alterthums.*

6. Williams, pp. 6–51.
7. See Montalembert, *The Monks of the West,* II, 210–14; Severe, *Vie de Saint Martin,* II, 737–66; Mantel, *Geschichte des Weihnachtsbaum;* Teirlinck, *Flora Diabolica;* Tille, *Die Geschichte der deutschen Weihnacht;* Detering, *Die Bedeutnung der Eiche seit der Vorzeit;* Marzell, *Die Pflanzen im deutschen Volksleben;* idem, *Volksbotanik, Die Pflanze im detuschen Brauchtum;* idem, *Himmelsbrot und Teufelsteiten: volkstürmliche Pflanzennamen aus Bayern;* and Rollinson, *Life and Tradition in the Lake District,* pp. 61–62. The best explication of tales concerning trees is Bynum, *The Daemon in the Wood;* see also Bettelheim, *The Uses of Enchantment;* Lüthi, *Once Upon a Time;* Mannhardt, *Wald und Feldkulte,* esp. I, 72–154; Porteous, *Forest Folklore, Mythology, and Romance;* Ralston, "Forest and Field Myths"; Grimm, *Deutsche Mythologie,* II, 539–45; Gordon, *Green Magic;* Davidson, "The Sword at the Wedding"; Butterworth, *The Tree at the Navel of the Earth;* and Schrade, *Baum und Wald in Bildern deutschen Maler.*
8. For Saint Paul's warning see 1 Timothy 4:7; see also James G. Frazier, *The Magic Art and the Evolution of Kings,* esp. II, chap. x, "Relics of Tree-Worship in Modern Europe," pp. 59–96 (see also pp. 7–55); Cook, *The Tree of Life;* and esp. Toynbee, "The Religious Background of the Present Environmental Crisis."
9. There exists no adequate study of European supranatural humanoids; but see Sikes, *British Goblins;* Dyer, *The Ghost World;* Gerard, *The Land Behind the Forest,* I, 319–24, II, 9–13; Lascault, *Le Monstre dans l'art occidental;* Landrin, *Les Monstres marins;* Bernheimer, *Wild Men in the Middle Ages;* Briggs, *The Anatomy of Puck.*
10. On the Old Religion see Davidson, *Gods and Myths of Northern Europe,* esp. pp. 191–215; Vries, *Altgermanische Religionsgeschichte;* Brown, "Some Examples of Post-Reformation Folklore in Devon"; Opie, "The Tentacles of Tradition"; Ryan, "Othin in England"; Markale, *Les Celtes et la Civilisation celtique;* and Herberstein, *Description of Moscow,* p. 36.
11. On Seville, see Dominguez-Ortíz, *The Golden Age of Spain, 1516–1659,* p. 323n. Benjamin Rudyerd's Parliament speech on the dark corners is given in his *Memoirs... Containing his Speeches,* pp. 135–38. John Dury's remarks are quoted in Christopher Hill, *Change and Continuity in Seventeenth-Century England,* p. 20; see also Burke, *Popular Culture,* p. 51, and Hall, *Funebria Florae, The Downfall of May Games.* For general background, see Banks, *British Calendar Customs,* and James, *Seasonal Feasts and Festivals.*
12. *Oxford English Dictionary,* II, 3778–3779; Kersey, *A New English Dictionary,* under *wilderness;* Hoskins, *The Making of the English Landscape,* pp. 95–103; Tuan, *Landscapes of Fear,* pp. 73–86.
13. Hector Boece's 1527 remarks concerning Garloch and Joan Blaeu's 1653 remarks concerning Loch Lomond are quoted in Costello, *In Search of Lake Monsters,* pp. 129, 130–31; see esp. pp. 128–37.

14. Boswell, *Journal of a Tour of the Hebrides* [1773], pp. 270–71. Some evidence suggests that "fish without fin" may be large or mutant eels (see Moriarty, *Eels*, pp. 20–29). For information concerning contemporary giant eels I am indebted to Roger Courtenay, Harvard University Graduate School of Design. See also Simpson, "Fifty British Dragon Tales: An Analysis," which emphasizes the aquatic habitat of many mythical and legendary British dragons.

15. Studies of the traditional, territorial *landschaft* are few. The best are Meitzen, *Siedelung und Agrarwesen der Westgermanen und Ostgermanen* (the atlas in vol. 4 is particularly useful), and Bader, *Das Mittelalterliche Dorf als Friedens- und Rechtsbereich, Dorfgenossenschaft und Dorfgemeinde,* and *Rechtsformen und Schichten der Liegenschaftsnutzung im Mittelalterlichen Dorf.* Also useful are Klaar, *Die Siedlungs- und hausformen des Wiener Waldes;* Bloch, *Land and Work in Medieval Europe;* Coulton, *The Medieval Panorama;* Schwarz, *Allgemeine Siedlungsgeographie,* esp. pp. 162–212; Addy, *Church and Manor;* Laslett, *The World We Have Lost;* and Grainge, *The Vale of Mowbray.* See several articles, all contained in *Geographie et historie agraires:* Helmut Jäger, "Die Ausdehnung der Wälder in Mitteleuropa über offenes Siedlungsland" (pp. 300–12), Rigmor Frimannslund, "A Cluster Settlement in Western Norway" (pp. 209–20), and M. M. de Planhol and J. Schneider, "Excursions in Lorraine Septentrionale" (pp. 37–46). See also Hager and Heyn, *Das alte Dorf;* Mejborg, *Das Bauernhaus im Herzogthum Schleswig und das Leben des schleswigischen Bauernstandes im 16, 17, und 18 Jahrhundert;* Worlidge, *Systema Agriculturae;* Dickinson, "Rural Settlement in the German Lands"; Uhlig, "Old Hamlets with Infield and Outfield Systems in Western and Central Europe"; Düring, *Das Siedlungsbild der Insel Fahman;* Bendermacher, *Dorfformen in Westfalen-Lippe;* Olsen, *Farms and Fanes of Ancient Norway;* Holmsen, "The Old Norwegian Peasant Community"; Frimanuslund, "Farm Community and Neighborhood Community"; and Gomme, *The Village Community with Special Reference to the Origin and Form of its Survivals in Britain.*

16. The hieroglyphs are analyzed in Müller, *Die Heilige Stadt.* For the smallness of the landschaft, see Bouchard, *Le Village Immobile,* esp. p. 352; Seebohm, *The English Village Community Examined in its Relations to . . . the Common or Open Field System of Husbandry;* and Laslett, p. 80.

17. Seebohm, *Customary Acres and their Historical Importance;* Field, *English Field Names, A Dictionary;* Shaw-Lefevre, *English and Irish Land Questions;* Epperlein, *Der Bauer im Bild des Mittelalters;* Giles, *History of the Parish and Town of Brampton,* esp. pp. 75–80; Slicker von Bath, *The Agrarian History of Europe A.D. 500–1850;* Cooter, "Ecological Dimensions of Medieval Agrarian Systems"; Boserup, *The Conditions of Agricultural Growth;* McLaskey, "English Open Fields as Behavior Towards Risk". The European *Haus-Vater* literature yields much information of landschaft agricultural spaces and systems (see esp. Glorez, *Vollständige Hauss- und Land Bibliothec;* for an introduction to this genre, see Güntz, *Handbuch der Landwirtschaftlichen Literatur*).

18. Addy, *The Evolution of the English House;* Atkinson, *Forty Years in a Moorland Parish,* esp. pp. 18–26; Pitkin, "Partible Inheritance and the Open Fields."

19. Henning, *Das Deutsche Haus in seiner Historischen Entwicklung;* Grimm, *Deutsche Rechtsalterthümer,* II, 539; Doyon and Hubrecht, *L'Architecture Rurale et Bourgeoise en France,* esp. pp. 83–101; Eberlein and Ramsdell, *Small Manor Houses and Farmsteads in France,* pp. 57, 128, 144–45.

20. Chaucer, "The Nun's Priest's Tale" [c. 1386–88], *Works,* p. 132 (ll. 4035–39); Andrews, *The Old English Manor,* pp. 82–119.

21. Hall, *Society in the Elizabethan Age* (this work offers two exquisite color facsimiles of an Elizabethan estate manuscript map, one showing house forms); Gomme, *Village Community,* pp. 116–46, 252–55. On housebreaking see also Palgrave, *The Rise and Progress of the English Commonwealth,* pt. ii, clxxii.

22. On defenses against supernatural evils, see William, "The Protection of the House: Some Iconographic Evidence from Wales"; Nattrass, "Witch Posts"; and Hayes and Rutter, *Cruck-Framed Buildings in Ryedale and Eskdale,* pp. 87–95. On breaking and entering, see His, *Das Strafrecht des deutschen Mittelatlers,* pp. 20–36.

23. "An Acte Againste erectinge and mayntayninge of Cottages" [Feb. 4 and Mar. 29, 1588–89], *Statutes of the Realm,* IV, ii, 804–05. Courts prosecuted men who broke the law (see Campbell, *The English Yeoman Under Elizabeth and the Early Stuarts,* pp. 96–98). The best survey of English domestic architecture of the period is Barley, *The English Farmhouse and Cottage.* See also Gailey, "The Peasant Houses of the South-west Highlands of Scotland: Distribution, Parallels, and Evolution."

24. On the circular form of the landschaft, see the excellent analysis by Thünen, *Der isolirte staat in beziehung auf landwirthschaft.*

25. On rolands, see Mejborg, p. 26, and Müller. For Puritan opposition, see especially Hall, *Funebria Florae,* esp. p. 3. See also Platt, *The English Medieval Town,* pp. 15–47, and Auerbach, "Befehlerles," *Schwarzwälder Dorfgeschichten,* pp. 133–58. For the popularity of Old Religion-related customs in early modern Europe, see Brand, *Observations on the Popular Antiquities of Great Britain;* Ladurie, *Carnival in Romans;* and especially Burke, *Popular Culture,* pp. 208–43.

26. The landschaft priest is quoted in Burke, pp. 50–51.

27. *German Folk Tales* [1857] offers an excellent collection of European folktales, many involving the landschaft–wilderness opposition.

28. On bandits see Burke, *Popular Culture,* pp. 165–69, and Hobsbawm, *Bandits.*

29. Bernheimer, *Wild Men in the Middle Ages;* Mannhardt, *Wald und Feldkulte,* I, 88.

30. For an introduction to the evolution of paths, roads, and highways, see Hitzer, *Die Strasse,* esp. pp. 105–85; Villefosse, *Histoire des grandes routes de France;* and Watkins, *The Old Straight Track.* On *strassenromantik,* Stephan, *Das Verkehrsleben in Altertum und Mittelalter;* for a collection of folksongs, see *Alte hoch- und niederdeutschen Volkslieder,* nos. 64–73, 260. Uhland tried his

hand at strassenromantik poetry himself (see his "Abschied" [1806], *Gedichte*, pp. 209-10). See also Lenau, "Der Postillion" [1833], *Sammtliche Werke*, I, 200-03. The old romance endures (see Vivante, "Crossroads," and Brownstein, "The U. P. S. Man").

31. Hampe, *Die Fahrende Leute in der Deutschen Vergangenheit;* Danckert, *Unehrliche Leute: Die Verfemten Berufe*, pp. 214-20; Stephan, *Geschichte der preussichen Post*. On the separation of road from landschaft, see De Quincey, "The English Mail Coach" [1849; rev. 1854], *Collected Writings*, XIII, 270-327.

32. Lelievre, *La Vie des Cités de l'Antiquité à nous Jours*, p. 11; Estienne, *Guides des chemins de France; La Guide des chemins pour aller et venir par tout le Royaume de France et autre pays circonuoisins*. On the growing anonymity of urban life, see Sennett, *The Fall of Public Man*, pp. 38-43.

33. Sargent, "Feudalism to Family Farms in France"; Fussell, *Village Life in the Eighteenth Century;* Blum, *End of the Old Order.*

34. Mumford, *The Culture of Cities*, pp. 13-86; Burke, pp. 245-50.

35. On grass growing in streets, see Fols, *Erinnerungen eines Schulmannes aus dem alten Danzig, 1822-1841*, p. 5.

36. On the uses of *landscape* see the *Oxford English Dictionary* under *landscape;* Grimm, *Deutsches Wörterbuch*, VI, 133-34; and Appleton, *The Experience of Landscape.*

37. Ruffin, "Observations Made During an Excursion to the Dismal Swamp"; Byrd, *Secret History of the Line* [1727], in *Prose Works*, esp. pp. 67-74. On early American attitudes toward wilderness, see Carroll, *Puritanism and the Wilderness;* Jones, *O Strange New World;* esp. pp. 1-70; and Nash, *Wilderness and the American Mind*. The European concept of wilderness endured for decades, especially when travelers surveyed the western parts of North America (see Möllhausen, *Wanderungen durch die Prärien und Wüsten*).

38. Mather, *A Short Essay to Preserve and Strengthen the Good Impression Produced by Earthquakes*, pp. 46-47 [appendix]; see also his *The Terror of the Lord*. On the 1755 earthquake, see Bakewell, *An Introduction to Geology*, esp. p. 251; on Missouri, see Flint, *Recollections*, pp. 212-20.

39. Trumbull, *Complete History*, II, 91-93; Barber, *Connecticut Historical Collections*, pp. 525-28.

40. Melville, "Letter to Nathaniel Hawthorne," *Letters*, p. 143; Geller, "Notes on Sea-Serpents of Coastal New England"; Thoreau, *Cape Cod*, pp. 87-88. On his almost drowning, see Watson, "When Thoreau was a Young Man in Plymouth."

41. At least two scholars have identified "wilderness evil" as a main theme in American culture. See Rourke, *The Roots of American Culture*, esp. p. 20: "Folk evil was present in our colonial settlements from an early period, drawing upon a common inheritance of medieval beliefs in daemonic powers, colored by an infiltration of Indian faith in strange earth spirits, and shaped by the terror of the wilderness." See also Hoffman, *Form and Fable in American Fiction*, esp. p. 8: "This lore is the detritus of Europe's pagan past, a

past which has lingered in country customs, seasonal festivals, the lore of witchcraft, and folk belief in revenants, stregas, fairies, and other un-Christian inhabitants of the world of spirit." Shaped land is always perceived—if only half-consciously—against the backdrop of wilderness.

42. Dwight, *Travels in New England;* Thoreau, "Walking" [1862], *Excursions,* pp. 161–214.

PLANTING

1. Dunton, *Letters Written from New England, 1686,* p. 52.
2. Defoe, *The Life and Strange Surprizing Adventures of Robinson Crusoe.*
3. Emerson, "Farming," *Society and Solitude,* pp. 147–48.
4. Chevalier, *La Formation des grands domaines au Mexique; Recopilación des leyes de los reynos de los Indias,* bk. IV, chaps. 5, 7, 12. See also "Royal Ordinances Concerning the Laying Out of New Towns," and *Colección de Documentos Ineditos Relativos Conquista y Organización de los Antiques Posesions Espanalos de America.* For the Spanish background of New Spain settlement, see Dominquez-Ortíz, *The Golden Age of Spain, 1516–1659;* see also Bancroft, *History of Arizona and New Mexico, 1530–1888.*
5. Conway, "Village Types in the Southwest"; Stanislawski, "Early Spanish Town Planning in the New World." The quotations are from Nuttall's translation of "Royal Ordinances."
6. Chevalier, pp. 29–40; McBride, *Land Systems of Mexico.*
7. *Historical Documents Relating to New Mexico, Nueva Vizcaya, and Approaches Thereto, to 1773,* I, 175–89; see also Viceroy Marques de Falces, "Land Ordinances," *The Spanish Tradition in America,* pp. 128–34.
8. On the *estensión* see Dusenberry, *The Mexican Mesta;* Moorhead, *The Presidio;* McWilliams, *North from Mexico;* and Reps, *The Making of Urban America,* pp. 26–54. See also Hardy, "La forma de las ciudades coloniales en Hispanoamerica"; Fagiolo, "La fondazione delle citta Latino-Americane Gli Archetipi della Giustizia E Della Fede"; and Cozzato, "Il Sistema Economico—Territoriale Nell' America Spagnola," all in *Psicon,* II (Oct.–Dec. 1975): 8–85 (this is an extremely valuable collection of articles).
9. Greenleaf, "Land and Water in Mexico and New Mexico"; Glick, *The Old World Background of the Irrigation System of San Antonio, Texas;* Simmons, "Spanish Irrigation Practices in New Mexico"; Hutchins, "The Community Acequia; Its Origin and Development"; Taylor, "Land and Water Rights in the Viceroyalty of New Spain."
10. Blackman, Spanish Institutions of the Southwest; Stanislawski, *The Anatomy of Eleven Towns in Michoacan;* Vassberg, "The Tierias Baldios: Community Property and Public Lands in Sixteenth-Century Castille"; Algier, "The Pueblo Mesta Ordinances of 1556 and 1560"; Weeks, "The Agrarian System of the Spanish Colonies," esp. 163. For general background on the Islamic contribution to New Spain water and common land rights, see Watt, *A*

History of Islamic Spain, and particularly Glick, *Irrigation and Society in Medieval Valencia.*

11. Bunting, *Taos Adobes,* and *Early Architecture in New Mexico;* Southwick, *Build with Adobe;* Adams, *The Architecture and Art of Early Hispanic Colorado;* Anderson, "The City is a Garden," *Landscape Papers,* pp. 58-63; West, "The Flat-Roofed Folk Dwelling in Rural Mexico." The best article is Jackson, "First Comes the House."

12. Gregg, *Scenes and Incidents in the Western Prairies,* pp. 148-53, 202-06; "Albuquerque and Galisteo: Certificate of their Founding, 1706."

13. "Instructions to Peralta by Vice-Roy [Martin-López de Gouna]."

14. Borhegyi, "The Evolution of a Landscape"; Burnett, "Madrid Plaza"; Field, "Sketches of Big Timber, Bent's Fort, and Milk Fort in 1839." There is no substitute for seeing Chimayo.

15. Carlson, "Rural Settlement Patterns in the San Luis Valley: A Comparative Study."

16. Chevalier, pp. 66-67; de Falces, p. 128.

17. Chaves, p. 181. On later Spanish colonization, see *The Spanish in the Mississippi Valley, 1752-1804,* and Weber, "Mexico's Far Northern Frontier, 1821-1845: A Critical Bibliography." Additional useful spatial information is found in Robertson, "Provincial Town Plans from Late Sixteenth-Century Mexico." For a comparative study, see Lockart, *Spanish Peru.* Old Spanish ideas endure (see Lomnitz, *Network and Marginality*).

18. *Winthrop Papers,* II, plates following p. 276; the essay is in III, pp. 181-85.

19. For an analysis, see Stilgoe, "The New England Town: Ideal and Reality." For an opposite interpretation, see Fries, *The Urban Idea in Colonial America,* pp. 48-49.

20. Winthrop, "A Modell of Christian Charity," *Winthrop Papers,* II, pp. 282-87.

21. Johnson, *Wonder-working Providence,* esp. pp. 90, 116, 189. On Andover, see Bailey, *Historical Sketches of Andover,* p. 33, and Greven, *Four Generations,* pp. 55-58.

22. Cotton, *A Brief Exposition,* p. 85. The 1642 quotation is in Miller, *The New England Mind,* p. 36. On dissension in Hingham, see Waters, "Hingham, Massachusetts, 1631-1661: An East Anglian Oligarchy in the New World," and Coolidge, "Hingham Builds a Meetinghouse."

23. Increase Mather, *An Earnest Exhortation to the Inhabitants of New England,* p. 9.

24. For a study of one early settlement process, see Powell, *Puritan Village,* pp. 92-101.

25. Ibid., pp. 108-24; Lockridge, *A New England Town,* pp. 10-16; Osgood, *The American Colonies in the Seventeenth Century,* I, 424-67.

26. Zuckerman, *Peaceable Kingdoms;* Daniels, "Connecticut's Villages Become Mature Towns."

27. Greven, pp. 175-258; Bushman, *From Puritan to Yankee.* Old ideas of nucleation lived on, however (see Barnard, *A Sermon Preached in Boston . . . for Encouraging Industry,* and *Records of the Governor and Company of the Massachusetts Bay,* I, 157, 291).

28. Clark, *The Eastern Frontier;* Weeden, *Economic and Social History of New England, 1620–1789.*
29. Freeman, *The Town Officer;* most New England town-record books mention commons. For an extended analysis of grazing and other common-land usage and greens, see Stilgoe, "Common, Close, and Village Green: The 'Meetinghouse Lot' in New England, 1620-1960"; Cushing, "Town Commons of New England, 1640-1840"; Felt, *Annals of Salem,* I, 336, 353, 357; II, 496; Perley, *History of Salem,* II, 204–05, 211, 436–38; and Adams, *The History of the Town of Fairhaven, Vermont,* pp. 192–93.
30. *Scituate Records,* I, 37, 39, 52–54; Forman, "Mill Sawing in Seventeenth-Century Massachusetts"; Candee, "Merchant and Millwright."
31. Symonds, "Letter [1637]."
32. Stevens, *Poems,* p. 21.
33. Hawthorne, *The Scarlet Letter,* and "Young Goodman Brown," *Mosses from an Old Manse,* pp. 89–106; Sewall, *Diary, 1674–1729,* I, 472, 513. On backcountry attitudes, see Taylor, *Poems,* and Stoddard, *An Answer to Some Cases of Conscience.*
34. Manuscript deeds offer excellent insights into the landscape and wilderness perceptions and ideals of New England husbandmen.
35. See the maps reproduced in Reps, *The Making of Urban America,* pp. 115–46.
36. Litchfield, "Diary, 1774–1775," p. 152.
37. Thoreau, *A Week on the Concord and Merrimack Rivers,* p. 160. See also his *Cape Cod* and *Main Woods.*
38. See Stilgoe, "Folklore and Graveyard Design," for an analysis of the shift. See also Sewall, *Diary,* I, 472; Increase Mather, *A Discourse Concerning the Uncertainty of the Times of Men;* and Drake, *The Town of Roxbury,* pp. 95–97.
39. Very little attention has been given to the frittering away of common land (see Greven, pp. 222–58, and the transaction cited in *Early Records of the Town of Providence,* V, 232).
40. Richeson, *English Land Measuring to 1800,* pp. 142–88. For an analysis of the cultural and spatial impact of mathematical surveying, see Stilgoe, "Jack-o-lanterns to Surveyors."
41. Tocqueville, *De la democratie en Amérique,* I, 1-7-111; the distinction is missed by most translators.
42. Dwight, *Travels in New England and New York,* I, 265, 123; Frost, "The Onset," *The Poetry of Robert Frost,* p. 226; Eliade, *The Sacred and the Profane,* pp. 26–27.
43. Donnelly, *The New England Meeting Houses of the Seventeenth Century;* Mather, *Magnalia Christi Americana,* I, frontispiece. One of the best ways of examining the seventeenth- and early eighteenth-century significance of meetinghouses is to study their depiction in common sketch maps. See, for example, "Proposed Site for Ipswich Meetinghouse" [1677], and Godsoe, "Plan of Division of John Hole's Dec'd., his Land" [Dec. 17, 1739]. The Godsoe manuscript map emphasizes the meetinghouse by depicting it oversize; the

Ipswich map emphasizes the centrality of the proposed site for a new meetinghouse. See also "A Plan of the Town of Northwood" [1805], and "Plan of a Portion of Wrentham, Massachusetts" [1762].

44. Beverly, *The History and Present State of Virginia,* pp. 15-16.
45. Alsop, *A Character of the Province of Maryland,* p. 36; Beverly, pp. 298-99.
46. Hammond, *Leah and Rachel, or the Two Fruitful Sisters, Virginia and Maryland,* p. 10. For general background see Bruce, *Economic History of Virginia in the Seventeenth Century,* I, 1-238.
47. Bruce, *Economic History,* I, 189-240.
48. Ibid., II, 512-30; "Instructions to Governor Yeardley, 1618," esp. 157.
49. Bruce, *Economic History,* I, 10; Phillips, *Life and Labor in the Old South,* pp. 112-18. See also *A Perfect Description of Virginia.*
50. Craven, *Soil Exhaustion as a Factor in the Agricultural History of Virginia and Maryland, 1606-1860;* Gray, *History of Agriculture,* I, 165-68. On holdings, see *Cavaliers and Pioneers.*
51. See such maps as Smith, "Map of Virginia," and the anonymous Dutch map, "Nova Virginiae Tabula." The Tidewater is shown quite clearly on Herman, "Virginia and Maryland"; see Wright, *The John Henry County Map.*
52. Gray, I, 141, 144-45, 140, 146-49; Bruce, I, 313; *The Colonial Records of North Carolina,* I, 222; Shrigley, *A True Relation of Virginia and Maryland,* p. 5; Franklin, "Agriculture in Colonial North Carolina."
53. Wilson, *An Account of the Province of Carolina* [1682], in *Narratives of Early Carolina, 1650-1708,* p. 171; Nairne, *A Letter from South Carolina,* p. 13. The *Gazette* is quoted in Dunbar, "Colonial Carolina Cowpens," 126.
54. Mason, "The Etymology of 'Buckaroo.'"
55. Jones, *The Present State of Virginia,* pp. 39, 77.
56. *Statutes at Large . . . of Virginia,* I, 352-53, and II, 244; Bruce, *Economic History,* I, 323, 554. On householders, see Clemens, "The Operation of an Eighteenth-Century Chesapeake Tobacco Plantation."
57. Lounsbury, "The Development of Domestic Architecture in the Albemarle Region"; Glassie, *Folk Housing in Middle Virginia;* Davidson, *Pine Log and Greek Revival;* Bonner, "Plantation Architecture of the Lower South on the Eve of the Civil War"; Forman, *The Architecture of the Old South; Early Mansion and Plantation Houses of Maryland,* and *Virginia Architecture in the Seventeenth Century.*
58. Mason is quoted at length in Morgan, *Virginians at Home,* pp. 53-54.
59. Blum, *The End of the Old Order in Rural Europe.*
60. Paulding, *Letters from the South,* p. 24.
61. Jefferson, *Farm Book.*
62. Phillips, *Life and Labor,* pp. 115-35.
63. Moore, *Mississippi Agriculture, 1770-1860;* Mitchell, *Commercialism and Frontier Perspectives in the Early Shenandoah Valley.*
64. Henning, *Statutes,* II, 172-77; *Virginia's Cure,* pp. 4-5, 8-10. On town schemes, see Riley, "The Town Acts of Colonial Virginia"; "Virginia Past

and Present," esp. pp. 195–96; and Olmsted, *A Journey in the Seaboard States in the Years 1853–1854,* I, 274–77.

65. Jefferson, *Notes on the State of Virginia,* p. 103. See also Jones, *The Dead Towns of Georgia,* and Bruce, *Economic History,* II, 523.

66. Earle and Hoffman, "Staple Crops and Urban Development in the Eighteenth-Century South"; on rolling, see Bruce, *Economic History,* vol. 1, p. 444.

67. Bruce, *Social Life of Virginia in the Seventeenth Century;* see also Morgan, and *The Correspondence of the Three William Byrds of Westover, Virginia, 1684–1776.*

68. Bruce, *Social Life,* p. 194; on racing, see Lefler and Powell, *Colonial North Carolina,* p. 189.

69. Schoepf, *Travels in the Confederation, 1783–1784,* II, 30, 47, 90.

70. Clark, *The Southern Country Store;* Atherton, *The Southern Country Store, 1800–1860.*

71. Olmsted, *A Journey Through Texas,* pp. 22–42, esp. 24, 28.

72. Clayton, *Letter to the Royal Society.* See also Grove, "Virginia in 1732."

73. Schoepf, II, 31–37, 89.

74. Craven, "Letter," *The Farmer's Register* [Richmond], pp. 150–152; Burnaby, *Travels through the Middle Settlements of North America in 1759 and 1760,* p. 29.

75. Zelinsky, *The Cultural Geography of the United States,* pp. 122–25.

76. Olmsted, *Journey in the Back Country,* is the best introduction to the prewar southern landscape.

77. For general background on Pennsylvania, see Brown, *William Penn's Holy Experiment.*

78. Penn, "Instructions"; for background on earlier techniques of urban land assignment, see Vance, "Land Assignment in the Precapitalist, Capitalist, and Postcapitalist City."

79. Lemon, "Urbanization and the Development of Eighteenth-Century Southeastern Pennsylvania and Adjacent Delaware."

80. Lemon, *The Best Poor Man's Country,* esp. pp. 118–49.

81. Mittelberger, *Journey to Pennsylvania,* p. 51.

82. For examples of the changing meaning of terms, see *Narratives of Early Pennsylvania, West New Jersey, and Delaware, 1630–1707.* See also, Ogden, *An Excursion into Bethlehem and Nazareth in Pennsylvania in the Year 1799.*

83. Tönnies, *Community and Society,* p. 43; Bacon, "Friendship," *Moral and Historical Works,* p. 74.

84. Steele, *The Spectator* [no. 49, Apr. 26, 1711], I, 228; Mather, *Bonifacius,* p. 57.

85. See, for example, Fordham, *Personal Narrative of Travels in Virginia, Maryland . . . and of a Residence in the Indian Territory, 1817–1818,* p. 128.

NATIONAL DESIGN

1. Cooper, *Notions of the Americans* [1829], I, 304.

2. Langeweische, *I'll Take the Highroad,* pp. 126–27, *A Flier's World,* and "The USA from the Air." Foreigners are especially intrigued by the grid

(Haefner, *Höhenstufen, offentliche Ländereien und private Landnutzung auf der Ostseite der Sierra Nevada,* and Glikson, *The Ecological Basis of Planning,* esp. p. 57).

3. Langeweische, *Highroad,* p. 127.

4. Bridenbaugh, *Cities in the Wilderness;* Albion, *The Rise of New York Port; The City in Southern History.* Most United States scholars totally ignore the cities of New Spain. For the early modern European background to New World urbanization, see Huellmann, *Stadtewesen des Mittelalters.*

5. Whitehill, *Boston,* esp. pp. 1-21.

6. Weeden, *Economic and Social History of New England, 1620-1789.*

7. On Rix, see Rutman, *Winthrop's Boston,* pp. 192-94.

8. Rutman; Johnson, *Wonder-Working Providence,* p. 71.

9. Wood, *New England's Prospect,* p. 59; on wharves, see Rutman, pp. 40, 83, 193, 207, 247-48; on churches, pp. 95-251.

10. On Charleston, see Nelson, "Walled Cities of the United States," esp. 254; on "forts and half moons," see *Statutes at Large of South Carolina, 1662-1838,* VII, 28-30.

11. Bridenbaugh, p. 66; Smith, "Charleston: The Original Plan and the Earliest Settlers"; Reps, *The Making of Urban America,* pp. 174-77.

12. Beverly, *The History and Present State of Virginia,* p. 105; Jones, *The Present State of Virginia,* pp. 25, 28; on Annapolis and Williamsburg, see also Reps, pp. 108-14.

13. Stevin, *Materiae Politicae Burgherliche Stoffen,* esp. "Van de ordening der Steden" [pagination is missing or erratic].

14. On Penn's possible drawing from the London fire plans, see Reps, p. 163.

15. *Annals of Pennsylvania from the Discovery of the Delaware,* pp. 505-13.

16. Penn, "Instructions"; Ellis, "Philadelphia in 1698"; Wolf, *Urban Village.*

17. Franklin, *Autobiography,* pp. 22, 23, 25.

18. On taverns, see Bridenbaugh, pp. 106-10, and Franklin, pp. 22-23, 25.

19. Gilpin, "Journal of a Tour from Philadelphia through the Western Counties of Pennsylvania in the Months of September and October, 1809"; Pearson, "Description of Lancaster and Columbia in 1801"; Penn, "Journal of a Visit to Reading, Harrisburg, Carlisle, and Lancaster in 1788"; Ogden, *An Excursion into Bethelem and Nazareth in Pennsylvania in the Year 1799;* see also Wade, *The Urban Frontier* (the Drake quotation is on p. 29). See also Reps, pp. 204-39, and Lewis, "Small Town in Pennsylvania."

20. For an introduction to the evolution of the grid, see Johnson, *Order Upon the Land,* "Rational and Ecological Aspects of the Quarter Section: An Example from Minnesota," and "The Orderly Landscape: Landscape Tastes and the United States Survey"; see also Jackson, "The Order of a Landscape: Reason and Religion in Newtonian America," *The Interpretation of Ordinary Landscapes,* pp. 153-63, and Whittlesey, "Origins of the American System of Land Surveys."

21. Green, *Boundary Lines of Old Groton,* p. 15; Ford, *Colonial Precedents of Our National Land System as it Existed in 1800,* p. 16.

22. Stilgoe, "Jack-o-Lanterns to Surveyors: The Secularization of Landscape Bounties"; Dean, *A Brief History of the Town of Stoneham, Massachusetts,* pp. 20–21.

23. Richeson, *English Land Measuring to 1800,* pp. 107–08, 122–29, 139–41; Nordon, *The Surveior's Dialogue;* Atwell, *The Faithful Surveyor;* Darby, "The Agrarian Contribution to Surveying in England"; Thrower, *Original Survey and Land Subdivision.*

24. Ford, p. 40; *Laws of the State of New York,* I, 720–21; *Acts and Resolves of Massachusetts, 1784–1785.*

25. Dwight, *Travels,* IV, 20–21.

26. Ford, pp. 64–66; Jefferson, *Writings,* XII, 391–95; III, 475–86.

27. Pickering, *Life,* I, 506–07.

28. Johnson, *Order Upon the Land,* pp. 116–50.

29. Carstensen, "Patterns on the American Land," *Surveying and Mapping;* Bruges, *A Journal of a Surveying Trip.*

30. Johnson, *Order Upon the Land,* pp. 168–77.

31. *Annals of Congress,* pp. 339, 336; see also pp. 328–31, 334–35, 338–42. On the contemporaneous significance of the grid, see Everett, "The Public Lands," and Hawes, *Manual of United States Surveying.*

32. Vattel, *The Law of Nations; or Principles of the Law of Nature,* pp. 80–82; Madison, "The Federalist, No. 14," *The Federalist, or The New Constitution,* pp. 81–87.

33. Coxe, "Address to the Honourable the Members of the Convention of Virginia"; Goodrich, "National Planning of Internal Improvements."

34. Stevens, *Albert Gallatin;* Gallatin, *Writings,* I, 334, 370.

35. Gallatin, "Report on Roads and Canals," I, 724–41; 742–921 are useful appendixes.

36. [Jared Sparks], "Internal Improvements of North Carolina," *North American Review;* see also *Speech of Mr. Miner on . . . Internal Improvements.*

37. Bridenbaugh, p. 172; Stevenson, *The World's Lighthouses Before 1820.*

38. Lewis, *Description of the Light Houses on the Coast of the United States;* Cohen, "Once There Was a Light"; Dodd, "The Wrecking Business on the Florida Reef, 1822–1860"; Gordon, *A Collection of the Laws of the United States Relating to Revenue, Navigation, and Commerce and Light-Houses.*

39. Wood, *The Turnpikes of New England and Evolution of the Same Through England, Virginia and Maryland,* esp. pp. 3–24.

40. Eshleman, "History of Lancaster County's Highway System, 1714–1760."

41. Wood.

42. Johnson, *Rural Economy,* pp. 231, 198, 200; "Ollapodiana," 351.

43. Fulton, *A Treatise on the Improvement of Canal Navigation,* p. 134; see also pp. 133, 135.

44. Stevenson, *Sketch of the Civil Engineering of North America,* pp. 192–93 (this is an excellent work). See also Calhoun, *The American Civil Engineer, 1792–1843.*

45. Stevenson, pp. 186–214. See also Camposeo, "The History of the Canal System Between New Haven and Northampton, 1822–1847"; Jones, *The Economic History of the Anthracite-Tidewater Canals;* and Tanner, *A Description of All Canals and Railroads of the United States.*

46. Welch, *Report on the Allegheny Portage Railroad; Life on the Chesapeake and Ohio Canal.*

47. Hawthorne, "Sketches from Memory," *Complete Works,* II, 484–85; see also "Ollapodiana," 344–53, and Fulton, *Report of the Practicability of Navigating with Steam Boats,* esp. pp. 1–2.

48. "Bill for Internal Improvements," 129–31.

49. Pope, *A Treatise on Bridge Architecture,* p. 127.

50. On French engineering see *La Grande Encyclopedie,* XVIII, 741–43.

51. Paisons, *Engineers and Engineering in the Renaissance.*

52. Calhoun, *The American Civil Engineer, 1792–1843,* esp. pp. ix–x, 3–47.

53. Webster, *An American Dictionary,* s.v. "engineer."

54. *Appleton's Cyclopedia of American Biography,* IV, 154; Stuart, *Lives and Works of Civil and Military Engineers of America,* esp. pp. 22–23, 98–99, 132–35, 213–17, 266–67; Calhoun, pp. 43–47; Miele and Miller, "Monocacy Aqueduct on the Chesapeake and Ohio Canal and the 'Principles of Economy, Usefulness, and Durability.'"

55. Mahon, *Civil Engineering for the Use of Cadets of the United States Military Academy,* p. 192; for another West Point textbook, see Sganzin, *Programme d'un cours de construction.*

56. Hill, *Roads, Rails and Waterways.*

57. Miller, "Standardized Specification for Building Stone Lock Keepers' Houses on the C. and O. Canal, Maryland"; Carroll, "Early Brick Law in Massachusetts."

58. Stevenson, pp. 223–36.

59. Whipple, *A Work on Bridge Building;* Haupt, *The General Theory of Bridge Construction.* For general background on late eighteenth-century American building, see Norman, *The Town and Country Builder's Assistant.*

60. Stevenson, pp. 309–16.

61. Shaler, *American Highways.*

62. Finlay, *Journal.*

63. Ibid., pp. 34, 62.

64. Ibid., pp. 67, 22, 61. See also such maps as Jefferys, "A Map of the Most Inhabited Part of New England," and Burr, "Map of Maine."

65. Catlett, "National Road to California"; Johnson, *The Stranger in America,* 465–70; Crosby, "El Camino Real in Baja California: Loreto to San Diego"; Eshleman, "History of Lancaster County's Highway System, 1714–1760"; Beeman, "Trade and Travel in Post-Revolutionary Virginia: A Diary of an Itinerant Peddler." On local control see Cooper, *Notions of the Americans,* I, 70, and Tocqueville, "Notebook E" [1831], *Journey to America,* pp. 272, 271; Wakefield [Bell], *Excursions in North America;* Gillespie, *A Manual of the Princi-*

ples and Practice of Road-Making; Potter, *The Road and the Roadside;* and Colles, *A Survey of the Roads of the United States of America.* On tyranny see Cooper, *Notions of the Americans,* I, 72–74.

66. Bushnell, *The Day of Roads,* pp. 8, 3.

AGRICULTURE

1. Crèvecoeur, *Letters from an American Farmer,* pp. 18–19.
2. Newbury, *The Yeoman's Prerogative, or the Honour of Husbandry,* p. 15; see also Markham, *The English Husbandman,* p. 3, and Martini, *Das Bauertum im detuschen Schriften von den Anfängen bis zum 16. Jahrhundert.*
3. Gregor, *Folklore of Scotland,* p. 181.
4. See especially, "Original"; "The Husbandman"; "The Importance of Agriculture"; Bement, "Rural Life"; Emerson, "Farming," *Society and Solitude,* pp. 147–48; and Crèvecoeur, *Letters,* p. 61.
5. Emerson, "Farming," p. 14. The phrase is Gates's in *The Farmer's Age: Agriculture, 1815–1860,* an excellent economic history.
6. *The Old Farmer's Almanac, 1979,* p. 76; *Farmer's Almanac, 1979,* p. 1. For background see also Shepherd, *An Almanack, 1752;* Shurtleff, "The Blight, Fact and Fiction"; and Addy, *Household Tales,* pp. 62–65. For an example of astrology in colonial almanacs, see Leeds, *The American Almanac;* on almanacs, see Kenney, "Jacob Taylor and His Almanacs." On agricultural folklore in general, see Burdick, *Magic and Husbandry.* On nineteenth-century New England, see Larcom, *A New England Girlhood,* pp. 82–84.
7. Estienne and Liebault, *Maison Rustique, or the Countrie Farme,* pp. 1–5, 36–37, 41–45, 208.
8. Ibid., pp. 208, 36–37, 665.
9. Passim and Bennett, "Changing Agricultural Magic in Southern Illinois"; *The Foxfire Book,* pp. 212–27. See especially Black, *God's Way.*
10. Evelyn, *A Philosophical Discourse of the Earth,* pp. 289, 292.
11. Ibid., p. 292.
12. Ibid., p. 298. Not every English plowman knew the signs (see Markham, *English Husbandman,* pp. 37, 95–98). I have been unable to learn about sixteenth- and seventeenth-century Spanish New World soil classifications.
13. Browne, "Letter to Sir Simonds D'Ewes" [1638]; "Letter" [1637], *Letters from New England,* pp. 226–27, 214.
14. Donck, "Description of New Netherlands," I, 148.
15. On tree beliefs in Europe see Gubernatis, *Mythologie des Plantes;* Grimm, *Deutsche Mythologie,* III, 539–45; and Vesley, "Legendes, Superstitions, and Coutumes." In America, see Acrelius, *A History of New Sweden,* pp. 171–75.
16. See, for example, Morton, *The New English Canaan,* pp. 182–87; Smith, *Remarkable Occurrences,* pp. 84–90; Hulbert, *Soil;* and Volney, *View of the Climate and Soil of the United States of America.*
17. Bayard, *Voyage dan l'interieur des États-Unis,* p. 65; Priest, *Travels in the*

United States, p. 35; Thomas, *Travels through the Western Country in the Summer of 1816*, pp. 13, 66–67, 105, 122, 166.

18. Harker, "Report About and From America, 49.

19. Wood, *New England's Prospect*, pp. 33–36; see also Markham, pp. 96–98; Lemon, *The Best Poor Man's Country*, pp. 42–70, 243n; Hulbert, p. 71; and Fletcher, *Pennsylvania Agriculture and Country Life, 1640–1840*, pp. 48–56.

20. "On the Nature of Soils"; *General Instructions to his Deputies*, p. 22. The best study of the prairies is McManis, *The Initial Evaluation and Utilization of the Illinois Prairies, 1815–1840*.

21. Dwight, *Travels*, III, 59–60; Thoreau, *Cape Cod*, pp. 122, 124, 80, 180–81.

22. Collot, "A Journey in North America in 1796," p. 291; Dana, *A Description of the Bounty Lands in the State of Illinois*, pp. 6–7.

23. Atwater, "On the Prairies and Barrens of the West."

24. Markham, pp. 25–26. On farmstead siting in Europe, see Gschwend, *Schweizer Bauernhäuser;* Doyon and Hubrecht, *Architecture Rurale et Bourgeoise en France;* Barbieri and Gambi, *La Casa Rurale in Italia;* Edallo, *Ruralistica;* Mejborg, *Das Bauerhaus im Herzogthum Schleswig;* and Burnett, "Madrid Plaza." Güntz, *Handbuch der Landwirtschaftlichen Literatur*, is a useful introduction to the nineteenth-century German literature.

25. Conway, "Southwestern Colonial Farms"; Adams, *The Architecture and Art of Early Hispanic Colorado;* Jackson, "A Catalog of New Mexico Farm Building Terms"; Carlson, "Rural Settlement in the San Luis Valley: A Comparative Study"; Field, "Sketches of Big Timber, Bent's Fort, and Milk Fort in 1839"; Conway, "A Northern New Mexico House Type and a Suggestion for Identifying Others."

26. Jans, *Ländliche Baukunst in den östlichen Niederlanden*, esp. pp. 14–21; Maaskant, *Oude Boerderijen.*

27. Little has been written on the cultural sources of Dutch-American architecture. See Fitchen, *The New World Dutch Barn;* Reynolds, *Dutch Houses in the Hudson Valley before 1776;* and Wacker, "Folk Architecture as an Indicator of Culture Areas and Culture Diffusion: Dutch Barns and Barracks in New Jersey."

28. Bordley, *Essays and Notes on Husbandry and Rural Affairs*, pp. 133–34; Arthur and Whitney, *The Barn*, pp. 84–113; *The Pennsylvania Barn;* Meynen, "Das pennsylvaniendeutsche Bauernland"; Cobbett, *A Year's Residence in America*, pp. 25–27; Glassie, "The Pennsylvania Barn in the South." On Pennsylvania German innovation and subsequent stagnation, see Bressler, "Agriculture Among the Germans in Pennsylvania During the Eighteenth Century." It is most illuminating to talk with owners of bank barns.

29. Lawton, "Ground Rules of Folk Architecture"; Jenkins, "Ground Rules of Welsh Houses."

30. On brace-frame construction see Salzman, *Building in England Down to 1540*, pp. 196, 200–06, and Joendl, *Die Landwirtschaftliche Baukunst*, III, 511–40. On the raising ceremony, see *Handwörterbuch des Deutschen Aberglaubens*, III, 1560–68; VI, 1016–18.

31. Hollweg, *Das Zünftige Richtfest.*
32. For the poem, see McDuffee, *History of the Town of Rochester,* I, 132.
33. *Scituate Town Records,* I, 139.
34. Halsted, *Barn Plans.*
35. Glassie, *Pattern in the Material Folk Culture,* pp. 9, 101, 209–12. For a contemporary corncrib specification, see Hylton, *Build it Better Yourself,* pp. 789–99.
36. No accurate, comprehensive study of American farmhouses exists. See Kaufman's *The American Farmhouse;* Glassie, *Folk Housing in Middle Virginia;* Lewis, "Common Houses, Cultural Spoor"; Gould, *The Early American House;* Chambart de Laurve, "Le Logement, le menage et l'espace familial"; Cobbett, p. 25; Kniffen and Glassie, "Building in Wood in the Eastern United States"; Kniffen, "Folk Housing: Key to Diffusion"; Lewis, "The Geography of Old Houses"; and Rickert, "House Facades of the Northeastern United States: A Tool of Geographic Analysis"; see also Arr, *New England Bygones,* and Johnson, *The Farmer's Boy.* I have found it useful to examine collections of old photographs.
37. Rutman, *Husbandmen of Plymouth;* Demos, *A Little Commonwealth.*
38. Beverly, *The History and Present State of Virginia,* p. 290.
39. Backus, "Some Hints Upon Farm Houses, p. 401.
40. Allen, *Rural Architecture,* p. 112. The interested reader should examine issues of *American Farmer, Southern Cultivator, Farmer's Register, American Cotton Planter, Southern Agriculturist, Soil of the South,* and *Southern Planter* for contemporaneous information on good and bad farmhouse design. See especially "Plans of Houses"; "Farm Buildings"; "Rural Architecture"; "A Farm Cottage"; "Plan of a Farm Dwelling House"; and Currier, "The Farmer's Home," 46. For general background, see Zelinsky, "The New England Connecting Barn"; Trewartha, "Some Regional Characteristics of American Farmsteads"; and Hubka, "The Connected Farm Buildings of Southwestern Maine."
41. "Rural Architecture," 73.
42. Downing, *The Architecture of Country Houses;* Riddell, *Architectural Designs for Model Country Residences;* Davis, *Rural Residences;* Allen, *Rural Architecture,* p. 82.
43. Allen, *Rural Architecture,* pp. 111–13.
44. On colonial planting, see Leighton, *Early American Gardens,* esp. 237, 267, 273, 332, 363, 405; Boland, *Gardener's Magic and Other Old Wives' Lore;* Marzell, *Volksbontanik, Die Pflanze im deutschen Brauchtum;* Gerard, *The Herbal or General History of Plants;* and Rhode, "The Folk-Lore of Herbals"; on later periods see "Stumbling Blocks in the Way of Our Farmers."
45. Strickland, *Journal of a Tour in the United States;* Shipton, *New England Life in the Eighteenth Century,* p. 213; for background on tree lore, see Detering, *Die Bedeutnung der Eiche seit der Vorzeit.*
46. Allen, *Rural Architecture,* p. 111.

47. Kocher, "Color in Early American Architecture with Special Reference to the Origin and Development of House Painting."

48. Kocher, "Color," 288; Williams, *Old American Houses*, pp. 203–06.

49. Benes, "Sky Colors and Scattered Clouds: The Decorative and Architectural Painting of New England Meeting Houses, 1738–1834"; *150th Anniversary of the First Church in Pomfret* [Connecticut], pp. 43–44; sextons and parish historians can offer much insight on these matters.

50. Reynolds, *Directions for House and Ship Painting.*

51. Cummings, *Architecture in Early New England*, p. 16; Newton, "On the Tradition of Polychromy and Paint of the American Dwelling from Colonial to Present Times"; Faulkner, *Architecture and Color*, esp. p. 3.

52. Rochefoucault-Liancourt, *Travels through the United States*, I, 396.

53. Crèvecoeur, *Letters*, p. 4. On housewifery, see also Tusser, *Five Hundred Pointes of Good Husbandrie;* Child, *American Frugal Housewife;* Cott, *The Bonds of Womanhood;* and De Pauw and Hunt, *Remember the Ladies: Women in America.*

54. Frost, *Poetry*, pp. 375–76.

55. The place-names are from New Mexico, Connecticut, Massachusetts, and New Hampshire. For an example of colonial law regulating the use of natural grassland, see *Scituate Town Records*, III, 82, 96, and *New Netherlands*, p. 148.

56. Jackson, "Ghosts at the Door"; see also Hoskins, *The Making of the English Landscape*, pp. 75–116; Lecoeur, *Esquisses du Bocage Normand;* Walcott, "Husbandry in Colonial New England"; Bidwell and Falconer, *History of Agriculture*, pp. 19–23, 101–04; and Gray, *History of Agriculture*, I, 3–126.

57. Symonds, "Letter."

58. Smith, *Advertisements for the Unexperienced Planters*, 38; Judd (*History of Hadley*, p. 432) notes the persistence of the immediate technique.

59. *Documentary History of New York*, IV, 30; the anonymous Pennsylvania settler is quoted in Gordon, *A Gazetteer of the State of Pennsylvania*, p. 32.

60. Strickland, *Journal of a Tour*, pp. 95–96.

61. For a description of England at this time, see Cobbett, *Rural Rides*. At least one early nineteenth-century American found girdled trees aesthetically displeasing (see Dwight, *Travels*, II, 83–84). For other aesthetic observations, see Reed and Matheson, *A Narrative of the Visit*, p. 104; Faux, *Memorable Days in America;* and Alexis de Tocqueville, *Journey to America*, pp. 337–38.

62. On *svedjebruket* see Grotenfelt, *Det primitiva jordbrukets metoder i Finland*, pp. 27–30, 36–39, 147–50, and Retzius, *Finnland Nordiska Museet*, pp. 35–40, which book appeared in authorized translation by C. Appel, *Finnland*, esp. 42–49; on folklore, see Vanberg, *Of Norwegian Ways*, pp. 138–40, 217–19. See also Johnson, *The Swedish Settlements on the Delaware*, II, 527–28; I have been unable to locate all Johnson's references on this subject, particularly no. 58 on II, 528. See also Grotenfelt, *Det primitiva jordbrukets.*

63. The quotation is from Retzius; I have translated from Appel's translation, p. 44.

64. The quotation from a Bedford County farmer is in Gordon, *Gazetteer*, p. 34. See also Shurtleff, *The Log Cabin Myth*, esp. pp. 163–85.

65. Woods, *Two Years Residence*, pp. 122–28; Newton and Pulliam-DiNapoli, "Log Houses as Public Occasions: A Historical Theory"; Glassie, *Pattern in the Material Folk Culture*, pp. 79–117; Kniffen and Glassie, "Building in Wood"; Woods, *Two Years Residence*, p. 125; William Oliver, *Eight Months in Illinois*, pp. 235–39; "A Winter in the South"; Harris, *Journal of a Tour*, p. 15.

66. "Specifications for Building a Log Courthouse in Maryville, Missouri"; Johnson, *A Home in the Woods*; Beck, "Taming the Land"; Nead, *The Pennsylvania German.*

67. *Documentary History of New York*, IV, 30. No distinctions concerning rates of clearing in different colonies exist.

68. On plows in the colonies, see Bidwell and Falconer, *History of Agriculture*, 35, 123, 208–10, 282–86, 303, and Gray, *History of Agriculture*, I, 26–27, 162, 169–70, 218, 326, 377, 555. On slaves and plows, see Gray, I, 402, 542, 564, 701–02, 708, 796; see also "Cultivation of Cleared Lands."

69. John Smith, *Advice*, p. 37.

70. "Letter to England", *Letters from New England*, pp. 214–15.

71. See Eliot, "Essays Upon Field Husbandry"; Deane, *New England Farmer*, pp. 187–91, 196; and Spurrier, *The Practical Farmer*, p. 173. See also *Grass*, pp. 6–25, 45–48, 351–53. The Pennsylvania Farm Museum of Landis Valley in Lancaster, Pennsylvania, cultivates colonial grasses.

72. *Grass*, pp. 13–14; Jefferson, *Notes on the State of Virginia*, p. 37; Carrier and Bart, "The History of Kentucky Bluegrass and White Clover in the United States."

73. Weeden, *Economic and Social History*. On haymaking and lightning, see "Effects of Lightning—Barn Burned."

74. Penn, "A Further Account of the Province of Pennsylvania." See also Fletcher, *Pennsylvania Agriculture;* Gray, *History of Agriculture*, I, 195, and Bidwell and Falconer, *History of Agriculture.*

75. Johnson, *Wonder-Working Providence*, p. 85.

76. Gray, *History of Agriculture*, I, 193–96.

77. "Letter," *The Farmer's Monthly Visitor*, 42.

78. Fletcher, *Pennsylvania Agriculture*, pp. 121, 129, 134, 135; "Tiilage Husbandry"; "Rotation of Crops." For general comments, see Parkinson, *The Experienced Farmer's Tour;* Russell, *North America;* and Strickland, *Observations on the Agriculture.*

79. Melville, *Israel Potter.*

80. Some estensión walls still exist, in La Cienega, New Mexico, and elsewhere, but barbed wire replaced most decades ago. On fences, see Bidwell and Falconer, *History of Agriculture*, pp. 21, 121, 271; Danhof, "The Fencing

Problem in the Eighteen Fifties"; Meredith, "The Importance of Fences to the American Pioneer"; Zelinsky, "Walls and Fences"; Larsen, "Peter Kalm's Observations on the Fences of North America"; Ferrall, *A Ramble for Six Thousand Miles,* p. 63; and Meredith, "The Nomenclature of American Pioneer Fences."

81. Oliver, *Eight Months,* pp. 239–40.
82. Mather and Hart, "Fences and Farms."
83. "Stone Walls"; "Stone Fencing."
84. The stone posts are preserved at the Pennsylvania Farm Museum of Landis Valley.
85. "Fences," *Boston Cultivator;* "Fences," *Soil of the South;* "Stone Walls." Issue numbering and pagination in many agricultural periodicals are extremely erratic; many journals suffered temporary lapses of publication as well.
86. Harper, "Changes in Forest Area of New England in Three Centuries"; Braun, *Deciduous Forests;* for background, see Deveze, *La Vie de la Forêt;* Boasen, *Wald und Bauertum;* and Glacken, *Traces on the Rhodian Shore,* pp. 318–30. See also Smith, "The Logging Frontier."
87. Henlein, *Cattle Kingdom,* pp. 1–8.
88. Power, *Planting Corn Belt Culture,* p. 96; Thomas, *Travels through the Western Country,* p. 104. On European cattle raising, see Carrier, *Water and Grass.*
89. Rouse, *The Criollo,* esp. pp. 40–46; Dacy, *Four Centuries of Florida Ranching;* Akerman, *Florida Cowman;* and Brand, "The Early History of the Range Cattle Industry in Northern Mexico."
90. Henlein, *Cattle Kingdom,* p. 21; Dunbar, "Colonial Carolina Cowpens."
91. Thompson, "The Beef Cattle Industry," 177; Henlein, "Early Cattle Ranges."
92. Henlein, *Cattle Kingdom,* pp. 104–29.
93. Peck, *A New Guide for Emigrants,* p. 263; this is a most valuable book.
94. See, for example, Towne and Wentworth, *Cattle and Men;* Dykstra, *The Cattle Towns;* Parsons, *Land and Cattle;* Knudtsen, *Here is Our Valley;* and Paul, *This Was Cattle Ranching.* The word *ranch,* as it is used in the contemporary West, means only the house and stables not the surrounding *spread* of pasture land.
95. "Stumbling Blocks in the Way of Our Farmers."
96. "Woods and Woodlands."
97. Winberry, "The Osage Orange."
98. Spurrier, *The Practical Farmer,* pp. 240–42. See the orchards at the Pennsylvania Farm Museum of Landis Valley.
99. "Shelter for Farms."
100. *Dream Life,* p. 50; see also, pp. 46, 82, 85–86, 91, 100, 160.
101. Thomas, "A Complete Country Residence," pp. 21–35; "Laying Out and Dividing Farms," 233–38; Walden, *Soil Culture.*
102. Jones, "Creative Disruptions in American Agriculture, 1620–1820," an excellent article. See also Secoy and Smith, "Superstitions and Social Prac-

tices." The nineteenth-century quotation is from "Cultivation of Cleared Lands."

103. Jones, "Creative Disruptions."
104. Loehr, "Self-Sufficiency on the Farm."
105. Dwight, *Travels*, IV, 20.
106. Judd, *Richard Edney and the Governor's Family*, p. 324.
107. Ibid., pp. 324, 325.

COMMUNITY

1. Tocqueville, *Journey to America*, p. 266.
2. Cazenove, *Journal*, p. 34; Flagg, "Letters," 143. See also Fordham, *Personal Narrative*, p. 128, and Flagg, *The Far West*.
3. Flagg, "Letters," 143; Flint, *Letters from America*, p. 95.
4. Imlay, *A Topographical Description*, pp. 29–30; Harker, "First Hand Observations in the Years 1848 and 1849," esp. 48–49.
5. Raumer, *Die Vereingten Staaten*, II, 414–15; see also Jakle, *Images of the Ohio Valley*, pp. 114–15.
6. Isle, *Atlas Nouveau*, this is an invaluable atlas. For the quotation, see Arena, "Land Settlement Policies and Practices in Spanish Louisana," p. 51.
7. No up-to-date spatial history of New France exists. See Franz, *Die Kolonisation des Mississippitales;* Harris, *The Seigneurial System;* Seguin, *La Civilisation Traditionelle,* idem, *Les Granges de Quebec;* Gauthier, *Les manoirs du Quebec;* Douville and Casanova, *Daily life;* Franquet, *Voyages et Memoires sur le Canada;* Alvord, *Illinois Country;* Finley, *The French in the Heart of America;* Trudel, *The Beginnings of New France;* Winsor, *The Mississippi Basin; The French in the Mississippi Valley;* Palm, *The Jesuit Missions;* and Hennepin, *Description de la Louisiane,* which has excellent maps. On Sainte Genevieve, see Peterson, "Early Ste. Genevieve and its Architecture," esp. 209–11.
8. Peterson, 208–12; and Dorrance, "The Survival of the French in the Old District of Sainte Genevieve," esp. 14–15.
9. Porterfield, "Ste. Genevieve, Missouri," *Frenchmen and French Ways in the Mississippi Valley,* pp. 140–78; on houses, see Gauthier-Larouche, *Evolution de la maison rurale;* on commons, see Beuckman, "The Commons of Kaskaskia, Cohokia, and Prairie du Rocher." Information concerning the commons of old Sainte Genevieve and Kaskaskia is difficult to obtain, as both commons washed into the Mississippi River.
10. Peterson, 212–13.
11. Ibid., 212–16.
12. Brackenridge, *Recollections of Persons and Places*, p. 22; Seguin, *L'equipement de la ferme Canadienne;* Derruau, "A l'origine du 'rang' Candien." On Spanish land law, see Arena, esp. pp. 57–59.
13. Arena, p. 58; "Ulloa sends an Expedition to the Spanish Illinois Country," *The Spanish Regime in Missouri,* I, 16–19; *Spanish in the Mississippi Valley,* ed. McDermott.

14. Rohrbaugh, *The Trans-Appalachian Frontier;* Bartlett, *The New Country.*
15. On liberalism, see Polanyi, *The Great Transformation,* Foster, *Their Solitary Way.*
16. Tocqueville, *Democracy in America,* p. 12. See also Blum, *The End of the Old Order.*
17. Imlay, p. 19.
18. Olmsted, *Journey in the Back Country,* p. 225; Hall, "Journal," 215, 219, 231, 241.
19. Hall, "Journal," 219, 231.
20. Saaz, *Der Ackerman von Böhmen;* Izquierdo, *Practica de los Exercicios;* Ariès, *Western Attitudes toward Death;* Morin, *L'Homme et la mort dan l'histoire;* Schweizer, *Kirchhof und Friedhof;* Stilgoe, "Folklore and Graveyard Design."
21. Davidson, "The Untilled Field"; Henderson, *Notes on the Folk Lore of the Northern Counties,* p. 241; Scott, *Demonology and Witchcraft,* p. 87.
22. Hueppi, *Kunst und Kult der Grab Stätten;* Holbein, *Les Images.*
23. Ditchfield, *The Old-Time Parson;* Puckle, *Funeral Customs;* Gasquet, *Parish Life.* On the east-facing siting, see Cooper, *Symbolism in the Bible and the Church,* pp. 242-43.
24. Adams, "Markers Cut By Hand." It is best to explore the graveyards, particularly those north of Chimayo.
25. Earle, *Customs and Fashions;* Coffin, *Death in Early America;* Cole, "Early New England Funeral Customs"; Fales, "The Early American Way of Death."
26. Prince, *The Grave and Death Destroyed,* pp. 5-9.
27. Drake, *The Town of Roxbury,* pp. 97-100.
28. Benes, *The Masks of Orthodoxy;* Forbes, *Gravestones of Early New England;* Deetz and Dethlefsen, "Death Heads, Cherubs, and Willow Trees"; Tashjian, *Memorials for Children of Change.*
29. Jackson, "The Vanishing Epitaph: From Monument to Place"; Kendall, *Travels through the Northern Parts,* I, 253-54.
30. Zelinsky, "Unearthly Delights."
31. Tarpley, "Southern Cemeteries."
32. Jeanne, "The Traditional Upland South Cemetery."
33. Benes, *Masks,* pp. 34-36; Woods, *Two Years Residence,* p. 117.
34. Shelton, "Rural Cemeteries."
35. M'Nemar, *The Kentucky Revival,* p. 24.
36. Boles, *The Great Revival;* Mead, *The Lively Experiment,* pp. 90-133; Cross, *The Burned-Over District.*
37. Armenius, "Account of the Rise and Progress of the Work of God," 273; Johnson, *The Frontier Camp Meeting,* pp. 50-65, 257-58; Pierson, *In the Brush.*
38. Finley, *Autobiography,* pp. 166-67; Johnson, p. 65.
39. Bruce, *And They All Sang Hallelujah,* pp. 50, 70; attendance estimates vary widely—I have tried to be conservative.
40. Raumer, *America and the American People,* pp. 343-44; M'Nemar, *Kentucky Revival,* p. 73; Marryat, *A Diary in America,* pp. 180-89; Long, *Pictures of*

Slavery in Church and State, pp. 157–60; Hall, "Journal," 221, 225; Ferrall, *A Ramble of Six Thousand Miles,* pp. 71–78.

41. Halliday, "Methodism in Southeastern Indiana," 180; Gorham, *Camp-Meeting Manual,* pp. 121–22, 134.

42. Gorham, pp. 125–30.

43. Ibid., pp. 125–27.

44. "Is the Modern Camp Meeting a Failure?"; Johnson, pp. 54–223.

45. Long, pp. 159–60; Johnson, p. 114.

46. Bruce, p. 111; Boles; Poesy, *The Baptist Church,* p. 89; Davidson, *History of the Presbyterian Church.*

47. Bruce, p. 50.

48. Remarkably little material exists on the design and uses of rural church buildings.

49. Rines, *Old Historic Churches of America,* esp. pp. 274–75; Julien and Hollis, *Look to the Rock; Colonial Churches.*

50. Rose, *The Colonial Houses of Worship.*

51. Porter, *The New England Meeting House;* Donnelly, *The New England Meeting Houses;* Dunham, *An Historical Discourse;* Brock, *Colonial Churches;* Rogers, *The Cane Ridge Meeting House;* Forrest, *Missions and Pueblos;* Prince, *Spanish Mission Churches;* Benes and Zimmerman, *New England Meeting House and Church.*

52. Europeans thought rural churches looked like houses (see Münch, "Über den Mangel des Romantischen in dem hiesigne Leben," *Gesammelte Schriften,* pp. 351–52).

53. *The Schoolmaster and Academic Journal,* I (May 8, 1834), 14, 7.

54. Burke, *Popular Culture;* Cremin, *American Education,* pp. 27–30; Bailyn, *Education in the Forming of American Society;* Sizer, *The Age of the Academies; A Study of the Rural Schools of Maine.*

55. *Records of the Governor and Company of the Massachusetts Bay in New England,* II, 203; Cremin, pp. 126–37.

56. *The Statutes at Large . . . of Virginia,* II, 517.

57. Reisner, *The Evolution of the Common School,* pp. 270–340, esp. pp. 278–80, 307–14.

58. Norton, "Early Schools and Pioneer Life"; Maurer, "Early Lutheran Education in Pennsylvania"; "School Houses."

59. "Sale of School Lands"; Dennenberg, "The Missing Link."

60. *Report on School Houses,* pp. 1–3.

61. Ibid., p. 3.

62. "The School Room."

63. Carney, *Country Life,* pp. 340–46; "Furniture of School-Houses."

64. "School Houses," *The Illustrated Annual Register;* "School Houses," *Wisconsin Farmer.*

65. Irving, "The Legend of Sleepy Hollow," *The Sketch-Book,* n.p.; Eggleston, *The Hoosier Schoolmaster;* Clemens, *The Adventures of Tom Sawyer;* the schoolmaster is typically a foolish character.

66. "Our Common Schools"; Merrick, "Claims of Common Schools Upon the Farmer."

67. Merrick, 88; see also his "The Art of Learning to Read."

68. Johnson, *The Country School;* Larcom, "The Old School-House," *Poems,* p. 13; Garland, *A Son of the Middle Border,* p. 95; Pattengill, *School Grounds; Rural School Architecture* (1901); *Rural School Architecture* (1880); Corbett, *The School Garden;* Bailey, *Hints on School Grounds;* Jenkins, "A Model Rural School-house"; Hall, *Tree Planting.*

69. Morse, *American Geography,* p. vii.

70. Ibid., pp. 286–87, 163, 415.

71. Ibid., p. 479.

72. Harris, "The General Store as an Outlet for Books on the Southern Frontier, 1800–1850," and "Books on the Frontier: The Extent and Nature of Book Ownership in Southern Indiana, 1800–1850"; McFadden, "A Hoosier General Store in 1847"; Peckham, "Books and Reading on the Ohio Valley Frontier"; Foght, *The American Rural School.*

73. Olmsted, *Journey in the Back Country,* p. 308.

74. Watson, *History of Agricultural Societies,* esp. pp. 115–20; Neely, *The Agricultural Fair,* esp. pp. 51–71.

75. Defoe, *Tour,* I, 89–95.

76. Watson, "Address Delivered Before the Schoharie Agricultural Society," *The Plough Boy;* Fessenden, "Address"; Nelson, "Address"; Everett, "The Husbandman, Mechanic, and Manufacturer," *Operations and Speeches,* III, 88–96; idem, "Agriculture," I, 442–58; Hesford, "Too Happy Husbandmen: Addresses Given to Middlesex Farmers from the 1820s to 1860." Every October and November throughout the nineteenth century, agricultural periodicals reprinted county-fair addresses.

77. "Fair of the Farmers' Agricultural Society"; "Trial of Stump Machines."

78. Gage, "Going to the Fair."

79. On village life see Atherton, *Main Street on the Middle Border;* Smith, *As A City Upon a Hill;* Shaw, "The Geography of a Small Trade Center in the Corn Belt"; Odell, *The Functional Pattern of Villages;* and Anderson, *The Country Town.*

80. Birkbeck, *Notes on a Journey in America,* p. 98.

81. Dickens, *The Life and Adventures of Martin Chuzzlewit,* I, 357–401.

82. On the speculation see Rohrbough, *The Land Office Business,* pp. 242–49; on Allegan, see C. C. Trowbridge, "Letter"; on Detroit, see Bates, "By-Gones of Detroit," esp. 379–80, and Atherton, *Main Street,* p. 3.

83. Bates, 379; Birkbeck, p. 99.

84. Farnham, *Life in Prairie Land.*

85. Atherton, *Main Street,* pp. 39–57.

86. On verticality, see Arnheim, *The Dynamics of Architectural Form,* pp. 76–87, and collections of nineteenth-century small-town newspapers.

87. Colles, *Survey of the Roads,* p. 163.

88. Raber, p. 56[?]; the only copy of this work I have seen is erratically paged.

ARTIFICE

1. Hawthorne, "The Artist of the Beautiful," *Complete Works,* II, 505.
2. Hawthorne, "Ethan Brand" [1851], *Complete Works,* III, 478; Bunyan, *The Pilgrim's Progress,* p. 112.
3. Sikes, *British Goblins,* pp. 26–31; Dalyell, *The Darker Superstititions of Scotland,* p. 534; Agricola, *De re metallica* [1556], p. 217; idem, *De animantibus subterraneis.* See also Blechschmidt, *De Silberne Rose;* Burton, *The Miners;* Samuel, *Miners, Quarrymen, and Saltworkers;* Fish, *The Folklore of the Coal Miners;* and Korson, *Black Rock.* Ask the steelworkers of Gary, Indiana, about the maiden or virgin of the open hearth; see Paul Sebillot, *Le travaux publics,* esp. pp. 387–589, for European background.
4. Burton, *The Anatomy of Melancholy,* p. 320.
5. Morse, *American Geography,* p. 479.
6. Browne, *Religio Medici,* p. 36 (the work was written about 1635). Browne may have been correct after all (see Gold and Soter, "Deep-Earth-Gas Hypothesis"). See also Hale, *The Primitive Origination of Mankind,* p. 89; see also pp. 76, 310, and Robert Boyle, *An Essay About the Origine and Virtues of Gems.*
7. Willard, *A Compleat Body of Divinity,* p. 117.
8. Paracelsus, *Hermetic and Alchemical Writings* [1628], I, 301. On the alliance of metals and planets, see Magnus, *Book of Minerals* [c. 1262], p. 168; Fevre, *A Compleat Body of Chymistry,* II, 168, 183; and Glaser, *The Compleat Chymist,* pp. 68–69, 77, 86, 113. Belief in the alliance died very slowly. See also Duncan, "The Natural History of Metals and Minerals"; on the essence of gold, see Collier, *Cosmogonies of Our Fathers,* p. 423.
9. On New England alchemy see Brewster, "Letter to John Winthrop, Jr., 1656," *Collections;* Wilkinson, "New England's Last Alchemists"; idem, "The Alchemical Library of John Winthrop, Jr. (1606–1676), and his Descendants in Colonial America"; and Morton, *Compendium Physicae,* pp. 117–19. For an indication of the power of the four-element thinking in seventeenth-century art, see Bradstreet, "The Four Seasons of the Year" [1678], *Works,* pp. 65–72, and Taylor, "Meditation 40" [1640], *Poems,* pp. 64–66.
10. Stiles, *Literary Diary,* III, 266–67. Mountains long fascinated educated Europeans. See, for example, Ruskin, *Modern Painters,* I, 274–308; Clark, *Landscape into Art,* pp. 44–46; Glacken, *Traces on the Rhodian Shore,* pp. 410–15; Nicholson, *Mountain Gloom;* Hyde, "The Ancient Appreciation of Mountain Scenery"; Adams, *The Birth and Development of the Geological Sciences,* pp. 329–98; and Rees, "The Scenery Cult: Changing Landscape Tastes over Three Centuries."
11. Milton, *Paradise Lost,* p. 12 (*Paradise Lost* appeared in 1667).
12. Megenberg, *Buch der Natur;* the translation is from Adams, *Birth of the Geological Sciences,* p. 404.

13. Kircher, *Mundus Subterraneus*, II, 90-103, 184-85, 187, 227, 256, 293, 322. On dragons in European folklore, see Scheuchzer, *Sive Itinera*, III, 353-401; "The Two Brothers," *German Folk Tales*, pp. 226-43; and Comenius, *Naturall Philosophie*, pp. 93, 146. See also Willard, p. 117, and "The Three Dwarfs in the Forest," *German Folk Tales*, pp. 50-55.

14. On alchemy as a spiritual search, see Jung, *Psychology and Alchemy*, esp. pp. 1-47, 225-340, and *Alchemical Studies*, esp. 109-250. Jung emphasizes the complex nature of mercury as matter and spirit (see esp. pp. 225-37). See also Maier, *Emblemata Nova De Secretis Naturae*, and *Chymisches Cabinet*. For the relation of the literature to popular thought, see Frei, "Magie und Psychologie," and Read, *Prelude to Chemistry*.

15. Espejo, "Report of an Expedition" [1585], *The Rediscovery of New Mexico*, pp. 213-31; see esp. pp. 222, 223, 224.

16. Ibid., p. 227. For accounts of Spanish searches for metals in northern New Spain, see *Spanish Exploration in the Southwest*. Few scholars have investigated this subject.

17. Eden, *The Decades of the New Worlde*, contains most of the *Pyrotechnia*, pp. 355-67, esp. pp. 355, 357, 363, 364.

18. Barba, *El Arte de los Metales* [c. 1637].

19. Plattes, *A Discovery of Subterraneall Treasure*, pp. 2, 4 (this is a neglected masterpiece of geological analysis).

20. Ibid., pp. 9-10; see also Agricola, *De Re Metallica*, p. 39.

21. Plattes, *A Discovery of Subterraneall Treasure*, pp. 12-13.

22. *The Proceedings of the English Colonies in Virginia* [1612], reprinted in *Narratives of Early Virginia, 1606-1625*, pp. 119-204; for the quotations see pp. 136-37. See also "Letter of Don Diego De Molina" [1613], pp. 218-24, esp. p. 218.

23. Oñate, "Account of the Discovery of the Mines" [1599], *Spanish Exploration in the Southwest*, pp. 239-49; for the quotations see pp. 246, 244; on timber, see p. 246; see also Luxan, "Account of the Antonio De Espejo Expedition into New Mexico" [1582], *The Rediscovery of New Mexico, 1580-1594*, pp. 153-212; for the quotations see pp. 171, 157.

24. For an introduction to late medieval and early modern mining, see Nef, "Mining and Metallurgy in Medieval Society," *The Cambridge Economic History of Europe*, II, 430-93; Lombard, *Les Metaux dans l'ancien monde*; Wilsdorf, *Georg Agricola*; Schreiber, *Der Bergbau; Beiträge zur Geschichte des Bergbaus*; Kirnbauer, *Schlägel und Eisen; Der Belehrende Bergman*; Wilsdorf, *Bergwerke und Hüttenanlagen*; Rouzaud, *Histoire d'une mine*; Hue, *Die Bergarbeiter*, esp. I, 70-332; Houghton, *Laws and Customs*; and Manlove, *The Liberties and Customes of the Lead Mines*.

25. Eden, *Decades*, p. 358; Houghton, *Rara Avis; Terris*; anyone learning mining from textbooks imbibed alchemy too.

26. Agricola, *De Re Metallica*, p. 24.

27. On definitions, see Brading, *Mines and Merchants*, p. 131, and West, *The*

Mining Community in Northern New Spain, p. 19. On mining codes, see Gamboa, *Comentarios a las orderanzas de minas.* On *real de minas,* see Mecham, "The *Real de Minas* as a Political Institution." See also Brading, "Mexican Silver-Mining in the Eighteenth Century"; Land, "New Spain's Mining Depression"; Brading and Cross, "Colonial Silver Mining in Mexico and Peru"; Fisher, *Minas y mineros;* and Bobb, *The Viceregency of Antonio Maria Bucareli,* pp. 172–204.

28. West, pp. 20–22.

29. Young, *Western Mining,* esp. 60–64; Dahlgren, *Historic Mines of Mexico;* Humboldt, *Political Essay,* III, 104–454. On abandoned mines see Bancroft, *History of Arizona and New Mexico,* pp. 303–04; Probert, *Lost Mines and Buried Treasures;* and Granger, *A Motif Index.*

30. Gregg, *Commerce of the Prairies* [1844], pp. 115–25; for the quotation see p. 116. Most abandoned mining towns in the Rocky Mountains still attract prospectors intrigued by legends of forgotten strikes. See also Bayard, "A Notice of Silver Ore."

31. Plattes's book was reprinted as *A Discovery of Subterraneal Treasure.* See also Richards, *A History of American Mining,* pp. 2–9.

32. Brock, "Early Iron Manufacture in Virginia, 1619–1776"; Beverly, *The History and Present State of Virginia,* p. 126 (see also pp. 54–55).

33. *A Perfect Description of Virginia,* sec. 29; Brock, 78; Stith, *History of the First Discovery and Settlements of Virginia* [1747], pp. 176, 218.

34. Bruce, *Virginia Iron Manufacture,* pp. 6–11.

35. Byrd, *A Progress to the Mines,* in *Prose Works,* pp. 339–78; see esp. pp. 347, 353.

36. Ibid., pp. 347, 348, 360.

37. Ibid., pp. 360, 348, 355, 367, 369.

38. Ibid., p. 369.

39. Ibid., pp. 366, 358, 364.

40. On African mining, see Cline, *Mining and Metallurgy,* esp. pp. 17–38; Christian, *Negro Ironworkers of Louisiana,* pp. 11–18; Clark, *History of Manufactures,* I, 399; Lewis, "Slave Families," and "The Use and Extent of Slave Labor"; and Smith, "Vesuvius Furnace Plantation."

41. Phelps, *History of Simsbury,* pp. 113–19; Phelps, *Newgate of Connecticut,* pp. 13–25 (for the quotation see p. 15); Dersch, "Copper Mining in Northern Michigan"; Long, "The Nickel Mines of Lancaster County"; Abbott, "Cornish Miners"; Perirgo, "The Cornish Miners." Cornish miners, recruited from one of the "dark corners" of the British Isles, kept alive many medieval beliefs.

42. Phelps, *Newgate,* pp. 18–20.

43. Woodward, *An Essay toward a Natural History of the Earth,* pp. 227–28; Phelps, *Newgate,* p. 19; Morse, *American Geography,* pp. 289–90; Wall, *The Chronicles of New Brunswick,* pp. 327–39.

44. Grammer, "Account of the Coal Mines," esp. 127–29; on cryptochemical jargon, see Crosland, *Historical Studies,* esp. 65–106.

45. Poe, "The Cask of Amontillado" [1846], *Best Known Works,* pp. 205; Lippard, *The Quaker City.* On Copper Hill as a tourist spot, see Egleston, "The Newgate of Connecticut." For subterranean horror improved for theological use, see Hollis, *The Mouth of the Pit.* See also Hardenberg [Novalis], *Heinrich von Ofterdingen* [1800] in his *Schriften,* I, 5–186, esp. 57–88; for the enduring connection between astrology and mining, see 82.

46. Plattes, p. 24.

47. Bining, *British Regulation,* pp. 25–27, 47–51.

48. Byrd, pp. 350, 348.

49. Sosa, "Report to the Viceroy," *Rediscovery of New Mexico,* p. 308; Barba, p. 173.

50. Walker, *Hopewell Village,* pp. 239–49; Pierce, *Iron in the Pines,* p. 92; Boyer, *Early Forges,* pp. 1–2; Kemper, "American Charcoal Making"; Sim and Weiss, *Charcoal-Burning,* pp. 9, 13, 21–22, 28, 32, 49; Gemmell, *The Charcoal Iron Industry.* See also Bining, *The Iron Plantations;* Spargo, *Iron Mining;* Sullivan, *The Industrial Worker;* Bining, *Pennsylvania Iron Manufacture;* Montgomery, "Early Furnaces and Forges"; Freiday, "Tinton Manor;" Rutsch, "The Colonial Plantation Settlement"; Bishop, *History of American Manufactures,* I, 465–631; Hartley, *Ironworks on the Saugus;* Lesley, *The Iron Manufacturer's Guide;* and Convention of Iron Masters, *Documents.*

51. Acrelius, *History of New Sweden,* p. 168; Grittinger, *Cornwall Furnace,* p. 16; Boyer, p. 1.

52. Nef, p. 44; Meister, "Die Anfänge des Eisenindustrie in der Grafschaft Mark."

53. Walker, pp. 14–56; Grittinger, pp. 18–19.

54. Agricola, *De Re Metallica,* p. 379; Walker, pp. 23, 26.

55. *Forges and Furnaces,* p. 181; see also Kerry, "The Long Pond Ironworks."

56. Walker, pp. 318–38.

57. Ibid., p. 154.

58. Ibid., pp. 219–24; Jones, *The Economic History of the Anthracite-Tidewater Canals.*

59. Walker, p. 223; "Coal, and the Coal-Mines of Pennsylvania"; *The Lonacoming Journals;* La Fayette, *Flaming Brands;* Paul, *California Gold;* Breton, "Mining Techniques."

60. Longfellow, *Complete Poetical Works,* pp. 14–15; Vautin's painting hangs at the Longfellow House, a museum operated by the National Park Service, in Cambridge, Massachusetts.

61. Gillbane, "Pawtucket Village Mechanics"; for the *Chronicle* quotation, see 4.

62. Rawson, *Handwrought Ancestors,* pp. 166–201; Davidson, "Weland the Smith"; Hegi, *Geschichte der Zukunft;* Krappe, "Zur Wielandssage," 9–23; Stevenson, *The Din of a Smithy;* Uhland, "Der Schmied," *Gedichte,* p. 99.

63. Bachelard, *The Psychoanalysis of Fire.* In "Snowbound," John Greenleaf Whittier quotes Agrippa (see *Poetical Works,* pp. 286-94). Whittier quoted correctly (see Agrippa, *Occult Philosophy or Magic,* p. 43).

64. Wigglesworth, "The Day of Doom," *Seventeenth-Century American Poetry,* pp. 55-113; for the quotations see pp. 107, 109, 110.

65. Edwards, "The Future Punishment of the Wicked," *Representative Selections,* pp. 144-54, 146, 150, 151-52; *Revelation,* 22:8; Salvator R. Tarnmoor [Herman Melville], "The Encantadas, or Enchanted Isles," for the quotation see 312.

66. Danckert, *Unehrliche Leute,* pp. 125-29.

67. Mitchell, *The Past in the Present,* pp. 149-51; Dalyell, *Darker Superstitions,* pp. 80-93; Eliade, *Sacred and Profane,* pp. 129-32; Tuan, *Topophilia,* pp. 23-24.

68. Danckert, pp. 129-30.

69. Ibid., pp. 131-35; "The Nixie in the Pond," *German Folk Tales,* pp. 585-90, concerns a typical greedy miller; Jacob, *Sechstausend Jahre Brot,* p. 158.

70. Danckert, p. 130; Saavedra, *El ingenioso hidalgo,* I, 189 n.1.

71. Bloch, "Avenement et Conquetes du Moulin à Eau"; White, *Medieval Technology,* pp. 80-89; Gille, "Le Moulin à eau"; Horwitz, "Uber das Aufkommen die erste Entwicklung und die Verbreitung von Windrädern"; Husslage, *Viere voor,* and *Windmolen.*

72. Howell, "Colonial Watermills," *America's Wooden Age,* pp. 120-59; Wailes, *The English Windmill;* Weiss, *Early Windmills.*

73. Information on La Cueva mill is best obtained locally; the mill may be made into a museum.

74. *Scituate Town Records,* I, 9, 19, 34, 41.

75. Howell and Keller, *The Mill at Philipsburg,* pp. 67-78.

76. *Scituate Town Records,* I, 19, 17-18.

77. Ibid., I, 18. Learning to build a mill, of course, accords with the theories developed by Ferguson, "The Mind's Eye: Non-verbal Thought in Technology"; see also Bridenbaugh, *The Colonial Craftsman,* pp. 18-20, 58-59.

78. *Scituate Town Records,* I, 18; Jaray, *The Mills;* Weiss and Sim, *Early Grist and Flouring Mills;* Rose, *Diary,* Jan. 26, 1751.

79. Plater, "Building the North Wales Mill"; Bridenbaugh, *Colonial Craftsman,* p. 20; Magee, *The Miller;* Jordon, "Evolution of the American Windmill."

80. Plater.

81. Howell and Keller, pp. 127-48.

82. Joshua Jacobs's record books are in the Norwell Historical Society, Norwell, Mass.

83. Evans, "Merchant Gristmills and Communities"; Swanson, *Old Mills;* Wilhelm, "The Blue Ridge Mill Complex"; Tyler, "Two Centuries of Technological Change"; Staughan, "The Old Mill."

84. Wigglesworth, "God's Controversy with New England," *Seventeenth-Century*

American Poetry, p. 43. On waste of timber, see Geller, *Pilgrims in Eden*, pp. 15-22.

85. Carroll, *The Timber Economy*, pp. 3-21, 57; Monson, *The Trades Increase;* Brown, *The Forests of England*, esp. p. 230.

86. *The Statutes at Large of Virginia*, I, 115; "Virginia Colonial Records," esp. 32; "Discourse of the Old Company"; Bruce, *Economic History of Virginia*, II, 428-31. On paltrok mills, see Stokhuyzen, *The Dutch Windmill*, p. 53. The pamphlet was Williams's *Virginia's Discovery of Silk Wormes*, appendix. For the 1623 suggestion, see the excellent article by Forman, "Mill Sawing in Seventeenth-Century Massachusetts," esp. 111; see also Pownall, *A Topographical Description*, pp. 25-26.

87. Beckman, *A History of Inventions*, I, 375-76; Winthrop, *The History of New England*, I, 116.

88. Byrd, "Letters," 233; Whiffen, *The Eighteenth-Century Houses*, p. 4, and *The Public Buildings of Williamsburg*, p. 21.

89. Byrd, *Secret Diary*, pp. 112, 158-59; Jones, *Present State of Virginia*, pp. 81, 142.

90. Forman, 112; Felt, *History of Ipswich*, pp. 95-96.

91. Forman; Byrd, "Letters," 233.

92. Carroll, pp. 101-19; Forman, 118.

93. Small, "Deposition," *New Hampshire Provincial Papers*, I, 45-46; Candee, "Merchant and Millwright," on Gorges, see 132; on Exeter, see *New Hampshire Provincial Papers*, I, 139.

94. Fitts, *History of Newfields*, p. 195; Candee; see also the map "A Survey of Piscataqua River."

95. Candee, esp. 137; Williamson, *The History of Maine*, II, 554-57.

96. Carroll, pp. 97-102.

97. Neal, *History of New-England*, II, 573-74.

98. *The Colonial Records of North Carolina*, VII, 429-30, 440-41; Kalm, *Travels in North America*, I, 282, 343.

99. Baxter, *Documentary History of the State of Maine*, p. 306.

100. Geller, pp. 31-39; Sclafert, "A Propos du Deboisement des Alpes du Sud," esp. 274; Felt, 25-26; Neal, II, 566-67.

101. Bolles, *Industrial History*, pp. 500-01.

102. Young, *History of Chautauqua County*, pp. 376-79; Defebaugh, *History of the Lumber Industry*, II, 440-44.

103. Blair, *A Raft Pilot's Log;* Weiss, *The Early Sawmills;* Wood, *A History of Lumbering in Maine;* Springer, *Forest Life and Forest Trees;* Curry, "Early Timber Operations in Southeast Arkansas." One of the best descriptions of lumbering camps is Kendall, *Travels Through the Northern Parts of the United States*, III, 73-84.

104. Leech, "Sharon Hollow: The Story of an Early Mulay Sawmill of Michigan"; Gray, "American Forest Trees."

105. Lillard, *The Great Forest,* pp. 138–44.
106. Greeley, *The Great Industries,* pp. 40–41.
107. Giedion, *Space, Time, and Architecture,* pp. 345–53; Field, "A Reexamination into the Invention of the Balloon Frame."
108. Robinson, "A Cheap Farmhouse."
109. Fowler, *A House for All,* pp. 28, 21, 5; Creese, "Fowler and the Domestic Octagon"; Carmer, *Dark Trees,* pp. 127–50.
110. Downing is quoted in Pierson, *American Buildings,* p. 270; see also pp. 271–317.
111. Melville, "The Paradise of Bachelors," *Great Short Works,* pp. 210–15; Marx, *The Machine in the Garden;* Williams, *The Country and the City,* pp. 214–47.
112. Hoskins, *One Man's England,* pp. 90–102, and *The Making of the English Landscape,* pp. 211–32.
113. Coleman, *The Transformation of Rhode Island,* pp. 3–85; Goodrich, *Historical Sketch of the Town of Pawtucket,* esp. p. 63; Pierson, "Notes on the Early Industrial Architecture in England."
114. Coleman, pp. 77–78.
115. James, "The Blackstone Valley," *On Geography,* pp. 132–80; Coleman, "Rhode Island Cotton Manufacturing"; Rivard, "Textile Experiments in Rhode Island"; Ware, *The Early New England Cotton Manufacture.*
116. Sande, "The Textile Factory"; Pierson, *American Buildings,* pp. 30–54.
117. Observation of mill structures is the best teacher; several days spent scrutinizing shapes and proportion can reveal a great deal.
118. Leyland, "Early Years of the Hope Cotton Manufacturing Company," 30; Keach, *Burrillville.*
119. Most of the houses survive, in use. See also especially Pierson, *American Buildings,* pp. 56–58, and Hitchcock, *Rhode Island Architecture,* pp. 36–43.
120. The quotations are found in White, *Memoir of Samuel Slater,* pp. 126–27 (see also pp. 86–142); LeBlanc, *Location of Manufacturing.*
121. White, p. 127.
122. Armstrong, *Factory Under the Elms,* p. 24 (this book is a thorough work); Wallace, *Rockdale,* p. 95; Leiper and Martin, *Report of the Committee.*
123. *Documents Relating to Manufactures.* For a contemporary view of early nineteenth-century factory villages, see Dunwell, *The Run of the Mill;* see also Sande, *Industrial Archaeology.*
124. Melville, *Great Short Works,* p. 221; Lieber, *Plantations;* Gersuny, "'A Devil in Petticoats.'"
125. *Cotton Was King.*
126. Emerson, "Farming," *Society and Solitude,* p. 138. On technique, see Barrett, *The Illusion of Technique.*
127. Wood, *New England's Prospect,* p. 14; Kendall, *Travels,* III, 84–85.
128. Poe, "The Gold Bug" [1843], *Best Known Works,* pp. 53–78; for the quotation see p. 63. For Poe's interest in landscape architecture, see his "The Domain of Arnheim," *Best Known Works,* pp. 287–306.

129. Milton, *Paradise Lost*, p. 7.
130. Chaucer, *The Canterbury Tales*, pp. 472-74; for the original version (c. 1387-1400) see *Works*, pp. 250-53 (this is an important antiartifice statement). On the nineteenth-century awakening, see Yoder, "Official Religion versus Folk Religion."
131. Zentler, *Americanischer Stadt und Land Calendar;* Raber, *The Devil and Some of his Doings;* Berg, *Abbadon and Mahanaim*. For the early years of advanced technology, see Bigelow, *Elements of Technology*. See also Winner, *Autonomous Technology*, and Ellul, *The Technological Society*.

CONCLUSION

1. Grund, *The Americans*, II, 263-64.
2. James, *The American Scene*, pp. 38, 442, 50. In his novels James writes lovingly about pedestrian places (see *The Ambassadors*, p. 24).
3. James, *American Scene*, pp. 105, 98, 122.
4. Ibid., pp. 73, 46, 49, 385.
5. For an analysis of the railroad view, see Percy, "The Man on the Train."
6. On lawns, see Jackson, "Ghosts at the Door," and Grigson, "The Room Outdoors."
7. On main streets and shopping malls, see Francaviglia, "Main Street U.S.A."

BIBLIOGRAPHY

ABBREVIATIONS

AAG	Association of American Geographers
ISHS	Illinois State Historical Society
MHS	Massachusetts Historical Society
MIT	Massachusetts Institute of Technology
NEQ	*New England Quarterly*
NMHR	*New Mexico Historical Review*
NYHS	New York Historical Society
USDA	United States Department of Agriculture
WMQ	*William and Mary Quarterly*

Abbott, Collamer M. "Cornish Miners in Appalachian Copper Camps." *Revue internationale d'histoire de la banque*, 7 (1973), 199-219.

Acrelius, Israel. *A History of New Sweden* [1759]. Trans. William M. Reynolds. Phil.: Historical Society of Pennsylvania, 1876.

Acts and Resolves of Massachusetts, 1784-1785. Boston: Adams, 1885.

Adams, Andrew N. *History of the Town of Fairhaven, Vermont.* Fairhaven: Author, 1870.

Adams, Frank Dawson. *The Birth and Development of the Geological Sciences.* Balt.: Williams, 1938.

Adams, Robert. *The Architecture and Art of Early Hispanic Colorado.* Boulder: Colorado Associated Univ. Press, 1974.

———. "Markers Cut by Hand." *American West,* 4 (1967), 59-64.

Addy, Sidney Oldall. *Church and Manor: A Study in English Economic History.* London: Allen, 1913.

———. *The Evolution of the English House* [1898]. Ed. John Summerson. London: Allen, 1933.

———. *Household Tales with other Traditional Remains Collected in the Counties of York, Lincoln, Derby, and Nottingham.* London: Nutt, 1895.

Agricola, Georg. *De re metallica* [1556]. Trans. Herbert Clark Hoover and Lou Henry Hoover. New York: Dover, 1950.

———. *De animantibus subterraneis.* Basel, Frobenium and Epicopium, 1549.

Agrippa, Henry Cornelius. *Occult Philosophy or Magic* [1533]. Ed. Willis F. Whitehead. Chicago: Hahn, 1898.

Akerman, Joe A. *Florida Cowman: A History of Florida Cattle Raising.* Kissimmee, Fla.: Fla. Cattlemen's Ass., 1976.

"Albuquerque and Galisteo: Certificate of the Founding, 1706." Ed. Lansing B. Bloom. *NMHR,* 10 (1935), 48-50.

Algier, Keith W., "The Puebla Mesta Ordinances of 1556 and 1560." *NMHR,* 44 (January 1969), 5-23.

Allen, Lewis F. *Rural Architecture.* New York: Moore, 1852.

Alsop, George. *A Character of the Province of Maryland* [1666]. Ed. Newton D. Mereness. Cleveland: Burrows, 1902.

Alte hoch- und niederdeutschen Volkslieder. Ed. Ludwig Uhland. Stuttgart: Cotta'scher, 1844-45.

Alvord, Clarence Walworth. *Illinois Country, 1673-1818.* Springfield: Illinois Centennial Comm., 1920.

America's Wooden Age: Aspects of its Early Technology. Ed. Brooke Hindle. Tarrytown, N.Y.: Sleepy Hollow, 1975.

Anderson, Edgar. *Landscape Papers.* Berkeley: Turtle Island, 1976.

Anderson, Wilbert L. *The Country Town: A Study of Rural Evolution.* New York: Baker, 1906.

Andrews, Charles M. *The Old English Manor: A Study in Economic History.* Balt.: Johns Hopkins Univ. Press, 1892.

Annals of Congress Washington, D.C.: Gales and Seaton, 1834-51.

3 8 1

Appleton, Jay. *Experience of Landscape.* New York: Wiley, 1975.

Appleton's Cyclopedia of American Biography. New York: Appleton, 1888.

Arena, C. Richard. "Land Settlement Policies and Practices in Spanish Louisiana." *The Spanish in the Mississippi Valley,* 79-94.

Ariès, Philippe. *Western Attitudes toward Death from the Middle Ages to the Present.* Balt.: Johns Hopkins Univ. Press, 1974.

Armenius, Theophilus. "Account of the Rise and Progress of the Work of God in the Western Country." *Methodist Magazine,* 2 (1819), 184-87, 221-24, 272-74, 304-08, 349-53, 393-96, 434-38.

Armstrong, John Borden. *Factory Under the Elms: A History of Harrisville, New Hampshire, 1774-1976.* Cambridge Mass.: MIT Press, 1976.

Arnheim, Rudolf. *The Dynamics of Architectural Form.* Berkeley: Univ. of Calif. Press, 1977.

Arr, E. H. *New England Bygones: Country Life in the 1840s.* Phil.: Lippincott, 1883.

Arthur, Eric, and Dudley White. *The Barn.* Greenwich, Conn.: New York Graphic Society, 1972.

Atherton, Lewis. *Main Street on the Middle Border* [1954] Chicago, Quadrangle, 1966.

————. *The Southern Country Store, 1800-1860.* Baton Rouge: Louisiana State University Press, 1949.

Atkinson, John C. *Forty Years in a Moorland Parish.* London: Macmillan, 1891.

Atwater, Caleb. "On the Prairies and Barrens of the West." *American Journal of Science,* 1 (1818), 116-25.

Atweel, George. *The Faithful Surveyour: Teaching How to Measure all manner of Ground Exactly.* Cambridge, England: William Nealand, 1658.

Auerbach, Berthold. *Schwarzwälder Dorfgeschichten.* Mannheim: Bassermann, 1846.

Baasen, Carl. *Wald und Bauertum.* Leipzig: S. Hirzel, 1940.

Bachelard, Gaston. *The Poetics of Space.* Trans. Maria Jolas. New York: Orion, 1964.

————. *The Psychoanalysis of Fire* [1938]. Trans. Alan C. M. Ross. Boston: Beacon, 1968.

Backus, Samuel D. "Some Hints Upon Farm Houses." *Report for 1859.* United States Commissioner of Patents. Washington, D.C.: Bowman, 1860.

Bacon, Francis. *Moral and Historical Works.* Ed. Joseph Devey. London: Bell, 1871.

Bader, Karl Siegfried. *Dorfgenossenschaft und Dorfgemeinde.* Cologne: Böhlaus, 1962.

————. *Das Mittelalterliche Dorf als Friedens- und Rechtsbereich.* Weimar: Böhlaus, 1957.

————. *Rechtsformen und Schichten der Liegenschaftsnutzung im Mittelalterlichen Dorf.* Vienna: Böhlaus, 1973.

Bailey, L. H. *Hints on School Grounds.* Ithaca: Cornell Univ. Press, 1901.

Bailey, M. W. *The English Farmhouse and Cottage.* London: Routledge, 1961.

Bailey, Sarah Loring. *Historical Sketches of Andover*. Boston: Houghton, 1880.

Bailyn, Bernard. *Education in the Forming of American Society*. Chapel Hill: Univ. of North Carolina Press, 1960.

Bakewell, Robert. *An Introduction to Geology*. New Haven: Howe, 1833.

Bancroft, Hubert H. *History of Arizona and New Mexico, 1530–1888*. San Francisco: History Co., 1889.

Banks, Mary Macleod. *British Calendar Customs*. London: Folk-Lore Society, 1937.

Barba, Alvaro Alonzo. *El Arte de los Metales* [1637]. Trans. Ross E. Douglas and E. P. Matthewson. New York: Wiley, 1923.

Barber, John Warner. *Connecticut Historical Collections*. New Haven: Durrie and Peck, 1836.

―――. *Historical Collections of Every Town in Massachusetts, with Geographical Descriptions*. Worchester: Lazell, 1848.

Barbieri, Guiseppe. *La Casa Rurale in Italia*. Florence: Olschki, 1970.

Barnard, Thomas. *A Sermon Preached in Boston*. Boston: S. Kneeland, 1758.

Barrett, William. *The Illusion of Technique: A Search for Meaning in a Technological Civilization* [1976]. Garden City, N.Y.: Anchor, 1979.

Bartlett, Richard A. *The New Country: A Social History of the American Frontier*. New York: Oxford, 1974.

Bates, George C. "By-Gones of Detroit." *Michigan Pioneer and Historical Collections*, 22 (1893), 305–404.

Bath, Bernard H. Slicker von. *The Agrarian History of Europe, A.D. 500–1850*. Trans. Olive Ordish. London: Arnold, 1963.

Baumgart, Wolfgang. *Der Wald in der deutschen Dichtung*. Berlin: De Gruyter, 1936.

Bayard, Charles J. "A Notice of Silver Ore on the Upper Platte in 1808." *Colorado Magazine*, 51 (Winter 1974), 43–51.

Bayard, Ferdinand. *Voyage dan l'interieur des États-Unis . . . dans la vallee de Shenandoah*. Paris: Cocheris, 1797.

Beck, Berton E. "Taming the Land." *Pennsylvania Folklife*, 14 (Spring 1965), 28–31.

Beckman, Johannes. *A History of Inventions and Discoveries*. Trans. William Johnston. London: J. Bell, 1797.

Beeman, Richard R. "Trade and Travel in Post-Revolutionary Virginia: A Diary of an Itinerant Peddler, 1807–1808." *Virginia Magazine of History and Biography*, 84 (April 1976), 174–88.

Beiträge zur Geschichte des Bergbaus, Huttenwesens, und der Montanwissenschaften 16, bis 20. Jahrhundert. Leipzig: Verlag für Gundstoffindustrie, 1964.

Belehrende Bergman: Ein sassliches Lese- und Bildungsbuch. Pirna: Friese, 1830.

Bement, C. N. "Rural Life." *American Quarterly Journal of Agriculture and Science*, 4 (July–December 1846), 84–89.

Bendermacher, Justinus. *Dorfformen in Westfalen-Lippe*. Troisdorf: Jarschel, 1977.

Benes, Peter. *The Masks of Orthodoxy: Folk Gravestone Carving in Plymouth County, Massachusetts: 1689-1805.* Amherst: Univ. of Mass. Press, 1977.

———. "Sky Colors and Scattered Clouds: The Decorative and Architectural Painting of New England Meeting Houses, 1738 to 1834." *Proceedings for 1979 Dublin Seminar for New England Folklife,* 35-47.

———, and Phillip D. Zimmerman. *New England Meeting House and Church, 1630-1850.* Boston: Boston Univ. Scholarly Publications, 1979.

Beresford, Maurice. *History on the Ground: Six Studies in Maps and Landscape.* Rev. ed. London: Methuen, 1971.

Berg, Joseph F. *Abbadon and Mahanaim: or, Demons and Guardian Angels.* Phil.: Higgins, 1856.

Bernheimer, Richard. *Wild Men in the Middle Ages: A Study in Art, Sentiment, and Demonology.* Cambridge: Harvard Univ. Press, 1952.

Benros, T. A. *Aus dem Walde.* Bern: Benteli, 1976.

Bettelheim, Bruno. *The Uses of Enchantment: The Meaning and Importance of Fairy Tales.* 1975. Reprint. New York: Vintage, 1977.

Beuckman, Frederic. "The Commons of Kaskaskia, Cahokia, and Prairie du Rocher." *Illinois Catholic Historical Review,* 1 (April 1919), 405-12.

Beverly, Robert. *The History and Present State of Virginia* [1705]. Ed. Louis B. Wright. Charlottesville: Univ. of Va. Press, 1968.

Bidwell, Percy Wells, and John Falconer. *History of Agriculture in the Northern United States, 1620-1860.* Washington, D.C.: Carnegie, 1925.

Bigelow, Jacob. *Elements of Technology.* Boston: Hilliard, 1829.

"Bill for Internal Improvements." *American Register,* 2 (1817), 128-48.

Bining, Arthur Cecil. *British Regulation of the Colonial Iron Industry.* Phil.: Univ. of Penn. Press, 1933.

———. *The Iron Plantations of Early Pennsylvania.* Phil.: Hist. Soc. of Penn., 1933.

———. *Pennsylvania Iron Manufacture in the Eighteenth Century.* Harrisburg: Penn. Historical Comm., 1938.

Biringuccio, Vannuccio. *Pyrotechnia* [1540]. Trans. Richard Eden [1555]. Ed. Edward Arber. *The First Three English Books on America.* Birmingham, England: Author, 1885.

Birkbeck, Morris. *Notes on a Journey in America.* London: Severn, 1818.

Bishop, J. Leander. *A History of American Manufactures, 1608 to 1860.* Phil.: Young, 1866.

Black, T. E. *God's Way: Based on the 12 Signs of the Zodiac and the Word of God . . . Correct Signs and Dates for Planting.* Andalusia, Ala.: Author, 1963.

Blackman, Frank W. *Spanish Institutions of the Southwest.* Balt.: Johns Hopkins Univ. Press, 1891.

Blair, Walter Acheson. *A Raft Pilot's Log: A History of the Great Rafting Industry on the Upper Mississippi, 1840 to 1915.* Cleveland: Clark, 1930.

Blechschmidt, Manfred. *Die Silberne Rose: Europäische Bergmannssagen.* Rudolstadt: Greifenverlag, 1974.

Bloch, Marc. "Avenement et conquetes du moulin à eau." *Annales d'histoire economique et sociale,* 7 (November 30, 1935), 538-63.

————. *Land and Work in Medieval Europe.* Trans. J. E. Anderson. 1963. Reprint. Berkeley: Univ. of Calif. Press, 1967.

Blum, Jerome. *The End of the Old Order in Rural Europe.* Princeton: Princeton Univ. Press, 1978.

Bobb, Bernard E. *The Viceregency of Antonio Maria Bucareli in New Spain, 1771–1779.* Austin: Univ. of Texas Press, 1962.

Boland, Bridget. *Gardener's Magic and Other Old Wives' Lore.* London: Bodley Head, 1977.

Boles, John B. *The Great Revival, 1787–1805: The Origins of the Southern Evangelical Mind.* Lexington: Univ. Press of Ky., 1972.

Bolles, Albert S. *Industrial History of the United States.* Norwich, Conn.: H. Bill, 1881.

Bonner, James C. "Plantation Architecture of the Lower South on the Eve of the Civil War." *Journal of Southern History,* 11 (August 1945), 370–88.

Bordley, J. B. *Essays and Notes on Husbandry and Rural Affairs.* Phil.: Dobson, 1801.

Borhegyi, Stephen F. de. "The Evolution of a Landscape." *Landscape,* 4 (Summer 1954), 24–30.

Boserup, Ester. *The Conditions of Agricultural Growth: The Economics of Agrarian Change under Population Pressure.* Chicago: Aldine, 1965.

Boswell, James. *Journal of a Tour of the Hebrides* [1773]. Ed. R. W. Chapman. Oxford: Oxford Univ. Press, 1924.

Bouchard, G. *Le Village immobile: Sennely-en-Sologne au 18^e Siecle.* Paris: Plon, 1972.

Boyer, Charles S. *Early Forges and Furnaces in New Jersey.* Phil.: Univ. of Penn. Press, 1931.

Boyle, Robert. *An Essay About the Origine and Virtues of Gems.* London: William Godbid, 1672.

Brackenridge, Henry M. *Recollections of Persons and Places in the West.* Phil.: Lippincott, 1868.

Brading, D. A. "Mexican Silver-Mining in the Eighteenth Century: The Revival of Zacatecas." *Hispanic-American Historical Review,* 50 (November 1970), 665–81.

————. *Miners and Merchants in Bourbon Mexico.* Cambridge, England: Cambridge Univ. Press, 1971.

————, and Harry E. Cross. "Colonial Silver Mining: Mexico and Peru." *Hispanic-American Historical Review* 52 (November 1972), 545–79.

Bradstreet, Anne. *Works.* Ed. Jeannie Hensley. Cambridge, Mass.: Harvard Univ. Press, 1967.

Brand, Donald D. "The Early History of the Range Cattle Industry in Northern Mexico." *Agricultural History,* 35 (July 1961), 132–39.

Brand, John. *Observations on the Popular Antiquities of Great Britain.* Ed. Henry Ellis. London: Bohn, 1849.

Braun, E. Lucy. *Deciduous Forests of Eastern Northern America.* Phil.: Blakiston, 1950.

Bressler, Leo. "Agriculture among the Germans in Pennsylvania during the Eighteenth Century." *Pennsylvania History,* 22 (April 1956), 102–33.

Breton, Roslyn, "Mining Techniques in the California Goldfields during the 1850s." *Pacific Historian,* 20 (Fall 1976), 286–302.

Brewster, Jonathan. "Letter to John Winthrop, Jr." *Collections,* MHS, 4th series, 7, 72–75.

Bridenbaugh, Carl. *Cities in the Wilderness: The First Century of Urban Life in America, 1625–1742.* New York: Ronald, 1938.

———. *The Colonial Craftsman.* New York: New York Univ. Press, 1950.

Briggs, K. M. *The Anatomy of Puck: An Examination of Fairy Beliefs among Shakespeare's Contemporaries and Successors.* London: Routledge, 1959.

Brock, Henry Irving. *Colonial Churches in Virginia.* Richmond, Va. Dale, 1930.

Brock, Robert Alonzo. "Early Iron Manufacture in Virginia." *Proceedings,* United States National Museum, 8 (April 23, 1885), 77–80.

Bronner, Edwin B. *William Penn's Holy Experiment: The Founding of Pennsylvania, 1681–1701.* New York: Greenwood, 1963.

Brown, John Croumbi. *The Forests of England and the Management of Them in Bye-Gone Times.* Edinburgh: Oliver and Boyd, 1883.

Brown, Theo. "Some Examples of Post-Reformation Folklore in Devon." *Folklore,* 72 (June 1961), 388–99.

Browne, Thomas. *Religio Medici* [1643]. London: Dent, 1920.

Brownstein, Michael. "The U.P.S. Man." *New Yorker,* 55 (November 19, 1979), 42–43.

Bruce, Dickson D. *And They All Sang Hallelujah: Plain-Folk Camp-Meeting Religion, 1800–1845.* Knoxville: Univ. of Tenn. Press, 1974.

Bruce, Kathaleen. *Virginia Iron Manufacture in the Slave Era.* New York: Century, 1931.

Bruce, P. A. *Economic History of Virginia in the Seventeenth Century.* Boston: Macmillan, 1895.

———. *Social Life of Virginia in the Seventeenth Century.* Richmond: Whittet and Shepperson, 1907.

Bunting, Bainbridge. *Early Architecture in New Mexico.* Albuquerque: Univ. of N.M. Press, 1976.

———. *Taos Adobes.* Sante Fe, N.M.: Fort Burgurin Research Center, 1964.

Bunyan, John. *The Pilgrim's Progress from this World to That Which is to Come* [1678]. New York: American, 1964.

Burdick, Lewis Dayton. *Magic and Husbandry: The Folk-Lore of Agriculture.* Binghamton, N.Y.: Osteningo, 1905.

Burges, George. *A Journal of a Surveying Trip* [1795]. Mount Pleasant, Mich.: John Cumming, 1955.

Burke, Peter. *Popular Culture in Early Modern Europe.* New York: Harper, 1978.

Burnaby, Andrew. *Travels through the Middle Settlements of North America.* London: T. Payne, 1798.

Burnett, Hugh B. "Madrid Plaza." *Colorado Magazine,* 42 (Summer 1965), 224–37.

Burr, David H. "Map of Maine . . . Exhibiting Post Offices, Roads, Canals, and Railroads." Boston: Burr, 1839.

Burton, Anthony. *The Miners*. London: Deutsch, 1976.

Burton, Robert. *The Anatomy of Melancholy*. Oxford: John Lichfield, 1621.

Bushman, Richard L. *From Puritan to Yankee: Character and the Social Order in Connecticut, 1690 to 1765*. Cambridge, Mass.: Harvard Univ. Press, 1967.

Bushnell, Horace. *The Day of Roads*. Hartford: Elihu Geer, 1846.

Butterworth, E. A. S. *The Tree at the Navel of the Earth*. Berlin: De Gruyter, 1970.

Bynum, David E. *The Daemon in the Wood: A Study of Oral Narrative Patterns*. Cambridge, Mass.: Center for the Study of Oral Literature, 1978.

Byrd, William. "Letters." Ed. W. G. Stanard. *Virginia Magazine of History and Biography*, 24 (June 1916), 225-37.

———. *Prose Works*. Ed. Louis B. Wright. Cambridge, Mass.: Harvard Univ. Press, 1966.

———. *Secret Diary for the Years 1709-1712*. Ed. Louis B. Wright. Richmond, Va.: Dietz, 1941.

Calhoun, Daniel H. *The American Civil Engineer, 1792-1843*. Cambridge, Mass.: MIT Press, 1960.

Campbell, Mildred. *The English Yeoman under Elizabeth and the Early Stuarts* [1942]. New York: Barnes and Noble, 1960.

Camposeo, James Mark. "The History of the Canal System Between New Haven and Northampton, 1822-1847." *Historical Journal of Western Massachusetts*, 10 (Fall 1977), 37-53.

Candee, Richard M., "Merchant and Millwright: The Water-powered Sawmills of the Piscataqua." *Old-Time New England*, 60 (July 1969–April 1970), 131-49.

Carlson, Alvar Ward. "Rural Settlement Patterns in the San Luis Valley: A Comparative Study." *Colorado Magazine*, 44 (Spring 1967), 109-28.

Carmer, Carl. *Dark Trees to the Wind*. New York: Sloane, 1949.

Carney, Michael. *Country Life and the Country School*. Chicago: Row, 1912.

Carrier, E. H. *Water and Grass: A Study in the Pastoral Economy of Southern Europe*. London: Christopher's, 1932.

Carrier, Lyman, and Katherine S. Bort. "History of Kentucky Bluegrass and White Clover in the United States." American Society of Agronomy, *Journal*, 8 (1916), 256-66.

Carroll, Orville W. "Early Brick Law in Massachusetts." Association for Preservation Technology *Bulletin*, 8 (1976), 20-23.

Carroll, Peter N. *Puritanism and the Wilderness: The Intellectual Significance of the Frontier, 1629-1700*. New York: Columbia Univ. Press, 1969.

———. *The Timber Economy of Puritan New England*. Providence: Brown Univ. Press, 1973.

Carstensen, Vernon. "Patterns on the American Land." *Surveying and Mapping*, 36 (December 1976), 303-09.

Castiglioni, Luigi. *Viaggio negli Stati Uniti dell America*. Milan: Marelli, 1790.

Catlett, H. G. "National Road to California" [pamphlet]. Victoria, Texas: n.p., 1847.

Cavaliers and Pioneers: Abstracts of Virginia Land Patents and Grants, 1623–1800. Ed. Nell Marion Nugent. Richmond, Va.: Dietz, 1934.

Cayrol, Jean. *De l'espace humain* (Paris: Seuil, 1968).

Cazenove, Theophile. *Journal* [1797]. Trans. Rayner Wickersham Kelsey. Haverford: Penn. History Press, 1922.

Cervantes, Miguel De. *El ingenioso hidalgo Don Quijote de la Mancha* [1615]. Ed. D. Clemencin. Madrid: Hernando, 1894.

Chamberlayne, Edward. *The Present State of England.* London: John Martyn, 1669.

Changing Rural Landscapes. Ed. Ervin H. Zube and Margaret J. Zube. Amherst: Univ. of Massachusetts Press, 1977.

Chaucer, Geoffrey. *The Canterbury Tales.* Ed. Nevil Coghill. Baltimore: Penguin, 1960.

———. *Works.* Ed. Alfred W. Pollard. London: Macmillan, 1901.

Chevalier, François. *La Formation des grands domaines au Mexique: Terre et societé aux XVIe-XVIIe siècles.* Paris: Institute d'Ethnologie, 1952.

Child, Lydia Maria. *American Frugal Housewife.* Boston: Carter and Hendee, 1835.

Christian, Marcus. *Negro Ironworkers of Louisiana.* Gretna, La.: Pelica, 1972.

Cipolla, Carlo M. *Clocks and Culture, 1300–1700.* London: Collins, 1967.

City in Southern History, The. Ed. Blaine A. Brownell. Port Washington, N.Y.: Kennikat, 1977.

Clark, Charles E. *The Eastern Frontier: The Settlement of Northern New England, 1610–1673.* New York: Knopf, 1970.

Clark, Kenneth. *Landscape into Art* [1949]. Boston: Beacon, 1961.

Clark, Thomas D. *The Southern Country Store* [1944]. Norman: Univ. of Oklahoma Press, 1974.

Clark, Victor S. *History of Manufactures in the United States.* New York: Peter Smith, 1949.

Clayton, John. *Letter to the Royal Society* [1688]. Washington, D.C.: Peter Force, 1836.

Clemens, Paul G. E. "The Operation of an Eighteenth-Century Chesapeake Tobacco Plantation." *Agricultural History,* 49 (July 1975), 517–31.

Clemens, Samuel L. *The Adventures of Tom Sawyer.* Hartford: America, 1876.

Cline, Walter. *Mining and Metallurgy in Negro Africa.* Menasha, Wis.: George Banta, 1937.

"Coal, and the Coal-Mines of Pennsylvania." *Harper's New Monthly Magazine,* 15 (September 1857), 451–63.

Cobbett, William. *Rural Rides* [1830]. Harmondsworth, England: Penguin, 1975.

———. *A Year's Residence in America* [1818]. Ed. John Freeman. London: Chapman, c. 1935.

Coffin, Margaret M. *Death in Early America.* New York: Nelson, 1976.

Cohen, Richard Bowman. "Once There Was A Light." *Virginia Cavalcade,* 27 (Summer 1977), 5–19.

Cole, Pamela. "Early New England Funeral Customs." *Journal of American Folklore,* 7 (1894), 217-23.

Colección de Documentos Ineditos Relativos al Descubrimiento Conquista y Organización de los Antiquas Posesiones Espanolas de America y Oceania, National Archives, Madrid.

Coleman, Peter J. "Rhode Island Cotton Manufacturing: A Study in Economic Coservatism." *Rhode Island History,* 23 (July 1964), 65-80.

————. *The Transformation of Rhode Island, 1790-1860.* Providence: Brown Univ. Press, 1969.

Colles, Christopher. *A Survey of the Roads of the United States* [1789]. Ed. Walter W. Ristow. Cambridge, Mass.: Harvard Univ. Press, 1961.

Collier, Katherine Brownell. *Cosmogonies of Our Fathers.* New York: Columbia Univ. Press, 1934.

Colonial Churches in the Original Colony of Virginia. Richmond: Southern Churchman Co., 1908.

Colonial Records of North Carolina. Ed. William L. Saunders. Goldsboro, N.C.: Nash, 1886.

Comenius, John Amos. *Naturall Philosophie Reformed by Divine Light.* London: Leybourn, 1651.

Convention of Iron Masters. *Documents Relating to the Manufacture of Iron in Pennsylvania.* Phil.: General Committee, 1850.

Conway, A. W. "A Northern New Mexico House-Type and a Suggestion for the Identifying of Others." *Landscape,* 1 (Autumn 1951), 20-21.

————. "Southwestern Colonial Farms." *Landscape,* 1 (Spring 1951), 6-9.

————. "Village Types in the Southwest." *Landscape,* 2 (Spring 1952), 14-19.

Cook, Robert. *The Tree of Life: Symbol of the Center.* London: Thames and Hudson, 1974.

Coolidge, John. "Hingham Builds a Meetinghouse." *NEQ,* 24 (1961), 435-61.

Cooper, Gilbert. *Symbolism in the Bible and the Church.* New York: Philosophical Library, 1959.

Cooper, James Fenimore. *Notions of the Americans* [1829]. Ed. Robert E. Spiller. New York: Ungar, 1963.

Cooter, William S. "Ecological Dimensions of Medieval Agrarian Systems." *Agricultural History,* 52 (October 1978), 458-77.

Corbett, L. C. *The School Garden.* Washington, D.C.: Government Printing Office, 1905.

Correspondence of the Three William Byrds of Westover, Virginia 1684-1776, The. Ed. Marion Tinling. Charlottesville: Univ. Press of Virginia, 1977.

Costello, Peter. *In Search of Lake Monsters.* New York: Coward, McCann, and Geoghegan, 1974.

Cott, Nancy F. *The Bonds of Womanhood: "Woman's Sphere" in New England, 1780-1835.* New Haven: Yale Univ. Press, 1977.

Cotton, John. *A Brief Exposition.* London: Ralph Smith, 1654.

Cotton Was King: A History of Lowell, Massachusetts. Ed. Arthur L. Eno, Jr. Lowell: Lowell Hist. Soc., 1976.

Coulton, G. G. *The Medieval Panorama: The English Scene from Conquest to Reformation*. Cambridge, England: Cambridge Univ. Press, 1938.

Coxe, Tench. "Address to the Honourable the Members of the Convention of Virginia." *American Museum*, 3 (1788), 426–30.

Cozzato, Vincenzo. "Il Sistema Economico—Territoriale Nell' America Spagnola." *Psicon*, 2 (October–December 1975), 65–85.

Craven, Avery O. *Soil Exhaustion as a Factor in the Agricultural History of Virginia and Maryland, 1606–1860*. Urbana: Univ. of Illinois Press, 1926.

Craven, John. "Letter." *Farmer's Register*, 1 (August 1833), 150–52.

Creese, Walter. "Fowler and the Domestic Octagon." *Art Bulletin*, 28 (June 1946), 89–102.

Cremin, Lawrence. *American Education: The Colonial Experience, 1607–1783*. New York: Harper, 1970.

Crèvecoeur, J. Hector St. John de. *Letters from an American Farmer* [1782]. Ed. Warren Barton Blake. New York: Dutton, 1957.

Crosby, Harry. "El Camino Real in Baja California: Loreto to San Diego." *Journal of San Diego History*, 23 (Winter 1977), 1–54.

Crosland, Maurice P. *Historical Studies in the Language of Chemistry* [1962]. New York: Dover, 1978.

Cross, Whitney R. *The Burned-Over District: The Social and Intellectual History of Enthusiastic Religion in Western New York, 1800–1850*. Ithaca: Cornell Univ. Press, 1950.

"Cultivation of Cleared Lands," *American Agriculturist*, 3 (January 1844), 3–4.

Cumming, Abbott L. *Architecture in Early New England*. Sturbridge, Mass.: Old Sturbridge Village Inc., 1958.

Currier, Moody. "The Farmer's Home." *Farmer's Monthly Visitor*, 12 (February 1852), 46.

Curry, Corliss C. "Early Timber Operations in Southeast Arkansas." *Arkansas Historical Quarterly*, 19 (Summer 1960), 111–18.

Cushing, John D. "Town Commons of New England, 1640–1840." *Old-Time New England*, 50 (1961), 86–94.

Dacy, George H. *Four Centuries of Florida Ranching*. St. Louis: Britt, 1940.

Dahlgren, Charles Bunker. *Historic Mines of Mexico*. New York: Author, 1883.

Dalyell, John Graham. *The Darker Superstitions of Scotland, Illustrated from History and Practice*. Edinburgh: Waugh and Innes, 1834.

Dana, Edmund. *A Description of the Bounty Lands in the State of Illinois*. Cincinnati: Looker, 1819.

Danckert, Werner. *Unehrliche Leute: Die Verfemten Berufe*. Munich: Frauche, 1963.

Danhof, Clarence H. "The Fencing Problem in the 1850s." *Agricultural History*, 18 (October 1944), 168–86.

Daniels, Bruce C. "Connecticut's Villages Become Mature Towns: The Complexity of Local Institutions, 1676 to 1776." *WMQ*, 34 (January 1977), 83–103.

Darby, H. C. "The Agrarian Contribution to Surveying in England." *Geographical Journal,* 82 (1933), 529–38.

Darthelmess, Alfred. *Wald Umwelt des Menschen.* Munich: Alber, 1972.

Davidson, H. R. Ellis. *Gods and Myths of Northern Europe.* Harmondsworth, England: Penguin, 1964.

————. "The Sword at the Wedding." *Folklore,* 71 (March 1960), 1–18.

————. "Weland the Smith." *Folklore,* 69 (September 1958), 145–59.

Davidson, Robert. *History of the Presbyterian Church in the State of Kentucky with a Preliminary Sketch of the Churches in the Valley of Virginia.* New York: R. Carter, 1847.

Davidson, T. D. "The Untilled Field." *Agricultural History Review,* 3 (1955), 20–25.

Davidson, William H. *Pine Log and Greek Revival: Houses and People of Three Counties in Georgia and Alabama.* Alexander City, Ala.: Outlook, 1965.

Davis, Alexander Jackson. *Rural Residences.* New York: Architect, 1837.

Dean, Silas. *A Brief History of the Town of Stoneham, Massachusetts.* Boston: Hart, 1843.

Deane, Samuel. *New England Farmer or Georgical Dictionary.* Boston: Wells, 1822.

Deetz, J., and E. Dethlefsen. "Death Heads, Cherubs, and Willow Trees: Experimental Archaelogy in Colonial Cemeteries." *American Antiquity,* 31 (1966), 502–10.

Defebaugh, James Elliott. *History of the Lumber Industry in America.* Chicago: American Lumberman, 1907.

Defoe, Daniel. *The Life and Strange Surprizing Adventures of Robinson Crusoe.* London: Taylor, 1719.

————. *A Tour Thro' the Whole Island of Great Britain.* London: S. Birt, 1753.

Demos, John. *A Little Commonwealth: Family Life in Plymouth Colony.* New York: Oxford, 1970.

Dennenberg, Dennis. "The Missing Link: New England's Influence on Early National Educational Policies." *NEQ,* 52 (June 1979), 219–33.

DePauw, Linda Grant, and Conover Hunt. *Remember the Ladies: Women in America, 1750–1815.* New York: Viking, 1976.

DeQuincey, Thomas. *Collected Writings.* Ed. David Masson. Edinburgh: Black, 1890.

Derriau, M. "A l'origine du 'rang' Canadien." *Cahiers de Geographie de Quebec,* 1 (October 1956), 39–47.

Dersch, Virginia Jonas. "Copper Mining in Northern Michigan: A Social History." *Michigan History,* 61 (Winter 1977), 290–321.

Detering, Alfred. *Die Bedeutnung der Eiche seit der Vorzeit.* Leipzig: Rabisch, 1938.

Deveze, Michael. *La Vie de la forêt Française au XVIe siècle.* Paris: École Pratique, 1961.

Dickens, Charles. *The Life and Adventures of Martin Chuzzlewit* [1844]. London: Chapman and Hall, c. 1870.

Dickinson, Robert E. "Landscape and Society." *Scottish Geographical Magazine,* 55 (January 1939), 1–15.

————. "Rural Settlement in the German Lands." AAG, *Annals*, 39 (December 1949), 239–63.

"Discourse of the Old Company." *Virginia Magazine of History and Biography*, 1 (October 1893), 155–67.

Ditchfield, P. H. *The Old-Time Parson*. London: Methuen, 1908.

Documentary History of the State of Maine. Ed. James Phinney Baxter. Portland: Thurston, 1897.

Documents Relating to Manufactures in the United States [1833]. Ed. Louis McLane. New York: Kelley, 1969.

Dodd, Dorothy. "The Wrecking Business on the Florida Reef, 1822–1860." *Florida Historical Quarterly*, 22 (1944), 171–99.

Dominquez-Ortíz, A. *The Golden Age of Spain, 1516–1659*. Trans. James Casey. London: Weidenfeld, 1971.

Donnelly, Marion Card. *The New England Meeting Houses of the Seventeenth Century*. Middletown, Conn.: Wesleyan Univ. Press, 1968.

Dorrance, Ward Allison. "The Survival of the French in the Old District of Sainte Genevieve." *University of Missouri Studies*, 10 (April 1935), 1–133.

Douville, R., and J. Casanova. *Daily Life in Early Canada*. London: Allen and Unwin, 1968.

Downing, Andrew Jackson. *The Architecture of Country Houses*. New York: Appleton, 1850.

Doyon, Georges, and Robert Hubrecht. *L'Architecture rurale et bourgeoise en France*. Paris: Vincent, 1957.

Drake, Francis S. *The Town of Roxbury: Its Memorable Persons and Places*. Boston: Municipal Printing Office, 1905.

Dunbar, Gary S. "Colonial Carolina Cowpens." *Agricultural History*, 35 (July 1961), 125–130.

Duncan, Edgar Hill. "The Natural History of Metals and Minerals in the Universe of Milton's *Paradise Lost*." *Osiris*, 11 (1954), 386–421.

Dunham, Samuel. *An Historical Discourse . . . One Hundred and Fiftieth Anniversary of the First Church in Brookfield*. Springfield, Mass.: Bowles, 1867.

Dunton, John. *Letters Written from New England, 1686*. Ed. W. H. Whitmore. Boston: Prince Society, 1867.

Dunwell, Steve. *The Run of the Mill*. Boston: Godine, 1978.

Düring, Kurt. *Das Siedlungsbild der Insel Fahman*. Stuttgart: Engelshorn, 1937.

Dusenberry, William H. *The Mexican Mesta: The Administration of Ranching in Colonial Mexico*. Urbana: Univ. of Illinois Press, 1963.

Dwight, Timothy. *Travels in New England and New York* [1821]. Ed. Barbara Miller Solomon. Cambridge, Mass.: Harvard Univ. Press, 1969.

Dyer, T. F. Thiselton. *The Ghost World*. London: Ward and Downey, 1893.

Dykstra, Robert R. *The Cattle Towns*. New York: Knopf, 1968.

Earle, Alice M. *Customs and Fashions in Old New England*. New York: Scribner's Sons, 1893.

Earle, Carville, and Ronald Hoffman. "Staple Crops and Urban Development in the Eighteenth-Century South." *Perspectives in American History*, 10 (1976), 7–80.

Early Records of the Town of Providence. Ed. Horatio Rogers. Providence, R.I.: Snow and Farnham, 1894.

Eberlein, Harold Donaldson, and Roger Wearne Ransdell, *Small Manor Houses and Farmsteads in France*. Phil.: Lippincott, 1926.

Ecology and Religion in History. Ed. David Spring and Eileen Spring. New York: Harper, 1974.

Edallo, Amos. *Ruralistica*. Milan: Hoepli, 1946.

Edwards, Jonathan. *Representative Selections*. Ed. Clarence H. Faust and Thomas H. Johnson. New York: American, 1935.

"Effects of Lightning—Barn Burned." *Monthly Genesee Farmer*, 3 (September 1838), 127.

Eggleston, Edward. *The Hoosier Schoolmaster*. New York: Judd, 1871.

Egleston, N. H. "The Newgate of Connecticut: The Old Simsbury Copper Mines." *Magazine of American History*, 15 (April 1886), 321–34.

Eliade, Mircea. *The Sacred and the Profane: The Nature of Religion*. Trans. Willard R. Trask. New York: Harcourt, 1959.

Eliot, Jared. "Essays upon Field Husbandry." Massachusetts Society for Promoting Agriculture, *Papers*, 2 (1811), 9–25.

Ellis, Rowland. "Philadelphia in 1698." *Pennsylvania Magazine of History and Biography*, 18 (July 1894), 245–48.

Ellul, Jacques. *The Technological Society*. Trans. John Wilkinson. New York: Knopf, 1964.

Emerson, Ralph Waldo. *Journals and Miscellaneous Notebooks*. Ed. William H. Gilman and Alfred R. Ferguson. Cambridge, Mass.: Harvard Univ. Press, 1963.

———. *Society and Solitude*. Boston: Houghton, 1884.

Epperlein, Siegfried. *Der Bauer im Bild des Mittelalters*. Leipzig: Vienna, 1975.

Eshleman, H. Frank. "History of Lancaster County's Highway System, 1714–1760." Lancaster County Historical Society, *Journal* 26 (March 1922), 37–80.

Espejo, Antonio. "Report of an Expedition" [1585]. *Rediscovery of New Mexico*, pp. 34–52.

Estienne, Charles. *Guides des chemins de France*. Lyon: Benoist, 1601.

———, and Charles Liebault. *Maison rustique, or The Countrie Farm* [1567]. Trans. Richard Sinflet. London: Stevens, 1616.

Evans, Priscilla Ann. "Merchant Gristmills and Communities, 1820–1880: An Economic Relationship." *Missouri Historical Review*, 68 (1973–74), 317–26.

Evelyn, John. *A Philosophical Discourse of the Earth*. London: John Martyn, 1678.

Everett, Edward. *Orations and Speeches on Various Occasions*. Boston: Little, Brown, 1859.

———. "The Public Lands." *American Almanac and Repository of Useful Knowledge*. Boston: Gray and Bowen, 1832, pp. 142–45.

Fagiolo, Marcello. "La fondazione delle citta Latino Americane Gli Archetipi della Guistizia E Della Fede." *Psicon,* 2 (October–December, 1975), 8–32.

"Fair at Rochester." *Cultivator,* 7 (November 1840), 179.

Fales, Martha G. "The Early American Way of Death." Essex Institute. *Historical Collections,* 100 (April 1964), 75–84.

"Farm Buildings." *American Agriculturist,* 1 (July 1842), 115–21.

"Farm Cottage." *Wisconsin Farmer,* 8 (September 1856), 389–90.

Farmer's Almanac, 1979. Lewiston, Me.: Almanac Publishing, 1978.

Farnham, Eliza W. *Life in Prairie Land.* New York: Harper, 1846.

Faulkner, Waldron. *Architecture and Color.* New York: Wiley, 1972.

Faux, William. *Memorable Days in America.* London: Simpkin, 1823.

Felt, Joseph B. *Annals of Salem.* Salem: Observer and Ives, 1827, 1849.

――――. *History of Ipswich, Essex, and Hamilton.* Cambridge, Mass.: Folsom, 1834.

"Fences." *Boston Cultivator,* 13 (April 12, 1851), n.p.

"Fences." *Soil of the South,* 4 (1854), 6.

Ferguson, Eugene S. "The Mind's Eye: Non-verbal Thought in Technology." *Science,* 197 (August 26, 1977), 827–36.

Ferrall, S. A. *A Ramble of Six Thousand Miles through the United States.* London: Effingham, 1832.

Fessenden, Thomas Green. "Address." *New England Farmer,* I (October 19, 1822), 89–92.

Field, John. *English Field Names: A Dictionary.* Newton Abbott: David and Charles, 1972.

Field, Matthew C. "Sketches of Big Timber, Bent's Fort, and Milk Fort in 1839." *Colorado Magazine,* 14 (May 1937), 102–08.

Field, Walker. "A Reexamination into the Invention of the Balloon Frame." American Society of Architectural Historians, *Journal,* 2 (October 1942), 3–29.

Finlay, Hugh. *Journal, 1773–1774.* Ed. Frank H. Norton. Brooklyn: Frank Norton, 1867.

Finley, James B. *Autobiography.* Ed. W. P. Strickland. Cincinnati: Methodist Book Concern, 1854.

Finley, John. *The French in the Heart of America.* New York: Scribner's, 1915.

Fitchen, John. *The New World Dutch Barn.* Syracuse: Syracuse Univ. Press, 1968.

Fischer, Otto. "Landscape as Symbol." *Landscape,* 4 (Spring 1955), 24–33.

Fish, Lydia M. *The Folklore of the Coal Mines of the Northeast of England.* Norwood Penn.: Norwood Editions, 1975.

Fisher, John Robert. *Minas y mineros en el Peru colonial, 1776–1824.* Lima: Instituto de Estudios Peruanos, 1977.

Fitts, James Hill. *History of Newfields, New Hampshire.* Concord, N.H.: Rumford, 1912.

Flagg, Edmund. *The Far West, or a Tour Beyond the Mountains.* New York: Harper, 1838.

Flagg, Gershom. "Letters." Ed. Solon J. Buck. ISHS, *Transactions,* 15 (1910), 143–49.

Fletcher, Stevenson Whitcomb. *Pennsylvania Agriculture and Country Life, 1640 – 1840*. Harrisburg: Pennsylvania Historical and Museum Commission, 1950.

Flint, James. *Letters from America*. Edinburgh: Tait, 1822.

Flint, Timothy. *Recollections of the Last Ten Years* [1826]. Ed. C. Hartley Grattan. New York: Knopf, 1932.

Foght, Harold Waldstein. *The American Rural School*. New York: Macmillan, 1910.

Fols, R. *Erinnerungen eines Schulmannes aus dem alten Danzig, 1822 –1841*. Danzig: Saunier, 1902.

Forbes, H. *Gravestones of Early New England and the Men Who Made Them: 1653 – 1800*. Boston: Houghton, 1927.

Ford, Amelia Clewley. *Colonial Precedents of Our National Land System as it Existed in 1800*. Madison: Univ. of Wisconsin Bulletins, 1910.

Fordham, Elias Pym. *Personal Narrative of Travels in Virginia, Maryland . . . and of a Residence in the Indian Territory, 1817 –1818*. Ed. Frederick A. Ogg. Cleveland: Clarke, 1906.

Forges and Furnaces in the Province of Pennsylvania. Phil.: Pennsylvania Society of the Colonial Dames of America, 1914.

Forman, Benno M. "Mill Sawing in Seventeenth-century Massachusetts." *Old-Time New England*, 60 (April–June 1970), 110–49.

Forman, Henry Chandlee. *The Architecture of the Old South: The Medieval Style, 1585 –1850*. Cambridge, Mass.: Harvard Univ. Press, 1948.

——. *Early Mansion and Plantation Houses of Maryland*. Easton, Md.: Author, 1934.

——. *Virginia Architecture in the Seventeenth Century*. Williamsburg, Va.: 350th Anniversary Celebration Corp., 1957.

Forrest, Earle R. *Missions and Pueblos of the Old Southwest*. Cleveland: Clark, 1929.

Foster, Stephen. *Their Solitary Way: The Puritan Social Ethic in the First Century of Settlement in New England*. New Haven: Yale Univ. Press, 1971.

Fowler, Orson Squire. *A Home for All*. New York: Fowler, 1851.

Foxfire Book, The. Ed. Eliot Wigginton. Garden City, N.J.: Doubleday, 1972.

Francaviglia, Richard V. "Main Street U.S.A.: The Creation of a Popular Image." *Landscape*, 21 (Spring 1977), 18–22.

Franklin, Benjamin. *Autobiography* [1789]. Ed. Russel B. Nye. Boston: Houghton, 1958.

Franklin, W. Neil. "Agriculture in Colonial North Carolina." *North Carolina Historical Review*, 3 (October 1926), 539–74.

Franquet, L. *Voyages et mémoires sur le Canada*. Montreal: Editions Elysée, 1974.

Franz, Alexander. *Die Kolonisation des Mississippi Tales bis zum ansgange der französischen Herrschaft*. Leipzig: Georg Wigand, 1906.

Frazier, James G. *The Magic Art and the Evolution of Kings*. London: Macmillan, 1911.

Frei, Gebhard. "Magic und Psychologie." *Neue Schweizer Rundschau*, 48 (1948/ 49), 680–88.

Freiday, Dean. "Tinton Manor: The Iron Works." New Jersey Historical Society *Proceedings,* 70 (October 1952), 250–61.

Fries, Sylvia. *The Urban Idea in Colonial America.* Phil.: Temple Univ. Press, 1977.

Frimanuslund, Rigmor. "Farm Community and Neighborhood Community." *Scandinavian Economic History Review,* 4 (1956), 62–81.

Frost, Robert. *Poetry.* Ed. Edward Connery Lathem. New York: Holt, 1969.

Fulton, Robert. *Report of the Practicability of Navigating with Steam Boats.* Phil.: Town, 1828.

––––––. *A Treatise on the Improvement of Canal Navigation.* London: Taylor, 1796.

"Furniture of School-Houses." *Farmer's Monthly Visitor,* 13 (March 1853), 88–90.

Fussell, George Edwin. *Village Life in the Eighteenth Century.* Worcester, England: Littlebury, 1947.

Gailey, Alan. "The Peasant Houses of the South-west Highlands of Scotland: Distribution, Parallels and Evolution." *Gwerin,* 3 (June 1962), 227–42.

Gallatin, Albert. "Report on Roads and Canals." *American State Papers,* Class 10 (Miscellaneous), I, 724–41.

––––––. *Writings.* Ed. Henry Adams. 1879. Reprint. New York: Antiquarian, 1960.

Gamboa, Francisco Xavier. *Comentarios a las ordenanzas de minas.* Madrid: J. Ibarra, 1761.

Garland, Hamlin. *A Son of the Middle Border.* New York: Macmillan, 1917.

Gasquet, Francis. *Parish Life in Medieval England.* London: Methuen, 1906.

Gates, Paul W. *The Farmer's Age: Agriculture, 1815–1860.* New York: Harper, 1960.

Gauthier, Raymonde. *Les manoirs du Quebec.* Quebec: Fides, 1975.

Gauthier-Larouche, G. *Evolution de la maison rurale traditionelle dans la region de Quebec.* Quebec: Laval, 1974.

Geller, Lawrence D. "Notes on Sea-Serpents of Coastal New England." *New York Folklore Quarterly,* 26 (June 1970), 153–60.

––––––. *Pilgrims in Eden: Conservation Policies at New Plymouth.* Wakefield, Mass.: Pride, 1974.

Gemmell, Alfred. *The Charcoal Iron Industry in the Perkiomen Valley.* Morristown, N.J.: Hartenstine, 1949.

General Instructions to his Deputies by the Surveyor General of the United States for the States of Ohio and Indiana and the Territory of Michigan. Cincinnati: Wood, 1833.

Geographie et histoire agraires. Nancy: Univ. de Nancy, 1959.

Gerard, E. *The Land Behind the Forest: Transylvania.* London: Blackwood, 1888.

Gerard, John. *The herbal or general history of Plants* [1633]. New York: Dover, 1975.

German Folk Tales. Ed. Jacob and Wilhelm Grimm. Trans. Francis P. Magoun and Alexander H. Krappe. Carbondale: Southern Illinois Univ. Press, 1960.

Gersung, Carl. "A Devil in Petticoats and Just Cause: Patterns of Punishment in Two New England Textile Factories." *Business History Review,* 50 (Summer 1976), 131–52.

Gibson, Charles. *The Spanish Tradition in America.* Columbia: Univ. of South Carolina Press, 1968.

Giedion, Sigfried. *Space, Time, and Architecture.* 4th ed. Cambridge, Mass.: Harvard Univ. Press, 1962.

Gilbane, Brendan F. "Pawtucket Village Mechanics—Iron, Ingenuity, and the Cotton Revolution." *Rhode Island History* 34 (February 1975), 2–11.

Giles, John Allen. *History of the Parish and Town of Brampton.* Brampton, England: Author, 1848.

Gille, B. "Le Moulin a eau, une revolution technique medievale." *Techniques et civilisations,* 3 (1954), 1–15.

Gillespie, William Mitchell. *A Manual of the Principles and Practice of Road-Making.* New York: Barnes, 1848.

Gilpin, Joshua. "Journal of a Tour from Philadelphia." *Pennsylvania Magazine of History and Biography,* 50 (1926), 64–78, 163–78, 380–82.

Glacken, Clarence. *Traces on the Rhodian Shore: Nature and Culture in Western Thought from Ancient Times to the End of the Eighteenth Century.* (Berkeley: Univ. of Calif. Press, 1967.

Glasser, Christophe. *The Compleat Chymist.* London: J. Starkey, 1677.

Glassie, Henry. *Folk Housing in Middle Virginia.* Knoxville: Univ. of Tennessee Press, 1975.

———. *Pattern in the Material Folk Culture of the Eastern United States.* Phil.: Univ. of Penn. Press, 1968.

———. "The Pennsylvania Barn in the South." *Pennsylvania Folklife,* 15 (Winter 1965–66), 8–19.

Glick, Thomas F. *Irrigation and Society in Medieval Valencia.* Cambridge, Mass.: Harvard Univ. Press, 1970.

———. *The Old World Background of the Irrigation System of San Antonio, Texas.* El Paso: Univ. of Texas at El Paso, 1972.

Glikson, Arthur. *The Ecological Basis of Planning.* Ed. Lewis Mumford. The Hague: Nijhoff, 1971.

Glorez, Andreas. *Vollständige Hauss- und Land- Bibliothec.* Regensburg: Q. Heyl, 1701.

Godsoe, John. "Plan of Division of John Hale's Dec'd, His Land." December 17, 1739, Whipple Family Papers, New Hampshire Historical Society.

"Going to the Fair." *New England Farmer,* 13 (November 1858), 68.

Gold, Thomas, and Steven Soter. "The Deep-Earth-Gas Hypothesis." *Scientific American,* 242 (June 1980), 154–61.

Gomme, George L. *The Village Community, with Special Reference to the Origin and Form of its Survivals in Britain.* London: Scott, 1890.

Goodrich, Carter. "National Planning of Internal Improvements." *Political Science Quarterly,* 63 (March 1948), 16–44.

Goodrich, Massena. *Historical Sketch of the Town of Pawtucket.* Pawtucket, R.I.: Nickerson, 1876.

Gordon, Lesley. *Green Magic: Flowers, Plants, and Herbs in Lore and Legend.* London: Ebury, 1977.

Gordon, Thomas Francis. *A Collection of the Laws of the United States relating to Revenue, Navigation, and Commerce, and Light-houses.* Phil.: Ashmead, 1844.
———. *A Gazetteer of the State of Pennsylvania.* Phil.: Belknap, 1832.
Gorham, B. Weed. *Camp Meeting Manual.* Boston: Degen, 1854.
Gould, Mary Earle. *The Early American House.* Rutland, Vt.: Tuttle, 1965.
Graham, John. "Account of the Coal Mines." *American Journal of Science,* 1 (1818), 125–30.
Grainge, William. *The Vale of Mowbray.* London: Simpkin, 1859.
Grande Encyclopedie. Paris: Societé Anonyme de la Grande Encyclopédie, n.d.
Granger, Byrd H. *A Motif Index for Lost Mines and Treasures.* Tucson: Univ. of Arizona Press, 1977.
Grass: The Yearbook of Agriculture. Washington, D.C. United States Department of Agriculture, 1948.
Grave, William Hugh. "Travel Journal." Ed. Gregory A. Stiverson and Patrick H. Butler. *Virginia Magazine of History and Biography,* 85 (January 1977), 18–44.
Gray, John. "American Forest Trees." *North American Review,* 44 (April 1837), 334–61.
Gray, Lewis C. *History of Agriculture in the Southern United States to 1860.* New York: Carnegie Institution, 1941.
Greeley, Horace et al. *The Great Industries of the United States.* Hartford: Burr, 1873.
Green, Samuel. *Boundary Lines of Old Groton.* Groton, Mass.: Author, 1885.
Greenleaf, Richard E. "Land and Water in Mexico and New Mexico." *NMHR,* 47 (April 1972), 85–112.
Gregg, Josiah. *Commerce of the Prairies* [1844]. Ed. Max L. Moorhead. Norman: Univ. of Oklahoma Press, 1954.
———. *Scenes and Incidents in the Western Prairies.* Phil.: Moore, 1857.
Gregor, Walter. *Folklore of Scotland.* London: Folk-Lore Society, 1881.
Greven, Philip J., Jr. *Four Generations: Population, Land, and Family in Colonial Andover, Massachusetts.* Ithaca: Cornell Univ. Press, 1970.
Grigson, Geoffrey. "The Room Outdoors." *Landscape,* 4 (Winter 1954–55), 25–29.
Grimm, Jacob. *Deutsche Mythologie.* Berlin: Dümmlers, 1876.
———. *Deutsche Rechtsalterthümer.* Ed. Andreas Heusler and Rudolf Hübner. Leipzig: Dieterich'sche, 1899.
———, and Wilhelm Grimm. *Deutsches Wörterbuch.* Leipzig: S. Hirzel, 1885.
Grittinger, Henry C. *Cornwall Furnace and the Cornwall Ore Banks.* Lebanon, Penn.: Lebanon Courier, 1901.
Grotenfelt, Gösta. *Det primitiva jordbrukets metoder i Finland under den historiska tiden.* Helsingfors: Simeli, 1899.
Grund, Francis J. *The Americans.* London: Longman, 1837.
Gschwend, Max. *Schweizer Bauernhäuser.* Bern: Haupt, 1971.
Gubernatis, Angelo. *Mythologie des plantes ou les legendes du regne vegetal.* Paris: Reinwald, 1878.

Guide des chemins pour aller et venir par tout le Royaume de France et autres pays circonuoisins. Lyon: Benoist Rigaud, 1596.

Güntz, Max. *Handbuch der Landwirtschaftlichen Literatur.* Leipzig: Voight, 1897.

Haefner, Harold. *Höhenstufen, offentliche Ländereien und private Landnutzung auf der Ostseite der Sierra Nevada.* Zurich: Juris, 1970.

Hager, Franziska, and Hans Heyn. *Das alte Dorf.* Rosenheim: Rosenheimer, 1977.

Hale, Matthew. *The Primitive Origination of Mankind Considered and Examined According to the Light of Nature.* London: W. Godbid, 1677.

Hall, Basil. *Forty Etchings.* Edinburgh: Cadell, 1829.

Hall, Hubert. *Society in the Elizabethan Age.* London: Swan, 1902.

Hall, Thomas. *Funebria Florae, The Downfall of May Games.* London: Henry Mortlock, 1660.

Hall, William. "Journal." Ed. Jay Monaghan. ISHS *Journal,* 39 (March 1946), 214–42.

Hall, William L. *Tree Planting on Rural School Grounds.* Washington, D.C.,: Government Printing Office, 1901.

Halliday, F. C. "Methodism in Southeastern Indiana." Ed. Allen Wiley. *Indiana Magazine of History,* 23 (June 1927), 3–64, 130–216, 239–332, 393–466.

Halsted, Byron. *Barn Plans and Outbuildings.* New York: Judd, 1898.

Hamerton, Philip Gilbert. *Landscape.* Boston: Roberts, 1890.

Hammond, John. *Leah and Rachel, or, the Two Faithful Sisters, Virginia and Maryland.* London: T. Mabb. 1656.

Hampe, Theodor. *Die Fahrenden Leute in Der Deutschen Vergangenheit.* Leipzig: Diederichs, 1902.

Handwörterbuch des Deutschen Aberglaubens. Ed. E. Hoffman-Krayer. Berlin: De Gruyter, 1927–42.

Hardoy, Jorge E. "La forma de las ciudades coloniales en Hispanoamerica." *Psicon,* 2 (October–December 1975), 8–30.

Harker, J. G. "First Hand Observations." Trans. Richard B. O'Connell. *Mississippi Valley Collection Bulletin,* 3 (Fall 1970), 1–74, and 4 (Spring 1971), 85–118.

Harper, Roland M. "Changes in Forest Area of New England in Three Centuries." *Journal of Forest History,* 16 (April 1918), 441–52.

Harris, Michael H. "Books on the Frontier: The Extent and Nature of Book Ownership in Southern Indiana, 1800–1850." *Library Quarterly,* 42 (October 1972), 416–30.

————. "The General Store as an Outlet for Books on the Southern Frontier, 1800–1850." *Journal of Library History,* 8 (July–October 1973), 124–32.

Harris, R. C. *The Seigneurial System in Early Canada.* Quebec: Laval, 1968.

Harris, Thaddeus M. *Journal of a Tour into the Territory Northwest of the Alleghany Mountains.* Boston: Manning, 1805.

Hart, John Fraser. *The Look of the Land.* Englewood Cliffs, N.J.: Prentice-Hall, 1975.

Hartley, E. N. *Ironworks on the Saugus.* Norman: Univ. of Oklahoma Press, 1957.

Haupt, Hermann. *The General Theory of Bridge Construction*. New York: Appleton, 1851.

Hawes, J. H. *Manual of United States Surveying*. Phil.: Lippincott, 1868.

Hawthorne, Nathaniel. *Complete Works*. Boston: Houghton, 1882.

_____. *Mosses from an Old Manse*. Boston: Houghton, 1883.

_____. *The Scarlet Letter*. Boston: Houghton, 1883.

Hayes, R. H., and J. G. Rutter. *Cruck-Framed Buildings in Ryedale and Eskdale*. Scarborough, England: Scarborough Arch. Soc., 1972.

Hazard, Samuel. *Annals of Pennsylvania*. Phil.: Hazard, 1850.

Hegi, Friedrich. *Geschichte der Zunft zur Schmiden*. Zurich: Druckerei Amberger, 1912.

Henderson, William. *Notes on the Folk Lore of the Northern Counties . . . and the Borders*. London: Longmans, 1866.

Henlein, Paul C. *Cattle Kingdom in the Ohio Valley, 1783–1860*. Lexington: Kentucky Univ. Press, 1959.

_____. "Early Cattle Ranges of the Ohio Valley." *Agricultural History*, 35 (July 1961), 150–54.

Hennepin, Louis. *Description de la Louisiane*. Paris: Sebastien Hure, 1683.

Henning, Rudolf. *Das Deutsche Haus in seiner historischen entwickelung*. Strassburg: Karl J. Trubner, 1882.

Herberstein, S. *Description of Moscow*. Trans. J. B. C. Grundy. London: Dent, 1969.

Herman, Augustine. *Virginia and Maryland*. London: John Seller, 1673.

Hermes, F. P. *Handbuch . . . Forst- Jagd- und Fischerei Gesetzgebung*. Aachen: La Ruelle, 1830.

Hesford, Walter. "Too Happy Husbandmen: Addresses Given to Middlesex Farmers from the 1820s to 1860." *Concord Saunterer*, 14 (Summer 1979), 17–18.

Hilf, Richard B., and Fritz Röhrig. *Wald und Weidwerk: in Geschichte und Gegenwart*. Potsdam: Akademische Verlagsgesellschaft, 1938.

Hill, Christopher. *Change and Continuity in Seventeenth-Century England*. Cambridge, Mass.: Harvard Univ. Press, 1975.

Hill, Forest G. *Roads, Rails, and Waterways: The Army Engineers and Early Transportation*. Norman: Univ. of Oklahoma Press, 1957.

Hine, Orlo D. *Early Lebanon*. Hartford: Brainard, 1880.

His, Rudolf. *Das Strafrecht des deutschen Mittelatlers*. Leipzig: Theodor Weicher, 1920.

Historical Documents Relating to New Mexico, Nueva Vizcaya, and Approaches Thereto, to 1773. Ed. Charles Hackett. *Spanish Tradition in America*, pp. 128–34.

Hitchcock, Henry Russell. *Rhode Island Architecture*. Cambridge, Mass.: MIT Press, 1968.

Hitzer, Hans. *Die Strasse: Vom Trampelpfad zur Autobahn*. Munich, Callwey, 1971.

Hobsbawm, E. J. *Bandits*. London: Weidenfeld, 1969.

Hoffman, Daniel. *Form and Fable in American Fiction*. New York: Norton, 1965.

Hoffman, I. "Minisink, N.J." *New York Magazine,* 5 (June 1794), 322.

——. "Pahaquarrie." *New York Magazine,* 5 (February 1794), 66.

Holbein, Hans (the younger). *Les Images de la mort.* Lyons: Frellon, 1547.

Hollis, Benjamin Samuel. *The Mouth of the Pit, or the Hartley Colliery Calamity: A Sermon.* London: n.p., 1862.

Hollweg, August. *Das Zunftige Richtfest.* Munster: Aschendorff, 1951.

Holmsen, Andreas. "The Old Norwegian Peasant Community." *Scandinavian Economic History Review,* 4 (1956), 17–32.

Horwitz, Hugo T. "Uber das Aufkommen, die erste Entwicklung und die Verbreitung von Windrädern." *Beiträge zur Geschichte der Technik und Industrie,* 22 (1933), 93–102.

Hoskins, W. G. *English Landscapes.* London: BBC, 1973.

——. *The Making of the English Landscape.* London: Hodder, 1955.

——. *One Man's England.* London: BBC, 1976.

Houghton, Thomas. *Rara Avis in Terris: or the Compleat Miner.* London: William Cooper, 1681.

Howell, Charles, and Allan Keller. *The Mill at Philipsburg Manor Upper Mills.* Tarrytown, N.Y.: Sleepy Hollow, 1977.

Hubka, Thomas C. "The Connected Farm Buildings of Southwestern Maine." *Pioneer America,* 9 (December 1977), 143–78.

Hue, Otto. *Die Bergarbeiter.* Stuttgart: Diek, 1910 and 1913.

Hueppi, Adolf. *Kunst und Kult der Grab Stätten.* Olten: Walter, 1968.

Hulbert, Archer Butler. *Soil: Its Influence on the History of the United States.* New Haven: Yale Univ. Press, 1930.

Hüllmann, Karl Dietrich. *Staedtewesen des Mittelalters.* Bonn: Marcus, 1826.

Humboldt, Alexander. *Political Essay on the Kingdom of New Spain.* Trans. John Black. London: Longman, 1811.

Husband, Timothy. *The Wild Man: Medieval Myth and Symbolism.* New York: Metropolitan Museum of Art, 1980.

"Husbandman." *Farmer's Cabinet,* 1 (July 1, 1836), 14.

Husslage, G. *Viere voor: Herinneringen van een Zaanse molenmaker.* Amsterdam: Heijnis, 1966.

——. *Windmolen.* Amsterdam: n.p., 1968.

Hutchins, Wells A. "The Community Acequia: Its Origin and Development." *Southwestern Historical Quarterly,* 31 (January 1928), 261–84.

Hyde, W. W. "The Ancient Appreciation of Mountain Scenery." *Classical Journal,* 11 (1915), 70–85.

Hylton, William H. *Build it Better Yourself.* Emmaus, Penn.: Rodale, 1977.

Imlay, Gilbert. *A Topographical Description of the Western Territory.* London: J. Debrett, 1797.

"Importance of Agriculture." *Farmer's Cabinet,* 1 (February 15, 1837), 225–26.

"Instructions to Governor Yeardley, 1618." *Virginia Magazine of History and Biography,* 2 (October 1894), 154–65.

"Instructions to Peralta by Viceroy." Trans. Ireneo L. Chaves. *NMHR*, (1929), 178–87.

Interpretation of Ordinary Landscapes, The. Ed. D. W. Meinig. New York: Oxford, 1979.

Irving, Washington. *The Sketch-Book.* New York: Van Winkle, 1819.

"Is the Modern Camp Meeting a Failure?" *Methodist Quarterly Review,* 13 (October 1861), 600–01.

Isle, Guillaume. *Atlas nouveau contenant toutes les parties du monde.* Amsterdam: Jean Covens, 1733.

Izquierdo, Sebastian. *Practica de los Exercicios.* Rome: Varese, 1675.

Jackson, John Brinckerhoff. *American Space: The Centennial Years: 1865–1876.* New York: Norton, 1972.

————. "Catalog of New Mexico Farm Building Terms." *Landscape, 1 (Winter 1952), 31–32.*

————. "First Comes the House." *Landscape,* 9 (Winter 1959-60), 26–32.

————. "Ghosts at the Door." *Landscape,* 1 (Autumn 1951), 3–9.

————. *Landscapes.* Amherst: Univ. of Mass. Press, 1970.

————. "The Meaning of *Landscape.*" *Kulturgeografi,* 88 (1965), 47–50.

————. *The Necessity for Ruins and Other Topics.* Amherst: Univ. of Mass. Press, 1980.

————. "The Order of a Landscape: Reason and Religion in Newtonian America." *Interpretation of Ordinary Landscapes,* pp. 153–63.

————. "The Vanishing Epitaph: From Monument to Place." *Landscape,* 17 (1967), 22–26.

Jacobs, Heinrich. *Sechstausend Jahre Brot.* Hamburg: Rowohlt, 1954.

Jacobs, Joshua. "Record Book." Norwell Historical Society Library, Norwell, Mass.

Jakle, John. *Images of the Ohio Valley: A Historical Geography of Travel, 1740 to 1860.* New York: Oxford, 1977.

James, Edwin O. *Seasonal Feasts and Festivals.* New York: Barnes and Noble, 1961.

James, Henry. *The Ambassadors* [1903]. New York: Norton, 1964.

————. *The American Scene.* New York: Harper, 1907.

Jans, Jan. *Landliche Baukunst in den östlichen Niederlanden.* Munster: Aschendorffsche, 1970.

Janson, Charles William. *The Stranger in America.* London: Albion, 1807.

Jaray, Cornell. *The Mills of Long Island.* Port Washington, N.Y.: Friedman, 1962.

Jeanee, Donald G. "The Traditional Upland South Cemetery." *Landscape,* 18 (Spring 1969), 39–41.

Jefferson, Thomas. *Farm Book.* Ed. Edwin M. Betts. Charlottesville: Univ. Press of Va., 1977.

————. *Notes on the State of Virginia* [1785]. Ed. Thomas Perkins Abernathy. New York: Harper, 1964.

————. *Writings.* Ed. Andrew A. Lipscomb. Washington, D.C.: Thomas Jefferson Memorial Ass., 1903.

Jefferys, Thomas. "A Map of . . . New England." London: Jefferys, 1755.

Jenkins, J. Marshall. "Ground Rules of Welsh Houses: A Primary Analysis." *Folk Life,* 5 (1967), 65–91.

Jenkins, W. H. "A Model Rural School-House." *Craftsman,* 20 (May 1911), 212–15.

Joendl, J. P. *Die Landwirtschaftliche Baukunst.* Prague: Schönfeld, 1829.

Johnson, Amandus. *The Swedish Settlements on the Delaware, 1638–1664.* Phil.: Univ. of Penn. Press, 1911.

Johnson, Charles A. *The Frontier Camp Meeting.* Dallas: Southern Methodist Univ. Press, 1955.

––––––. "The Frontier Camp-Meeting: Contemporary and Historical Appraisals." *Mississippi Valley Historical Review,* 37 (1950), 91–110.

Johnson, Clifton, *The Country School in New England.* New York: Appleton, 1893.

––––––. *The Farmer's Boy.* New York: Appleton, 1894.

Johnson, Edward. *Wonder-working Providence* [1654]. Ed. J. F. Jameson. New York: Scribner's, 1910.

Johnson, Hildegard Binder. *Order Upon the Land: The United States Rectangular Land Survey and the Upper Mississippi Country.* New York: Oxford Univ. Press, 1976.

––––––. *The Orderly Landscape: Landscape Tastes and the United States Survey.* Minneapolis: James Ford Bell Library, 1977.

––––––. "Rational and Ecological Aspects of the Quarter Section: An Example from Minnesota." *Geographical Review,* 47 (1957), 330–48.

Johnson, Oliver. *A Home in the Woods.* Indianapolis: Indiana Historical Soc., 1951.

Johnson, S. W. *Rural Economy.* New York: Riley, 1806.

Jones, Charles C. *The Dead Towns of Georgia.* Savannah: Morning News, 1878.

Jones, Chester Lloyd. *The Economic History of the Anthracite-Tidewater Canals.* Phil.: Univ. of Penn. Press, 1908.

Jones, E. L. "Creative Disruptions in American Agriculture, 1620–1820." *Agricultural History,* 43 (October 1974), 510–28.

Jones, Howard Mumford. *O Strange New World: American Culture, The Formative Years.* New York: Viking, 1967.

Jones, Hugh. *The Present State of Virginia* [1753]. Ed. Richard L. Morton. Chapel Hill: Univ. of N.C. Press, 1956.

Jordan, Terry G. "Evolution of the American Windmill: A Study in Diffusion and Modification." *Pioneer America,* 5 (July 1973), 3–12.

Judd, Sylvester (1813–1853). *Richard Edney and the Governor's Family: A Rus-urban Tale.* Boston: Phillips, Sampson, 1850.

Judd, Sylvester (1789–1860). *History of Hadley.* Springfield, Mass.: Huntting, 1905.

Julien, Carl, and Daniel W. Hollis. *Look to the Rock: One Hundred Ante-Bellum Presbyterian Churches of the South.* Richmond, Va.: Knox, 1961.

Jung, C. G. *Alchemical Studies.* Trans. R. F. C. Hull. Princeton: Princeton Univ. Press, 1970.

_____. *Psychology and Alchemy.* Trans. R. F. C. Hull. Princeton: Princeton Univ. Press, 1968.

Kalm, Peter. "Observations on the Fences of North America." Trans. Esther L. Larsen. *Agricultural History,* 21 (1947), 75–78.

_____. *Travels in North America* [1749]. Ed. Adolph B. Benson. New York: Dover, 1937.

Kaufman, Henry J. *The American Farmhouse.* New York: Hawthorne, 1975.

Keach, Horace A. *Burrillville, As It Was, and As It Is.* Providence: Knowles, 1856.

Kemper, Jackson. "American Charcoal Making in the Era of the Cold-Blast Furnace." *Regional Review,* 5 (July 1940), 3–15.

Kendall, Edward Augustus. *Travels Through the Northern Parts of the United States.* New York: Riley, 1809.

Kenney, William H. "Jacob Taylor and His Almanacs." *Pennsylvania Folklife,* 14 (Spring 1965), 32–35.

Kerry, Theodore W. "The Long Pond Ironworks: A North Jersey Plantation." *Pioneer America,* 2 (July 1970), 11–19.

Kersey, John. *A New English Dictionary.* London: Bonwicke, 1702.

Kircher, Anthanasius. *Mundus subterraneus.* Amsterdam: Janssonium, 1664.

Kirnbauer, Franz. *Schlägel und Eisen und andere Symbole der Berg- und Hüttenleute.* Vienna: Montan-Verlag, 1975.

Klaar, Adalbert. *Die Siedlungs- und hausformen des Wiener Waldes.* Stuttgart: Engelhorns, 1936.

Kniffen, Fred. "Folk Housing: Key to Diffusion." AAG, *Annals,* 55 (December 1965), 549–77.

Kniffen, Fred, and Henry Glassie. "Building in Wood in the Eastern United States: A Time-Place Perspective." *Geographical Review,* 56 (1966), 48–65.

Knudtsen, Molly Flagg. *Here is Our Valley.* Reno: Agricultural Experiment Station, 1975.

Kocher, A. Lawrence. "Color in Early American Architecture with Special Reference to the Origin and Development of House Painting." *Architectural Record,* 64 (October 1928), 278–90.

Korson, George Gershon. *Black Rock: Mining Folklore of the Pennsylvania Dutch.* Balt.: Johns Hopkins Univ. Press, 1960.

Köstler, J. N. *Wald-Mensch-Kultur.* Hamburg: Parey, 1967.

Krappe, Alexander Haggerty. "Zur Wielandssage." *Archiv für das Studium der neueren Sprachen und Literaturen,* 158 (1930), 9–23.

Ladurie, Le Roy. *Carnival in Romans.* Trans. Mary Feeney. New York: Braziller, 1979.

LaFayette, Kenneth D. *Flaming Brands: Fifty Years of Iron Making in the Upper Peninsula of Michigan, 1848–1898.* Marquette: Northern Michigan Univ. Press, 1977.

Lanaconing Journals: The Founding of a Coal and Iron Community. Ed. Katherine A. Harvey. Phil.: American Philosophical Society, 1977.

Landrin, Armand. *Les Monstres marins.* Paris: Hachette, 1867.

Lang, M. F. "New Spain's Mining Depression and the Supply of Quicksilver from

Peru, 1600–1700." *Hispanic-American Historical Review,* 48 (November 1968), 632–41.

Langewiesche, Wolfgang. *A Flier's World.* New York: McGraw-Hill, 1951.

———. *I'll Take the High Road.* New York: Harcourt, 1930.

———. "The U.S.A. from the Air." *Harper's,* 21 (October 1950), 176–88.

Larcom, Lucy. *A New England Girlhood* [1889]. New York: Corinth, 1961.

———. *Poems.* Boston: Houghton, 1888.

Lascault, Gilbert. *Le Monstre dans l'art occidental.* Paris: Klineksieck, 1973.

Laslett, Peter. *The World We Have Lost: England Before the Industrial Age.* New York: Scribner's, 1971.

Lauwe, P. H. Chombart. "Le logement, le menage et l'espace familial." *Information Sociales,* 9 (1955), 956–80.

Laws and Customs of the Mines in the Forest of Dean. Ed. T. Houghton. London: Wm. Cooper, 1687.

Laws of the State of New York. Albany: Weed, Parsons, 1886.

Lawton, Arthur. "The Ground Rules of Folk Architecture." *Pennsylvania Folklife,* 23 (Autumn 1973), 13–19.

"Laying Out and Dividing Farms." *Illustrated Annual Register of Rural Affairs for 1855-6-7.* Albany: Luther Tucker, 1873, 233–38.

LeBlanc, R. G. *Location of Manufacturing in New England in the Nineteenth Century.* Hanover, N.H.: Geography Publications at Dartmouth, 1969.

Lecoeur, Jules. *Esquisses du Bocage Normand.* Conde-sur Noireau: L. Morel, 1883.

Leech, Carl Addison. "Sharon Hollow: Story of an Early Mulay Sawmill of Michigan." *Michigan Historical Magazine,* 17 (Summer 1933), 377–92.

Leeds, Daniel. *The American Almanac.* New York: Bradford, 1705.

LeFevre, Nicholas. *A Compleat Body of Chymistry.* London: Octavian Pulleyn, 1664.

Lefler, Hugh T., and William S. Powell. *Colonial North Carolina: A History.* New York: Scribner's, 1973.

Leighton, Ann. *Early American Gardens.* Boston: Houghton, 1970.

Leiper, G. G., and W. Martin. *Report of the Committee . . . on . . . Manufactories.* Chester, Penn.: Lescure, 1826.

Lelievre, Pierre. *La Vie des cités de' l'antiquité à nous jours.* Paris: Bourrelier, 1950.

Lemon, James T. *The Best Poor Man's Country: A Geographical Study of Early Southeastern Pennsylvania.* New York: Norton, 1976.

———. "Urbanization and the Development of Eighteenth-Century Southeastern Pennsylvania and Adjacent Delaware." *WMQ,* 3d ser., 24 (1967), 501–24.

Lenau, Nicholas. *Sammtliche Werke.* Stuttgart: Cotta'scher, 1855.

Lesley, J. P. *The Iron Manufacturer's Guide to the Furnaces . . . of the United States.* New York: Wiley, 1859.

"Letter." *Farmer's Monthly Visitor,* 12 (February 1852), 42.

Letters from New England: The Massachusetts Bay Colony, 1629–1638. Ed. Everett Emerson. Amherst: Univ. of Mass. Press, 1976.

Lewis, Peirce. "Axioms of the Landscape: Some Guides to the American Scene." *Journal of Architectural Education,* 30 (September 1976), 6–9.

———. "Common Houses, Cultural Spoor." *Landscape,* 19 (January 1975), 1–22.

_____. "Geography of Old Houses." *Earth and Mineral Sciences,* 39 (February 1970), 33–37.

_____. "Small Town in Pennsylvania." AAG *Annals,* 62 (1972), 323–51.

Lewis, Ronald L. "Slave Families at Early Chesapeake Ironworks." *Virginia Magazine of History and Biography,* 86 (April 1978), 169–79.

_____. "The Use and Extent of Slave Labor in the Virginia Iron Industry: The Ante-Bellum Era." *West Virginia History,* 38 (January 1977), 141–56.

Lewis, Winslow. *Description of the Light Houses on the Coast of the United States.* Boston: T. G. Bangs, 1817.

Leyen, F. von der, and A. Spamer. *Die Altdeutschen Wandteppiche in Regensburger Rathaus.* Regensburg: Habbel, 1910.

Leyland, Herbert T. "Early Years of the Hope Cotton Manufacturing Company." *Rhode Island History,* 25 (January 1966), 25–32.

Lieber, Francis. *Plantations for Slave Labor the Death of Yeomanry.* Phil.: C. Sherman, 1863.

Life on the Chesapeake and Ohio Canal [1859]. Ed. Ella E. Clark and Thomas F. Hahn. York, Penn.: American Canal and Transportation Center, 1975.

Lillard, Richard G. *The Great Forest.* New York: Knopf, 1948.

Lipchitz, Joseph W. "The Golden Age." *Cotton Was King,* pp. 80–104.

Lippard, George. *The Quaker City.* Phil.: Peterson, 1845.

Litchfield, Israel. "Diary." Ed. Richard Brigham Johnson. *New England Historical and Genealogical Register,* 129 (April, July, October 1975), 150–71, 250–69, 361–78.

Lockart, James. *Spanish Peru: A Colonial Society.* Madison: Univ. of Wisconsin Press, 1968.

Lockridge, Kenneth A. *A New England Town: The First Hundred Years: Dedham, Massachusetts, 1636–1736.* New York: Norton, 1970.

Loehr, Rodney C. "Self-Sufficiency on the Farm, 1759–1819." *Agricultural History,* 26 (April 1952), 37–42.

Lombard, Maurice. *Les metaux dans l'ancien monde du Ve au XIe siècle.* Paris: Mouton, 1974.

Lomnitz, Larissa Adler. *Networks and Marginality: Life in a Mexican Shantytown.* New York: Academic, 1977.

Long, John D. "The Nickel Mines of Lancaster County." Lancaster County Historical Society, *Journal,* 80 (1976), 157–76.

Long, John Dixon. *Pictures of Slavery.* Phil.: Author, 1857.

Longfellow, Henry Wadsworth. *Complete Poetical Works.* Boston: Houghton, 1914.

Lounsbury, Carl. "The Development of Domestic Architecture in the Albemarle Region." *North Carolina Historical Review,* 54 (Winter 1977), 17–18.

Lovejoy, Arthur O. "The First Gothic Revival and the Return to Nature." *Modern Language Notes,* 23 (1932), 419–46.

Lüthi, Max. *Once Upon a Time: On the Nature of Fairy Tales.* Trans. Lee Chadeayne and Paul Gottwald. Bloomington: Indiana Univ. Press, 1976.

Luxan, Diego Perez. "Account of the Antonio De Espejo Expedition into New Mexico" [1582]. *The Rediscovery of New Mexico*, pp. 153–212.

Maaskant, A. A. C. *Oude Boerderijen.* Uitgeverig: N. Klawer, 1969.

Madison, James. "No. Fourteen." *The Federalist.* Washington, D.C.: Gideon, 1818, pp. 81–87.

Magee, Henry. *The Miller in Eighteenth-Century Virginia.* Williamsburg: Colonial Williamsburg Foundation, 1958.

Magnus, Albertus. *Book of Minerals* [1262]. Trans. Dorothy Wyckoff. Oxford: Clarendon, 1967.

Mahon, D. H. *Civil Engineering for the Use of Cadets.* New York: Wiley, 1852.

Maier, Michael. *Chymisches Cabinet.* Frankfurt: Oehrling, 1708.

_____. *Emblemata Nova de secretis naturae.* Oppenheim: H. Galleri, 1618.

Manlove, Edward. *The Liberties and Customes of the Lead Mines within the Wapentake of Wirksworth.* London [?]: n.p., 1653.

Mannhardt, Wilhelm. *Wald- und Feldkulte.* Berlin: Borntraeger, 1875.

Mantel, Kurt. *Geschichte des Weihnachtsbaum.* Hannover: Schoper, 1975.

Markale, Jean. *Les Celtes et la Civilisation celtique.* Paris: Payot, 1976.

Markham, Gervase. *The English Husbandman.* London: William Sheares, 1635.

Marryat, Frederick. *A Diary in America.* London: Longman, 1839.

Martini, Fritz. *Das Bauertum im deutschen Schriften von den Anfängen bis zum 16. Jahrhundert.* Halle: Niemeyer, 1944.

Marx, Leo. *The Machine in the Garden: Technology and the Pastoral Ideal in America.* New York: Oxford Univ. Press, 1969.

Marzell, Heinrich. *Himmelsbrot und Teufelsleiten: Volkstürmliche Pflanzennamen aus Bayer.* Munich: Bayerische Heimatsforschung, 1951.

_____. *Die Pflanzen im deutschen Volksleben.* Jena: Diederichs, 1925.

_____. *Volksbotanik, Die Pflanze im deutschen Brauchtum.* Berlin: Enckehaus, 1935.

Mason, Julian. "The Etymology of 'Buckaroo.'" *American Speech,* 35 (February 1960), 51–55.

Mather, Cotton. *Bonifacius: An Essay Upon the Good* [1710]. Ed. David Levin. Cambridge, Mass.: Harvard Univ. Press, 1966.

_____. *Magnalia Christi Americana.* London: Parkhurst, 1702.

_____. *A Short Essay to Preserve and Strengthen the Good Impressions Produced by Earthquakes.* Boston: S. Kneeland, 1727.

_____. *The Terror of the Lord: Some Account of the Earthquake that Shook New England in the Night.* Boston: S. Kneeland, 1727.

Mather, Eugene Cotton, and John Fraser Hart. "Fences and Farms." *Geographical Review,* 44 (April 1945), 201–23.

Mather, Increase. *A Discourse Concerning the Uncertainty of the Times of Men.* Boston: B. Green, 1697.

_____. *An Earnest Exhortation to the Inhabitants of New England.* Boston: John Foster, 1676.

Maurer, Charles Lewis. "Early Lutheran Education in Pennsylvania." Pennsylvania German Society, *Proceedings,* 40 (n.d.), 1–285.

McCourt, Desmond. "The Outshot House-Type and its Distribution in County Londonderry." *Ulster Folklife*, 2 (1956), 27–34.

McBride, George McCutchen. *The Land Systems of Mexico*. New York: American Geographical Society, 1923.

McDermott, John Francis. *The French in the Mississippi Valley*. Urbana: Univ. of Illinois Press, 1965.

McDuffee, Franklin. *History of the Town of Rochester, New Hampshire*. Manchester, N.H.: Clarke, 1892.

McFadden, I. M. "A Hoosier General Store in 1847." *Indiana Magazine of History* 35 (September 1939), 299–302.

McLean, Albert S. Jr. "Thoreau's True Meridian: Natural Fact and Metaphor." *American Quarterly*, 20 (Fall 1968), 566–79.

McLoskey, Donald N. "English Open Fields as Behavior Toward Risk." *Research in Economic History*, 1 (1976), 124–70.

McManis, Douglas. *The Initial Evaluation and Utilization of the Illinois Prairie*. Chicago: Univ. of Chicago Dept. of Geography, 1964.

McNemar, Richard. *The Kentucky Revival: or a Short History of the Late Extraordinary Outpouring of the Spirit of God in the Western States of America*. Pittsfield, Mass.: Allen, 1808.

McWilliams, Carey. *North from Mexico*. New York: Greenwood, 1968.

Mead, Sidney E. *The Lively Experiment: The Shaping of Christianity in America*. New York: Harper, 1963.

Mecham, J. C. "The *Real de Minas* as a Political Institution." *Hispanic-American Historical Review*, 27 (1927), 45–83.

Megenberg, Conrad. *Buch der Natur*. Augsberg: Johann Bämler, 1475.

Meinig, D. W., ed. *The Interpretation of Ordinary Landscapes*. New York: Oxford, 1979.

Meister, A. "Die Anfänge des Eisenindustrie in der Grafschaft Mark." *Beiträge zur Geschichte Dortmunds und der Grafschaft Mark*, 4 (1909), 130–49.

Metizen, August. *Siedelung und Agrarwesen der Westgermanen und Ostgermanen*. Berlin: Hertz, 1895, 4 vols.

Mejborg, Reinhold Frederick Severin. *Das Bauernhaus im Herzogthum Schleswig und das Leben des schleswigischen Bauernstandes*. Schleswig: Bergas, 1896.

Melville, Herman [Salvator R. Tarnmoor]. "The Encantadas, or Enchanted Isles." *Putnam's Monthly Magazine*, 3 (March, April, May 1854), 311–19, 345–55, 460–66.

———. *Great Short Works*. Ed. Warner Berthoff. New York: Harper, 1971.

———. *Israel Potter: His Fifty Years of Exile* [1854]. New York: Warner, 1974.

———. *Letters*. Ed. Merrell R. Davis and William H. Gilman. New Haven: Yale Univ. Press, 1960.

Meredith, Mamie J. "The Importance of the Fence to the American Pioneer." *Nebraska History*, 32 (1951), 94–107.

———. "The Nomenclature of American Pioneer Fences." *Southern Folklore Quarterly*, 15 (June 1951), 109–51.

Merrick, J. M. "The Art of Learning to Read." *Farmer's Monthly Visitor*, 12 (September 1852), 280–82.

———. "Claims of Common Schools Upon the Farmer." *Farmer's Monthly Visitor*, 12 (January, February, March 1852), 21–22, 54–56, 87–88.

Meynen, Emil. "Das pennsylvaniendeutsche Bauernland." *Deutsches Archiv für Landes- und Volksforschung*, 3 (1939), 253–92.

Miele, John R., and Hugh C. Miller. "Monocacy Aqueduct on the Chesapeake and Ohio Canal and the 'Principles of Economy, Usefulness, and Durability.'" Association for Preservation Technology, *Bulletin*, 5 (1973), 71–83.

Miller, Perry. *The New England Mind: From Colony to Province* [1953]. Boston: Beacon, 1961.

Milton, John. *Paradise Lost and Selected Poetry and Prose*. Ed. Northrop Frye. New York: Holt, 1951.

Mitchell, Arthur. *The Past in the Present: What is Civilisation?* Edinburgh: Douglas, 1880.

Mitchell, Donald G. *Dream Life* [1851]. New York: Scribner, 1857.

———. "Fences and Divisions of Farm Lands." Connecticut Board of Agriculture *Report* (1875), 171–90.

Mitchell, Robert D. *Commercialism and Frontier Perspectives in the Early Shenandoah Valley*. Charlottesville: Univ. Press of Virginia, 1977.

Mittelberger, Gottlieb. *Journey to Pennsylvania* [1756]. Trans. Oscar Handlin and John Clive. Cambridge, Mass.: Harvard Univ. Press, 1960.

Molina, Diego. "Letter" [1613]. *Narratives of Early Virginia, 1606–1625*. Ed. Lyon Gardiner Tyler. New York: Scribner's, 1907.

Möllhausen, Baldwin. *Wanderungen durch die Prärien und Wüsten des Westlichen Nordamerika*. Leipzig: Mendelsohn, 1860.

Monson, William. *Naval Tracts, or The Trade's Increase* [1615]. London: Churchill, 1703.

Montalembert, Count de. *The Monks of the West, from St. Benedict to St. Bernard*. London: Nimmo, 1896.

Montgomery, Morton L. "Early Furnaces and Forges of Berks County, Pennsylvania." *Pennsylvania Magazine of History and Biography*, 8 (March 1884), 56–81.

Moore, John Hebron. *Mississippi Agriculture, 1770–1860*. Atlanta: Emory Univ. Press, 1955.

Moorhead, Max L. *The Presidio: Bastion of the Spanish Borderlands*. Norman: Univ. of Oklahoma Press, 1975.

Morgan, Edmund S. *Virginians at Home: Family Life in the Eighteenth Century*. Williamsburg: Colonial Williamsburg Foundation, 1952.

Moriarty, Christopher. *Eels: A Natural and Unnatural History*. New York: Universe, 1978.

Morin, Edgar. *L'Homme et la mort dans l'histoire*. Paris: Correa, 1951.

Morse, Jedidiah. *The American Geography*. Elizabethtown: Shepard Kollock, 1789.

Morton, Charles. *Compendium Physicae*. Ed. Samuel E. Morison. Colonial Society of Massachusetts, Publications, 33 (1940).

Morton, Thomas. *The New English Canaan* [1637]. Ed. Charles *Francis Adams.* Boston: Prince Society, 1883.

Müller, Werner. *Die Heilige Stadt.* Stuttgart: Kahlhammer, 1961.

Mumford, Lewis. *The Culture of Cities.* Rev. ed. New York: Harcourt, 1970.

Münch, Friedrich. *Gesammelte Schriften.* St. Louis: C. Witter, 1902.

Myers, Albert Cool. *Narratives of Early Pennsylvania, West New Jersey, and Delaware, 1630–1707.* New York: Scribner's 1912.

Nairne, Thomas. *A Letter from South Carolina.* London: A. Baldwin, 1710.

Narratives of Early Carolina, 1650–1708. Ed. Alexander S. Salley, Jr. New York: Scribner's, 1911.

Narratives of Early Virginia, 1606–1625. Ed. Lyon Gardiner Tyler. New York: Scribner's, 1907.

Nash, Roderick. *Wilderness and the American Mind.* New Haven: Yale Univ. Press, 1967.

Nattrass, Mary. "Witch Posts." *Gwerin,* 3 (June 1962), 254–67.

Nead, Daniel W. *The Pennsylvania German in the Settlement of Maryland.* Lancaster, Penn.: New Era, 1914.

Neal, Daniel. *History of New-England.* London: J. Clark, 1720.

Neely, Wayne Caldwell. *The Agricultural Fair.* New York: Columbia Univ. Press, 1935.

Nef, John Ulric. *The Conquest of the Material World.* Chicago: Univ. of Chicago Press, 1964.

Nelson, Albert. "Address." *New England Farmer,* 15 (November 10, 1836), 145–47.

Nelson, Howard J. "Walled Cities of the United States." AAG, *Annals,* 51 (March 1961), 1–22.

New Hampshire Provincial Papers. Ed. Nathaniel Bouton. Concord, N.H.: Jenks, 1867.

Newbury, Nathanael. *The Yeomans Perogative, or the Honour of Husbandry.* London: J. Moxon, 1652.

Newton, Milton B., and Linda Pulliam-DiNapoli. "Log Houses as Public Occasions: A Historical Theory." AAG, *Annals,* 67 (September 1977), 360–83.

Newton, Roger Hale. "On the Tradition of Polychromy and Paint of the American Dwelling from Colonial to Present Times." Society of Architectural Historians, *Journal,* 3 (July 1943), 21–25, 43.

Nicholson, Marjorie Hope. *Mountain Gloom and Mountain Glory.* New York: Norton, 1962.

Norden, John. *The Surveiors Dialogue: Very Profitable for all Men to Peruse.* London: Thomas Snodham, 1618.

Norman, John. *The Town and Country Builder's Assistant.* Boston: Norman, 1786.

Norton, J. M. "Early Schools and Pioneer Life." Michigan Pioneer and Historical Society, *Collections,* 28 (1900), 107–10.

"Nova Virginiae Tabula." Amsterdam: Henrici Hondii, c. 1635.

Novalis [Friedrich Ludwig von Hardenberg]. *Schriften.* Ed. Ludwig Tieck and Friederich von Schlagel. Berlin: Reimer, 1826.

Odell, Clarence B. *The Functional Pattern of Villages in a Selected Area of the Corn Belt.* Chicago: Univ. of Chicago Libraries, 1939.

O'Ferrall, Simon A. *A Ramble of Six Thousand Miles.* London: Wilson, 1832.

Ogden, John C. *An Excursion into Bethelem and Nazareth in Pennsylvania.* Phil.: Grist, 1800.

Old Farmer's Almanac, 1979. Dublin, N.H.: Yankee, 1978.

Oliver, William. *Eight Months in Illinois.* Newcastle-upon-Tyne: Mitchell, 1843.

"Ollapodiana." *Knickerbocker,* 8 (September 1836), 344-53.

Olmsted, Frederick Law. *Journey in the Back Country* [1860]. New York: Schocken, 1970.

———. *A Journey in the Seaboard Slave States in the Years 1853-1854.* Ed. William P. Trent. New York: Putnam's Sons, 1904.

———. *A Journey Through Texas.* New York: Dix, 1857.

Olsen, Magnus. *Farms and Fanes of Ancient Norway.* Cambridge, Mass.: Harvard Univ. Press, 1928.

On Geography. Ed. D. W. Meinig. Syracuse: Syracuse Univ. Press, 1971.

"On the Nature of Soils." *Farmer's Cabinet,* 1 (October 1, 1836), 81-82.

Oñate, Juan. "Account of the Discovery of the Mines" [1599]. *Spanish Exploration in the Southwest,* pp. 32-41.

One-Hundred-and-Fiftieth Anniversary of the First Church in Pomfret. Danielson, Conn.: Transcript, 1866.

Opie, Peter. "The Tentacles of Tradition." *Folklore,* 74 (Winter 1963), 507-26.

"Original." *The Plough Boy,* 1 (December 11, 1819), 1-2.

Ortíz, A. Dominguez. *The Golden Age of Spain: 1516-1659.* Trans. James Casey. London: Weidenfeld, 1971.

Osgood, Herbert L. *The American Colonies in the Seventeenth Century.* New York: Macmillan, 1904.

"Our Common Schools." *Wisconsin Farmer,* 8 (September 1856), 412-14.

Oxford English Dictionary. Oxford, England: Oxford Univ. Press, 1971.

Palgrave, Francis. *The Rise and Progress of the English Commonwealth.* London: John Murray, 1832.

Palm, Mary Borgias. *The Jesuit Missions of the Illinois Country, 1673-1763.* St. Louis: St. Louis Univ. Press, 1931.

Paracelsus. *Heretic and Alchemical Writings* [1628]. Trans. A. E. Waite. London: Eliott, 1894.

Parkinson, Richard. *The Experienced Farmer's Tour in America.* London: John Stockdale, 1805.

Paul, Rodman W. *California Gold: The Beginnings of Mining in the Far West.* Magnolia, Mass.: Peter Smith, 1947.

Paulding, James Kirk. *Letters from the South.* New York: James Eastburn, 1817.

Parsons, Jack. *Land and Cattle: Conversations with Joe Pankey, a New Mexico Rancher.* Albuquerque: Univ. of New Mexico Press, 1978.

Parsons, William Barclay. *Engineers and Engineering in the Renaissance.* Balt.: Williams, 1939.

Passim, Herbert, and John W. Bennett. "Changing Agricultural Magic in Southern Illinois." *The Study of Folklore.* Ed. Alan Dundes. Englewood Cliffs, N.J.: Prentice-Hall, 1965, pp. 114–26.

Paul, Virginia. *This Was Cattle Ranching.* Seattle: Superior, 1973.

Pearson, John. "Description of Lancaster and Columbia in 1801." Lancaster County Historical Society, *Journal,* 61 (1957), 49–61.

Peck, J. M. *A New Guide for Emigrants to the West.* Boston: Gould, 1837.

Peckham, Howard H. "Books and Reading on the Ohio Valley Frontier." *Mississippi Valley Historical Review,* 44 (March 1958), 649–63.

Penn, John. "Journal of a Visit to Reading, Harrisburg, Carlisle, and Lancaster in 1788." *Pennsylvania Magazine of History and Biography,* 3 (1879), 284–95.

Penn, William. "Instructions" [1681]. Historical Society of Pennsylvania, *Memoirs,* 2 (1827), 213–21.

Pennant, Thomas. *A Tour in Scotland.* London: B. White, 1769.

Pennsylvania Barn, The. Ed. Alfred C. Shoemaker. Kutztown: Pennsylvania Folklife Society, 1959.

Percy, Walker. "The Man on the Train: Three Existential Modes." *Partisan Review,* 23 (Fall 1956), 478–94.

Perfect Description of Virginia. London: Richard Wodenoth, 1649.

Peringo, Lynn. "The Cornish Miners of Early Gilpin County." *Colorado Magazine,* 14 (May 1937), 91–101.

Perley, Sidney. *History of Salem, Massachusetts.* Salem, Mass.: Author, 1926.

Peterson, Charles E. "Early Ste. Genevieve and its Architecture." *Missouri Historical Review,* 35 (January 1941), 207–32.

Phelps, Noah A. *History of Simsbury, Granby and Canton from 1642 to 1845.* Hartford: Tiffany, 1845.

———. *Newgate of Connecticut.* Hartford: American, 1876.

Phillips, U. B. *Life and Labor in the Old South.* Boston: Little, Brown, 1929.

Pickering, Timothy. *Life.* Ed. Octavius Pickering. Boston: Little, Brown, 1867.

Pierce, Arthur D. *Iron in the Pines: The Story of New Jersey's Ghost Towns and Bog Iron.* New Brunswick: Rutgers Univ. Press, 1957.

Pierson, Hamilton W. *In the Brush; or, Old-Time Social, Political, and Religious Life in the Southwest.* New York: Appleton, 1881.

Pierson, William H. *American Buildings and their Architects: Technology and the Picturesque, the Corporate and the Early Gothic Styles.* Garden City, N.Y.: Doubleday, 1978.

———. "Notes on the Early Industrial Architecture in England." Society of Architectural Historians, *Journal,* 8 (January–June 1949), 1–32.

Pitkin, Donald S. "Partible Inheritance and the Open Fields." *Agricultural History,* 35 (April 1961), 65–69.

"Plan of a Farm Dwelling House." *Cultivator,* 7 (April 1840), 76–77.

"Plan of a Portion of Wrentham, Massachusetts" [1762]. Suffolk County Plans, Suffolk County Courthouse, Boston.

"Plan of Irasburgh" [1792]. Bailey Howe Library, University of Vermont.

"Plan of the Town of Northwood" [1805]. New Hampshire State Library.

"Plans of Houses." *Cultivator*, 8 (August 1857), 249.

Plater, David D. "Building the North Wales Mill of William Allason." *Virginia Magazine of History and Biography*, 85 (January 1977), 45–50.

Platt, Colin. *The English Medieval Town*. New York: McKay, 1976.

Plattes, Gabriel. *A Discovery of Subterraneall Treasure*. London: Jasper Emery, 1639.

———. *A Discovery of Subterraneal Treasure*. Phil.: Bell, 1784.

Poe, Edgar Allan. *Best Known Works*. Ed. Hervey Allen. New York: Blue Ribbon, 1927.

Polanyi, Karl. *The Great Transformation: The Political and Economic Origins of Our Time*. New York: Farrar, 1944.

Pope, Thomas. *Treatise on Bridge Architecture*. New York: Niven, 1811.

Porteous, Alexander. *Forest Folklore, Mythology, and Romance*. New York: Macmillan, 1928.

Porter, Noah. *The New England Meeting House*. New Haven: Tercentenary Commission, 1933.

Porterfield, Neil H. "Ste. Genevieve, Missouri." *Frenchmen, French Ways in the Mississippi Valley*. Ed. John Francis McDermott. Urbana: Univ. of Illinois Press, 1969, pp. 140–78.

Posey, Walter Brownlaw. *The Baptist Church in the Lower Mississippi Valley, 1776–1845*. Lexington: Univ. of Kentucky Press, 1957.

Potter, Burton Willis. *The Road and the Roadside*. Boston: Little, Brown, 1893.

Pownall, T. *A Topographical Description of . . . North America*. London: Almon, 1776.

Powell, Sumner Chilton. *Puritan Village: The Formation of a New England Town*. Garden City, N.Y.: Doubleday, 1965.

Power, Richard Lyle. *Planting Corn Belt Culture: The Impress of the Upland Southerner and Yankee in the Old Northwest*. Indianapolis: Indiana Historical Society, 1953.

Priest, William. *Travels in the United States*. London: Johnson, 1802.

Prince, L. Bradford. *Spanish Mission Churches of New Mexico*. Cedar Rapids, Ia.: Torch, 1915.

Prince, Thomas. *The Grave and Death Destroyed*. Boston: S. Gerrish, 1728.

Probert, Thomas. *Lost Mines and Buried Treasures of the West*. Berkeley: Univ. of Calif. Press, 1977.

Proceedings of the English Colonies in Virginia [1612]. *Narratives of Early Virginia*, pp. 119–204.

"Proposed Site for Ipswich Meetinghouse" [1677]. Massachusetts State Archives, Boston.

Puckle, Bertram S. *Funeral Customs: Their Origin and Development*. London: T. Werner Laurie, 1926.

Quinby, Ian M. *Material Culture and the Study of American Life*. New York: Norton, 1978.

Raber, William B. *The Devil and Some of His Doings.* Dayton, Ohio: United Brethern in Christ, 1855.

Ralston, W. R. S. "Forest and Field Myths." *Contemporary Review,* 31 (February 1878), 520–31.

Raumer, Frederick. *America and the American People.* Trans. William W. Turner. New York: Langley, 1846.

Rawson, Marion Nicholl. *Handwrought Ancestors.* New York: Dutton, 1936.

Read, J. *Prelude to Chemistry: An Outline of Alchemy, its Literature, and Relationships.* New York: Macmillan, 1937.

Recopilación de Leyes de los Reynos de Los Indias. Madrid: Ortega, 1774.

Records of . . . Massachusetts Bay. Ed. Nathaniel B. Shurtleff. Boston: White, 1853–54.

Rediscovery of New Mexico, 1580–1594. Ed. George P. Hammond and Agapito Rey. Albuqueque: Univ. of New Mexico Press, 1966.

Reed, Andrew, and James Matheson. *A Narrative of the Visit to the American Churches.* New York: Harper, 1835.

Rees, Ronald. "The Scenery Cult: Changing Landscape Tastes over Three Centuries." *Landscape,* 19 (May 1975), 39–47.

Reisner, Edward H. *The Evolution of the Common School.* New York: Macmillan, 1930.

Report on School Houses. Newburyport, Mass.: Hiram Tozer, 1833.

Reps, John W. *The Making of Urban America: A History of City Planning in the United States.* Princeton: Princeton Univ. Press, 1965.

Retzius, Gustaf. *Finland: Nordiska Museet.* Stockholm: Beijers, 1881.

————. *Finnland: Schilderungen aus Seiner Natur, Seiner Alten Kultur, und Seinem Heutigen Volksleben.* Berlin: George Reimer, 1885.

Reynolds, Helen. *Dutch Houses in the Hudson Valley before 1776.* New York: Dover, 1965.

Reynolds, Hezekiah. *Directions for House and Ship Painting.* New Haven: Hudson, 1812.

Richeson, A. W. *English Land Measuring to 1800.* Cambridge, Mass.: MIT Press, 1966.

Rickard, Thomas A. *A History of American Mining.* New York: McGraw-Hill, 1932.

Rickert, John E. "House Facades of the Northeastern United States: A Tool of Geographic Analysis." *AAG, Annals,* 57 (June 1967), 211–38.

Riddell, John. *Architectural Designs for Model Country Residences.* Phil.: Lippincott, 1864.

Riley, Edward M. "The Town Acts of Colonial Virginia." *Journal of Southern History,* 16 (August 1950), 306–23.

Rines, Edward Francis. *Old Historic Churches of America.* New York: Macmillan, 1936.

Rivard, Paul E. "Textile Experiments in Rhode Island." *Rhode Island History,* 33 (May 1974), 35–45.

Robertson, Donald. "Provincial Town Plans from Late Sixteenth Century Mexico." *Verhandlungen des 37th Internationalen Amerikanstenkongresses,* 4 (n.d.), 123-29.

Robinson, Solon. "A Cheap Farmhouse." *American Agriculturist,* 5 (February 1846), 57-58.

Rochefoucault-Liancourt, Duc. *Travels through the United States.* London: R. Phillips, 1799.

Rogers, James R. *The Cane Ridge Meeting House in Bourbon County.* Cincinnati: Standard, 1910.

Rohde, Eleanour Sinclair. "The Folk-Lore of Herbals." *Folk-Lore,* 33 (1922), 243-64.

Rohrbaugh, Malcolm. *The Land Office Business.* New York: Oxford, 1968.

––––––. *The Trans-Appalachian Frontier.* New York: Oxford, 1978.

Rollinson, William. *Life and Tradition in the Lake District.* London: Dent, 1974.

Rose, Harold W. *The Colonial Houses of Worship in America.* New York: Hastings, 1963.

Rose, Robert. *Diary,* located at Colonial Williamsburg, Inc., Williamsburg, Virginia.

"Rotation of Crops." *Farmer's Cabinet* 4 (September 1, 1836), 49-52.

Rourke, Constance. *The Roots of American Culture.* Ed. Van Wyck Brooks. New York: Harcourt, 1942.

Rouse, John E. *The Criollo: Spanish Cattle in the Americas.* Norman: Univ. of Oklahoma Press, 1977.

"Royal Ordinances Concerning the Laying Out of New Towns." Ed. Zelia Nuttall. *Hispanic-American Historical Review,* 5 (May 1922), 249-54.

Rudyerd, Benjamin. *Memoirs . . . Containing his Speeches.* Ed. J. A. Manning. London: Boone, 1841.

Ruffin, Edmund. "Observations Made During an Excursion to the Dismal Swamp." *Farmer's Register,* 4 (January 1, 1837), 513-24.

"Rural Architecture." *Cultivator,* 4 (March 1847), 73-74.

"Rural Cemeteries." *Knickerbocker,* 11 (December 1838), 535-37.

Rural School Architecture. Springfield, Ill.: Dept. of Public Instruction, 1901.

Rural School Architecture. Washington, D.C. Bureau of Education, 1880.

Ruskin, John. *Modern Painters.* New York: Wiley, 1885.

––––––. *Praeterita* [1889]. Ed. Kenneth Clark. London: Rupert Hart-Davis, 1949.

Russel, Robert. *North America: Its Agriculture and Climate.* Edinburgh: Black, 1857.

Rutman, Darrett B. *Husbandmen of Plymouth.* Boston: Beacon, 1967.

––––––. *Winthrop's Boston: A Portrait of a Puritan Town, 1630-1649.* 1965. Reprint. New York: Norton, 1972.

Rutsch, Edward S. "The Colonial Plantation Settlement Pattern in New Jersey: Iron and Agricultural Examples." *Fifth Annual New Jersey Historical Symposium* (December 1973), 11-23.

Ryan, J. S. "Othin in England." *Folklore,* 74 (Autumn 1963), 460-80.

Saaz, Johann. *Der Ackerman von Böhmen*. Esslingen: K. Fyner, 1474.

"Sale of School Lands." Alton *Spectator* [Lower Alton, Ill.]. 1 (November 5, 1834), 3.

Salzman, L. F. *Building in England Down to 1540: A Documentary History*. Oxford: Oxford Univ. Press, 1952.

Samuel, Raphael. *Miners, Quarrymen, and Saltworkers*. London: Routledge, 1977.

Sande, Theodore Anton. *Industrial Archeology: A New Look at the American Heritage*. Brattleboro, Vt.: S. Greene, 1976.

_____. "The Textile Factory in Pre-Civil War Rhode Island." *Old-Time New England*, 66 (Summer–Fall 1975), 13–31.

Sargent, Frederic O. "Feudalism and Family Farms in France." *Agricultural History*, 35 (October 1961), 193–201.

Scheuchzer, Johann Jacob. *Sive Itinera per Helvetiae alpinas regiones*. Leyden: Petri Vander, 1723.

Schmithüsen, Josef. "Was ist eine Landschaft?" *Erdkundliches Wissen*, 9 (1964), 7–24.

Schoepf, J. D. *Travels in the Confederation, 1783–1784*. Trans. Alfred J. Morrison. Phil.: Campbell, 1911.

School Grounds, School House Architecture, and Outbuildings. Lansing, Mich.: R. Smith, 1894.

"School Houses." *Farmer's Monthly Visitor*, 13 (February 1853), 51–52.

"School Houses," *Illustrated Annual Register of Rural Affairs for 1855-6-7*. Albany: Luther Tucker and Sons, 1873, 156–61.

"School Houses." *Wisconsin Farmer*, 8 (March 1856), 127–28.

"School Room." *Farmer's Monthly Visitor*, 13 (June 1853), 187.

Schoolmaster and Academic Journal, The. Ed. B. F. Morris. Oxford, Ohio: Author, 1834.

Schrade, Hubert. *Baum und Wald in Bildern deutscher Maler*. Munich: Länger, 1937.

Schreiber, G. *Der Bergbau in Geschichte, Ethos, and Sakralkultur*. Berlin: Opladen, 1962.

Schwarz, Gabriele. *Allgemeine Siedlungsgeographie*. Berlin: De Gruyter, 1966.

Schweizer, Johannes. *Kirchhof und Friedhof: Eine Darstellung der beiden Haupttypen europäischer Begrabnisstätten*. Linz-an-der-Donau: Oberosterreichischer Landesverlag, 1956.

Scituate Town Records. Scituate Town Hall, Scituate, Mass.

Scott, Walter. *Demonology and Witchcraft* [1830]. New York: Bell, 1970.

Sebillot, Paul. *Les Trauvaux publics et les mines dans les traditions et les superstitions de tours les pays*. Paris: Rothschild, 1894.

Secoy, D. M., and A. E. Smith. "Superstitions and Social Practices Against Agricultural Pests." *Environmental Review*, 3 (May 1978), 2–18.

Seebohm, Frederic. *Customary Acres and Their Historical Importance*. London: Longmans, 1914.

_____. *The English Village Community Examined in its Relations to . . . the Common or Open Field System*. London: Longmans, 1890.

Seguin, R-L. *La Civilisation traditionelle de l''habitant' aux 17 ^e et 18 ^e siècle.* Montreal: Fides, 1967.

———. *L'equipement de la ferme Canadienne aux XVII ^e et XVIII ^e siècles.* Montreal: Ducharme, 1959.

———. *Les Granges de Quebec.* Ottawa: National Museum, 1963.

Seidenstickes, August. *Waldgeschichte des Alterthums.* Frankfurt: Trowitzsch, 1886.

Sennett, Richard. *The Fall of Public Man.* New York: Knopf, 1977.

Seventeenth-Century American Poetry. Ed. Harison T. Meserole. Garden City, N.Y.: Anchor, 1968.

Severe, Sulpice. *Vie de Saint Martin* [c. 400]. Paris: Cerf, 1968.

Sewall, Samuel. *Diary, 1674–1729.* Ed. M. Halsey Thomas. New York: Farrar, 1973.

Sganzin, J. M. *Elementary Course of Civil Engineering.* Boston: Hilliard, 1837.

Shaler, Nathaniel. *American Highways.* New York: Century, 1896.

Shaw, E. B., "The Geography of a Small Trade Center in the Corn Belt." Geographical Society of Philadelphia, *Bulletin,* 29 (1931), 265–79.

Shaw-Lefevre, George John. *English and Irish Land Questions.* London: Cassell, 1881.

"Shelter for Farms." *Cultivator,* 2 (October 1854), 297–98.

Shepherd, Job. *Almanack for 1752.* Newport, R.I.: Franklin, 1751.

Shipton, Clifford K. *New England Life in the Eighteenth Century.* Cambridge, Mass.: Harvard Univ. Press, 1963.

Shrigley, Nathaniel. *A True Relation of Virginia and Maryland.* London: Tho. Milbourne, 1669.

Shurtleff, Harold. *The Log Cabin Myth: A Study of the Early Dwellings of the English Colonists of North America.* Ed. Samuel Eliot Morison. Cambridge, Mass.: Harvard Univ. Press, 1939.

Shurtleff, M. C. "The Blight, Fact and Fiction." *Agricultural Chemicals,* 29 (1971), 22–24.

Sikes, Wirt. *British Goblins: Welsh Folk-Lore, Fairy Mythology, Legends, and Traditions.* London: Low, 1880.

Sim, Robert J., and Harry B. Weiss. *Charcoal-Buring in New Jersey from Early Times to the Present.* Trenton: New Jersey Agricultural Society, 1955.

Simmons, Marc. "Spanish Irrigation Practices in New Mexico." *NMHR,* 47 (1972), 103–39.

Simpson, Jacqueline. "Fifty British Dragon Tales: An Analysis." *Folk-Lore,* 89 (1978), 79–93.

Sizer, Theodore. *The Age of the Academies.* New York: Columbia Univ. Press, 1964.

Small, Francis. "Deposition." *New Hampshire Provincial Papers,* I, 45–46.

Smith, David C. "The Logging Frontier." *Journal of Forest History,* 18 (October 1974), 96–106.

Smith, Elizabeth Simpson. "Vesuvius Furnace Plantation." *Historic Preservation,* 28 (April–June 1976), 24–27.

Smith, Henry A. "Charleston: The Original Plan." *South Carolina Historical and Genealogical Magazine,* 9 (January 1908), 12–27.

Smith, James. *An Account of the Remarkable Occurrences . . . 1755–1759.* Cincinnati: Robert Clark, 1870.

Smith, John. *Advertisements for the Unexperienced Planters of New England, or any where,* MHS, *Collections,* 3d ser., 3 (1833), 1–54.

———. "Map of Virginia." Oxford: William Hale, 1612.

Smith, Page, *As a City Upon a Hill: The Town in American History.* Cambridge, Mass.: MIT Press, 1966.

Sosa, Castano. "Report to the Viceroy, July 27, 1591." *Rediscovery of New Mexico,* pp. 50–63.

Southwick, Marcia. *Build with Adobe.* Chicago: Sundlow, 1965.

Spanish Exploration in the Southwest, 1542–1706. Ed. Henry E. Bolton. New York: Scribner's, 1916.

Spanish in the Mississippi Valley, 1752–1804. Ed. John Francis McDermott. Urbana: Univ. of Illinois Press, 1974.

Spanish Regime in Missouri, The. Ed. Louis Houck. Chicago: Donnelley, 1909.

Spanish Tradition in America, The. Ed. Charles Gilson. Columbia: Univ. of South Carolina Press, 1968.

Spargo, John. *Iron Mining and Smelting in Bennington, Vermont, 1786–1842.* Bennington, Vt.: Historical Museum, 1938.

Sparks, Jared. "Internal Improvements of North Carolina." *North American Review,* 12 (January 1821), 16–37.

"Specifications for Building a Log Courthouse." Ed. Paul Goeldner. Association for Preservation Technology *Bulletin,* 5 (1973), 75.

Speech of Mr. Miner on . . . Internal Improvements. Washington, D.C.: Gales and Seaton, 1828.

Springer, John S. *Forest Life and Forest Trees: Comprising Winter Camp-Life Among the Loggers.* New York: Harper, 1851.

Spurrier, John. *The Practical Farmer.* Wilmington, Del.: Brynberg and Andrews, 1793.

"Standardized Specifications for Building Stone Lock Keepers' Houses." Ed. Hugh C. Miller. Association for Preservation Technology, *Bulletin,* 5 (1973), 69–74.

Stanislawski, Dan. *The Anatomy of Eleven Towns in Michoacan.* Austin: Univ. of Texas Press, 1950.

———. "Early Spanish Town Planning in the New World." *Geographical Review,* 38 (January 1947), 94–105.

Statutes at Large of South Carolina, 1662–1838. Ed. Thomas Cooper and David J. McCord. Columbia, S.C.: Johnston, 1836–41.

Statutes at Large . . . of Virginia. Ed. William Waller Henning. New York: Bartow, 1823.

Statutes of the Realm. London: n.p., 1819.

Steele, Richard. *The Spectator.* Ed. N. Ogle. London: Whittaker, 1827.

Stenton, Doris M. *English Society in the Early Middle Ages.* Harmondsworth, England: Penguin, 1951.

Stephan, Heinrich. *Geschichte der preussichen Post.* Berlin: R. Decker, 1859.

————. *Das Verkehrsleben in Altertum und Mittelalter.* Goslar: Herzog, 1967.

Stevens, John Austin. *Albert Gallatin.* Boston: Houghton, 1883.

Stevens, Wallace. *Poems.* New York: Vintage, 1959.

Stevenson, D. Alan. *The World's Lighthouses Before 1820.* London: Oxford Univ. Press, 1959.

Stevenson, David. *Sketch of the Civil Engineering of North America.* London: John Weale, 1838.

Stevenson, J. A. R. *The Din of a Smithy.* London: Chapman, 1932.

Stevin, Simon. *Materiae Politica: Burgherlicke Stoffen.* Leyden: Iustus Livius, 1649.

Stiles, Ezra. *Literary Diary.* Ed. Franklin B. Dexter. New York: Scribner's, 1901.

Stilgoe, John R. "Common, Close, and Village Green: The 'Meetinghouse Lot' in New England, 1620–1960." *Common Ground.* Ed. Ronald L. Fleming. Cambridge, Mass.: Townscape Institute, 1981.

————. "Folklore and Graveyard Design." *Landscape,* 22 (Spring 1978), 22–28.

————. "Jack-o-lanterns to Surveyors: The Secularization of Landscape Boundaries." *Environmental Review,* 1 (Autumn 1976), 14–31.

————. "A New England Coastal Wilderness." *Geographical Review,* 71 (January 1981), 33–50.

————. "The Puritan Townscape: Ideal and Reality." *Landscape,* 20 (Spring 1976), 3–7.

Stith, William. *History of the First Discovery and Settlement* of Virginia [1747]. New York: Sabin, 1865.

Stokhuyzen, Frederick. *The Dutch Windmill.* Trans. Carry Dikshourn. London: Merlin, 1963.

Stoddard, Solomon. *An Answer to Some Cases of Conscience.* Boston: Green, 1722.

"Stone Fencing." *New England Farmer,* 10 (November 1858), 496–97.

"Stone Walls." *Farmer's Cabinet,* 1 (September 1, 1836), 57.

Straughan, Walter C. "The Old Mill of Guilford." *Pioneer America,* 4 (July 1972), 44–49.

Strickland, William. *Journal of a Tour in the United States of America, 1794–1795.* Ed. J. E. Strickland. New York: New York Historical Society, 1971.

————. *Observations on the Agriculture of the United States.* London: Bulmer, 1800.

Stuart, Charles B. *Civil and Military Engineers of North America.* New York: Van Nostrand, 1871.

Study of the Rural Schools of Maine, A. Augusta: State Superintendent of Common Schools, 1895.

"Stumbling Blocks in the Way of Our Farmers." *Farmer's Monthly Visitor,* 13 (February 1852), 41–43.

Sullivan, William A. *The Industrial Worker in Pennsylvania, 1800–1840.* Harrisburg: Penn. Historical and Museum Commission, 1955.

"Survey of Piscataqua River" [c. 1700]. At Public Record Office, London.

"Susan Miller." *Mind Amongst the Spindles.* Ed. C. Knight. London: Charles Knight, 1844.

Symonds, Samuel. "Letter" [1637]. MHS, *Collections,* 4th ser., 8 (n.d.), 118–20.

Tanner, Henry S. *A Description of All Canals.* New York: Tanner, 1840.

Tarpley, Fred A. "Southern Cemeteries: Neglected Archives for the Folklorist." *Southern Folklore Quarterly,* 27 (1963), 323–33.

Tashjian, Dickran, and Ann Tashjian. *Memorials for Children of Change; the Art of Early New England Stonecarving.* Middletown, Conn.: Wesleyan Univ. Press, 1974.

Taylor, Edward. *Poems.* Ed. Donald E. Stanford. New Haven: Yale Univ. Press.

Taylor, William B. "Land and Water Rights in the Viceroyalty of New Spain." *NMHR,* 50 (July 1975), 189–212.

Teirlinck, I. *Flora diabolica: de plant in de demonologie.* Antwerp: Mees, 1924.

Tienhoven, Cornelius. *Information Relative to Taking Up Land in New Netherlands* [1650], *Documentary History of the State of New York.* Ed. E. B. O'Callagan. Albany: Van Benthuysen, 1851, IV, 25–36.

"Tillage Husbandry." *Cultivator,* 1 (March 1834), 38–41.

Tille, Alexander. *Die Geschichte der deutschen Weihnacht.* Leipzig: Keil, 1893.

Thomas, David. *Travels through the Western Country.* Auburn, N.Y.: David Ramsey, 1819.

Thomas, J. J. "A Complete Country Residence." *Illustrated Annual of Rural Affairs.* Albany: Luther Tucker, 1858, 21–35.

Thompson, James Westfall. "The Beef Cattle Industry in Ohio Prior to the Civil War." *Ohio Historical Quarterly,* 64 (April, July 1955), 168–94, 287–319.

Thoreau, Henry David. *Cape Cod.* Boston: Ticknor, 1865.

———. *Excursions.* Ed. Leo Marx. New York: Corinth, 1962.

———. *Maine Woods.* Boston: Ticknor, 1864.

———. *A Week on the Concord and Merrimack Rivers* [1849]. Ed. Denham Sutcliffe. New York: New American Library, 1961.

Thrower, N. *Original Survey and Land Subdivision.* Chicago: Rand, 1966.

Thünen, Johann Heinrich. *Der isolirte staat in beziehung auf landwirthschaft.* Rostock: Leopold, 1842–63.

Tocqueville, Alexis. *De la democratie en Amerique.* Paris: Freres, 1864.

———. *Democracy in America.* Trans. George Lawrence. Ed. J. P. Mayer. Garden City, N.Y.: Doubleday, 1969.

———. *Journey to America.* Trans. George Lawrence. Ed. J. P. Mayer. New Haven: Yale Univ. Press, 1959.

Tönnies, Ferdinand. *Community and Society* [1887]. Trans. Charles P. Loomis. New York: Harper, 1963.

Towne, Charles Wayland, and Edward N. Wentworth. *Cattle and Men.* Norman: Univ. of Oklahoma Press, 1955.

Toynbee, Arnold. "The Religious Background of the Present Environmental Crisis." *Ecology and Religion in History.* Ed. David Spring and Eileen Spring. New York: Harper, 1974, pp. 137–49.

Trewartha, Glenn T. "Some Regional Characteristics of American Farmsteads." AAG, *Annals,* 38 (Fall 1948), 169–225.

"Trial of Stump Machines." *Cultivator,* 5 (April 1857), 128.

Trowbridge, C. C. "Letter." *Michigan Pioneer and Historical Collections,* 4 (1881), 173–76.

Trudel, Marcel. *The Beginnings of New France, 1524–1663.* Trans. Patricia Claxton. Toronto: McClelland, 1973.

Trumbull, Benjamin. *A Complete History of Connecticut.* New Haven: Maltby, 1818.

Tuan, Yi-Fu. *Landscapes of Fear.* New York: Pantheon, 1979.

————. *Space and Place: The Perspective of Experience.* Minneapolis: Univ. of Minnesota Press, 1977.

————. *Topophilia: A Study of Environmental Perception, Attitudes, and Values.* Englewood Cliffs, N.J.: Prentice-Hall, 1974.

Tusser, Thomas. *Five Hundred Pointes of Good Husbandrie, mixed in everie month with huswiferie.* London: H. Denham, 1580.

Tyler, John. "Two Centuries of Technological Change Reflected in a Cumberland County Mill." *Pioneer America,* 2 (January 1970), 1–6.

Uhland, Ludwig. *Gedichte.* Stuttgart: Cotta'scher, 1853.

Uhlig, Harold. "Old Hamlets with Infield and Outfield Systems in Western and Central Europe." *Geografiska Annaler,* 43 (1961), 285–312.

Vanberg, Bert. *Of Norwegian Ways.* Minneapolis: Dillon, 1974.

Vance, James E. "Land Assignment in the Precapitalist, Capitalist, and Post-capitalist City." *Economic Geography,* 47 (1971), 103–120.

Vassberg, David E. "The Tierras Baldias: Community Property and Public Lands in 16th Century Castille." *Agricultural History,* 48 (July 1974), 383–401.

Vattel, Emmerich. *The Law of Nations, or Principles of the Law of Nature.* Dublin: Luke White, 1781.

Vesly, Leon. "Legendes, superstitions, and coutumes." *Bulletin de la société libre d'emulation d'commerce et de l'industrie de la Seine Inferieure,* 54 (1892), 226–43.

"View from Bushongo Tavern." *Columbian Magazine,* 2 (July 1788), 354.

Villee, H. W. *Der Bauer als Landmesser, oder der Practische Feldmesskunst.* Reading, Penn.: J. Ritter, 1824.

Villefosse, René Heron. *Histoire des grandes routes de France.* Paris: Librairie Academique, 1975.

"Virginia Colonial Records." *Virginia Magazine of History and Biography,* 15 (July 1907), 26–43.

"Virginia Past and Present." *Putman's Monthly Magazine,* 2 (August 1853), 195–201.

Virginia's Cure. London: W. Godbid, 1662.

Vivante, Arturo. "Crossroads." *New Yorker,* 54 (April 17, 1978), 34–37.

Vries, Jan. *Altgermanische Religionsgeschichte.* Berlin: De Gruyter, 1956.

Wacker, Peter O. "Folk Architecture as an Indicator of Culture Areas and Culture Diffusion: Dutch Barns and Barracks in New Jersey." *Pioneer America,* 5 (July 1973), 37-47.

Wade, Richard C. *The Urban Frontier: The Rise of Western Cities, 1790-1830.* Cambridge, Mass.: Harvard Univ. Press, 1959.

Wailes, Rex. *The English Windmill.* London: Routledge, 1954.

Wakefield, Priscilla. *Excursions in North America.* London: Darton, 1810.

Walcott, Robert R. "Husbandry in Colonial New England." *NEQ,* 9 (1936), 218-52.

Walden, J. H. *Soil Culture.* New York: Chappell, 1858.

Walker, Joseph. *Hopewell Village: A Social and Economic History of an Iron-Making Community.* Phil.: Univ. of Pennsylvania Press, 1966.

Wall, John P. *The Chronicles of New Brunswick, New Jersey.* New Brunswick: Thatcher-Anderson, 1931.

Wallace, Anthony F. C. *Rockdale.* New York: Knopf, 1978.

Ware, Caroline. *The Early New England Cotton Manufacture.* Boston: Houghton, 1931.

Waters, John J. "Hingham, Massachusetts, 1631-1661: An East Anglian Oligarchy in the New World." *Journal of Social History,* 1 (1967-68), 353-70.

Watkins, Alfred. *The Old Straight Track.* London: Methuen, 1925.

Watson, Elkanah. "Address." *The Plough Boy,* 1 (no. 26), 205-06; (no. 27), 213-14; (no. 28), 220-22.

———. *History of Agricultural Societies on the Modern Berkshire System.* Albany: Steele, 1820.

Watson, Ellen. "When Thoreau was a Young Man in Plymouth." MS. Box B, folder 14, Hillside Collection, Pilgrim Society Library, Plymouth, Mass.

Watt, W. Montgomery. *A History of Islamic Spain.* Edinburgh: University Press, 1965.

Webster, Noah. *An American Dictionary.* New York: Converse, 1828.

Weeden, William B. *Economic and Social History of New England, 1620-1789.* Boston: Houghton, 1891.

Weeks, David. "The Agrarian System of the Spanish Colonies." *Journal of Land and Public Utility Economics,* 23 (May 1947), 153-68.

Weiss, Harry B[ischoff]. *The Early Sawmills of New Jersey.* Trenton: New Jersey Agricultural Society, 1968.

———, and Robert J. Sim. *Early Grist and Flouring Mills of New Jersey.* Trenton: New Jersey Agricultural Society, 1956.

———, and Grace M. Weiss. *Early Windmills of New Jersey and Nearby Sites.* Trenton: New Jersey Agricultural Society, 1969.

Welch, Sylvester. *Report on the Allegheny Portage Railroad* [1833]. Ed. William H. Shank. York, Penn.: American Canal and Transportation Center, 1975.

West, Robert C. "The Flat-Roofed Folk Dwelling in Rural Mexico." *Geoscience and Man,* 5 (June 10, 1974), 111-32.

———. *The Mining Community in Northern New Spain: The Parral Mining District.* Berkeley: Univ. of California Press, 1949.

Whiffen, Marcus. *The Eighteenth Century Houses of Williamsburg.* Williamsburg: Colonial Williamsburg Corp., 1960.

_____. *The Public Buildings of Williamsburg.* Williamsburg: Colonial Williamsburg, 1958.

Whipple, Squire. *A Work on Bridge Building.* New York: Van Nostrand, 1847.

White, George Savage. *Memoir of Samuel Slater.* Phil.: Carpenter, 1836.

White, Lynn, Jr. *Medieval Technology and Social Change.* New York: Oxford Univ. Press, 1962.

Whitehill, Walter Muir. *Boston: A Topographical History.* Cambridge, Mass.: Harvard Univ. Press, 1968.

Whittier, John Greenleaf. *Poetical Works.* Boston: Houghton, 1892.

Whittlesey, Charles. "Origins of the American System of Land Surveys." Association of Engineering Societies *Journal,* 3 (September 1884), 275-80.

Wigglesworth, Michael. "God's Controversy with New England." *Seventeenth-Century American Poetry,* pp. 42-53.

Wilhelm, E. J. "The Blue Ridge Mill Complex." *Pioneer America,* 1 (January 1969), 17-21.

Wilkinson, Ronald Sterne. "The Alchemical Library of John Winthrop, Jr. (1606-1676) and his Descendants in Colonial America." *Ambix,* 11 (February 1963), 2-48.

_____. "New England's Last Alchemists." *Ambix,* 10, (October 1962), 128-38.

Willard, Samuel. *A Compleat Body of Divinity.* Boston: B. Green and S. Kneeland, 1726.

Williams, Edward. *Virginia's Discovery of Silk Wormes.* London: John Stephenson, 1650.

Williams, Eurwyn. "The Protection of the House: Some Iconographic Evidence from Wales." *Folklore,* 89 (1978), 148-53.

Williams, George H. *Wilderness and Paradise in Christian Thought.* New York: Harper, 1960.

Williams, H. L., and O. K. Williams. *Old American Houses.* Garden City, N.Y.: Doubleday, 1946.

Williams, Raymond. *The Country and the City.* New York: Oxford, 1975.

Williamson, W. D. *The History of Magic.* Hallowell, Penn.: Glazier, 1852.

Wilsdorf, Helmut. *Bergwerke und Hüttenanlagen der Agricola-Zeit.* Berlin: Deutsches Verlag der Wissenschaften, 1971.

_____. *Georg Agricola und seine Zeit.* Berlin: Deutsches Verlag der Wissenschaften, 1956.

Wilson, Samuel. *An Account of the Province of Carolina* [1682], *Narratives of Early Carolina, 1650-1708,* pp. 156-79.

Winberry, John. "The Osage Orange." *Pioneer America,* 11 (August 1979), 134-41.

Winner, Langdon. *Autonomous Technology: Technics-out-of-Control as a Theme in Political Thought.* Cambridge, Mass.: MIT Press, 1977.

Winsor, Justin. *The Mississippi Basin: The Struggle in America Between England and France, 1697-1763.* Boston: Houghton, 1895.

"Winter in the South." *Harper's New Monthly Magazine,* 15 (September, October, November 1857), 433–50, 594–606, 721–40.

Winthrop, John. *The History of New England.* Ed. James Savage. Boston: Little, Brown, 1853.

Winthrop Papers. Boston: MHS, 1931.

Wolf, Stephanie Grauman. *Urban Village: Community and Family in Germantown, Pennsylvania, 1683–1800.* Princeton: Princeton Univ. Press, 1976.

Wood, Frederick J. *The Turnpikes of New England and Evolution of the Same Through England, Virginia, and Maryland.* Boston: Marshall Jones, 1919.

Wood, Richard George. *A History of Lumbering in Maine, 1820–1861.* Orono: University of Maine Press, 1935.

Wood, William. *New England's Prospect* [1634]. Ed. Alden T. Vaughan. Amherst: Univ. of Massachusetts Press, 1977.

Woods, John. *Two Years Residence . . . in the Illinois Country.* London: Longman, 1822.

"Woods and Woodlands." *New England Farmer,* 24 (December 17, 1845), 197.

Woodward, John. *An Essay toward a Natural History of the Earth and Terrestrial Bodies.* London: Bettesworth, 1723.

Worlidge, John. *Systema Agriculturae.* London: Samuel Speed, 1669.

Wright, Louis B. *The John Henry County Map of Virginia, 1770.* Charlottesville: Univ. Press of Virginia, 1977.

Yoder, Don. "Official Religion versus Folk Religion." *Pennsylvania Folklife,* 15 (Winter 1965–66), 36–52.

Young, Andrew White. *History of Chautauqua County.* Buffalo: Matthews and Warren, 1875.

Young, Otis E. *Western Mining from Spanish Times to 1893.* Norman: Univ. of Oklahoma Press, 1970.

Zaroulis, Nancy. "Daughters of Freemen: The Female Operatives and the Beginning of the Labor Movement." *Cotton was King,* pp. 105–26.

Zelinsky, Wilbur. *The Cultural Geography of the United States.* Englewood Cliffs, N.J.: Prentice-Hall, 1973.

————. "The New England Connecting Barn." *Geographical Review,* 48 (October 1958), 540–53.

————. "Unearthly Delights: Cemetery Names as a Key to the Map of the Changing American Afterworld." *Geographies of the Mind: Papers in Honor of John K. Wright.* Ed. Martyn Bowden and David Lowenthal. New York: Oxford Univ. Press, 1975, pp. 171–96.

————. "Walls and Fences." *Landscape,* 8 (Spring 1959), 14–20.

Zentler, Conrad. *Americanischer Stadt und Land Calendar.* Phil.: Zentler, 1824.

Zube, Ervin H., and Zube, Margaret J., eds. *Changing Rural Landscapes.* Amherst: University of Massachusetts Press, 1977.

Zuckerman, Michael. *Peaceable Kingdoms: New England Towns in the Eighteenth Century.* New York: Random House, 1970.

EAST HAMPTON LIBRARY

3 0625 00061 7116

973   1
Stilgoe, J.

Common landscape of
America...

973   1

3 0625 00061 7116

Common landscape of
America...   29.95

AUG 23 83   8743
JAN 3 84   H.B.N. 1923
JUL 2 85
JUL 10 87   N 2202
APR 6 90   12772

PLEASE NOTE
To save dollars ...

No overdue notice(s) will be sent on this
material.   You are responsible for
returning by date on card in pocket.
Otherwise you will be billed.

Board of Managers
East Hampton Free Library
159 Main Street
East Hampton, NY 11937
324-0222